MASTER VISUALLY™

HTML 4 and XHTML™ 1

Visual

by Kelly Murdock

IDG
BOOKS

From

maranGraphics™

IDG Books Worldwide, Inc.
An International Data Group Company
Foster City, CA • Indianapolis • Chicago • New York

Master VISUALLY™ HTML 4 and XHTML™ 1

Published by
IDG Books Worldwide, Inc.
An International Data Group Company
919 E. Hillsdale Blvd., Suite 400
Foster City, CA 94404
www.idgbooks.com (IDG Books Worldwide Web Site)
Original text and Illustrations Copyright © 2000 IDG Books Worldwide, Inc.

Certain of the text and illustrations are Copyright © 1992-2000 maranGraphics Inc. and are used with maranGraphics' permission.

Design Copyright © 1992-2000 maranGraphics, Inc.
     5755 Coopers Avenue
     Mississauga, Ontario, Canada
     L4Z 1R9

Library of Congress Control Number.: 00-107555

ISBN: 0-7645-3454-8

Printed in the United States of America

10 9 8 7 6 5 4 3 2 1

1O/QY/QZ/QQ/IN

Distributed in the United States by IDG Books Worldwide, Inc.

Distributed by CDG Books Canada Inc. for Canada; by Transworld Publishers Limited in the United Kingdom; by IDG Norge Books for Norway; by IDG Sweden Books for Sweden; by IDG Books Australia Publishing Corporation Pty. Ltd. for Australia and New Zealand; by TransQuest Publishers Pte Ltd. for Singapore, Malaysia, Thailand, Indonesia, and Hong Kong; by Gotop Information Inc. for Taiwan; by ICG Muse, Inc. for Japan; by Intersoft for South Africa; by Eyrolles for France; by International Thomson Publishing for Germany, Austria and Switzerland; by Distribuidora Cuspide for Argentina; by LR International for Brazil; by Galileo Libros for Chile; by Ediciones ZETA S.C.R. Ltda. for Peru; by WS Computer Publishing Corporation, Inc., for the Philippines; by Contemporanea de Ediciones for Venezuela; by Express Computer Distributors for the Caribbean and West Indies; by Micronesia Media Distributor, Inc. for Micronesia; by Chips Computadoras S.A. de C.V. for Mexico; by Editorial Norma de Panama S.A. for Panama; by American Bookshops for Finland.

For corporate orders, please call maranGraphics at 800-469-6616.

For general information on IDG Books Worldwide's books in the U.S., please call our Consumer Customer Service department at 800-762-2974. For reseller information, including discounts and premium sales, please call our Reseller Customer Service department at 800-434-3422.

For information on where to purchase IDG Books Worldwide's books outside the U.S., please contact our International Sales department at 317-572-3993 or fax 317-572-4002.

For consumer information on foreign language translations, please contact our Customer Service department at 1-800-434-3422, fax 317-572-4002, or e-mail rights@idgbooks.com.

For information on licensing foreign or domestic rights, please phone +1-650-653-7098.

For sales inquiries and special prices for bulk quantities, please contact our Order Services department at 800-434-3422 or write to the address above.

For information on using IDG Books Worldwide's books in the classroom or for ordering examination copies, please contact our Educational Sales department at 800-434-2086 or fax 317-572-4005.

For press review copies, author interviews, or other publicity information, please contact our Public Relations department at 650-653-7000 or fax 650-653-7500.

For authorization to photocopy items for corporate, personal, or educational use, please contact Copyright Clearance Center, 222 Rosewood Drive, Danvers, MA 01923, or fax 978-750-4470.

Screen shots displayed in this book are based on pre-released software and are subject to change.

Trademark Acknowledgments

ABOUT IDG BOOKS WORLDWIDE

Welcome to the world of IDG Books Worldwide.

IDG Books Worldwide, Inc., is a subsidiary of International Data Group, the world's largest publisher of computer-related information and the leading global provider of information services on information technology. IDG was founded more than 30 years ago by Patrick J. McGovern and now employs more than 9,000 people worldwide. IDG publishes more than 290 computer publications in over 75 countries. More than 90 million people read one or more IDG publications each month.

Launched in 1990, IDG Books Worldwide is today the #1 publisher of best-selling computer books in the United States. We are proud to have received eight awards from the Computer Press Association in recognition of editorial excellence and three from Computer Currents' First Annual Readers' Choice Awards. Our best-selling ...For Dummies® series has more than 50 million copies in print with translations in 31 languages. IDG Books Worldwide, through a joint venture with IDG's Hi-Tech Beijing, became the first U.S. publisher to publish a computer book in the People's Republic of China. In record time, IDG Books Worldwide has become the first choice for millions of readers around the world who want to learn how to better manage their businesses.

Our mission is simple: Every one of our books is designed to bring extra value and skill-building instructions to the reader. Our books are written by experts who understand and care about our readers. The knowledge base of our editorial staff comes from years of experience in publishing, education, and journalism — experience we use to produce books to carry us into the new millennium. In short, we care about books, so we attract the best people. We devote special attention to details such as audience, interior design, use of icons, and illustrations. And because we use an efficient process of authoring, editing, and desktop publishing our books electronically, we can spend more time ensuring superior content and less time on the technicalities of making books.

You can count on our commitment to deliver high-quality books at competitive prices on topics you want to read about. At IDG Books Worldwide, we continue in the IDG tradition of delivering quality for more than 30 years. You'll find no better book on a subject than one from IDG Books Worldwide.

John Kilcullen
Chairman and CEO
IDG Books Worldwide, Inc.

*Eighth Annual
Computer Press
Awards ≥ 1992*

*Ninth Annual
Computer Press
Awards ≥ 1993*

*Tenth Annual
Computer Press
Awards ≥ 1994*

*Eleventh Annual
Computer Press
Awards ≥ 1995*

IDG is the world's leading IT media, research and exposition company. Founded in 1964, IDG had 1997 revenues of $2.05 billion and has more than 9,000 employees worldwide. IDG offers the widest range of media options that reach IT buyers in 75 countries representing 95% of worldwide IT spending. IDG's diverse product and services portfolio spans six key areas including print publishing, online publishing, expositions and conferences, market research, education and training, and global marketing services. More than 90 million people read one or more of IDG's 290 magazines and newspapers, including IDG's leading global brands — Computerworld, PC World, Network World, Macworld and the Channel World family of publications. IDG Books Worldwide is one of the fastest-growing computer book publishers in the world, with more than 700 titles in 36 languages. The "...For Dummies®" series alone has more than 50 million copies in print. IDG offers online users the largest network of technology-specific Web sites around the world through IDG.net (http://www.idg.net), which comprises more than 225 targeted Web sites in 55 countries worldwide. International Data Corporation (IDC) is the world's largest provider of information technology data, analysis and consulting, with research centers in over 41 countries and more than 400 research analysts worldwide. IDG World Expo is a leading producer of more than 168 globally branded conferences and expositions in 35 countries including E3 (Electronic Entertainment Expo), Macworld Expo, ComNet, Windows World Expo, ICE (Internet Commerce Expo), Agenda, DEMO, and Spotlight. IDG's training subsidiary, ExecuTrain, is the world's largest computer training company, with more than 230 locations worldwide and 785 training courses. IDG Marketing Services helps industry-leading IT companies build international brand recognition by developing global integrated marketing programs via IDG's print, online and exposition products worldwide. Further information about the company can be found at www.idg.com.   1/26/00

maranGraphics is a family-run business
located near Toronto, Canada.

At maranGraphics, we believe in producing great computer books – one book at a time.

maranGraphics has been producing high-technology products for over 25 years, which enables us to offer the computer book community a unique communication process.

Our computer books use an integrated communication process, which is very different from the approach used in other computer books. Each spread is, in essence, a flow chart – the text and screen shots are totally incorporated into the layout of the spread. Introductory text and helpful tips complete the learning experience.

maranGraphics' approach encourages the left and right sides of the brain to work together – resulting in faster orientation and greater memory retention.

Above all, we are very proud of the handcrafted nature of our books. Our carefully-chosen writers are experts in their fields, and spend countless hours researching and organizing the content for each topic. Our artists rebuild every screen shot to provide the best clarity possible, making our screen shots the most precise and easiest to read in the industry. We strive for perfection, and believe that the time spent handcrafting each element results in the best computer books money can buy.

Thank you for purchasing this book. We hope you enjoy it!

Sincerely,

Robert Maran
President
maranGraphics

Please visit us on the Web at:
www.maran.com

CREDITS

Acquisitions, Editorial, and Media Development

Project Editor
Darren Meiss

Acquisitions Editor
Martine Edwards

Associate Project Coordinator
Lindsay Sandman

Copy Editor
Tim Borek

Proof Editor
Dwight Ramsey

Technical Editor
Allen Wyatt

Permissions Editor
Carmen Krikorian

Associate Media Development Specialist
Megan Decraene

Editorial Manager
Rev Mengle

Media Development Manager
Heather Heath Dismore
Laura Carpenter

Editorial Assistant
Candace Nicholson

Production

Book Design
maranGraphics

Project Coordinators
Valery Bourke
Cindy Phipps

Layout
Kelly Hardesty
Todd Klemme
Seth Conley
Anna Rohrer
Brian Massey

Editorial Graphics Production
Ronda David-Burroughs
Craig Dearing
David Gregory
Mark Harris
Jill Johnson

Proofreaders
Angel Perez
Charles Spencer
York Production Services, Inc.

Indexer
York Production Services, Inc.

Special Help
Dana Lesh
Angie Hunckler
Mary Jo Richards
Clint Lahnen
Brent Savage
Shelley Norris
Brian Kramer
Ted Cains

GENERAL AND ADMINISTRATIVE

IDG Books Worldwide, Inc.: John Kilcullen, CEO

IDG Books Technology Publishing Group: Richard Swadley, Senior Vice President and Publisher; Walter R. Bruce III, Vice President and Publisher; Joseph Wikert, Vice President and Publisher; Mary Bednarek, Vice President and Director, Product Development; Andy Cummings, Publishing Director, General User Group; Mary C. Corder, Editorial Director; Barry Pruett, Publishing Director

IDG Books Consumer Publishing Group: Roland Elgey, Senior Vice President and Publisher; Kathleen A. Welton, Vice President and Publisher; Kevin Thornton, Acquisitions Manager; Kristin A. Cocks, Editorial Director

IDG Books Internet Publishing Group: Brenda McLaughlin, Senior Vice President and Publisher; Sofia Marchant, Online Marketing Manager

IDG Books Production for Branded Press: Debbie Stailey, Director of Production; Cindy L. Phipps, Manager of Project Coordination, Production Proofreading, and Indexing; Tony Augsburger, Manager of Prepress, Reprints, and Systems; Laura Carpenter, Production Control Manager; Shelley Lea, Supervisor of Graphics and Design; Debbie J. Gates, Production Systems Specialist; Robert Springer, Supervisor of Proofreading; Trudy Coler, Page Layout Manager; Troy Barnes, Page Layout Supervisor, Kathie Schutte, Senior Page Layout Supervisor; Michael Sullivan, Production Supervisor

Packaging and Book Design: Patty Page, Manager, Promotions Marketing

The publisher would like to give special thanks to Patrick J. McGovern, without whom this book would not have been possible.

ABOUT THE AUTHOR

Kelly Murdock has been involved in numerous Internet-related titles including, most recently, *JavaScript visual blueprints, HTML 4 Unleashed, Using FrontPage* and *FrontPage Bible*. He also works full-time managing a Web development team for Big Planet and is the creative force behind the children's Web site at www.animabets.com.

AUTHOR'S ACKNOWLEDGEMENTS

There are several individuals and organizations that I'd like to thank for their support on this project. First of all is my family. Thanks to my wife, Angela, for her encouragement and support. Thanks to Eric and Thomas for being understanding while Dad was so busy.

Thanks to Chris Murdock for his work on the Animabets characters that are featured prominently throughout the book.

Thanks to Martine Edwards for directing me to this project and a big thanks to the host of editors and project managers that oversaw this project including: Darren Meiss, Rev Mengle, Tim Borek, Dana Lesh, and many others. Thanks also to all other IDG employees who were responsible for copy editing, proofreading, indexing, designing the cover, and producing the CD.

Thanks also to all the contributors who added value to the book's CD including:

Michelle Gallina of Ulead Systems

Dan Conway and Leona Lapez of Macromedia

Zeke Tamez of Coffee Cup Software

Al Jensen of Scream Design

Albert Wiersch of CSE HTML Validator

Thank you for being such a good son. I love you.

To Thomas, 2000

HTML 4 AND XHTML™

HTML EDITOR

Hook into the Big One

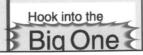

the World

1

HTML AND THE WEB

1) INTRODUCING THE WORLD WIDE WEB BROWSERS

2) INTRODUCING HTML

TABLE OF CONTENTS

3) INTRODUCING XML AND HTML

2 GETTING STARTED

4) COMPOSING AND EDITING HTML

5) BASIC HTML STRUCTURE

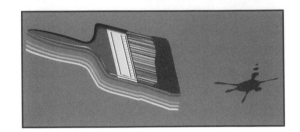

3

WORKING WITH TEXT, LISTS, AND LINKS

TABLE OF CONTENTS

8) FORMATTING TEXT

9) CREATING LISTS

4   *ADDING IMAGES*

TABLE OF CONTENTS

12) WORKING WITH GIF IMAGES

13) WORKING WITH JPEG AND PNG IMAGES

14) BUILDING IMAGE MAPS

5

15) CREATING TABLES

16) USING FRAMES

6

COLLECTING DATA WITH FORMS

17) BUILDING FORMS

18) CAPTURING FORM DATA

7 ADDING EMBEDDED OBJECTS

TABLE OF CONTENTS

8   INTERACTIVITY WITH JAVASCRIPT

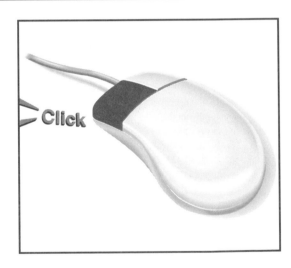

TABLE OF CONTENTS

26) WORKING WITH THE DOCUMENT OBJECT MODEL

27) JAVASCRIPT TECHNIQUES

9 BUILDING STYLE SHEETS

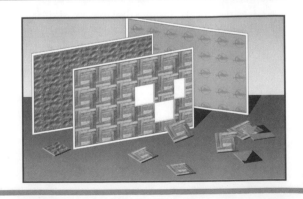

TABLE OF CONTENTS

10

USING DYNAMIC HTML

11 PUBLISHING WEB PAGES

TABLE OF CONTENTS

12

ADVANCED HTML TOPICS

SECTION 1

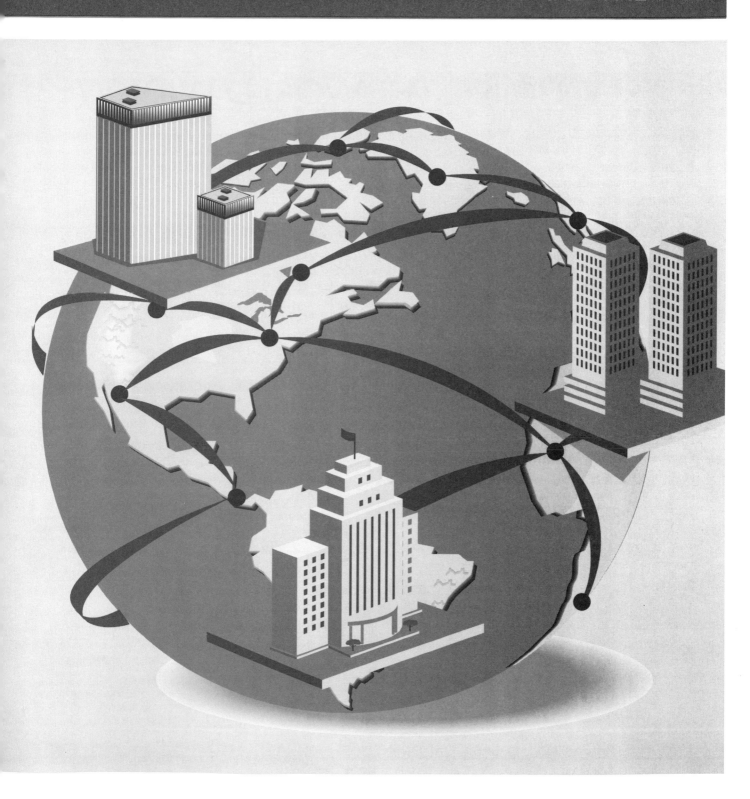

INTRODUCING THE WORLD WIDE WEB

Everywhere you look today, from billboards to television commercials, you see Internet addresses. These addresses specify the location on the Internet of pages that present information about the company or group.

Most of these addresses begin with WWW, which is an acronym for *World Wide Web*. The World Wide

Web is the part of the Internet that includes these informational pages. These pages can include text, graphics, and even multimedia elements. Other parts of the Internet include file repositories (*FTP* sites) and *e-mail*.

One key difference between these Internet information pages, often referred to as *Web pages*, and

standard brochures, is that these pages can be accessed by a connected computer from anywhere in the world. These pages can also link to other Web pages, providing an easy and efficient way to move from one page to another.

INTRODUCING THE WORLD WIDE WEB

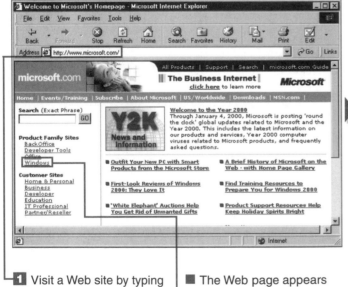

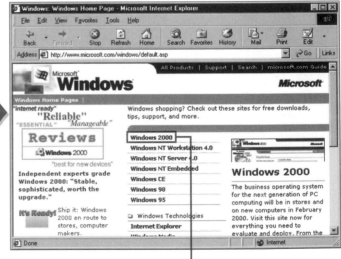

1 Visit a Web site by typing the site name (URL) and pressing Enter.

■ The Web page appears displaying text and many links to other pages.

2 Click an underlined link.

■ Another Web page appears. Pages can also include images.

3 Click another link.

Note: Links can take on different forms including text and images.

How can I find the information you need if don't know a Web address?

✔ Many Web pages such as www.yahoo.com, www.excite.com and www.alta-vista.com, offer search capabilities that let you locate Web pages with specific information by typing keywords into the search field. The subject of searching for Web pages is covered later in this chapter.

If I see a Web address in a magazine, to which Web page does it point?

✔ Every Web page on the Web can have a separate Web address. Most of these addresses are relative to the top-most Web page. The published Web address that appears within magazines typically points this top-most page. From this top level page, you can access all other pages within the Web site.

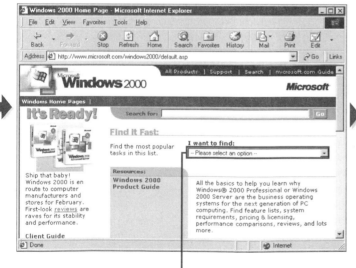

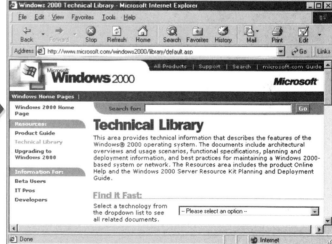

■ Another Web page appears. This page includes a drop-down list.

4 Clicking a link from a drop-down list works the same way as the other links described in this section.

■ The Web page you chose from the drop-down list appears.

CONNECT TO THE WEB

Before you can view Web pages on your computer, you need to be connected to the Internet. This connection can be made using a modem in your computer over standard phone lines.

To establish the connection, you need to dial in to a computer that

gives you access to the World Wide Web. Companies known as *Internet service providers* (ISPs) maintain these access computers.

Several large ISPs, such as America Online (AOL), are available across the country and the world, but you

may opt for one of the local ISP companies in your area.

An ISP can help you get set up and connected by providing you with the software you need and the dial-in phone numbers.

CONNECT TO THE WEB

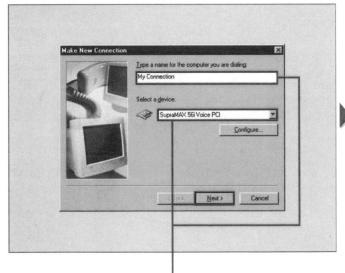

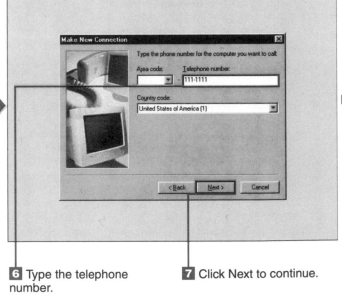

1 Click Start⇨ Programs⇨Accessories⇨ Communications⇨Dial-Up Networking.

2 Double-click the Make New Connection icon.

■ The Make New Connection Wizard begins.

3 Type a name.

4 Select the modem.

5 Click Next to continue.

6 Type the telephone number.

7 Click Next to continue.

What speed of modem do I need to connect to the Internet?

✔ You can connect to the Internet using whichever modem speed your ISP supports. Most ISPs support a broad range of modem speeds. Faster modems enable you to download and view Web pages more quickly than slower modems. Logically, larger Web pages take longer to download than smaller ones do.

What other national ISPs are available?

✔ Other national and international ISPs include Microsoft Network (MSN), AT&T WorldNet, and MCI WorldCom. This book's CD includes the setup software for DotPlanet, another national ISP. Using the CD, you can sign up and connect to the Internet.

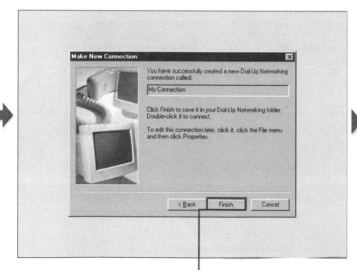

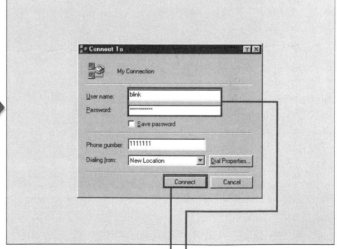

■ The final step of the Make New Connection Wizard appears.

8 Click Finish to complete the connection and create a shortcut on the desktop.

9 Double-click the new shortcut created for this connection.

■ The Connect To dialog box appears.

10 Type your username and password.

11 Click Connect.

UNDERSTANDING WEB BROWSERS

The software program that is used to view Web pages is called a *browser*. Browsers have been created to run on many types of computers and operating systems.

You can download the latest browsers from the Internet, but until you connect, you cannot download them. However, most ISPs give you a CD-ROM

containing a copy of the latest browser that you can install.

Although many different browsers exist, the two most popular Web browsers are Internet Explorer, made by Microsoft, and Navigator, made by Netscape. These two browsers are similar in function and are used by a large majority of the users.

As you look at each of these browsers, note the similar features. You can also customize the browser using the Options dialog box.

This book features the Microsoft Internet Explorer browser prevalently. Occasionally Netscape Navigator is used to demonstrate some features that do not work in Internet Explorer.

UNDERSTANDING WEB BROWSERS

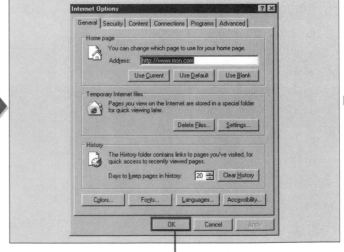

1 Open the Internet Explorer browser.

■ The home page opens.

2 Click Tools.

3 Click Internet Options.

■ The Internet Options dialog box opens. It enables you to customize Internet Explorer.

4 Click OK to close and save your changes.

What are the home pages for each browser?

✔ Each browser automatically connects with its designated home page when you launch the browser. For Microsoft Internet Explorer, the default home page is the Microsoft Network (MSN) page; for Netscape Navigator, the default home page is Netcenter. Each of these portals offers a broad range of information including stock quotes, shopping, and news headlines. "Set the Home Page," later in this chapter, shows you how to change the home page.

What can I customize on my browser?

✔ You can customize your browser in many different ways. You can set the home page, change the default colors and fonts, and set security levels. Customization can be set using the Internet Options dialog box in Internet Explorer. Clicking Tools⇨Internet Options opens the dialog box.

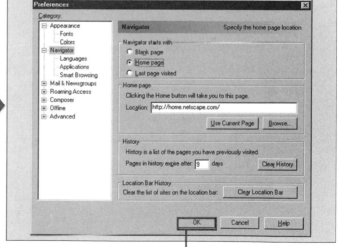

5 Open the Netscape Navigator browser.

■ The home page opens.

6 Click Edit.

7 Click Preferences.

■ The Preferences dialog box opens. It enables you to customize Navigator.

8 Click OK to close the window and save your changes.

UPGRADE MICROSOFT INTERNET EXPLORER

The CD-ROM that you receive from your ISP may not have the latest browser version, but you can use this browser to download the latest version of Internet Explorer from Microsoft's Web site.

The latest browser includes new features designed to make the Web pages more interactive and easier to use.

To see which version of Internet Explorer you are using, choose Help⇨About Internet Explorer.

To update your version to the latest version, visit www.microsoft.com/windows/ie and click the download link. The instructions walk you through the update process.

UPGRADE MICROSOFT INTERNET EXPLORER

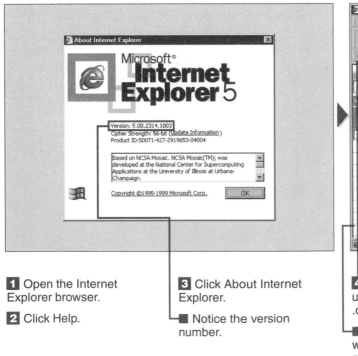

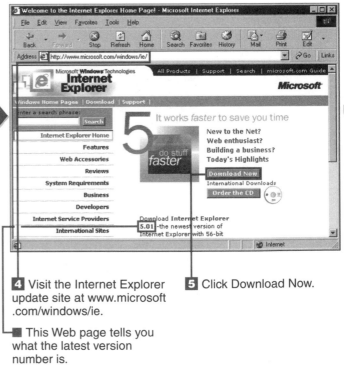

1 Open the Internet Explorer browser.

2 Click Help.

3 Click About Internet Explorer.

■ Notice the version number.

4 Visit the Internet Explorer update site at www.microsoft .com/windows/ie.

■ This Web page tells you what the latest version number is.

5 Click Download Now.

How crucial is it that you use the latest version of a browser?

✔ Most of the browser upgrades are intended to make the browser easier to use. If you plan on taking advantage of the latest Web technologies, such as online shopping, you should be sure to have the latest version. If you are not concerned with the latest Web improvements, you could view the Web with older browser versions.

How often does Microsoft create a new version of IE?

✔ When IE was first introduced, Microsoft released a new version every year or so, but as the software becomes more mature, Microsoft updates it less often. Currently, Microsoft updates IE about every two years.

Do older Web page files work on the newer browsers?

✔ Older Web pages are compliant to the HTML standard. Most older pages work on the newer browsers, but some later features do not work.

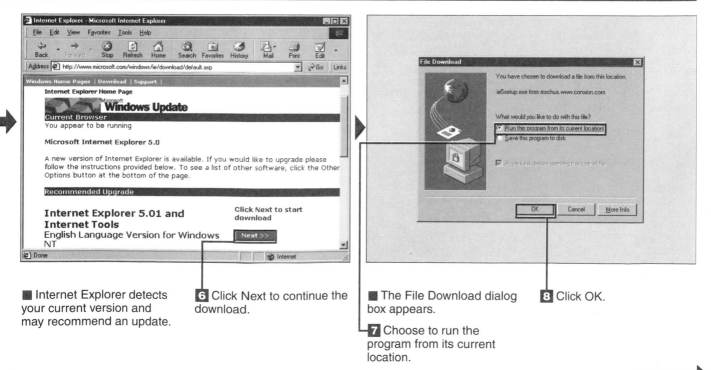

■ Internet Explorer detects your current version and may recommend an update.

6 Click Next to continue the download.

■ The File Download dialog box appears.

7 Choose to run the program from its current location.

8 Click OK.

CONTINUED

UPGRADE MICROSOFT INTERNET EXPLORER CONTINUED

The update version that you download from the Microsoft Web site is fairly small. The file you download is actually only a wizard that is used to connect to the Microsoft Web site and download the complete version.

You need to connect to the Internet before running this downloaded file.

The installation package is around 15MB and takes a considerable amount of time to download and install. The wizard is designed to download and install the software automatically, so you do not need to watch it as it downloads.

The installation includes a mail client for checking and sending e-mail, multimedia extensions for playing various multimedia elements in the browser, and the browser itself.

UPGRADE MICROSOFT INTERNET EXPLORER

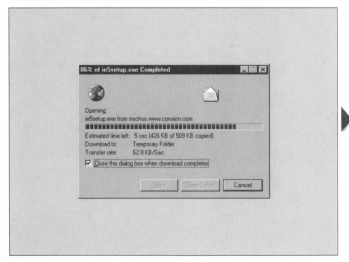

■ The update file downloads. The status bar indicates the level of completion.

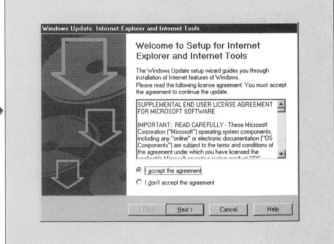

■ If you selected to run the program from its current location, the update dialog box appears.

Besides downloading the browsers, where can I get the browser software?

✔ Many CDs are available from ISPs that include the browser software. The CD for this book also includes browser software. These versions do not necessarily contain the latest browser versions.

Where can I upgrade the Netscape Navigator browser?

✔ The Netscape Navigator browser includes a menu command that starts the update process. To check your version number, select Help⇨About Communicator and to update your version of Netscape Navigator, select the Help⇨Software Updates command.

Does the entire installation need to be downloaded in one session?

✔ If the browser installation quits in the middle of the process, the downloaded files are saved to the local hard drive. The next time you connect, the installation files continue to download from the point where the connection was terminated.

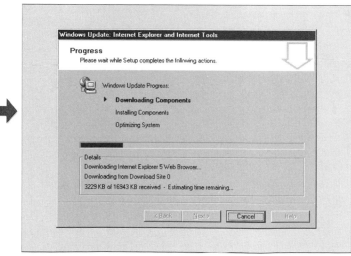

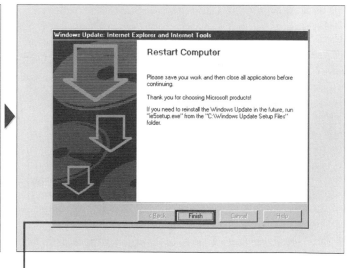

■ The Update Wizard automatically downloads and installs the needed components.

9 When the Update Wizard completes, click the Finish button to restart your computer.

LOCATE A WEB ADDRESS

After you have installed a browser, you may want to check out one of the many addresses that exist on the Web. These Web addresses can be entered into the Address field at the top of the browser window, beneath the toolbar buttons. If you type a Web address into this field and press the Enter key, the browser attempts to load the Web page found at that address.

In front of the Web address in the Address field, you see the protocol definition of http (short for Hypertext Transport Protocol). This tells the browser the technology to use to load the Web pages. If you do not enter this, the browser puts it in automatically.

The technical name for a Web address is *Universal Resource Locator* (URL). This notation is used throughout the book.

LOCATE A WEB ADDRESS

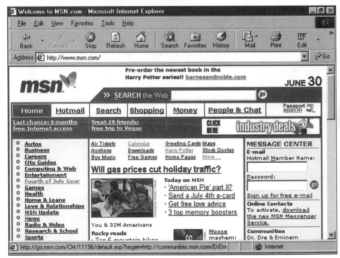

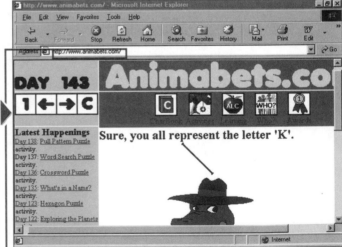

1 Open a browser.

2 Enter the URL for a Web page.

3 Press the Enter key.

■ The Web page is displayed in the browser.

What happens if I misspell the URL?

✔ If you misspell the Web address in the Address field, the browser attempts to find the Web pages at the location that you requested. If a domain exists that has the misspelling, those pages are loaded. With the vast number of pages on the Web, there is a good chance that if you misspell a Web address that the wrong pages will appear. Many companies on the Web will also obtain the misspelled domains to help users that misspell the correct domain still find their site. If a domain for the misspelling does not exist, the browser will display a "Not Found" error.

How else can I locate a Web address?

✔ Another way to access a Web page is to click a link that points to the Web page. Search engines will present Web pages as a link, and clicking a link loads the Web page.

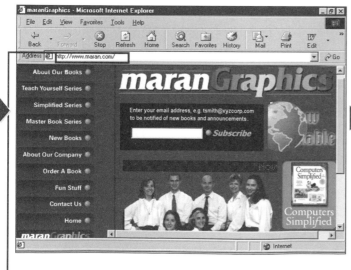

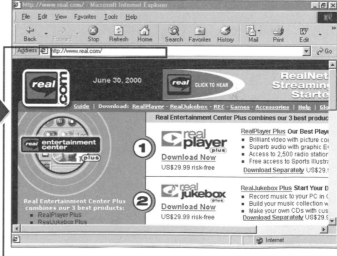

4 Enter another URL for a Web page.

5 Press the Enter key.

■ The Web page is displayed in the browser.

6 Enter another URL for a Web page.

7 Press the Enter key.

■ The new Web page is displayed in the browser.

STOP A DOWNLOAD

When you request a Web page by typing in its URL, the browser contacts the server that contains the page and automatically begins loading each piece of the Web page including text, graphics, and any other elements.

As you move about the Web, especially if you are using a slower modem, you likely will not always want to wait for the current Web page to load in its entirety.

You can stop the process of loading a Web page by clicking the Stop button located on the browser's

toolbar. Another way to stop the page download is to press the Esc key.

When the Stop button is clicked, the content that has already been downloaded does not disappear, but any additional content is stopped from downloading.

STOP A DOWNLOAD

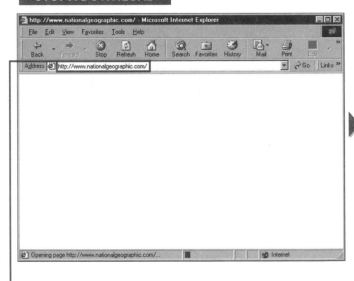

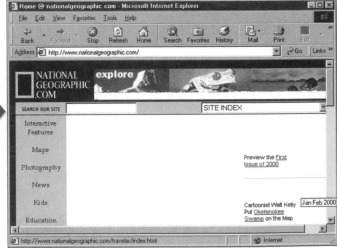

1 Enter a Web site in the Address bar.

2 Press the Enter key.

■ The blue progress bar on the status bar of the browser shows how much of the Web page has downloaded.

■ As the Web page continues to download, more and more images appear.

How can I tell when the Web page is completely loaded?

✔ In the upper-right corner of the browser is an icon with the Windows logo on it. This icon becomes animated when any download activity is occurring. When the page has finished downloading, this icon animation stops. Also, when the browser has finished the current download piece, such as a graphic, the word *Done* appears on the browser status bar. The status bar appears at the bottom of the browser window. If the status bar is not visible, you can make it visible by clicking View➪Status Bar.

Which pieces of content download first?

✔ Typically, text appears first as a page is downloaded, and images and multimedia elements then appear more slowly. Text does not require much file space and can be downloaded very quickly. Images are considerably larger and take longer to download depending on their size.

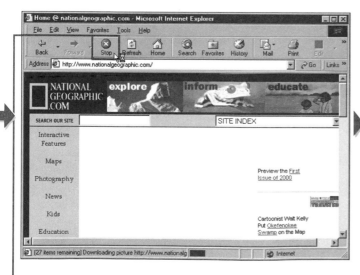

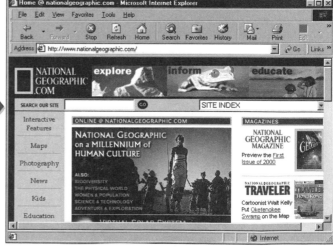

3 Click the Stop button on the browser toolbar.

■ The page download stops and several images are missing.

4 Load the page again until the entire page is loaded.

■ Now all the images are visible.

REFRESH A PAGE

Many Web pages include dynamic content, such as stock quotes. Every time you visit these sites, different information is presented. The browser provides an easy way for you to request the current page again.

At any time, you can reload the current page using the Refresh button. This button causes the current page to be reloaded from the server. This action updates the Web page content with the latest information.

When the Refresh button is clicked, the current Web page does not disappear, but the server where the Web pages are located is contacted and the Web pages are downloaded once again. If the page contains some dynamic content, that content is updated automatically.

REFRESH A PAGE

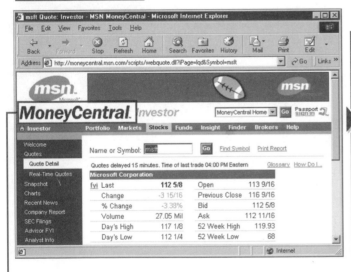

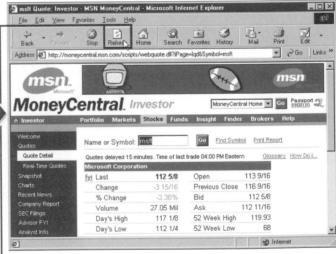

1 Visit a Web site with dynamic content such as a site that displays stock quotes.

■ The page displayed here is MoneyCentral on the MSN site.

2 Click the Refresh button on the top toolbar.

Can I make the browser reload all elements of a Web page including the graphics?

✔ The Refresh button typically only reloads the text of the page and not the graphics, because the graphics take much longer to download. There is a way to force the graphics of a Web page to be downloaded also and that is to hold down the Shift key while clicking the Refresh button.

Can I make the toolbar buttons disappear?

✔ You can make the toolbar buttons at the top of the browser disappear if you select View⇨Toolbars⇨Standard Buttons. You can also right-click any of the buttons and select the Standard Buttons option in the pop-up menu. These commands are toggles that will turn the buttons on or off. You can also make the Address bar and Links bar disappear.

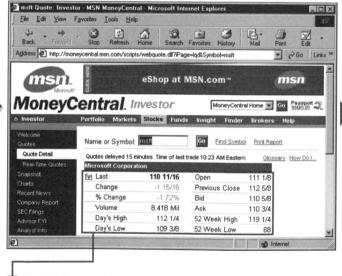

■ The Web page is reloaded with new information.

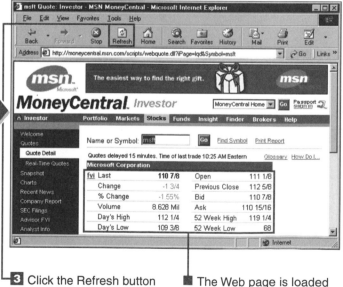

3 Click the Refresh button again.

■ The Web page is loaded again and new information is displayed.

USING BACK AND FORWARD BUTTONS

As you travel about the Web moving from one link to another, the browser remembers each page that you have visited and enables you to move backwards through the history of pages you have visited.

All the pages you visit are kept in a list called the *history*. Clicking the

Back button moves you sequentially through the history one page at a time. After you've used the Back button, the Forward button becomes active. This button enables you to move forward through the history list.

Click the small downward-pointing arrow to the right of the Back or

Forward buttons to see the next several pages in the history list. You can select any of these pages to load that page, which lets you jump to any page that exists in the history list.

USING BACK AND FORWARD BUTTONS

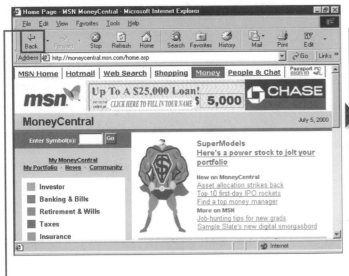

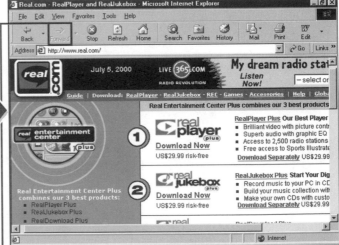

1 Click the Back button in the browser toolbar.

■ The previous page is displayed.

2 Click the Forward button to return to the former page again.

Can I see a more detailed history list?

✔ If you click the History button, a complete history list for the day and previous weeks is displayed in a sidebar on the left side of the screen. Navigating through these menu options, you can locate the exact page that you visited several days or weeks ago. To close the history list, click the X button in the upper-right-hand corner of the sidebar.

Can I search through the history list?

✔ When the History sidebar is open, you can click the Search button at the top of the sidebar to display a Search box where you can enter a keyword to find. Clicking the Search Now button searches the pages in the history for the keyword that was entered. All matches are displayed in the sidebar. Selecting a page in the sidebar makes that Web page appear in the browser.

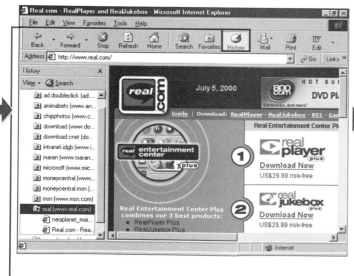

3 Click the History button on the browser toolbar.

■ The History sidebar is shown to the left of the browser.

4 Click a site listed in the History sidebar.

■ The site opens.

SET THE HOME PAGE

When you first install a browser, the default home page is set to the default for the browser, but you can change your home page to any page you'd like using the Internet Options dialog box.

The toolbar at the top of the browser also includes a Home button. Clicking this button automatically loads your designated home page. This is useful if you ever want to quickly return to a familiar page. The home page is loaded when you first open the browser.

To open the Internet Options page in Internet Explorer, select Tools⇨Internet Options. Enter the URL of your desirewd home page in the Address field at the top of the General panel.

The Internet Option page also includes a button called Use Current to make the current Web page the home page.

SET THE HOME PAGE

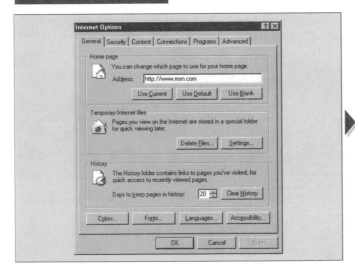

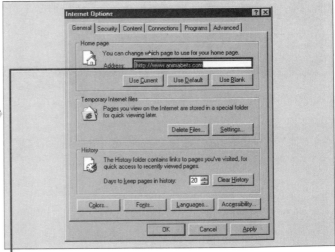

1 In the Internet Explorer window, click Tools.

2 Click Internet Options.

■ The Internet Options dialog box opens.

3 Enter a different URL in the Address field.

How do I set a specific home page if I do not know the URL?

✔ If you do not know the URL for a site that you want to make your home page, simply locate the site in your browser, open the Internet Options dialog box, and then click the Use Current button below the Address field. This loads the current URL into the Address field and makes the loaded page your new home page.

What other home pages can I use?

✔ The Internet Options dialog box also includes a button labeled Use Default. This button will set the home page to Internet Explorer's default home page, www.msn.com. There is also a button labeled Use Blank that changes the home page to a blank page.

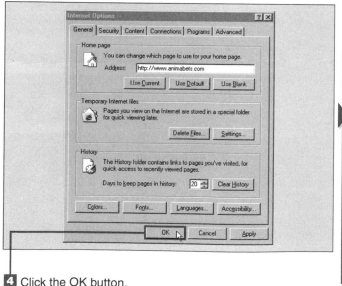

4 Click the OK button.

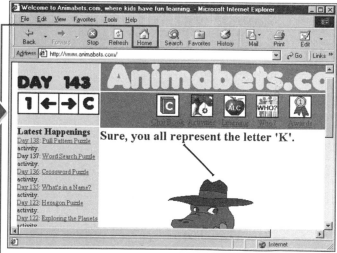

5 Click the Home button on the browser toolbar.

■ The new designated home page is loaded.

SEARCH THE WEB

If you are new to the Web, finding the Web pages that you want to look at can be difficult. Luckily, many different Web page search sites, also known as *search engines,* can help you find just what you are looking for.

Internet Explorer includes one of these search engines within its

interface. Clicking the Search button opens a Search sidebar to the left of the browser. This sidebar includes a search field where you can type in the keywords to search for. Pressing the Search button in the sidebar begins the search.

A listing of potential matches displays in the sidebar as links. Clicking any of these links takes you directly to that page. The links are all listed in order with the most likely matches coming first.

SEARCH THE WEB

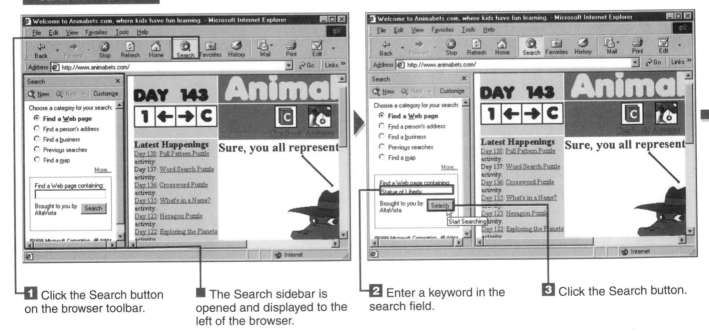

1 Click the Search button on the browser toolbar.

■ The Search sidebar is opened and displayed to the left of the browser.

2 Enter a keyword in the search field.

3 Click the Search button.

Is there an easier way to search for Web sites?

✔ Another way to search for Web sites is to type the search keywords directly in the Address field and press the Enter key. Doing this performs the search and returns the results in the Search sidebar.

Are there other search sites?

✔ The Web is full of indexed sites and sites that make it easy to find specific Web pages. Some of the more popular such sites are www.yahoo.com, www.excite.com, and www.lycos.com.

Are there techniques for narrowing the search?

✔ It can be difficult to locate the exact Web page that you want. Search engines offer features that help you to narrow the search, such as using quotes or searching within a search list. See the various search engine Web sites for more information on their searching features.

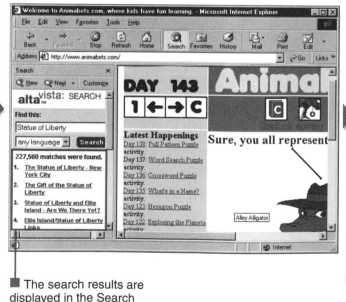

■ The search results are displayed in the Search sidebar.

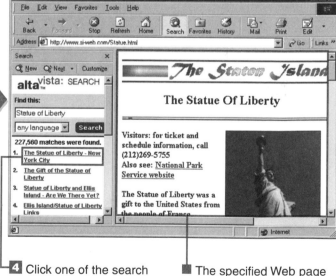

4 Click one of the search result links.

■ The specified Web page loads.

USING FAVORITES AND BOOKMARKS

If you find a Web page that you want to remember, you could have the browser store this page in its list of favorites. You can then easily return to that Web page by opening the list and clicking the selection.

These lists of favorites are contained within the Favorites sidebar that is opened when the Favorites button is clicked. Netscape Navigator uses a similar metaphor, but refers to them as bookmarks.

There is also a Favorites menu in Internet Explorer that can be used to add Web pages to the favorites list and to access your favorite Web pages. To add a Web page to the list of favorites, choose Favorites⇨Add to Favorites.

The Favorites⇨Organize Favorites command opens the Organize Favorites dialog box where you can create, move, rename, and delete folders.

USING FAVORITES AND BOOKMARKS

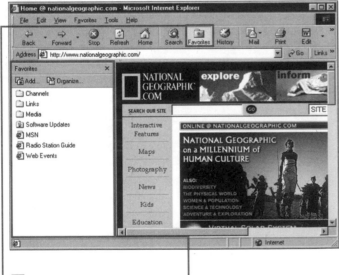

1 Click the Favorites button to open the Favorites sidebar.

■ The Favorites list is displayed in the sidebar.

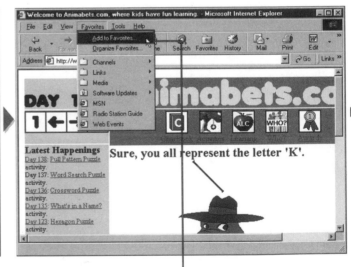

2 Locate a Web site that you wish to add to your Favorites list.

3 Click Favorites.

4 Click Add to Favorites.

Can I organize your favorites list using just the Favorites sidebar?

✔ You can organize your favorites list using the Favorites sidebar if you drag and drop the site icons. You can also create, cut, copy, paste, rename, and delete folders by right-clicking the folder icon. This presents a pop-up menu of options. You can also create folders that can be used to organize your favorite links.

How do I add the current Web page to a new folder in the favorites menu?

✔ If you locate a Web page that you want to add to your favorites list in a new folder, select Favorites⇨Add to Favorites in Internet Explorer. This command box opens the Add Favorite dialog box, whewre you can create a new folder by clicking the New Folder button. After naming the folder, click OK to add the current Web page to this folder.

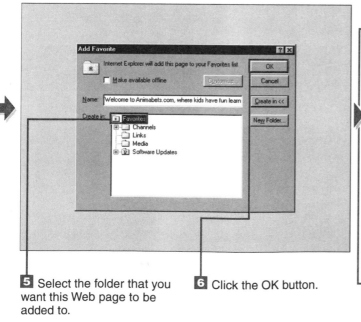

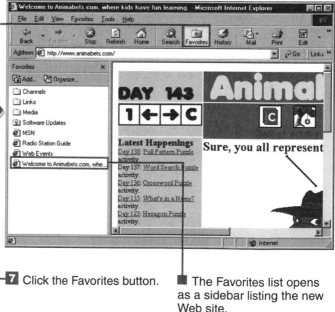

5 Select the folder that you want this Web page to be added to.

6 Click the OK button.

7 Click the Favorites button.

■ The Favorites list opens as a sidebar listing the new Web site.

PRINT A WEB PAGE

When a Web page is being viewed in a browser, you can send the page to the printer to create a hard copy of the Web page. The browser interface is not printed, but the contents of the page are.

You can print the current page by clicking the Print button on the

toolbar or by selecting File⇨Print. This opens the Print dialog box, where you can select the printer to use, the print range, and the number of copies.

If the site is divided into frames, the Print dialog box offers the options to print all frames, only the

selected frame, or each frame individually.

Internet Explorer also includes a Page Setup dialog box, which can be accessed by selecting File⇨Page Setup. This dialog box lets you select the paper size, header and footer, margin, and orientation.

PRINT A WEB PAGE

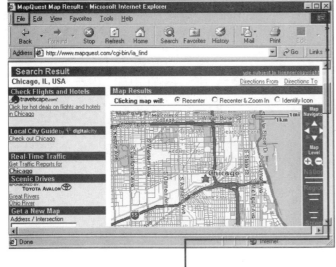

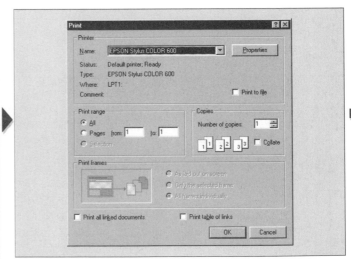

1 Open a page that you'd like to send to the printer.

2 Click File.

3 Click Print.

■ The Print dialog box opens.

Even though a Web page is displayed in color, can I set it to print in black and white?

✔ Clicking the Properties button in the Print dialog box opens the Properties dialog box specific to the selected printer. Using these options, you can choose to print in black and white.

Is there an option to change the page dimensions?

✔ Selecting File⇨Page Setup, you can access the Page Setup dialog box. Its options enable you to specify the paper size, the margins, the orientation and the header and footer of the page.

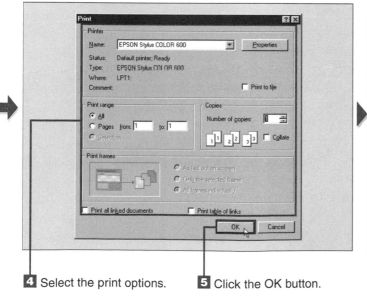

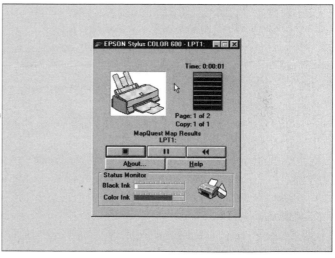

4 Select the print options.

5 Click the OK button.

■ The Web page is sent to the printer.

OPEN A LOCAL PAGE

If a Web page is saved to your local computer, you can view those pages in a browser by selecting File⇨Open.

This command calls up the Open dialog box, where you can browse to the file that you wish to open in the browser.

The big advantage of this is that you don't need to be connected to the Internet to view the page, which is especially helpful when creating new Web pages. You get a chance to view the Web pages as you work on them. However, any external links in the local Web page will not work unless you are

connected to the Internet, but you can test the links to other locally saved pages.

Using this book's CD, you can view all the examples created in this book in a browser without being connected to the Internet.

OPEN A LOCAL PAGE

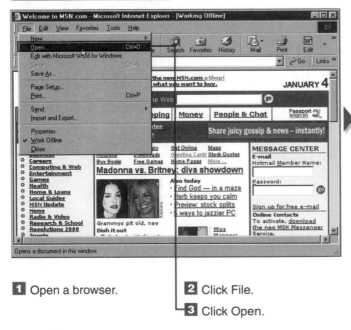

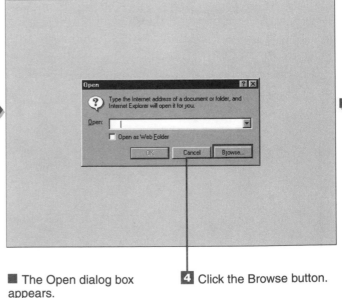

1 Open a browser.

2 Click File.

3 Click Open.

■ The Open dialog box appears.

4 Click the Browse button.

If there an easier way to open local Web pages in the browser?

✔ An easier way to open local Web pages within the browser is to drag them from Windows Explorer and drop them on the browser. If a local Web file or image is dropped anywhere on the browser, that element loads within the browser.

Can Web pages be downloaded from the Internet for viewing after I have disconnected?

✔ Using the File⇨Save As command, you can save a Web page to your local hard drive. When you save a Web page, all the image files are downloaded and saved along with the HTML file. To view the Web page in the local browser, you need to open the file with the .html extension. The Save As Type option lets you select to download just the HTML file or the complete Web page.

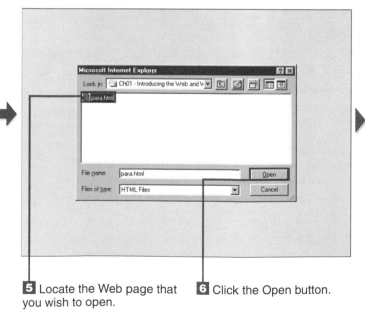

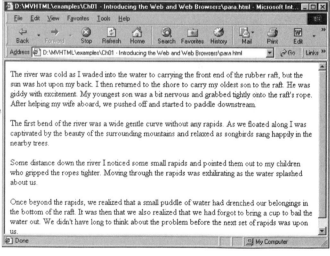

5 Locate the Web page that you wish to open.

6 Click the Open button.

■ The local Web page is opened within the browser.

VIEW HTML SOURCE

The remainder of this book focuses on the creating of HTML files that can be viewed in a browser. The browser offers a way to view the HTML code used to create the Web page. This provides a useful way to learn how different pages are created.

Selecting View⇨Source opens a separate window that displays the HTML code used to create the Web page. When this command is used, the source is opened by default into the Windows Notepad application. Using this application, you can edit and save the file.

As you learn and use HTML, the Web itself is a great source of knowledge. You can learn many new and interesting techniques by finding a site that is using the trick you want to learn and viewing the source to see how they accomplished it.

VIEW HTML SOURCE

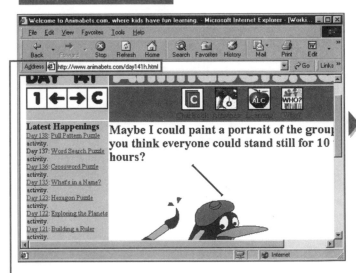

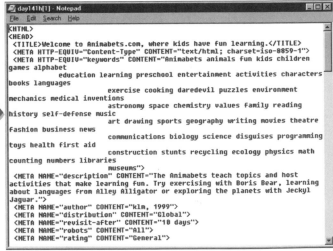

1 Open a Web page in a browser.

2 Click View.

3 Click Source.

■ A separate window is opened that displays the HTML code used to create the Web page.

Can I copy and paste sections of code from other Web pages into your own Web pages?

✔ If you want to work with HTML code that you've found on the Web using the View⇨Source command, you can save a copy of it to your local computer, or you can cut and paste sections of it into your own Web pages. However, code that is taken off the Web should be modified. Keep in mind that Web pages on the Internet are copyrighted by their respective owners.

How can I edit the Web page file?

✔ Internet Explorer includes a command that enables you to edit the source file for a Web page. This command is File⇨Edit in Notepad. If you select the Programs tab in the Internet Options dialog box, you can change the default editing program. The default editing options include Notepad and FrontPage Editor, which is a visual editing tool.

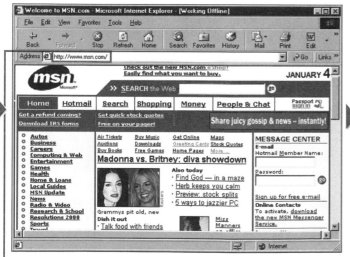

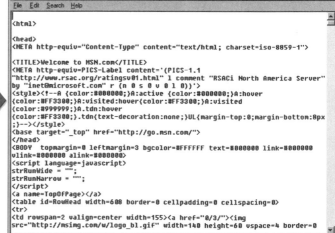

4 Open another Web page in the browser.

5 Click View.

6 Click Source.

■ A separate window is opened that displays the HTML code used to create the Web page.

HTML—THE LANGUAGE OF THE WEB

When you surf the Web, you can see a lot of variety in the Web pages. All these pages have one thing in common, and that is the language that was used to produce them. This language is Hypertext Markup Language, or HTML.

HTML Web pages can include many different elements. Some of the HTML elements of a Web page are described here.

Text and Lists

The easiest and most versatile communication medium that Web pages can use is text. Since Guttenberg developed the printing press, text has been an efficient means of spreading thoughts and ideas. Web pages continue this tradition in the electronic frontier.

In HTML, text can display in a browser without the cost of a traditional printer. Web page text can also be formatted in a variety of ways ranging from standard bold and italics to numerous colors and visual effects, such as flashing.

Lists organize textual information in a browser. HTML supports several different list types, including bulleted lists and numbered lists. Text and list elements, along with all the text formatting options, are covered in Chapters 7, 8, and 9.

Hyperlinks

Hyperlinks tie together different Web pages through a series of clicks. Each click on a link opens a new page in the browser. Hyperlinks can be linked to pages within a single site or to any site on the Web. Linking several Web pages together with hyperlinks provides easy navigation among Web pages. Using hyperlinks is like traditional footnotes taken to the next level.

Standard text can be made into hyperlinks. These hyperlinks appear different from the rest of the text. Images can also be made into hyperlinks. Chapter 10 introduces you to creating hyperlinks.

Images

Adding images to a book by using traditional printing methods greatly increases the complexity and cost of the project. Today, with inexpensive scanners and a plethora of software graphic tools, adding images to a Web page is easy.

Images on a Web page make the page more interesting. Images can be used in a number of different ways to add variety and interest to the Web page. Part IV covers working with images and the various image formats.

Tables

HTML tables provide an easy way to organize data using rows and columns. These tables include a variety of options for controlling how the table is formatted. For example, you can control the alignment of the text within each individual table cell.

Tables are also frequently used to position objects on the Web page. Using HTML tables, you can precisely set the dimensions of each cell. Chapter 15 shows how tables are built.

Frames

HTML frames are an alternative way of displaying several Web pages in a browser at the same time. This is done by splitting the browser window into several different frames. Each frame can then hold a separate Web page.

Frames are useful for creating sidebar navigation templates that allow the user to click in one frame and update content in a separate frame. They are also helpful for adding a header or footer to the Web page. Chapter 16 covers frames.

CONTINUED

HTML—THE LANGUAGE OF THE WEB
CONTINUED

HTML includes support for several dynamic interactive elements, including those listed in this section.

Forms

Forms enable users to enter information into a Web page.
Form elements can include text fields, buttons, drop-down lists, and radio and checkbox buttons. These elements let you create

customized forms for user input. This captured information can then be e-mailed to the Webmaster or stored in a database. Part VI discusses the building and use of forms.

Multimedia

Although multimedia is not native to HTML Web pages, browsers will support sound, music, video, and other interactive multimedia elements by using plug-in modules. Adding

multimedia to a Web page enables you to include elements not possible in printed books. Part VII covers adding various multimedia elements to a Web page.

Java Applets

Java applets can be embedded within Web pages to extend their functionality and usefulness. *Applets* are programs written using the Java language. These programs can be sophisticated pieces of software that help you calculate your taxes or explore advanced mathematical functions. See Chapter 24 for more information on Java applets.

Style Sheets

Style sheets enable you to build consistent, transportable, and well-defined style templates. These templates can be linked to several different Web pages, making it easy to maintain and change the look and feel of all the Web pages within a site. Part IX covers the use of style sheets.

JavaScript

JavaScript is a scripting language that cohabitates with HTML inside Web pages. Using JavaScript, you can have a Web page check its contents, perform simple calculations, and interact with a user. Part VIII presents JavaScript in detail.

Dynamic HTML

Dynamic HTML provides a way to move and interact with various HTML elements, making Web pages come alive. Although there are inconsistencies between the various browsers in the way that Dynamic HTML is implemented, with help from JavaScript, it can be used to create some interesting presentations. See Part X for more on using Dynamic HTML.

UNDERSTANDING THE HTML SPECIFICATION

The World Wide Web Consortium (W3C) governs the official HTML specification. The official specification can be found at www.w3c.org.

This organization has also developed many new and upcoming Web specifications including style sheets, XHTML, and XML. The W3C also produces software products like the Amaya browser and the Jigsaw Web server to test these specifications.

All of the specifications are developed by committees. These committees follow a standard adoption process that allows members, and eventually the general public, to comment on the proposed specification. As the specification moves through this process, it is given a version number. The most current version of the HTML specification is 4.01.

The W3C is essential to the Web because it ensures that consistent syntax is used to develop Web pages. Without this organization, each browser producers would create commands that would only work within their own browsers.

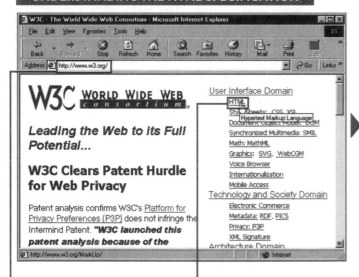

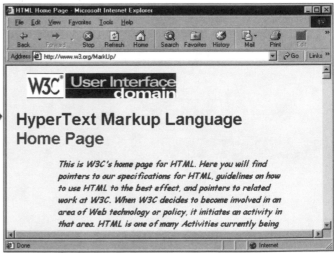

1 Open a Web page for the World Wide Web Consortium, at www.w3c.org, in a browser.

2 Click the link to the HTML specification.

■ The HTML home page is displayed.

How close do the browsers adhere to the HTML specification?

✔ The official specification is the accepted standard, but Netscape and Microsoft, as the makers of the browsers, lag the official specification somewhat. In the past, they have also taken the liberty to include some proprietary features that only work within their browsers. These proprietary tags have for the most part been unused by the majority of Web page users. Although differences between the official specification and the browsers exist, they are becoming closer as time progresses.

How can you obtain the software that the W3C produces?

✔ All of the software that the W3C produces is available for download from their Web site. Many of these products support features that have not been implemented in the more popular browsers.

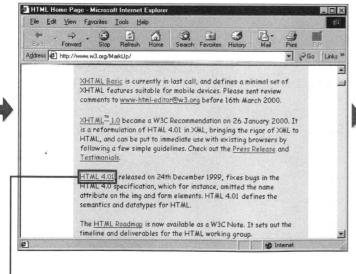

3 Scroll down the page and click the HTML 4.01 link.

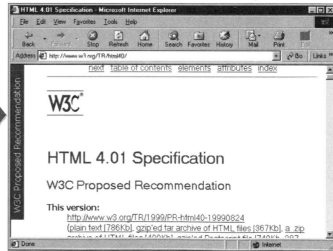

■ This is the official HTML 4.01 Specification.

USING HTML TAG SETS

The way to format text in HTML is with *tags*. The tags themselves are text, but browsers detect them because they are surrounded with the less than (<) and greater than (>) symbols. There should be no spaces between these symbols and the tag name.

HTML tags usually come in pairs with an opening tag and a closing tag. The text appearing between the tags affect these two tags. The closing tag is different from the opening tag because it includes a slash symbol (/) after the opening less than symbol (<). For example,

the tag for marking text as bold is the <b> tag, so surrounding the text with opening and closing <b> tags makes the text within these tags appear bold in the browser. In HTML code, it would appear like this: <b>this text is bold</b>.

1 Create a new file in Notepad.

2 Type a simple line of text.

3 Save the file as first.html.

4 Open the file first.html in a browser.

■ The line of text displays in the browser.

What if there is no text between the tags?

✔ If there is no text between the tags, then there is nothing to format, so no formatting will appear. Some tags, especially tags without a closing tag like the image (`<img/>`) tag, do not need any text between them.

Can you apply several sets of tags to the same line of text?

✔ Several different tags can affect a single line of text, but you should always be careful not to overlap tag pairs. For example, a line of text that is surrounded by both `<b>` and `<i>` tags appears both bold and italicized.

What happens if you overlap sets of tags?

✔ If two sets of HTML tags are overlapped, only the first tag will be recognized. You should look for this type of error if your text isn't being displayed properly.

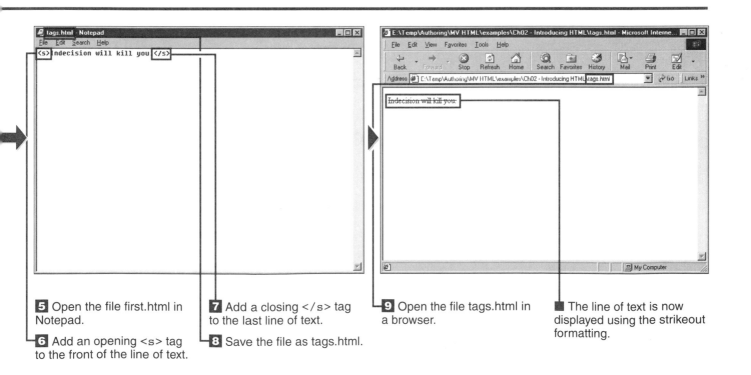

5 Open the file first.html in Notepad.

6 Add an opening `<s>` tag to the front of the line of text.

7 Add a closing `</s>` tag to the last line of text.

8 Save the file as tags.html.

9 Open the file tags.html in a browser.

■ The line of text is now displayed using the strikeout formatting.

USING SINGLE HTML TAGS

Some HTML tags do not require a closing tag. These tags are formatted a little differently. They include the slash symbol (/) after the tag name and before the greater-than symbol (>).

An example of this tag type is the image tag, which is represented as <img/>. The image tag only specifies the image name and where the image to display is located; therefore, the tag does not require any text, so no ending tag is needed.

Other single tag elements include the line break tag (<br/>), the horizontal rule tag (<hr/>), the frame tag (<frame/>), the meta data tag (<meta/>), and the form element tag (<input/>).

If a single HTML tag is added to the middle of a line of text, the element represented by the single tag appears between the lines of text.

USING SINGLE HTML TAGS

```
single.html - Notepad
File  Edit  Search  Help
<s>Indecision will kill you.</s>
<hr/>
```

```
D:\MVHTML\examples\Ch02 - Introducing HTML\single.html - Microsoft Internet Explorer
File  Edit  View  Favorites  Tools  Help
Back  Forward  Stop  Refresh  Home  Search  Favorites  History  Mail  Print  Edit
Address  D:\MVHTML\examples\Ch02 - Introducing HTML\single.html

Indecision will kill you.
_____

Done                                     My Computer
```

1 Open the tags.html file (created in the section, "Using HTML Tag Sets") in Notepad.

2 Type a single HTML tag below the line of text, such as **<hr/>**.

3 Save the file with a new name.

4 Open the file in a browser.

■ A horizontal rule appears under the line of text.

Do some tags allow the closing tag to be optional?

✔ Several tags make the closing tag optional, such as the tags for defining table rows and cells, `<tr>` and `<td>`. For these tags, the browser is smart enough to know that the row ends where the next one starts. However, it is a good idea to always include the closing tag for clarity and to make the document well-formed.

Besides table rows and cells, which other tags have an optional closing tag?

✔ The closing paragraph tag (`</p>`) is also optional. A new paragraph automatically marks the end of the previous paragraph. The closing tag for individual list elements (`</dt>`,`</dd>`, and `</li>`) are also optional. For tables, cell headings (`</th>`) and table sections (`</thead>`, `</tbody>`, and `</tfoot>`) are also optional.

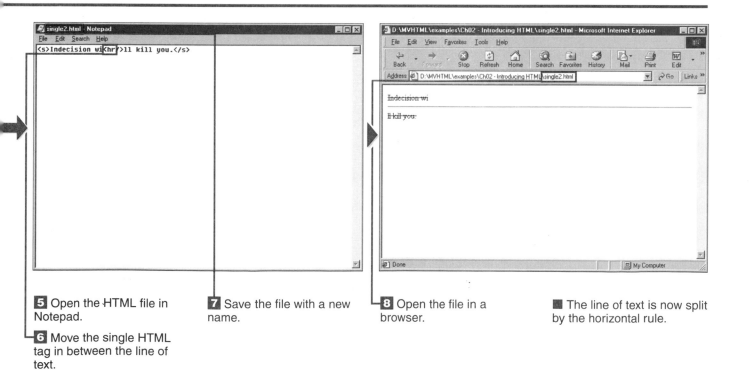

5 Open the HTML file in Notepad.

6 Move the single HTML tag in between the line of text.

7 Save the file with a new name.

8 Open the file in a browser.

■ The line of text is now split by the horizontal rule.

USING HTML ATTRIBUTES

For added settings, tags can include attributes. These attributes are positioned within the brackets of the opening tag and are usually set to a value using the equal sign (=). The value should also be included in quotes. For example, `<p align="center">` causes the text that follows to be centered in the browser window.

For single HTML tags, the attributes come between the end of the tag name and the slash symbol. For example, `</img href="image.gif">`.

Some tags have multiple attributes. Multiple attributes can be included within a tag by separating them with a single space. For example, `</hr align="center"`

`width="20"`. Other tags have no attributes. Some attributes, such as `nowrap`, don't accept a value.

Each attribute has a default value that is used if the attribute is not included with the tag. For example, the default `align` attribute value is `left`.

USING HTML ATTRIBUTES

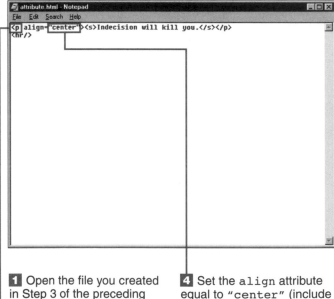

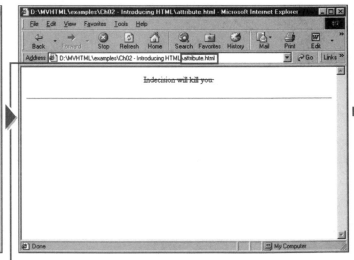

1 Open the file you created in Step 3 of the preceding section in Notepad.

2 Type **<p>**.

3 Between the letter p and the >, type a space and **align**.

4 Set the `align` attribute equal to "center" (include the quotation marks).

5 Add a closing `</p>` tag to the end of the line.

6 Save the file.

7 Open the file in a browser.

■ The line of text is now centered in the browser window.

Can attribute values be set to anything or are there specific values that they accept?

✔ Some attribute values can be set to only predefined values. For example, the `align` attribute can only be set to `left`, `right`, `center`, or `justify`. Other attributes, such as `width`, can accept any numerical value that represents the number of pixels to use for the width of the horizontal rule.

Where can I find out which attributes and values can be used with each tag?

✔ Throughout this book, all the attributes used with a tag and its valid values are mentioned. Also, reference indexes list all the tags, attributes, and values. For a definitive list, check the actual HTML specification found on the W3C's site at www.w3c.org.

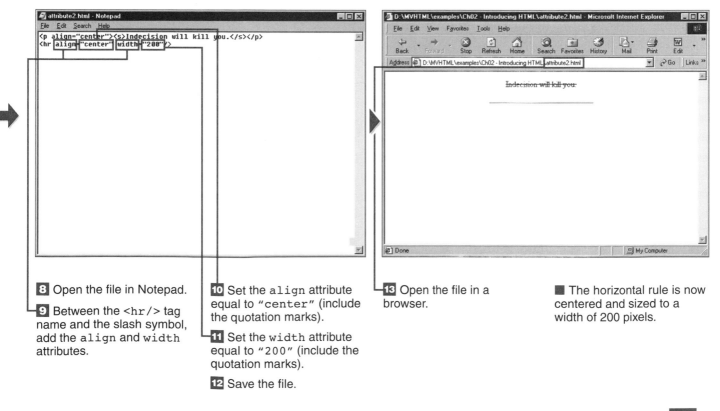

8 Open the file in Notepad.

9 Between the `<hr/>` tag name and the slash symbol, add the `align` and `width` attributes.

10 Set the `align` attribute equal to `"center"` (include the quotation marks).

11 Set the `width` attribute equal to `"200"` (include the quotation marks).

12 Save the file.

13 Open the file in a browser.

■ The horizontal rule is now centered and sized to a width of 200 pixels.

USING ENTITIES

Many symbols are frequently published that do not appear on the standard English keyboard, such as the cent and copyright symbols. In HTML, these are called *character entities*. Character entity symbols also include language diacritical marks and mathematical symbols.

HTML enables you to include these symbols in a Web page by typing an ampersand symbol (&), followed by a keyword or number, and then a semicolon (;). When the browser sees this character entity value, it replaces it with the appropriate symbol.

For example, to have a browser display the copyright symbol (©), you need to type **©** or **©** in an HTML file.

For a complete view of the available character entities, load the EntitiesChart.html file in a browser. This Web page interactively displays all the supported character entities.

USING ENTITIES

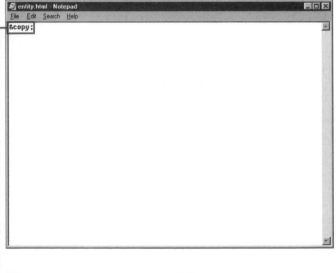

1 Open a new file in Notepad.

2 Type the character entity value for the copyright symbol (**©**).

3 Save the file as an HTML file.

4 Open the file in a browser.

■ The copyright symbol is displayed.

Why are there both numerical and named character entity values?

✔ The numerical values are taken from the ASCII values for the various characters, but these can be difficult to remember, so the named character entity values were created to make it easier for Web page authors to use. It is more likely that numerical values will be visible than named values. Numerical values are different than the Unicode symbol values for many characters.

Why does the EntitiesChart.html file not display many of the character entities as boxes?

✔ Many of the character entities cannot be displayed when the operating system that the browser is running on does not support the characters. These characters are displayed as boxes.

If the user's operating system does not support the needed character, how can the symbol be represented?

✔ If their operating system does not support a particular character, you can display the character as an image.

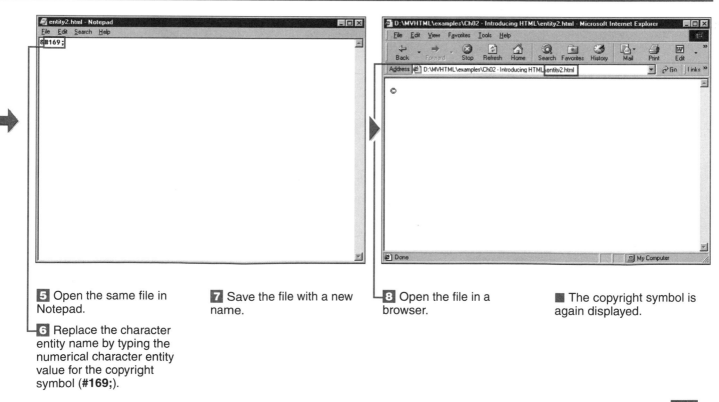

5 Open the same file in Notepad.

6 Replace the character entity name by typing the numerical character entity value for the copyright symbol (**#169;**).

7 Save the file with a new name.

8 Open the file in a browser.

■ The copyright symbol is again displayed.

FIND ENTITY VALUES

Named entity values make it easier to remember the code for displaying a specific symbol, but even they can be difficult to remember if they are not used frequently.

Using JavaScript, you can create a simple application that displays all the symbols and their entity

values. This book's CD-ROM contains a file that does this, called EntitiesChart.html. Using this file makes it easy to visually select the symbol you need.

The file includes a chart that displays all the character entities listed as part of the HTML 4.01 specification. The file uses

JavaScript commands to display the keyword and numerical values as the mouse is moved over the top of the various entities.

Keep in mind also that not every symbol is available on every system. Many of the symbols on my particular system are displayed as simple boxes.

FIND ENTITY VALUES

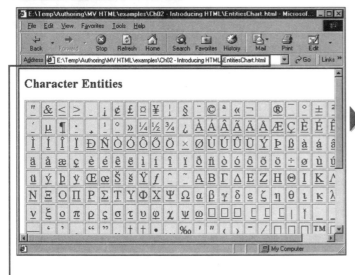

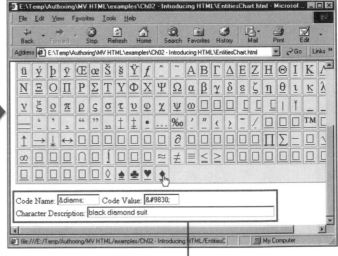

1 Open the EntitiesChart.html file in a browser. You can find this file on the book's CD-ROM with the content for this chapter.

■ All the character entities are displayed in a chart.

2 Scroll to the bottom of the chart.

■ The text fields show the code name and value and a description of the entity on which the mouse is positioned.

The characters display differently in the various browsers. Why do the browsers display only some of the character entities?

🖝 The browsers rely on the system character mappings to display the character entities. If the system does not include the correct configuration, some character entities cannot be displayed.

How can I know what each character is?

🖝 The chart includes a description field that lists a description of the selected character. These descriptions can help identify the various symbols.

What if all the characters look unfamiliar?

🖝 The characters are used to represent different pronunciations in various languages. They also include the uppercase and lowercase Greek alphabets that are frequently used to represent mathematical equations. If you do not recognize the symbol, chances are you do not need to use it.

Which character entities are used most often?

🖝 The nonbreaking space character (nbsp;) is used frequently to separate elements. Most other characters are specialized.

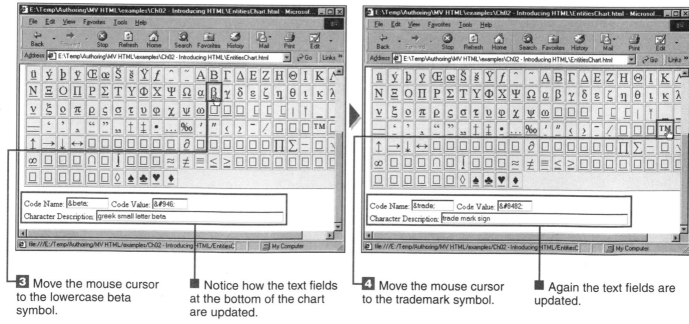

3 Move the mouse cursor to the lowercase beta symbol.

■ Notice how the text fields at the bottom of the chart are updated.

4 Move the mouse cursor to the trademark symbol.

■ Again the text fields are updated.

UNDERSTANDING XML AND XHTML

XML stands for *Extensible Markup Language*. It can be used to extend HTML to meet specific needs. Many Web page creators need support for tags that tell more about the text they mark.

For example, to display a person's name and address in a Web page, you simply need to include the text within an HTML file and maybe surround it with a paragraph tag (<p>). This displays the text in a browser, but provides no information about what kind of text is being displayed. For this example, XML could extend HTML by defining <fname>, <lname>, <street>, <city>, <state>, and <zipcode> tags. These tags would then give the data some meaning. This intelligent data could then easily be pulled into a database or moved between different applications.

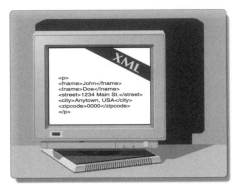

The tags and attributes and their meanings are defined in a separate document called a *Document Type Definition,* or DTD for short. The current Web browsers compare HTML documents by default against the HTML 4 DTD. Using the <!doctype> tag, you can specify which DTD to use. Chapter 5 explains the <!doctype> tag in more detail.

Other available DTDs are discussed in the next section, "Understanding the XHTML DTDs." If the specified DTD for a Web page is an XML DTD, then the Web page will be able to use the additional tags and attributes that are defined in the DTD.

You can find more specifics about XML and some examples of XML documents in Chapter 40.

One of the requirements of XML documents is that they are *valid*. This means that they strictly adhere to the rules specified in the DTD.

Browsers that load HTML Web pages are very forgiving. If you accidentally leave an ending tag off or overlap tag sets, the browser most of the time can still display the content correctly. This helps explain why HTML has been so widely accepted; anyone can see results quickly with only a little bit of knowledge.

In many ways, HTML is a "quick-and-dirty" way to publish Web pages. Serious Web page developers have demanded a more robust language that overcomes the limitations of HTML. XML is the answer to these demands, but you should not expect XML to supplant HTML.

In the near future, browsers will support XML documents as well as HTML documents. To load XML and HTML documents using the same browser, you will need to clean up the HTML code so that it reaches the same standards of validity as XML documents. XHTML is a specification that imposes XML-like rules on standard HTML documents.

UNDERSTANDING THE XHTML DTDS

XHTML provides for essentially three different DTDs. These are *Strict, Transitional,* and *Frameset.* The same three types are also exist for HTML 4.

The Strict DTD is a stickler, requiring clean tag markup and use of the latest tags throughout the document. The Transitional DTD is the most widely used DTD, because it includes support for many older tags, such as the `bgcolor` attribute to the `<body>` tag, that are still being used. The Frameset DTD is used when you want to break your Web pages up into frames.

You can see all of these DTDs online at www.w3.org/TR/xhtml1/#dtds.

Within each of these DTD documents is a public line of text that shows the correct syntax that should be used to include the DTD in the `<!doctype>` tag.

UNDERSTANDING THE XHTML DTDS

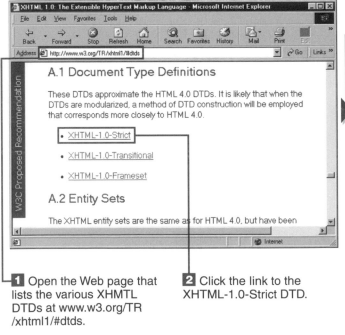

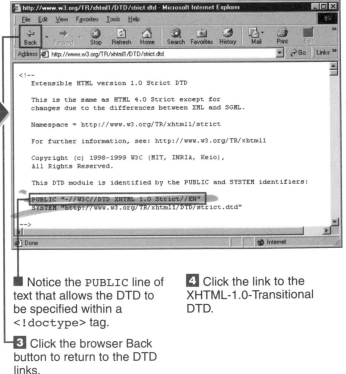

1 Open the Web page that lists the various XHMTL DTDs at www.w3.org/TR/xhtml1/#dtds.

2 Click the link to the XHTML-1.0-Strict DTD.

■ Notice the PUBLIC line of text that allows the DTD to be specified within a `<!doctype>` tag.

3 Click the browser Back button to return to the DTD links.

4 Click the link to the XHTML-1.0-Transitional DTD.

What other DTDs can be used?

✔ Besides the HTML 4.01 and XHTML 1.0 DTDs, you can select to use older DTDs for HTML version 2.0 and 3.2. A number of XML DTDs are beginning to appear. Chapter 39 covers several of these DTDs.

Why would I want to use the XHTML specification instead of the HTML specification?

✔ The DTD that you use depends on your future plans. If the HTML files that you are creating will someday be used alongside XML content, it is in your best interest to make your code adhere to the XHTML specification. However, if you can be sure that your HTML files will never be used on an XML browser, the HTML specification will suffice.

When will XML browsers begin to appear?

✔ The W3C already has a browser that can interpreted a limited set of XML applications. In the future, you can expect more XML-capable browsers to appear.

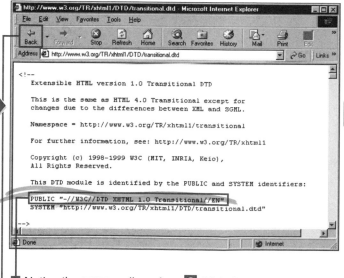

■ Notice the PUBLIC line of text that allows the DTD to be specified within a `<!doctype>` tag.

5 Click the browser Back button to return to the DTD links.

6 Click the XHTML-1.0-Frameset link.

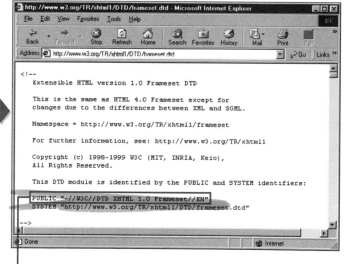

■ Notice the PUBLIC line of text that allows the DTD to be specified within a `<!doctype>` tag.

EXPLORE DIFFERENCES BETWEEN HTML AND XHTML

XHTML documents must follow several rules to be considered valid. These rules are not necessarily required for standard HTML documents.

The first rule is that all tag sets must have a closing tag: They must include a slash symbol (/) before the last greater than symbol (>) if they are a single HTML tag. Tag sets must also not overlap one another.

Another rule is that all tags and attributes must be lowercase. Standard HTML did not care if a tag was uppercase, lowercase, or a combination, but XHTML documents are case-sensitive.

In XHTML documents, all attribute values must be in quotes. This even includes attributes that do not require a value, such as the `nowrap` attribute. These attributes must be set as the value, such as `nowrap="nowrap"`.

Sections of an XHTML document can be marked to be ignored by the browser. These sections include the `CDATA` keyword. This keyword needs to include comments and brackets on either end, beginning with `<![CDATA[` and ending with `]]>`. These markings should surround all `<script>` and `<style>` tags included in the document.

EXPLORE DIFFERENCES BETWEEN HTML AND XHTML

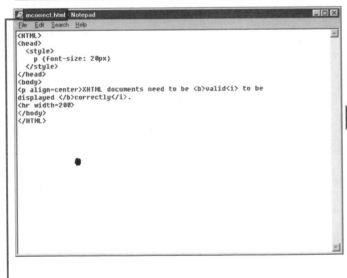

1 Open incorrect.html from the CD in Notepad.

■ Notice how this standard HTML file is not valid.

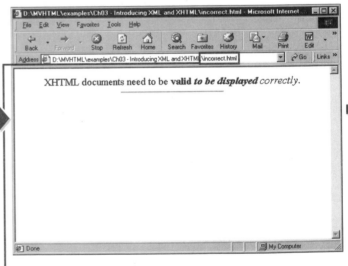

2 Open the incorrect.html file in a browser.

■ The document is displayed without errors in the browser.

Is there a way to see an error with an XHTML document?

✔ If you were to check an invalid XHTML document in an XML browser, you would see some errors generated, but the current HTML browsers are still forgiving to invalid XHTML documents. Until XML browsers are available, you can use HTML Tidy to check your documents for validity. This utility is covered in the next section.

Why do <script> and <style> tag sets need to be commented out with the <![CDATA[tag?

✔ The <script> tags are used to contain JavaScript statements, and <style> tags are used to contain style sheet definitions. Both JavaScript and style sheets are extensions to the original HTML specification. The XHTML specification needs a way to identify such sections that are not included in the specification. Even though these sections are commented out, the browser still recognizes and uses them.

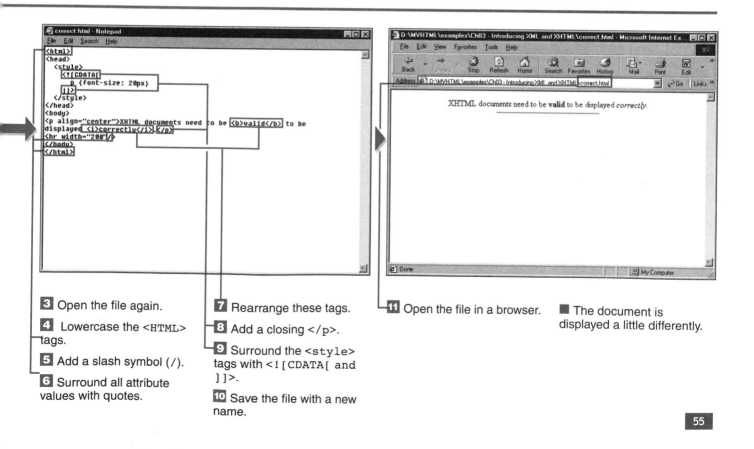

3 Open the file again.

4 Lowercase the <HTML> tags.

5 Add a slash symbol (/).

6 Surround all attribute values with quotes.

7 Rearrange these tags.

8 Add a closing </p>.

9 Surround the <style> tags with <![CDATA[and]]>.

10 Save the file with a new name.

11 Open the file in a browser.

■ The document is displayed a little differently.

CONVERT HTML DOCUMENTS INTO XHTML WITH HTML TIDY

Dave Raggett, a member of the World Wide Web Consortium, has created a utility called HTML Tidy that can check for invalid problems that exist with a Web page. This utility can be used to help you convert standard HTML documents into XHTML documents.

HTML Tidy is run from the command line, such as a DOS window. To check a document using this utility, type **tidy.exe** and the name of the file to check. If you include the −errors option, Tidy displays a report of errors.

HTML Tidy can also indent the entire document using the −indent flag, to make it easier to read and maintain.

Using the −asxml option, you can convert an HTML document to an XHTML document.

CONVERT HTML DOCUMENTS INTO XHTML WITH HTML TIDY

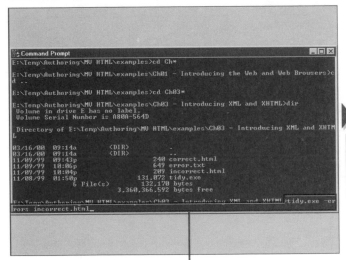

1 Select Start⇨Programs⇨ MS-DOS Prompt to open an MS-DOS window.

2 Open a DOS Prompt window and locate the Tidy.exe program on the book's CD-ROM.

3 Type **Tidy.exe -errors incorrect.html** at the DOS prompt, and then press Enter.

■ The error report is generated and displayed.

Are there any other options available for HTML Tidy?

✔ HTML Tidy includes several additional options. All available commands can be viewed using the tidy.exe **-help** option. The **–config** option, when followed by a filename, loads the options from the designated file. The **–indent** option formats the file by indenting the text to make it more readable. The **–omit** option eliminates all the optional end tags.

The **–upper** option forces all tags to appear in uppercase characters. The **–clean** option automatically replaces all font and center tags with style sheets. The **–numeric** option uses numeric character entities instead of named character entities. The **–modify** option enables the original file to be modified. The **–errors** option shows only errors. The **–asxml** option converts the HTML file to a well-formed XML document.

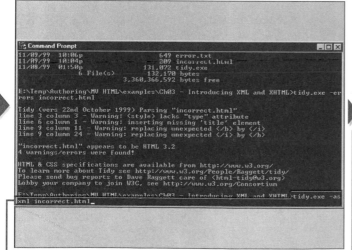

4 Type **Tidy.exe -asxml incorrect.html** after the DOS prompt in the DOS window, and then press Enter.

■ The changes needed by the file are displayed.

VIEW HTML SOURCE CODE

As you write HTML pages and load them in a browser, you can immediately see the results. As you browse the Web and look at other pages, the browsers include a feature that lets you look at the HTML code that generates the page. Using this feature, you can look at the source code for any page on the Web.

In Internet Explorer, you can view the HTML code with the View⇨Source command. In Netscape Navigator, you can use the View⇨Page Source command. Both of these commands open the HTML code in a different window.

This browser feature can be a great learning tool. As you see interesting HTML techniques, you can view the page source. By reading through the source, you can understand and learn how the author was able to produce the Web page.

VIEW HTML SOURCE CODE

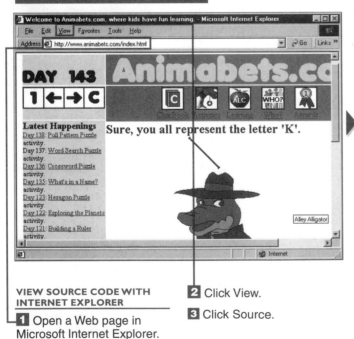

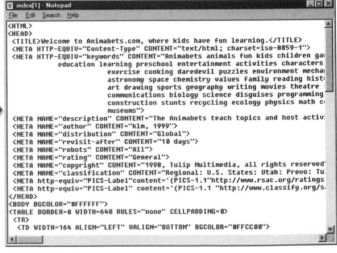

VIEW SOURCE CODE WITH INTERNET EXPLORER

1 Open a Web page in Microsoft Internet Explorer.

2 Click View.

3 Click Source.

■ Windows Notepad opens with the HTML source for the page.

Why does the code sometimes look like it is writing over itself?

✔ Depending on the system used to generate the HTML code, the line returns can cause the two lines of code to appear on top of each other in Notepad. To fix this, select Edit⇨Word Wrap.

Is there any way to hide your HTML source code from being viewed by users?

✔ There is no way with standard HTML to hide your source code from users. Some sites are able to hide their source code using Java applets. Viewing the source for these sites will still show the HTML for including the applet. There are other creative solutions using JavaScript, but they are not foolproof.

Can you copy HTML source code into your own pages?

✔ When you view the source of a Web page, you can copy the source to your own document. Remember, however, that pages on the Web are copyrighted.

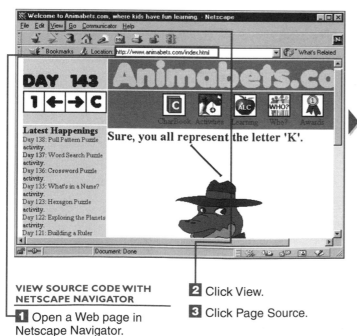

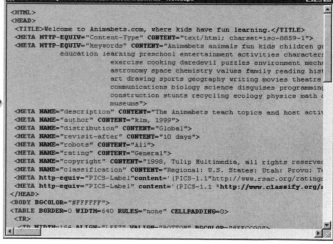

VIEW SOURCE CODE WITH NETSCAPE NAVIGATOR

■1 Open a Web page in Netscape Navigator.

■2 Click View.

■3 Click Page Source.

■ A separate window appears displaying the HTML source code.

EDIT WEB PAGES WITH INTERNET EXPLORER

Using Microsoft Internet Explorer, you can edit the cached version of a Web page. This provides a great opportunity to experiment with pages taken straight off the Web.

When you visit a page on the Web, a copy of the page is downloaded to your local machine and saved in a *disk cache*. This saved copy is kept

on your hard disk, so that if you visit the page again, you will not have to wait for the entire page to download all over again.

This cached copy can also be edited and viewed on your local computer. However, you will not be able to send the modified page back to the server to replace the existing page.

Using the File menu in Internet Explorer, you can edit cached Web pages with Notepad, Microsoft Word, or FrontPage, depending on the software that is installed on your computer. The default HTML editor can be set in the Internet Options dialog box.

EDIT WEB PAGES WITH INTERNET EXPLORER

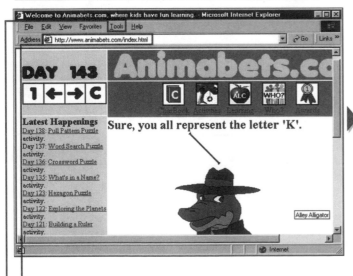

1 Open a Web page in Microsoft Internet Explorer.

2 Click Tools⇨Internet Options to open the Internet Options dialog box.

3 Click the Programs tab and then select Windows Notepad as the HTML editor.

4 Click OK to close the Internet Options dialog box.

5 Click File.

6 Click Edit with Windows Notepad.

■ Windows Notepad opens with the HTML source for this page.

7 Click Edit.

8 Click Word Wrap in Notepad.

If I edit a page a Web page and save the file, will the changes be visible to everyone on the Web?

✔ When a Web page is downloaded, a copy of the page is saved to your hard drive. This copy is a cached copy. If the browser gets another request for a cached page, it can display it quickly without having to download it. When you edit pages using the browser, it is this cached copy that is changed. The changes are only visible on your computer.

Are Web pages copyrighted?

✔ Web pages taken from the Web are automatically copyrighted. You can explicitly state this in the head of your Web pages using a `<meta>` tag. Even if a Web page doesn't specifically include a copyright statement, you still cannot freely copy and use the code.

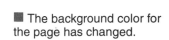

9 Scroll down the window until you find the `<BODY BGCOLOR="#FFFFFF">` tag.

10 Change #FFFFFF to #FF00FF.

11 Click File.

12 Click Save.

■ The saved file overwrites the local cached copy of the page.

13 Return to your browser and click View.

14 Click Refresh.

■ The background color for the page has changed.

EDIT WEB PAGES WITH NETSCAPE NAVIGATOR

Netscape Navigator also offers an option for editing Web pages. When you select File⇨Edit Page, a separate program called Netscape Composer loads the page in a visual editor.

Visual editors let you edit Web pages without seeing the HTML code. In many ways this approach

is more intuitive, but it lacks the flexibility of working directly with the HTML code.

Netscape Composer lets you see the HTML code used to generate the Web page with the View⇨Page Source command. This feature opens the source code in a separate

window, but does not let you edit the code.

To edit the HTML code, you can select Tools⇨HTML Tools⇨Edit HTML Source. This command displays the HTML source code in a separate window, where you can edit it.

EDIT WEB PAGES WITH NETSCAPE NAVIGATOR

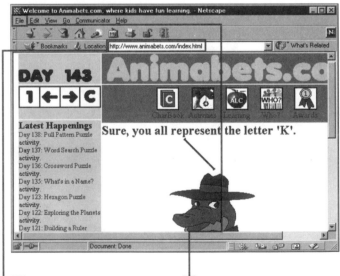

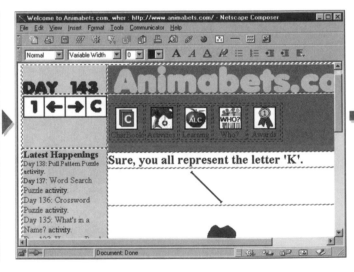

1 Open a Web page in Netscape Navigator.

2 Click File.

3 Click Edit Page.

■ Netscape Composer appears with the Web page ready for editing.

MASTER IT

How can I publish the edited page to the Web?

✔ Once you save a local copy of the edited page, you can publish it to the Web using the process described in Chapter 38.

What are the advantages and disadvantages of using a visual editing tool like Netscape Composer?

✔ Visual editors are more like desktop publishing packages, which makes them easier to use when laying out an HTML page. For example, visual editors make creating tables very easy. However, when using them, the editor has a specific way that it generates source code, which may lead to problems. For example, when you select text and increase its size, the editor could do this using a `<font>` tag or a different level of heading tag. Not knowing how the editor does this could lead to problems if you need to change the size.

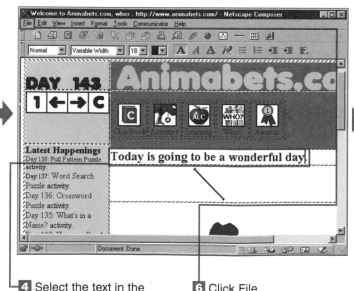

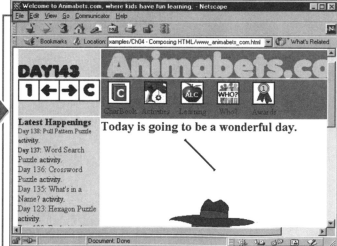

4 Select the text in the center of the Composer window.

5 Enter a new line of text.

6 Click File.

7 Click Save to save a copy of the file to your hard drive.

8 Return to the browser and click File.

9 Click Open Page.

10 Locate the saved page and load it in the browser.

■ The edited Web page is displayed.

WRITE AND SAVE HTML WITH NOTEPAD

HTML is a text-based markup language and as such requires no specialized development environment. Although many different HTML editors exist, all you really need to create Web pages is a simple text editor like Windows Notepad.

HTML source code can be entered by simply typing the content into

the text editor. HTML files should be saved as standard text files with the .html extension. You can also save files with the .htm extension. This abbreviated extension is compatible with both the 8.3 DOS convention and current file-naming standards

After the HTML source is entered into a text editor and saved, you

can open the file in a browser to view the results.

All the examples throughout this book were created using Windows Notepad. This program provides a common utility that can be used on any system.

WRITE AND SAVE HTML WITH NOTEPAD

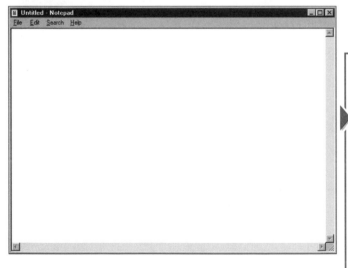

1 Click the Windows Start button.

2 Select Programs.

3 Select Accessories.

4 Click Notepad.

■ The Notepad window appears.

5 Type several lines of text into the Notepad window.

Can I use a standard word processor to create and save Web pages?

✔ Any word processor can be used to write HTML code, but you must remember to save the file using a plain text format. Standard word-processing formats, such as the Microsoft Word .doc format, include special header sections that display as junk in a browser. Many word processors, include Microsoft Word, can export documents with limited formatting as an HTML document. You should always check the exported document in a browser before publishing it on the Web.

Does a Web page need any other files to be viewed in a browser?

✔ If the Web page only contains text, the .HTML file is all that is needed. If the Web page references any external files like images or audio files, those files should also be with the .HTML file.

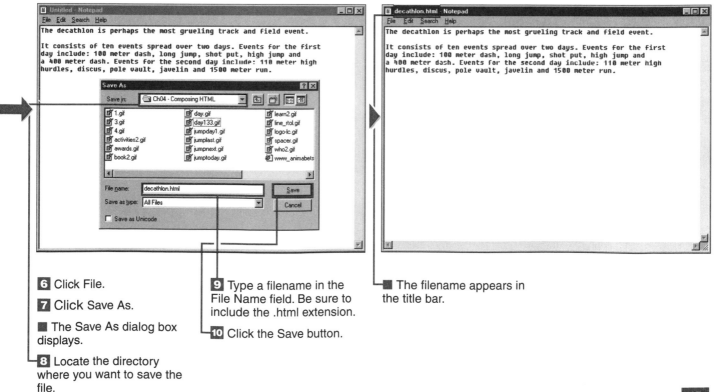

6 Click File.

7 Click Save As.

■ The Save As dialog box displays.

8 Locate the directory where you want to save the file.

9 Type a filename in the File Name field. Be sure to include the .html extension.

10 Click the Save button.

■ The filename appears in the title bar.

INTRODUCING HTML EDITORS

If you find that typing and editing HTML tags is mundane and tiresome, you can look into using one of many HTML editors that are available. These editors automatically enter the tags for you, using standard menus and dialog boxes.

These editors can show you how the page looks without having to open it in a browser, but they still allow you to edit the HTML code directly.

A variety of different commercial and shareware HTML editors are available. The following list includes many of the more popular editors.

Claris Home Page

Claris Home Page includes a powerful set of features. The package includes several assistants that can automatically accomplish tasks such as creating multipage Web sites and linking to FileMaker Pro databases. It also includes a broad collection of clip art and templates.

Home Page is available for Windows and Macintosh platforms. You can find more information at www.claris.com.

Allaire HomeSite

Allaire HomeSite is another full-featured HTML editor with support for Dynamic HTML, style sheets, and JavaScript. HomeSite also includes tools to help you manage your entire Web site, including a link checker, HTML validator, and a spell-checking engine.

HomeSite is available for the Windows 95/98 and NT platforms. You can find more information at www.allaire.com.

Hot Dog Professional

Hot Dog Professional by Sausage Software is another popular HTML editor. This package automates the tasks of working with HTML code and offers many time-saving shortcuts.

Hot Dog Professional is available for the Windows platform. You can find more information at www.sausage.com.

SoftQuad HoTMetaL PRO

HoTMetaL PRO, created by SoftQuad Software, is an excellent HTML editor and site management tool. It is also customizable and extensible. SoftQuad Software also offers an XML editor called XMetaL.

HoTMetaL and XMetaL are available for the Windows platform. Learn more at www.sq.com.

BBEdit

BBEdit by Bare Bones Software is the most popular HTML editor available for the Macintosh platform. It works directly with HTML text and offers many different features for controlling and manipulating the code.

BBEdit is only available for the Macintosh platform. You can find more information at www.barebones.com.

INTRODUCING VISUAL WEB PAGE EDITORS

If you find that working directly with HTML code is confusing, you should consider using a visual Web page editor. These editors let you create Web pages without having to look at the HTML code.

Visual editors let you add tags, attributes, and values using menus and dialog boxes. Many elements, such as images and tables, can be positioned using drag and drop features. These editors are similar in many ways to desktop publishing packages.

Another helpful aspect of these packages is their ability to manage and publish entire Web sites by including features such as link checkers and FTP capabilities.

Microsoft FrontPage 2000

Microsoft FrontPage 2000 is a new product that is part of the Office 2000 Premium Suite. In many ways, this product looks and feels like the rest of the Office applications.

FrontPage 2000 works on the Windows platform. Find out more at www.microsoft.com/frontpage.

Macromedia Dreamweaver

Macromedia's Dreamweaver is an advanced Web site development tool that is widely extensible. It includes support for many new and existing technologies.

Dreamweaver is available for Windows and Macintosh platforms. You can find more information at www.macromedia.com/software/dreamweaver.

Adobe GoLive

Adobe GoLive is a design tool that offers unequaled control over how items get placed on the Web page. This professional tool combines the best design tools with the power of HTML editing.

Adobe GoLive is available for Windows and Macintosh platforms. For more information, go to www.adobe.com/products/golive.

NetObjects Fusion

NetObjects Fusion uses a unique template paradigm to control the reusability of Web page elements.

Fusion is available for Windows and Macintosh platforms. You can find more information at www.netobjects.com.

BUILD A WEB PAGE SKELETON

Now that you have learned what tags are, you are ready to build the skeleton of a Web page. The start and end of every Web page is marked with opening and closing <html> tags.

Within the <html> tags are two major sections—*head* and *body*, marked with their respective tags. The head section includes information about the Web page that is not displayed in the browser.

The body section includes all the content that is displayed in the browser. Each of these sections is covered in more detail in later tasks.

Does the <html> tag have any attributes?

✔ The <html> tag has a version attribute where you specify the URL of a Document Type Definition document. This provides the same function as the <!doctype> tag that is covered in the next task. The <html> tag can also hold the dir and lang attributes that are common to all tags. These tags are discussed in Chapter 39.

BUILD A WEB PAGE SKELETON

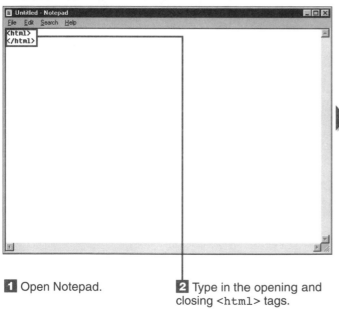

1 Open Notepad.

2 Type in the opening and closing <html> tags.

3 Between the <html> tags, add opening and closing tags for the <head> tag.

4 After the <head> tags, add the <body> opening and closing tags.

5 Click File.

6 Click Save As.

7 Type **skeleton.html** in the File Name box.

8 Click the Save button.

SPECIFY A DOCUMENT TYPE DEFINITION

A Document Type Definition (DTD) document includes all the tags, attributes, and rules that govern the Web page. Each version of HTML has a separate DTD that it uses to validate the HTML syntax.

Using the `<!doctype>` tag, you can specify which HTML version and DTD the Web page should adhere to. This tag, if used, should be the first line of the Web page.

Valid HTML versions include 2, 3.2, 4, and 4.01. You can also specify XHTML versions.

Is this tag optional?

✔ The `<!doctype>` isn't required. Most browsers will display the Web page without this tag using its own default DTD.

How can I specify an XHTML document?

✔ To make the Web page conform to the XHTML standard, type **public "-//w3c//dtd xhtml 1.0 strict//en"** within the `<!doctype>` tag.

SPECIFY A DOCUMENT TYPE DEFINITION

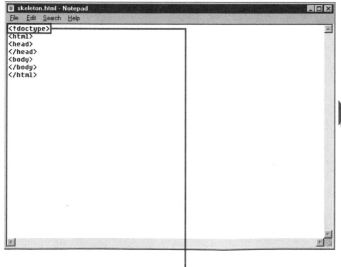

1 Open an HTML file in Notepad.

■ This example shows the file skeleton.html from the CD.

2 Add the `<!doctype>` tag to the first line of the file.

3 Between the doctype text and the closing bracket, type **html public "-//w3c//dtd html 4.01//en"**.

4 Save the file with a new name.

BUILD A HEAD SECTION

The head section can include information about the Web page that isn't displayed in the browser. Search engines and other automatic agents can use this information to identify and classify Web pages.

Tags found within the head section can include the <title>, <base>, <meta>, <link>, <script>, and <style> tags. Each of these tags is covered in the tasks and chapters that follow.

The <head> tag can include the profile attribute. This attribute specifies the URL for the location of a separate file of meta data. Using this attribute, you can reference a single file that holds the meta data for numerous Web pages.

That head section can also include blocks of JavaScript (identified by the <script> tag) and style sheet

MASTER IT

Can the <head> tag be positioned below the <body> tag?

✔ The <head> tag must appear after the opening <html> tag and before the body section.

definitions (identified by the <style> tag).

BUILD A HEAD SECTION

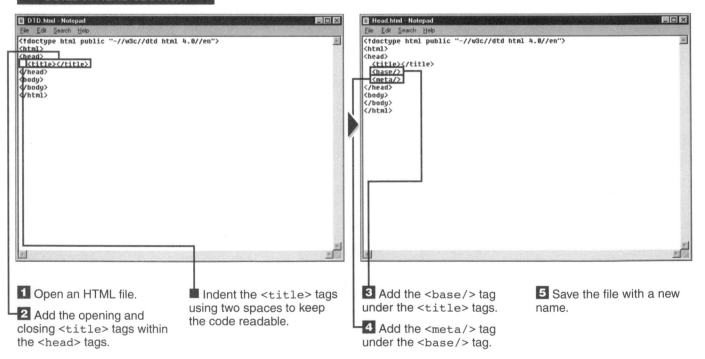

1 Open an HTML file.

2 Add the opening and closing <title> tags within the <head> tags.

■ Indent the <title> tags using two spaces to keep the code readable.

3 Add the <base/> tag under the <title> tags.

4 Add the <meta/> tag under the <base/> tag.

5 Save the file with a new name.

GIVE A PAGE A TITLE

The `<title>` tag identifies the Web page. This title appears in the title bar of the browser when the Web page is loaded.

The title text is also used to reference the page when saved as a bookmark. Many search engines also use Web page titles as a way to identify a Web page.

Each Web page can include only a single `<title>` tag.

What happens if I forget to include a title?

✔ If the browser does not find a `<title>` tag, it displays the filename in the title bar.

What if the title text is longer than the browser's title bar?

✔ The browser displays as much of the title text as will fit within the title bar. If the title text exceeds the length of the title bar, the later portion of the title will be truncated.

GIVE A PAGE A TITLE

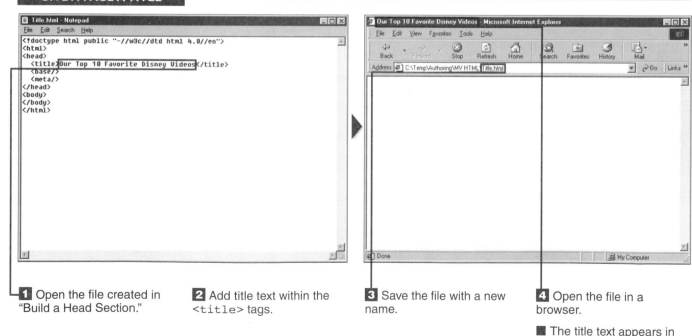

1 Open the file created in "Build a Head Section."

2 Add title text within the `<title>` tags.

3 Save the file with a new name.

4 Open the file in a browser.

■ The title text appears in the browser's title bar.

SET BASE VALUES FOR LINKS

The `<base/>` tag can be used to define the base URL for all links on the page. The single attribute for this tag is `href`, which holds the base URL. Base URLs need to include the protocol and server name, like this: http://www.mykite.com.

After a `<base/>` tag is set, all links on the page are relative to the base URL. Relative links include additional path information that is combined with the base value to complete the link.

By default, all relative links are determined based on the URL for the current page. For example, if a Web page is located at www.mykite.com/bluekites, then a link of /squarekites/diamond.html would actually link to www.mykites.com/bluekites/square kites/diamond.html. If all links for the site are found on the www.mykites.com site, you can set the `<base/>` tag to this to avoid having to type it for every link.

SET BASE VALUES FOR LINKS

```
<!doctype html public "-//w3c//dtd html 4.0//en">
<html>
<head>
  <title>Our Top 10 Favorite Disney Videos</title>
  <base href="http://www.myfamily.com/disneyvideos"/>
  <meta/>
</head>
<body>
</body>
</html>
```

```
<!doctype html public "-//w3c//dtd html 4.0//en">
<html>
<head>
  <title>Our Top 10 Favorite Disney Videos</title>
  <base href="http://www.myfamily.com/disneyvideos"/>
  <meta/>
</head>
<body>
  <a href="favorites.html">favorites</a>
  <a href="http://www.elsewhere.com/favorites.html">elsewhere</a>
</body>
</html>
```

1 Open the file created in "Give a Page a Title" in Notepad.

2 Add the `href` attribute.

3 Set the `href` attribute equal to "http://www.myfamily.com/disneyvideos".

4 Within the `<body>` tags, add a simple relative link by typing **<a href="favorites.html">favorites</a>**.

5 Under the first link, add a second link by typing **<a href="http://www.elsewhere.com/favorites.html">elsewhere</a>**.

6 Save the file with a new name.

If the <base/> tag is included, can you still specify a different URL?

✔ If an absolute URL including the protocol and domain name is part of a link, then the base link value is ignored.

Does the base URL need to point to a location on the same server as the Web pages?

✔ The base URL can point to any location on the Web. To point to a different location, you need to include the protocol, domain name and any additional path information, such as http://www.mysite.com/images.

How does the <base/> tag differ from the <link/> tag?

✔ The <base/> tag defines the relative link base, but the <link/> tag provides links to external files used by the Web page such as style sheets and scripts. The <link/> tag is discussed in Chapter 29.

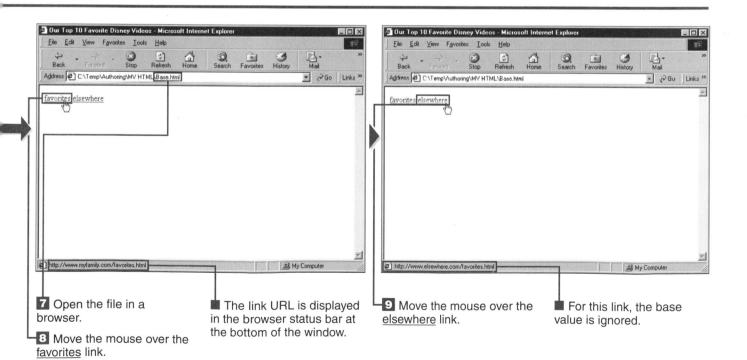

7 Open the file in a browser.

8 Move the mouse over the favorites link.

■ The link URL is displayed in the browser status bar at the bottom of the window.

9 Move the mouse over the elsewhere link.

■ For this link, the base value is ignored.

USING META TAGS

The `<meta/>` tag is used to add nondisplayable information about the Web page. This information can include the author, creation date, keywords, and other types of information.

Search engines look for this information and use it to categorize the contents of the Web page. The `<meta/>` tag is placed in the head section so that search engines do not need to search the entire page for the information they need.

The common attributes that are used to define the Web page include `http-equiv`, `name`, and `content`. The `http-equiv` attribute actually adds the information to the response header that accompanies the page request.

MASTER IT

Do search engines only use `<meta/>` tags to categorize a Web page?

✔ There are many different search engines and many different ways that they obtain Web page information. Some search engine agents also use the page title, as well as the content of the Web page.

The `name` and `content` attributes make the information available for reference.

USING META TAGS

1 Open the Base.html file from the CD.

2 Add two `<meta/>` tags with the `http-equiv` and `content` attributes.

3 Add three more `<meta/>` tags with the `name` and `content` attributes.

4 Save the file with a new name.

INCLUDE SITE INFORMATION FOR SEARCH ENGINES

Many search engines use a Web page's meta data to get information about how to list the page in their search directory. Although the `<meta/>` tag is not required, it is to your advantage to use it because this information helps users find your page.

Any type of information can be included in a `<meta/>` tag, but common data types include keywords, reply-to, author, description, and copyright.

Can additional values be used with the http-equiv and name attributes?

✔ The values used with the `http-equiv` and `name` attributes in this section are not the only values that can be used. Other values include `pub-date`, `mod-date`, `content-type`, `distribution`, `revisit-after`, `expires`, `robots`, `rating`, and `classification`.

INCLUDE SITE INFORMATION FOR SEARCH ENGINES

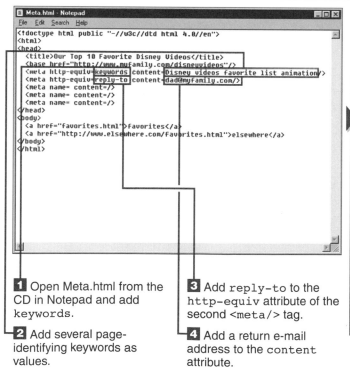

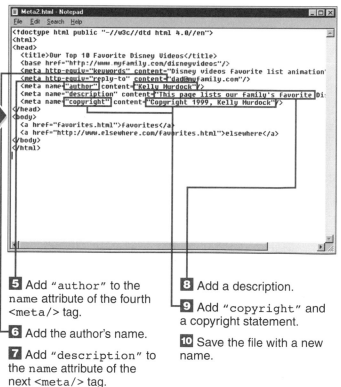

1 Open Meta.html from the CD in Notepad and add keywords.

2 Add several page-identifying keywords as values.

3 Add reply-to to the http-equiv attribute of the second `<meta/>` tag.

4 Add a return e-mail address to the content attribute.

5 Add "author" to the name attribute of the fourth `<meta/>` tag.

6 Add the author's name.

7 Add "description" to the name attribute of the next `<meta/>` tag.

8 Add a description.

9 Add "copyright" and a copyright statement.

10 Save the file with a new name.

SET A PAGE EXPIRATION DATE

The *cache* is where copies of downloaded Web pages are kept locally so they do not need to be downloaded if the page is loaded again. This local storage helps Web pages to appear in the browser quicker, but if the page has been updated, the cached copy could be older than the updated Web page.

A <meta/> tag can be used to set the expiration date for a Web page.

This helps ensure that visitors will see the latest version. The expiration date is the date after which the browser will always request a new version from the server.

To set an expiration date, set the value of the name attribute to expires and the content attribute to the expiration date in Greenwich Mean Time. This format

uses three characters for the day followed by the date, month, year, and time—for example, Mon, 11 October 1999 08:00:00 GMT.

To disable caching altogether, set the <meta/> tag's name attribute to pragma and its content attribute to no-cache. This prevents the Web page from being cached.

SET A PAGE EXPIRATION DATE

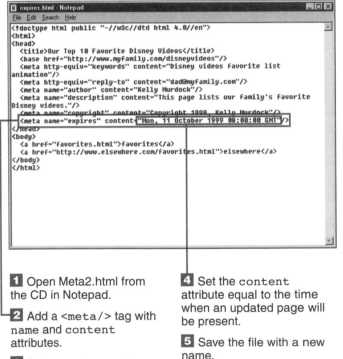

1 Open Meta2.html from the CD in Notepad.

2 Add a <meta/> tag with name and content attributes.

3 Set name to "expires".

4 Set the content attribute equal to the time when an updated page will be present.

5 Save the file with a new name.

DISABLE CACHING

1 Open the Meta2.html file from the CD in Notepad.

2 Add a <meta/> tag with the name and content attributes.

3 Set the name attribute equal to "pragma".

4 Set the content attribute equal to "no-cache".

5 Save the file.

INSTRUCT SEARCH PAGE ROBOTS

Search engines need to be updated regularly and to accomplish this task, many search engines use robots. A *robot* is a specialized program that periodically browses the Web looking for new and updated Web pages. When it finds a new Web page, it reads the page's meta data and indexes the information for the search engine.

Using a <meta/> tag, you can prevent robots from indexing your Web pages. To do this, set the name attribute to robots and the content attribute to none.

If you want the robot to index your page, set the name attribute to robots and the content attribute to all, follow. This instructs the robot to include all the links on your Web page in its indexing process.

Can I instruct a robot to index all your Web pages without following your links?

✔ To instruct robots to index your page, but not follow any links, set the value of the content attribute to **all, nofollow.**

INSTRUCT SEARCH PAGE ROBOTS

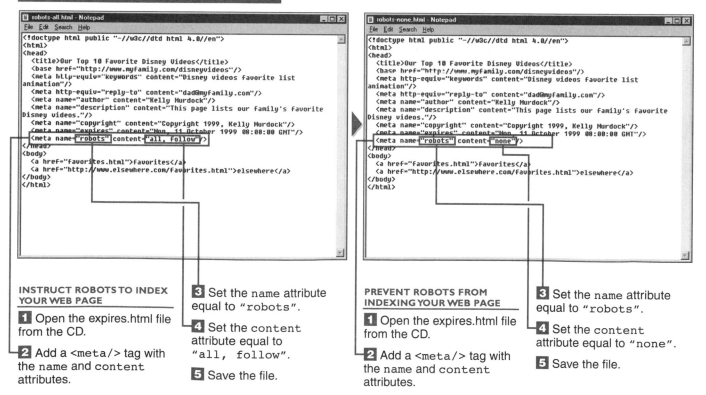

INSTRUCT ROBOTS TO INDEX YOUR WEB PAGE

1 Open the expires.html file from the CD.

2 Add a <meta/> tag with the name and content attributes.

3 Set the name attribute equal to "robots".

4 Set the content attribute equal to "all, follow".

5 Save the file.

PREVENT ROBOTS FROM INDEXING YOUR WEB PAGE

1 Open the expires.html file from the CD.

2 Add a <meta/> tag with the name and content attributes.

3 Set the name attribute equal to "robots".

4 Set the content attribute equal to "none".

5 Save the file.

RATE YOUR SITE

The W3C has created the Platform for Internet Content Selection (PICS) specification, which is used to rate Web page content. The rating can be included in a `<meta/>` tag, which filtering software can use to regulate Internet pages.

Several different Web sites include forms that can generate valid `<meta/>` tags that conform to the PICS standard. One such site is the Vancouver Webpages Rating Service, found at http://vancouver-webpages.com/VWP1.0/.

This form asks content producers to rate their sites in several categories include multiculturalism, educational content, environmental awareness, tolerance, violence, sex, profanity, safety, and gambling. The site also lists a detailed description of each rating level from which you can select the appropriate rating.

You need to include a contact name and e-mail address where users can send feedback on your ratings.

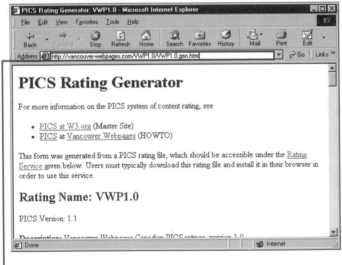

1 In a browser, visit the PICS Rating Generator at http://vancouver-webpages.com/VWP1.0/VWP1.0.gen.html.

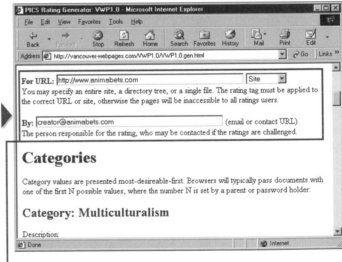

2 Scroll down and enter the URL and contact information.

MASTER IT

What other PICS rating-generating Web sites are available?

✔ Another organization that helps build PICS-compatible meta data is SafeSurf, which can be found at www.safesurf.com. Another site is the Safe for Kids site at www.Weburbia.com/safe.

Are there other rating systems?

✔ The Internet Content Rating Association (ICRA) site, found at www.icra.org, enables you to register your Web site using the popular RSACi rating system. This rating system provides ratings for the sex, nudity, language, and violence. This standard is also based on the PICS standard.

How can I use these ratings to protect viewers?

✔ To enable content filtering on the Internet Explorer browser, open the Internet Options dialog box, click the Content tab, and then click the Enable button. This sequence opens the Content Advisor dialog box, where you can set the rating levels for your browser.

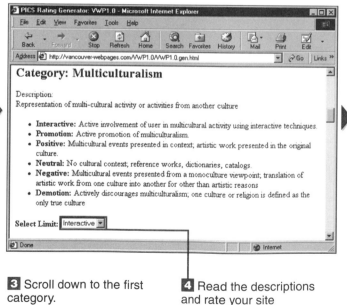

3 Scroll down to the first category.

4 Read the descriptions and rate your site appropriately.

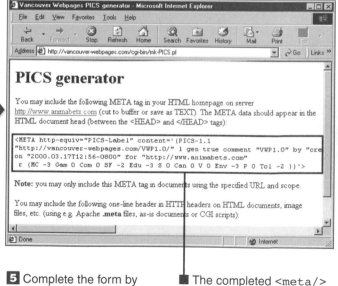

5 Complete the form by rating all categories.

6 Click the Generate Rating Tags button at the bottom of the form.

■ The completed `<meta/>` tag is generated and displayed.

7 Copy the `<meta/>` tag into your Web pages.

REFRESH A PAGE

You can also use a `<meta/>` tag to cause a page to refresh after a given number of seconds. This is accomplished by setting the `http-equiv` attribute to **refresh**. The `content` attribute holds the time in seconds before the page is refreshed.

When the `http-equiv` attribute is set to `refresh`, it can also be

used to load a separate URL in a process that is called *client-pull*. To load a separate URL, you need to include a semicolon and the URL address after the time value. For example, 5; url=http://www.mykites .com loads the home page at www.mykites.com after 5 seconds.

The client-pull technique can be used to generate Web site tours by pulling one page after another. If several sequential pages include this attribute in their `<meta/>` tags, the pages continually load one after another creating a kiosk of sorts.

REFRESH A PAGE

```
meta-refresh.html - Notepad
File Edit Search Help
<html>
<head>
<meta http-equiv="refresh" content="5; url=meta-refresh2.html"/>
</head>
<body>
What is the difference between a sick cow and an angry crowd?
</body>
</html>
```

```
meta-refresh2.html - Notepad
File Edit Search Help
<html>
<head>
</head>
<body>
One moos badly and the other boos madly.
</body>
</html>
```

1 Open skeleton.html from the CD in Notepad.

2 Add a `<meta/>` tag with the `http-equiv` and `content` attributes.

3 Set the `http-equiv` attribute to "refresh".

4 Set content "5; url=meta-refresh2.html".

5 Add some text between the `<body>` tags.

6 Save the file with a new name.

7 Open the skeleton.html file from the CD in Notepad.

8 Add a line of text between the `<body>` tags to identify the intro page that appears after the refresh.

9 Save the file with a new name.

How can the client-pull technique be used?

✔ The next task shows you how to create a slide show using this technique. Another common use is to notify users when a Web page address has changed. The older page contains a message that tells the user the page has changed and the refresh URL takes them to the new page. If your Web page contains dynamic content such as stock quotes, the refresh value can be used to reload the page at regular intervals.

Can client-pull be used to create animations?

✔ You can create animations using the client-pull technique, but this relies heavily on the server, and network traffic could make the time between successive frames sporadic. Delayed frames will prevent your animation from displaying smoothly. Other alternatives for animation, such as the GIF animation format, are more reliable.

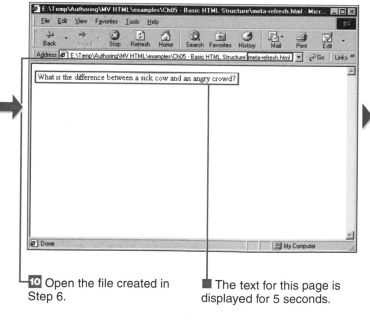

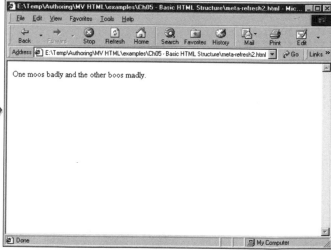

10 Open the file created in Step 6.

■ The text for this page is displayed for 5 seconds.

■ After 5 seconds, the page saved in Step 9 loads automatically.

CREATE A CLIENT-PULL SLIDE SHOW

By stringing together several Web pages that use the refresh <meta/> tag, you can create a simple slide show of pages or images. This technique is too sporadic to be used for animations, but is a useful technique for displaying several images in consecutive order.

If the last page in the sequence refers to the first one, the sequence will loop indefinitely. This can be useful for presentations that need to run independent without interaction from any users.

You can also vary the times between each successive page by

modifying the time value for each page.

Another nice advantage of this technique is that it doesn't require any JavaScript. The interactivity is accomplished completely using only standard HTML tags. Similar results can be produced in a single page using JavaScript.

CREATE A CLIENT-PULL SLIDE SHOW

1 Open the skeleton.html file from the CD in Notepad and add a title.

2 Add a <meta/> tag with the http-equiv and content attributes.

3 Add "refresh" and "5; url=slide2.html".

4 Add <img src="vacation1.jpg">.

5 Save the file with a new name.

6 Create and save an additional page for each successive slide. Be sure to change the refresh URL to point to the next page. You also need to change the source image.

7 Open the file from Step 5 in a browser.

■ The first image appears.

MASTER IT

What happens if I use the Back button?

✔ The browser's Back button causes the previous slide page to load. The previous slide will once again count the allotted refresh time and load the next page. Therefore, the use of the browser's Back button will only temporarily pause the sequence.

Is there any way to stop the slide show before it finishes?

✔ The slide show sequence can be stopped at any time by clicking the Stop button in the browser. The sequence can be restarted at any time using the Refresh button.

If I create a presentation using this technique, can I pause the next page from loading until a key on the keyboard is pressed?

✔ Unless you use the browser's Stop and Refresh buttons, there isn't a way to specify an action as the result of a key press. JavaScript, however, does have this ability.

■ After 5 seconds, the second image appears.

■ This slide show continues until all pages have been displayed.

BUILD A BODY SECTION

The body section of a Web page contains all the information that is displayed in the browser. The <body> tag itself includes several attributes that define the general nature of the Web page. These attributes include the page background color, a background image, and the text and link colors. These attributes are covered in more detail in Chapter 6.

The <body> tag can also hold the onload and onunload JavaScript events. These events are covered in Section VIII.

Is the <body> tag always required?

✔ The <body> tags should always be included in a Web page, but if a Web page uses frames, the <body> tags are replaced with the <frameset> tags. These tags are covered in Chapter 16.

BUILD A BODY SECTION

■1 Open skeleton.html from the CD in Notepad.

■2 Between the <body> tags, add several lines of text that end with a <br/> tag.

■3 Save the file with a new name.

■4 Open the file in a browser.

■ Notice that all the text included between the <body> tags is displayed in the browser.

ADD HTML COMMENTS

As you add content to your Web page, there will be times when you want to add a comment about the Web page content that will not be displayed in the browser.

To mark text as a comment, you need to enclose the text with the `<!--` and `-->` tags. There must be a space between the opening tag and the first letter. These tags can span multiple lines.

What will happen if you nest comments?

✔ If you nest comment blocks, the text between two ending tags is displayed. The browser will recognize the first comment tag and ignore all others until it finds the first ending tag. All text after this first ending tag will be displayed.

ADD HTML COMMENTS

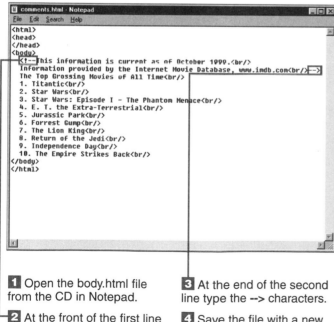

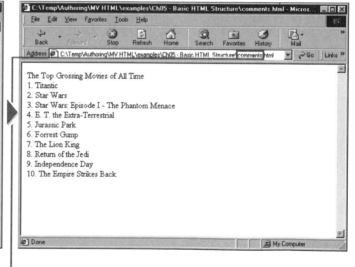

1 Open the body.html file from the CD in Notepad.

2 At the front of the first line of text type the `<!--` characters.

3 At the end of the second line type the `-->` characters.

4 Save the file with a new name.

5 Open the file in a browser.

■ Notice that the commented lines of text are not displayed in the browser.

USING NAMED COLORS

The easiest way to reference colors is to use the actual color names. HTML actually recognizes 16 color names: black, white, silver, gray, maroon, red, purple, fuchsia, green, lime, olive, yellow, navy, blue, teal, and aqua.

In addition to these HTML-defined colors, Netscape Navigator and Microsoft Internet Explorer recognize 140 standard color names.

Among these 140 named colors are many of the standard colors, including red, blue, white, orange, green, blue, pink, yellow, and black. The list also includes specialized colors such as burlywood, goldenrod, salmon, orchid, and indigo.

Some color names include a combination of words such as orangered, darkviolet, and mediumseagreen. Although these are separate words, the color name when used in an HTML document, shouldn't contain any spaces. Color names are also not case-sensitive, so powderblue and PowderBlue will both work.

USING NAMED COLORS

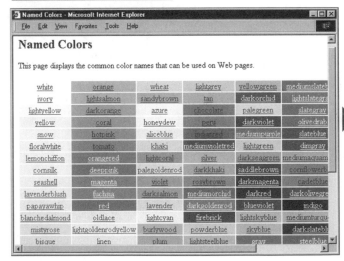

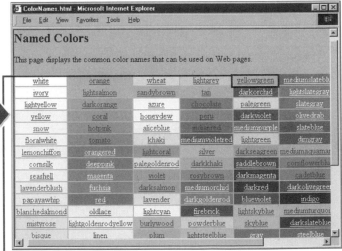

1 Open the ColorNames.html file from the content for this chapter found on the book's CD.

■ All of the valid named colors are visible.

2 Click the yellowgreen link.

■ The background changes to yellow-green.

What are the named colors?

✔ Some named colors include: white, orange, wheat, lightgrey, yellowgreen, mediumslateblue, forestgreen, ivory, lightsalmon, sandybrown, tan, darkorchid, lightslategray, lightseagreen, lightyellow, darkorange, azure, chocolate, palegreen, slategray, dodgerblue, yellow, coral, honeydew, peru, darkviolet, olivedrab, midnightblue, snow, hotpink, aliceblue, indianred, mediumpurple, slateblue, cyan, floralwhite, tomato, khaki, mediumvioletred, lightgreen, dimgray, aqua, lemonchiffon, orangered, lightcoral, silver, darkseagreen, mediumaquamarine, springgreen, darkgoldenrod, blueviolet, indigo, lightcyan, firebrick, lightskyblue, mediumturquoise, darkcyan, mistyrose, lightgoldenrodyellow, burlywood, powderblue, skyblue, darkslateblue, teal, bisque, linen, plum, lightsteelblue, gray, steelblue, green, moccasin, olive, royalblue, darkgreen, navajowhite, salmon, crimson, greenyellow, purple, turquoise, blue, peachpuff, ghostwhite, palevioletred, lightblue, maroon, mediumseagreen, mediumblue, gold, mintcream, goldenrod, darkgray, aquamarine, limegreen, darkblue, pink, whitesmoke, orchid, brown, chartreuse, darkslategray, navy, lightpink, beige, and black.

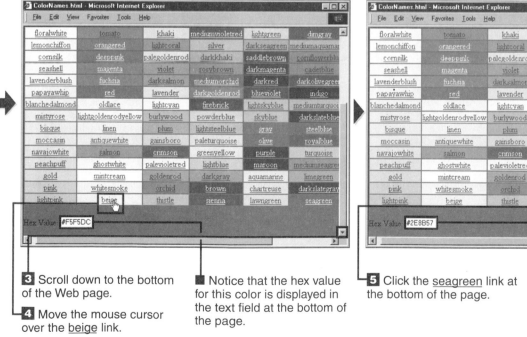

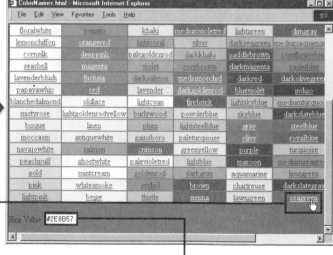

3 Scroll down to the bottom of the Web page.

4 Move the mouse cursor over the beige link.

■ Notice that the hex value for this color is displayed in the text field at the bottom of the page.

5 Click the seagreen link at the bottom of the page.

■ Notice that the background color changes to seagreen and the hex value is updated.

SPECIFY HEX COLOR VALUES

Another way to specify colors is to use a six-digit hexadecimal value that represents the amounts of red, green, and blue. The first two digits represent the amount of red, the second two represent green, and the final two represent blue. For each color, these values can range from 00 for no color to FF for full color.

For example, red is represented as FF0000, green is 00FF00, and blue is 0000FF. Combining red and blue creates magenta with a value of FF00FF, and combining green and blue creates cyan with a value of 00FFFF. Black is 000000, white is FFFFFF, and gray is 808080.

To identify a hexadecimal color value, the browser requires that the value be preceded with the number symbol (#).

SPECIFY HEX COLOR VALUES

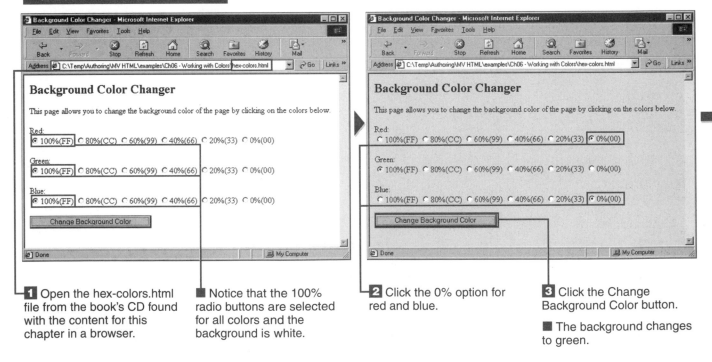

1 Open the hex-colors.html file from the book's CD found with the content for this chapter in a browser.

■ Notice that the 100% radio buttons are selected for all colors and the background is white.

2 Click the 0% option for red and blue.

3 Click the Change Background Color button.

■ The background changes to green.

What is the hexadecimal number system?

✔ Hexadecimal numbers are based on 16 values instead of 10 like the decimal system. Counting in hexadecimal continues with the letters A through F after reaching 9.

Why is the hexadecimal number system used?

✔ Computers are good at counting, and it does not matter if the number system has 10 or 16 numbers. The hexadecimal numbers from 00 to FF equate to the decimal numbers 0 through 255. Using the hexadecimal system is more efficient because 256 values can be represented using only two hexadecimal digits instead of three.

How many different colors are possible?

✔ For hex color values, red, green, and blue all have 256 possible values, which can produce 256 times 256 times 256 (or 16.7 million) different colors.

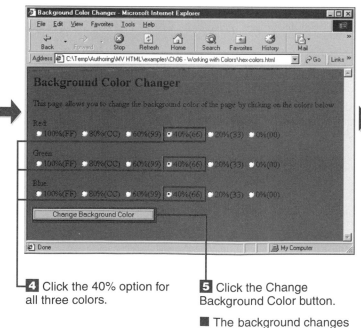

4 Click the 40% option for all three colors.

5 Click the Change Background Color button.

■ The background changes to gray.

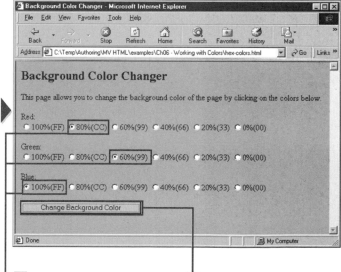

6 Click the 80% option for red, 60% for green, and 100% for blue.

7 Click the Change Background Color button.

■ The background changes to a light purple.

USING BACKGROUND COLORS

To set the background color of a Web page, you must be familiar with the <body> tag. One of its attributes, bgcolor, sets the background color for the Web page. The value for this attribute can be either a named color or a hexadecimal color value.

For most browsers, the default background color is white or gray, but this color can be changed using the bgcolor attribute.

For example, <body bgcolor="blue"> changes the background color to blue, and <body bgcolor="#FF0000">

changes the background color to red.

When you change the background color, you should be careful to make sure that it is different from the text color. If the text color and the background color are the same, the text will not be visible.

USING BACKGROUND COLORS

```
<html>
<head>
</head>
<body bgcolor="violet">
</body>
</html>
```

1 Open the skeleton.html file from the book's CD in Notepad.

2 Add the bgcolor attribute to the <body> tag.

3 Set the bgcolor value to violet.

4 Save the file with a new name.

5 Open the file in a browser.

■ The background color for this page is violet.

Are there other ways to add background color to a Web page?

✔ There are other ways to add background color to a Web page using tables and style sheets. Each table cell can be colored separate from the background color and style sheets enable more control over color. Tables and style sheets are covered in later chapters.

What is the best way to choose a color?

✔ There are several ways to visually select a color to use. The ColorNames.html file included on the book's CD provides a good interactive color selector. You can also view the source of a Web page with a color that interests you.

Is it better to use color names or hexadecimal color values?

✔ Using hexadecimal color values, you can create any one of 16.7 million different colors. Many of these will not be distinguishable from its neighboring colors. The color names, however, are easy to remember and use.

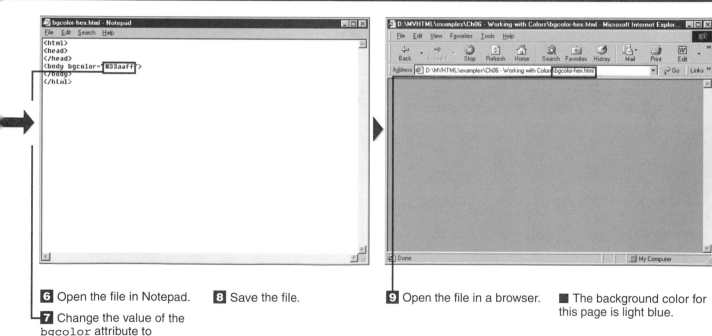

6 Open the file in Notepad.

7 Change the value of the bgcolor attribute to #33aaff.

8 Save the file.

9 Open the file in a browser.

■ The background color for this page is light blue.

SPECIFY PAGE TEXT AND LINK COLORS

Because the default background color is white, it makes sense that the default text color would be black. So what happens when you change the background color to black? If you don't change the text color, the text on the page will not be visible.

Text color can be specified using the `text` attribute within the

`<body>` tag. For example, `<body text="purple">`-displays a white background with purple text.

In addition to text color, you can also specify the color used for links, visited links, and active links. The attributes for specifying link colors are `link`, `vlink`, and `alink`. For example,

`<body link="green" vlink="lightgreen">` colors the links green and the visited links light green.

The default color for links and active links is blue, and the default color for visited links is purple.

SPECIFY PAGE TEXT AND LINK COLORS

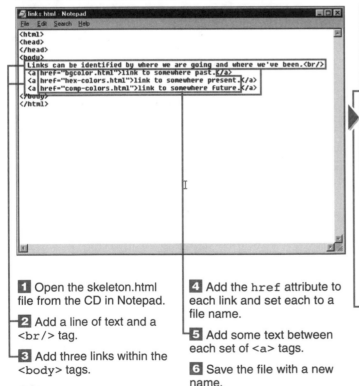

1 Open the skeleton.html file from the CD in Notepad.

2 Add a line of text and a `<br />` tag.

3 Add three links within the `<body>` tags.

4 Add the `href` attribute to each link and set each to a file name.

5 Add some text between each set of `<a>` tags.

6 Save the file with a new name.

7 Open the file in a browser.

8 Click the first link.

9 Click the Back button in the browser to return the links.html page.

10 Click the mouse over the second link without releasing the click.

■ The first link has changed to purple and the next two links are blue.

How are active links different from normal links?

✔ The default color for normal and active links is blue. Some browsers recognize an active link when the mouse cursor is placed over the link; other browsers recognize active links when the link has the focus. You can set the focus with the Tab key. For example, if you have a Web page with different colors specified for normal links and active links, the active link on the Web page appears a different color. This color moves to the next link whenever the Tab key is pressed.

Is there a way to reset all the visited links?

✔ In your browser's option settings dialog box, you can locate a control for resetting all the visited links. In Internet Explorer, open the Internet Options dialog box by selecting Tools⇨Internet Options and then clicking the Clear History button.

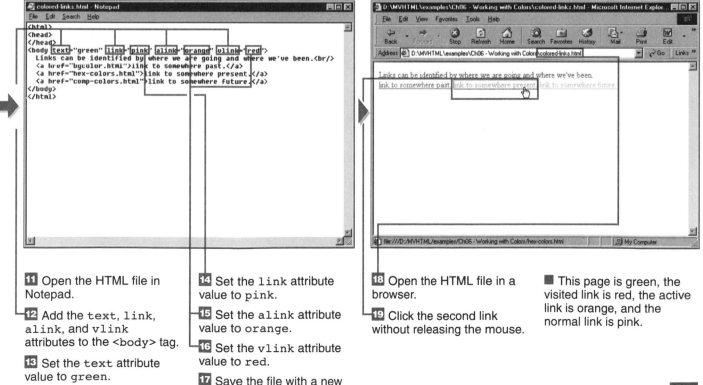

11 Open the HTML file in Notepad.

12 Add the `text`, `link`, `alink`, and `vlink` attributes to the `<body>` tag.

13 Set the `text` attribute value to `green`.

14 Set the `link` attribute value to `pink`.

15 Set the `alink` attribute value to `orange`.

16 Set the `vlink` attribute value to `red`.

17 Save the file with a new name.

18 Open the HTML file in a browser.

19 Click the second link without releasing the mouse.

■ This page is green, the visited link is red, the active link is orange, and the normal link is pink.

SELECT COMPLEMENTARY COLORS

Selecting colors is easy enough, but selecting complementary colors can be tricky. The biggest Web faux pas is to use text and background colors that do not have enough contrast. This makes the text difficult to read.

Graphic designers use complementary colors to give their

Web pages a consistent and aesthetically pleasing color theme. For example, a Web page with a black background should use light complementary colors for the text on the page.

Complementary colors can also be used to enhance the site. For example, a color that is close to the

hue of the background color can be used for borders to accent the Web page.

The book's CD includes an HTML file named comp-colors.html that will help you select an aesthetically pleasing color scheme.

SELECT COMPLEMENTARY COLORS

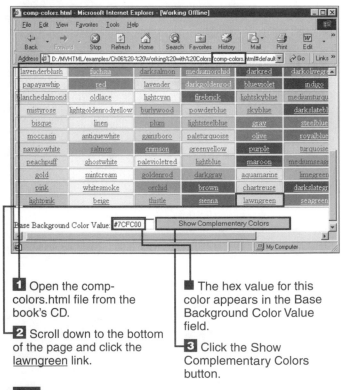

1 Open the comp-colors.html file from the book's CD.

2 Scroll down to the bottom of the page and click the lawngreen link.

■ The hex value for this color appears in the Base Background Color Value field.

3 Click the Show Complementary Colors button.

■ A new window pops up displaying all the complementary colors for lawngreen.

How do I use these complementary colors?

✔ The text should have a high contrast to the background color. The opposite or split complementary colors are good choices for text colors. *Analogous* and *monochromatic* colors are good supporting and secondary colors. The *triadic* colors provide a good combination of colors when used together.

What is the significance of the colors that only use 00, 33, 66, 99, CC, and FF?

✔ When you build a Web page using a subtle color on one computer, the same color may look different on another type of computer. To resolve this, Netscape has identified 216 system colors that are common between Windows and Macintosh machines. These are called the *palette-safe colors*, and they only use the above values. Using these colors guarantees that the color will be displayed consistently on all machines regardless of the operating system or browser.

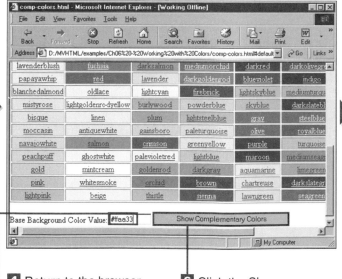

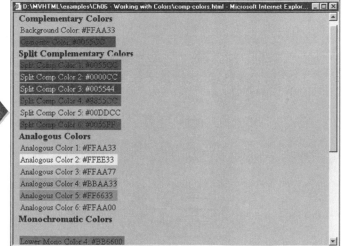

4 Return to the browser displaying the comp-colors.html file.

5 Type **#ffaa33** in the Base Background Color Value box.

6 Click the Show Complementary Colors button.

■ The pop-up window is updated with new complementary colors.

ADD NORMAL TEXT

One of the first things you will want to place on your Web page is text, which turns out to be one of the easiest tasks to do.

Any text that is placed between the <body> tags is displayed in the browser. The text wraps to automatically fit within the browser window. If the browser window changes size, the text is reloaded to fit within the resized window.

Will text ever appear outside of the browser window?

✔ By default, the text is wrapped to appear within the browser window. If, however, the text is part of a table cell with a defined width, the text could extend beyond the browser window.

ADD NORMAL TEXT

1 Open the skeleton.html file from the CD in Notepad.

2 Between the <body> tags, add a section of text.

3 Save the file with a new name.

4 Open the file in a browser.

■ Notice how the text appears in the browser.

ADD A LINE BREAK

Text that is included between the `<body>` tags is not formatted. To add formatting to the text, you need additional tags.

The `<br/>` is used to add a line break to the text. Multiple `<br/>` tags can appear simultaneously.

Are `<br/>` tags the only way to separate sections of text?

✔ The `<br/>` tag is only one way to separate lines of text. Other tags, like the `<p>` and `<blockquote/>` tags, also separate sections of text.

ADD A LINE BREAK

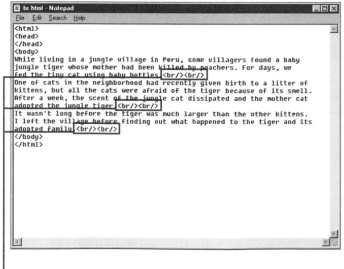

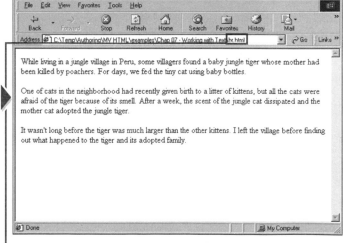

1 Open the text.html file from the CD into Notepad.

2 At the end of each paragraph, add two `<br/>` tags.

3 Save the file with a new name.

4 Open the new file in a browser.

■ Notice how the line breaks appear between each paragraph.

UNDERSTANDING WHITE SPACE

There are many different ways to separate text, including spaces, tabs, and returns. All of these are collectively called *white space* because they add space between text. However, when the browser encounters several consecutive white space characters, it collapses it to a single space.

You can use the <pre> tag to maintain the spaces. The task "Using Preformatted Text" discusses the <pre> tag in detail.

What is the advantage of collapsing white space?

✔ Because the browser collapses multiple spaces into a single space, you can indent lines of text without worrying about multiple spaces. This enables you to organize the HTML code into a much more readable format.

UNDERSTANDING WHITE SPACE

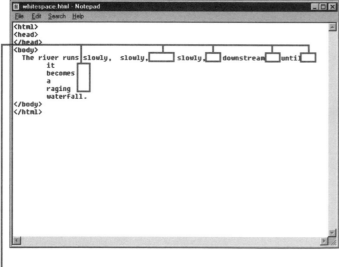

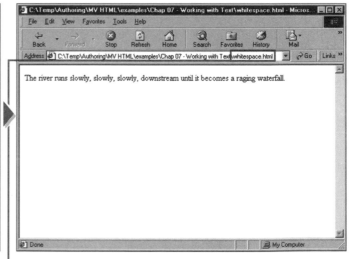

1 Open the skeleton.html file from the CD into Notepad.

2 Within the <body> tags, add a sentence of text that includes multiple spaces, tabs, and returns.

3 Save the file with a new name.

4 Open the file in a browser.

■ Notice how all the white space has been collapsed.

USING PREFORMATTED TEXT

Using the `<pre>` tags, you can maintain the white space as typed. Browsers display preformatted text using a monospace font.

The `<pre>` tag includes a `width` attribute that can be used to set the width of the text block measured in pixels.

How can the `<pre>` tags be used?

✔ The `<pre>` tags provide another way to position text on the page. Many existing documents already include the necessary white space, and, using the `<pre>` tags, you can maintain this work. You can also use `<pre>` tags as an alternative to tables.

USING PREFORMATTED TEXT

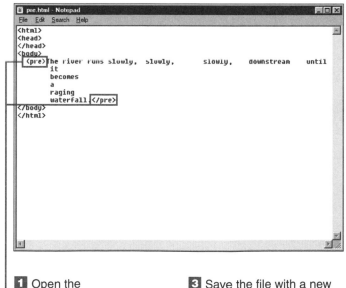

1 Open the whitespace.html file from the preceding task.

2 Enclose the text within opening and closing `<pre>` tags.

3 Save the file with a new name.

4 Open the new file in a browser.

■ Notice how the white space has been maintained.

DIVIDE TEXT INTO PARAGRAPHS

Paragraphs of text can be defined using the `<p>` tags. This tag is different from the `<br/>` tag in that it encloses the entire paragraph.

The `<p>` tag can also include the `align` attribute, which is covered in the next task.

MASTER IT

Can other tags be placed within the `<p>` tags?

✔ Paragraphs of text can hold additional formatting tags as long as the tags don't overlap.

DIVIDE TEXT INTO PARAGRAPHS

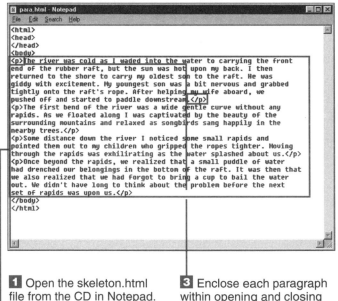

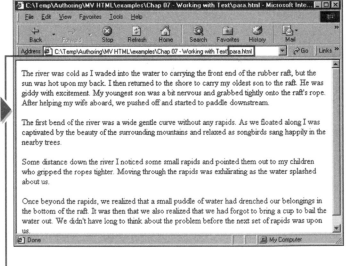

1 Open the skeleton.html file from the CD in Notepad.

2 Between the `<body>` tags, add several paragraphs of text.

3 Enclose each paragraph within opening and closing `<p>` tags.

4 Save the file with a new name.

5 Open the file in a browser.

■ Notice how the text has been split into separate paragraphs.

ALIGN PARAGRAPHS OF TEXT

The <p> tag includes a single attribute that is used to align the text. Acceptable values for the align attribute include left, center, right, or justify.

Another way to center blocks of text is to use the <center> tags. These tags automatically center all the text that comes between them. The <center> tags can cause unexpected results when used with style sheets and are therefore not recommended with them.

What is the default alignment for paragraphs?

✓ Each section of text marked with the <p> tag is automatically aligned to the left unless specified otherwise.

ALIGN PARAGRAPHS OF TEXT

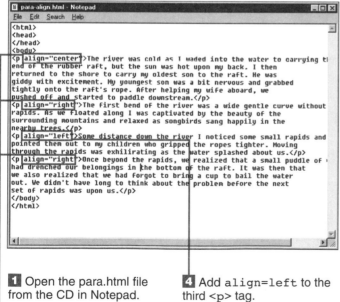

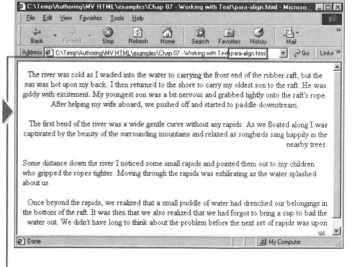

1 Open the para.html file from the CD in Notepad.

2 Add align=center to the first paragraph tag.

3 Add align=right to the second and fourth <p> tags.

4 Add align=left to the third <p> tag.

5 Save the file with a new name.

6 Open the file in a browser.

■ Notice how each paragraph is aligned differently.

ADD HEADINGS

Headings are useful for creating headlines above sections of text. HTML includes several different heading levels. Some of these levels are actually smaller than normal text, but all headings will appear as bold.

Headings can be added to a Web page using one of six different heading tags, represented by <h1>, <h2>, <h3>, <h4>, <h5>, and <h6>. The different heading tags represent the size of the heading with <h1> being the largest heading size, and <h6> being the smallest.

Heading tags can also include the `align` attribute. The `align` attribute is used to set the heading's horizontal alignment. This attribute can accept values including, `left`, `center`, `right`, or `justify`.

Headings, like the <p> tag, always start a new line, so two heading tags next to each other will appear on different lines.

ADD HEADINGS

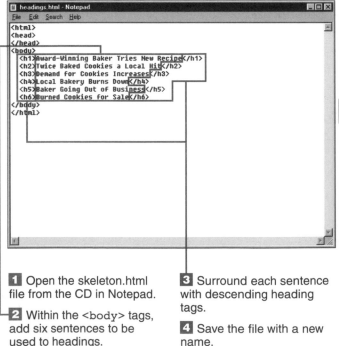

1 Open the skeleton.html file from the CD in Notepad.

2 Within the <body> tags, add six sentences to be used to headings.

3 Surround each sentence with descending heading tags.

4 Save the file with a new name.

5 Open the file in a browser.

■ Notice how each successive heading is smaller in size.

Do headings get any special formatting?

✔ Although the size of the various headings levels is different, all headings are displayed using a bold format.

How big is the `<h1>` heading, and how small is the `<h6>` heading?

✔ The actual point size of headings differ from browser to browser, but an `<h1>` heading is about two to three times the height of normal body text, and an `<h6>` heading is slightly smaller than normal body text.

Are heading sizes different for different browsers?

✔ Depending on your browser settings and the browser that you are using, the size of your headings will be different. The relative sizes of the various heading levels, however, remain constant.

Can headings be used to create an outline?

✔ Using headings to create an outline is a good use of the heading tags. You can also indent the headings using `<pre>` tags.

ADD HEADINGS WITH ATTRIBUTES

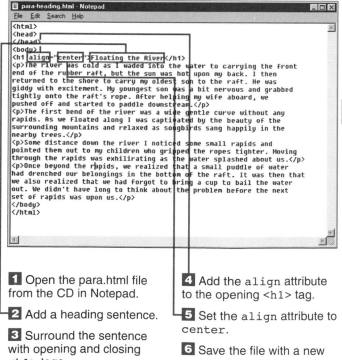

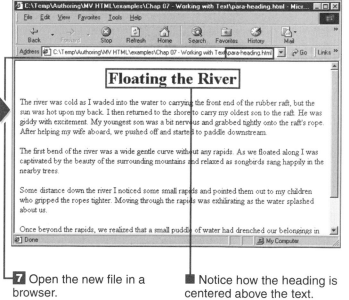

■1 Open the para.html file from the CD in Notepad.

■2 Add a heading sentence.

■3 Surround the sentence with opening and closing `<h1>` tags.

■4 Add the `align` attribute to the opening `<h1>` tag.

■5 Set the `align` attribute to `center`.

■6 Save the file with a new name.

■7 Open the new file in a browser.

■ Notice how the heading is centered above the text.

SEPARATE SECTIONS WITH HORIZONTAL RULES

A nother way to separate sections of text is with the `<hr/>` tag. This tag stands for horizontal rule and displays a line in the browser.

This tag also includes the `align` attribute that can be used to align the rule to the left, right, or center.

Another attribute, `noshade`, is used to disable shading of the rule. The default style is a shaded rule, but using the `noshade` attribute causes the rule to be displayed as a solid line.

MASTER IT

Why can the align attribute not be set to justify?

✔ `justify` is a valid value, but it really isn't an option because the rule width is set by the `width` attribute discussed in the task "Changing Rule Size and Width."

SEPARATE SECTIONS WITH HORIZONTAL RULES

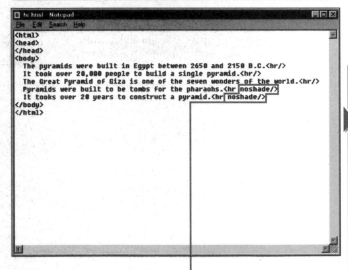

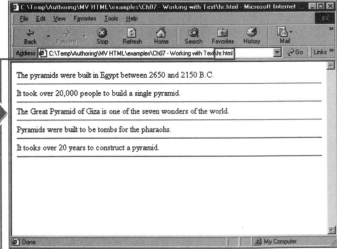

1 Open the skeleton.html file from the CD in Notepad.

2 Add several sentences of text between the `<body>` tags.

3 After each sentence add an `<hr/>` tag.

4 Add the `noshade` attribute to the last two `<hr/>` tags.

5 Save the file.

6 Open the file in a browser.

■ Notice how horizontal rules have been added between each sentence.

CHANGE RULE SIZE AND WIDTH

The `<hr>` tag also includes attributes that can be used to change the width and size of a horizontal rule.

These attributes are typically measured in pixels, but you can also specify size and width as a percentage of the browser window. To do this, add a percent symbol (%) after the value.

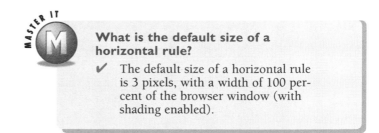

MASTER IT

What is the default size of a horizontal rule?

✔ The default size of a horizontal rule is 3 pixels, with a width of 100 percent of the browser window (with shading enabled).

CHANGE RULE SIZE AND WIDTH

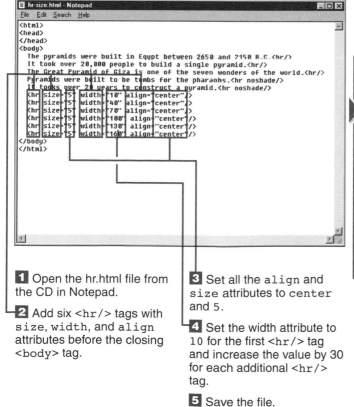

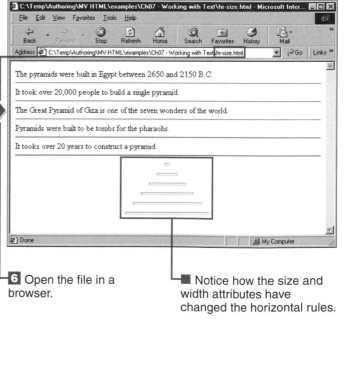

1 Open the hr.html file from the CD in Notepad.

2 Add six `<hr/>` tags with `size`, `width`, and `align` attributes before the closing `<body>` tag.

3 Set all the `align` and `size` attributes to `center` and `5`.

4 Set the width attribute to `10` for the first `<hr/>` tag and increase the value by 30 for each additional `<hr/>` tag.

5 Save the file.

6 Open the file in a browser.

■ Notice how the size and width attributes have changed the horizontal rules.

CHANGE TEXT SIZE

Although the recommended way to change text size is with style sheets, a quick method for changing text size is to use the `<font>` tag with the `size` attribute.

The `size` attribute can have values that range from 1 to 7, with 7 being the largest value. You can also place a plus (+) or minus (−) sign in front of the size value to incrementally increase or decrease the current size value from the

default font size, which is 3 unless declared differently in the `<basefont/>` tag. The `<basefont/>` tag is described in the section "Set the Base Font Attributes."

CHANGE TEXT SIZE

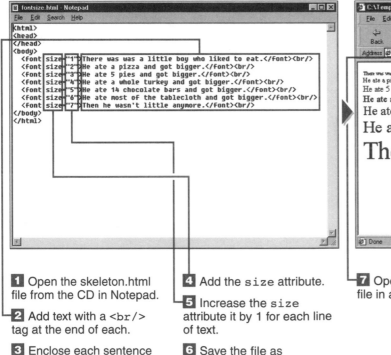

1 Open the skeleton.html file from the CD in Notepad.

2 Add text with a `<br/>` tag at the end of each.

3 Enclose each sentence with opening and closing `<font>` tags.

4 Add the `size` attribute.

5 Increase the `size` attribute it by 1 for each line of text.

6 Save the file as fontsize.html.

7 Open the fontsize.html file in a browser.

■ Notice how each line of text is larger than the last one.

Can the <font> tag be applied to individual letters?

✔ The <font> tag and its attributes affect the text that it surrounds. This applies to paragraphs, sentences, words, or even individual letters. For example, the statement <font size="+2">H</font>ello displays the word *hello* with a capital letter that is two levels larger than the rest of the text.

Can the <font> tag be applied multiple times to a section of text?

✔ If the <font> tag is applied multiple times to a single section of text, only the attribute that is closest to the text is applied. For example, the statement <font size="7"><font size="1">H</font></font>ello sizes the capital *H* letter to a level 1 and the level 7 attribute is ignored. This order includes relative attribute values that include a plus or minus sign.

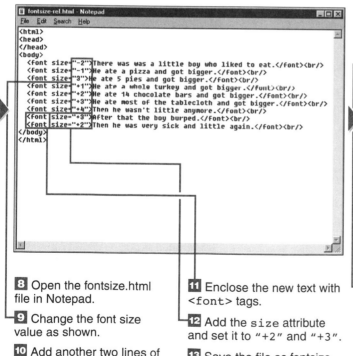

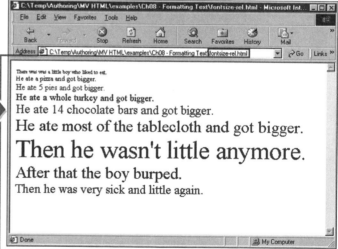

8 Open the fontsize.html file in Notepad.

9 Change the font size value as shown.

10 Add another two lines of text to the file. Include <br/> tags at the end of these lines.

11 Enclose the new text with <font> tags.

12 Add the size attribute and set it to "+2" and "+3".

13 Save the file as fontsize-rel.html.

14 Open the fontsize-rel.html file in a browser.

■ Notice how the relative size differences are visible.

FORMAT TEXT BIG OR SMALL

Another way to change the size of text is with the `<big>` and `<small>` tags. These tags simply need to surround the text that you want to make bigger or smaller.

What is the basis for the resulting size of the `<big>` and `<small>` tags?

✔ The size of text marked with the `<big>` and `<small>` tags is left to the browser to decide appropriate sizes, but it is based on the default text size defined by the `<basefont/>` tag.

FORMAT TEXT BIG OR SMALL

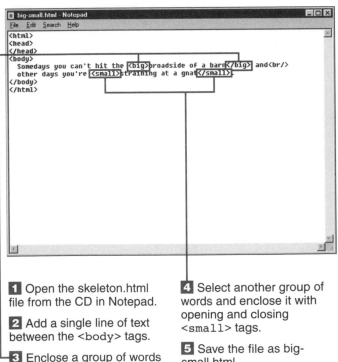

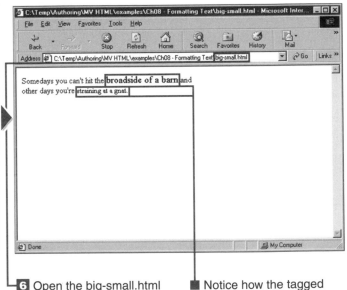

1 Open the skeleton.html file from the CD in Notepad.

2 Add a single line of text between the `<body>` tags.

3 Enclose a group of words with opening and closing `<big>` tags.

4 Select another group of words and enclose it with opening and closing `<small>` tags.

5 Save the file as big-small.html.

6 Open the big-small.html file in a browser.

■ Notice how the tagged words are larger or smaller.

CREATE DROP CAPS

Many books make the first letter in the opening paragraph considerably larger than the rest of the text. This technique is called a *drop cap,* and can be created by surrounding the first letter with the `<font>` tag and setting the `size` attribute to be larger than the normal text.

MASTER IT

Can this same technique be done with style sheets?

✔ Style sheets include all the features of the `<font>` tag plus many more. For this reason, style sheets are the preferred method for defining style.

How can I add an ornate drop cap to the opening paragraph?

✔ If you replace the first letter of the paragraph with an image, you can make the initial capital as ornate as you want. (See Chapter 12.)

CREATE DROP CAPS

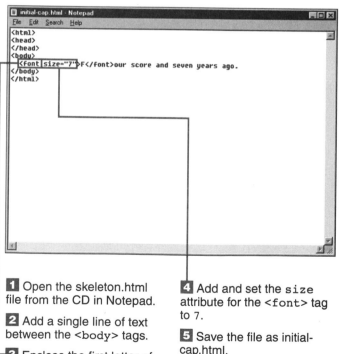

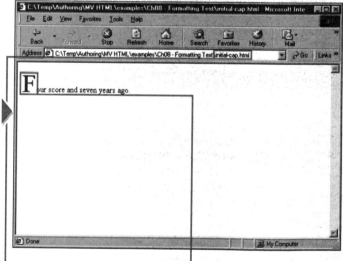

1 Open the skeleton.html file from the CD in Notepad.

2 Add a single line of text between the `<body>` tags.

3 Enclose the first letter of the sentence with `<font>` tags.

4 Add and set the `size` attribute for the `<font>` tag to 7.

5 Save the file as initial-cap.html.

6 Open the initial-cap.html file in a browser.

■ Notice how the first capital is larger than the rest of the sentence.

CHANGE TEXT COLOR

The `<font>` tag also has a color attribute, which can be used to change the text color. Acceptable colors can be the browser-recognized named color or any color value designated by three hex color values.

What do I do if my text disappears?

✔ If your text has disappeared, then chances are that the color of the text is the same as the background color. If the background and text colors are the same, then the text appears to have disappeared. You must change the text's `color` attribute in the HTML file so that it is different from the background color.

CHANGE TEXT COLOR

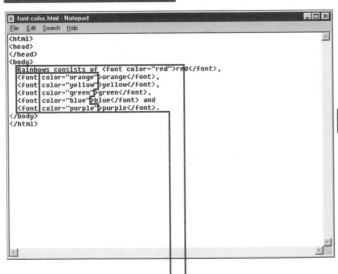

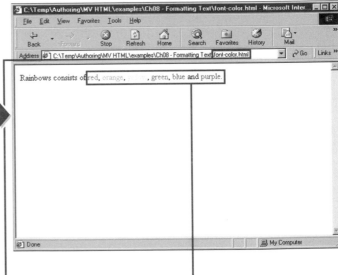

1 Open the skeleton.html file from the CD in Notepad.

2 Add a single line of text between the `<body>` tags with several color names.

3 Enclose each color with opening and closing `<font>` tags.

4 Add the `color` attribute to each `<font>` tag and use a named color as its value.

5 Save the file as font-color.html.

6 Open the font-color.html file in a browser.

■ Notice how the tagged words are different colors.

CHANGE TEXT FACE

The `<font>` tag also includes a face attribute. This attribute can be used to change the font used to display the text.

You can also stack different face names by separating them with a comma. The browser then uses the first font that it recognizes to display the text, searching from left to right.

Arial, Book Antiqua, Bookman Old Style, Century Schoolbook, Courier, Courier New, Garamond, Times New Roman, and Verdana are all acceptable font categories for the Windows system. Macintosh font categories include Chicago, Courier, Geneva, Helvetica, Monaco, New York, Palatino, and Times.

MASTER IT

What will the browser display if it cannot find any of the specified font faces?

✔ If the specified font faces are not available, the text is displayed in the default font face, the same as normal text.

CHANGE TEXT FACE

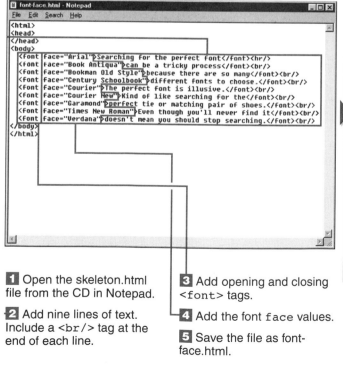

1 Open the skeleton.html file from the CD in Notepad.

2 Add nine lines of text. Include a `<br/>` tag at the end of each line.

3 Add opening and closing `<font>` tags.

4 Add the font face values.

5 Save the file as font-face.html.

6 Open the font-face.html file in a browser.

■ Notice how each line of text uses a different font.

SET THE BASE FONT ATTRIBUTES

The `<basefont/>` tag can be used to set the default size, color, and face to be used for a Web page. Unless specifically noted, all normal text will use the default values set by the `<basefont/>` tag.

Several `<basefont/>` tags can be included in a Web page. Each tag defines the font attributes for all text below it.

Does the `<font>` or `<basefont/>` tag take precedence?

✔ If a section of text is enclosed with the `<font>` tags, the attributes specified in the `<font>` tag take precedence over the `<basefont/>` tag.

SET THE BASE FONT ATTRIBUTES

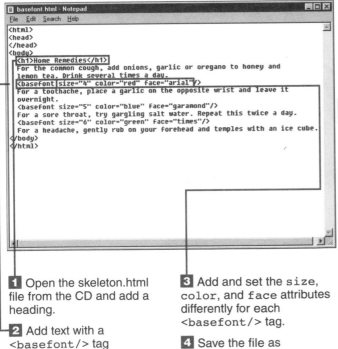

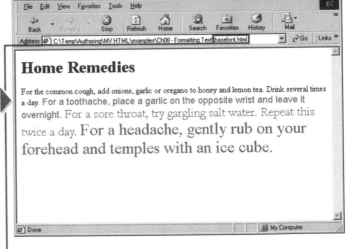

1 Open the skeleton.html file from the CD and add a heading.

2 Add text with a `<basefont/>` tag beginning the latter sections.

3 Add and set the `size`, `color`, and `face` attributes differently for each `<basefont/>` tag.

4 Save the file as basefont.html.

5 Open the basefont.html file in a browser.

■ Notice how the font, size, and color is different for each section.

APPLY ITALICS AND BOLD STYLES

The `<b>` and `<i>` tags can be used to mark text that should be formatted in bold and in italics.

These formatting tags can be combined, but you should be careful not to overlap tags. For example, `<b><i>King Arthur</i></b>` formats the text as both bold and italics, but `<i><b>King Arthur</i></b>` may produce irregular results.

If bold and italics tags are both used on a section of text, does it matter which one comes first?

✔ If a section of tags is wrapped within `<b>` and `<i>` tags, it does not matter which tag comes first. The order if both are applied can be left to your preference.

APPLY ITALICS AND BOLD STYLES

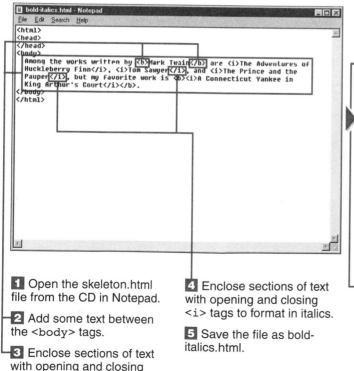

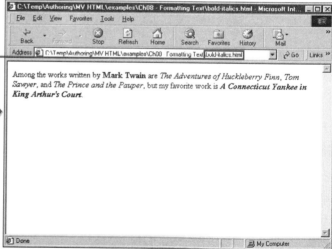

1 Open the skeleton.html file from the CD in Notepad.

2 Add some text between the `<body>` tags.

3 Enclose sections of text with opening and closing `<b>` tags to format in bold.

4 Enclose sections of text with opening and closing `<i>` tags to format in italics.

5 Save the file as bold-italics.html.

6 Open the bold-italics.html file in a browser.

■ Notice how marked sections of text are bold or italics or both.

APPLY UNDERLINE AND STRIKETHROUGH

The `<u>` tag works just like the bold and italics tags. It marks text that should be underlined.

There are two ways to mark text that should be struck out— `<strike>` and `<s>`.

Why are there two ways to format strikethrough text?

As HTML evolved, both Netscape and Microsoft proposed different methods of doing the same thing. In the case of the `<s>` and `<strike>` tag, both were accepted. The former is easier to type, but the latter is more intuitive.

APPLY UNDERLINE AND STRIKETHROUGH

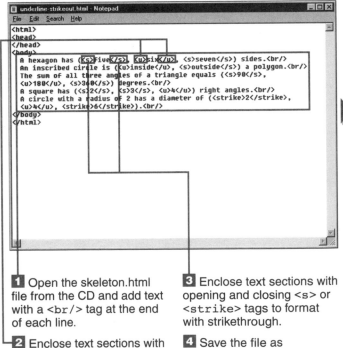

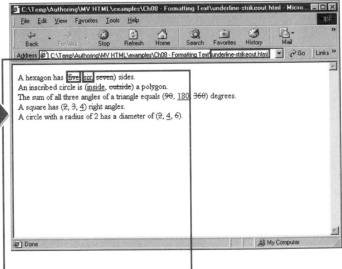

1 Open the skeleton.html file from the CD and add text with a `<br/>` tag at the end of each line.

2 Enclose text sections with opening and closing `<u>` tags to format with underline.

3 Enclose text sections with opening and closing `<s>` or `<strike>` tags to format with strikethrough.

4 Save the file as underline-strikeout.html.

5 Open the underline-strikeout.html file in a browser.

■ Notice how the marked text is formatted with underline or strikethrough.

APPLY SUBSCRIPTS AND SUPERSCRIPTS

Subscripts and superscripts can be marked using the `<sub>` and `<sup>` tags. Text marked as subscripts appears slightly below the default text in a browser window. Superscript, on the other hand, appears slightly above the default text.

These tags can be combined with the `<small>` tag to reduce the size of the sub and superscripts.

If I include several consecutive `<sub>` or `<sup>` tags, will the text be higher or lower than using only one tag set?

✔ Placing two sets of `<sub>` or `<sup>` tags around some text has the same result as if a single set is included.

APPLY SUBSCRIPTS AND SUPERSCRIPTS

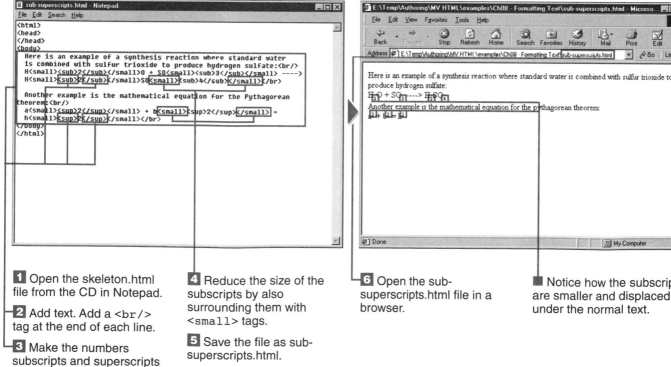

1 Open the skeleton.html file from the CD in Notepad.

2 Add text. Add a `<br/>` tag at the end of each line.

3 Make the numbers subscripts and superscripts with `<sub>` or `<sup>` tags.

4 Reduce the size of the subscripts by also surrounding them with `<small>` tags.

5 Save the file as sub-superscripts.html.

6 Open the sub-superscripts.html file in a browser.

■ Notice how the subscripts are smaller and displaced under the normal text.

121

APPLY TYPEWRITER TEXT

HTML includes a tag that can format text to look like it was created using a typewriter. The `<tt>` tag stands for teletype. This text is *monospaced* and provides another way to highlight text such as code or keywords. Monospaced text spaces each letter an equal width, so that the letter *w* occupies the same width as the letter *i*.

What is the benefit of using a monospaced font?

✔ Every letter of a monospaced font has the same width, so the letter *i* has the same width as *w*. The advantage of this is that it lines up the text into straight columns. It also makes it easy to justify the text.

USING TYPEWRITER TEXT

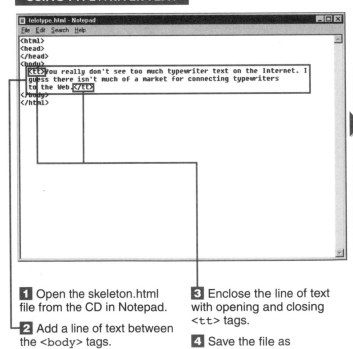

1 Open the skeleton.html file from the CD in Notepad.

2 Add a line of text between the `<body>` tags.

3 Enclose the line of text with opening and closing `<tt>` tags.

4 Save the file as teletype.html.

5 Open the teletype.html file in a browser.

■ The text is displayed in a monospaced font as if typed on a typewriter.

APPLY EMPHASIS

The `<b>`, `<i>`, `<s>`, and `<u>` tags are all examples of physical tags. Using these markup tags, you can get exactly what you specify. Another type of tags exists called *logical tags*. These tags let you specify the function of the tag and let the browser decide how to format them.

Two logical tags for adding emphasis and strong emphasis are `<em>` and `<strong>`. Using these tags, you

can identify text that you want emphasized. In Part IX, which discusses style sheets, you can find

out how to define what type of formatting gets applied to the emphasized text.

What is the default formatting for the `<em>` and `<strong>` tags?

✔ The default `<em>` tag makes text appear exactly like the `<i>` tag, and the default `<strong>` tag makes text appear just like the `<b>` tag.

APPLY EMPHASIS

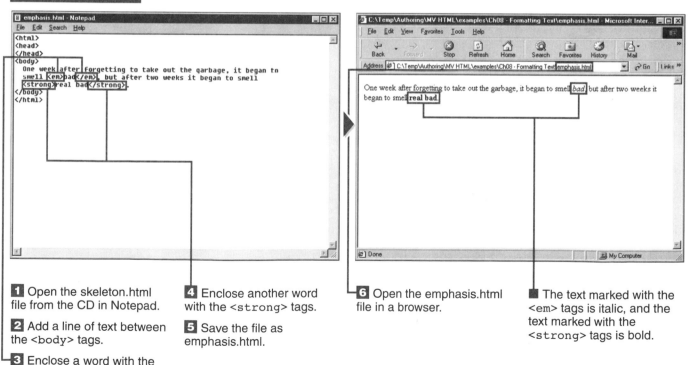

1 Open the skeleton.html file from the CD in Notepad.

2 Add a line of text between the `<body>` tags.

3 Enclose a word with the `<em>` tags.

4 Enclose another word with the `<strong>` tags.

5 Save the file as emphasis.html.

6 Open the emphasis.html file in a browser.

■ The text marked with the `<em>` tags is italic, and the text marked with the `<strong>` tags is bold.

CITE TEXT

HTML also includes several *logical tags*. The name of a logical tag matches the type of text that it uses to format. The `<cite>` tag is used to mark citations, and so on. The default for this tag formats the text in italics.

MASTER IT

Can the formatting used with the `<cite>` tag be changed?

✔ Style sheets can be used to define different formatting that is applied to various tags.

CITE TEXT

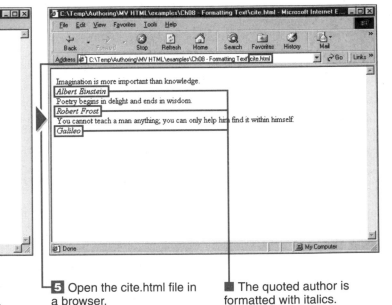

1 Open the skeleton.html file from the CD in Notepad.

2 Add several citations between the `<body>` tags. End each line with a `<br/>` tag.

3 Enclose the quote's author in `<cite>` tags.

4 Save the file as cite.html.

5 Open the cite.html file in a browser.

■ The quoted author is formatted with italics.

APPLY BLOCK QUOTES

The `<blockquote>` tags are similar to the `<p>` tag in that they separate sections of text. Sections of text enclosed within the `<blockquote>` tags are indented from the left and edge of the browser window.

The `<blockquote>` tags can also be nested to increase the indent amount. This provides a quick way to change the margins for a section of text.

For smaller quotes, such as a single line, you can use the `<q>` tags. This marks quotes like the `<blockquote>` but is reserved for inline use and does not indent the text.

Both the `<blockquote>` and `<q>` tags have a `cite` attribute that can be set equal to the reference URL.

If the `<blockquote>` tag is similar to the `<p>` tag, does it have an align attribute?

✔ Because the `<blockquote>` tag controls the indentation of a section of text, it is always aligned.

APPLY BLOCK QUOTES

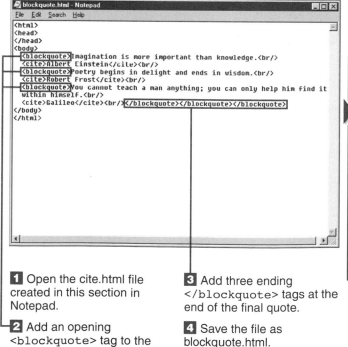

1 Open the cite.html file created in this section in Notepad.

2 Add an opening `<blockquote>` tag to the front of each quote.

3 Add three ending `</blockquote>` tags at the end of the final quote.

4 Save the file as blockquote.html.

5 Open the blockquote.html file in a browser.

■ Each successive quote is indented farther than the quote above it.

125

DEFINE ACRONYMS

Acronyms can be defined using the <acronym> tags. You can also use the `title` attribute to hold the acronym meaning. These titles become visible if you hold the mouse over the acronym in the Internet Explorer browser.

Defining acronyms becomes important when you are trying to support audio browsers. By identifying acronyms, you can instruct an audio browser to spell the acronyms instead of trying to pronounce them.

MASTER IT

Can I make the title text visible when the mouse is over it in browsers other than Internet Explorer?

✔ Using JavaScript, you can make the title text appear when the mouse rolls over the acronym. This is covered in the rollover section in Chapter 25.

DEFINE ACRONYMS

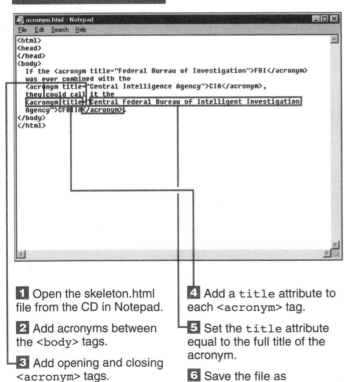

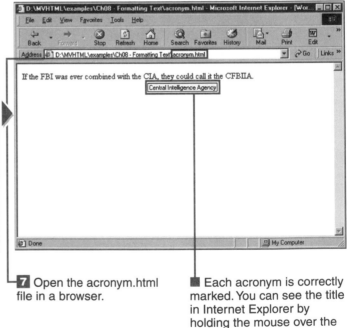

1 Open the skeleton.html file from the CD in Notepad.

2 Add acronyms between the <body> tags.

3 Add opening and closing <acronym> tags.

4 Add a `title` attribute to each <acronym> tag.

5 Set the `title` attribute equal to the full title of the acronym.

6 Save the file as acronym.html.

7 Open the acronym.html file in a browser.

■ Each acronym is correctly marked. You can see the title in Internet Explorer by holding the mouse over the acronym.

FORMAT AN ADDRESS

A ddresses can be marked with the <address> tag. These can include street addresses or e-mail addresses. Browsers display these in italics.

MASTER IT

Does the <address> tag make the address appear on a new line?

✔ The <address> tag is similar to the <p> tag in that it starts the address on a new line. Separate lines within the address need to include line breaks, but the beginning and ending lines of the address do not need any <br/> tags.

FORMAT AN ADDRESS

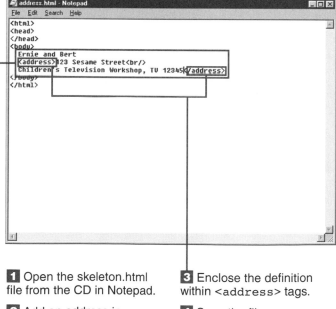

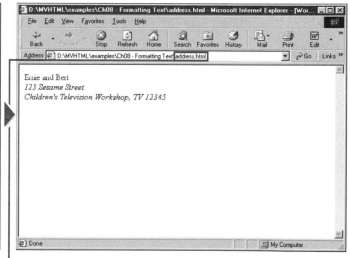

1 Open the skeleton.html file from the CD in Notepad.

2 Add an address in between the <body> tags.

3 Enclose the definition within <address> tags.

4 Save the file as address.html.

5 Open the address.html file in a browser.

■ The address appears in italics.

MARK INSERTED AND DELETED TEXT

HTML includes two tags that enable you to edit online documents. The <ins> tags are used to mark text that has been inserted into a source document, and <del> is used to mark text that has been deleted from the source document. Take care so that these tags do not overlap.

For example, inserted text is marked like <ins>this is inserted text</ins> and deleted text is marked like <del>this is deleted text</del>.

In the browser, deleted text is displayed with strikethrough formatting, and inserted text is displayed with underline formatting.

Both of these tags include site and datetime attributes. The site attribute is used to include the URL of the source document. The datetime attribute is set equal to the date and time when the marked section was changed.

MARK INSERTED AND DELETED TEXT

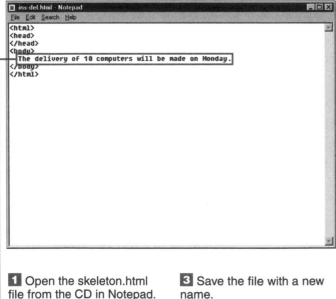

1 Open the skeleton.html file from the CD in Notepad.

2 Type a line of text within the <body> tags.

3 Save the file with a new name.

4 Open the file in a browser.

■ The text appears in the browser.

What is the proper format for the datetime attribute?

✔ The **datetime** attribute should conform to the ISO8601 standard. This standard lists the year, month, and date separated by dashes; then *T*, hours, minutes, and seconds; then the hours and minutes that the current time zone is ahead or behind Greenwich Mean Time.

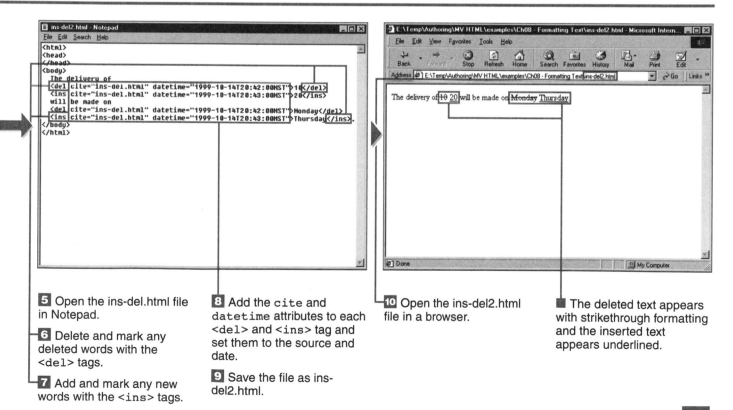

5 Open the ins-del.html file in Notepad.

6 Delete and mark any deleted words with the <del> tags.

7 Add and mark any new words with the <ins> tags.

8 Add the cite and datetime attributes to each <del> and <ins> tag and set them to the source and date.

9 Save the file as ins-del2.html.

10 Open the ins-del2.html file in a browser.

■ The deleted text appears with strikethrough formatting and the inserted text appears underlined.

MARK CODE TEXT

HTML also includes several tags that are used to mark various types of programming text. The first is the `<code>` tag that marks programming syntax. There is also a `<var>` tag that is used to mark variables. The `<kbd>` and `<samp>` tags are used to mark text to be typed in and sample output text.

Within the browser, all code-marked text appears in a plain monospaced font. Variables are italicized.

What if the code does not display correctly?

✔ Code syntax includes lots of special symbols, such as < and > that are used by HTML tags. Be sure to use escape characters like the / to make these symbols visible.

MARK CODE TEXT

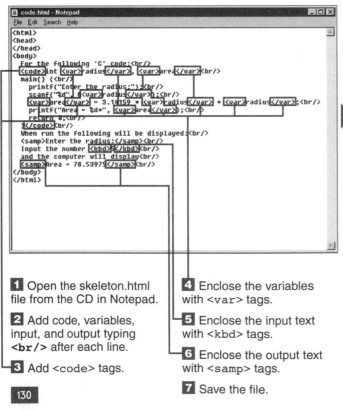

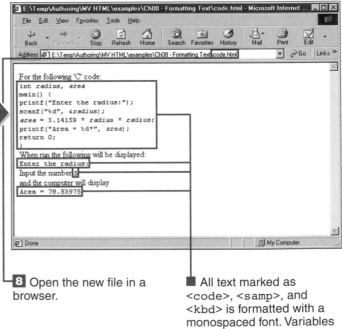

1 Open the skeleton.html file from the CD in Notepad.

2 Add code, variables, input, and output typing `<br/>` after each line.

3 Add `<code>` tags.

4 Enclose the variables with `<var>` tags.

5 Enclose the input text with `<kbd>` tags.

6 Enclose the output text with `<samp>` tags.

7 Save the file.

8 Open the new file in a browser.

■ All text marked as `<code>`, `<samp>`, and `<kbd>` is formatted with a monospaced font. Variables are italicized.

MARK DEFINITIONS

Definitions in HTML can be marked with the <dfn> tag. Definitions marked in this way will appear in italics in the browser.

How can I highlight the definition term?

✔ You can emphasize the definition term using the <b>, <em>, or <strong> tags.

MARK DEFINITIONS

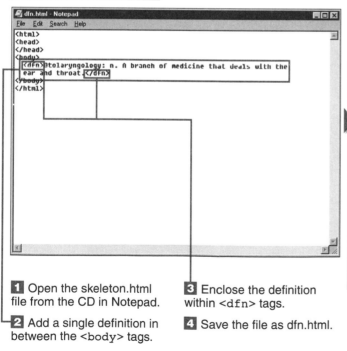

1 Open the skeleton.html file from the CD in Notepad.

2 Add a single definition in between the <body> tags.

3 Enclose the definition within <dfn> tags.

4 Save the file as dfn.html.

5 Open the dfn.html file in a browser.

■ The definition appears in italics.

BUILD AN ORDERED LIST

HTML supports several different types of lists. One of these types is the *ordered list*. Ordered lists sequentially number each element in the list.

To create an ordered list, start with the opening and closing <ol> tags. Then, mark each element of the list with an <li/> tag. The first element will be numbered 1 and so

forth. The <li/> tag does not need an ending tag.

For example, the following statement creates an ordered list with four elements: <ol><li/>item 1<li/>item 2<li/>item 3<li/>item 4</ol>. If you indent each element within the <ol> tags, the list elements are easier to see.

Ordered lists can include several attributes that are used to set the numbering type and start number. These attributes are included within the opening <ol> or the <li/> tags. They are presented in subsequent tasks later in this chapter.

BUILD AN ORDERED LIST

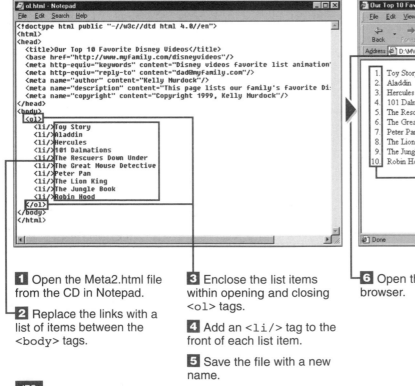

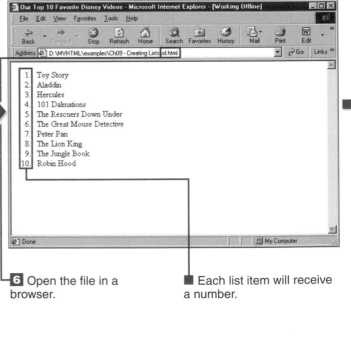

1 Open the Meta2.html file from the CD in Notepad.

2 Replace the links with a list of items between the <body> tags.

3 Enclose the list items within opening and closing <ol> tags.

4 Add an <li/> tag to the front of each list item.

5 Save the file with a new name.

6 Open the file in a browser.

■ Each list item will receive a number.

Do the list elements need a closing `<li>` tag?

✔ The closing `<li>` tag is optional. The browser will imply that the next list element starts where the former one ends. If you do not use the closing `<li>` tag, make sure that you include a forward slash (/) in the opening tag to be XHTML compliant.

Can the `<li/>` tag accept any attributes?

✔ The `<li>` tag can accept the **type** and **value** attributes. These attributes can be used to change the numbering style and the value of the current list item. I cover these attributes in more detail later in this chapter.

Can you include a closing `</li>` tag?

✔ The ending `</li>` tag is optionally. If you include it will add some additional tags to the HTML file, but it can make reading the existing list elements much easier.

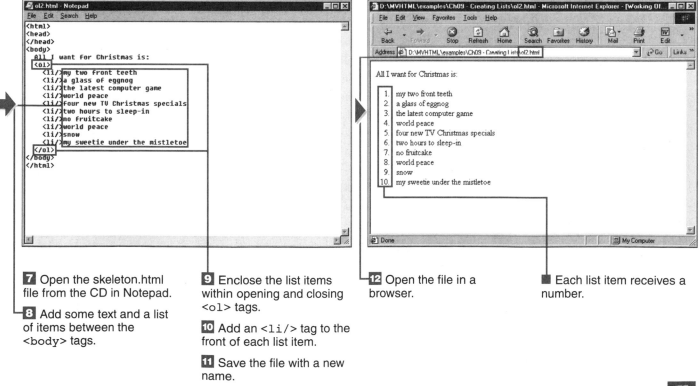

7 Open the skeleton.html file from the CD in Notepad.

8 Add some text and a list of items between the `<body>` tags.

9 Enclose the list items within opening and closing `<ol>` tags.

10 Add an `<li/>` tag to the front of each list item.

11 Save the file with a new name.

12 Open the file in a browser.

■ Each list item receives a number.

CHANGE NUMBERING STYLE

The <ol> tag includes a type attribute that can be used to change the number style. This attribute lets you specify the numbering style to use. The choices include upper- and lowercase letters, Arabic numbers, and upper- and lowercase Roman numerals.

The type attribute values can include a standard Arabic number

(1), lowercase alphabet (a), uppercase alphabet (A), lowercase Roman numeral (i), and uppercase Roman numeral (I).

For example, the statement <ol type="1" specifies that the ordered list use Arabic numbers. The statement <ol type="a"> creates a list using lowercase alphabet letters.

The type attribute can also be used with other types of lists like an unordered list. Unordered lists can accept different values that determine the type of bullet to use for the list.

CHANGE NUMBERING STYLE

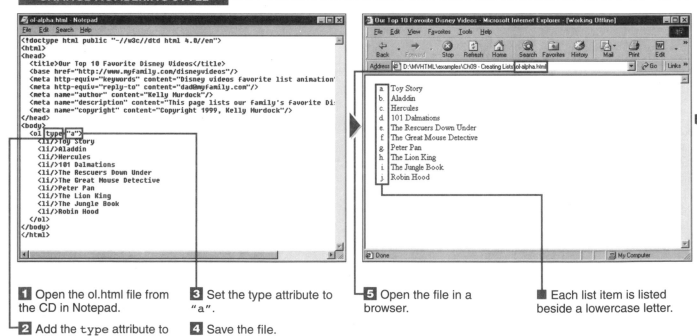

■1 Open the ol.html file from the CD in Notepad.

■2 Add the type attribute to the opening <ol> tag.

■3 Set the type attribute to "a".

■4 Save the file.

■5 Open the file in a browser.

■ Each list item is listed beside a lowercase letter.

How can I change the number type in the middle of the list?

✔ The `<li/>` tag includes two attributes—`type` and `value`. The `type` attribute can be used to change the numbering type for any list item. The `value` attribute can change the number index. This affects all list items below the change as the section "Set the First List Value" shows.

Can directory, definition, and menu lists include the type attribute?

✔ The `type` attribute works only with ordered and unordered lists. It cannot be used with directory, definition, or menu lists.

What happens if the number style does not match the list type?

✔ If the number style specified with `type` attribute does not match the list type, the browser uses the default list type value to display the list. For example, if you have an ordered list that uses uppercase Roman numerals and you set the `type` attribute for a list element to `"disc"`, the default Arabic numbering will be used for this list element.

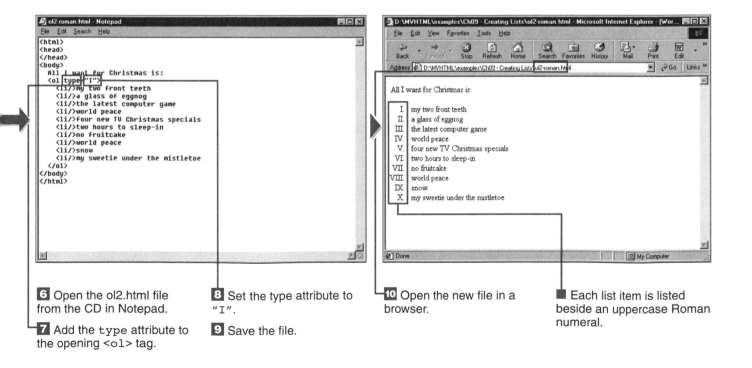

6 Open the ol2.html file from the CD in Notepad.

7 Add the `type` attribute to the opening `<ol>` tag.

8 Set the type attribute to `"I"`.

9 Save the file.

10 Open the new file in a browser.

■ Each list item is listed beside an uppercase Roman numeral.

SET THE FIRST LIST VALUE

O rdered lists can also include the start attribute that can be used to set the value of the first element in the list.

If the start attribute is used with a <li/> tag, the list begins counting from that point on using the start value.

MASTER IT

How can I use the uppercase alphabet type and start the list with the letter *B*?

✔ The type attribute controls which numbering type the list uses, but the start attribute needs an Arabic number to determine the starting value. For example, to start an uppercase alphabet list with the letter *B*, you need to set the start attribute to 2.

SET THE FIRST LIST VALUE

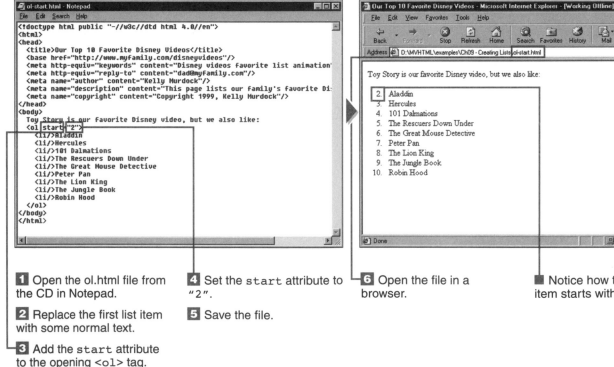

1 Open the ol.html file from the CD in Notepad.

2 Replace the first list item with some normal text.

3 Add the start attribute to the opening <ol> tag.

4 Set the start attribute to "2".

5 Save the file.

6 Open the file in a browser.

■ Notice how the first list item starts with number 2.

LIST NONSEQUENTIAL NUMBERS

Using the start attribute, you can change the number for the first list item, but the `<li/>` tag's value attribute can be used to change the numbering for all other list items.

If you specify the value for each individual list item, you can nonsequentially number the list items.

If the numbering type is different, should the values still be Arabic numbers?

✔ Regardless of what the numbering type is, the value attribute should always include Arabic numbers. For example, if you specify the type attribute as uppercase alphabetical, you can start the list with a *c* if the start value is set to '3'.

CREATE A LIST OF NONSEQUENTIAL NUMBERS

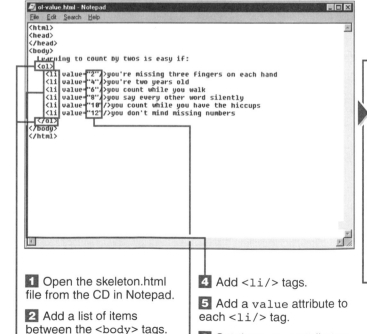

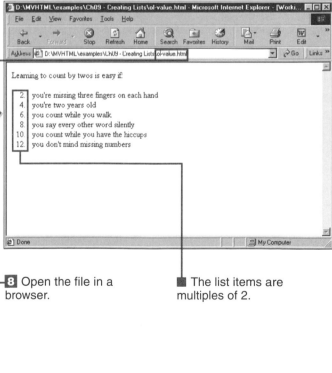

1 Open the skeleton.html file from the CD in Notepad.

2 Add a list of items between the `<body>` tags.

3 Enclose the list items within opening and closing `<ol>` tags.

4 Add `<li/>` tags.

5 Add a value attribute to each `<li/>` tag.

6 Set the value attributes to multiples of 2.

7 Save the file.

8 Open the file in a browser.

■ The list items are multiples of 2.

BUILD AN UNORDERED LIST

Another common type of list is the *unordered list.* This list is commonly called a *bulleted list.* It can be created using the <ul> tag with individual list items marked again with the <li/> tag. A bullet appears in front of each list item.

To create an unordered list, start with the opening and closing <ul> tags. Then, mark each element of

the list with an <li/> tag. The <li/> tag does not need an ending tag. When viewed in a browser, each item in the list will have a bullet in front of it. The default bullet is the solid disc.

For example, the following statement creates an unordered list with four elements: <ul><li/>item 1<li/>item 2<li/>item 3<li/>item

4</ul>. If you indent each element within the <ul> tags, the list elements are easier to see.

Unordered lists can include the type and start attributes. You can include these attributes within the opening <ol> or within the <li/> tags. They are presented in subsequent tasks later in this chapter.

BUILD AN UNORDERED LIST

1 Open the ol.html file from the CD in Notepad.

2 Change the <ol> tags to <ul> tags.

3 Save the file.

4 Open the file in a browser.

■ Each list item now begins with a bullet.

Can I mix ordered and unordered lists?

✔ You cannot make numbers appear as part of an unordered list and vice versa, but you can nest lists to make bulleted items appear next to numbered items. See the section "Create a Nested List" for an example of nesting lists.

Can I create an empty list?

✔ Lists should contain at least one item. If no `<li/>` tags are found within the `<ul>` tags, the browser ignores the tags.

What bullet types are available?

✔ With ordered lists, you can select to use a number of different list types including alphabetical and Roman numerals. The **type** attribute for unordered lists can be set to `disc`, `square`, or `circle`. The section "Change Bullet Style" shows this more detail.

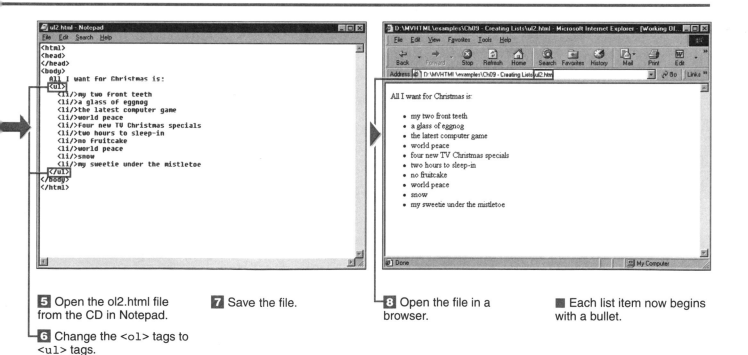

5 Open the ol2.html file from the CD in Notepad.

6 Change the `<ol>` tags to `<ul>` tags.

7 Save the file.

8 Open the file in a browser.

■ Each list item now begins with a bullet.

CHANGE BULLET STYLE

Just like you can change the numbering style for an ordered list, you can change the bullet style for an unordered list using the `type` attribute. Changing the opening `<ul>` tag's `type` attribute changes the bullet type for all list elements.

The `type` attribute can be set to `disc`, `square`, and `circle`. The `disc` type is simply a solid circle. This is the default type. The `square` type is a solid square, and the `circle` type is a ring.

For example, the statement `<ul type="square"><li/>item` `1<li/>item 2<li/>item 3<li/>item 4</ul>` creates a unordered list with four elements. Each bullet in the list includes a square bullet.

You can also change the bullet type for individual list items with the `type` attribute of the `<li/>` tag.

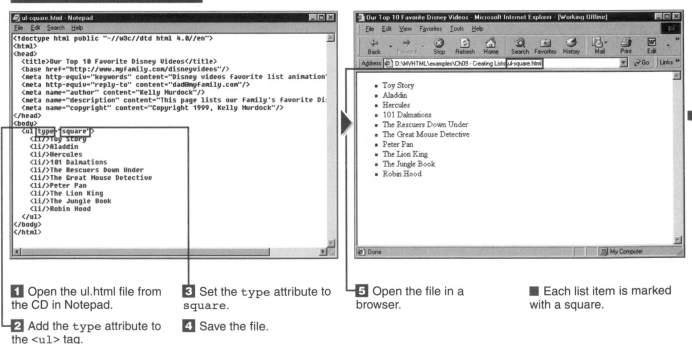

1 Open the ul.html file from the CD in Notepad.

2 Add the `type` attribute to the `<ul>` tag.

3 Set the `type` attribute to `square`.

4 Save the file.

5 Open the file in a browser.

■ Each list item is marked with a square.

Does the value attribute do anything when used in an unordered list?

✔ The `value` attribute works only when included as part of an ordered list. If it is included as part of an unordered list, the values are ignored.

Is the bullet color always the same as the text color?

✔ The bullet colors will be the same color as the text in the page. If you change the text color using the `text` attribute of the `<body>` tag, the bullet color changes.

Can I change the color of the bullets?

✔ The bullet color is always be the same color as the first character in the list item. If you surround the `<li/>` and the first character with a set of `<font>` tags with the `color` attribute set, the bullet color and the first character will be a different color from the text.

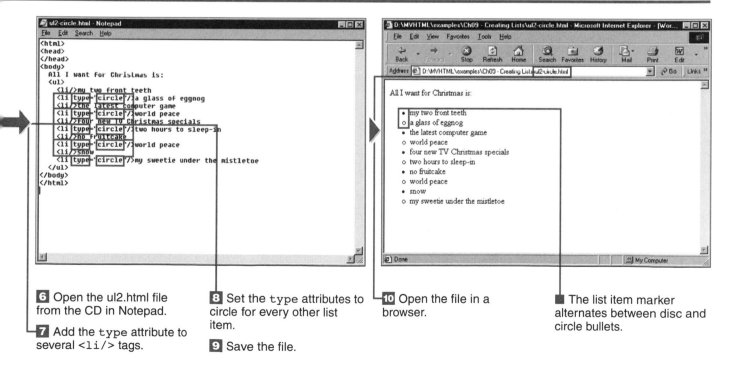

6 Open the ul2.html file from the CD in Notepad.

7 Add the `type` attribute to several `<li/>` tags.

8 Set the `type` attributes to circle for every other list item.

9 Save the file.

10 Open the file in a browser.

■ The list item marker alternates between disc and circle bullets.

CREATE A NESTED LIST

One of the key advantages of using lists is that you can *nest* one within another so that the nested list appears to be contained within the first list. This is convenient for creating outlines. Be careful not to overlap opening and closing list tags for the different lists.

For example, you can create an outline with Roman numerals that

contains a bulleted list if you nest both ordered and unordered lists. The code for this would look like
`<ol type="I"><li/>top level 1<ul><li/>item 1<li/>item 2<li/>item 3<li/>item 4</ul><li/>top level 2<ul><li/>item 1<li/>item 2<li/>item 3<li/>item 4</ul></ol>`.

This example would create two Roman numeral top-level heads. Within each top-level head would be a four element unordered list.

Nested lists can be created with different types of lists or with the same type of lists.

CREATE A NESTED LIST

```
<html>
<head>
</head>
<body>
<h1>Best Places to Live</h1>
<ol>
  <li/>Buffalo, New York
  <li/>Phoenix, Arizona
  <li/>Louisville, Kentucky
</ol>
</body>
</html>
```

Best Places to Live

1. Buffalo, New York
2. Phoenix, Arizona
3. Louisville, Kentucky

1 Open the skeleton.html file from the CD in Notepad.

2 Add a header using the `<h1>` tags.

3 Add a list of items between the `<body>` tags.

4 Enclose the items within opening and closing `<ol>` tags.

5 Add an `<li/>` tag to the front of each list item.

6 Save the file.

7 Open the file in a browser.

■ A single ordered list is displayed.

What do I need to do to indent the nested lists?

✔ Any lists that are nested within another list are automatically indented.

How can I tell which list elements belong to which list?

✔ Every list item created with an `<li/>` tag belongs to the list type that isn't closed that appears directly above it. For example, both ordered lists and unordered lists use the `<li/>` tag. If you identify a list element and look at the list type that it is contained within, you can learn the list type.

Is there any way to keep list elements straight?

✔ By using indents, you can keep the list elements straight. If you indent each subnested list in further than the parent list that contains it, you can at a glance determine the various lists and the elements that it contains.

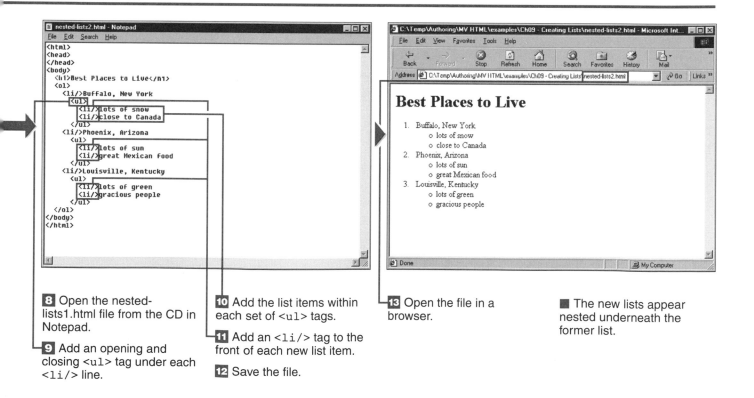

8 Open the nested-lists1.html file from the CD in Notepad.

9 Add an opening and closing `<ul>` tag under each `<li/>` line.

10 Add the list items within each set of `<ul>` tags.

11 Add an `<li/>` tag to the front of each new list item.

12 Save the file.

13 Open the file in a browser.

■ The new lists appear nested underneath the former list.

USING A DEFINITION LIST

Another type of list is the *definition list*. This type of list can be used to create a glossary or link list.

Definition lists are surrounded by <dl> tags. Inside these tags are <dt/> and <dd/> tags. The word or phrase can be marked with the <dt/> tag, and its definition is marked with the <dd/> tag.

Should the <dt/> tag always appear before the <dd/> tag?

✔ The <dd/> tag will always be indented, regardless of whether it comes first or second in the list.

Does the definition list need to have an equal number of <dt/> and <dd/> tags?

✔ Each definition list can include any number of <dt/> and <dd/> tags.

USING A DEFINITION LIST

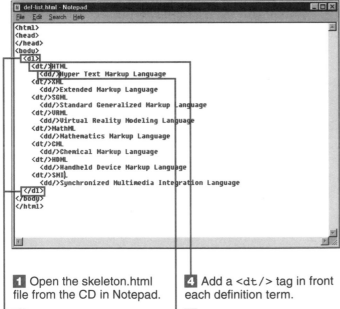

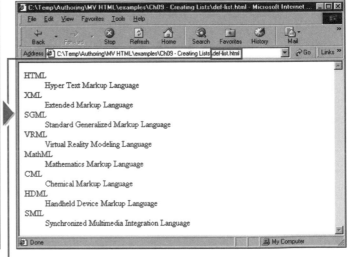

1 Open the skeleton.html file from the CD in Notepad.

2 Add opening and closing <dl> tags.

3 Add the list of definition terms and definitions within the <dl> tags.

4 Add a <dt/> tag in front each definition term.

5 Add a <dd/> tag in front each definition.

6 Save the file.

7 Open the file in a browser.

■ The definitions are indented underneath each term.

USING DIRECTORY AND MENU LISTS

HTML includes two additional list types that are not used much anymore. Directory lists are created with the `<dir>` tag, and menu lists are created with the `<menu>` tag. Like the other list types, individual list items are specified with `<li/>` tags.

The results of both these list types look just like an unordered list.

What is the difference between the directory and menu lists and the unordered list?

✔ The key difference is that the directory and menu lists do not include attributes for changing the bullet style.

USING DIRECTORY AND MENU LISTS

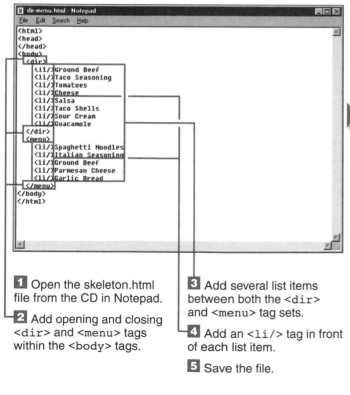

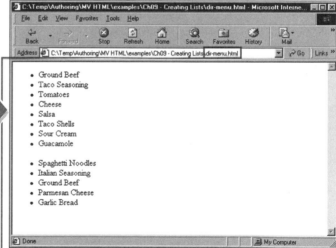

1 Open the skeleton.html file from the CD in Notepad.

2 Add opening and closing `<dir>` and `<menu>` tags within the `<body>` tags.

3 Add several list items between both the `<dir>` and `<menu>` tag sets.

4 Add an `<li/>` tag in front of each list item.

5 Save the file.

6 Open the file in a browser.

■ Notice how both list types resemble an unordered list.

WORK WITH TEXT LINKS

Linking is what makes the World Wide Web "wide." By linking to pages within your site and on other sites, users can quickly and easily navigate between many different Web pages.

Creating a text link is accomplished surrounding some text with the <a> tags. Within the

<a> tag, the href attribute holds the address that the link connects to.

For example, the statement <a href="www.lycos.com">This is a link to Lycos</a> displays the text, "This is a link to Lycos" in the browser. Clicking this link takes the user to the Web page found at www.lycos.com.

Links appear blue by default in a browser unless the link attribute of the <body> tag specifies a different color. The link attribute is covered in Chapter 6.

WORK WITH TEXT LINKS

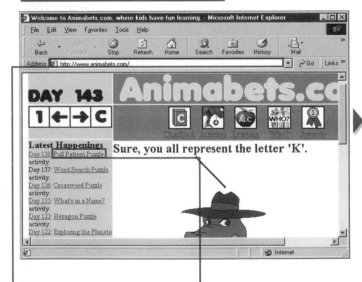

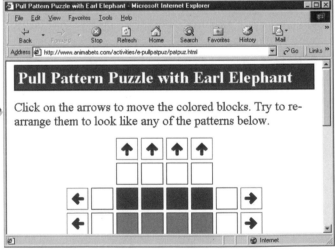

1 In a browser, type the address **www.animabets.com** in the Address bar and press Enter.

■ The Animabets.com home page loads.

2 Click the Pull Pattern Puzzle link on the left.

■ The Pull Pattern Puzzle page loads.

3 Scroll to the bottom of the page.

Why are all links colored blue and underlined?

✔ By giving links a different color and formatting, it makes them easy to recognize and access. First-time users learn very quickly that to navigate the Web they need to click these blue links.

Can I link from other HTML elements such as images?

✔ Anything within the <a> tags is considered a link. This can include text and images. Creating image links is covered in Chapter 11. Another way to link with images is to use image maps. These are covered in Chapter 14.

Can a single text link point to two different Web pages?

✔ The <a> tag can accept only a single href attribute, and it can point to only a single Web page.

■ At the bottom of the page are some additional links.

4 Click the CharBook link.

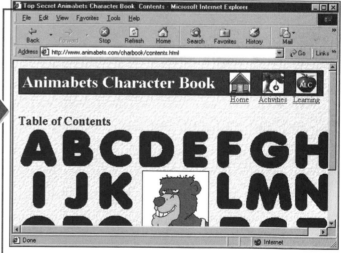

■ The Character Book Web page loads.

CREATE INTERNAL LINKS

Links to pages within your own Web site are known as *internal links*. These links can be either *absolute* or *relative*. Absolute links include the complete Web address for the Web page such as http://www.mySite.com/page1.html. Relative links locate Web pages within the same directory or

subdirectory that can be defined from the current position such as store/saleItems.html.

For example, if I have two Web pages in the same directory—one called page1.html—I can construct a link by calling the filename as the `href` attribute value.

Subdirectory paths can be specified using a slash (/) and the subdirectory name. You can also specify the directory above the current directory using two dots and a slash (../).

CREATE INTERNAL LINKS

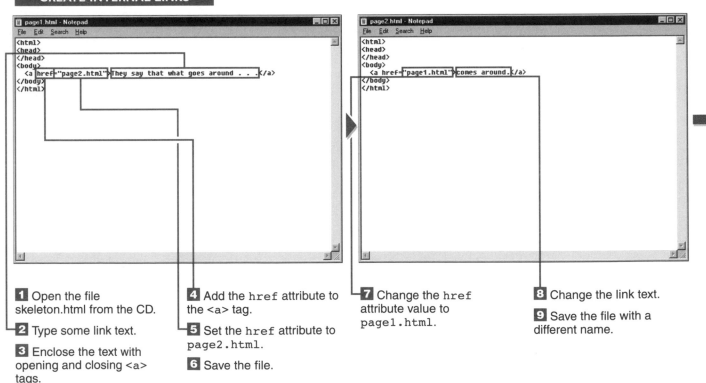

1 Open the file skeleton.html from the CD.

2 Type some link text.

3 Enclose the text with opening and closing <a> tags.

4 Add the `href` attribute to the <a> tag.

5 Set the `href` attribute to page2.html.

6 Save the file.

7 Change the `href` attribute value to pagel.html.

8 Change the link text.

9 Save the file with a different name.

How do I create links to sections within the same page?

✔ Links to sections within the same page are called *anchors*. These can also be created using the **<a>** tag, but they are referenced using the number symbol (#). This is covered later in the task "Link to Sections within a Page."

What is the advantage of using relative links versus using absolute links?

✔ If you open a local file in a browser, you can view the Web page even if you're not connected to the Internet, but links on the local Web page file work only if they are relative. Absolute links make a request to the server to retrieve the linked Web page. Relative links can be found relative to the current Web page.

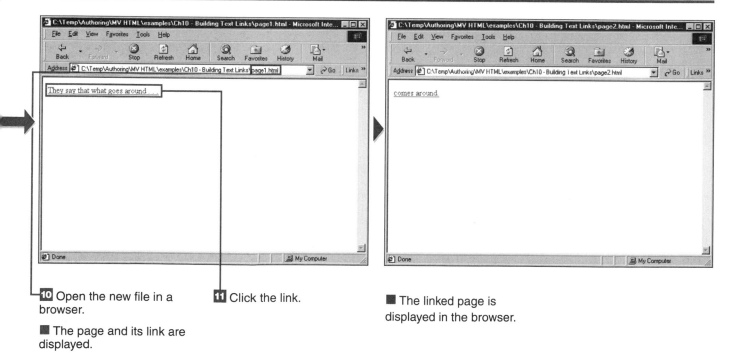

10 Open the new file in a browser.

■ The page and its link are displayed.

11 Click the link.

■ The linked page is displayed in the browser.

CREATE EXTERNAL LINKS

Links outside of your own Web site are known *as external links*. These links must always be *absolute*. An absolute link can include a protocol, such as HTTP, a domain name, such as www.myfamily.com, and a filename.

Each directory in an absolute link is separated by a slash symbol (/).

Note that this symbol is different from the backslash (\) that is used in Windows and DOS to separate directories.

Entering the protocol is optional for Internet Explorer. If you enter a Web address into the Address bar of the browser without a specified protocol, the browser automatically assumes that this address points to a Web page and includes the HTTP protocol.

Web page links, therefore, do not need to include the protocol. For example, a link with the href attribute set to "www.hello.com" finds the page.

---

1 Open the file skeleton.html on the CD in Notepad.

2 Type two titles of external pages to which you want to link. Add a <br /> tag to the end of each line.

3 Add <a> tags.

4 Add the href attribute to the <a> tags and set them to the Web page addresses.

5 Save the file as a new HTML file.

6 Open the new HTML file in a browser.

7 Click the first link.

■ The page shows two links.

Is there any way to tell where a link goes before clicking it?

✔ If you move the mouse over a link, the link address appears in the status bar of the browser. This helps you know where the link will take you before you visit it.

Can I use the backslash in place of the forward slash when specifying links?

✔ The backslash is used on Windows machines to designate the various directories, but for HTML links, you need to use the forward slash in order for the link to work.

What happens if I misspell the address of a link?

✔ If you misspell the Web address of a link, the linked Web page will most likely not be found. Chapter 38 shows how to use some utilities to check the links on a site.

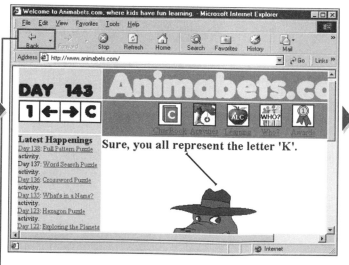

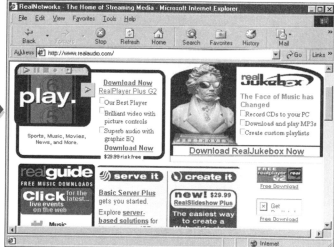

■ This link takes you to the Animabets.com Web page.

■ The previous page is loaded.

■ The RealAudio.com Web page loads.

8 Click the Back button in the browser.

9 Click the second link.

NAME ANCHORS

The `<a>` tag can also be used to name anchor points within a Web page. These anchor points can be referenced within a link and will automatically scroll the browser so the anchor's location is displayed at the top of the browser.

The `name` attribute is used to designate and name these anchors. The anchor name does not require a closing `<a>` tag because it is only marking a position. So, `<a name="top"/>` would be a valid anchor.

Does the `<a>` tag always require a closing tag?

✔ When the `</a>` tag is used to name anchors, the closing tag is not needed, but you should include a / to be compliant with the XHTML standard. However, when a set of `<a>` tags is used to create a link, make sure you include both opening and closing `<a>` tags.

NAME ANCHORS

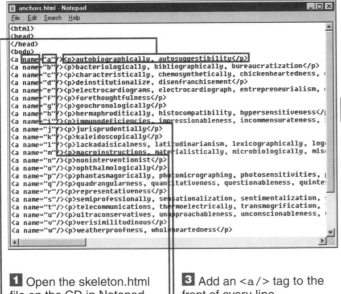

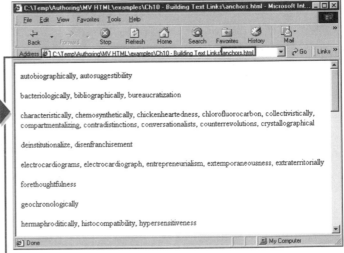

1 Open the skeleton.html file on the CD in Notepad.

2 Type in several sections of text in between the `<body>` tags. Enclose each line with `<p>` tags.

3 Add an `<a/>` tag to the front of every line.

4 Add the `name` attribute.

5 Set the value of the `name` attribute to the anchor title.

6 Save the file as a new HTML file.

7 Open the new HTML file in a browser.

■ Notice how the addition of anchor titles does not change the text in any way.

LINK TO SECTIONS WITHIN A PAGE

To link to an anchor name, you must include the number symbol (#) in front of the anchor name.

For example, if you create an anchor named Top, you can link to this anchor with the code `<a href="#Top">`.

What if the number symbol (#) is left off?

✔ If the number symbol (#) is left off, then the browser looks for a Web page with the anchor name. The number symbol (#) tells the `<a>` tag to look for an anchor tag.

LINK TO SECTIONS WITHIN A PAGE

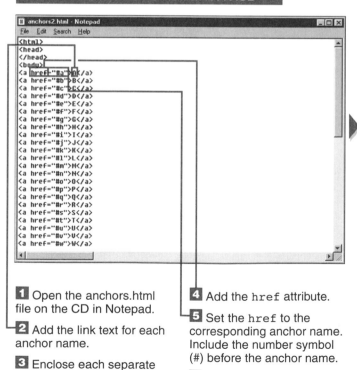

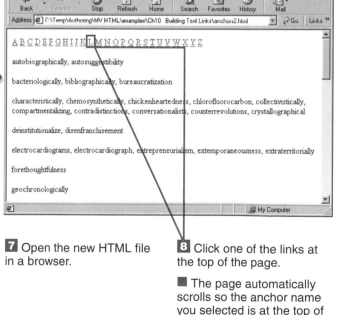

1 Open the anchors.html file on the CD in Notepad.

2 Add the link text for each anchor name.

3 Enclose each separate link text with opening and closing `<a>` tags.

4 Add the `href` attribute.

5 Set the `href` to the corresponding anchor name. Include the number symbol (#) before the anchor name.

6 Save the file as a new HTML file.

7 Open the new HTML file in a browser.

8 Click one of the links at the top of the page.

■ The page automatically scrolls so the anchor name you selected is at the top of the browser.

USING MAILTO LINKS

A large majority of the links you create will link to Web pages, but links do not always need to point to a Web page. Another way to use links is to point to a user's e-mail address.

Using the mailto protocol instead of HTTP, you can link to an e-mail address. When a user clicks the e-mail link, the system's e-mail client is opened with the address entered.

You can also automatically tell the client where to send the e-mail and what the e-mail subject and message should say using the subject and body keywords.

The format should look like this: mailto:jerry@myfamily.com ?subject=hello&body=my message. The question mark (?) lets you add variables that can be interpreted by the mail client. The ampersand (&) separates the various variables.

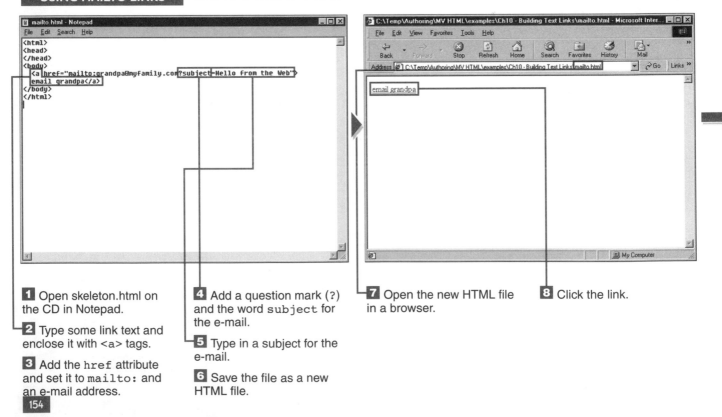

1 Open skeleton.html on the CD in Notepad.

2 Type some link text and enclose it with <a> tags.

3 Add the href attribute and set it to mailto: and an e-mail address.

4 Add a question mark (?) and the word subject for the e-mail.

5 Type in a subject for the e-mail.

6 Save the file as a new HTML file.

7 Open the new HTML file in a browser.

8 Click the link.

154

The subject keyword can be used to add a subject to the message. Are there any other keywords that add content to the e-mail?

✔ If you add an ampersand (&) after the first parameter like `subject`, additional parameters can be added to the link. Another useful parameter is the `body` keyword. This keyword can be set to the text that will appear in the body of the message. For example, the statement `mailto:grandpa@ myfamily.com?subject=hello& body=this is a message` automatically fills the address, subject, and body of the e-mail.

Are there any other protocols that can be used in the same way as the mailto protocol?

✔ In addition to the HTTP and `mailto` protocols, you can link to a newsgroup with the `news` protocol. This works by setting the `href` value to `news` and listing the newsgroup name. For example, `href="news: comp.pcs.videocards"`. The tasks "Using FTP Links" and "Link to Files" cover other link types including `ftp` and `file`.

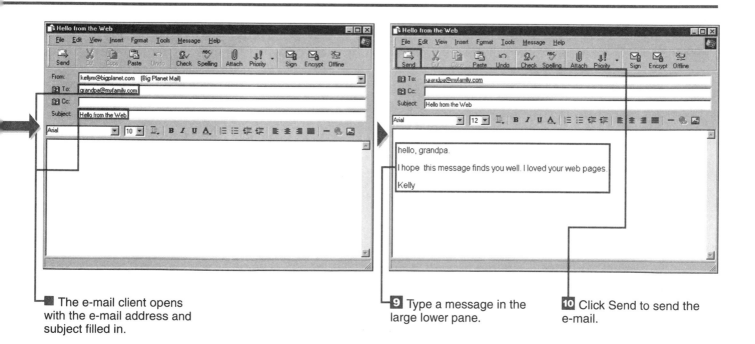

■ The e-mail client opens with the e-mail address and subject filled in.

⑨ Type a message in the large lower pane.

⑩ Click Send to send the e-mail.

USING FTP LINKS

FTP stands for File Transfer Protocol. An FTP site usually contains directories of files that provide an easy way to locate and download files. Most FTP sites require a username and password to access the site.

To make an FTP link, type **ftp** followed by the username and password (separated by a colon),

the at sign (@), and then the site location. For example, href= "ftp://user23:password1@ flowers.com/roses/ bloom.txt would access the file bloom.txt in the roses directory on the flowers.com FTP site. Be warned that this link makes your username and password visible in the source.

Many FTP sites do not require a username or password. For these sites, the link can be simply ftp:// and the domain name, as the example in this section shows.

The following example uses the file skeleton.html, which is included on the CD that comes with this book.

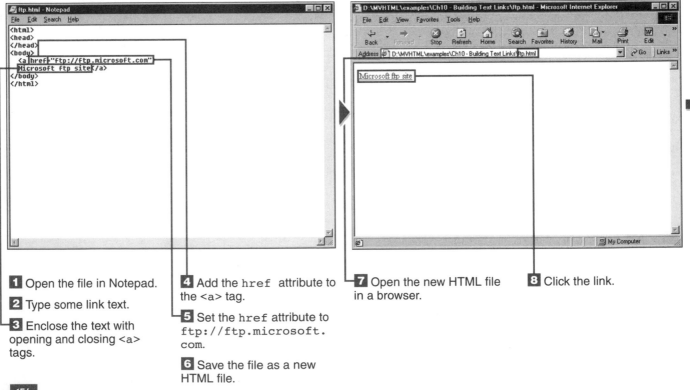

■1 Open the file in Notepad.

■2 Type some link text.

■3 Enclose the text with opening and closing <a> tags.

■4 Add the href attribute to the <a> tag.

■5 Set the href attribute to ftp://ftp.microsoft. com.

■6 Save the file as a new HTML file.

■7 Open the new HTML file in a browser.

■8 Click the link.

What if you do not have a username or password for an FTP site?

✔ If you do not have a username or password for an FTP site, contact the site manager and ask him or her for one. Many sites, such as Microsoft.com, enable you to use the username anonymous and your e-mail address as the password.

Is there a security risk if I include the username and password to the FTP site within the link?

✔ If you include the username and password to the FTP site within the link, this information becomes available to anyone who views the source to the Web page. The username and password will also be displayed on the browser's status bar whenever a user moves the mouse over the link. This is a security risk to your FTP site and should be used with caution.

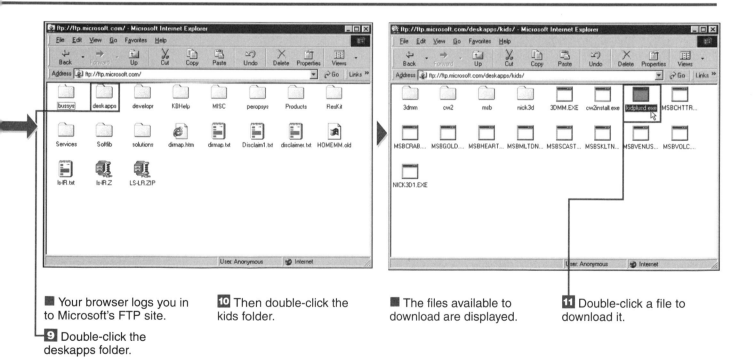

■ Your browser logs you in to Microsoft's FTP site.

9 Double-click the deskapps folder.

10 Then double-click the kids folder.

■ The files available to download are displayed.

11 Double-click a file to download it.

LINK TO FILES

Web pages are visible because they are posted to servers connected to the Web, but you can also view and link to files that are on your local computer.

The easiest way to load a local file into a browser is to drag it from a file manager like Windows Explorer and drop it on the browser window. This action loads the Web page within the browser.

To link to a local file, use the `file:` protocol and include the directory and filename for the file to open.

For example, a link with the `href` attribute set to `"file://C| temp/hello.html"` links to a file named hello.html located on the C drive in the temp directory.

LINK TO FILES

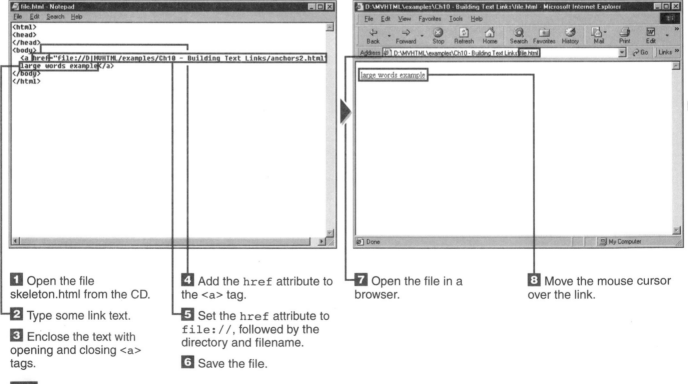

1 Open the file skeleton.html from the CD.

2 Type some link text.

3 Enclose the text with opening and closing <a> tags.

4 Add the `href` attribute to the <a> tag.

5 Set the `href` attribute to `file://`, followed by the directory and filename.

6 Save the file.

7 Open the file in a browser.

8 Move the mouse cursor over the link.

How can I indicate a different local hard drive?

✔ To indicate a different local hard drive, you need to add the hard drive letter followed by the pipe symbol (|) after the `file` keyword. For example, `href="file://D|temp/hello.html"` loads the file named hello.html from the temp directory on the D hard drive.

How do I represent spaces if the file directory name includes spaces?

✔ If you are trying to link to a local file that includes spaces in the name or spaces in any of the directory names, you should replace the spaces with '`%20`'. When the server encounters the '`%20`' symbols, it automatically replaces them with a space. This process is called *URL encoding*, and it is covered in Chapter 38.

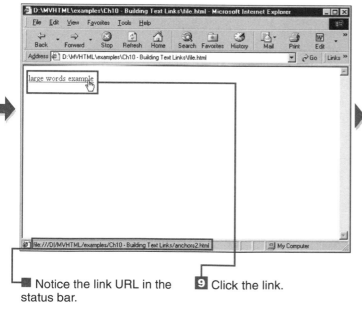

■ Notice the link URL in the status bar.

9 Click the link.

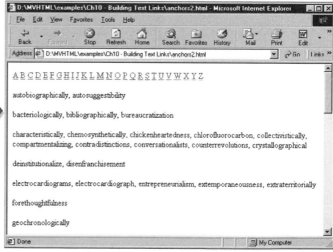

■ The linked page loads.

11) ADDING IMAGES

12) WORKING WITH GIF IMAGES

13) WORKING WITH JPEG AND PNG IMAGES

14) BUILDING IMAGE MAPS

UNDERSTANDING IMAGE TYPES

Web page browsers cannot use just any old format. They require that you use one of three specific formats that the browsers recognize. These acceptable formats include GIF, JPEG, and PNG.

All these formats include features that enable them to be optimized to produce small file sizes. The smaller the image file, the quicker the download.

Each of the formats is slightly different, and they each have advantages and disadvantages.

GIF Images

GIF (Graphics Interchange Format) images are the most common image format found on the Web. This format supports 256 separate colors and includes some additional features such as transparency, interlacing, and animation capabilities. Chapter 12 covers each of these unique features in more detail.

GIF images are compressed using a "lossless" compression algorithm. This algorithm looks for sections of the image that are similar. For example, if an image has a white section where the next 200 pixels are all white, then instead of saving the value of white 200 times, the format simply saves the information that the next 200 pixels are all white. This dramatically reduces the amount of information needed to represent the image, and no image information is lost.

Because of the way GIF images are compressed, they provide a suitable format for line drawings such as cartoons and for images with large sections of solid colors like company logos.

GIF images, however, are not a good choice for images with a lot of colors, such as gradients or photographs. Because the GIF format only supports 256 colors, any additional colors are mapped to one of these 256.

JPEG Images

The JPEG (Joint Photographic Experts Group) format supports 16.7 million colors and provides a good format to use for photographs and images that include a broad range of colors.

The compression algorithm used to compress JPEG images enables you to specify the amount of compression. The trade-off is between image quality and file size. JPEG compression is a "lossy" algorithm, which means that some of the image information is lost during the compression process.

The JPEG format also includes a progressive feature that is similar to interlacing GIF images. Chapter 13 covers this and other JPEG features.

PNG Images

The PNG (Portable Network Graphics) format is a relatively new format being used on the Web. In many respects, it combines the best of both GIF and JPEG formats.

The PNG format, like the JPEG format, supports 16.7 million colors, but its compression algorithms are "lossless." This means that the graphical information isn't removed from the image during the compression calculations.

See Chapter 13 for more details on the PNG format.

ADD IMAGES TO A WEB PAGE

Images can do a lot for making your Web pages more interesting, and there are many different techniques that use images. The tasks in this chapter show you how to add and control images on your Web pages. These images are sometimes called *inline images*.

Images are added to a Web page using the `<img/>` tag. The URL of the image to include is specified in the `src` attribute. This URL could be simply the filename of the image if the image is located in the same directory as the Web page. It could also be an absolute URL pointing to an image anywhere on the Web.

The polar bear image used in this example was provided by Art Today. Found at www.ArtToday.com, they provide a large repository of online images.

ADD IMAGES TO A WEB PAGE

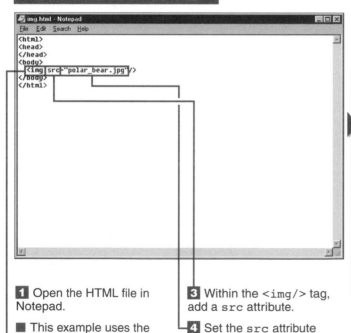

1 Open the HTML file in Notepad.

■ This example uses the skeleton.html file from the book's CD.

2 Within the `<body>` tags, add an `<img/>` tag.

3 Within the `<img/>` tag, add a `src` attribute.

4 Set the `src` attribute equal to the image filename.

5 Save the file under a new name.

6 Open the HTML file in a browser.

■ The image is displayed in the browser.

Can the src attribute point to an FTP site or a local file?

✔ URLs using the file and FTP keyword count as URLs and can be used to load an image on a Web page. Keep in mind that local files are not accessible to other people on the Web.

Are there any other image formats that can be used?

✔ Microsoft's Internet Explorer browser recognizes the BMP image format, but Netscape Navigator does not.

What can I do if I am using an image other than a GIF, JPG, or PNG?

✔ If you've created an image and saved it in a format other than GIF, JPEG or PNG, you need to convert the image file to one of the above formats. Most graphics programs let you save images in these formats.

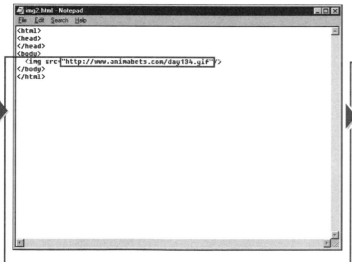

7 Open the new HTML file in Notepad.

8 Change the `src` attribute to be an absolute URL for an image on the Web.

9 Save the file with a new filename.

10 Open the new HTML file in a browser.

■ The Web image is displayed in the browser.

SPECIFY IMAGE DIMENSIONS

The <img/> tag also includes attributes for setting the dimensions of the image. These attributes are width and height.

If these attributes are missing, the browser displays the image with its default dimensions. The default dimensions are the size of the image when it was initially saved. The benefit of including these

attributes is that the browser knows the exact size of the image and can continue with the page layout even if the entire image hasn't finished downloading. Including the width and height attributes can actually make the Web page download and appear faster.

If the width and height values are different than the actual image

dimensions, the image is resized to the specified dimensions.

You can find the dimensions of any Web page image by right-clicking the image and selecting Properties from the pop-up menu. This command opens the Properties dialog box where the image dimensions are displayed.

SPECIFY IMAGE DIMENSIONS

1 Open the HTML file in Notepad.

■ This example uses the skeleton.html file from the book's CD.

2 Within the <body> tags, add an <img/> tag.

3 Within the <img/> tag, add width and height attributes.

4 Set the width attribute and the height attribute measured in pixels.

5 Save the file with a new filename.

6 Open the HTML file in a browser.

■ Notice how the browser uses the width and height attributes to allocate the space for the image.

What happens if I use dimension values that are different from the image's actual dimensions?

✔ If you use image dimensions that are different from the image's actual dimensions, the image is resized to the dimensions you specify. This can be used to your advantage to size a single-pixel image to a large block of color as shown in the section "Add Color Using Single-Pixel Images," in the next chapter. If used with graphic images, however, the image could be stretched or squashed disproportionately.

Does reducing the display size of an image speed up my Web page?

✔ The entire image is downloaded regardless of the size that is specified in the width and height attributes, so the images do not download any quicker if the width and height attributes are reduced. This also means that the image download will not increase if the image is sized larger.

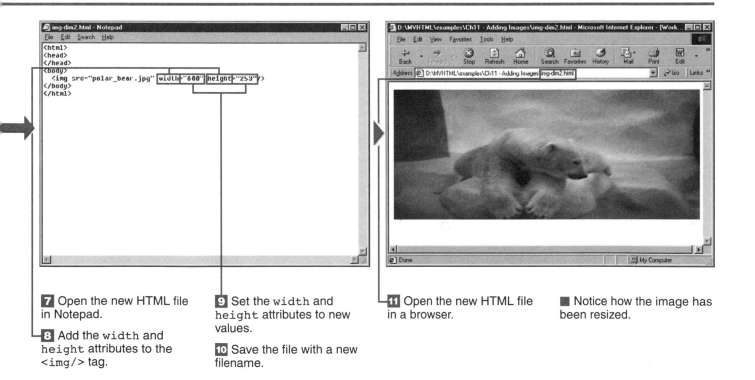

7 Open the new HTML file in Notepad.

8 Add the width and height attributes to the <img/> tag.

9 Set the width and height attributes to new values.

10 Save the file with a new filename.

11 Open the new HTML file in a browser.

■ Notice how the image has been resized.

ALIGN IMAGES

It can be tricky to position images exactly where you want them in the browser. By default, a single image added to a Web page is positioned in the upper-left corner of the browser, but you can change the horizontal or vertical alignment of images using the `align` attribute.

The options for horizontal alignment include `left` (the default) or `right`. For vertical alignment, the options are `top`, `middle`, and `bottom`.

The vertical alignment is based on the text to the side of the image. For example, if an image is placed to the right of a paragraph of text and the `align` attribute is set to `top`, the last line of the paragraph will be aligned with the top of the image. If the `align` attribute is set to `bottom`, the last line of text will be aligned with the bottom edge of the image.

Using dynamic HTML, you can control with more detail the exact placement of images on a Web page. See Part X, "Using Dynamic HTML," for more on this subject.

ALIGN IMAGES

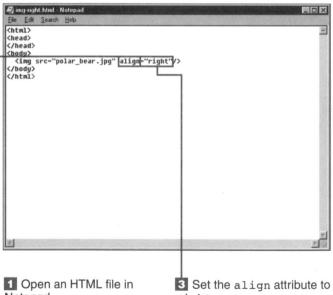

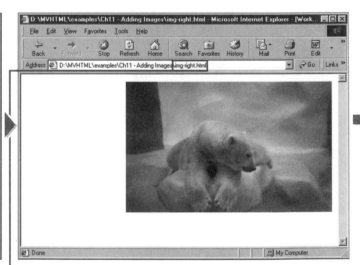

1 Open an HTML file in Notepad.

■ This example uses the img.html file from the book's CD.

2 Within the `<img/>` tag, add the `align` attribute.

3 Set the `align` attribute to `right`.

4 Save the file with a new filename.

5 Open the HTML file in a browser.

■ The image is aligned to the right in the browser.

Can I center an image in the browser?

✔ For the `align` attribute of the `<img/>` tag, center is not an option. You can surround the image with opening and closing `<center>` tags. These tags center in the browser all items that are included within the them. Another technique is to use tables to position the image. Items within tables can be centered within the table cells. Using tables is covered in Chapter 15.

What other options are available for positioning images?

✔ In addition to the `<center>` tags and tables, you can use style sheets to position images. Style sheets include many different alignment options including the ability to position Web page elements anywhere within the browser. Style sheets are covered in Part IX of this book. Style sheets are actually the preferred method for aligning Web page elements.

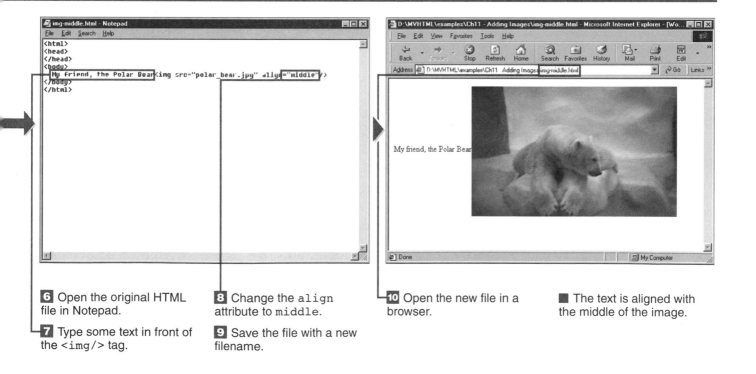

6 Open the original HTML file in Notepad.

7 Type some text in front of the `<img/>` tag.

8 Change the `align` attribute to `middle`.

9 Save the file with a new filename.

10 Open the new file in a browser.

■ The text is aligned with the middle of the image.

ADD SPACE BETWEEN IMAGE AND TEXT

Many Web pages use text and images together. HTML provides several options for defining how the text and images are laid-out. These options are specified using attributes that are added to the `<img/>` tag.

When a large section of text is positioned next to an image, text is pushed up to the very edge of the

image. Using the `vspace` and `hspace` attributes, you can define the amount of space that appears between the text and the image. Both these attributes are set equal to the number of pixels of space that should appear between the image and the text.

For example, if an image is specified using a tag like `<img src="myImage.gif"`

`hspace=10 vspace=20/>`, 10 pixels of space will be displayed on each side of the image and 20 pixels of space will appear above and below the image.

This is a good attribute to use because it makes the page appear cleaner and sets the images off from the text. The `vspace` and `hspace` attribute values are measured in pixels.

ADD SPACE BETWEEN IMAGE AND TEXT

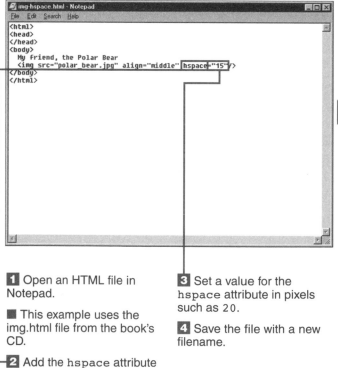

1 Open an HTML file in Notepad.

■ This example uses the img.html file from the book's CD.

2 Add the `hspace` attribute to the `<img/>` tag.

3 Set a value for the `hspace` attribute in pixels such as `20`.

4 Save the file with a new filename.

5 Open the new HTML file in a browser.

■ The image is separated from the text by the number of pixels you designate.

Can I use negative values for the hspace and vspace attributes to position the text over the image?

✔ If you specify a negative value for the `hspace` and `vspace` attributes, the browser will simply interpret these values as zero and display no space between the text and image. If you want to position text on top of an image, you can use Dynamic HTML to accomplish this. This topic is covered in Part X, "Using Dynamic HTML."

Is the space always symmetrical on both sides of the image?

✔ Using the `hspace` and `vspace` attributes will add space symmetrically around the image. The `hspace` attribute adds space to both sides of the image, and the `vspace` attribute adds equivalent space to both the top and bottom of the image. These attributes offer no way for you to specify unequal space to the image.

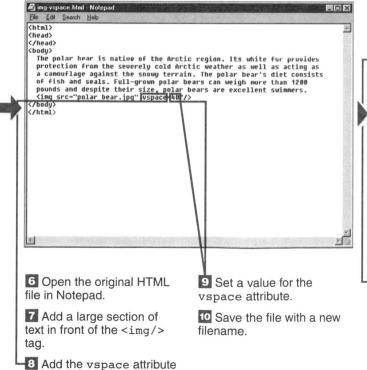

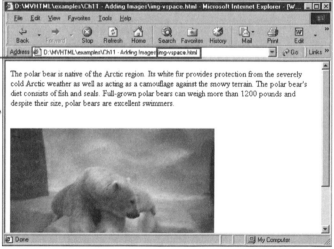

6 Open the original HTML file in Notepad.

7 Add a large section of text in front of the `<img/>` tag.

8 Add the `vspace` attribute to the `<img/>` tag.

9 Set a value for the `vspace` attribute.

10 Save the file with a new filename.

11 Open the new file in a browser.

■ The image is separated vertically from the text by the number of pixels you designate.

WRAP TEXT AROUND AN IMAGE

Another advantage of the `align` attribute is to cause the text to wrap around the image. If text comes below an image that uses the `align` attribute set to either `left` or `right`, the text wraps around the image on either the left or right side.

When text is wrapped around the image, you can also use the `hspace` and `vspace` attributes to separate the image from the text.

For example, if a paragraph is text is followed with the statement `<img src="myimage.gif" align="right"/>`, the text will wrap around the right side of the image.

The text can flow around the image, but if the browser window isn't wide enough to include the image, the space designated by the `hspace` value, and the text, then the text will be displayed below the image without any wrapping.

WRAP TEXT AROUND AN IMAGE

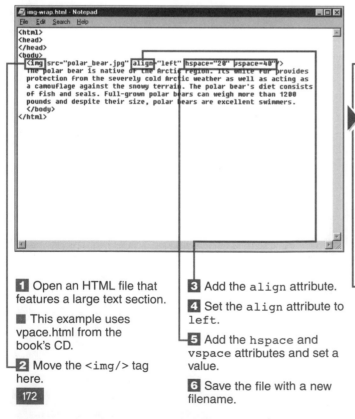

1 Open an HTML file that features a large text section.

■ This example uses vpace.html from the book's CD.

2 Move the `<img/>` tag here.

3 Add the `align` attribute.

4 Set the `align` attribute to `left`.

5 Add the `hspace` and `vspace` attributes and set a value.

6 Save the file with a new filename.

7 Open the HTML file in a browser.

■ The text wraps to the right of the image.

172

Because left is the default alignment, do I still get text wrapping if I do not specify the align attribute?

✔ Although left is the default alignment value, if the `align` attribute is missing, the image will be aligned to the left, but the text will appear below the image. If the `align` attribute is included and set to `left`, the text will wrap to the right of the image.

Are there any other ways to align images and wrap text?

✔ Tables can be used to position text and images. Another useful way to wrap text around an image is to use style sheets. Style sheets offer many unique options for working with text and images such as specifying text alignment, indents and letter and word spacing. Style sheets are covered in Part IX.

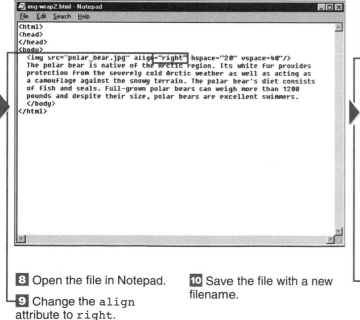

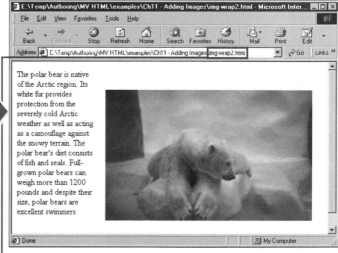

8 Open the file in Notepad.

9 Change the `align` attribute to `right`.

10 Save the file with a new filename.

11 Open the new HTML file in a browser.

■ The text wraps to the left of the image.

ADD AN IMAGE BORDER

Another way to define the space that the image occupies is to add a border around the image. Borders are also useful to set off the image from the rest of the page.

Image borders are created using the border attribute. The value for this attribute is the width of the

border, which is measured in pixels.

For example, the statement <img src="myImage.gif" border= "10"/> creates a 10-pixel border around the entire image.

The default color for the image border is the same as the text color. If the image is made into a link, as

shown in the "Create an Image Link" task that appears later in this chapter, the border color will be the same as the link color, which is blue by default.

If the border attribute is missing or set to 0, no borders will appear around the image.

ADD AN IMAGE BORDER

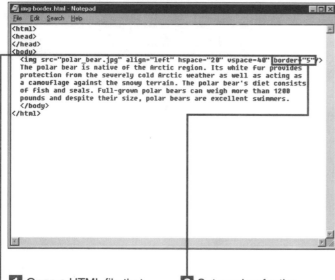

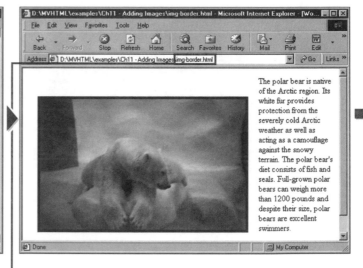

1 Open a HTML file that features a large text section in Notepad.

■ This example uses the img-border.html file from the book's CD.

2 Add the border attribute.

3 Set a value for the border attribute.

4 Save the file with a new filename.

5 Open the new file in a browser.

■ A border of the pixel thickness you designated surrounds the image.

Can I color the border?

✔ The border is always colored the same color as the text in the Web page, unless it is a link. Linked images will be colored the same color as text links. The text and link colors can be changed using the `text` and `link` attributes of the `<body>` tag. Chapter 6 shows how these attributes work. A work-around to this is to add a colored border to the actual image. This can be done using an image-editing package.

Can style sheets be used to create image borders?

✔ Style sheets, covered in Part IX, can add borders to images. Style sheet image borders can vary in style, color and width. You can even apply a different borders to each side of the image independently.

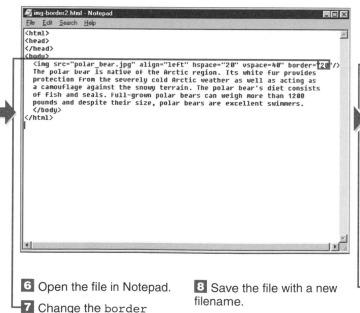

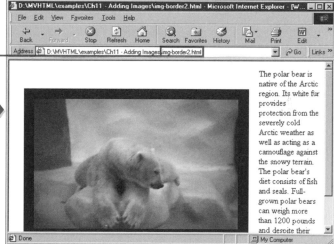

6 Open the file in Notepad.

7 Change the `border` attribute value.

8 Save the file with a new filename.

9 Open the file in a browser.

■ A border with a different thickness surrounds the image.

MAKE AN ALTERNATIVE TEXT LABEL

lternative text is a line of text that is associated with an image. This text is displayed if the user moves and stops the mouse cursor over the top of the image.

If a user stops the browser before the entire page is downloaded, chances are they will not get to see the images associated with the

page, but the alternative text will be visible.

Using the alt attribute, you can specify alternative text that displays if the mouse cursor is positioned over the image that's fully downloaded or in the image's place if the entire image is not downloaded.

For example the statement <img src="myImage.gif" alt="This is my favorite image."/> displays the alternative text if the image could not load into the browser.

If the alt attribute is missing, the image will appear fine, but it will not have a title.

MAKE AN ALTERNATIVE TEXT LABEL

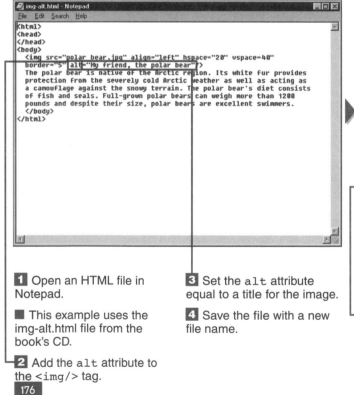

1 Open an HTML file in Notepad.

■ This example uses the img-alt.html file from the book's CD.

2 Add the alt attribute to the <img/> tag.

3 Set the alt attribute equal to a title for the image.

4 Save the file with a new file name.

5 Open the new HTML file in a browser.

6 Move the mouse cursor over the image.

■ The text specified in the alt attribute is displayed.

Is there ever a time when the alt attribute should not be included?

✔ In Chapter 12, I describe how to use single-pixel images and image spacers to help you position images and text within the browser. Single-pixel images and image spacers would not need to use the `alt` attribute.

Should I use alt attributes all the time?

✔ Another major reason to include the `alt` attribute for every image is for browsers built for the blind. These browsers read the alt text to the user, so you need to be specific about what the image shows. Browsers can be configured to not show any images. Users will select this option to make the Web pages download quicker. If this setting is enabled, the alternative text can be used to explain to the user what the image is showing.

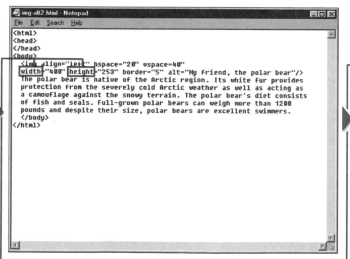

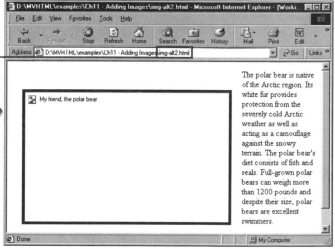

7 Open the HTML file in Notepad.

8 Add the `width` and `height` attributes to the `<img/>` tag.

9 Set values for the `width` attribute.

10 Remove the `src` attribute from the `<img/>` tag.

■ Removing the `src` attribute causes the image to fail to load in the browser.

11 Save the file with a new filename.

12 Open the file in a browser.

■ The space for the image is shown with the alt text.

CREATE AN IMAGE LINK

Images often make better, more-intuitive hyperlinks than text. Many navigation schemes use images for their links instead of text. Chapter 10 shows how text can be made into hyperlinks.

Just as text can be used as a link as, an image can also be used as a

link. To make an image into a link, simply surround the complete `<img/>` tag with opening and closing `<a>` tags and set the `href` attribute to where you want the link to go. Image links, like text links, can be either relative or absolute.

Different parts of an image can also be set to link to different places if you create an image map. Image maps are discussed in Chapter 14.

If a linked image includes a border, then the border will be the same color as the text links.

CREATE AN IMAGE LINK

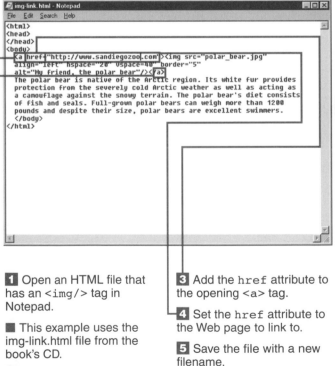

1 Open an HTML file that has an `<img/>` tag in Notepad.

■ This example uses the img-link.html file from the book's CD.

2 Add `<a>` tags.

3 Add the `href` attribute to the opening `<a>` tag.

4 Set the `href` attribute to the Web page to link to.

5 Save the file with a new filename.

6 Open the file in a browser.

■ The border color has changed to blue.

178

Is there any way to identify an image as a link if the borders are turned off?

✔ If an image does not include any borders, the only way to tell if the image is a link is to move the mouse cursor over the top of the image and look at the browser's status bar to see if there is a link URL.

Can image links be used to link to an e-mail or an FTP site?

✔ Image links, since they use the <a> tag are exactly the same as text links. To link to an e-mail address, you simply need to add the mailto:// protocol to the front of the e-mail address. To link to an FTP site, you need to use the ftp:// protocol in front of the FTP site address.

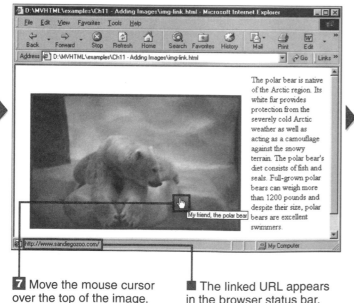

7 Move the mouse cursor over the top of the image.

■ The linked URL appears in the browser status bar.

8 Click the image.

■ The Web page that the image is linked to opens.

CREATE THUMBNAIL IMAGES

One of the difficulties inherent with working with large images is that they take a considerably longer amount of time to download. One way to resolve this issue is to present the user with several thumbnail images.

Thumbnail images are smaller versions of the original. Being smaller, they can download much more quickly. Thumbnail images give the user an idea of what the image looks like and lets them decide whether to download the larger image.

The smaller thumbnail images could then be linked to the larger image. To create an image link, see the previous task, "Create an Image Link."

Be cautious to not just change the `width` and `height` attribute values. Changing these values will still cause the entire large image to download and be resized by the browser. To gain quicker download speeds, the thumbnail needs to be a separate image.

CREATE THUMBNAIL IMAGES

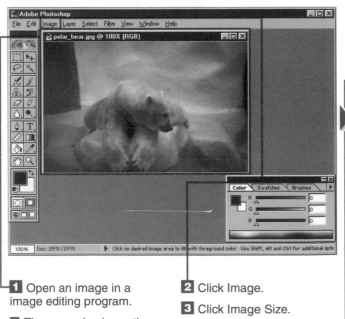

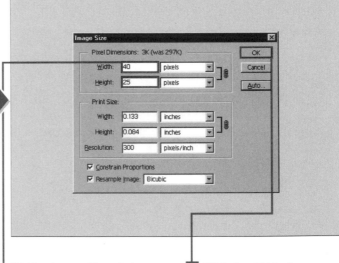

1 Open an image in a image editing program.

■ The example shows the polar_bear.jpg image in Photoshop.

2 Click Image.

3 Click Image Size.

■ The Image Size dialog box opens.

4 Type a width measurement in the Width field.

■ The Height field automatically updates to maintain the same height to width ratio.

5 Click the OK button.

■ The image is resized.

6 Save the file with a new name.

What size should thumbnail images be?

✔ The size of your thumbnails depends on the size of your original image. You should always look closely at your thumbnails to see if they are a good representation of the original image. You can also reduce the size of your thumbnails by reducing the number of colors used.

Are there any other ways to create thumbnails?

✔ Another thumbnail method is to simply crop (or cut) a small section of the original image and use that as a thumbnail.

Should I tell readers how big the actual image file is before they click the thumbnail?

✔ It is a really good idea to let the users know the size of large image. This helps them decide whether they want to take the time to download the larger image.

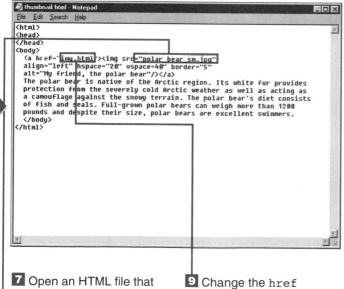

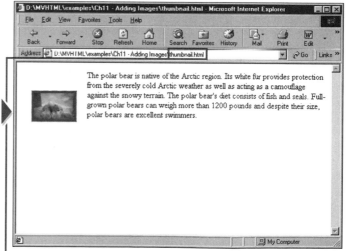

7 Open an HTML file that has an `<img/>` tag in Notepad.

■ This example uses the thumbnail.html file from the book's CD.

8 Change the `src` attribute to the thumbnail filename.

9 Change the `href` attribute of the `<a>` tag to link to another Web page.

10 Save the file with a new filename.

11 Open the thumbnail file in a browser.

■ The thumbnail image is linked to a Web page with the full image.

LOAD A BACKGROUND IMAGE

The Web page background is one of the first items that is loaded when a Web page is accessed. The background offers the first impression of a Web page.

Chapter 6 shows how to change the background color of a Web page with the bgcolor attribute added

to the opening <body> tag. The <body> tag includes another attribute that you can use to load an image into the background of a Web page.

This attribute is background, and it accepts the URL of an image to load into the background.

Any text added to the page is drawn over the top of the background image, so you should try to use background images that are mostly solid colors if you want your Web pages to be legible. You should also be careful that the color of the background image does not match the text color.

LOAD A BACKGROUND IMAGE

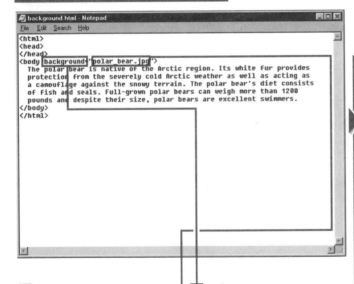

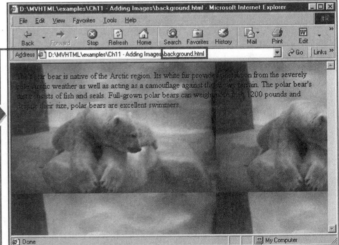

1 Open the an HTML file in Notepad.

■ This example uses the background.html file on the CD.

2 Remove any <img/> tags.

3 Add the background attribute to the <body> tag.

4 Set the background attribute to filename for an image.

5 Save the file with a new filename.

6 Open the new file in a browser.

■ The image loads into the background, and the text appears on top of the image.

182

Can I load an HTML file as the background?

✔ The only file types that are accepted by the `background` attribute are the GIF, JPEG, and PNG image formats. If you specify a Web page, the background loads as the default white color.

Can I use style sheets to get the same result as using the background attribute?

✔ Style sheets can be used to control many aspect of the background including its color, the background image's position, and how it repeats. Style sheets are covered in Part IX.

How do I create a good background image?

✔ Background images can be created using an image editing package. If the details of the background image make it difficult to see the text on the Web page, try fading the image to improve legibility.

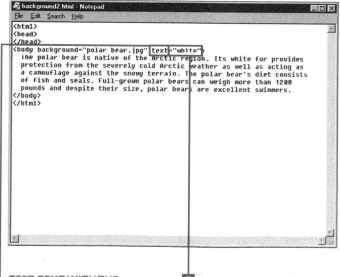

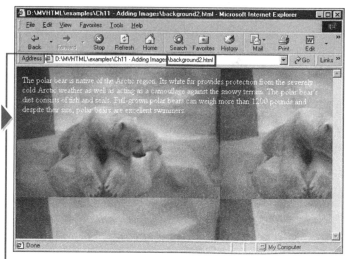

TEST TEXT WITH THE BACKGROUND

1 Open the HTML file in Notepad.

2 Add the text attribute to the <body> tag.

3 Set the `text` attribute to another color.

4 Save the file with a new filename.

5 Open the new file in a browser.

■ The text is now easier to read across the background image.

TILE A BACKGROUND IMAGE

When you load a background image using the steps outlined in "Loading a Background Image," the image is *tiled* to fill the entire browser window. Because browser windows can change sizes, browsers compensates for this by tiling the background image as

many times as it takes to cover the browser window.

You can use this feature to your advantage if you use a seamless tile image as your background. A *seamless tile* is one whose left edge matches its right edge and whose top edge matches the bottom edge. This way the image (or pattern) is

repeated to look like one continuous background.

The background pattern used in the example below was provided by Andy's Art Attack, which can be found at www.screamdesign.com. They offer a large assortment of Web graphics.

TILE A BACKGROUND IMAGE

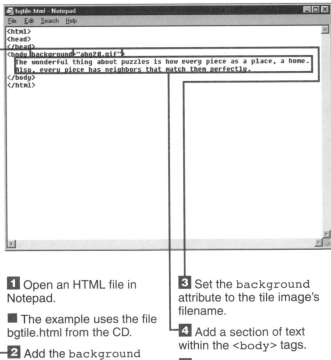

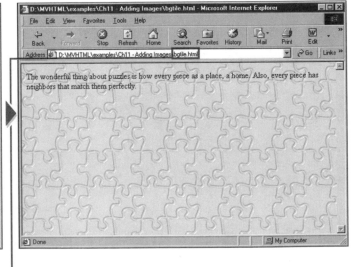

1 Open an HTML file in Notepad.

■ The example uses the file bgtile.html from the CD.

2 Add the background attribute to the <body> tag.

3 Set the background attribute to the tile image's filename.

4 Add a section of text within the <body> tags.

5 Save the file with a new filename.

6 Open the file in a browser.

■ The background tiles seamlessly to create a pattern.

CREATE MARGIN BACKGROUNDS

Although background images will tile if they do not fill the entire window space, you do not always want the background image to be tiled. For these cases, there is a trick that you can use.

If the background image is larger than the browser window, the browser will simply show as much

of the background image as it can. The trick to not tiling the background is to create an image that is larger than the browser window could ever be. That way the browser will not tile the image.

You can use these large images to create margin backgrounds that have some color on one end and white for the rest of the page.

To create the image used in this example, I created an image 1 pixel by 2000 and colored the leftmost pixels. When loaded as a background, the image tiles vertically, but not horizontally, thereby creating the background image.

CREATE MARGIN BACKGROUNDS

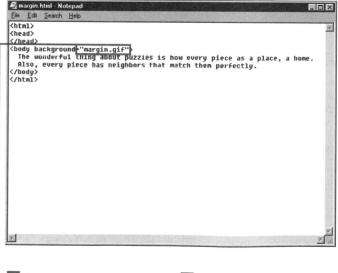

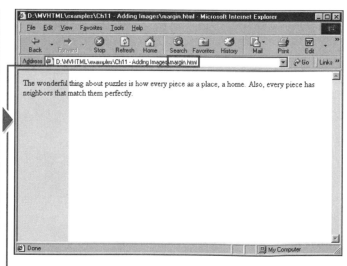

1 Open an HTML file in Notepad.

■ The example uses margin.html from the CD.

2 Change the `background` attribute value to an image.

3 Save the file with a new filename.

4 Open the new file in a browser.

■ A background margin appears to the left of the browser window.

USING TRANSPARENT GIF IMAGES

GIF images are perhaps the most common image format on the Web. They have many unique features that make them a good choice to work with when building Web sites.

One of the features of the GIF image format is that you can select one color within the image to be transparent. This transparent color lets the background show through

the image when viewed in a browser. This transparency lets your image be visible without showing its bounding box.

Because GIF images include 256 indexed colors, the designated transparent color becomes transparent regardless of where the color appears in the image. For example, if you have an image of a snowman set on a white

background and you select the color white as your transparent color, all white pixels in the entire image, including the interior of the snowman, will be transparent.

This tasks uses two images from the book's CD—tyrone.gif and tyrone-t.gif. The latter includes transparency. The section "Create a Transparent GIF Image" shows how to create a transparent GIF image.

USING TRANSPARENT GIF IMAGES

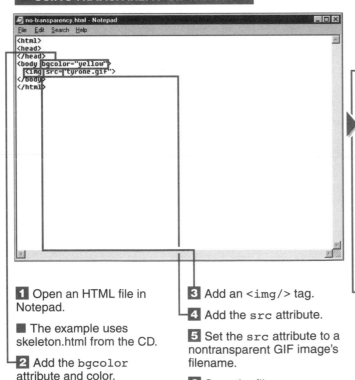

1 Open an HTML file in Notepad.

■ The example uses skeleton.html from the CD.

2 Add the bgcolor attribute and color.

3 Add an <img/> tag.

4 Add the src attribute.

5 Set the src attribute to a nontransparent GIF image's filename.

6 Save the file.

7 Open the file in a browser.

■ The white background of the image is visible.

Does the transparency affect only the background color?

✔ When you select a color to be the transparent color, it makes all pixels colored with that color transparent. Notice in the task example that the white eyes of the dinosaur character also appear transparent along with the white background.

What is the difference between the GIF87a and GIF89a standards?

✔ Of the two GIF standards—GIF87a and GIF89a, only the latter allows transparency.

How do I specify the transparent color?

✔ Image-editing programs like Photoshop or Paint Shop Pro can be used to specify a transparent color. The section "Create a Transparent GIF Image" shows you how to do this.

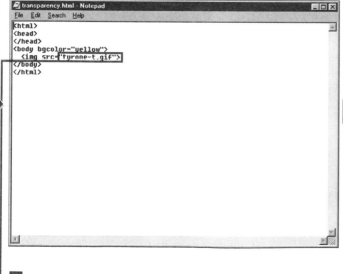

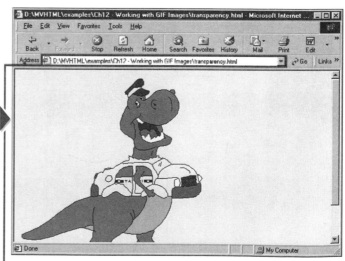

8 Open the file in Notepad.

9 Change the `src` attribute of the `<img/>` tag to a transparent GIF's filename.

■ This example uses tyrone-t.gif from the CD.

10 Save the file as with a new filename.

11 Open the file in a browser.

■ The white background of the image is transparent.

CREATE A TRANSPARENT GIF IMAGE

Most image editors that allow images to be saved in the GIF format, like Photoshop and Paint Shop Pro, offer a way to select a transparent color for the image. This process is usually interactive, accomplished by clicking the color to be made transparent.

You should always preview the image to make sure that you have selected the correct color. Some image editors enable you to preview the image within the software package.

When viewed in a browser, the transparent image lets the background show through the places in the image where the transparent color exists.

CREATE A TRANSPARENT GIF IMAGE

1 Open a GIF file in an image-editing program.

■ The example shows tyrone.gif from the CD being edited in Photoshop.

2 Click File⇨Export⇨GIF 89a Export.

■ The GIF 89a Export Options dialog box opens.

3 Click the eyedropper tool.

4 Click the color in the preview pane that you want to make transparent.

Can I make an entire image transparent?

✔ If the entire image is a single color and you make that color transparent, none of the image will be visible in a browser. This is a good technique to use for spacer images because it ensures that the image is never seen. Spacer images are covered later in this chapter in the section "Using Graphical Spacers."

Can I make two colors in an image transparent?

✔ The GIF format only supports a single transparent color. You cannot select two colors that are transparent.

Can JPEG images be transparent?

✔ JPEG images do not support transparency. If you want to use transparency, you must use the GIF image format.

What do I do if the background color also appears as part of the image?

✔ All pixels that are the same as the designated transparent color will be transparent. If there are pixels within the image that you don't want to be transparent, you should change their color before selecting a transparent color.

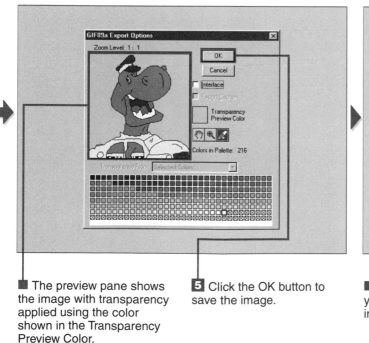

■ The preview pane shows the image with transparency applied using the color shown in the Transparency Preview Color.

5 Click the OK button to save the image.

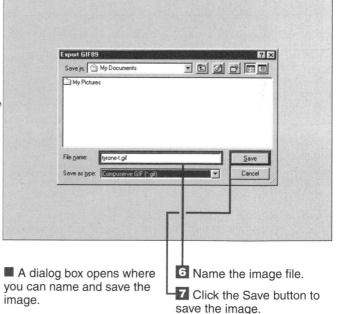

■ A dialog box opens where you can name and save the image.

6 Name the image file.

7 Click the Save button to save the image.

CREATE AND USE INTERLACED GIF IMAGES

GIF images can be saved as *interlaced* images. Interlaced images appear line by line in the browser as they are downloaded. The benefit of interlaced GIF images is that the user can see a representation of the image without having to wait for the entire image to download.

The image appears without much detail initially, but the details fill in as the image downloads.

Interlacing is good to use for larger images that take longer to download. Saving an image as an interlaced image does not make the image any smaller, but it creates

the illusion of the image loading more quickly within the browser.

To make an image interlaced, you simply need to select the interlace option when saving the GIF image in an image-editing package. This option is available as part of the Options dialog box when the image is saved.

CREATE AND USE INTERLACED GIF IMAGES

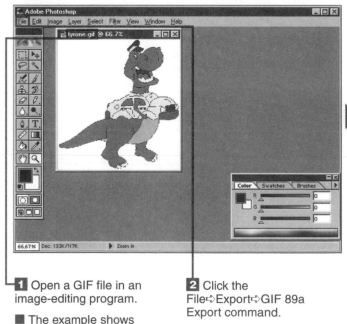

■1 Open a GIF file in an image-editing program.

■ The example shows tyrone.gif from the CD being edited in Photoshop.

■2 Click the File⇨Export⇨GIF 89a Export command.

■ The GIF 89a Export Options dialog box opens.

■3 Click the Interlace checkbox to select it.

■4 Click the OK button.

■5 Give the file a new filename.

■6 Click the Save button.

Can a GIF image include both transparency and interlace features?

✔ Any GIF image can be both interlaced and transparent. In Photoshop, you can select the Interlace option and pick a transparent color in the GIF 89a Export Options dialog box. See "Create a Transparent GIF Image" for more information.

Can I remove interlacing for an image?

✔ Interlacing can be removed from an image. To do this, you need to resave the image with the interlace option deselected. This enables you to save the image without any interlacing. To enable interlacing again, you would need to once again save the image to the GIF format.

Can I use interlacing on JPEG images?

✔ The JPEG format does not support interlacing, but it does support a similar feature known as progressive JPEG. Chapter 13 covers progressive JPEG images.

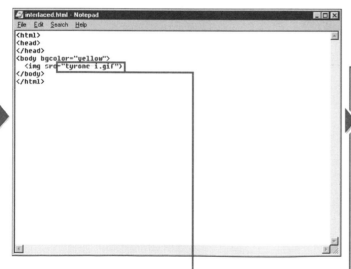

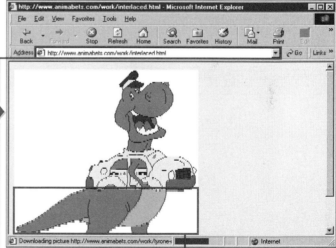

7 Open an HTML file in Notepad.

■ The example shows the transparency.html file from the CD.

8 Within an `<img/>` tag, set an `src` attribute equal to the GIF filename.

9 Save the HTML file with a new filename.

10 Open the HTML file in a browser.

■ Notice how the image appears in pieces as it downloads.

ADD COLOR USING SINGLE-PIXEL IMAGES

One way to add splashes of color to a Web page without requiring large downloads is to load a single-pixel image and resize it to any size you need using the width and height attributes.

Single-pixel image files are very small and download almost immediately. Typical single-pixel image files are less than 1K in size.

For example, if you use an image-editing program to create a 1-pixel-by-1-pixel colored GIF image named small.gif, you could use it the following tag to resize it: `<img src="small.gif" width="200" height="100"/>`. This code creates a colored bar that is 200 pixels wide and 100 pixels in height.

Another technique is to use GIF images with several pixels arranged in a pattern. Images with 4 pixels —or even 20 pixels—are still very small.

ADD COLOR USING SINGLE-PIXEL IMAGES

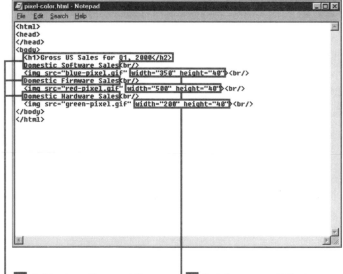

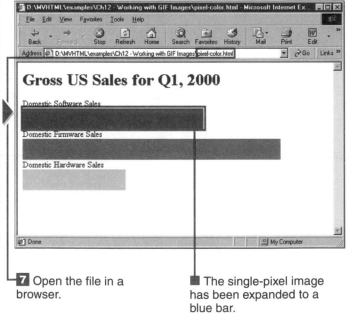

1 Add a heading and three lines of text to an HTML file.

2 Add `<br/>` and `<img/>` tags after each line of text.

3 Add `src`, `width`, and `height` attributes to each `<img/>` tag.

4 Set the `src` attributes for each `<img/>` tag to a single-pixel image.

5 Set the `width` and `height` attributes to the desired dimensions.

6 Save the file.

7 Open the file in a browser.

■ The single-pixel image has been expanded to a blue bar.

What if I use 2- or 4-pixel images?

✔ The browser will resize the image to fit the new dimensions regardless of the number of pixels it includes. The reason for using a single pixel is to save file size. If the desired block of color is going to be a single color, there is no reason to include extra pixels.

Are there any drawbacks to using single-pixel images?

✔ One drawback of this technique is that the color sections are always rectangular, but you can combine these rectangular images with some other images that have the same color to get some interesting results.

Can I use single-pixel JPEG images?

✔ Single-pixel JPEG images can be used to create blocks of color just like GIF images. The advantage of using GIF images is that they can be compressed smaller than JPEG images for single-color images.

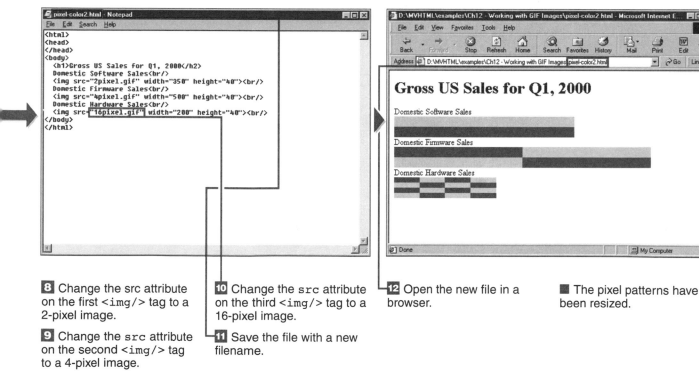

8 Change the src attribute on the first `<img/>` tag to a 2-pixel image.

9 Change the src attribute on the second `<img/>` tag to a 4-pixel image.

10 Change the src attribute on the third `<img/>` tag to a 16-pixel image.

11 Save the file with a new filename.

12 Open the new file in a browser.

■ The pixel patterns have been resized.

USING GRAPHICAL SPACERS

Although images include the vspace and hspace attributes, other elements such as tables and paragraphs of text, do not have any way to add white space around them.

One solution for these elements for adding white space is to use tables to add the extra space. See Chapter 15, "Creating Tables," for more on tables.

You can also use a GIF image that matches the background color, or a transparent single-pixel GIF image as a spacer to place white space around Web page elements. By positioning a spacer between two elements, you can then change the spacer's width and height attributes to move apart the elements.

To minimize the space that the spacer occupies, set either its width or height value to 1, depending on whether you want to space elements horizontally or vertically.

USING GRAPHICAL SPACERS

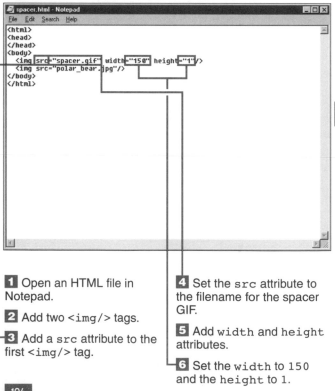

1 Open an HTML file in Notepad.

2 Add two <img/> tags.

3 Add a src attribute to the first <img/> tag.

4 Set the src attribute to the filename for the spacer GIF.

5 Add width and height attributes.

6 Set the width to 150 and the height to 1.

7 Save the file.

8 Open the file in a browser.

■ Notice how the regular image is positioned exactly 150 pixels from the left edge of the browser.

MASTER IT

Why does the vertical spacer need a <br/> after it?

✔ Because the width of the vertical space is only 1, the image fits nicely to the right side of the spacer without the <br/> tag. Adding the <br/> tag, however, forces the image to appear on a new line below the spacer image.

Can JPEG images be used as graphical spacers?

✔ JPEG images can be used to create spacer images just like GIF images. The advantage of using GIF images is that they can be compressed smaller than JPEG images for single-color images.

Can the same spacer be referenced throughout the Web page?

✔ If an image is downloaded and saved in cache, it doesn't need to be downloaded again. Because spacers are made to seen, you can reference a single spacer throughout the Web page rather than separate spacer image files.

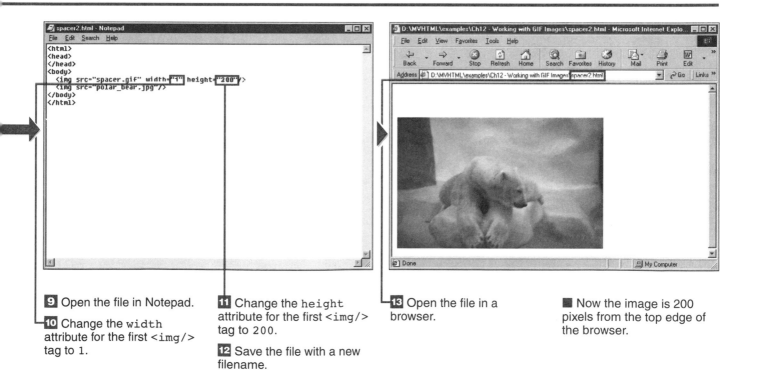

9 Open the file in Notepad.

10 Change the width attribute for the first <img/> tag to 1.

11 Change the height attribute for the first <img/> tag to 200.

12 Save the file with a new filename.

13 Open the file in a browser.

■ Now the image is 200 pixels from the top edge of the browser.

ADD A DROPPED CAPITAL

Chapter 8 gives an example of creating a fancy initial capital by changing the size of the first letter or a paragraph of text.

You can also use an image-editing program to create an image of a fancy initial capital. You can then add this image to the front of the paragraph.

When using this technique with a paragraph of text, be sure to include the `align` attribute with the `<img>` tag and set it to `left`, so that text wraps to the side of the dropped capital. See Chapter 11 for more information on align images and text.

The capital letter in the example below was created in Photoshop using 36-point VivaldiD font and saved as a GIF image.

ADD A DROPPED CAPITAL

1 Open an HTML file in Notepad that has a `<body>` tag that features text.

■ The example shows initial-cap.html from the CD.

2 Add an `<img/>` tag before the text.

3 Add a `src` attribute and set it to the filename for the initial cap you created in an image-editing program.

4 Save the file with a new filename.

5 Open the file in a browser.

■ The first capital is now a fancy image.

Note: You can also use this technique to add images within paragraphs of text. Just position the `<img/>` tag next to the text that it should be by, and remember to use the align attribute.

USING A GRAPHICAL HORIZONTAL RULE

The `<hr/>` tag can add standard horizontal rules to the page, but you can also use the `<img>` tag to add graphical horizontal rules. Normal horizontal rules are covered in Chapter 7.

Graphical horizontal rules are nothing more than long skinny images, but by using images, you can enhance your Web pages beyond what the normal `<hr/>` tags.

The horizontal rule used in the example below is part of Andy's Art Attack and can be found on the scream design Web site at `www.screamdesign.com`.

USING A GRAPHICAL HORIZONTAL RULE

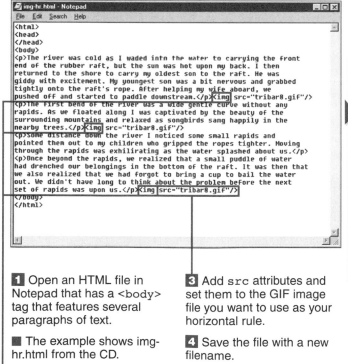

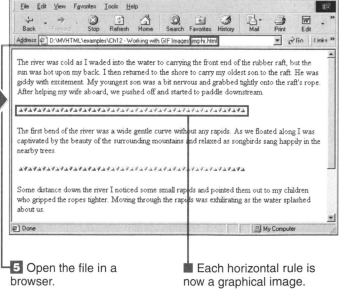

1 Open an HTML file in Notepad that has a `<body>` tag that features several paragraphs of text.

■ The example shows img-hr.html from the CD.

2 Add `<img/>` tags.

3 Add `src` attributes and set them to the GIF image file you want to use as your horizontal rule.

4 Save the file with a new filename.

5 Open the file in a browser.

■ Each horizontal rule is now a graphical image.

USING CUSTOM BULLETS

The standard disc, square, and circle bullet types add some variety to your Web page, but not much. The standard bullet types are covered in Chapter 9. To create more eye-catching lists, you can use images to create custom bullets for your Web pages.

You can use image-editing software to create a custom bullet and save it as a GIF image. The bullets can

be placed in front of the elements of a bulleted list using an <img/> tag with the src attribute set equal to the name of the custom bullet image.

The drawback of using custom bullets is that you cannot use the standard list structures with images. You will need to create the list by hand by using <br/> tags. You can control the spacing of the

list items by setting the height of your bullet images. Creating lists is covered in Chapter 9.

The custom bullet image used in the following example was created in Photoshop using a character taken from the Wingdings font. The image was then saved as a GIF image.

USING CUSTOM BULLETS

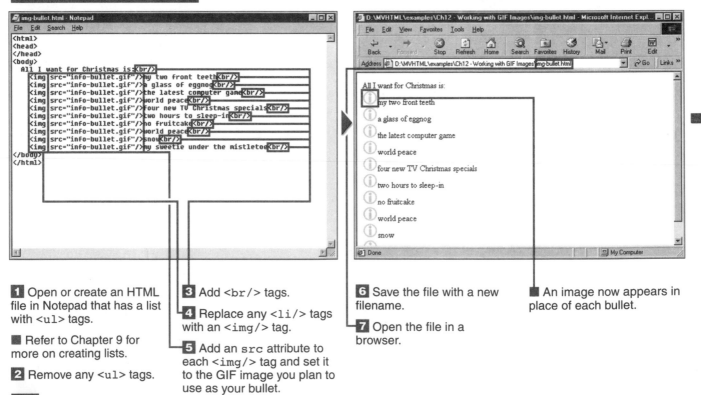

1 Open or create an HTML file in Notepad that has a list with <ul> tags.

■ Refer to Chapter 9 for more on creating lists.

2 Remove any <ul> tags.

3 Add <br/> tags.

4 Replace any <li/> tags with an <img/> tag.

5 Add an src attribute to each <img/> tag and set it to the GIF image you plan to use as your bullet.

6 Save the file with a new filename.

7 Open the file in a browser.

■ An image now appears in place of each bullet.

Can I use the other align attribute values also?

✔ To align bullets, the `left` and `right` `align` attribute values will cause the list items to wrap around the bullet image. You can also specify a vertical alignment using the `top`, `middle`, and `bottom` values.

Where can I find custom bullet images that can be used with a bulleted lists?

✔ You can certainly draw your own custom bullet images using an image editing program. You may also want to use a character taken from a graphical font like Wingdings.

Can custom bullet images use transparency?

✔ It is a good idea to make the background color of the custom bullet images transparent. Transparency allows the Web page background to display around the edges of bullet image.

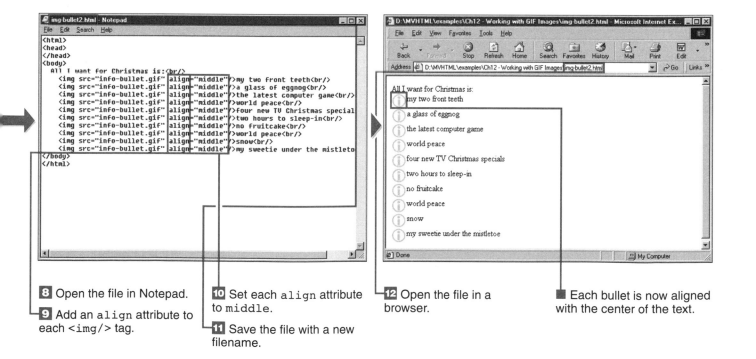

8 Open the file in Notepad.

9 Add an `align` attribute to each `<img/>` tag.

10 Set each `align` attribute to `middle`.

11 Save the file with a new filename.

12 Open the file in a browser.

■ Each bullet is now aligned with the center of the text.

USING ANIMATED GIF IMAGES

A *nimated GIF images* enable simple animations by combining several images (known individually as *frames*) together and displaying them in succession.

Animated GIF images are another feature of the GIF format. They are typically created using an application that can combine the various frames together.

After animated GIF images are saved, they can be displayed within a browser just like standard GIF images. When the image is completely loaded, the animation begins and plays through to the end. You can specify that the animation loop several times or even loop indefinitely.

Animated GIF images can increase the file size of an image many times. For example, an animated GIF image with six frames will be about six times the size of each original image. Each frame of an animated GIF needs to have the same dimensions and colors.

USING ANIMATED GIF IMAGES

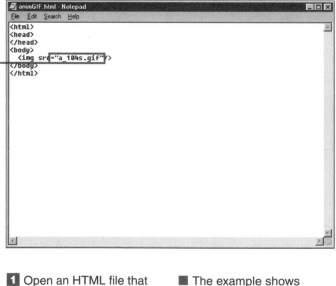

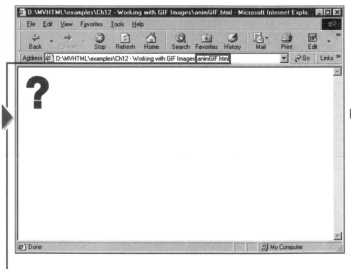

1 Open an HTML file that features in `<img/>` tag.

2 Set the `src` attribute to filename for the animated GIF.

■ The example shows a_104s.gif, which is available on the CD.

3 Save the file with a new filename.

4 Open the file in a browser.

■ The animated GIF image is displayed.

Where can animated GIF images be used on a Web page?

✔ You can include animated GIF images anywhere in a Web page that a normal GIF image can, except it cannot be included as a background.

Can JPEG images be animated?

✔ The JPEG format doesn't support animation. Only GIF images can be animated.

Where can I find animated GIF images?

✔ Many different sites across the Web offer free animated GIF files. Some sites allow you to use these images on your own Web site.

How can I avoid having animated GIFs slow down my Web page?

✔ Animated GIFs can slow down your Web site. You should be careful to use animated GIFs sparingly. Another helpful idea is to limit the number of times that an animated GIF loops.

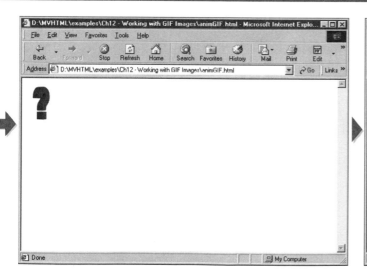

■ This screen shows another frame of the animated GIF image.

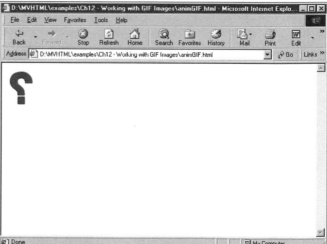

■ This screen shows another frame of the animated GIF image.

CREATE ANIMATED GIF IMAGES WITH ULEAD GIF ANIMATOR

The easiest way to create animated GIF images is by using a tool such as Ulead GIF Animator. Products such as this make it easy to create animated GIFs. A demo of this product can be found on the book's CD or at www.ulead.com.

When using a tool such as GIF Animator, you can set which images appear in the animation and in what order. You can also control the spacing between each frame and how often the animation repeats.

To create an animated GIF image, you need to create all the frames to be combined in the animated GIF beforehand. These images can then be opened and combined to produce the final animated GIF. Before saving the file, you can set the options like spacing and looping and preview the animation. When you are satisfied with the results, you can save the file.

CREATE ANIMATED GIF IMAGES WITH ULEAD GIF ANIMATOR

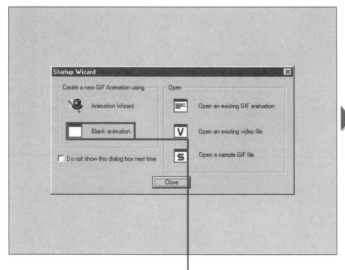

1 Open Ulead GIF Animator.

■ The Startup Wizard dialog box appears.

2 Click the Blank Animation option.

■ The GIF Animator interface appears with a blank animation.

3 Click Layer.

4 Click Add Images.

Can I convert video files to animated GIFs?

✔ GIF Animator provides a way to load video files in AVI, FLC, or MPEG format and convert them to animated GIFs. These files are opened using the File menu or they can be dragged from the Explorer and saved to the GIF format. GIF Animator will convert the files automatically.

Can I optimize animated GIF images to make them smaller?

✔ GIF Animator also includes an option for optimizing the animated GIF files before saving them. The optimized files look for specified colors that are not used and delete their index.

Does GIF Animator include any effects that automatically create animations?

✔ GIF Animator also includes several custom animation effects such as stretch, roll, and wipe. They can be used to make some graphical text stretch, roll, and wipe across the screen.

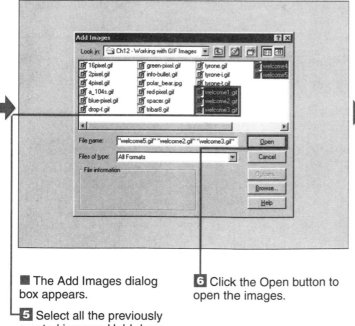

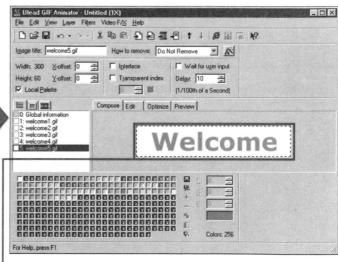

■ The Add Images dialog box appears.

5 Select all the previously created images. Hold down the Shift key as you click multiple images.

6 Click the Open button to open the images.

■ The images are loaded into GIF Animator.

CONTINUED

CREATE ANIMATED GIF IMAGES
WITH ULEAD GIF ANIMATOR CONTINUED

GIF Animator is a powerful package that lets you also specify transparency and interlace options.

Another nice feature of GIF Animator is the ability to work with layers. Photoshop supports layers and these layers can be imported directly into GIF Animator.

GIF Animator also includes an Animation Wizard that takes you step by step through the creation process. This is the easiest way to create an animated GIF image. All you need to do is follow the steps and the program automatically saves the file for you.

When you complete an animated GIF, you can preview the file within the application without having to

load the image in a browser. This convenient feature saves you the trouble of loading the image within a browser every few minutes when you want to check your progress.

GIF Animator also includes another wizard called the Optimization Wizard. This wizard helps reduce the overall file size. This is useful because animated GIF images can be large files.

CREATE ANIMATED GIF IMAGES WITH ULEAD GIF ANIMATOR

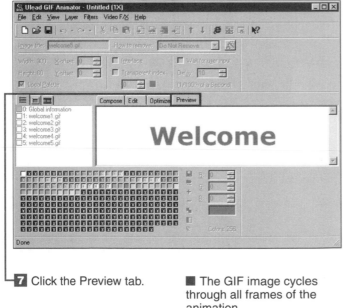

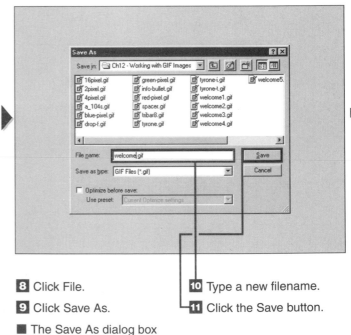

7 Click the Preview tab.

■ The GIF image cycles through all frames of the animation.

8 Click File.

9 Click Save As.

■ The Save As dialog box appears.

10 Type a new filename.

11 Click the Save button.

What other animated GIF tools are available?

✔ GIF Animator is not the only tool available for creating animated GIF images. Paint Shop Pro comes with a tool called Animation Shop that can be used to create animated GIF images. Another option is the GIF Construction Set, created by Alchemy Mindworks. For the Macintosh platform, check out GIF Builder. There are also many shareware animated GIF creation tools available. Check out www.download.com to find out more information about these products.

Is there a limit to the number of frames that I include in an animated GIF?

✔ The more frames that are included in an animated GIF file, the larger the file size. There really is no limit to the number of frames in each file, but it is to your advantage to keep the number of frames to a minimum.

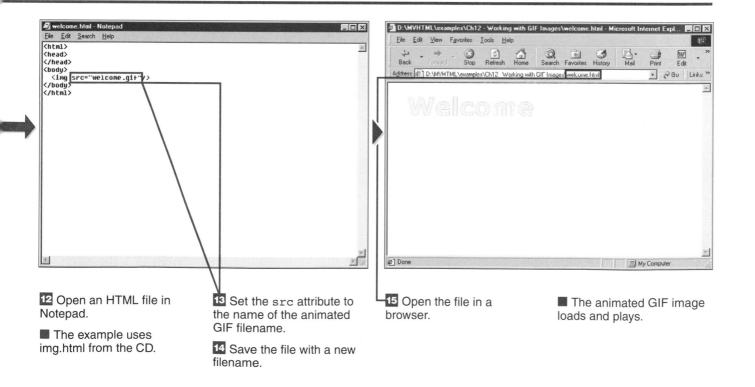

12 Open an HTML file in Notepad.

■ The example uses img.html from the CD.

13 Set the `src` attribute to the name of the animated GIF filename.

14 Save the file with a new filename.

15 Open the file in a browser.

■ The animated GIF image loads and plays.

USING SCANNED IMAGES

You can use images saved in the JPEG and PNG formats, in addition to GIF images. Both of these formats allow 16.7 million colors. Because both the JPEG and PNG formats support millions of colors, they are good formats to use for photographs and other realistic images.

Two good ways to obtain photographs include using a scanner or a digital camera. Scanners enable you to import directly from a physical image printed on paper into the computer. Digital cameras work like normal cameras, but capture a digital version of the image that can be uploaded to a computer.

Each scanner and digital camera has its own interface software for loading images into the computer. After you scan or load an image, it can be saved to the JPEG format for use on the Web. Some interfaces enable you to save images to the PNG format.

USING SCANNED IMAGES

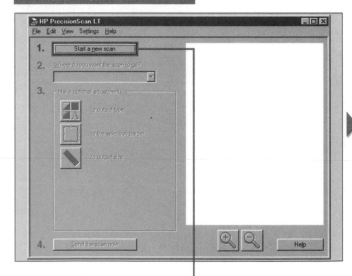

1 Open your scanning software.

■ This example uses HP PrecisionScan LT.

2 Click the Start a New Scan button (or some similar button for your software).

■ The image is scanned into the computer.

3 Click File.

4 Click Save As.

How can you save a scanned image as a PNG file?

✔ The PNG format is still relatively new, but many scanning and image editing programs support the format. To save an image as a PNG image, click the PNG file type in the Save as Type list and click Save.

Can scanned images be saved as GIF images?

✔ Many scanner interfaces can save images using the GIF format. If an image such as a photograph is saved using the GIF format, only 256 unique colors can be used to represent the image. This color limit can severely degrade the quality of the image. For photographs, the JPEG format with its 16.7 million colors is the preferred image format.

When would I want to save scanned images as GIF images?

✔ If you are scanning a drawing or an image with less than 256 colors, the GIF format provides better results and will usually download faster than a JPEG image.

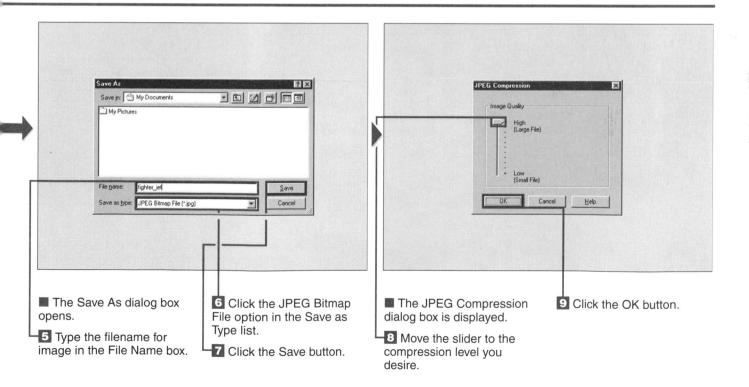

■ The Save As dialog box opens.

5 Type the filename for image in the File Name box.

6 Click the JPEG Bitmap File option in the Save as Type list.

7 Click the Save button.

■ The JPEG Compression dialog box is displayed.

8 Move the slider to the compression level you desire.

9 Click the OK button.

OPTIMIZE JPEG IMAGES

When saving a JPEG image, you can specify the quality level to use. These quality levels range from 0 (maximum compression) to 100 (minimum compression). Almost every tool that supports the JPEG format provides this option.

Lower-quality JPEG images can be compressed to a smaller file size

than higher-quality images. These smaller-sized images download more quickly to a Web page. Higher-quality JPEG images have a larger file size and download more slowly.

JPEG images are *lossy*, which means that information is lost as the image is compressed. The more

compression that is applied, the more data that is lost.

If a JPEG image is saved at a lower quality level, the original quality level cannot be obtained from the lower-quality image. For this reason, you should always keep a copy of the original image before downgrading its quality level.

OPTIMIZE JPEG IMAGES

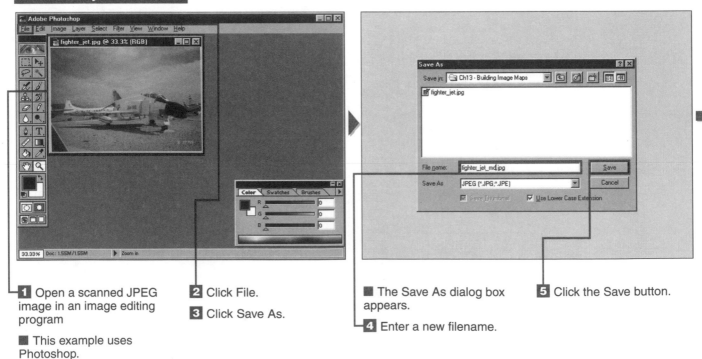

1 Open a scanned JPEG image in an image editing program

■ This example uses Photoshop.

2 Click File.

3 Click Save As.

■ The Save As dialog box appears.

4 Enter a new filename.

5 Click the Save button.

How much compression can I expect if I use the lowest quality setting?

✔ The amount of compression is different for every image depending on the amount of detail in the image. JPEG images such as clouds and forests can compress a lot better than images of machinery or people.

Can I use compressed JPG files instead of thumbnails to speed up download time?

✔ Maximum-compressed JPEG image files often appear fuzzy and distorted. This is the quality trade-off for the small file size. In many cases, you will be better off with thumbnails rather than maximum-compressed JPEG images. Another advantage of thumbnails is that many thumbnail images can appear on a single Web page.

What is the preferred JPEG setting that ensures quality and small file sizes?

✔ The prefererred JPEG settings really depend on the individual images. Some images are fine with a 40 percent compression setting, but others show some degradation at only 80 percent.

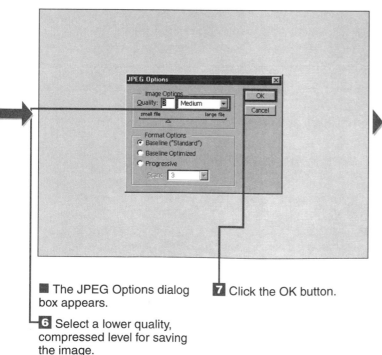

■ The JPEG Options dialog box appears.

6 Select a lower quality, compressed level for saving the image.

7 Click the OK button.

8 Open the image file in a browser.

■ Notice that the compressed version of this image is still very clear.

■ In the example, the file size for the original image was 465 kilobytes (K) and the compressed version was only 58K.

CREATE A PROGRESSIVE JPEG IMAGE

Another feature that is built into the JPEG format is a feature called *progressive JPEG*.

Progressive JPEG images are similar to interlaced GIF images in that they display in the browser a piece at a time as they download. For more on interlaced GIFs, see Chapter 12.

The difference between interlaced GIF images and progressive JPEGs is in how they download. While interlaced GIF images download one horizontal line at a time, progressive JPEGs download one block at a time.

These blocks will appear in the browser starting with the upper left quadrant and progressing to the lower-right quadrant. Each

quadrant is then individually divided into quadrants, and so on, until the entire image is rendered.

Progressive JPEGs are useful when you have large images that download slowly. Using progressive JPEG images enables the user to get an idea of what the image looks like before the entire image downloads.

CREATE A PROGRESSIVE JPEG IMAGE

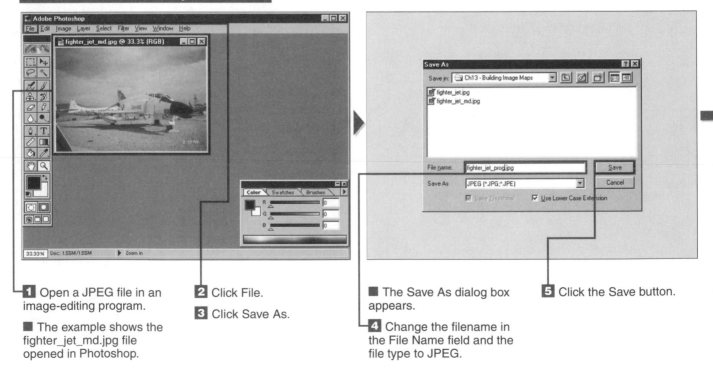

1 Open a JPEG file in an image-editing program.

■ The example shows the fighter_jet_md.jpg file opened in Photoshop.

2 Click File.

3 Click Save As.

■ The Save As dialog box appears.

4 Change the filename in the File Name field and the file type to JPEG.

5 Click the Save button.

JPEG images have a feature similar to interlacing. What other features do they have?

✔ Progressive rendering is the only additional feature that the JPEG format supports. JPEG images do not support transparency or animation.

Why should I use progressive JPEGs on my Web page?

✔ Progressive JPEGs are useful if your site includes many large JPEG images, because progressive JPEG images enable the user to see the image as it downloads. The image will initially appear blurry and blocky, but more details will appear as the file continues to download.

Can GIF images be saved like progressive JPEG images?

✔ GIF images support interlacing instead of progressive features. The rendering method is different between these two features.

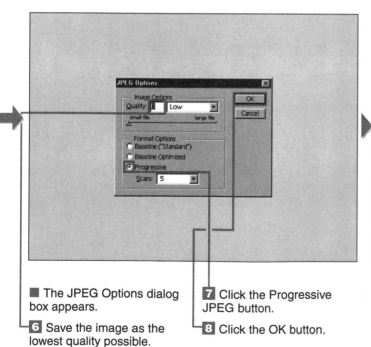

■ The JPEG Options dialog box appears.

6 Save the image as the lowest quality possible.

■ For example, the Quality value is set at 0.

7 Click the Progressive JPEG button.

8 Click the OK button.

9 Open the JPG file in a browser.

■ The image appears gradually one block at a time.

CREATE SEAMLESS BACKGROUND TEXTURES

JPEG images work well as backgrounds and can be made seamless to tile across the entire space of the browser window. GIF images, covered in Chapter 12, can also be used as background images. GIF images are better for patterns that include regular colors and JPEG images are better for backgrounds that include gradients and many colors.

To create a *seamless* background, you need to use an image-editing package such as Photoshop to carefully create images that match up when laid down next to each other, or *tiled*. You can manually create seamless images by painstakingly aligning the pixels on every edge with the pixels on the opposite edge. This way the background will be seamless from

edge to edge as the tile to fill the background of the browser.

Another way to align pixels is to use tools that make the process automatic such as tools in Photoshop and plug-ins for Photoshop such as Kai's Power Tools.

CREATE SEAMLESS BACKGROUND TEXTURES

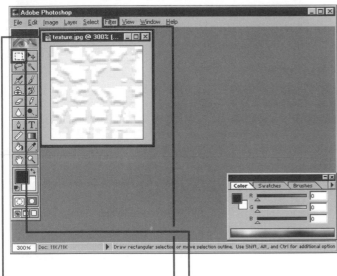

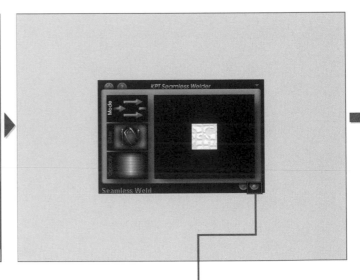

1 Open a JPG file in an image editing program.

■ The examples shows texture.jpg opened in Photoshop.

2 Click the Rectangular Marquee tool and drag a box within the perimeter of the image.

3 Select the seamless filter, such as KPT's Seamless Welder.

■ The KPT Seamless Welder interface appears.

4 Click the button to apply the seamless weld function.

Can I create a seamless background using a GIF image?

✔ GIF images can be used to create seamless background images. The JPEG format was used on this example because the image was detailed and better suited for the JPEG format.

Where can I find background images?

✔ In addition to creating seamless background tiles yourself, you can find many different sites and graphics collections on the Web that offer seamless background images.

If the background image is detailed, how can I be sure that the text on the page will be legible?

✔ If you fade the background image, then the text on the page will be legible. Most image-editing packages include a fade filter that does this automatically. Another way to fade an image is to change the brightness and contrast settings.

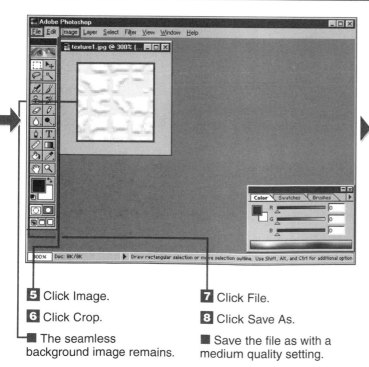

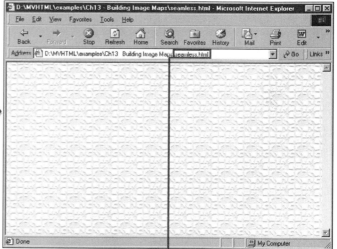

5 Click Image.

6 Click Crop.

■ The seamless background image remains.

7 Click File.

8 Click Save As.

■ Save the file as with a medium quality setting.

9 Open an HTML file in Notepad.

10 Add a background attribute to the <body> tag and set it to a filename for the seamless background texture.

11 Save the file.

12 Open the file in a browser.

■ The seamless background tiles horizontally and vertically across the entire browser window.

USING IMAGE MAPS

Chapter 11 shows you how to create an image link. This method works well, but each image can only be linked to a single location.

Image maps, on the other hand, let you link to many different pages using a single image. The linking is accomplished by defining shapes within the image called *hotspots*.

Each image can have several hotspots; each linked to a different Web page.

Image maps can be implemented on both the server and the client. This chapter focuses mainly on working with client-side image maps because they are much easier to work with and are more common than server-side image maps, but

server-side image maps are also covered at the end of the chapter.

Two differing standards exist for implementing server-side image maps—NCSA and CERN. The next example uses server-side image maps.

USING IMAGE MAPS

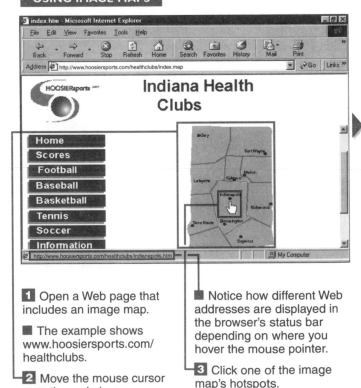

1 Open a Web page that includes an image map.

■ The example shows www.hoosiersports.com/healthclubs.

2 Move the mouse cursor over the main image.

■ Notice how different Web addresses are displayed in the browser's status bar depending on where you hover the mouse pointer.

3 Click one of the image map's hotspots.

■ A Web page associated with the hotspot is loaded.

4 Click the browser's Back button.

How are the coordinates in the status bar of the browser window measured?

✔ The numbers that appear in the status bar of the browser window when you move the mouse cursor over an image map are the number of pixels to the left and down from the upper-left corner of the image. The browser uses these values to match the position clicked with the list of associated links. Creating these links is covered in the next task.

What types of images make good image maps?

✔ Images that have clearly defined sections that can be easily selected for a hotspot region typically make good image maps.

Are image maps any larger than normal images?

✔ Image maps include additional information used to define the hotspots and links, but this information is minimal and doesn't add much size to the file.

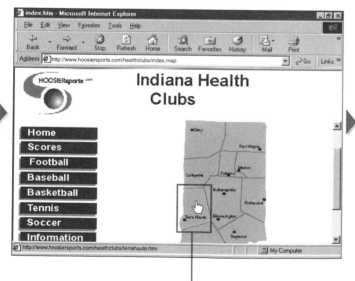

■ The page with the image map is reloaded.

5 Click a different hotspot on the image map.

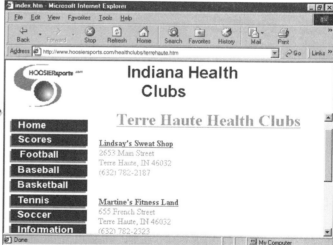

■ A different Web page is loaded.

CREATE IMAGE MAPS

The major benefit of client-side image maps is that all the code to make them work is contained within the Web page.

Adding the usemap attribute to the <img/> tag can make any image into an image map. You then set this attribute equal to a named anchor, such as #name, where the mapping coordinates are located.

Mapping coordinates specify the area of the hotspot.

The mapping coordinates are all included within the <map> tags. The opening <map> tag should include a name attribute set equal to the anchor name that also matches the image reference. For example, if the image tag looks like <img src="myImage.gif"

usemap="#map1"/>, the <map> tag associated with that image looks like <map name="map1">.

Within the <map> tags, several <area/> tags can appear—one for each hotspot. These <area/> tags include the shape, coordinates, and link URL for the hotspot.

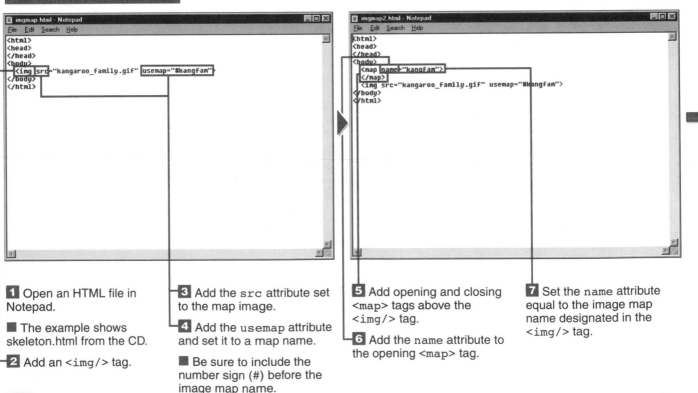

1 Open an HTML file in Notepad.

■ The example shows skeleton.html from the CD.

2 Add an <img/> tag.

3 Add the src attribute set to the map image.

4 Add the usemap attribute and set it to a map name.

■ Be sure to include the number sign (#) before the image map name.

5 Add opening and closing <map> tags above the <img/> tag.

6 Add the name attribute to the opening <map> tag.

7 Set the name attribute equal to the image map name designated in the <img/> tag.

Can I see the hotspot in the browser?

✔ If you click and hold the mouse button down over an image map in an Internet Explorer browser screen, the hotspot under the mouse cursor displays as lines on top of the image. This feature is a useful way to see hotspot boundaries.

What other shape attributes can I designate?

✔ In addition to the rectangular shape, image maps can use circular and polygonal shaped hotspots. The task "Specifying Hotspot Shape and Coordinates" covers these different hotspot shapes. The Each different shape needs a different number of coordinates. Rectangular hotspots need four values, circular hotspots need three values, and polygonal shaped hotspots can include any number of coordinates.

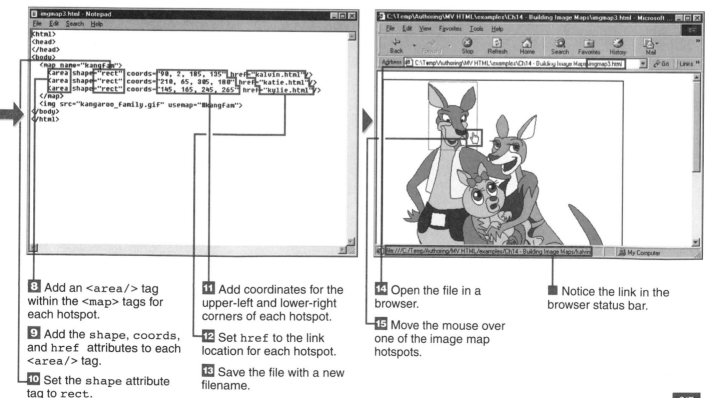

8 Add an `<area/>` tag within the `<map>` tags for each hotspot.

9 Add the `shape`, `coords`, and `href` attributes to each `<area/>` tag.

10 Set the `shape` attribute tag to `rect`.

11 Add coordinates for the upper-left and lower-right corners of each hotspot.

12 Set `href` to the link location for each hotspot.

13 Save the file with a new filename.

14 Open the file in a browser.

15 Move the mouse over one of the image map hotspots.

■ Notice the link in the browser status bar.

SPECIFY HOTSPOT SHAPE AND COORDINATES

Hotspot shapes can be rectangular (rect), circular (circle), or polygonal (poly). The shape attribute in the <area/> tag determines the hotspot shape that is used. The type of shape determines the number of coordinates needed. The default shape is rectangular.

Rectangular shapes require four coordinate values. These values

correspond to the hotspot's upper-left and lower-right corners.

Circular shapes require three coordinate values—two for the center location and a third for the radius of the circle.

The polygonal shape can have any number of coordinates. The last coordinate pair automatically connects to the first coordinate pair.

Coordinates need to be separated with a comma and/or a single space. For example, the statement <area shape="rect" coords="20, 20, 60, 60/> defines a hotspot that stretches from a corner 20 pixels from the top and 20 pixels from the left, down to a corner 60 pixels from the top and 60 pixels from the left edge of the image.

SPECIFY HOTSPOT SHAPE AND COORDINATES

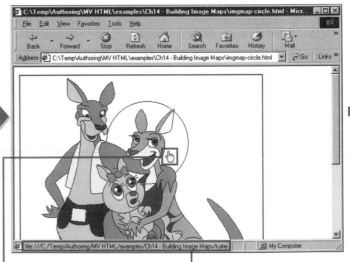

1 Open an HTML file in Notepad that features an image map.

2 Set the shape attribute for each <area/> to circle.

3 Update the coords attributes to include the coordinates of the circle center and radius.

4 Save the file with a new filename.

5 Open the file in a browser.

6 Move the mouse over one of the image map hotspots.

■ Notice the link in the browser status bar.

What happens if the coordinates of two hotspots overlap?

✔ If two hotspots overlap, the overlapped section is linked to the hotspot that appears first in the `<map>` tags.

Can I indent the line of code that includes the coordinates?

✔ The coordinate values included as part of the `coords` attribute need to include a single comma and/or a single space between them. The inclusion of additional spaces or returns will confuse the browser and produce irregular hotspots.

How do I know what coordinates to select?

✔ The coordinates that you select define the hotspot shape. Identifying the right coordinates is crucial to the image map. If the coordinates are off, the hotspot links will not match the image. The next task shows how to identify exact coordinates.

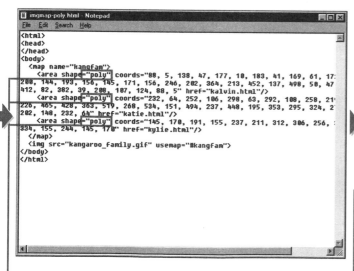

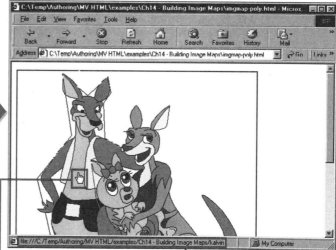

7 Open the file in Notepad.

8 Set the `shape` attribute for each `<area/>` to `poly`.

9 Update the `coords` attributes to include the coordinates for each point of a polygon that surrounds each hotspot.

10 Save the file with a new filename.

11 Open the file in a browser.

12 Move the mouse over one of the image map hotspots.

■ Notice the link in the browser status bar.

IDENTIFY IMAGE MAP COORDINATES

Identifying mapping coordinates can be tricky, but most image-editing programs display an image's coordinates as the mouse cursor is moved over an image. You can use these programs to identify various locations in the image. You can then write down the coordinates and input them into the `<area/>` tag.

You can identify hotspot coordinates by using your browser.

To do so, add the `ismap` attribute with the `<img/>` tag and surround the `<img/>` tag with `<a>` tags. You can set the `<a>` tag's `href` attribute to anything because it is removed after you obtain the coordinates.

When you open the Web page file containing the `<a>` tags in a browser, the coordinates of the image will appear in the status bar.

You can then hover the cursor over the hotspot and write down the hotspot's coordinates for inclusion in the `<area/>` tag.

The process of using the browser to obtain coordinates not only works for client-side image maps, but is also how you set up a server-side image maps. See "Create Server-Side Image Maps" for more information.

IDENTIFY IMAGE MAP COORDINATES

1 Open an image file in an image-editing program such as Paint Shop Pro.

2 Move the mouse cursor over the top of the image.

■ Notice that the coordinates are displayed on the status bar for the current cursor location.

3 Move the mouse cursor to a different location on the image.

■ The coordinates change as the mouse cursor moves.

4 Write down the values for each desired hotspot coordinate.

Why does the <img/> tag need to be included within a <a> tag in order for the browser to display the coordinates?

✔ You use the `ismap` attribute to create server-side image maps. The `ismap` attribute causes the mapping coordinates to be sent to the server for processing. The `usemap` attribute makes an image into a link; because the `ismap` attribute does not, the image needs to be made into a link so that it is recognized as one.

Is there an easier way to create an image map?

✔ Although the browser and an image-editing program can be used to obtain coordinate values, an easier way to create image maps is to use an image map creation program like Image Mapper++. This program lets you select hotspots by dragging the mouse over the image. I discuss Image Mapper++ in the task "Build Image Maps with Image Mapper++."

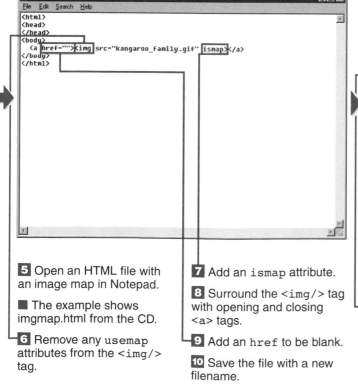

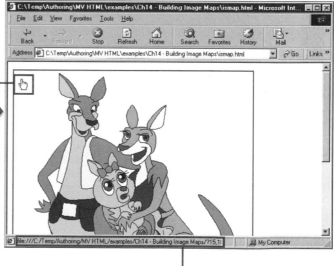

5 Open an HTML file with an image map in Notepad.

■ The example shows imgmap.html from the CD.

6 Remove any `usemap` attributes from the `<img/>` tag.

7 Add an `ismap` attribute.

8 Surround the `<img/>` tag with opening and closing `<a>` tags.

9 Add an `href` to be blank.

10 Save the file with a new filename.

11 Open the file in a browser.

12 Move the mouse cursor over the image.

■ Notice how the coordinates are displayed in the browser's status bar.

13 Write down the coordinates for each desired hotspot corner.

SPECIFY ALTERNATIVE TEXT

As you add numerous hotspots to an image, determining which hotspots correspond with which links can become difficult. To solve this problem, you can describe each hotspot link with a title using the alt attribute.

Using alt attributes with hotspot links works just like using alt attributes with normal images. You can include descriptive text that the browser displays when the mouse cursor is over the top of the hotspot.

The alt attribute displays only the descriptive text for areas that make up a hotspot, but you can also set up some descriptive text that displays for all areas that aren't

part of a hotspot. To do this, set the last <area/> tag in the list to a rectangle shape whose coordinates include the entire image and then add the nohref and alt attributes to the <area/> tag and set the alt attribute to the descriptive text for the background.

SPECIFY ALTERNATIVE TEXT

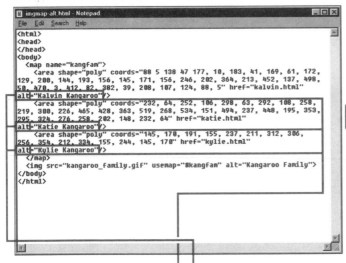

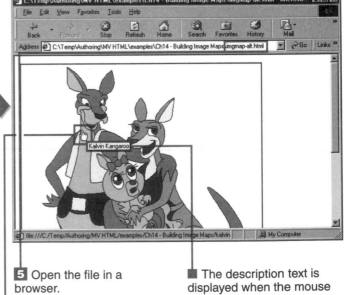

1 Open an HTML file that has an image map with several <area/> tags in Notepad.

■ The example shows imgmap-poly.html from the CD.

2 Add the alt attribute to the each <area/> tag.

3 Set the alt attribute equal to the descriptive text you desire.

4 Save the file with a new filename.

5 Open the file in a browser.

6 Move the mouse cursor over the image.

■ The description text is displayed when the mouse cursor is over the hotspot.

If you include an alt attribute as part of both the <img/> and <area/> tags, which one will be displayed?

✔ If the alt attribute is included with both the image and the hotspots, the description text for the hotspots takes precedence over the image descriptive text. The image description text displays when the mouse cursor is over any section of the image that isn't part of a hotspot if a background nohref <area/> tag isn't included.

Should the alt attribute be included with all <area/> tags?

✔ It is a good idea to include the alt attribute and some alternative text with every <area/> tag. This precaution ensures that a description of the link is always available even if the image cannot load for some reason.

SPECIFY MARGINS

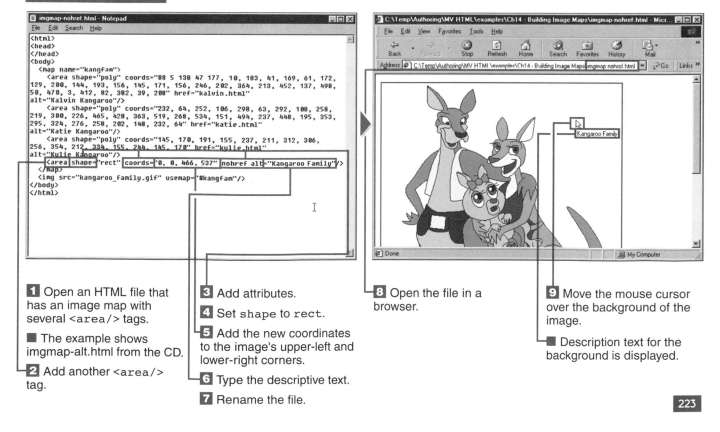

1 Open an HTML file that has an image map with several <area/> tags.

■ The example shows imgmap-alt.html from the CD.

2 Add another <area/> tag.

3 Add attributes.

4 Set shape to rect.

5 Add the new coordinates to the image's upper-left and lower-right corners.

6 Type the descriptive text.

7 Rename the file.

8 Open the file in a browser.

9 Move the mouse cursor over the background of the image.

■ Description text for the background is displayed.

BUILD IMAGE MAPS WITH IMAGE MAPPER++

Writing down a list of coordinates and entering them correctly into your HTML document is tedious process, prone to introducing errors. To eliminate possible errors, you can use one of the many image map creation tools.

One such tool is called Image Mapper++, created by CoffeeCup

Software. You can find this tool at www.coffeecup.com. This tool is also available on the book's CD.

This tool lets you load images, select and edit hotspots using the mouse, and save the resulting image map. The tool also automatically generates the necessary HTML code, complete with all the required coordinates.

This code can then be copied and pasted into your HTML file. Image Mapper++ also provides a way to quickly preview the results of your image map.

Other image map creation products exist, but the steps within this task are fairly representative of how most of these utilities work.

BUILD IMAGE MAPS WITH IMAGE MAPPER++

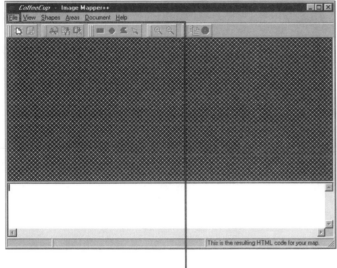

■1 Start your image-map-generating software.

■ The example shows Image Mapper++.

■2 Click File from the menu bar.

■3 Click Map Wizard.

■ Step 1 of the Map Wizard appears.

■4 Click the Create a New Map option button.

■5 Click the Next button.

Do I have to use the Map Wizard?

✔ The Map Wizard is provided for convenience only. Of the many image map tools that are available, some include wizards and other do not. Image Mapper++ offers the Map Wizard as an easy way to open an image and specify the descriptive text that should accompany the image map. You can search for other available utilities at www.download.com.

What other image mapping software can I use?

✔ Many different image-mapping software programs exist, including MapEdit and Mini Mapper. In addition to shareware and stand-alone utilities, many of the major Web editing applications like FrontPage and HomeSite offer image-mapping features. These features are built into the Web editing interface.

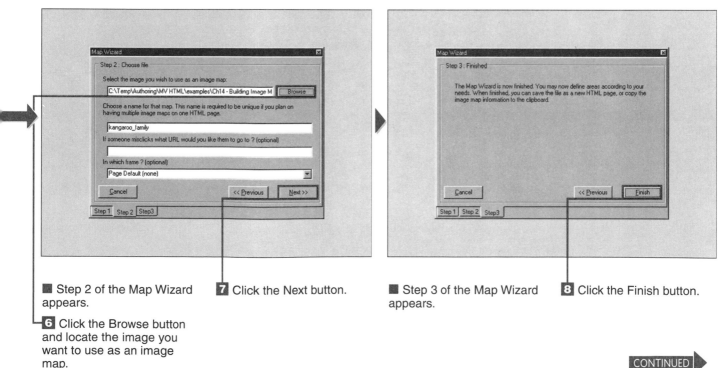

■ Step 2 of the Map Wizard appears.

6 Click the Browse button and locate the image you want to use as an image map.

7 Click the Next button.

■ Step 3 of the Map Wizard appears.

8 Click the Finish button.

CONTINUED

BUILD IMAGE MAPS WITH IMAGE MAPPER++ CONTINUED

The Image Mapper++ interface includes two panes. The top one displays the image and the bottom one displays the generated HTML code.

Within the top pane, you can interactively define hotspots by clicking and dragging on top of the image. You can select to make rectangular, circular, or polygonal hotspots.

After you create a hotspot, a dialog box appears that asks you to enter the link URL for the associated hotspot.

Each hotspot is displayed in the upper pane in red and each coordinate point is marked with a square. By moving these squares, you can edit the position of each coordinate.

Any changes you make in the upper window are automatically reflected in the code displayed in the lower pane. When you finish editing the hotspots, you can select and copy the code onto the Clipboard and paste it into your Web page file.

BUILD IMAGE MAPS WITH IMAGE MAPPER++

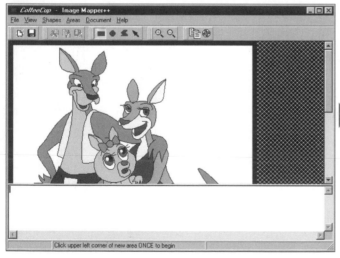

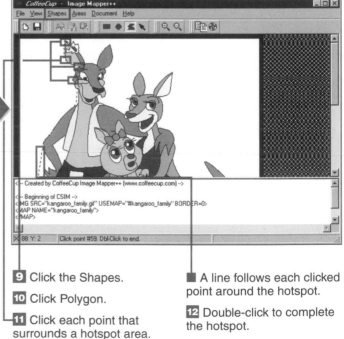

■ The image specified in Step 2 of the Map Wizard appears in the top pane.

9 Click the Shapes.

10 Click Polygon.

11 Click each point that surrounds a hotspot area.

■ A line follows each clicked point around the hotspot.

12 Double-click to complete the hotspot.

MASTER IT

The output from the Image Mapper++ tool listed some HTML tags in all capital letters. Is this correct?

✔ The creators of this tool obviously preferred the style of capitalizing all HTML tags. Capitalization does not affect normal HTML browsers, but to be compliant with XHTML browsers, all capitalized tags need to be changed to lowercase. You also need to add a slash mark at the end of `<img>` and `<area>` tags to be XHTML-compliant, because they do not have closing tags. More information on XHTML can be found in Chapter 3.

What other image map tools are available?

✔ Many of the larger Web-page-editing tools such as Microsoft FrontPage and Macromedia Dreamweaver have built-in image map creation tools. Standalone image map creation tools include MapEdit and CuteMap. These can be found online at www.download.com.

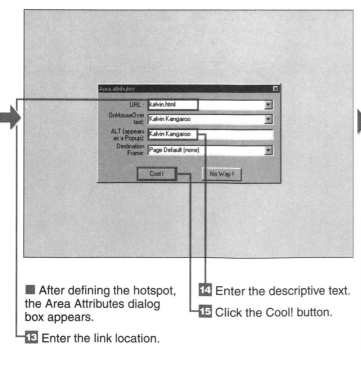

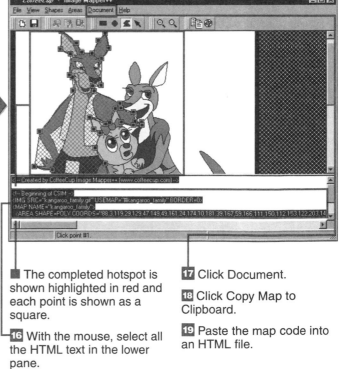

■ After defining the hotspot, the Area Attributes dialog box appears.

13 Enter the link location.

14 Enter the descriptive text.

15 Click the Cool! button.

■ The completed hotspot is shown highlighted in red and each point is shown as a square.

16 With the mouse, select all the HTML text in the lower pane.

17 Click Document.

18 Click Copy Map to Clipboard.

19 Paste the map code into an HTML file.

CREATE SERVER-SIDE IMAGE MAPS

Another way to create image maps is to let the server handle all the processing. *Server-side image maps* require that the image map information be included in a separate file with a .map extension. These map files are processed using a CGI script.

Two main standards govern server-side image maps, and each of these

standards requires the map file in a different format. The NCSA format lists the hotspot shape first, followed by the link URL and then the coordinates. The CERN format lists the hotspot shape, the coordinates with parenthesis around each coordinate pair, and finally the link URL.

NCSA map files need to be copied on the server into the cgi-bin/imagemap directory. CERN map files need to be copied into the cgi-bin/htimage directory.

The following takes you through the process of creating map files for both NCSA and CERN formats.

CREATE SERVER-SIDE IMAGE MAPS

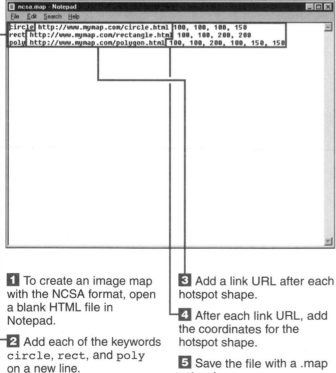

1 To create an image map with the NCSA format, open a blank HTML file in Notepad.

2 Add each of the keywords circle, rect, and poly on a new line.

3 Add a link URL after each hotspot shape.

4 After each link URL, add the coordinates for the hotspot shape.

5 Save the file with a .map extension.

6 Open a new HTML file in Notepad.

7 Add an <img/> tag with src and ismap attributes.

8 Set the src attribute to the URL for the map image.

9 Enclose the <img/> tag with <a> tags.

10 Add the href attribute to the <a> tag and set it equal to the URL of the NCSA map file.

11 Save the file.

MASTER IT

Which server-side standard is most popular?

✔ Actually server-side image maps have been replaced to a large degree with client-side image maps. The type of format you use really depends on the type of server you are using. Of the two types, NCSA is more common and closer to the client-side image map syntax. If you choose to use server-side image maps, you should check with your ISP to see which format they support.

Is there an advantage to using server-side image maps verses client-side image maps?

✔ The advantage of server-side image maps is that they live on the server. This requires additional bandwidth for processing, but some clients, such as WebTV, can access image maps only if they are on the server.

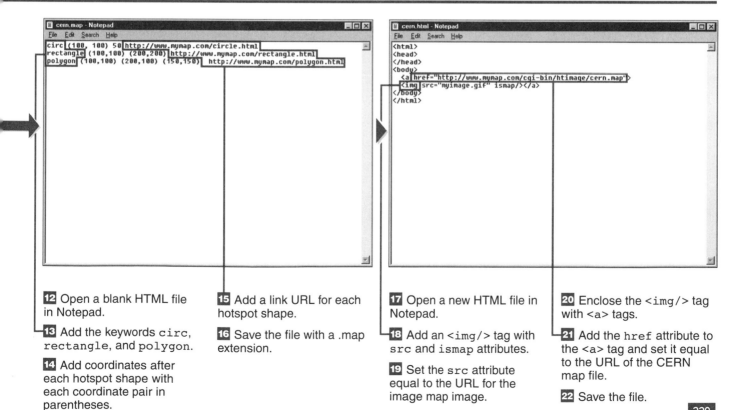

12 Open a blank HTML file in Notepad.

13 Add the keywords `circ`, `rectangle`, and `polygon`.

14 Add coordinates after each hotspot shape with each coordinate pair in parentheses.

15 Add a link URL for each hotspot shape.

16 Save the file with a .map extension.

17 Open a new HTML file in Notepad.

18 Add an `<img/>` tag with `src` and `ismap` attributes.

19 Set the `src` attribute equal to the URL for the image map image.

20 Enclose the `<img/>` tag with `<a>` tags.

21 Add the `href` attribute to the `<a>` tag and set it equal to the URL of the CERN map file.

22 Save the file.

SECTION V

The **Bear Facts** – The Web Site for Bear Lovers

| Physical Characteristics | Hunting & Fishing | Habitat/ Daily Life |

Click on thumbnails for larger pictures and some fun facts!

BUILD A BASIC TABLE

HTML tables are a common way of presenting information. Table information is organized into rows and columns. Each row and column can have a heading that identifies the type of information contained in the row or column.

You create simple tables by using the <table>, <tr>, and <td> tags. The <table> tag marks the beginning and end of the table, the <tr> tags mark the beginning of each new row and the <td> tags mark each new cell within a row.

These tags can include attributes that let you control the alignment, spacing, and even the background color of the table cells.

In addition to presenting data, you can use tables to position objects within the Web page. An example of using tables to position objects is covered later in the chapter.

BUILD A BASIC TABLE

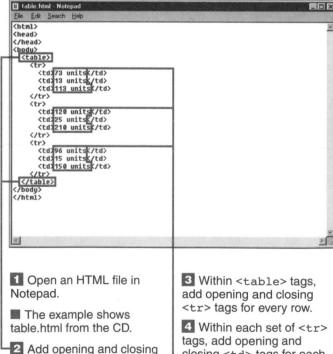

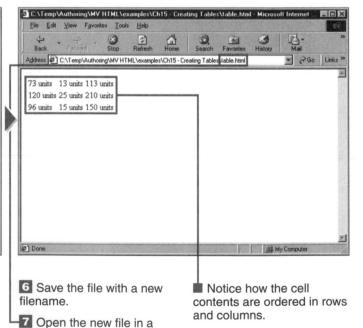

1 Open an HTML file in Notepad.

■ The example shows table.html from the CD.

2 Add opening and closing <table> tags.

3 Within <table> tags, add opening and closing <tr> tags for every row.

4 Within each set of <tr> tags, add opening and closing <td> tags for each cell in the row.

5 Add the cell content.

6 Save the file with a new filename.

7 Open the new file in a browser.

■ Notice how the cell contents are ordered in rows and columns.

ADD A NEW TABLE ROW

You can add new table rows at any place within a table by adding new `<tr>` tags to an existing table. These `<tr>` tags need to appear between the `<table>` tags.

The `<tr>` tags are only used to mark a new row and should not contain any content. The content needs to be positioned between the opening and closing `<td>` tags, which are within the `<tr>` tags.

The number of sets of `<tr>` tags within the `<table>` tags determines the number of rows for the table. The number of sets of `<td>` tags within a set of `<tr>` tags determines the number of cells in a single row.

ADD A NEW TABLE ROW

1 Open an HTML file with a `<table>` tag.

■ The example shows the HTML file created in "Build a Basic Table."

2 Copy the last set of `<tr>` tags and paste it just above the closing `<table>` tag.

3 Change the cell content located between the `<td>` tags.

4 Save the file with a new filename.

5 Open the new file in a browser.

■ Notice how the new row has been added to the bottom of the table.

ADD A TABLE BORDER

Although the cell contents within a table are positioned in rows and columns, you will not see the actual cells unless you specify to display borders.

To display borders, you need to add the `border` attribute to the opening `<table>` tag. The border value is the width of the border in

pixels. The border value defines the border thickness for the entire table.

For example, if you add the `border` attribute to the `<table>` tag and set it equal to 10, a 10-pixel border will be displayed around the outside of the entire table.

The default for tables is to not display any borders. Setting the `border` attribute to any non-zero value automatically enables borders between the cells as well as a border around the entire table. However, increasing the `border` value higher than 1 affects only the table border and not the cell borders.

ADD A TABLE BORDER

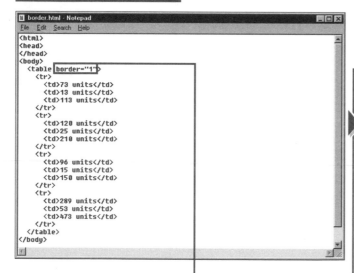

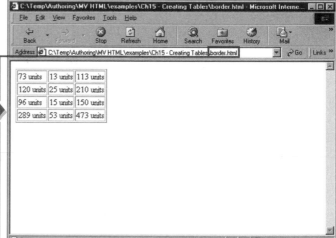

1 Open a HTML file with a `<table>` tag.

■ The example shows the file created in "Add a New Table Row."

2 Add the `border` attribute to the `<table>` tag and set its value to 1.

3 Save the file with a new filename.

4 Open the new file in a browser.

■ Notice how borders have been added to the table.

Can I make only part of the table border visible?

✔ You can make only part of the frame border visible if you add the `frame` attribute to the `<table>` tag. This attribute can be set to `void`, `above`, `below`, `hsides`, `vsides`, `lhs`, `rhs`, `box`, or `border`. The default is `void`. `above` and `below` make only the top or bottom edge of the border appear. `hsides` and `vsides` make only the horizontal or vertical edges appear. `lhs` and `rhs` will make the left- or right-hand side appear. `box` and `border` both make the all edges appear.

Can I set specific colors for table borders?

✔ You can specify a border colors using style sheets, but the color for a table that does not use style sheets will be the same as the text color. Style sheets are covered in Part IX.

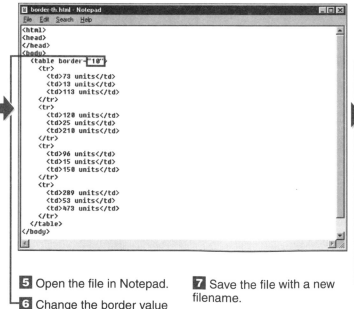

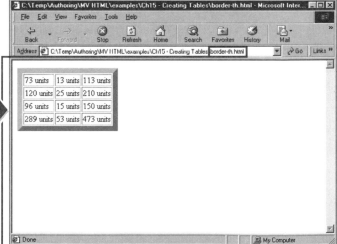

5 Open the file in Notepad.

6 Change the border value to 10.

7 Save the file with a new filename.

8 Open the new file in a browser.

■ Notice how the table border has increased in thickness, while the cell borders have maintained their original thickness.

ADD CELL BORDERS

The rules attribute of the `<table>` tag offers a way to control the display of the borders between the cells. You can set the rules attributed to `all`, `none`, `groups`, `rows`, or `cols`.

The default value is `none`. The `all` setting displays all internal borders, the same as if the `border` attribute were set. The `rows` and `cols` settings display borders to separate only the rows or columns. The `group` setting displays borders according to the specified row or column groups. Table groups are covered later in this chapter.

For example, if you set up a table and do not include the `border` attribute, but include the `rules` attribute and set it to `all`, each cell of the table will include a border. The whole table, however, will not include a border.

ADD CELL BORDERS

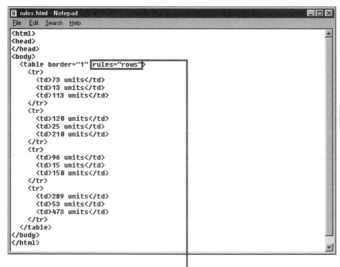

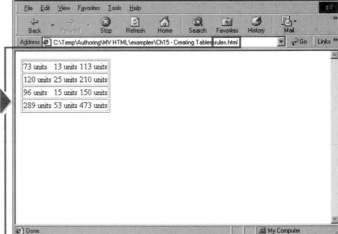

1 Open an HTML file with a `<table>` tag.

■ The example shows the file created in "Add a New Table Row."

2 Add the `rules` attribute to the `<table>` tag and set its value to `rows`.

3 Save the file with a new filename.

4 Open the new file in a browser.

■ Notice how horizontal borders separate the rows.

What is the relationship between the border and rules attributes?

✔ Default cell borders, with a thickness of 1 pixel, are automatically added between cells if the border attribute is set to a nonzero value. Likewise, if the `border` attribute is not included, a default 1-pixel border appears if the `rules` attribute is added to the `<table>` tag.

Can the border width between cells be changed?

✔ The default cell border thickness is 1 pixel. This appears whenever the `rules` or `border` attributes are used. This width cannot be changed using the either of these attributes, but adding the `cellpadding` attribute to the `<table>` tag can change the space between cells and therefore the border width. See the section "Set Cell Width and Height" in this chapter for more information.

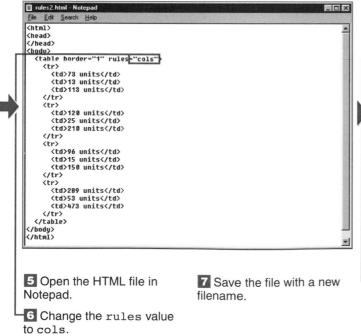

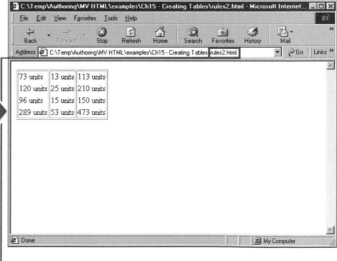

5 Open the HTML file in Notepad.

6 Change the `rules` value to `cols`.

7 Save the file with a new filename.

8 Open the file in a browser.

■ Notice how vertical borders separate the columns.

SET TABLE WIDTH

Unless specified, the content contained within the individual cells determines the width of the entire table. If enough cell content exists, the table is automatically sized to fit within the browser window, and the cell content will wrap within the individual cells. If the cell content includes no white space in which the text can wrap, however, the width of the table extends beyond the browser window.

You can set the entire table width using the width attribute in the <table> tag. This attribute can be specified in pixels or as a percentage of the browser window.

For example, if the width value is said to 400, the table will be set to exactly 400 pixels. But if the width attribute is set to 50%, the table is sized to fit exactly half the browser window.

SET TABLE WIDTH

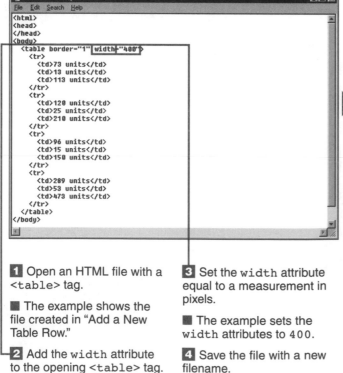

1 Open an HTML file with a <table> tag.

■ The example shows the file created in "Add a New Table Row."

2 Add the width attribute to the opening <table> tag.

3 Set the width attribute equal to a measurement in pixels.

■ The example sets the width attributes to 400.

4 Save the file with a new filename.

5 Open the file in a browser.

■ The width for the entire table is set to the designated number of pixels.

Are there times when a table width will be overridden?

✔ Any attributes specified within the `<table>` tags are automatically overridden by any attributes within the `<table>` tags, such as the `<tr>`, `<th>`, and `<td>` tags. The section "Set Cell Spacing and Padding" describes the `width`, `height`, `cellpadding`, and `cellspacing` attributes. If these attributes are set to values that add up to be greater than the specified width, the `width` value is ignored.

Can I disable text cell wrapping?

✔ If the `nowrap` attribute is added to the `<td>` tag, cell wrapping is disabled, and all the text appears in the cell without wrapping. This attribute does not need a value. Including the `nowrap` attribute overrides the `width` attribute in the `<table>` tag.

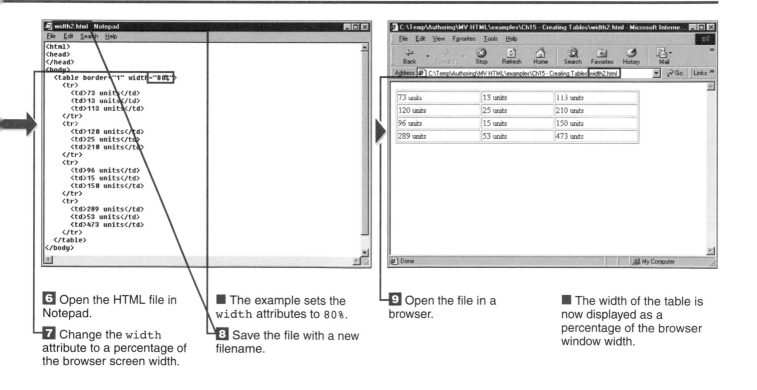

6 Open the HTML file in Notepad.

7 Change the `width` attribute to a percentage of the browser screen width.

■ The example sets the `width` attributes to `80%`.

8 Save the file with a new filename.

9 Open the file in a browser.

■ The width of the table is now displayed as a percentage of the browser window width.

SET TABLE ALIGNMENT AND WRAPPING TEXT

Chapter 11 explains how you can wrap text around an image. You can use the same technique to wrap text around tables.

Using the `align` attribute, you can align the table to the left or right edge of the browser. The default alignment is to the left.

If you want the text that comes after the closing `<table>` tag to wrap to the side of the table, you must include the `align` attribute. Even left-aligned tables require the `align` attribute if you wish the text to wrap around the table.

If the table is wider than the browser, the text will not wrap

around the edge of it. The text will only wrap around the table if the table width is less than the browser width. The width of a table by default is set by the width of the content within the table cells. It can also be set with the `width` attribute.

SET TABLE ALIGNMENT AND WRAPPING TEXT

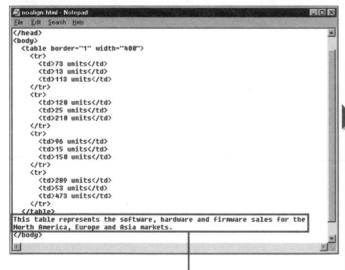

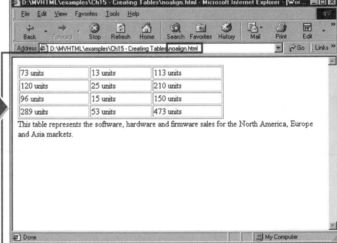

1 Open an HTML file with a `<table>` tag.

■ The example shows the file created in "Set Table Width."

2 Add a section of text under the closing `<table>` tag.

3 Save the file with a new filename.

4 Open the file in a browser.

■ Notice how the text appears underneath the table.

Can I add some space between the wrapping text and the table?

✔ You can use the `hspace` attribute to separate wrapping text from an image that it is next to, but no such attribute exists for tables. To separate wrapping text from tables, you can use a graphical spacer as discussed in Chapter 12. You can also add space using the nonbreaking space (` `) text definition.

Can <table> tags be positioned within other <table> tags?

✔ When one table appears within another table, it is called a *nested table*. A nested table example appears in the section "Build Nested Tables" later in this chapter. The size of a nested table will be determined by the outermost table.

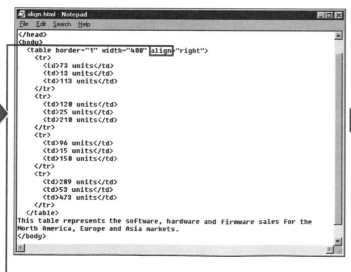

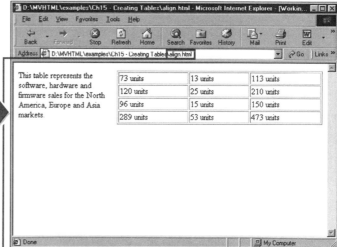

5 Open the HTML file in Notepad.

6 Add the `align` attribute to the opening `<table>` tag.

7 Set the `align` attribute equal to `left` or `right`.

■ The examples shows the `align` attribute set to `right`.

8 Save the file with a new filename.

9 Open the file in a browser.

■ The text now appears to the left of the table.

USE ROW AND COLUMN HEADINGS

After you now how to add cells to a table, you may want to add headings your tables. Table headings help you understand what the various rows and columns of data mean.

You can add table headings to a table by replacing the <td> tags with <th> tags. All attributes and

values between the <th> and <td> tags are identical. However, when text marked with a <th> tag is displayed in a browser, the text is bold.

For column heads, all <th> tags are included in a single row. Changing the first <td> tag in each row to a <th> tag can create row heads.

The <th> tags do not need to be placed on the cells appearing at the edge of the table. They can actually be placed anywhere within the table, but it makes more sense to have them appear at the top of the columns or at the start or end of a row.

USE ROW AND COLUMN HEADINGS

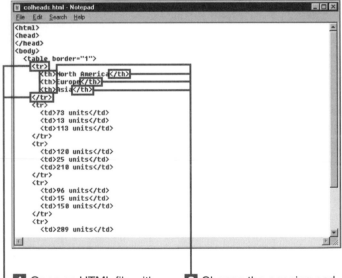

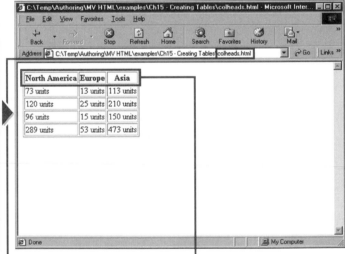

1 Open an HTML file with a <table> tag.

■ The example shows the file created in "Add a New Table Row."

2 Copy and past a set of <tr> tags.

3 Change the opening and closing <td> tags to <th> tags.

4 Change the content between the <th> to be column headers.

5 Save the file with a new filename.

6 Open the HTML file in a browser.

■ Notice the column heads that have been added to the table.

Do <th> tags always need to come at the start of a row or column?

✔ Any <tr> tag can be changed to a <th> tag. This causes the text contained within the <th> tag to be displayed as bold in the browser. Although <th> tags are mainly used for headings, they do not need to be used exclusively for headings.

Do I always need to include closing <tr> and <td> tags?

✔ Most browsers do not require closing <tr> or <td> tags. They can tell where the next cell or row starts from the opening tags. To be compliant with XHTML, however, you should include either a closing tag or a slash along with the opening tag. Also, style sheets, covered in Part IX, require closing tags in order to display correctly.

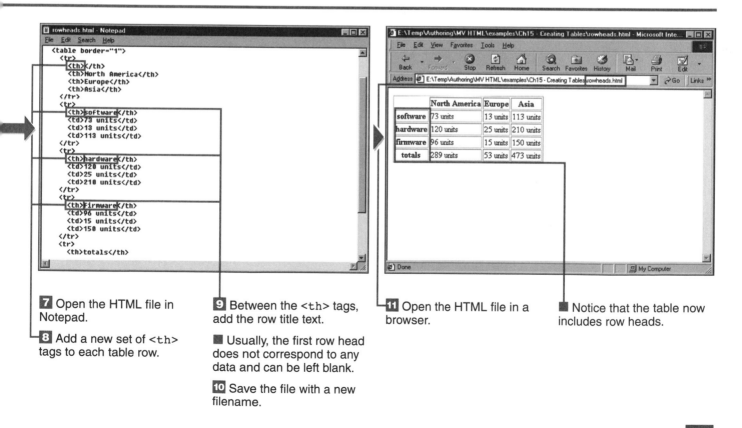

7 Open the HTML file in Notepad.

8 Add a new set of <th> tags to each table row.

9 Between the <th> tags, add the row title text.

■ Usually, the first row head does not correspond to any data and can be left blank.

10 Save the file with a new filename.

11 Open the HTML file in a browser.

■ Notice that the table now includes row heads.

SET CELL WIDTH AND HEIGHT

Adding the width attribute to the <table> tag enables you to specify the width for the entire table, but the height of the table is determined by the content of the various cells.

However, you can set the width and height of individual table cells by adding the width and height attributes to the <td> or <th> tags. You can set these attributes to either pixels or a percentage of the browser window.

Keep in mind that the size of an individual cell will affect the size of all the cells in the same row and column as the resized cell. For example, if a single cell is sized to have width and height values of 100 pixels, all cells within the same column will have widths of 100 pixels and all cells within the same row will have a heights of 100 pixels.

SET CELL WIDTH AND HEIGHT

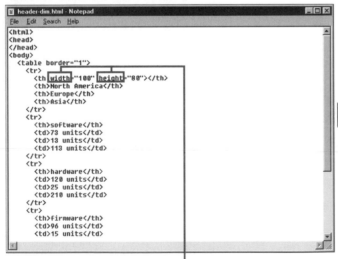

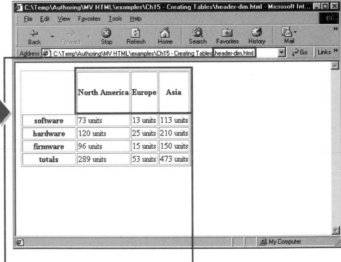

1 Open an HTML file that has a <table> tag and row and column heads in Notepad.

■ The example shows the file created in "Use Row and Column Headings."

2 Add width and height attributes.

3 Set the width and height attributes. The example shows these set at 100 and 80.

4 Save the file with a new filename.

5 Open the HTML file in a browser.

■ The size of the cells on the top row cells is larger.

If the width value for individual cells is greater than the width value for the table, which value is used?

✔ The value set for individual cells always overrides the value set for the entire table.

What happens if a cell includes a width value and the nowrap attribute?

✔ If a cell has a specified width and includes the `nowrap` attribute, the specified width is used as long as the cell text does not exceed the specified width. If the text does exceed the specified width, the width value is ignored. The `nowidth` attribute is discussed in the section "Set Table Width" earlier in the chapter.

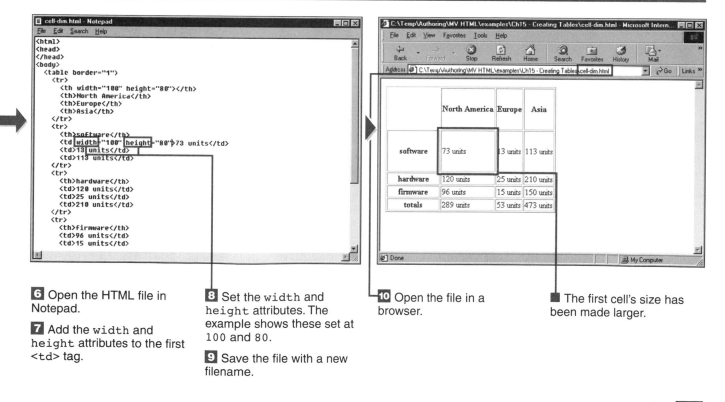

6 Open the HTML file in Notepad.

7 Add the `width` and `height` attributes to the first `<td>` tag.

8 Set the `width` and `height` attributes. The example shows these set at `100` and `80`.

9 Save the file with a new filename.

10 Open the file in a browser.

■ The first cell's size has been made larger.

SET CELL ALIGNMENT

By default, any content that is added within a cell is centered vertically and horizontally. However, you can control the alignment of the content within the cell by moving it to the edge of the cell.

The align attribute for the <table> tag sets the alignment for the entire table, but you can also control the alignment of individual cells using the align and valign attributes in the <tr>, <th>, and <td> tags.

The align attribute for the individual cell takes precedence over the align attribute for the entire table. For example, if the align attribute for the <table> is set to center and the align attribute for the <td> tag is set to right, the cell will be right-aligned.

You can set the align attribute to left, right, center, justify, or char. The valign attribute can be set to top, middle, bottom, or baseline.

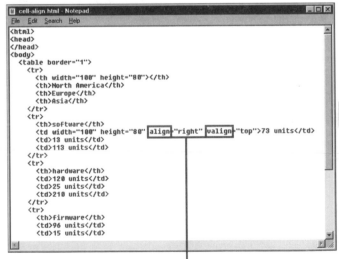

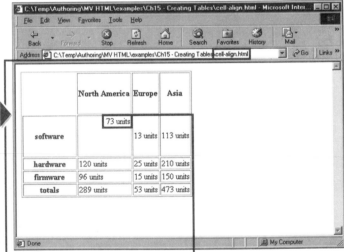

1 Open an HTML file that has a <table> tag and row and column heads in Notepad.

■ The example shows the file created in "Set Cell Width and Height."

2 Add the align and valign attributes.

3 Set the align and valign attributes. The example shows the attributes set to right and to top.

4 Save the file.

5 Open the HTML file in a browser.

■ The text in the first cell is displayed where you set the alignment. In the example the text appears in the upper-right corner of the cell.

What does the align attribute's char value do?

✔ If the `align` attribute is set to `char`, the contents of each column is aligned using a single character defined by the `char` attribute. The default character is the decimal point (`.`). You can also offset the alignment with the `charoff` attribute. The `charoff` value is measured in pixels or a percentage of the total length.

What does the valign attribute's baseline value do?

✔ The `baseline` value of the `valign` attribute causes all cells with this attribute within a row to be aligned.

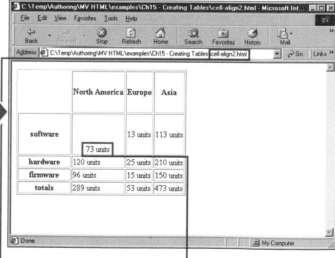

6 Open the file in Notepad.

7 Change the `align` and `valign` attributes. The examples shows the attributes set to `center` and to `bottom`.

8 Save the file with a new filename.

9 Open the HTML file in a browser.

■ The text is now centered along the bottom of the cell.

SET BACKGROUND COLORS

Chapter 6 shows you how you can use the bgcolor attribute of the <body> tag to change the background color of a Web page. Tables can also take advantage of the bgcolor attribute.

Using the bgcolor attribute, you can set the background color for the entire table or for individual

rows or cells. The bgcolor attribute can be added to the <table>, <td>, <th>, and <tr> tags.

Acceptable color values include the browser-recognized named colors like blue and darkgreen and RGB hexadecimal color values like #002cff. Remember that hexadecimal color values need to

begin with the number sign (#). Colors are discussed in Chapter 6.

For example, if the <table> tag includes the bgcolor attribute set to yellow and the first <tr> tag also includes the bgcolor attribute that is set to orange, the table cells will be yellow, except for the first row, which would be orange.

SET BACKGROUND COLORS

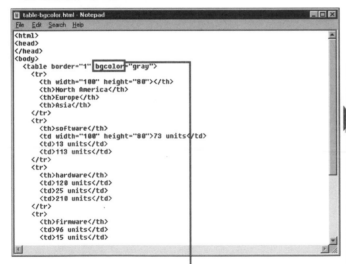 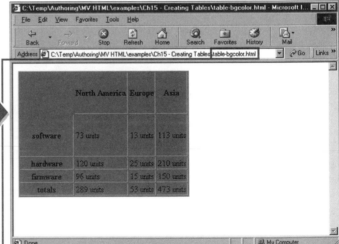

1 Open an HTML file that has a <table> tag and row and column heads in Notepad.

■ The example shows the file created in "Set Cell Width and Height."

2 Add the bgcolor attribute.

3 Set the bgcolor attribute to browser-recognized named colors. The example shows the attribute set to gray.

4 Save the file.

5 Open the HTML file in a browser.

■ The background color for the entire table is changed to the selected color.

Can you also use the background attribute to make an image appear as a table background?

✔ Support for the `background` attribute depends on the browser, but the major browsers do support this. To set the table background as a tileable image, simply set the `background` attribute equal to the URL for the image. See Chapter 11 for more information.

How can I describe a table?

✔ You can use the `<caption>` tag as a way to add a caption to the table (see the section "Add a Table Caption"). Another way to describe the table is with the `summary` attribute. This description is used for nonvisual browsers, such as audio browsers, to describe the table. Audio browsers are discussed along with aural style sheets in Chapter 39.

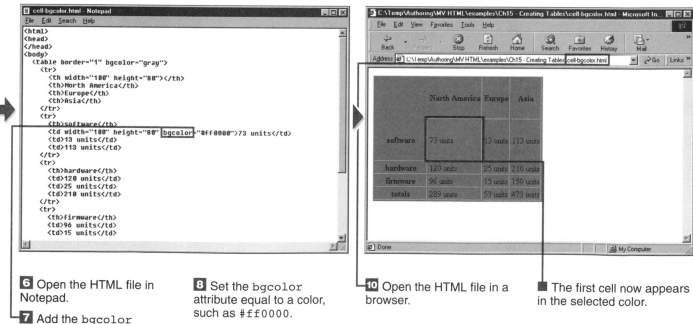

6 Open the HTML file in Notepad.

7 Add the `bgcolor` attribute to the first `<td>` tag.

8 Set the `bgcolor` attribute equal to a color, such as `#ff0000`.

9 Save the file with a new filename.

10 Open the HTML file in a browser.

■ The first cell now appears in the selected color.

SET CELL SPACING AND PADDING

Although there is no easy way to add space between a table and normal text, you can add space between a cell's content and its edges and also between adjacent cells.

The <table> tag can include two attributes that you can use to add some space around the content of a cell and between cells.

The cellpadding attribute adds space between the cell text and the edges of the cell. The cellspacing attribute adds space between each cell.

The values of the cellpadding and cellspacing attributes are measured in pixels.

For example, if you add a <table> tag with cellpadding and cellspacing attributes set to 10 and 20, 10 pixels will be placed between the edge of the cell and the cell content and 20 pixels will be placed between each cell.

SET CELL SPACING AND PADDING

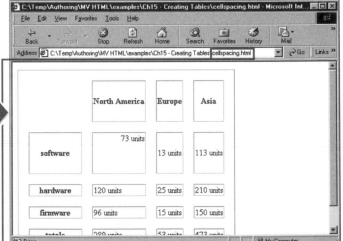

1 Open an HTML file that has a <table> tag and row and column heads in Notepad.

■ The example shows the file created in "Set Cell Width and Height."

2 Add the cellspacing attribute.

3 Set the cellspacing attribute to a desired value. The example shows the attribute set to 20.

4 Save the file with a new filename.

5 Open the HTML file in a browser.

■ The space between each cell has increased.

MASTER IT

How do the cellpadding and cellspacing attributes affect the cell's width?

✔ The cellpadding and cellspacing values are both independent of the cell's width. The cell's width exactly defines the space allotted for the content. cellspacing and cellpadding values do, however, affect the overall table width. For example, if the cell's width is said to be 100 pixels and the table's cellspacing and cellpadding values are set to 20 pixels, the end result for a two-column table would be a table width of 340 pixels.

What is the default values for the cellpadding and cellspacing attributes?

✔ The cell will not include any extra space if the cellpadding and cellspacing attributes are not included. This is the same affect if the cellpadding and cellspacing attributes were included and set to 0.

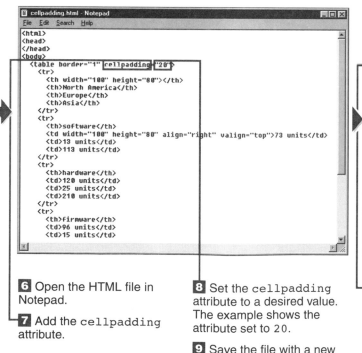

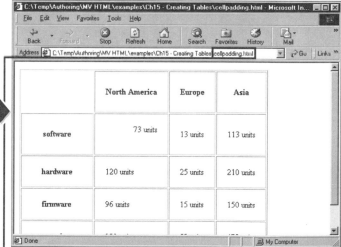

6 Open the HTML file in Notepad.

7 Add the cellpadding attribute.

8 Set the cellpadding attribute to a desired value. The example shows the attribute set to 20.

9 Save the file with a new filename.

10 Open the HTML file in a browser.

■ Space is added between the cell text and the cell edges.

SPAN SEVERAL CELLS

When you design tables, you sometimes want to combine two or more adjacent cells into one. You can do this with the rowspan and colspan attributes. The difference between these attributes is that rowspan combines at least two vertical cells,

and colspan combines at least two horizontal cells.

These attributes need to appear in the <td> or <th> tags. The value should be set to the number of rows or columns you want to span. The number of rows or columns to span includes the current cell.

For example, if you add the rowspan to a <td> tag and set its value to 4, the next three rows from the current cell will be spanned resulting in a single cell that covers four rows.

SPAN SEVERAL CELLS

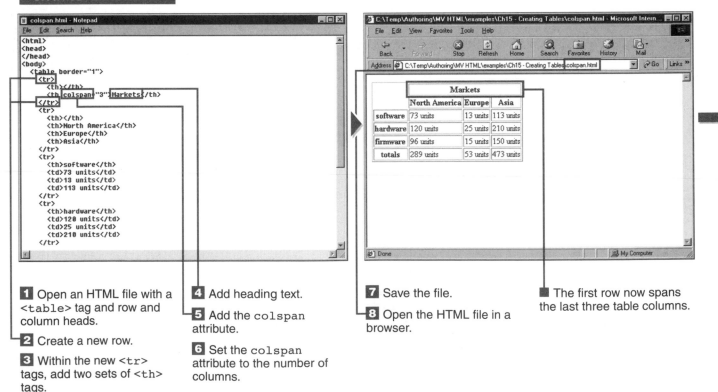

1 Open an HTML file with a <table> tag and row and column heads.

2 Create a new row.

3 Within the new <tr> tags, add two sets of <th> tags.

4 Add heading text.

5 Add the colspan attribute.

6 Set the colspan attribute to the number of columns.

7 Save the file.

8 Open the HTML file in a browser.

■ The first row now spans the last three table columns.

What happens if I forget to remove cells to account for a row or column span?

✔ When you add a row or column span to an existing table, you eliminate the need for several cells. For the table to display properly, the unneeded cells need to be identified and removed. If these cells are not removed, the unneeded cells after the span will still be displayed, expanding the table and misaligning the cells.

When should I use row and column spans?

✔ Row and column spans are useful when the content you wish to place within a cell will not fit. By spanning several cells, you can fit more text into the cell without altering the overall table.

What happens if the colspan or rowspan value is larger than the available cells?

✔ If you specify a row or column span that is larger than the available cells, the row or column will extend as far as it can, but it will not add any new cells to the table.

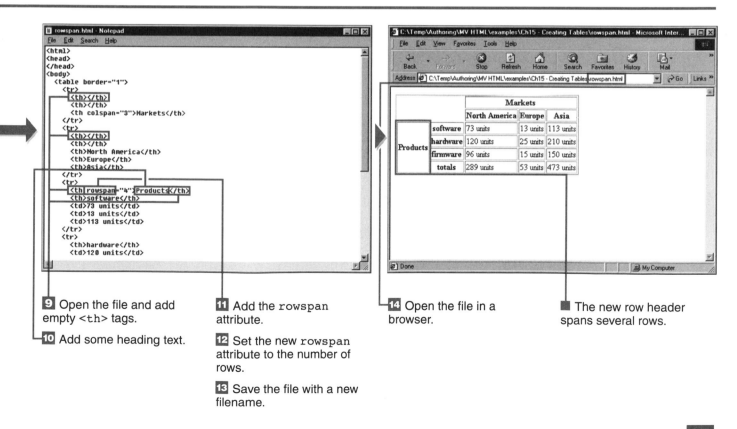

9 Open the file and add empty `<th>` tags.

10 Add some heading text.

11 Add the `rowspan` attribute.

12 Set the new `rowspan` attribute to the number of rows.

13 Save the file with a new filename.

14 Open the file in a browser.

■ The new row header spans several rows.

ADD A TABLE CAPTION

When you see a table in a book, it typically includes a caption positioned above or below the table. The caption tells you about the information that appears in the table.

You can add captions to tables using the `<caption>` tag. This tag can appear anywhere within the `<table>` tags as long as you include both opening and closing tags.

Captions can be displayed above or below the table using the `align` attribute set to `top` or `bottom`. The `align` attribute can also be set to `left`, `center`, or `right`.

The default is centered at the top of the table. For more about the `align` attribute, see Chapter 11.

For example, if the statement `<caption align="bottom">Sales Forecast</caption>` is placed within a set of `<table>` tags, a caption will appear directly below the table.

ADD A TABLE CAPTION

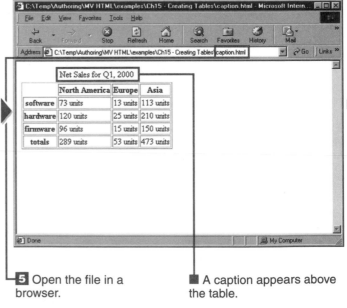

1 Open an HTML file that has a `<table>` tag and row and column heads in Notepad.

■ The example shows the file created in "Set Cell Width and Height."

2 Add opening and closing `<caption>` tags.

3 Add the caption text within the `<caption>` tags.

4 Save the file with a new filename.

5 Open the file in a browser.

■ A caption appears above the table.

Is there a way to include two caption position values like right and bottom?

✔ Using the `<caption>` tag, you can only include a single value for the `align` attribute. If you want to position the caption to the bottom right of the table, you can use a second set of table tags with no borders whose `align` attribute is set to `right`.

Why should I use a table caption rather than regular text?

✔ The advantage of using table captions created with the `<caption>` tag is that caption definition is included with the table. If the table gets moved or repositioned within the HTML file, the caption will be moved along with the table. Using text for captions enables more formatting and alignment options.

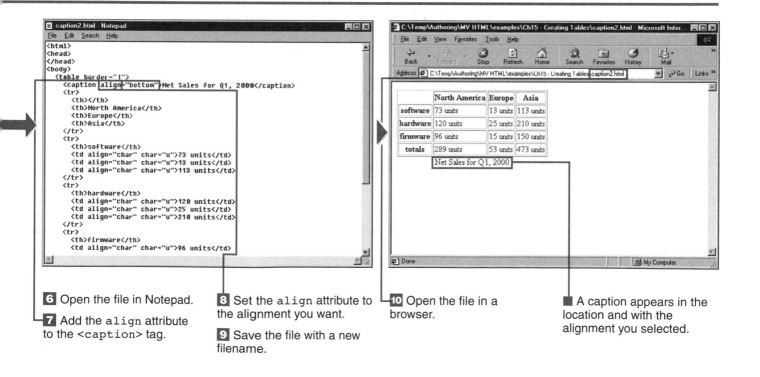

6 Open the file in Notepad.

7 Add the `align` attribute to the `<caption>` tag.

8 Set the `align` attribute to the alignment you want.

9 Save the file with a new filename.

10 Open the file in a browser.

■ A caption appears in the location and with the alignment you selected.

USE TABLE GROUPS

If a table has many cells that you want to align to the right, adding the align attribute to every <td> tag would be a lot of work. You can reduce this number by adding it to only the <tr> tags, but even this requires a lot of effort. A quicker way to handle this task is to use *table groups*. All attributes you add to a group tag are automatically applied to all cells within that group.

You can group rows into different sections using the <thead>, <tbody>, and <tfoot> attributes. All of these tags can use the align, valign, char, and charoff attributes.

You can group columns by using the <colgroup> and <col/> tags. These tags can also use the align, valign, char, and charoff attributes. They also

include a width attribute and the span attribute that can apply the defined settings to several columns at the same time.

For example, if a <colgroup> includes an width attribute set to 200 and a span attribute set to 4, the next four columns all have a width of 200 pixels.

USE TABLE GROUPS

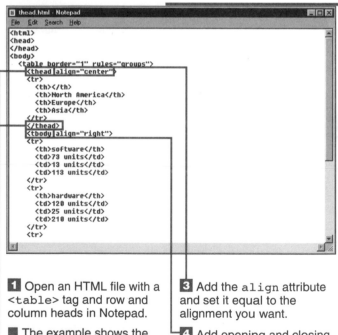

1 Open an HTML file with a <table> tag and row and column heads in Notepad.

■ The example shows the file created in "Set Cell Width and Height."

2 Add <thead> tags.

3 Add the align attribute and set it equal to the alignment you want.

4 Add opening and closing <tbody> tags.

5 Add the align attribute to the opening <tbody> tag and set it to the alignment you want.

6 Add a rules attribute to the <table> tag. Set it to groups.

7 Save the file.

8 Open the file in a browser.

■ All cells within the <thead> tags and all tags within the <tbody> tags align as you selected.

If the cell is in both a row and column group in which one takes precedence?

✔ If a cell belongs to both the row and a column group with conflicting attributes, the cell will be formatted with the attribute values that are closest to the actual cell content. So, for example, if the cell is included in both `<tbody>` and `<colgroup>` tags, the attribute values used to format the cell are taken from the later tag.

Why should I use table groups?

✔ Table groups enable you to set the attributes of a group of cells quickly and easily without having to change the attributes for each individual cell. For example, you could set the alignment of a `<thead>` tag to center and all the cells within the group will be centered-aligned.

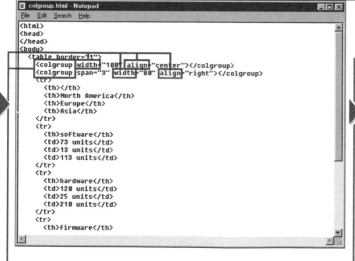

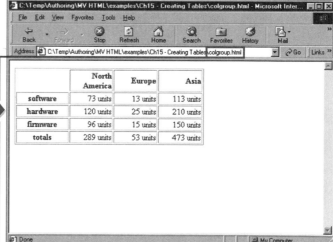

9 Open an HTML file with a `<table>` tag and row and column heads.

10 Add two `<colgroup>` tag sets.

11 Add `width` and `align` attributes.

12 For the first `<colgroup>` tag, set the width to `100` and the align value to `center`.

13 For the second `<colgroup>` tag, set the width to `80` and the align value to `right`.

14 Add the `span` attribute to the second `<colgroup>` tag and set it to 3.

15 Save the file.

16 Open the file in a browser.

■ The first column has a width of 100 pixels with centered text.

■ The next three columns have a width of 80 pixels with right-aligned text.

BUILD NESTED TABLES

To build more complex table structures, you can create a nested table. *Nested tables* result from placing an entire new table as the content of a table cell.

For example, if you have a four by four cell table created and within

the first set of `<td>` tags, you add another set of `<table>` tags, the second table will be nested within the first. When displayed, the inner table will exist within a cell of the outer table.

Be careful as you create nested tables that you keep the individual

table tags separated. Overlapping table tags will produce unexpected results. One easy way to keep the various opening and closing tags aligned is to indent every successive table tag.

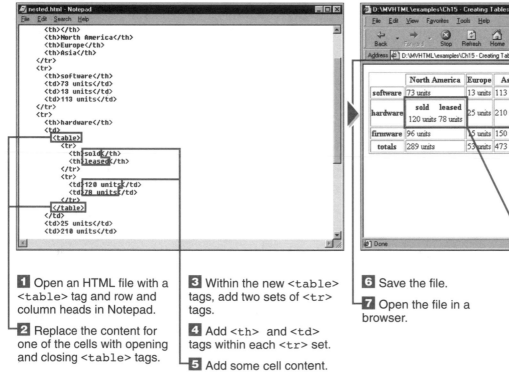

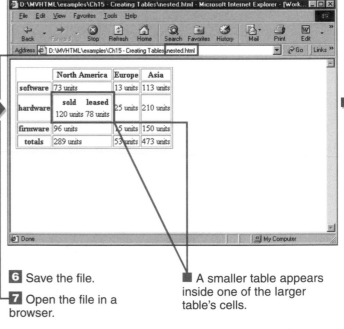

1 Open an HTML file with a `<table>` tag and row and column heads in Notepad.

2 Replace the content for one of the cells with opening and closing `<table>` tags.

3 Within the new `<table>` tags, add two sets of `<tr>` tags.

4 Add `<th>` and `<td>` tags within each `<tr>` set.

5 Add some cell content.

6 Save the file.

7 Open the file in a browser.

■ A smaller table appears inside one of the larger table's cells.

Does a nested table inherit attributes from its parent table?

✔ When a nested table appears within another table, it uses the default values for creating a table. The nested table does not to inherit the attributes from the parent table. You need to specify all attributes for the nested table.

Is there a limit to the number of tables that I can nest within one another?

✔ As long as you do not overlap tables, there is no limit to the number of tables that you can nest within one another.

When is a nested table appropriate to use?

✔ Nesting several tables within one another can be confusing and is not recommended. If you use tables to position object on your Web page, however, placing a nested table within the parent layout table would be acceptable.

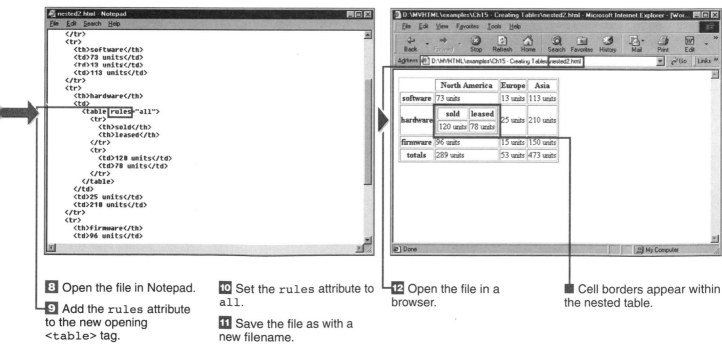

8 Open the file in Notepad.

9 Add the `rules` attribute to the new opening `<table>` tag.

10 Set the `rules` attribute to `all`.

11 Save the file as with a new filename.

12 Open the file in a browser.

■ Cell borders appear within the nested table.

POSITION OBJECTS WITH TABLES

Tables enable you to have a lot of control over the position of the various cells. You can also use table to your advantage for positioning objects on a Web page. By positioning objects in table cells, you can control precisely where they are positioned on the page, how much space comes

between elements, and how they are aligned.

Using the width attribute of the <table> tag, you can specify exactly the position of elements on either side of the table. You can also place graphical spacers, covered in Chapter 12, within a

table cell to control the width of individual cells.

As an example of using tables to position objects on a Web page, consider a navigation toolbar. Each icon of the toolbar can be placed in a separate cell of a single table row, with each icon centered and aligned.

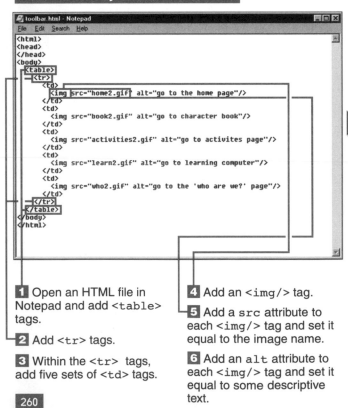

1 Open an HTML file in Notepad and add <table> tags.

2 Add <tr> tags.

3 Within the <tr> tags, add five sets of <td> tags.

4 Add an <img/> tag.

5 Add a src attribute to each <img/> tag and set it equal to the image name.

6 Add an alt attribute to each <img/> tag and set it equal to some descriptive text.

7 Repeat Steps 4-6 for the remaining sets of <td> tags.

8 Save the file with a new filename.

9 Open the file in a browser.

■ The images are positioned next to one another in a line.

10 Open the file in Notepad.

Using the cellpadding attribute adds both vertical and horizontal space around the icon. Can I space only the icons horizontally?

✔ One advantage of using the `cellpadding` attribute is that you only need to add it once to the `<table>` tag to apply it to all cells. If you want to space the icons only horizontally or vertically, you can add the `hspace` or `vspace` attributes to the `<img/>` tag. This only works for images, but you can use it to add either vertical or horizontal space in only one dimension between elements.

How do I center objects within tables?

✔ Once a table is created and used to position elements, you can also align those elements using the align attribute of the `<table>` or `<td>` tags.

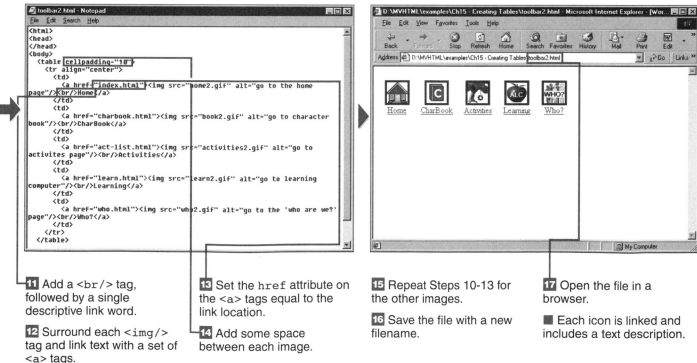

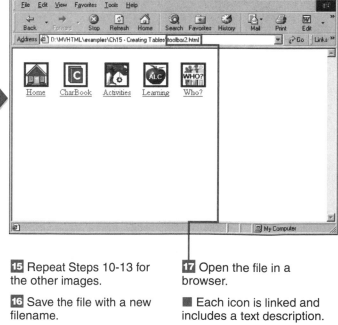

11 Add a `<br/>` tag, followed by a single descriptive link word.

12 Surround each `<img/>` tag and link text with a set of `<a>` tags.

13 Set the `href` attribute on the `<a>` tags equal to the link location.

14 Add some space between each image.

15 Repeat Steps 10-13 for the other images.

16 Save the file with a new filename.

17 Open the file in a browser.

■ Each icon is linked and includes a text description.

CREATE TEXT COLUMNS

A common way to use tables is to split up a Web page into columns like a newspaper. You can create columns by using a table with a single row and two cells.

For example, the following code would create a page that is 600 pixels wide with two columns:

```
<table
width="600"><tr><td></td>
<td></td></tr></table>.
```

To fill these two columns, you simply need to add content within the two sets of <td> tags.

You can add extra columns to the page by including more sets of <td> tags. You can also specify the gutter that exists between the columns and the margins on either side using the cellpadding attribute to the <table> tag.

CREATE TEXT COLUMNS

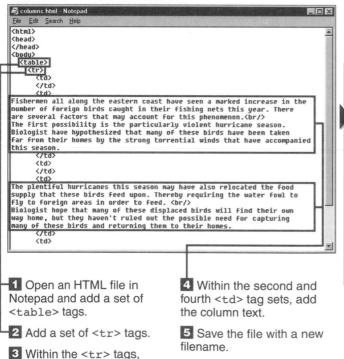

1 Open an HTML file in Notepad and add a set of <table> tags.

2 Add a set of <tr> tags.

3 Within the <tr> tags, add a five sets of <td> tags.

4 Within the second and fourth <td> tag sets, add the column text.

5 Save the file with a new filename.

6 Open the HTML file in a browser.

■ The text is aligned within two columns that span the entire browser window.

7 Open the file in Notepad.

MASTER IT

Can you add more than two columns to a page?

✔ The number of columns that you include using this technique is unlimited. To add additional columns, you simply need to add additional cells to the table.

Can I add images to a column?

✔ You can add images at any place within that column text by using the `<img/>` tag. Keep in mind that if you want to wrap the column text around the image, you need to include the `align` attribute as part of the `<img/>` tag.

Can I break up the columns like those in a newspaper?

✔ By adding additional rows to the table, you can break up the columns and switch between two and three column sections.

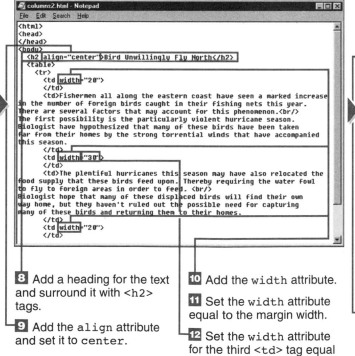

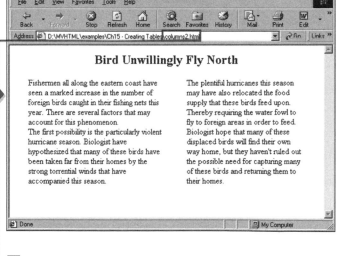

8 Add a heading for the text and surround it with `<h2>` tags.

9 Add the `align` attribute and set it to `center`.

10 Add the `width` attribute.

11 Set the `width` attribute equal to the margin width.

12 Set the `width` attribute for the third `<td>` tag equal to the space between the columns.

13 Save the file with a new filename.

14 Open the file in a browser.

■ A header and increased margins appear as part of the Web page layout.

USING FRAMES

Using *frames,* you can split the browser window into several individual frames that can each display a separate Web page.

Frames are useful for including sidebars, navigation, link lists, headers, or footers.

Each frame can include links to other pages. These linked pages can be opened in the existing frame or in another one.

Frames are defined by a parent Web page called a *frameset.* This frameset can include two or more frames. When frames are defined, you can specify the size of the frame and where it is located. All the frames together should account for 100 percent of the browser window.

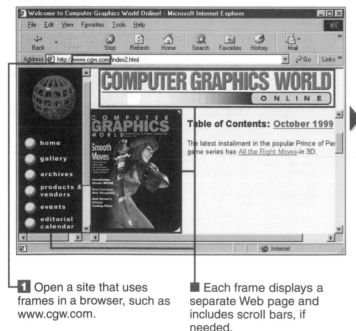

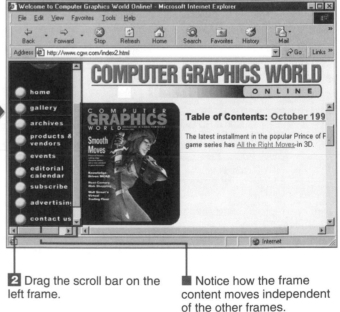

1 Open a site that uses frames in a browser, such as www.cgw.com.

■ Each frame displays a separate Web page and includes scroll bars, if needed.

2 Drag the scroll bar on the left frame.

■ Notice how the frame content moves independent of the other frames.

Why do many people not like to use frames?

✔ Many Web users feel that using frames limits the already restricted browser window space. The drawback of working with frames is the extra space that they take, especially if the browser window is fairly small to start with. If you choose to use frames, you should learn to use them judiciously. Many sites enable you to view their site with frames or without frames.

When are frames appropriate to use?

✔ Frames can make navigating a site much easier. If the main links to the site are located in a frame that appears at the top or along the edge of the browser, the content for those links can be displayed in the remainder of the browser window. Using this setup, the navigation links would be visible at all times for all pages within the site.

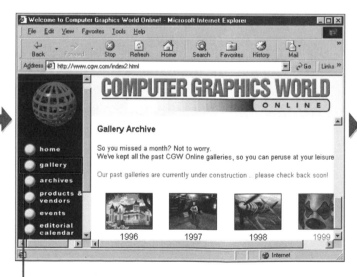

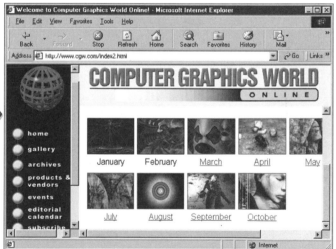

3 Click a link in the left-hand navigational frame.

■ The example shows result of clicking the Gallery link.

■ Notice how the right frame content updates independent of the other frames.

4 Click a link in the right frame.

■ Notice how the content in the right frame updates.

BUILD A FRAMESET

The set of tags that hold all the individual frames is called a *frameset*. The `<frameset>` tags replace the `<body>` tags and act as a container. Within the `<frameset>` tags, you can include one or many `<frame/>` tags used to actually define individual frames.

A frameset can divide frames vertically or horizontally. The `rows` attribute divides a frameset horizontally into rows, and the `cols` attribute divides a frameset vertically into columns.

The number of values included with the `rows` or `cols` attribute determines the number of frames included in a frameset. These values are a percentage of the total browser window.

For example, if the `cols` attribute is set to `50%, 25%, 25%`, the browser displays three vertical frames with the leftmost frame being twice as big as the remaining two.

The number of `<frame/>` tags included within the frameset should match the number of values contained within the `rows` or `cols` attribute.

BUILD A FRAMESET

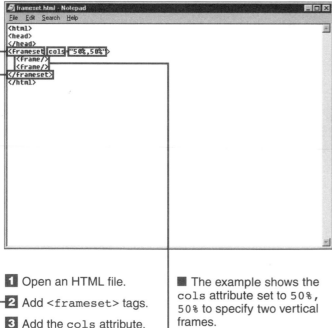

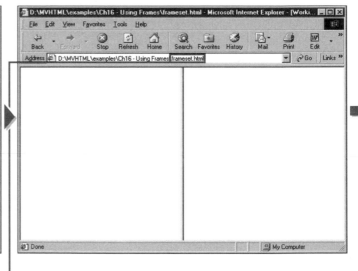

1 Open an HTML file.

2 Add `<frameset>` tags.

3 Add the `cols` attribute.

4 Set the `cols` attribute equal to the width percentages for the frames.

■ The example shows the `cols` attribute set to `50%, 50%` to specify two vertical frames.

5 Within the `<frameset>` tags, add two `<frame/>` tags.

6 Save the file with a new filename.

7 Open the HTML file in a browser.

■ The browser window is now divided into two vertical frames.

What happens if the number of values in the rows or cols attribute doesn't match the number of `<frame/>` tags?

✔ When each frame in the frameset is defined with a `<frame/>` tag, the frame is displayed in the browser using the default white background. If a `<frame/>` tag is missing, its space is still allocated but is left blank and displayed as an empty gray space.

What happens if the number of values in the rows or cols attribute doesn't add up to 100 percent?

✔ If the percentage values specified in the `rows` or `cols` attribute add up to more or less than 100 percent, the browser sizes the frames relative to the total sum of the values. For example, if the `cols` attribute is set to `100%, 200%`, the browser displays two vertical frames with the second being twice as big as the first.

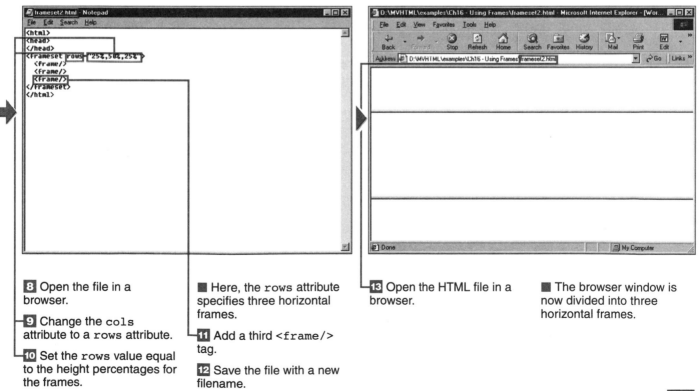

8 Open the file in a browser.

9 Change the `cols` attribute to a `rows` attribute.

10 Set the `rows` value equal to the height percentages for the frames.

■ Here, the `rows` attribute specifies three horizontal frames.

11 Add a third `<frame/>` tag.

12 Save the file with a new filename.

13 Open the HTML file in a browser.

■ The browser window is now divided into three horizontal frames.

SPECIFY FRAME CONTENT

Y ou can use the <frame/> tag to specify the content that should be displayed in each frame. This content is contained within a separate Web page. It is specified in the <frame/> tag using the src attribute. This attribute can point to a Web page file that exists in the same

directory as the frameset file, or it could point to a URL that could be anywhere on the Web.

The <frame/> tag can also include a name attribute. This attribute can be used to name the frame so it can be referenced by other Web page elements.

For example, an <a> tag can reference a specific frame using its name to cause the linked page to open within the specified frame. Links to other frames within a frameset are covered later in this chapter.

SPECIFY FRAME CONTENT

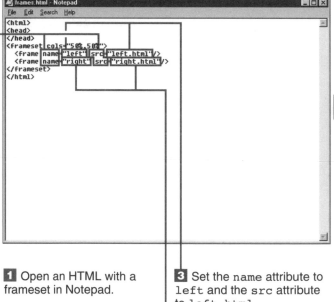

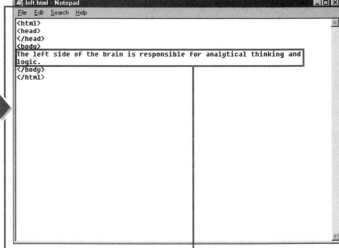

1 Open an HTML with a frameset in Notepad.

■ The example shows the file created in "Build a Frameset."

2 Add the name and src attributes.

3 Set the name attribute to left and the src attribute to left.html.

4 Set the name attribute to right and the src attribute to right.html.

5 Save the file.

6 Open a new HTML file in Notepad.

■ The example shows skeleton.html from the CD.

7 Between the <body> tags, add some text for the left frame.

8 Save the file as left.html.

Does the src attribute have to be a Web page, or can it be set another Web element such as a GIF image?

✔ The `src` attribute of a `<frame/>` tag can be set to any type of element that a browser can display. These elements includes Web pages, images, sound files, video files, and so on. The benefit of a Web page is that the Web page will fill the entire frame.

Can I specify the dimensions of a frame?

✔ The `<frameset>` tags can include the `rows` and `cols` attributes. These attributes are used to specify the dimensions of the various frames. The next section presents these attributes indetail.

Can I enable or disable any other features on frames?

✔ For frames, you can enable or disable frame borders, margins, and scroll bars. Read more about these topics later in this chapter.

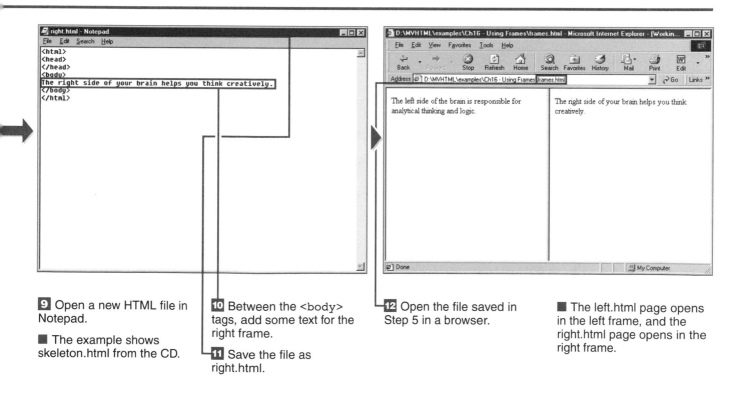

9 Open a new HTML file in Notepad.

■ The example shows skeleton.html from the CD.

10 Between the `<body>` tags, add some text for the right frame.

11 Save the file as right.html.

12 Open the file saved in Step 5 in a browser.

■ The left.html page opens in the left frame, and the right.html page opens in the right frame.

SPECIFY EXACT FRAME PIXEL WIDTHS

Within the opening `<frameset>` tag, you can specify exact frame widths in pixels instead of percentages. To do this, just type in numbers and leave off a percentage (%) symbol from the value.

You can also use the asterisk (*) to specify a frame that should take up the remaining space.

Pixel and percentage values can be combined within a single attribute.

For example, if a `cols` attribute is set to `200, *, 30%`, the browser makes the first frame exactly 200 pixels wide. The third frame is 30 percent of the browser window, and the middle frame occupies the remaining space.

Another way to space frames is to use *relative values*. Relative values include a number followed by the asterisk. For example, the values `1*, 2*, 3*` would make the widths of the frames to be— $\frac{1}{6}$, $\frac{1}{3}$, and $\frac{1}{2}$ the browser window.

SPECIFY EXACT FRAME PIXEL WIDTHS

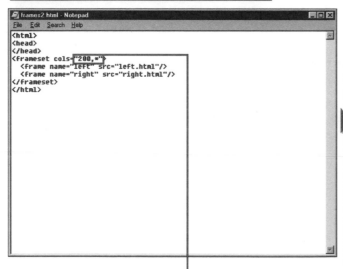

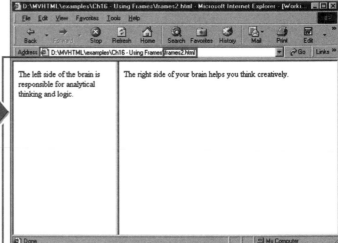

1 Open an HTML file that has two frames in Notepad.

■ The example shows the file created in "Specifying Frame Content."

2 Change the `cols` attribute of the `<frameset>` tag to `200, *`.

3 Save the file with a new filename.

4 Open the HTML file in a browser.

■ The left frame is now exactly 200 pixels wide.

Is including a 1 in front of the asterisk the same a single asterisk?

✔ The asterisk (*) represents the remaining available browser window space. If several asterisk symbols are included, the remaining space is divided equally among them. Any numbers appearing in front of them make those particular frames proportionally larger. A single asterisk produces the same results as an asterisk with a 1 in front of it.

What happens if the number of frames specified in the cols or rows attribute does not match the number of <frame/> tags?

✔ If the number of frames specified in the **<frameset>** tag exceeds the number of **<frame/>** tags, the extra space will be reserved, but no frame is visible. If the number of frames specified in the **<frameset>** tag is less than the number of the **<frame/>** tags, the extra frames are ignored.

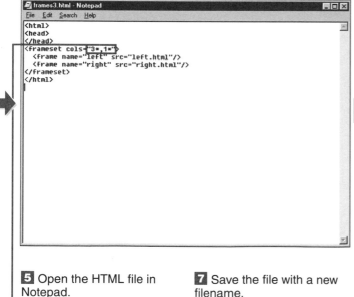

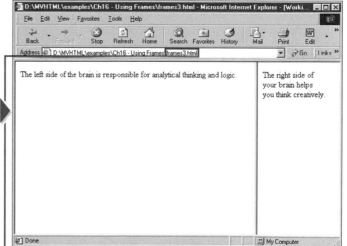

5 Open the HTML file in Notepad.

6 Change the `cols` attribute value to `3*, 1*`.

7 Save the file with a new filename.

8 Open the HTML file in a browser.

■ The first frame occupies 25 percent of the browser window, and the second frame occupies 75 percent.

REMOVE FRAME BORDERS

When frames are displayed in a browser, the browser automatically includes borders between the individual frames. You can remove these borders by using the frameborder attribute.

You can set the frameborder attribute equal to either 0 for no border or 1 to include a border. If the border value is set to a number greater than 2, the frames border displays, but the size is not any bigger. The default is for the browser is to display borders between every frame.

The frameborder attribute applies to the individual frame with which it is included. The border only disappears if the frameborder attribute is set to 0 for both frames connected to that border. If one adjacent <frame/> tag is not set, the frame border appears lighter.

REMOVE FRAME BORDERS

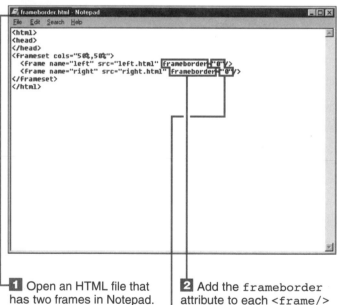

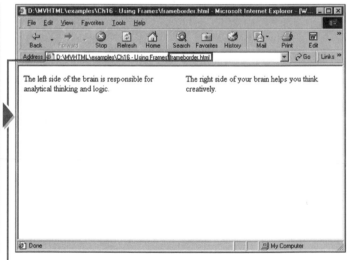

1 Open an HTML file that has two frames in Notepad.

■ The example shows the file created in "Specify Frame Content."

2 Add the frameborder attribute to each <frame/> tag.

3 Set the frameborder value to 0.

4 Save the file with a new filename.

5 Open the HTML file in a browser.

■ The frames are not separated with a frame border.

SET FRAME MARGINS

The `<frame/>` tag also includes a couple of attributes that set the margins for the frame. The `marginwidth` attribute sets the margins for both the left and right side margins. The `marginheight` attribute sets the margins for the top and bottom frame edges.

The `marginwidth` and `marginheight` attributes accept values that represent the margin width in pixels.

If you specify a margin width value that is larger than the frame width, the frame content will not be visible, but scroll bars will enable you to scroll and better view the frame content.

SET FRAME MARGINS

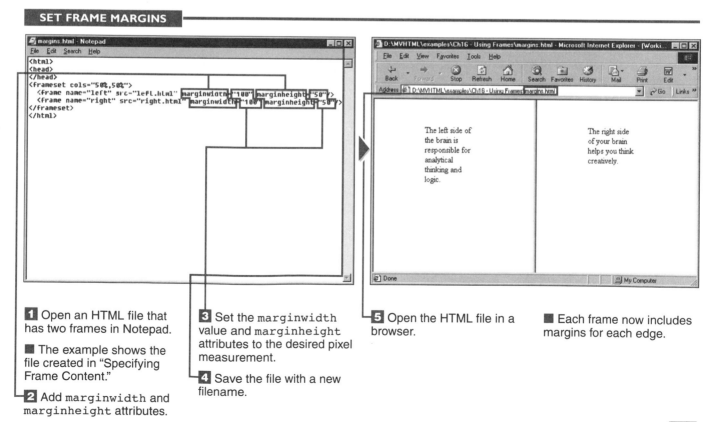

1 Open an HTML file that has two frames in Notepad.

■ The example shows the file created in "Specifying Frame Content."

2 Add `marginwidth` and `marginheight` attributes.

3 Set the `marginwidth` value and `marginheight` attributes to the desired pixel measurement.

4 Save the file with a new filename.

5 Open the HTML file in a browser.

■ Each frame now includes margins for each edge.

DISABLE THE RESIZE OPTION

Regardless of the specified width, you can resize frames in a browser window by dragging on the frame border. When the mouse cursor is over the top of a border, it changes to indicate that the frame can be resized.

You may not want to allow the user to resize the frames. For instance, if the layout of the Web pages is based on the frame sizes, the content will not be displayed correctly when the frames are resized.

Adding the `noresize` attribute to the `<frame/>` tag prevents the frames from being resized. This attribute is a keyword and it needs no value. If the keyword exists in the tag, the frame cannot be resized. If the word is missing, the frame can be resized.

For example, the statement `<frame src="myFrame.html" noresize/>` creates a frame that is loaded with the Web page named, myFrame.html. This frame can not be resized.

DISABLE THE RESIZE OPTION

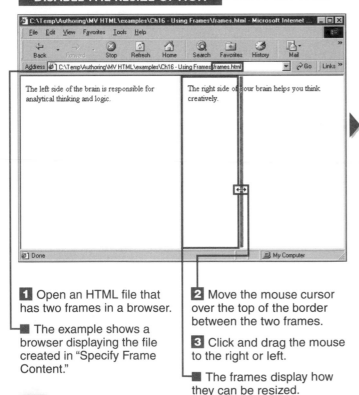

1 Open an HTML file that has two frames in a browser.

■ The example shows a browser displaying the file created in "Specify Frame Content."

2 Move the mouse cursor over the top of the border between the two frames.

3 Click and drag the mouse to the right or left.

■ The frames display how they can be resized.

4 Release the mouse button.

■ The frames are resized.

Can you resize a frame that does not have a border?

✔ Although it is hard to identify, you can still resize frames that don't have a border. To do this, move the cursor over the location where the border would be and watch for the cursor to change.

What if both <frame/> tags do not include the noresize attribute?

✔ A frame can not be resized if any of the frames bordering the border include the **noresize** attribute.

Is the noresize attribute XHTML compliant?

✔ XHTML documents require that all attributes include quote marks. In order to be XHTML compliant, you can set the **noresize** attribute to itself. For example, **noresize= "noresize"** is XHTML compliant.

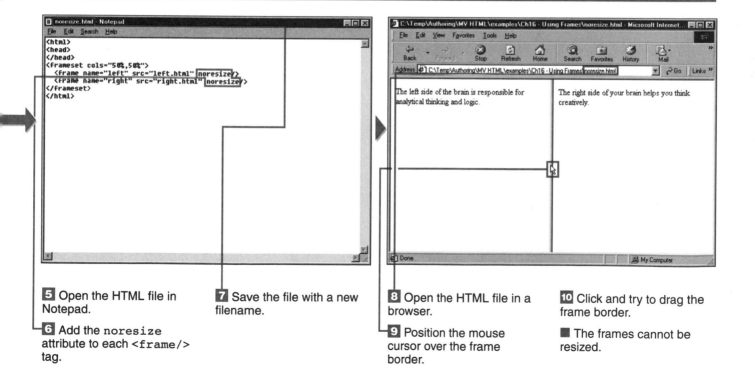

5 Open the HTML file in Notepad.

6 Add the **noresize** attribute to each **<frame/>** tag.

7 Save the file with a new filename.

8 Open the HTML file in a browser.

9 Position the mouse cursor over the frame border.

10 Click and try to drag the frame border.

■ The frames cannot be resized.

CONTROL SCROLL BARS

If the browser window is sized so that the content in a frame exceeds the size of the frame, a scroll bar appears that enables you to scroll within the frame. A scroll bar along the bottom edge of a frame lets you scroll horizontally, and a scroll bar along the right edge of a frame lets you scroll vertically.

Adding the `scrolling` attribute to a `<frame/>` tag lets you control whether a scroll bar appears for the frame. The `scrolling` attribute can accept the values of `yes`, `no`, and `auto`.

The default for frames is the `auto` setting. This setting displays scroll bars when they are needed. If they are not needed, the scroll bars are not displayed.

The `yes` and `no` values force the scroll bar to be present or not present.

CONTROL SCROLL BARS

scrolling.html - Notepad

```
<html>
<head>
</head>
<frameset cols="50%,50%">
  <frame name="left" src="left.html" scrolling="yes"/>
  <frame name="right" src="right.html" scrolling="yes"/>
</frameset>
</html>
```

The left side of the brain is responsible for analytical thinking and logic.

The right side of your brain helps you think creatively.

1 Open an HTML file that has two frames in Notepad.

■ The example shows the file created in "Specify Frame Content."

2 Add the `scrolling` attribute to each `<frame/>` tag.

3 Set each `scrolling` attribute equal to `yes`.

4 Save the file with a new filename.

5 Open the file in a browser.

■ Notice how scroll bars have been added to each frame even though they are not needed.

Will a scroll bar appear if the frameborder attribute is set to 0?

✔ Scroll bars appear according to the `scrolling` attribute, independent of the `frameborder` attribute. If you know that a frame is going to need a scroll bar, you can save some space by setting the `frameborder` value to 0.

When is it appropriate to hide the scroll bars for a frame?

✔ If you are setting the `border` attribute to 0 to hide frame borders, you may also want to disable scroll bars. If you hide the scroll bars, beware that the browser window could be reduced to the point where some of the content in the frame is not visible to the user.

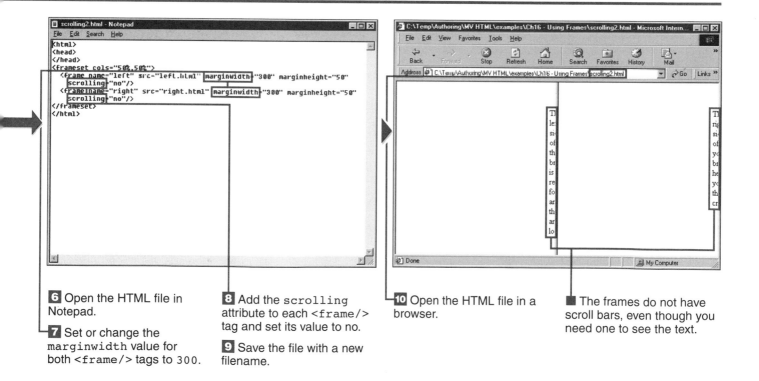

6 Open the HTML file in Notepad.

7 Set or change the `marginwidth` value for both `<frame/>` tags to `300`.

8 Add the `scrolling` attribute to each `<frame/>` tag and set its value to no.

9 Save the file with a new filename.

10 Open the HTML file in a browser.

■ The frames do not have scroll bars, even though you need one to see the text.

BUILD NESTED FRAMESETS

For more complex frame structures, you can nest `<frameset>` tags. *Nested framesets* allow you to break a framed row into several columns or a framed column into several rows.

To nest a frameset within another frameset, you just need to replace one of the `<frame/>` tags with a set of `<frameset>` tags. The new

`<frameset>` tags can then include several additional `<frame/>` tags.

For example, a nested frameset could include three frames like this: `<frameset rows="50%, 50%"><frame src="topframe. html"/><frameset cols= "50%, 50%"><frame src= "leftframe.html"/> <frame src="rightframe.html"/></`

`frameset></frameset>`. This code would create a single frame across the top of the browser and two side-by-side frames under the top frame.

For the following, use an HTML file that has two frames. The example use the file created in the section "Specify Frame Content" as its basis.

BUILD NESTED FRAMESETS

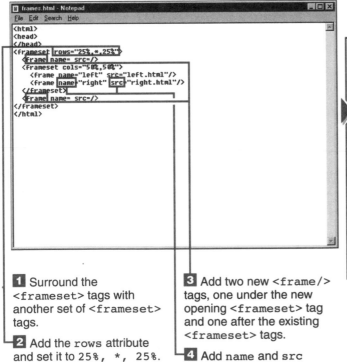

1 Surround the `<frameset>` tags with another set of `<frameset>` tags.

2 Add the `rows` attribute and set it to `25%, *, 25%`.

3 Add two new `<frame/>` tags, one under the new opening `<frameset>` tag and one after the existing `<frameset>` tags.

4 Add `name` and `src` attributes to the new `<frame/>` tags.

5 Set the `name` attribute to `title` and the `src` attribute to `title.html` for the first new `<frame/>` tag.

6 Set the `name` attribute to `question` and the `src` attribute to `question.html` for the second new `<frame/>` tag.

7 Save the file as `nested.html`.

Is there a limit to the number of framesets that can be nested?

✔ There is no limit to the number of framesets that can be nested within one another. Be warned, however, that too many frames in a page annoys users and makes navigating your site difficult. The rule of thumb is to never use more than four frames unless you have a compelling design.

How can I change the background of a frame?

✔ The background of a frame is determined by the individual Web page that loads within the frame. Because the `<frameset>` tags replace the `<body>` tags, you cannot add the background or `bgcolor` attributes to a frameset. Chapter 6 discusses setting the background color for a Web page.

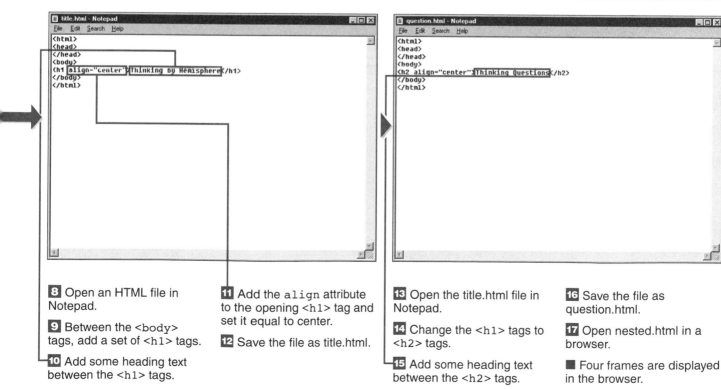

8 Open an HTML file in Notepad.

9 Between the `<body>` tags, add a set of `<h1>` tags.

10 Add some heading text between the `<h1>` tags.

11 Add the `align` attribute to the opening `<h1>` tag and set it equal to center.

12 Save the file as title.html.

13 Open the title.html file in Notepad.

14 Change the `<h1>` tags to `<h2>` tags.

15 Add some heading text between the `<h2>` tags.

16 Save the file as question.html.

17 Open nested.html in a browser.

■ Four frames are displayed in the browser.

SET THE FRAME TARGET

Frames divide the browser window into multiple windows. If you include a link on a Web page that is loaded in the frame, when that link is clicked the linked Web page will load into the frame where the link is located. This arrangement could be exactly what you want, but the

`target` attribute sets the linked page to load into one of the other frames.

If you add the `target` attribute to the `<a>` tag that creates the link within a frame, and set it equal to a frame name, the linked page loads into the named frame.

Each target value needs to match to a named frame. If the target value does not match a named frame, the browser automatically spawns a new browser window and loads the Web page into it.

SET THE FRAME TARGET

```
left1.html - Notepad
File  Edit  Search  Help
<html>
<head>
</head>
<body>
The left side of the brain is responsible for analytical thinking and
logic.
<a href="question1.html" target="question">View a question</a>
</body>
</html>
```

```
right1.html - Notepad
File  Edit  Search  Help
<html>
<head>
</head>
<body>
The right side of your brain helps you think creatively.
<a href="question2.html" target="question">View a question</a>
</body>
</html>
```

1 Open an HTML file with text and add a set of `<a>` tags after the text.

2 Between the `<a>` tags, add some link text.

3 Add the `href` and `target` attributes.

4 Set `href` to `question1.html`.

5 Set `target` to `question`.

6 Save the file as left1.html.

7 Open an HTML file with text and add a set of `<a>` tags after the text.

8 Add some link text.

9 Add the `href` and `target` attributes to the `<a>` tag.

10 Set the `href` attribute to `question2.html`.

11 Set the `target` attribute equal to `question`.

12 Save the file as right1.html.

Which target names are acceptable?

✔ The only target names that are acceptable are the names specified within the current frameset.

Do I need to include the target attribute with every link?

✔ If you include the `target` attribute as part of the `<base>` tag in the `<head>` section, all links are automatically directed to the specified frame unless otherwise noted. The `<base>` and `<head>` tags are covered in Chapter 5.

If the frame has been manually resized, will the Web page reset the frame to its original size when a new page loads?

✔ If a frame has been manually resized, it remains that same size as new pages are loaded into it. If the browser page is refreshed, however, then the frame returns to its original specified size.

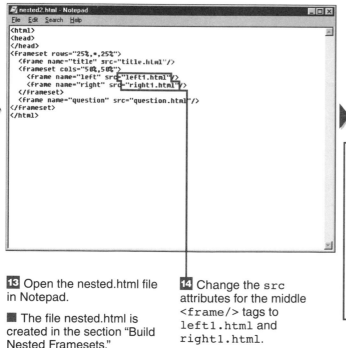

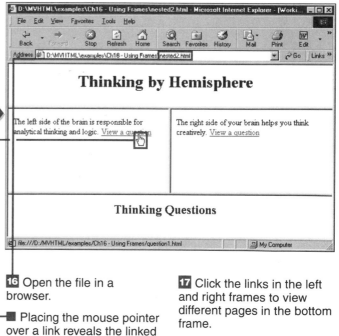

13 Open the nested.html file in Notepad.

■ The file nested.html is created in the section "Build Nested Framesets."

14 Change the `src` attributes for the middle `<frame/>` tags to `left1.html` and `right1.html`.

15 Save the file with a new file name.

16 Open the file in a browser.

■ Placing the mouse pointer over a link reveals the linked page in the status bar.

17 Click the links in the left and right frames to view different pages in the bottom frame.

USING SPECIAL TARGETS

Several special target names enable you to specify where the targeted content gets loaded. These special target names enable you to reset a frameset, load the content into a new window, or load the content into the top frame. You can use several *special target names* with the target attribute. These special target names are easy to identify because they begin with the underscore (_) character.

The special target names include the following:

• _blank loads the Web page into a new browser window without any frames.

• _self loads the Web page into the current frame. This same result happens if the target attribute is not included.

• _parent loads the Web page

into the current frames immediate parent frame thereby eliminating some of the frames.

• _top loads the page without any frames. It is a good target to use for any links leaving your site because it breaks out of frames.

The example uses the files created in "Set the Frame Target."

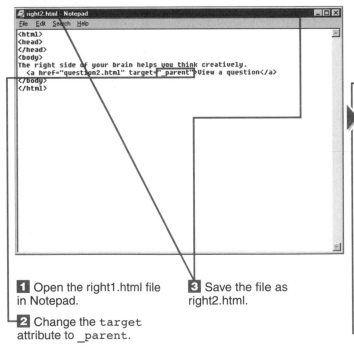

1 Open the right1.html file in Notepad.

2 Change the target attribute to _parent.

3 Save the file as right2.html.

4 Open the file saved in Step 15 of "Set the Frame Target" in Notepad.

5 Change the src attribute on the third <frame/> tag to right2.html.

6 Save the file with a new name.

Are there any other special target names?

✔ These are the only special target names that are recognized by the prominent browsers.

Why is it a good idea to reset a frameset?

✔ In some cases, you may want to maintain the logo from a different site, but the big reason to break out of frames is to reclaim the space used by the frame. Even a frame containing a small logo becomes annoying if the browser window is too small. Users typically do not like to scroll to move around a Web page.

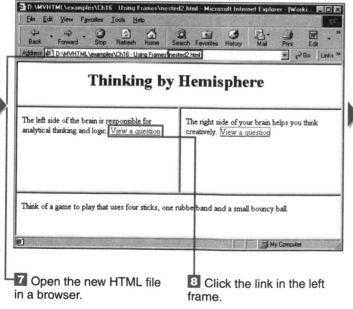

7 Open the new HTML file in a browser.

8 Click the link in the left frame.

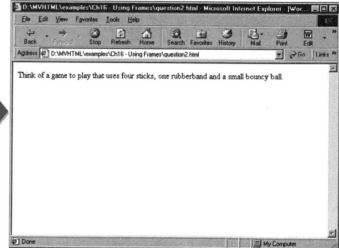

■ The page loads into the browser without any frames.

SECTION VI

SET UP A FORM

A Web page form can consist of many different form elements. These form elements can include elements such as text fields, radio buttons, drop-down lists, and submit and reset buttons.

The beginning and end of a form is noted by a set of <form> tags. All form elements must appear within these tags to belong to the form. A single Web page may have several forms, each with a unique name.

Each form can be named by using the name attribute. This name is used by languages such as JavaScript to refer to the form and its elements. Controlling form elements with JavaScript is covered in Part VIII, "Interactivity with JavaScript."

The <form> tag also includes attributes that you can use to specify how and where the form data gets passed (action, method, and enctype). Chapter 18 explains these attributes and how to use them.

SET UP A FORM

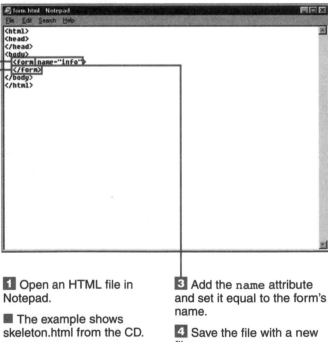

1 Open an HTML file in Notepad.

■ The example shows skeleton.html from the CD.

2 Add a set of <form> tags.

3 Add the name attribute and set it equal to the form's name.

4 Save the file with a new filename.

Note: This file can be used as a template for a form.

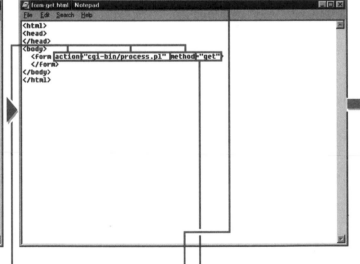

5 Open the file in Notepad.

6 Add the action and method attributes.

7 Set the action attribute to the URL of the form-processing script, like cgi-bin/process.pl.

8 Set the method attribute to get.

9 Save the file with a new filename.

Note: This file can be used as a template for a form that uses the get method.

Can `<form>` tags be nested within each other?

✔ You cannot nest `<form>` tags within each other. Each set of `<form>` tags should appear independent of all other `<form>` tag sets.

To what value should I set the enctype attribute?

✔ The `enctype` attribute by default is `application/x-www-form-urlencoded`. This is the content type that is used by all Web forms. You don't need to set this attribute unless you want to specifically define it. If you plan on e-mailing the form results, you need to set the `enctype` attribute to `multipart/form-data`.

What is the difference between the get and post methods?

✔ The `get` method tacks data onto the end of the URL to pass it to the server. The `post` method includes the form data as part of the HTTP request.

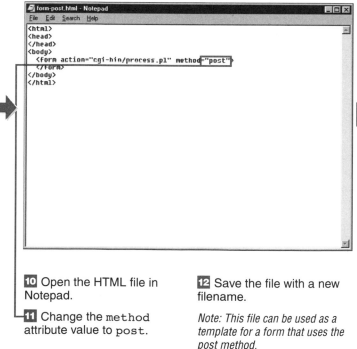

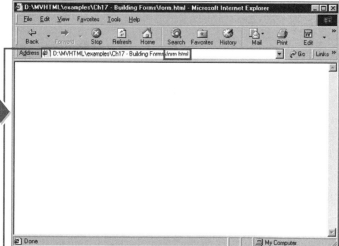

10 Open the HTML file in Notepad.

11 Change the `method` attribute value to `post`.

12 Save the file with a new filename.

Note: This file can be used as a template for a form that uses the post method.

13 Open the HTML file in a browser.

■ Nothing displays because no form elements have been added to the form.

CREATE FORM BUTTONS

You can build forms with a variety of elements, but all these elements are useless without a way to submit the form data to the server. The mechanism for submitting form data is with a submit button. This button can appear anywhere within the form. When a visit clicks the Submit button, the data is sent to the URL specified in the action attribute.

To create a submit button, you can use the <button> tag. The text that comes between the opening and closing <button> tags appears on the button face.

The <button> tag can also include the name and type attributes. The name attribute lets you name the button, and the type

attribute can be set to submit, reset, or button. The submit type sends the data for processing when clicked. The reset type clears all text fields and resets all other form elements to their default value. The button type is a generic button that you can use with JavaScript to trigger a script.

CREATE FORM BUTTONS

■1 Open an HTML file with a form in Notepad.

■ This file is created in "Set Up a Form."

■2 Add <button> tags.

■3 Add a button title.

■4 Add name and type attributes.

■5 Set name to a reference name.

■6 Set type equal to submit.

■7 Save the file.

■8 Open the HTML file in a browser.

■ The submit button appears in the browser.

288

How can I add some space between two buttons?

✔ To separate two buttons, you can add a *graphical spacer*, which is discussed in Chapter 12, or you can add some nonbreaking space character entities. These entities should be inserted using the   form. You need to add an character entity for every space appearing between the buttons. Nonbreaking spaces are covered in Chapter 7.

Is there another way to create buttons?

✔ You can also create buttons by using the <input/> tag. For these buttons, you can set the type attribute to submit, reset, or button. You can also change the text on the button face with the value attribute. The sections that follow give you more information on the <input/> tag.

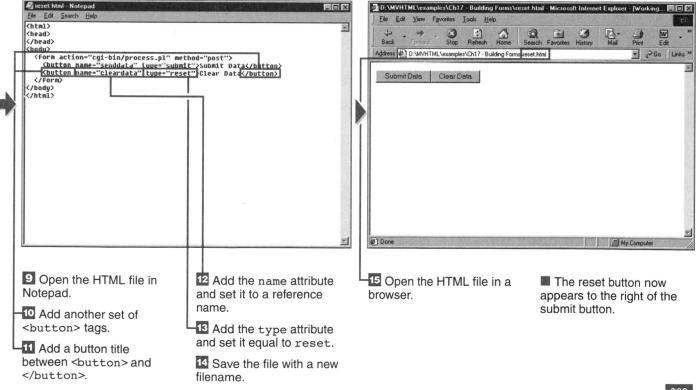

9 Open the HTML file in Notepad.

10 Add another set of <button> tags.

11 Add a button title between <button> and </button>.

12 Add the name attribute and set it to a reference name.

13 Add the type attribute and set it equal to reset.

14 Save the file with a new filename.

15 Open the HTML file in a browser.

■ The reset button now appears to the right of the submit button.

CREATE FORM TEXT FIELDS

*T*ext fields are very common form elements. They enable the user to enter characters or a single line of text into a text field.

You can create text fields by using the <input/> tag. You can also use this tag to create other form elements, depending on the type attribute. For text fields, the type attribute is set to type.

The <input/> tag can also include the name attribute for referencing the text field. The value attribute is used to set the text that initially appears in the text field, but the user can change this text.

The size attribute sets the width of the text field, measured in the number of characters. You can use the maxlength attribute to set the maximum number of characters that a user can enter into a text field.

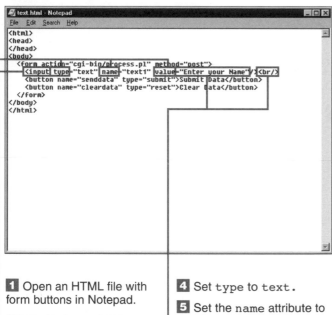

1 Open an HTML file with form buttons in Notepad.

■ This file is created in "Create Form Buttons."

2 Add an <input/> tag.

3 Add attributes.

4 Set type to text.

5 Set the name attribute to a reference name.

6 Set the value attribute to the text you want to initially appear in the text field.

7 Add a <br/> tag.

8 Save the file.

9 Open the HTML file in a browser.

■ A text field now appears before the two buttons.

What are the default values for the value, size, and maxlength attributes?

✔ If the `value`, `size`, and `maxlength` attributes are not included in the `<input/>` tag, their default values are used. If the `value` attribute is left off, no text initially displays in the text field. The default size for a text field is around 13 characters, and the default `maxlength` value allows an infinite number of characters.

What are the limits of the text field size?

✔ The default size of a text field is around 13 characters, but if you include the `size` attribute, you can set the `size` value to be as low as 1. The maximum size value will be determined by the browser width. If the `size` attribute is set to 0, the size will be set to the default size of 13 characters.

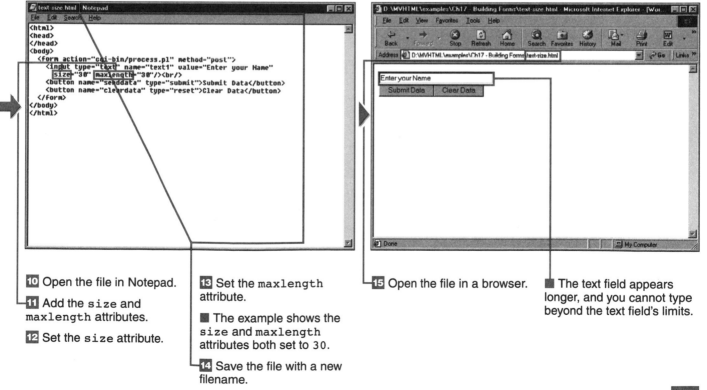

■0 Open the file in Notepad.

■1 Add the `size` and `maxlength` attributes.

■2 Set the `size` attribute.

■3 Set the `maxlength` attribute.

■ The example shows the `size` and `maxlength` attributes both set to 30.

■4 Save the file with a new filename.

■5 Open the file in a browser.

■ The text field appears longer, and you cannot type beyond the text field's limits.

CREATE FORM PASSWORD FIELDS

Password fields are similar to text fields, except that when the user enters text in a password field, the text is displayed as asterisk symbols (*).

Password fields are useful for letting users enter a password or a secure piece of text without letting those around them see the text on the screen.

The password field is similar to the text field—it is created using the `input` tag with the `type` attribute set to password.

The password field can use the `name`, `value`, `size`, and `maxlength` attributes the same as with a text field. See the section "Create Form Text Fields" for more information.

The password and text type `<input/>` elements also support the `readonly` attribute. This attribute makes the text field unchangeable. A password field that includes the `readonly` attribute can be viewed but not altered.

CREATE FORM PASSWORD FIELDS

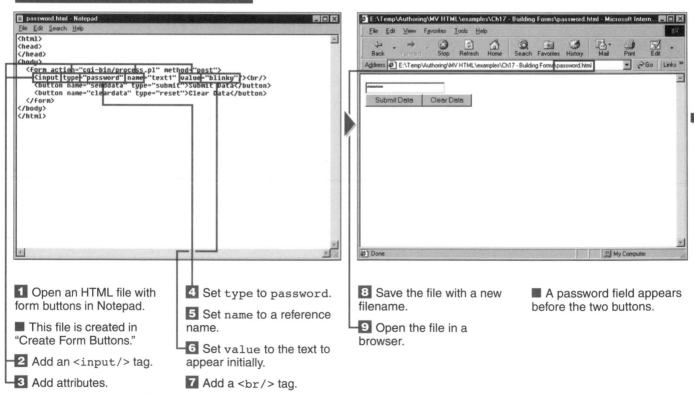

1 Open an HTML file with form buttons in Notepad.

■ This file is created in "Create Form Buttons."

2 Add an `<input/>` tag.

3 Add attributes.

4 Set `type` to `password`.

5 Set `name` to a reference name.

6 Set `value` to the text to appear initially.

7 Add a `<br/>` tag.

8 Save the file with a new filename.

9 Open the file in a browser.

■ A password field appears before the two buttons.

Can I change the symbol that is displayed for password fields?

✔ The default symbol that is displayed in a password field is the asterisk symbol (*). There is no way using the standard attributes to change this symbol, but using JavaScript, you can capture the text that is typed into a text field and replace them with any symbol you desire. JavaScript is explained in Part VIII.

Does using the password field make transaction secure over the Internet?

✔ The password field only shields the text that you are typing in from the eyes of those around you; it does not make the data secure. To make data secure, you need to create a secure link between the browser and the server.

Can I copy and paste text from a password field?

✔ If you copy the text entered into a password field, it will not be saved on the clipboard to be pasted elsewhere.

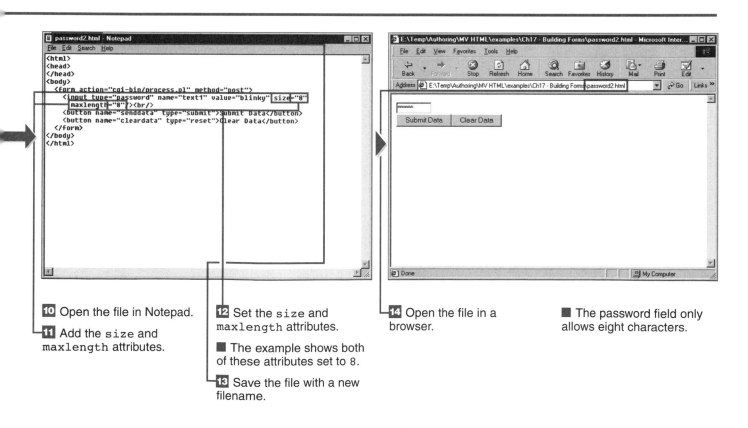

🔟 Open the file in Notepad.

1️⃣1️⃣ Add the `size` and `maxlength` attributes.

1️⃣2️⃣ Set the `size` and `maxlength` attributes.

■ The example shows both of these attributes set to 8.

1️⃣3️⃣ Save the file with a new filename.

1️⃣4️⃣ Open the file in a browser.

■ The password field only allows eight characters.

CREATE FORM TEXT AREAS

Text fields are great for entering a single line of text, but they do not work very well when you need the user to enter several lines of text. To enable the user to enter several lines of text, you can use the *textarea element*.

To create a textarea element, you can use the `<textarea>` tags. The

text between these tags is displayed when the element initially loads. This text appears exactly as it is typed, including all white space.

You can set the dimensions of the textarea field using the `rows` and `cols` attributes. These attributes refer to the number lines of text

and character width of the text area field.

You can also name test areas by using the `name` attribute. To keep the text in the textarea from being changed, you can add the `readonly` attribute to the `<textarea>` tag.

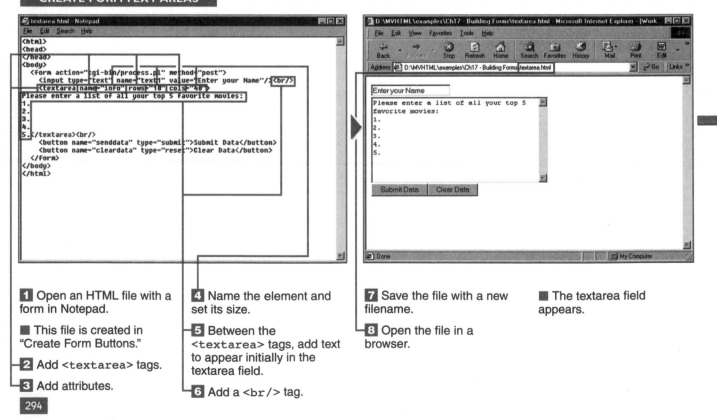

1 Open an HTML file with a form in Notepad.

■ This file is created in "Create Form Buttons."

2 Add `<textarea>` tags.

3 Add attributes.

4 Name the element and set its size.

5 Between the `<textarea>` tags, add text to appear initially in the textarea field.

6 Add a `<br/>` tag.

7 Save the file with a new filename.

8 Open the file in a browser.

■ The textarea field appears.

Can I wrap the contents of a text area field?

✔ A `<textarea>` tag can include the `wrap` attribute for controlling how the text wraps in the text area. The default value for the wrap attribute is `off`. This keeps all text on a single line until the Enter key is pressed. The soft (or virtual) value automatically wraps the text within the text area field, but the text goes to the server as a single line of text. The hard (or physical) value causes the text to be wrapped within the text area field and also sends the line return characters to the server.

How large can I make a text area field?

✔ Text area fields can be as large as the memory of computer. The size of text area fields isn't restricted by the size of the browser window. If the text area field exceeds the size of the browser window, scroll bars appear to let the user see the entire text area field.

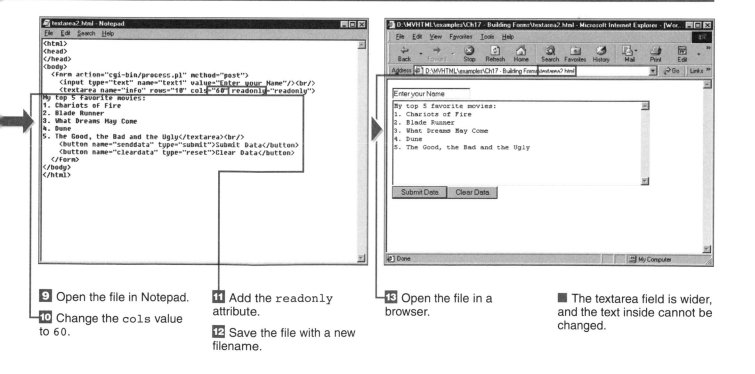

9 Open the file in Notepad.

10 Change the `cols` value to `60`.

11 Add the `readonly` attribute.

12 Save the file with a new filename.

13 Open the file in a browser.

■ The textarea field is wider, and the text inside cannot be changed.

LABEL A FORM ELEMENT

A s you start to add elements to a form, you can also include *labels* that explain what type of information is expected for each element.

You can create labels by simply adding text in front of each form element, but the correct way to label form elements is with the `<label>` tag.

The `<label>` tag can either encompass the form element that it labels, or it can identify the name of the element for which it is a label using the `for` attribute.

The text that makes up the label needs to be positioned between the two `<label>` tags.

The purpose of the `<label>` tag becomes important when you start to work with the *tab order* and *focus*. When a label element gets the focus, it shares it with the element that it labels. See the section "Control Tab Order" for more about tab order.

LABEL A FORM ELEMENT

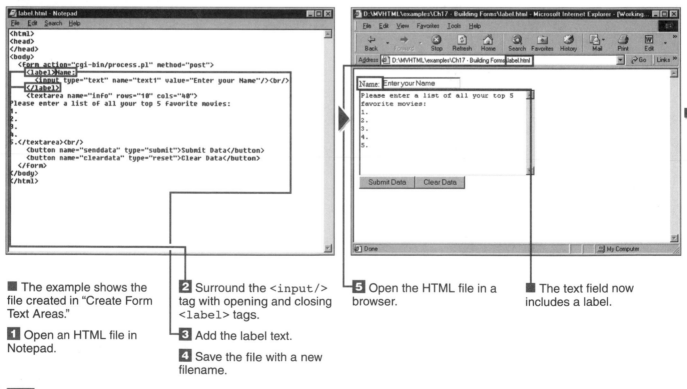

■ The example shows the file created in "Create Form Text Areas."

1 Open an HTML file in Notepad.

2 Surround the `<input/>` tag with opening and closing `<label>` tags.

3 Add the label text.

4 Save the file with a new filename.

5 Open the HTML file in a browser.

■ The text field now includes a label.

Can I separate the label from the form element?

✔ The text that appears between the two label tags works the same way as normal text in the Web page. You can add spaces and white space, but these will only display as a single space. You can also include line breaks within the `<label>` tags with an `<br/>` tag.

When should I label form elements?

✔ For elements like radio and checkbox buttons, labels can be very helpful. Radio and checkbox buttons can be labeled by placing normal text in front of the `<input/>` tag, but a more controlled way to label radio and checkbox buttons is with the `<label>` tag.

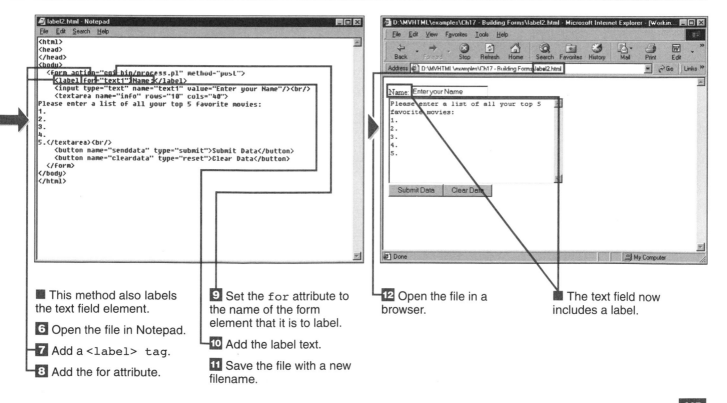

■ This method also labels the text field element.

6 Open the file in Notepad.

7 Add a `<label>` tag.

8 Add the for attribute.

9 Set the `for` attribute to the name of the form element that it is to label.

10 Add the label text.

11 Save the file with a new filename.

12 Open the file in a browser.

■ The text field now includes a label.

CREATE FORM CHECKBOXES

Y̶ou can use *form checkboxes* to mark a selection as true if checked or false if left unchecked. The default is to leave checkboxes unchecked. Checkboxes are typically displayed in groups.

You also use the <input/> tag to create checkbox elements by setting

the type attribute equal to checkbox.

You can name checkboxes with the name attribute. All checkbox elements that have the same name value belong to the same group.

The value attribute can be set to help identify the checkbox when the data is passed to the server.

The text that appears next to the checkbox can be regular text.

To initially mark a checkbox as checked, you can include the checked attribute.

The example shows the file created in the section "Label a Form Element."

CREATE FORM CHECKBOXES

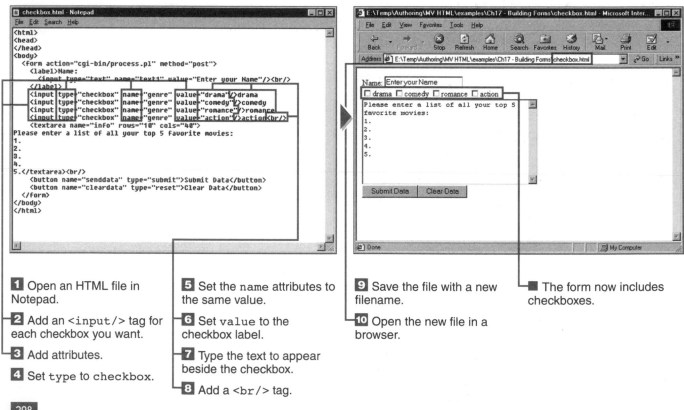

1 Open an HTML file in Notepad.

2 Add an <input/> tag for each checkbox you want.

3 Add attributes.

4 Set type to checkbox.

5 Set the name attributes to the same value.

6 Set value to the checkbox label.

7 Type the text to appear beside the checkbox.

8 Add a <br/> tag.

9 Save the file with a new filename.

10 Open the new file in a browser.

■ The form now includes checkboxes.

What is the advantage of grouping several checkboxes together?

✔ Although checkboxes don't affect one another, grouping checkboxes together only helps to organize them. The following section, which discusses radio buttons, explains how the group only allows one radio button at a time to be selected.

Do all checkbox buttons on the Web page need to belong to the same group?

✔ Checkbox buttons can have their own name and do not need to belong to a group. A single Web page can have many different groups of checkboxes.

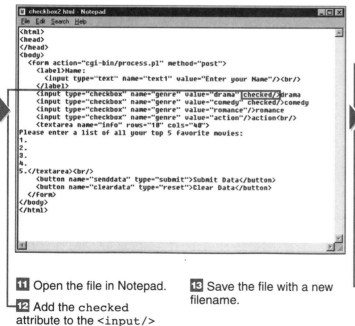

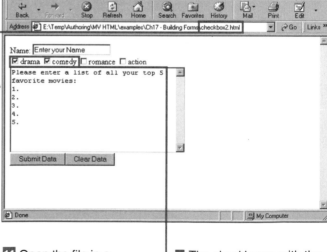

11 Open the file in Notepad.

12 Add the `checked` attribute to the `<input/>` tags that you want initially checked.

13 Save the file with a new filename.

14 Open the file in a browser.

■ The checkboxes with the checked attribute are initially checked.

CREATE FORM RADIO BUTTONS

*R*adio buttons are similar to checkboxes, except that they are mutually exclusive. This means that for a group of radio buttons, only one may be selected at a time.

You can use the <input/> tag to create radio buttons by setting the type attribute equal to radio.

You can use the name attribute to identify the radio button's group.

All radio button elements that have the same name attribute value belong to the same group.

The text that appears next to a radio button is included after the <input/> tag. The value attribute can be set to help identify the radio button when the data is passed to the server for processing.

To initially mark a radio button as selected, you can include the checked attribute. This attribute can only be added to a single <input/> tag in the group.

The example shows the file created in the section "Create Form Checkboxes."

CREATE FORM RADIO BUTTONS

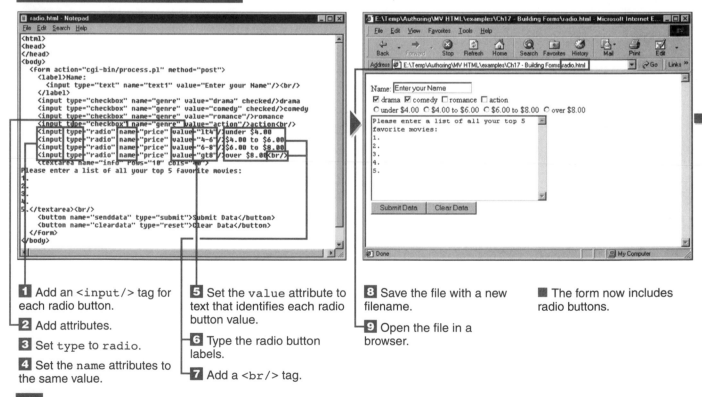

1 Add an <input/> tag for each radio button.

2 Add attributes.

3 Set type to radio.

4 Set the name attributes to the same value.

5 Set the value attribute to text that identifies each radio button value.

6 Type the radio button labels.

7 Add a <br/> tag.

8 Save the file with a new filename.

9 Open the file in a browser.

■ The form now includes radio buttons.

What happens if the checked attribute is added to several <input/> tags in a group?

✔ If the `checked` attribute is added to several <input/> tags in a single group, the last <input/> tag that includes the `checked` attribute is initially selected.

If none of the <input/> tags include the checked attribute, which radio button is selected?

✔ If none of the <input/> tags include a `checked` attribute, none of the radio buttons are initially selected.

Why do I set the name attribute to the same value?

✔ All radio buttons that share the same `name` value belong to the same group. Only one radio button within the group may be selected at a time. If a radio button has a different `name` value, it belongs to a different group.

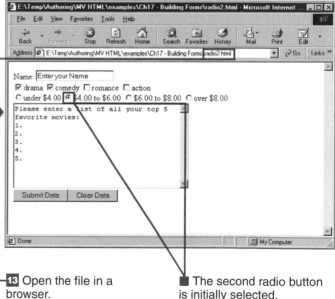

10 Open the file in Notepad.

11 Add the `checked` attribute to one radio button.

12 Save the file with a new filename.

13 Open the file in a browser.

■ The second radio button is initially selected.

CREATE FORM IMAGE BUTTONS

You can create buttons using the `<button>` or `<input>` tags, but these buttons use the system's default gray-colored buttons. To create a button that is unique, you can use a graphical image as the button. Doing so enables you to create a button with any look you can imagine.

To create a form image button, use an `<input/>` tag and set the `type` attribute to `image`. With the type set to `image`, you can also include the `src` attribute. Set this `attribute` equal to the filename of the image to load for the button.

The function of an image button is the same as that for a submit button. This button can also include a name attribute.

CREATE FORM IMAGE BUTTONS

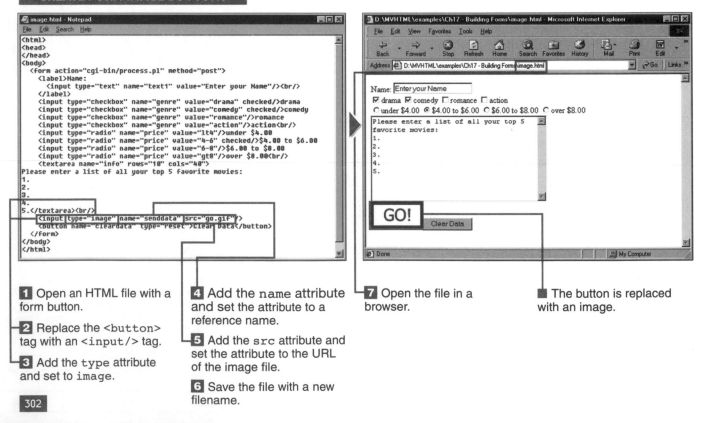

1 Open an HTML file with a form button.

2 Replace the `<button>` tag with an `<input/>` tag.

3 Add the `type` attribute and set to `image`.

4 Add the `name` attribute and set the attribute to a reference name.

5 Add the `src` attribute and set the attribute to the URL of the image file.

6 Save the file with a new filename.

7 Open the file in a browser.

■ The button is replaced with an image.

USE HIDDEN FIELDS

You may sometimes want to pass data that is not visible on the Web page along with the user input. This data can be passed through a *hidden field*. Hidden fields include data that is submitted for processing but not displayed in the browser.

You can create hidden fields by using the `<input/>` tag with the type attribute set to hidden. These fields should always include the name and value attributes. Use the name and value attributes to set the data passed to the server.

When the form is submitted, the name and value attributes of a hidden field are passed along with the rest of the data.

USE HIDDEN FIELDS

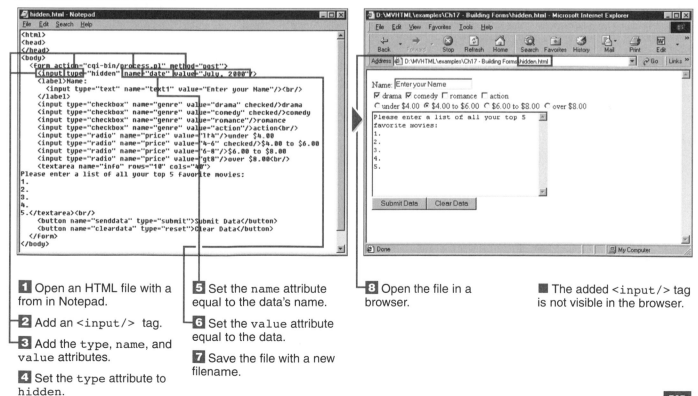

1 Open an HTML file with a from in Notepad.

2 Add an `<input/>` tag.

3 Add the type, name, and value attributes.

4 Set the type attribute to hidden.

5 Set the name attribute equal to the data's name.

6 Set the value attribute equal to the data.

7 Save the file with a new filename.

8 Open the file in a browser.

■ The added `<input/>` tag is not visible in the browser.

CREATE A SELECTION LIST

A *selection list* is a form element that can contain several items in a list. These list are often called *drop-down lists*.

You can create these lists by using two tags: The `<select>` tag creates the list container, and the `<option>` tag is used to specify the specific list items.

The `<select>` tag can include the `name` attribute for naming the selection list. It can also include a `size` attribute that specifies the number of list choices that are visible.

All `<option>` tags must be included within the opening and closing `<select>` tags. The text

that appears in the selection list should be placed between the opening and closing `<option>` tags.

The first `<option>` tag that includes the `selected` attribute is initially selected when this list displays.

CREATE A SELECTION LIST

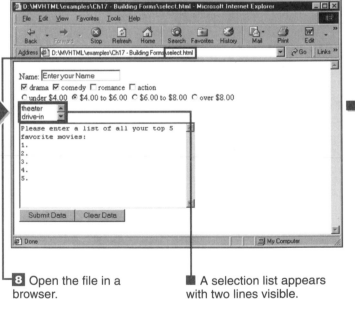

1 Open an HTML with a form in Notepad.

2 Add `<select>` tags.

3 Name the list.

4 Specify the number of options you want displayed.

5 Add and label the list options.

6 Add a `<br />` tag.

7 Save the file with a new filename.

8 Open the file in a browser.

■ A selection list appears with two lines visible.

How is the width of the selection list determined?

✔ The selection list width is determined by the length of the longest single line of text included in an `<option>` tag.

What happens if several `<option>` tags include the selected attribute?

✔ If several `<option>` tags include the `selected` attribute, the selection list initially selects only the last `<option>` tag that includes the `selected` attribute.

Can I set a width for a selection list?

✔ The width of the selection list will be as wide as the longest list item. No separate attribute can set the width of a selection list.

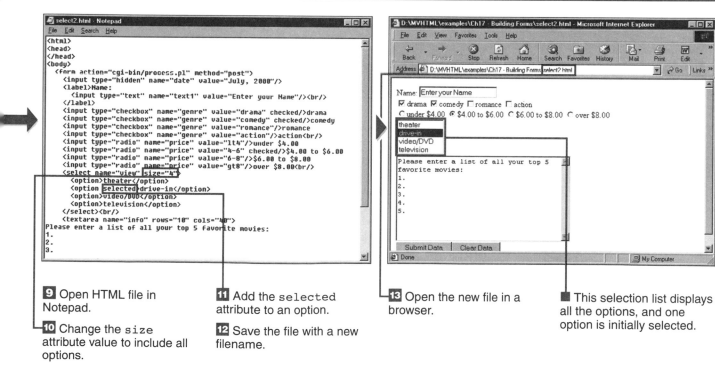

9 Open HTML file in Notepad.

10 Change the `size` attribute value to include all options.

11 Add the `selected` attribute to an option.

12 Save the file with a new filename.

13 Open the new file in a browser.

■ This selection list displays all the options, and one option is initially selected.

ALLOW MULTIPLE SELECTIONS

The default setup for a selection list only allows users to select one item at a time from the list, but you can specify that multiple items can be selected.

The <select> tag can also include the multiple attribute. If the multiple attribute is included, multiple items on the list can be selected at the same time. To select multiple items, the user needs to hold down the Ctrl or Shift key while clicking the list items.

Holding down the Ctrl key causes each additional clicked item to be added to the selection set. If an item is already selected when clicked, the item is removed from the selection set. Holding down the Shift key causes all items between the last selection and the current selection to be selected.

If multiple items can be selected, any or all the <option> tags can also include the selected attribute to mark them as initially selected.

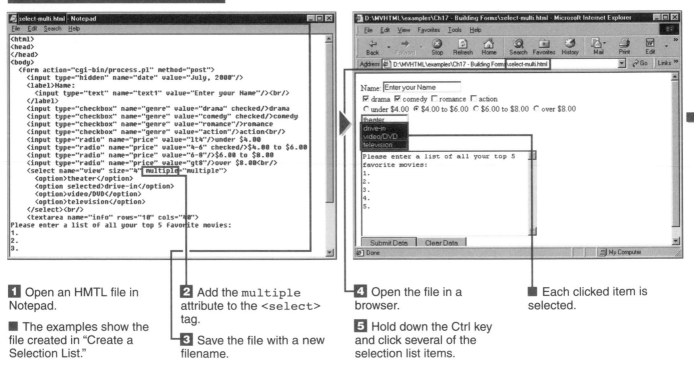

1 Open an HMTL file in Notepad.

■ The examples show the file created in "Create a Selection List."

2 Add the multiple attribute to the <select> tag.

3 Save the file with a new filename.

4 Open the file in a browser.

5 Hold down the Ctrl key and click several of the selection list items.

■ Each clicked item is selected.

Is the size attribute necessary when the multiple attribute is included?

✔ The default for a selection list if the `multiple` and `size` attributes are not included is to display a single-line drop-down list. If the `multiple` attribute is included without the `size` attribute, the selection list is displayed as a box with all the items visible. If the `size` attribute is included, the selection list is displayed as specified.

Can I make list items appear selected by default?

✔ If individual list items include the `selected` attribute, the list item appears selected when the list is displayed.

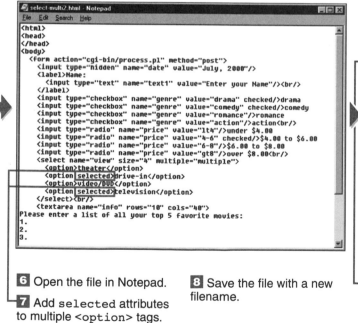

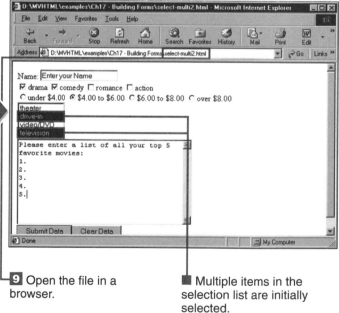

6 Open the file in Notepad.

7 Add `selected` attributes to multiple `<option>` tags.

8 Save the file with a new filename.

9 Open the file in a browser.

■ Multiple items in the selection list are initially selected.

CONTROL TAB ORDER

Moving between several form elements on a Web page by using only a mouse can be difficult. An alternate way to move between form elements is using the Tab key to move between different form elements. The Enter key can then be used to select an item.

The *default tab order* follows the order that the form elements appear on the Web page, but you can change this order using the `tabindex` attribute.

The `tabindex` attribute can be used with `<button>`, `<input>`, `<select>`, and `<textarea>` tags.

The value of the `tabindex` attribute is simply a number. The browser moves through the form elements, starting at the element with the lowest tabindex and proceeding in order to the form element with the highest tabindex value.

Elements can be removed from the tab sequence by setting their tabindex value to a negative number.

CONTROL TAB ORDER

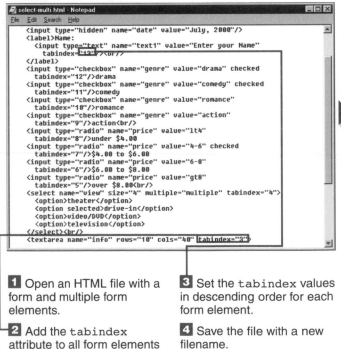

1 Open an HTML file with a form and multiple form elements.

2 Add the `tabindex` attribute to all form elements except for any hidden fields.

3 Set the `tabindex` values in descending order for each form element.

4 Save the file with a new filename.

5 Open the file in a browser.

6 Press the tab key several times.

■ Notice how the focus moves backwards from the bottom form elements to the top form elements.

What if two form elements have the same tabindex values?

✔ If two **separate** form elements have the same tabindex value, the tab order for those two elements follows the order that they are listed in the Web page, with the first one receiving the focus first.

If the tabindex is not specified for a form element, where does it fall in the order?

✔ If the **tabindex** isn't specified for a form element, that element is included in the tab order after all the specified elements.

What happens if my tabindex values skip numbers?

✔ If the **tabindex** values skip a number, the order follows the next sequential value. For example, if **tabindex** values are 3, 5, 7, and 8, the tab order follows the order of the numbers.

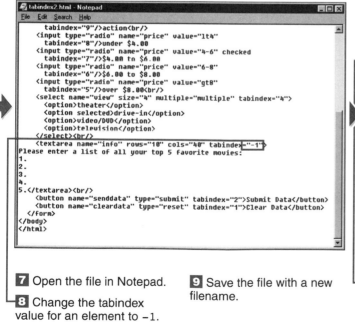

7 Open the file in Notepad.

8 Change the tabindex value for an element to -1.

9 Save the file with a new filename.

10 Open the file in a browser.

11 Press the Tab key several times.

■ Notice how the element you assigned a negative value to never gets the focus.

DISABLE FORM ELEMENTS

If you have a standard form and certain elements do not apply, you can disable the element. Disabled form elements are still visible, but appear in a lighter color.

Form elements can be *disabled,* or turned off, by using the `disabled` attribute. Disabled elements do not allow the user to enter any data.

Disabled elements are displayed differently than elements that are not disabled. The disabled elements are grayed out to show that they have been disabled. Disabled elements are also skipped in the tab order.

The `disable` attribute can be applied to the `<input/>`, `<select>`, `<option>`,

`<textarea>`, `<label>`, and `<button>` tags.

To disable a form element, you simply need to include the `disabled` attribute. The `disabled` attribute does not need a value.

DISABLE FORM ELEMENTS

1 Open an HTML file with a form and multiple form elements.

2 Add the `disabled` attribute to a form element.

3 Save the file with a new filename.

4 Open the file in a browser.

5 Click the disable element.

■ You can no longer do anything with the element.

What happens if only one radio button element or one checkbox element in a group is disabled?

✔ If only a single checkbox or radio button element is disabled, all elements except the disabled one will be available. Disabled checkboxes or radio buttons are not available for selection. They are also be skipped from the tab order.

Can the entire form be disabled?

✔ If you add the `disabled` attribute to the opening `<form>` tag, all the elements contained within the form are disabled.

How can I re-enable a form element that has been disabled?

✔ To re-enable a form element that has been disabled with the `disabled` attribute, all you need to do is to remove the `disabled` attribute from the form element.

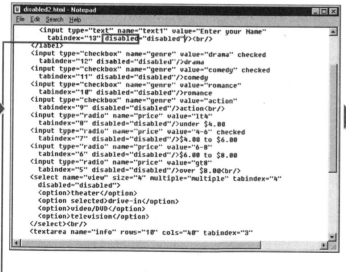

6 Open the file in Notepad.

7 Add the `disabled` attribute to the `<select>` tag.

8 Save the file a with a new filename.

9 Open the new file in a browser.

10 Click the various form elements.

■ Notice how all the form elements are disabled and grayed out.

GROUP ELEMENTS INTO A FIELDSET

For purposes of organizing a form, you can group sections of form elements into a group called a *fieldset*. Fieldsets are displayed in the browser within thin rectangular borders.

To group several form elements into a fieldset, you need to surround all the form elements with opening and closing `<fieldset>` tags.

You can label fieldsets by using a set of `<legend>` tags. These tags are placed inside the `<fieldset>` tags. The title for the fieldset can be included within the `<legend>` tags.

This `<legend>` tag can also include the `align` attribute for setting the alignment of the legend

title. The align attribute can be set to `left`, `center`, or `right`.

For example, the statement `<fieldset><legend>Name Field</legend><input type="text" value="name"/></fieldset>` creates a fieldset around the text field and label it a legend.

GROUP ELEMENTS INTO A FIELDSET

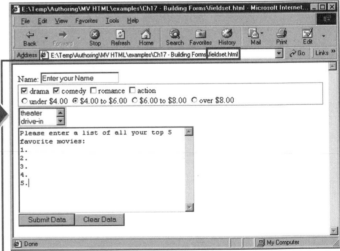

1 Open an HTML file with a form and multiple form elements.

2 Surround two form elements with opening and closing `<fieldset>` tags.

■ The example shows the `<fieldset>` tags around the checkbox and radio button form elements.

3 Save the file with a new filename.

4 Open the file in a browser.

■ The selected form elements are surrounded with a border.

Can I format the legend text?

✔ The fieldset legend text can be formatted by including the `<legend>` tags with a set of formatting marks such as `<b>` or `<i>`.

Can I increase the width of the fieldset border?

✔ There are no attributes that can be used to increase the width of the fieldset border.

Can I include a fieldset that does not have any form elements within it?

✔ If you include an opening and closing `<fieldset>` tag next to each other, a fieldset box will displays, but it does not contain any elements.

When is it appropriate to use a `<fieldset>` tag?

✔ `<fieldset>` tags are useful for dividing and labeling sections of a form, making it easier to refer to the various parts of a form.

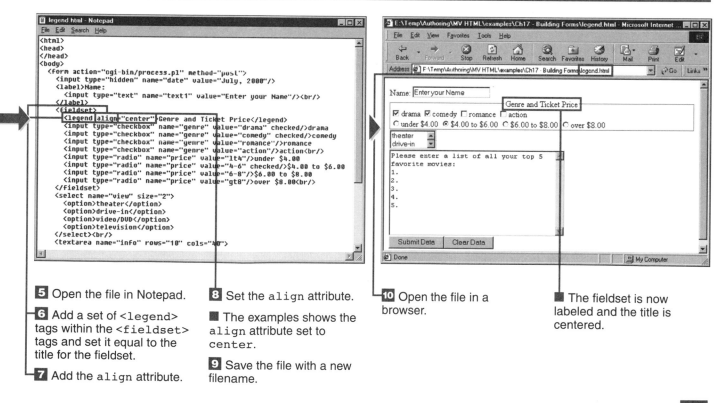

5 Open the file in Notepad.

6 Add a set of `<legend>` tags within the `<fieldset>` tags and set it equal to the title for the fieldset.

7 Add the `align` attribute.

8 Set the `align` attribute.

■ The examples shows the `align` attribute set to `center`.

9 Save the file with a new filename.

10 Open the file in a browser.

■ The fieldset is now labeled and the title is centered.

313

HANDLE FORM DATA

For form data to be sent to a server for processing, the form must include a submit button. When a user clicks this button, the form data is passed to the server.

The two attributes that you use to handle the form data are the

action and method attributes, found in the opening <form> tag. These two tags determine where and how the form data is sent.

The action attribute can be set to the URL of an application that can process the form data. These applications are typically *Common*

Gateway Interface (CGI) programs. Chapter 19 covers a sampling of CGI programs.

The CGI program that is called in the action attribute processes the data on the server and cannot be run from your local machine.

HANDLE FORM DATA

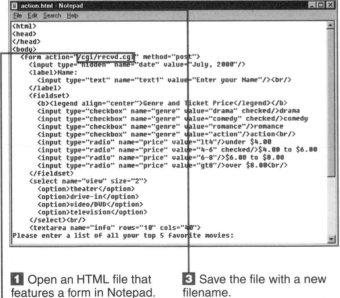

1 Open an HTML file that features a form in Notepad.

2 Set the action attribute of the <form> tag to the filename for the CGI program.

3 Save the file with a new filename.

4 Open an FTP program.

■ The FTP client used here is WS/FTP.

Note: Uploading files using an FTP client is discussed in Chapter 37.

5 Copy the CGI program into the cgi-bin directory.

6 Copy the Web page to the server.

MASTER IT

Can I test CGI programs on my local machine?

✔ If you install a Web server on your local machine, you can test CGI programs locally. Many Web editing tools, like Microsoft FrontPage and Macromedia Dreamweaver, include a stripped-down version of a Web server that you can use for this purpose.

Can I set the message that appears when my server receives data?

✔ The CGI program that accepts the form data returns the message that the browser displays. Composing a CGI program is covered in the "Post Form Data" section that appears later in the chapter.

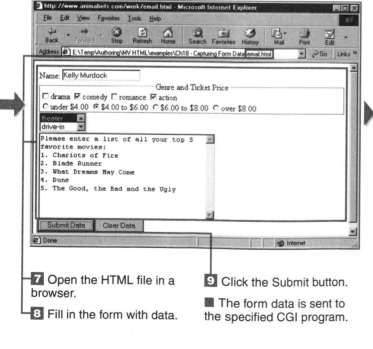

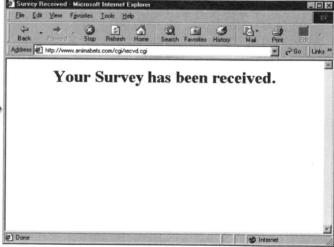

7 Open the HTML file in a browser.

8 Fill in the form with data.

9 Click the Submit button.

■ The form data is sent to the specified CGI program.

■ The CGI program processes the form data and returns a message to the browser.

E-MAIL FORM RESULTS

The server can also route the form data to an e-mail address for you. This is a convenient way to handle form data. This routing is accomplished by setting the action attribute to an e-mail address. Doing so causes all the form data to be e-mailed to the specified address.

In front of the e-mail address in the action attribute, you should add the mailto: text.

For this technique to work, you should set the method attribute to post. This sends the names and values to the specified e-mail address.

If you set the enctype to multipart/form-data, each piece of data is sent as a separate text file. If the enctype is not set, the form data is sent as a URL-encoded document. Not setting the enctype makes the document difficult to decipher. URL encoding is discussed later in the chapter.

E-MAIL FORM RESULTS

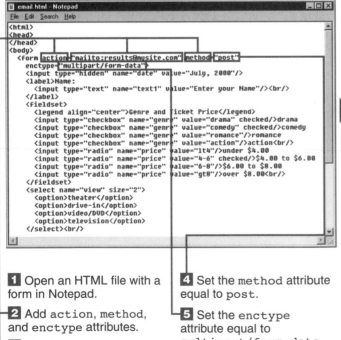

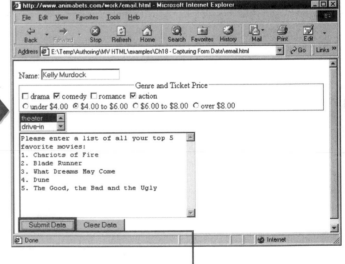

1 Open an HTML file with a form in Notepad.

2 Add action, method, and enctype attributes.

3 Set the action attribute to mailto: and add the recipient's e-mail address.

4 Set the method attribute equal to post.

5 Set the enctype attribute equal to multipart/form-data.

6 Save the file with a new filename.

7 Open the file in a browser.

8 Fill in the form with data.

9 Click the Submit button.

■ The form data is sent to the specified e-mail address.

How is the e-mail sent?

✔ If you include an e-mail address in the `action` attribute, the server automatically sends the form data to the e-mail address by using the server's `sendmail` function. If you load the page locally, the submit button attempts to open the e-mail client with the e-mail address listed.

Can I specify any e-mail address to receive the form data?

✔ The server will route the form data to the e-mail address specified in the `action` attribute. This address can be any valid e-mail address.

What will happen if the specified e-mail address does not exist?

✔ If the e-mail address does not exist, the server will generate an error that will appear in the server logs, but no information will be sent to the Web client and the form data will be lost.

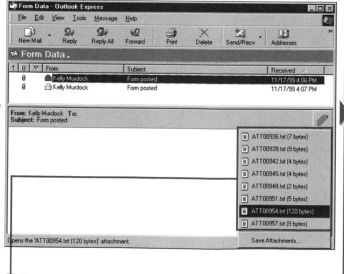

■ The form data is sent to the e-mail client as a series of separate text files, one for each form element.

10 Open one of the text files.

■ The form data for a text area element appears.

POST FORM DATA

The `method` attribute defines how the form data gets passed to the CGI program specified in the `action` attribute. The `method` attribute can be set to two different values—`get` and `post`.

The `get` method occurs when the `method` attribute of the `<form>` tag is set to `get`. It is a little different than the `post` method.

With the `get` method, the form data is attached to the end of the URL and passed to the CGI program. If the `get` method is used, the CGI program needs to access the form data using the `QUERY_STRING` environment variable.

The `get` method may be problematic if the browser limits how long the URL line can be. If the data attached to the URL is longer than the browser limits, some of the data may get truncated. As long as the data being passed is minimal, however, truncated data is not a problem.

POST FORM DATA WITH GET

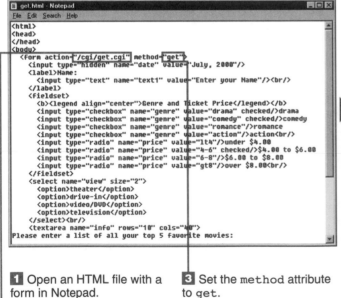

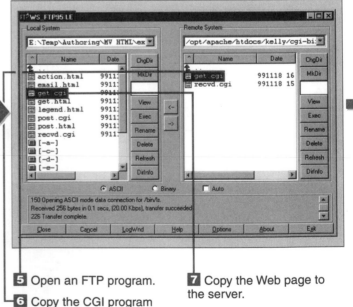

1 Open an HTML file with a form in Notepad.

2 Set the `action` attribute to name of the form handling CGI program such as get.cgi.

3 Set the `method` attribute to get.

4 Save the file with a new filename.

5 Open an FTP program.

6 Copy the CGI program specified in the HTML document into the cgi-bin directory.

7 Copy the Web page to the server.

What is the default method that is used if the method attribute is missing?

✔ If the `method` attribute is missing from the `<form>` tag, the `get` method is used to submit the form data.

Why does the browser URL line include extra information when the CGI script is run?

✔ Using the `get` method, the form data is attached to the end of the URL line. A question mark (`?`) separates the actual URL address and the name/value pairs. Each name/value pair is separated from the other with the ampersand symbol (`&`).

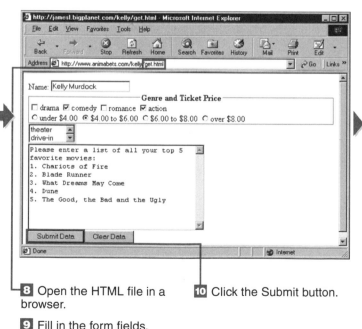

■ 8 Open the HTML file in a browser.

■ 9 Fill in the form fields.

■ 10 Click the Submit button.

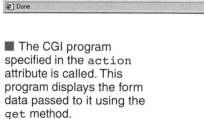

■ The CGI program specified in the `action` attribute is called. This program displays the form data passed to it using the `get` method.

POST FORM DATA (CONTINUED)

The post method for passing data to a CGI program is more common and more browser compatible. The post method sends all the form element's nameS and values to the standard input channel. The CGI program can then access this data and process it.

The default enctype attribute is application/x-www.form.urlencoded. This type is used if the enctype attribute is missing from the opening <form> tag.

Both the get and post methods URL-encode the form data, so the CGI program needs to be able to decode the URL to process the data.

Because the post method sends the form data to a standard input channel, you do not need to worry about the form data exceeding the browser limits. The post method can handle a large amount of data.

POST FORM DATA WITH POST

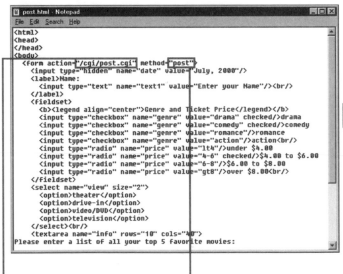

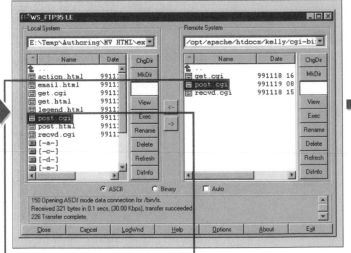

1 Open an HTML file with a form in Notepad.

2 Set the action attribute to the name of the form handing CGI program, such as post.cgi.

3 Set the method attribute to post.

4 Save the file with a new filename.

5 Open an FTP program.

6 Copy the CGI program specified in the html document into the cgi-bin directory.

7 Copy the Web page to the server.

How can a CGI program tell whether the form data is sent using the get or post method?

✔ CGI programs can get information about the form data from the environment variables that are passed along with the form data. These environment variables tell the CGI program the parameters of the form data. One of these environment variables, **REQUEST_METHOD**, tells the CGI program the value of the **method** attribute.

Can I use both the get and post method on the same form to pass data?

✔ Forms can only accept a single **method** attribute. This attribute must be set to either **get** or **post**. You cannot pass form data from a single form using both methods. A single Web page can have multiple forms though.

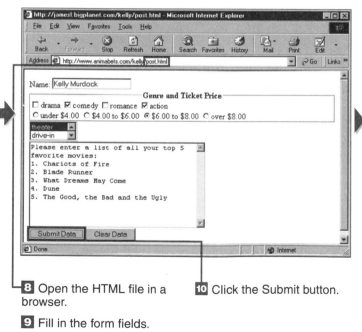

8 Open the HTML file in a browser.

9 Fill in the form fields.

10 Click the Submit button.

■ The CGI program specified in the **action** attribute is called This program displays the form data passed to it using the **post** method.

URL ENCODING

URLs and form data passed to the server can be very picky about the specific characters that they use. For example, if you include a space in your Web page filename, the browser may look for a file named the first word and will not be able to find the correct page.

When data is passed to the server, it is encoded to prevent this

problem. This encoding process is called *URL encoding*.

When data is URL encoded, spaces are changed to plus signs (+) and other characters that cause problems are preceded with the percent symbol (%) followed by the hexadecimal ASCII value that identifies the character. This essentially tells the browser to

replace the character with the specified symbol.

For example, a browser would interpret the URL http://www.myfamily.com/Favorite%20Videos as having a space between Favorite and Videos.

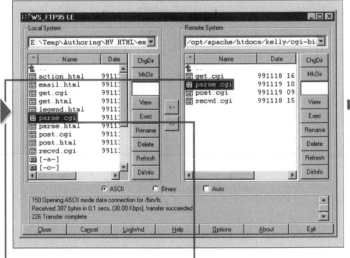

1 Open the an HTML file with a form in Notepad.

2 Set the action attribute to the name of the form-handling CGI program, such as parse.cgi.

3 Set the method attribute to post.

4 Save the file with a new filename.

5 Open an FTP program.

6 Copy the CGI program specified in the HTML file into the cgi-bin directory.

7 Copy the Web page to the server.

Besides the space symbol, which other symbols are encoded, and what are their encoded values?

✔ Most of the nonstandard symbols are encoded when passed as part of the URL line. Some of these symbols and their encoded values include the ampersand symbol (%26), the question mark (%3F), the percent symbol (%25), quotation marks (%22), the number sign (%23), the at symbol (%40), the colon symbol (%3A), the forward slash symbol (%2F), and the equal sign (%3D).

Does URL encoding make a URL secure?

✔ URL encoding will not make a URL or a Web site secure. URL encoding only puts the URL in a form that the server can recognize and easily interpret.

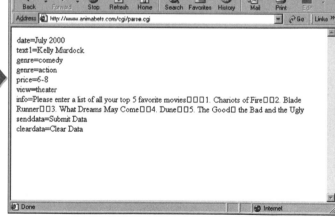

-8 Open the HTML file in a browser.

-9 Fill in the form fields.

-10 Click the Submit button.

■ The CGI program specified in the `action` attribute is called. This program parses the form data and displays it as name/value pairs.

UNDERSTANDING CGI APPLICATIONS

*C*GI stands for Common Gateway Interface. CGI applications run on the server and provide an interface between the client and server. The client and server can be different hardware configurations running different software. The interface ensures that, regardless of the different systems, data can still pass between the client and the server.

CGI applications provide another key benefit in that they can be developed by using a variety of languages including Perl, C, Visual Basic, or even AppleScript.

Regardless of the scripting language you use, the interface communicates between the client and server by passing data using *headers*. Data is passed to the server as a request header and is received from the server as a *response header*.

These headers store data as environment variables. For example, the REMOTE_HOST environment variable holds the hostname of the client,

REQUEST_METHOD lets you know whether the form was submitted using either the get or post method, and QUERY_STRING holds the form data/value pairs if the form was submitted using the get method.

When the server receives data from the client, you can use the script to process the data and return a response back to the client. The typical response returned to the client is an HTML page that explains to the user how the data was processed.

At the top of the script, you need to identify the scripting language. The scripting language needs to be installed on the server for the script to work. For the Perl scripting language, the first line should identify where the Perl modules are installed. For example, for my server, the first line of the Perl script is `#!/usr/bin/perl`.

SCRIPT AN HTML RESPONSE

Chapter 18 explains how to send form data to a CGI program using the `<form>` tag's `action` attribute. When the CGI program receives this data, you want to send a response back to the client to let the user know that the server received the data.

Using the Perl scripting language, you can send text back to the client by using the `print` keyword. For the browser to recognize the response text as HTML, you need to include the Multipurpose Internet Mail Extensions (MIME) type before any text. The `Content-type:` label, followed by the MIME type, enables you to do this. The MIME type for standard HTML is text/plain.

At the end of every HTML line, you should include the new line (`\n`) command, except for the `Content-type:` line, which should include two new line (`\n`) commands. You should place a semicolon (`;`) at the end of every line.

SCRIPT AN HTML RESPONSE

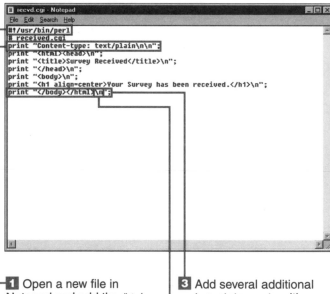

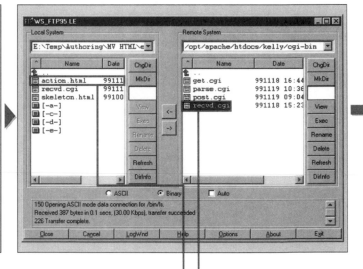

1 Open a new file in Notepad and add the `#!/usr/bin/perl` definition to the top of the file.

2 Type "**print Content-type: text/plain /n /n**".

3 Add several additional `print` statements with HTML statements in quotes.

4 Add a `\n` syntax within the quotes.

5 Save the file as recvd.cgi.

6 Open an FTP program.

■ This example shows WS/FTP.

7 Copy recvd.cgi into the cgi-bin directory on the server.

8 Copy the Web page that references this script to the server.

Can other MIME types be used instead of text/plain?

✔ A CGI script can respond back to the browser a number of content types. To do this, you need to specify a different MIME type. Sample MIME types include image/gif for GIF images, image/jpeg for JPEG images, audio/x-wav for WAV files, or video/x-msvideo for AVI video files.

What exactly are MIME types?

✔ Multipurpose Internet Mail Extensions (MIME) types were defined extensions that enabled different types of data to be sent over standard e-mail protocols. The same extensions have been included in HTML as a way to include alternative data in a Web page.

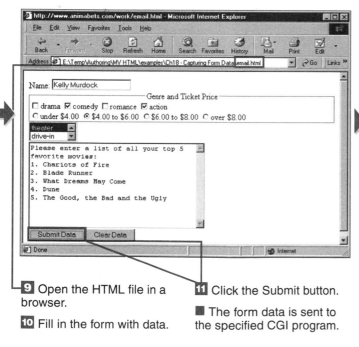

9 Open the HTML file in a browser.

10 Fill in the form with data.

11 Click the Submit button.

■ The form data is sent to the specified CGI program.

■ The CGI program processes the form data and returns a message to the browser.

VIEW ENVIRONMENT VARIABLES

*E*nvironment variables hold information about the client when the CGI script is called. The variables can be used to interface with the client. For example, the REMOTE_ADDR environment variable can identify the Web address of the Web page that called the CGI script and the REQUEST_METHOD environment variable identifies the method attribute of the form.

Common environment variables include REMOTE_ADDR, REMOTE_HOST, HTTP_ACCEPT, HTTP_USER_AGENT, REQUEST_METHOD, CONTENT_LENGTH, QUERY_STRING, and PATH_INFO.

When a form is passed to a CGI script using the get method, the form data is stored in the QUERY_STRING environment variable.

To look at the environment variables in the browser, you can print the ENV keyword followed by the environment variable in brackets and single quotes. A dollar sign ($) in front of the ENV keyword identifies Perl variables. For example, the statement $ENV{'REMOTE_ADDR'} accesses the remote address environment variable.

VIEW ENVIRONMENT VARIABLES

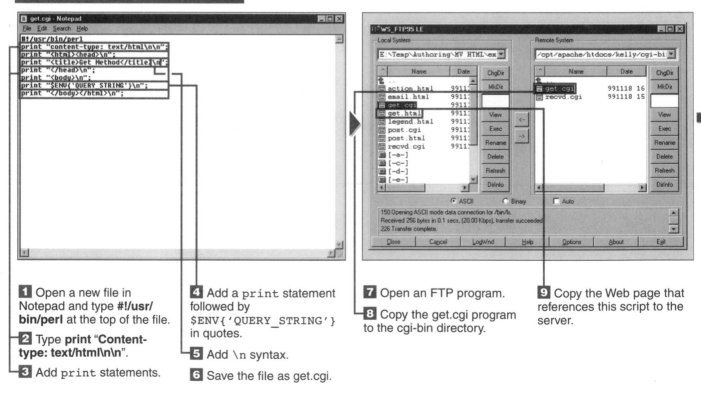

1 Open a new file in Notepad and type **#!/usr/bin/perl** at the top of the file.

2 Type print "**Content-type: text/html\n\n**".

3 Add print statements.

4 Add a print statement followed by $ENV{'QUERY_STRING'} in quotes.

5 Add \n syntax.

6 Save the file as get.cgi.

7 Open an FTP program.

8 Copy the get.cgi program to the cgi-bin directory.

9 Copy the Web page that references this script to the server.

Is there an easy way to see all the environment variables?

✔ All of the environment variables are stored in the %ENV array. You can print all the environment variables by looping through this array. For example, if you enter the Perl statements `foreach $env_vars (keys %ENV) { print "$env_vars = $ENV{$env_vars}\n";`, all environment variables display.

Which environment variable is used the most?

✔ The QUERY_STRING environment variable is probably used more often than the other environment variables because it contains the form data that is passed from the Web page. This form data includes the form element name and its associated value for each form element. For example, a form that includes a text field named text1 that has the text "hello" entered by the user would send "text1=hello" to the server.

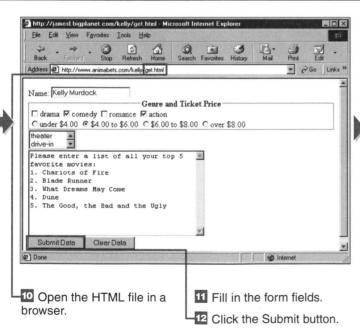

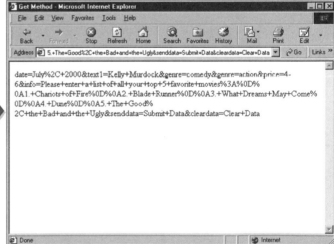

-10 Open the HTML file in a browser.

11 Fill in the form fields.

-12 Click the Submit button.

■ The CGI program specified in the action attribute is called.

■ This program displays the form data passed to it using the get method.

VIEW FORM DATA

When data is passed to a CGI script using the post method, the data is sent to *standard input*. By accessing the form data via the standard input, you can manipulate and use the data as needed to tabulate the results or log the information into a database.

All scripting languages have a standard input and a standard output. The standard input is the place within the CGI script where the Web page input can be received. For the Perl scripting language, you can access this input using the STDIN keyword.

To view the encoded form data, you need to read the data into a temporary variable and then output the contents of that variable to the browser.

The CONTENT_LENGTH environment variable holds the length of the form data. You can use this environment variable to read the form data. For example, in Perl you would read the standard input into a buffer with a statement like this, read(STDIN,$buffer, $ENV{'CONTENT_LENGTH'}).

VIEW FORM DATA

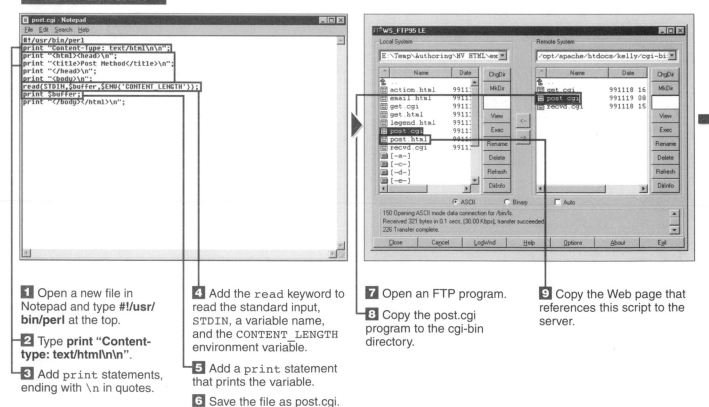

1 Open a new file in Notepad and type **#!/usr/bin/perl** at the top.

2 Type **print "Content-type: text/html\n\n"**.

3 Add print statements, ending with \n in quotes.

4 Add the read keyword to read the standard input, STDIN, a variable name, and the CONTENT_LENGTH environment variable.

5 Add a print statement that prints the variable.

6 Save the file as post.cgi.

7 Open an FTP program.

8 Copy the post.cgi program to the cgi-bin directory.

9 Copy the Web page that references this script to the server.

For both the get and post methods, the form data is URL encoded. Can the data be unencoded?

✔ By default, all data passed to a CGI script is URL encoded. You can include the logic within the CGI script to unencode the form data. This process is handled by *parsing* the data. There are many example scripts on the Web that will parse form data for you.

Are parsing functions used frequently in CGI scripts?

✔ Almost every CGI script that is used on the Web includes a parsing routine. These routines change the data into a useable form that can be moved to a database or presented back to the user. If you at www.scripts.com, you can find several Perl parsing libraries already created for your benefit.

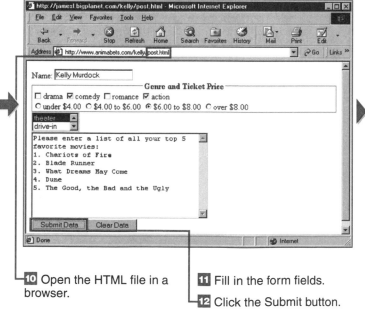

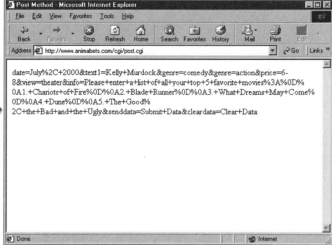

⑩ Open the HTML file in a browser.

⑪ Fill in the form fields.

⑫ Click the Submit button.

■ The CGI program specified in the action attribute is called.

■ This program displays the form data passed to it using the post method.

CREATE A PAGE HIT COUNTER

Another useful way to use CGI scripts is to create a counter to keep track of the number of times that the Web page has been opened. These counters are referred to as *page hit counters*. They are useful as a way to keep track of visitors internally.

The way this script works is to have the script run every time the

Web page is loaded. The script includes statements that open a file on the server that contains the count value. The count value is read from the file, the count value is then incremented, and finally, the count value is saved again to the file where it can be loaded and read the next time the Web page is loaded. By doing this, the counter

gets incremented every time the page is loaded.

You can find the count value by looking at the count variable in the server file or by printing the value to the browser.

CREATE A PAGE HIT COUNTER

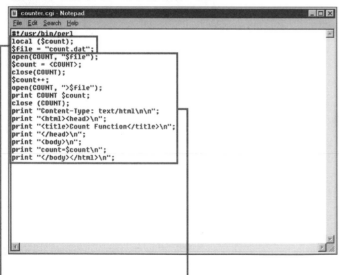

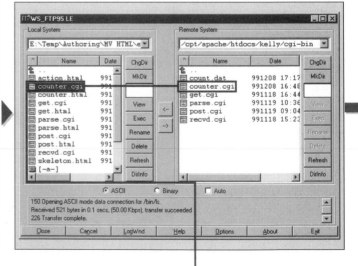

1 Open a new file in Notepad.

2 Type **#!/usr/bin/perl** at the top of the file.

3 Declare a local variable for the count and a filename.

4 Type the remaining code shown in the figure to open the file, increment the count variable, and display to the browser the count value.

5 Save the file as counter.cgi.

6 Open an FTP program.

7 Copy the counter.cgi program to the cgi-bin directory.

How can I add the counter CGI script to a Web page?

✔ You can add the counter CGI script to your Web page by using a server-side `include` statement. This statement included the `#exec` keyword followed by `cgi=` and the path and filename in quotes. The entire statement needs to be made into a comment so that it does not display in the browser. For example, at the place in the Web page where you want the counter to appear, type `<!--#exec cgi="/cgi-bin/counter.cgi" -->`.

What is the benefit of displaying the form data in the browser?

✔ By displaying the form data back to the browser where it came from, you can have the reader verify the correctness of the data, which enables the user to correct the data if it is incorrect. This step could save some processing time and effort by preventing errors before they occur.

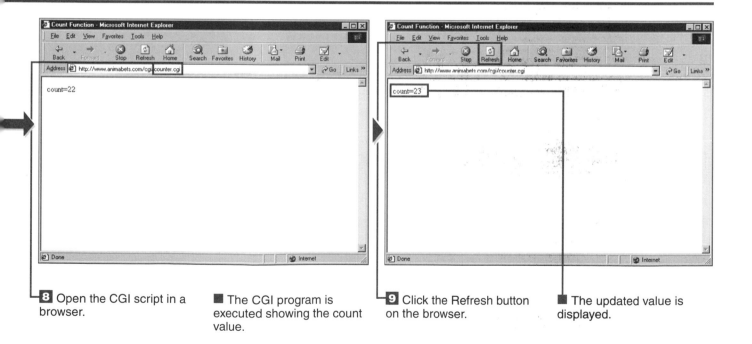

8 Open the CGI script in a browser.

■ The CGI program is executed showing the count value.

9 Click the Refresh button on the browser.

■ The updated value is displayed.

ENABLE PASSWORD ACCESS

Because CGI scripts run on the server, you can use them to restrict access to certain sections of your site.

You can control access to sections of your site in several ways. One common method is to let the user submit a form. The server could then compare the host name environment variable with an accepted list of hosts.

Another common approach is to assign a password to the user that is e-mailed to them separately. When the user then wants to access the site, let them enter a password into a form field. This password can then be compared on the server to valid passwords.

If a password is used, you can create a simple form with a text field that lets the user enter the

password and submit it to the server.

The passwords or valid domains can be included in a file like the counter example in "Create a Page Hit Counter."

ENABLE PASSWORD ACCESS

```
auth.cgi - Notepad
File  Edit  Search  Help
#!/usr/bin/perl
local ($valid);
$valid = $ENV{'REMOTE_HOST'};
if ($valid eq "animabets.com") {
    print "Content-Type: text/html\n\n";
    print "<html><head>\n";
    print "<title>Access Granted</title>\n";
    print "</head>\n";
    print "<body>\n";
    print "Access Granted. Welcome to the site.\n";
    print "</body></html>\n";
}
else {
    print "Content-Type: text/html\n\n";
    print "<html><head>\n";
    print "<title>Invalid Domain</title>\n";
    print "</head>\n";
    print "<body>\n";
    print "Invalid Domain $valid\n";
print "$ENV{'REMOTE_HOST'}\n";
print $valid;
    print "</body></html>\n";
}
```

```
Access Granted - Microsoft Internet Explorer
File  Edit  View  Favorites  Tools  Help
Back  Forward  Stop  Refresh  Home  Search  Favorites  History  Mail  Print  Edit
Address  http://www.animabets.com/cgi/auth.cgi

Access Granted. Welcome to the site.
```

1 Open a new file in Notepad and type **#!/usr/bin/perl** at the top of the file.

2 Define a local variable and set it equal to the REMOTE_HOST environment variable.

3 Check the variable with the valid host name and display the appropriate message.

4 Save the file as auth.cgi.

5 Use an FTP program to send the file to the server.

6 Open the auth.cgi script in a browser.

■ For this domain, the site is valid and a valid message appears.

How else can I use CGI scripts?

✔ This chapter shows only a few simple examples of how you can use CGI scripts. More complex examples include integrating with databases, processing orders, site search engines, form validation, and more.

I am unfamiliar with Perl. Where can I learn more about Perl and scripting?

✔ The purpose of this book is to teach you HTML, not Perl. Other books, including Paul Hoffman's *Perl For Dummies*, 2nd Edition, are available to teach you the details of programming with Perl. For these examples, follow the code that is included on the book's CD.

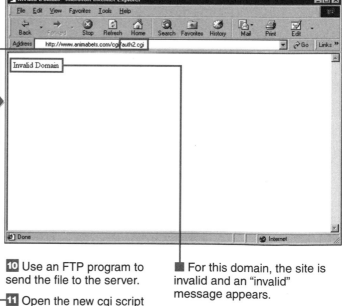

7 Open the auth.cgi file in Notepad.

8 Change the valid host name.

9 Save the file with a new filename.

10 Use an FTP program to send the file to the server.

11 Open the new cgi script in a browser.

■ For this domain, the site is invalid and an "invalid" message appears.

20) ADDING SOUND AND MUSIC

21) ADDING VIDEO

22) USING PLUG-INS

23) ADDING MULTIMEDIA WITH FLASH

24) EMBEDDING JAVA APPLETS

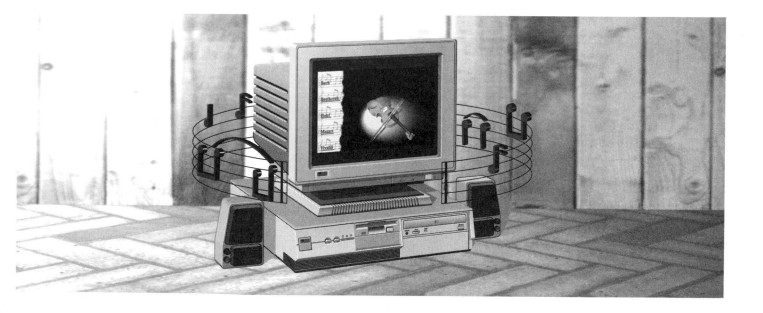

SOUND AND MUSIC FORMATS

Adding sound to your Web page can be very helpful. Ambient music playing softly in the background can set the mood for your site. Also, including

simple clicks and audio clues to actions, such as clicking buttons, provide valuable feedback to the user.

However, including sound on your Web page can be very expensive, not in terms of cost but in terms of the file size and download time.

Big Sound = Big File

Sound files can be some of the largest elements of a Web page; therefore, use them with care.

The reason sound files are so large is that quality sound requires a high sampling rate. *Sampling rate* is the number of times per second the sound is recorded, or sampled. This means that data for every audible frequency needs to be stored in the file many times each second.

You can also specify the size of the data to be 8-bit or 16-bit. Audio files recorded at 16-bit use 16 bits of memory to store the recorded sound. This is twice the size of 8-bit sound resulting in more detail and higher quality sound. Selecting 16-bit sound doubles the size of the file. Also, if the sound is recorded in stereo, the file size doubles.

Sound files with a lower sampling rate are of lower quality, but they have smaller file sizes. For example, an 8-bit, mono sound recorded with an 11,025 Hz sampling rate requires 22 kilobytes (K) for each second. This quality level is comparable to sound heard through a telephone. On the other hand, CD-quality sound is 16-bit stereo with a 44,100 Hz sampling rate, which requires 172K for each second.

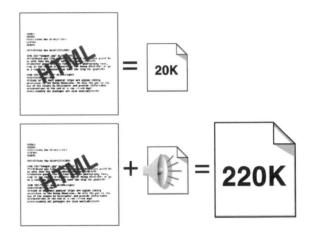

When a sound file is added to a Web page, the browser cannot play the sound, but it can pass the file off to a separate application that can play it. The information that enables the browser to identify the file type and pass it off to a separate program is the *MIME type*, which stands for Multipurpose Internet Mail Extensions. When the browser encounters a file with a known MIME type, it looks for the appropriate helper application that can handle the file.

If the browser encounters a file with an unknown MIME type , it displays a "File Not Found" error page. The ability for a user to hear the sound file on your Web page depends on the capabilities of the user's system.

Luckily many different audio formats are available. Each of these formats has different advantages and disadvantages.

AU Format

The AU audio format is the default audio format used by the UNIX and Linux systems. The AU format is common on the Internet because the low sound quality, thereby resulting in small file sizes. The MIME type for AU files is audio/basic.

AIFF Format

The AIFF audio format is used with Macintosh computers and offers a high-quality audio option, but the file sizes can be very large. The MIME type for AIFF files is audio/aiff.

WAV Format

The WAV audio format is another high-quality audio option with large file sizes that is commonly found on Windows machines. The MIME type for WAV files is audio/wav.

MIDI Format

The MIDI format is different than the other audio formats. Instead of storing sound frequencies, this format stores the notes that are played. The main advantage of this format is that it produces relatively tiny files, but the disadvantage is that they can be used only for music and not for speech or sounds.

RECORD SOUND FILES

Before you can add a sound file to a Web page, you need to obtain the sound file. You can find repositories of sound files throughout the Web, but perhaps the best source for obtaining sound files is to record them yourself using your computer's sound card and a microphone.

Most operating systems, such as Windows and the Mac OS, include utilities that can record sound files. These utilities are simple, easy-to-use applications that resemble a tape recorder.

To record sound, you need to plug a microphone into the sound card. Then, click the Record button and

speak into the microphone. When you finish recording, click the Stop button and save the sound file.

For sound files that are to be played on the Web, your best bet is to save the sound with low-quality mono settings.

RECORD SOUND FILES

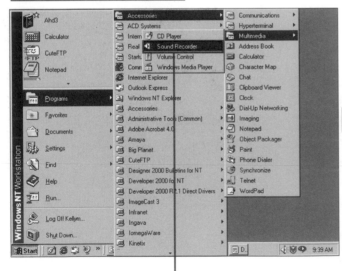

1 Click Start.

2 Select Programs.

3 Select Accessories.

4 Select Multimedia.

5 Click Sound Recorder.

■ The Sound Recorder application opens.

6 Make sure a microphone is attached to your system.

7 Click the Record button.

8 Speak into the microphone.

9 Click the Stop button when finished.

Can I use Sound Recorder to save the sound file as other formats, such as AU and AIFF?

✔ Sound Recorder is a program that works only with WAV files, but plenty of other programs can convert between the various audio formats. These programs include CoolEdit, Sonic Forge, and Goldwave. Later in this chapter, in "Convert between Sound Formats," you see an example of converting between different sound formats.

I noticed the Effects menu option. What effects are possible?

✔ The effects are fairly simple. They include increasing or decreasing the volume, increasing or decreasing the playback speed, adding an echo, and reversing the sound.

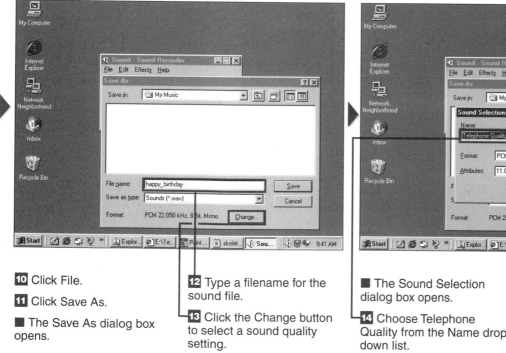

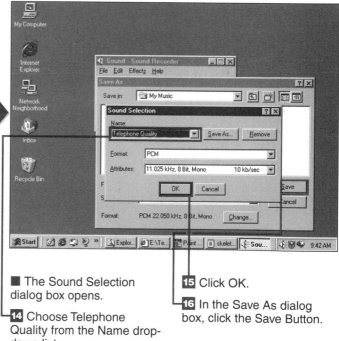

10 Click File.

11 Click Save As.

■ The Save As dialog box opens.

12 Type a filename for the sound file.

13 Click the Change button to select a sound quality setting.

■ The Sound Selection dialog box opens.

14 Choose Telephone Quality from the Name drop-down list.

15 Click OK.

16 In the Save As dialog box, click the Save Button.

ADD SOUND FILES AS LINKS

After you have a sound file, you can add it to a Web page in one of several ways. The easiest way to add a sound file to your Web page is by using the <a> tag. This way works just like linking to another Web page, except the sound filename replaces the Web page filename as the value for the href attribute. Standard text links are covered in Chapter 10.

For example, if you add the <a> tag and set the href attribute equal to a file called mysound.wav, this audio file loads when the user clicks the link.

If the user's system does not recognize this audio file type, the browser generates a file not found error.

If the user's system recognizes the sound file, then the required audio player application loads and automatically plays the sound.

This example uses the skeleton.html file from this book's CD, but the steps can be applied to any situation.

ADD SOUND FILES AS LINKS

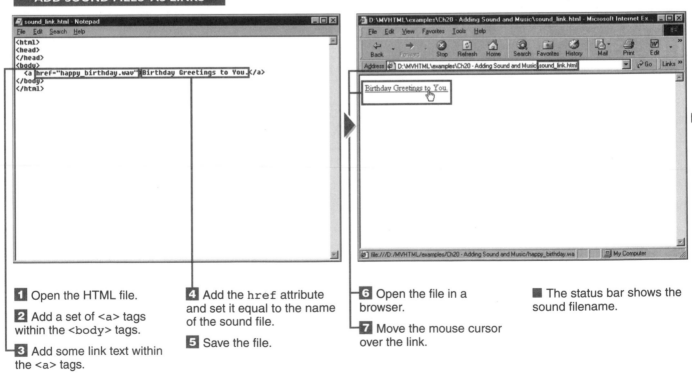

1 Open the HTML file.

2 Add a set of <a> tags within the <body> tags.

3 Add some link text within the <a> tags.

4 Add the href attribute and set it equal to the name of the sound file.

5 Save the file.

6 Open the file in a browser.

7 Move the mouse cursor over the link.

■ The status bar shows the sound filename.

What happens when a Macintosh user clicks a link to a WAV file?

✔ The default audio application for the Mac OS is QuickTime. This application can play WAV files as well as many other audio formats, including MP3. If the system does not recognize the file type, then the click is ignored or a file not found error page loads. To prevent this, you can convert the sound file into several different formats and include a link for each format.

Why does my audio player look different from the one in the figure?

✔ For my system, the associated audio player for WAV files is the Windows Media Player, but you may have a different application set to play audio files.

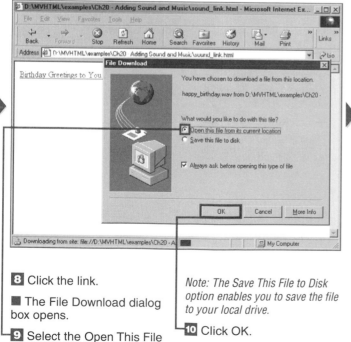

8 Click the link.

■ The File Download dialog box opens.

9 Select the Open This File from Its Current Location option.

Note: The Save This File to Disk option enables you to save the file to your local drive.

10 Click OK.

■ The default audio player loads and automatically plays the sound file.

ADD SOUND FILES AS OBJECTS

A more robust way to add sound files to your Web page is by using the `<object>` tag. This tag includes many more attributes that enable you to control the behavior of the sound file. The `<object>` tag loads the sound file immediately without waiting for a user to click a link for the sound file to play.

Alternative text for the object can be placed between the `<object>`

tags. This text displays if the object cannot load.

You can also include `<object>` tags within each other as a way to provide multiple possible solutions. If several `<object>` tags are included within each other, the browser looks at each successive `<object>` tag and loads the first one that it recognizes.

When using an `<object>` tag, you can also include `<param/>` tags within the `<object>` tags. These `<param/>` tags let you specify additional parameter values to the object. The next chapter gives an example of using the `<param/>` tag.

This example uses the skeleton.html file from this book's CD, but the steps can be applied to any situation.

ADD SOUND FILES AS OBJECTS

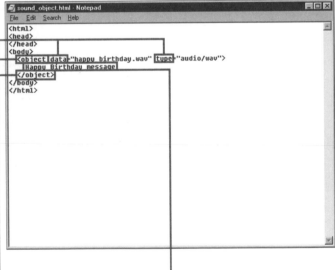

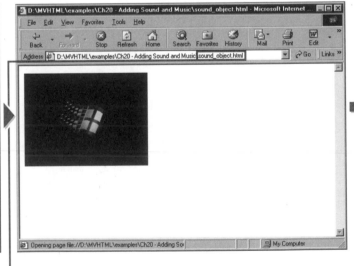

1 Open the HTML file and add `<object>` tags.

2 Type **data** and **type**.

3 Set the `data` attribute equal to the sound filename.

4 Set the `type` attribute equal to the MIME type for the sound format.

5 Add descriptive text.

6 Save the file.

7 Open the file in a browser.

■ The browser displays an area reserved for the object, but because it is a sound file, the Windows logo is displayed.

Can I resize the sound application icon in the Web page?

✔ When a sound file is loaded on my system using the `<object>` tag, the Media Player icon, shown as the Windows logo on a black background, in the browser is displayed as a 240 x 180 pixel icon. Other audio players may include different sized icons. You can resize this icon by using the width and height attributes. You can also make this icon disappear by setting the width and height attributes to 0.

When is the text inside the innermost `<object>` tag visible?

✔ The alternate text that is placed within the innermost `<object>` tag is only displayed in the browser if none of the specified sound files can be opened.

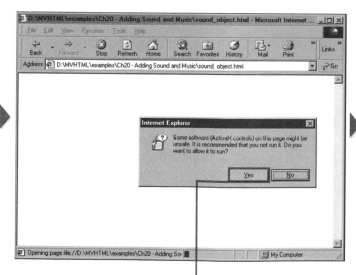

■ The browser then displays a warning message stating that it received a request to load the external application, which may be a virus.

8 Click Yes.

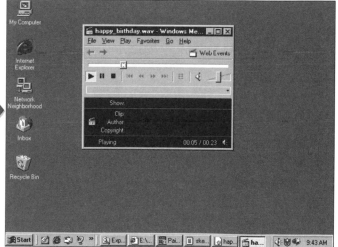

■ The default audio application loads and automatically plays the sound file.

EDIT SOUND FILES WITH SOUND FORGE

When recording sounds to use on a Web page, you may want to edit the sound files before including them. You can use many different tools to edit individual sound files.

These tools let you do things like adding effects, increasing the sound volume, and cropping the sound file to just the needed sounds.

One of these tools is Sound Forge. When a sound file loads into Sound Forge, it appears as a graph of sound volume or amplitude over time. This makes it easy to see where the sound's blank sections are located.

You can reduce the sound's file size by eliminating these blank sections. These sections typically appear

before and after the recorded sound, because it is difficult to click the Record and Stop buttons at exactly the right time.

These same steps can be repeated for just about any sound-editing program.

EDIT SOUND FILES WITH SOUND FORGE

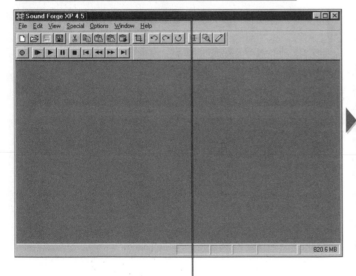

■1 Launch your sound-editing program.

■ The program's window appears; in this example, Sound Forge.

■2 Click File.

■3 Click Open.

■ The Open dialog box appears.

■4 Locate and select a sound file.

■5 Click the Open button.

Rather than deleting unwanted sections of sound, can I add sections of sound?

✔ By using the Cut, Copy, and Paste functions, you can select a section of sound from another sound file, copy it, and paste it into another sound file. Using this method, you can add sound sections to another sound file.

What other sound-editing tools are available?

✔ Many various sound-editing tools have similar features. Sound Forge is available as a commercial product. You can get more information at www.sonicfoundary.com. Another popular sound-editing tool is CoolEdit by Syntrillium Software. You can download a demo from www.syntrillium.com. If you want a shareware version, try Goldwave at www.goldwave.com.

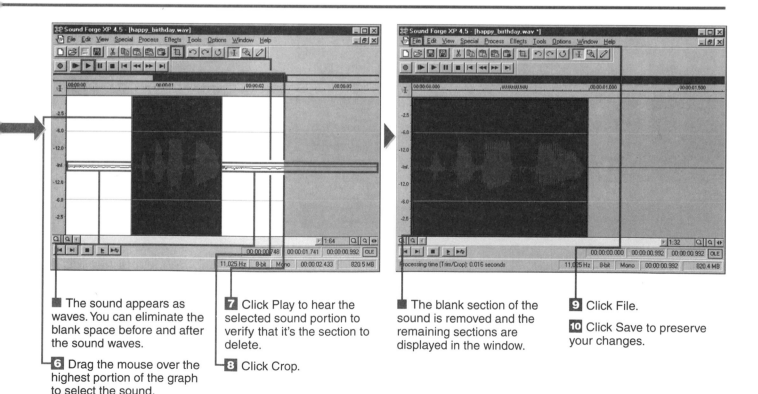

■ The sound appears as waves. You can eliminate the blank space before and after the sound waves.

6 Drag the mouse over the highest portion of the graph to select the sound.

7 Click Play to hear the selected sound portion to verify that it's the section to delete.

8 Click Crop.

■ The blank section of the sound is removed and the remaining sections are displayed in the window.

9 Click File.

10 Click Save to preserve your changes.

CONVERT A SOUND FILE TO A DIFFERENT FORMAT

You can use sound-editing tools, such as Sound Forge, to convert between the different sound formats. Saving a sound file in several different formats enables users of many different types of systems to access your sound files. Using the `<object>` tag, you can include all these formats together.

To save a file in a different format, simply load the sound file and choose File⇨Save As to save it as a different type file.

If you open the Save As dialog box and select the File Type drop-down list, you see a large number of different formats, but the most common for the Web include the WAV, AU, and AIFF formats. Sound Forge can also save sound files in the RealAudio (ra) and Advanced Streaming Format (asf) formats, which enable sounds to be streamed across the Web. Streaming audio is covered later in this chapter in "Streaming Audio."

Most sound-editing utilities enable you to convert between various formats.

CONVERT A SOUND FILE TO A DIFFERENT FORMAT

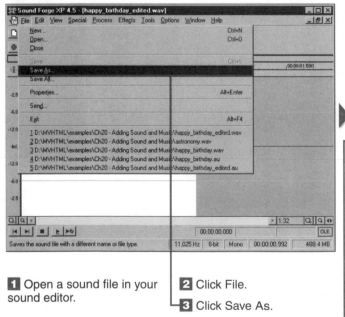

1 Open a sound file in your sound editor.

2 Click File.

3 Click Save As.

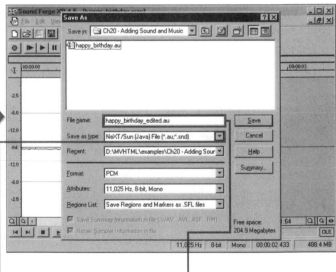

■ The Save As dialog box opens.

4 Choose a different file format in the Save as Type drop-down list.

5 Name the sound file.

MASTER IT

When should the streaming audio formats be used?

✔ If the sound file that you wish to include in your Web page includes a paragraph or more of spoken audio, then streaming audio would be the preferred format to use. A paragraph of spoken audio saved in the WAV format would be too large to include on a Web page.

Can I have music that loops (or plays over and over again)?

✔ If you wish to include music loops indefinitely, you should look into using MIDI files. These files are composed of simple notations that tell which notes to play and how long to play them. The file sizes for MIDI files are very small and they can be set to loop indefinitely. MIDI files are covered in the next section.

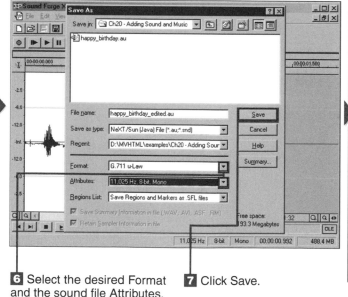

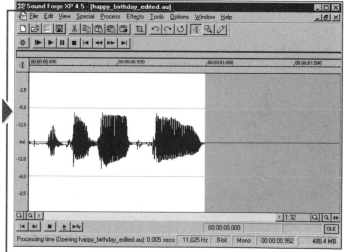

6 Select the desired Format and the sound file Attributes.

7 Click Save.

■ The name of the audio file is displayed in the title bar with its new extension.

ADD BACKGROUND MUSIC

The best format to use when adding background music to a Web page is the MIDI format. This format stores musical notation that is interpreted by the browser. This results in a fairly small sound file.

You can add background music to a Web page by using the `<a>` tag or the `<object>` tag, as shown earlier in this chapter. The MIME type for MIDI files is audio/midi.

You can also use Microsoft's proprietary tag that works only in Microsoft's Internet Explorer browser to add background sounds. The `<bgsound/>` tag includes a `src` attribute set to the sound filename and a `loop` attribute set to the number of times the sound file should loop.

The MIDI file used in the example below is an original composition provided by Cami Jensen.

ADD BACKGROUND MUSIC

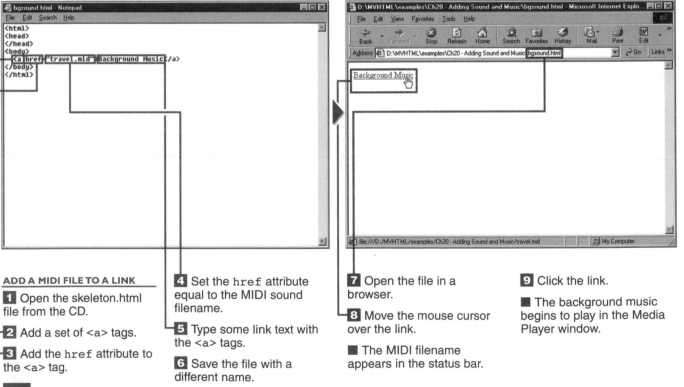

ADD A MIDI FILE TO A LINK

■1 Open the skeleton.html file from the CD.

■2 Add a set of `<a>` tags.

■3 Add the `href` attribute to the `<a>` tag.

■4 Set the `href` attribute equal to the MIDI sound filename.

■5 Type some link text with the `<a>` tags.

■6 Save the file with a different name.

■7 Open the file in a browser.

■8 Move the mouse cursor over the link.

■ The MIDI filename appears in the status bar.

■9 Click the link.

■ The background music begins to play in the Media Player window.

Can I make the background music loop indefinitely?

✔ To make the background music loop indefinitely, set the `loop` attribute equal to `infinite`. This causes the background music to play continuously until the user clicks the browser's Stop button.

Does the <bgsound/> tag work in the Netscape browser?

✔ Because the `<bgsound>` tag is proprietary, it works only in Microsoft Internet Explorer. This tag does not work when used in the Netscape Navigator browser.

Does Netscape Navigator support a tag that is similar to the <bgsound> tag?

✔ Netscape Navigator doesn't support a similar background sound tag. To include sound for Navigator, you need to use a link or the `<object>` tag.

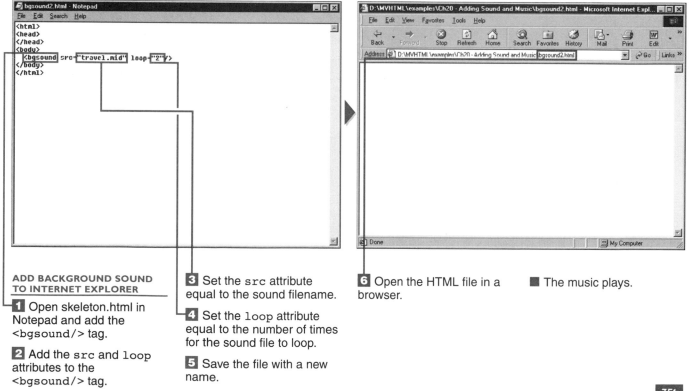

ADD BACKGROUND SOUND TO INTERNET EXPLORER

■1 Open skeleton.html in Notepad and add the `<bgsound/>` tag.

■2 Add the `src` and `loop` attributes to the `<bgsound/>` tag.

■3 Set the `src` attribute equal to the sound filename.

■4 Set the `loop` attribute equal to the number of times for the sound file to loop.

■5 Save the file with a new name.

■6 Open the HTML file in a browser.

■ The music plays.

USING STREAMING AUDIO

Streaming audio is a technology that plays a sound file as it downloads, which enables large audio files to be played in the browser.

One of the drawbacks of using sound files on a Web page is that the entire sound file must be downloaded in its entirety before any sound can be heard. Because sound files are so large, you cannot include any sound file longer than several seconds long.

To overcome this problem, several products, such as RealAudio, QuicktTime, and Microsoft's Streaming Format have been developed. These formats are capable of playing a sound file before the entire file has been downloaded.

Streaming sound files download into a buffer and then play while more sound is downloaded. This

process streams the sound file from its location to the user's browser.

These streaming audio formats require a proprietary audio player in order to hear the sound. Both Internet Explorer and Navigator browsers can automatically detect some of these formats and launch the appropriate audio player, provide you have it installed.

USING STREAMING AUDIO

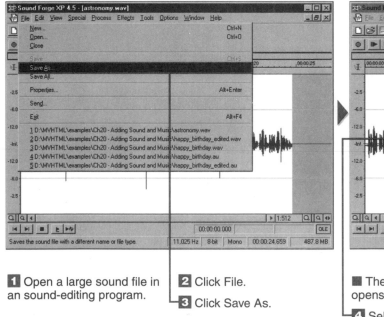

1 Open a large sound file in an sound-editing program.

2 Click File.

3 Click Save As.

■ The Save As dialog box opens.

4 Select the Advanced Streaming Format option from the Save as Type drop-down list.

5 Enter a filename for the sound file.

6 Click Save.

What are the different streaming formats?

✔ Two very popular streaming formats are the RealAudio (ra) format developed by RealNetworks. You can find more information about their format and download RealPlayer at www.realaudio.com. Microsoft has worked with many different companies in the industry to develop the Advanced Streaming Format (asf). Apple has advanced its QuickTime product to handle streaming audio.

Can these same streaming formats be used to stream video as well as audio?

✔ RealNetworks has a sister product called RealVideo that can be used to stream video files. The Advanced Streaming Format and QuickTime formats also support streaming video. Video is covered in more depth in Chapter 21.

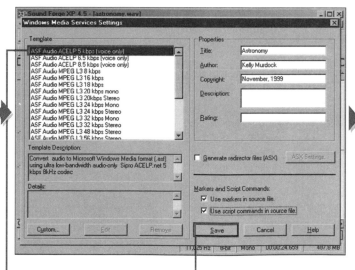

■ The Windows Media Services Settings dialog box opens.

7 Select a standard setting from the list.

8 Click Save.

■ When the file streams to the user, the title and author appear.

VIDEO FORMATS

Although the size of sound files can be very large, they are still small compared with the size of the video files. The reason that video files are so much larger is that they include both audio and video portions together.

Because of their size, many video files do not feasibly work on Web pages. However, if you use video files carefully, they can be an effective means of presenting information and adding excitement to your Web page.

You can obtain video files from the Web from one of the various video repositories, or you could use a video camera and a video capture card to shoot your own videos.

You can use several different video formats on the Web. Each of these formats requires a video player on the user's computer to view it.

MPEG Format

The Motion Picture Experts Group (MPEG) developed the MPEG format as a cross-platform video solution. The MIME type for the MPEG format is video/mpeg.

AVI Format

The AVI format is the default video format for the Windows operating system. The MIME type for the AVI format is video/avi.

QuickTime (MOV) Format

The QuickTime format is the default format used on Macintosh systems. The QuickTime plug-in enables Web browsers to play QuickTime movies. The MIME type for the QuickTime format is video/quicktime.

Advanced Streaming Format (ASF)

The Advanced Streaming Format is a streaming format developed by Microsoft with wide industry support. The MIME type for the ASF format is video/asf.

ADD VIDEO FILES AS LINKS

Including videos on a Web page can add some spice and flare to the site. It can also help the user see motion that would not be possible with normal images. Video files, however, can be very large because they include images and audio.

You can add a video file to a Web page using the <a> tag. To do this,

you simply need to set the href attribute to the video filename.

Which video format to use depends on the capabilities of the user's computer. When the user clicks the link, the video player associated with the file type loads, if available, and plays the video file.

If the file type is not recognized, the link is ignored or the user sees a "File Not Found" error page.

This example uses the skeleton.html file from this book's CD, but the steps can be applied to any situation.

ADD VIDEO FILES AS LINKS

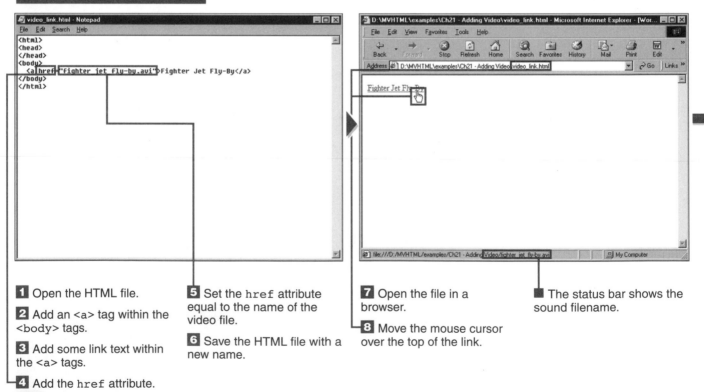

1 Open the HTML file.

2 Add an <a> tag within the <body> tags.

3 Add some link text within the <a> tags.

4 Add the href attribute.

5 Set the href attribute equal to the name of the video file.

6 Save the HTML file with a new name.

7 Open the file in a browser.

8 Move the mouse cursor over the top of the link.

■ The status bar shows the sound filename.

What happens if a Macintosh user clicks a link to an AVI file?

✔ When a browser on a Macintosh computer accesses a link to an AVI file, it tries to load the AVI if the default video player that can play this format. If no such video player exists, the browser opens a "File Not Found" error page. Luckily, QuickTime is the default video player and more recent versions of the QuickTime Player can load and play AVI files.

What happens if a Windows user clicks a link to an QuickTime file?

✔ If the default Windows video player can play the QuickTime file, the file loads into the player and plays. If the default Windows video player cannot play the QuickTime file, the "File Not Found" error page loads. Recent versions of Windows Media Player can play QuickTime videos.

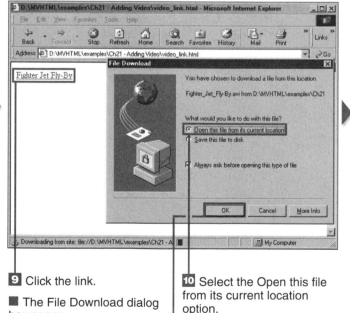

9 Click the link.

■ The File Download dialog box opens.

10 Select the Open this file from its current location option.

11 Click OK.

■ The Windows Media Player application loads and automatically plays the video file.

ADD VIDEO FILES AS OBJECTS

Another way to add video files to your Web page is with a set of <object> tags. Using the <object> tag gives Web page designers greater control over the file's appearance and behavior.

The content included within the <object> tags is displayed if the video format is not recognized. This content can be descriptive text or another video format within an <object> tag for the system to try.

The <object> tag includes many attributes that offer control over the video file, such as the width and height attributes for setting video dimensions. The <object> tag can also include align, border, vspace, and hspace attributes. These attributes work the same as those attributes for the <img/> tag, which is covered in Chapter 11.

The <object> tags can also contain <param/> tags that are used to load parameters. One such parameter is the hidden parameter, which hides the video player controls. To view the video player controls, set the name attribute of the <param/> tag to hidden and the value attribute to false. This displays the controls, enabling the user to play, stop, and pause the video.

This example uses the skeleton.html file from this book's CD, but the steps can be applied to any situation.

ADD VIDEO FILES AS OBJECTS

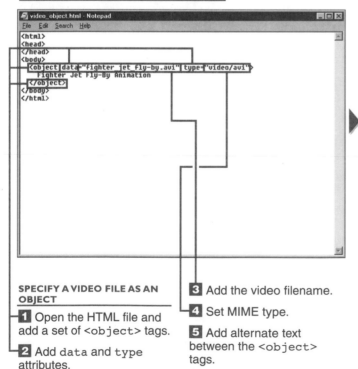

SPECIFY A VIDEO FILE AS AN OBJECT

1 Open the HTML file and add a set of <object> tags.

2 Add data and type attributes.

3 Add the video filename.

4 Set MIME type.

5 Add alternate text between the <object> tags.

6 Save the file.

7 Open the file in a browser.

■ The Windows Media Player application loads and automatically plays the video file.

Can I load several different formats of a video file using several <object> tag sets?

✔ In order to support a wide range of systems, you can include several **<object>** tags within one another. Each **<object>** tag can specify different video files in different formats. The browser then looks at each **<object>** tag in order from top to bottom and displays the first format that it recognizes.

Can I include an <img/> tag inside of the <object> tags instead of just plain text?

✔ Any HTML code that is included within the **<object>** tags will be displayed if the specified video file cannot load and play. This code could be descriptive formatted text, an image file, or any other HTML element.

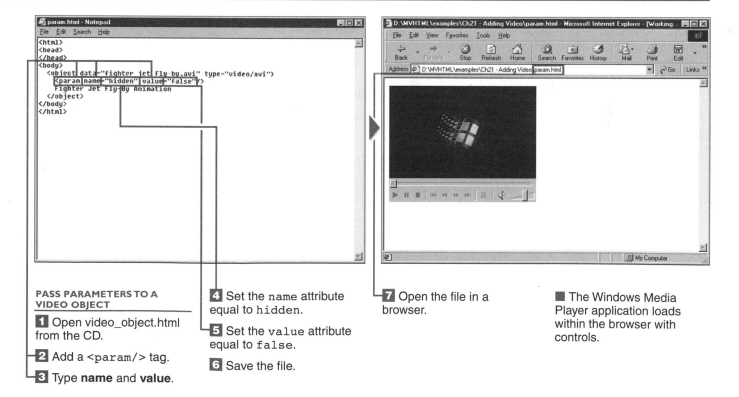

PASS PARAMETERS TO A VIDEO OBJECT

1 Open video_object.html from the CD.

2 Add a <param/> tag.

3 Type **name** and **value**.

4 Set the name attribute equal to hidden.

5 Set the value attribute equal to false.

6 Save the file.

7 Open the file in a browser.

■ The Windows Media Player application loads within the browser with controls.

REDUCE VIDEO FILE SIZE

The main problem with video files is their large file sizes. You can do several things to help reduce the size of video files.

The first file size reduction technique is to make the onscreen playback area smaller. The bigger the video size, the more file space it takes. You can also reduce the video's file size by reducing the length of the video.

Another technique works with colors. The fewer colors the video file has, the smaller the file size. For example, converting a video file to grayscale dramatically reduces its file size.

Many different video-editing tools enable you to reduce file size by changing the video size, length, and number of colors. Video-editing packages can also be used to crop the video to a reasonable size.

Adobe's Premiere is the product that is used in this example.

REDUCE VIDEO FILE SIZE

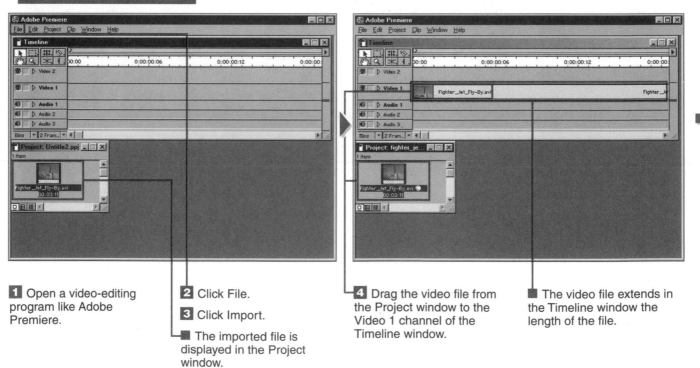

1 Open a video-editing program like Adobe Premiere.

2 Click File.

3 Click Import.

■ The imported file is displayed in the Project window.

4 Drag the video file from the Project window to the Video 1 channel of the Timeline window.

■ The video file extends in the Timeline window the length of the file.

Is the optimization step really necessary?

✔ Although optimization of a video file reduces the size, length, or quality of the video file, it truly is necessary because most browsers cannot handle large file sizes.

What other video-editing packages are available?

✔ Adobe produces a popular high-end video-editing package called Premiere. Ulead Systems has a package called MediaStudio Pro. An example of a shareware package is Personal AVI Editor. For Macintosh systems, check out QuickTime Plus or Apple's iMovie products.

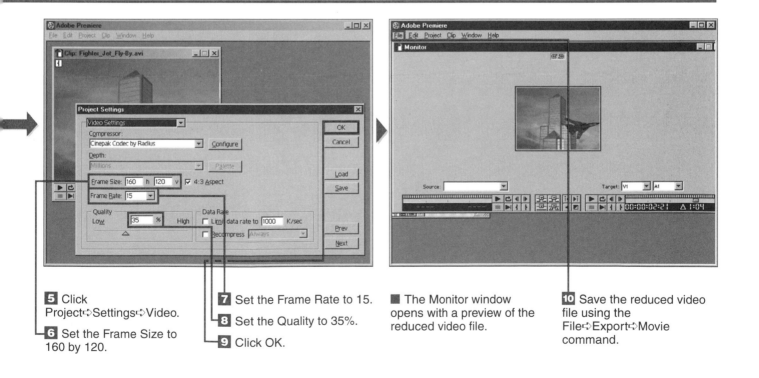

5 Click Project➪Settings➪Video.

6 Set the Frame Size to 160 by 120.

7 Set the Frame Rate to 15.

8 Set the Quality to 35%.

9 Click OK.

■ The Monitor window opens with a preview of the reduced video file.

10 Save the reduced video file using the File➪Export➪Movie command.

CONVERT VIDEO TO ANIMATED GIFS

Another drawback of video files is that they require a video player or a plug-in to work within the browser. This is not a problem for animated GIF files. Animated GIF files do not require a separate video player to be displayed in a browser. They can play in the browser without any help from an external program.

One way to ensure that your video file will be seen is to convert it to an animated GIF file. Many animated GIF programs, such as GIF Animator, offer an option to convert to standard video formats to animated GIF files. Once converted, an animated GIF file can then be added to a Web page using the <img/> tag.

Animated GIF files support only 256 colors, so they are not a good option for photorealistic video sequences.

GIF Animator is the software that is used for this example.

CONVERT VIDEO TO ANIMATED GIFS

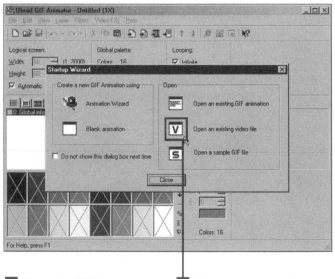

1 Open the GIF Animator program.

■ The Startup Wizard dialog box appears.

2 Click the Open an Existing Video icon.

3 In the Open Video File dialog box, locate and select the video file to open.

4 Click the Open button.

How do animated GIF file sizes compare to video files?

✔ Video files are compressed using algorithms that detect changes between various frames of a video file, but animated GIF files consist of multiple images all attached to each other. For this reason, compressed video files without a lot of motion will be much smaller than the same file converted to an animated GIF file. Animated GIF files are best used for animations with relatively few colors and large sections of similar color.

Is there a limit to the number of animated GIFs that can be included on a Web page?

✔ You can use any number of animated GIFs on a Web page. Keep in mind, however, that using too many animated GIFs detracts from the site's message. It is good style to use animated GIFs in moderation.

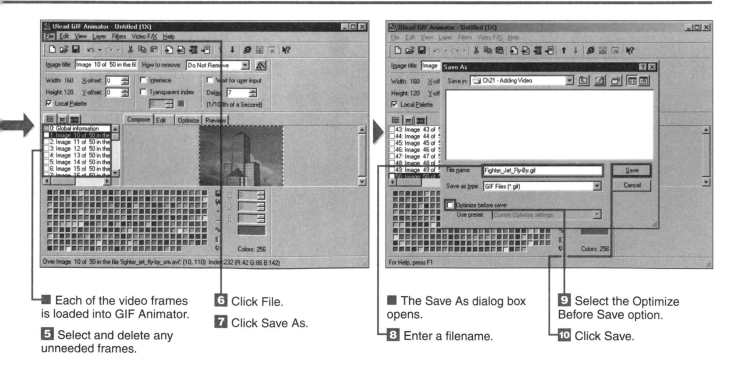

■ Each of the video frames is loaded into GIF Animator.

5 Select and delete any unneeded frames.

6 Click File.

7 Click Save As.

■ The Save As dialog box opens.

8 Enter a filename.

9 Select the Optimize Before Save option.

10 Click Save.

USING PLUG-INS

Plug-ins are external programs that you can add to the browser to enhance its capabilities. They enable browsers to be much more powerful and to support many more file types than they would otherwise.

Several plug-ins have become very popular and are continually being updated and supported. These plug-ins allow the browser to view specialized content, such as animation, published content, virtual reality worlds, and streaming audio and video.

This chapter highlights some of these popular plug-ins and explains how to use them.

Adobe Acrobat Reader

The Adobe Acrobat program plug-in lets you take existing documents produced with a word processor or desktop publishing program and save them as PDF files. The advantage of PDF files is that the exact look and layout of the original document is maintained. To view these documents on a Web page, you need to download the Acrobat Reader 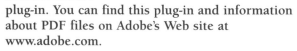 plug-in. You can find this plug-in and information about PDF files on Adobe's Web site at www.adobe.com.

RealAudio and RealVideo

RealAudio and RealVideo are popular streaming formats that enable you to see and hear large audio and video files even on a dialup modem connection. A streaming format is one that plays the content as it is downloaded. For example, you could listen to a live concert using streaming formats. Information and the RealPlayer plug-in are available at www.real.com.

QuickTime

Apple's streaming video format is the default standard for Macintosh systems. QuickTime is also available

for Windows computers. The plug-in and information can be found at www.apple.com/quicktime.

Shockwave and Flash

Macromedia has several plug-ins that enable files generated with their commercial products, such as Director and Flash, to

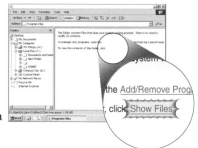

be displayed on the Web. Using these formats, you can create interactive multimedia presentations that include sound and animation. Information on these formats can be found at Macromedia's Web site at www.macromedia.com.

VRML

VRML stands for the Virtual Reality Modeling Language. This language is similar to HTML and can create three-dimensional virtual worlds. Using a VRML plug-in, you can load and navigate around these three-dimensional worlds inside a browser.

For example, you could enter a VRML world and move around as if you were in the world. You can choose from several different VRML plug-ins. To find more

information about this format and download a VRML plug-in, visit the Web 3D Consortium at www.vrml.org.

DOWNLOAD PLUG-INS

You enable a plug-in for a browser by downloading and installing the plug-in program. After you install the plug-in, the browser recognizes the file types that use these plug-ins and loads them within the browser window or launches an external application to view the content.

Many different types of plug-ins exist, and some of them come bundled with the various browsers. For example, Netscape browsers include plug-ins for Apple QuickTime video format and for Macromedia Flash format. For more information on Flash, see Chapter 23.

If a required plug-in is not available, the browser detects this and offers a dialog box enabling the user to download and install the required plug-in.

After you download the plug-in, you need to install it. The site from which you download the plug-in will have installation instructions.

DOWNLOAD PLUG-INS

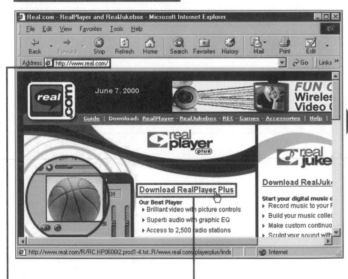

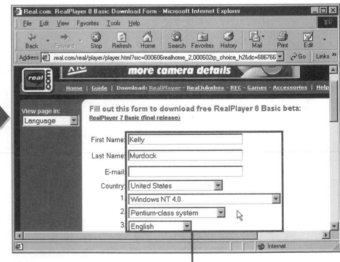

1 Open a Web page that includes a link to the plug-in that you wish to download, such as www.real.com.

2 Click a link to the plug-in.

■ Many companies ask that you fill out some information before downloading.

3 Fill in the information.

4 Click the button to begin the download.

How do I install the plug-in if I saved the file to my hard drive?

✔ The downloaded plug-in file is an installation program. To install it, you need to locate it on your hard drive and double-click the file. This starts the installation process that takes you through the setup. After setup is complete, you need to restart your browser to use the plug-in to view specialized content.

Where can I find a list of available plug-ins?

✔ Several plug-in Web sites exist that provide a comprehensive list of plug-ins. One such list is at http://browserwatch.internet.com/plug-in.html. These plug-in hubs offer you the ability to download most of the plug-ins you need without having to visit the home Web site of each plug-in.

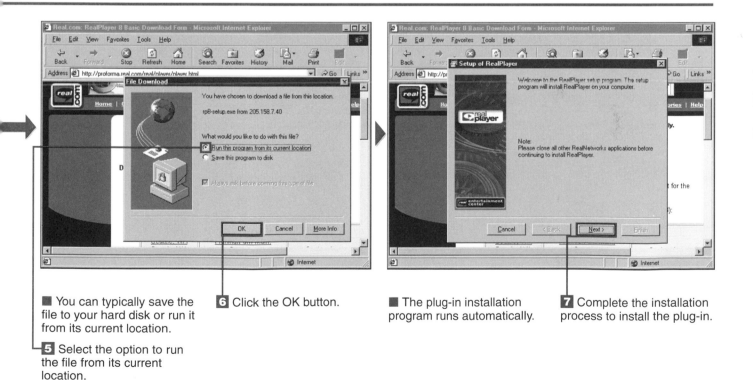

■ You can typically save the file to your hard disk or run it from its current location.

5 Select the option to run the file from its current location.

6 Click the OK button.

■ The plug-in installation program runs automatically.

7 Complete the installation process to install the plug-in.

USING PLUG-INS TO VIEW CONTENT

After you download and install a plug-in, you can view Web content that the plug-in can handle by simply clicking a link to that content. Doing so causes the plug-in to load within the browser and the content to be displayed.

For example, if you install the Acrobat Reader plug-in to view PDF files, you can click a link to a PDF file and the Acrobat Reader plug-in automatically loads within the browser with the link content displayed. The Acrobat Reader interface includes additional buttons and controls.

Some plug-ins do not load within the browser; they open a separate application in which you can view the content. For example, the RealPlayer plug-in opens a separate application that can play audio and video formats.

USING PLUG-INS TO VIEW CONTENT

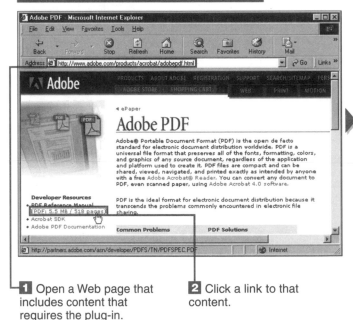

1 Open a Web page that includes content that requires the plug-in.

2 Click a link to that content.

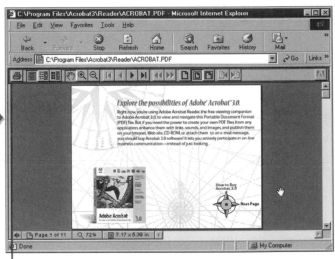

■ The plug-in loads within the browser with additional controls.

Can I view PDF files outside of a browser?

✔ Adobe Acrobat Reader installs both a browser-based version and a standalone version of the Reader. Using the standalone version, you can view PDF files without being connected to the Web or using a browser.

Do plug-ins always have their own interfaces?

✔ Installed plug-ins typically have their own interfaces. These interfaces include additional buttons and controls that are used to work with the specific content that the plug-in can play. For example, the RealPlayer plug-in interface includes buttons toplay, stop, pause, and rewind audio and video files. These buttons are unique and not found in the standard browser.

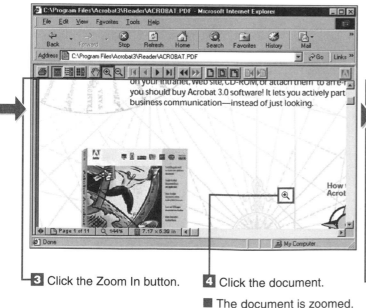

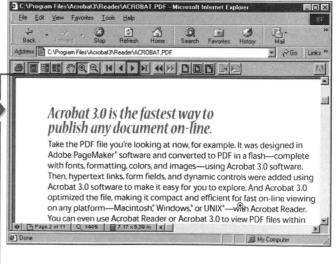

3 Click the Zoom In button.

4 Click the document.

■ The document is zoomed.

5 Click the Next Page button.

■ The next page in the document is loads.

ADD PLUG-IN CONTENT AS OBJECTS

You can add plug-in content to your Web page by using the <object> tag. Within the <object> tag, the data attribute is set to the filename for the content and the type attribute sets the MIME type for the plug-in application. The type is the necessary information that enables the browser to access the plug-in.

Any text between the <object> tags loads into the browser if the necessary plug-in is unavailable. You may want to use this text as a link to the Web site where the user can download the plug-in.

If you place the content within a Web page, you can also control the size of the content by using the height and width attributes.

The <object> tags can also contain <param/> tags that are used to load parameters into the plug-in. Check with the plug-in documentation to learn about accepted parameters.

This example uses the skeleton.html file, which you can find on the CD for the book.

ADD PLUG-IN CONTENT AS OBJECTS

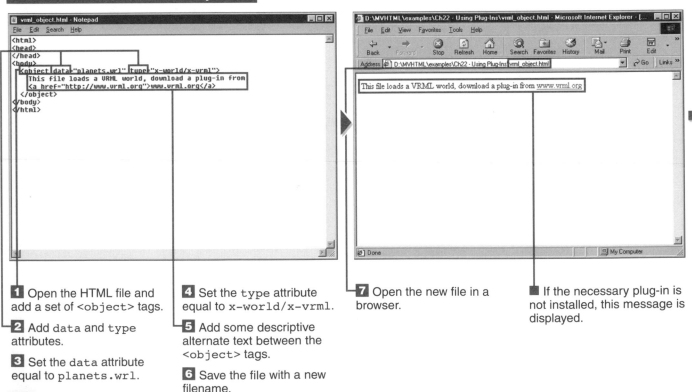

1 Open the HTML file and add a set of <object> tags.

2 Add data and type attributes.

3 Set the data attribute equal to planets.wrl.

4 Set the type attribute equal to x-world/x-vrml.

5 Add some descriptive alternate text between the <object> tags.

6 Save the file with a new filename.

7 Open the new file in a browser.

■ If the necessary plug-in is not installed, this message is displayed.

Can I add plug-ins to a Web page using standard links?

✔ You can add plug-ins to your Web page using standard links, but the `<object>` tag enables you to include the `type` attribute to tell the browser exactly which plug-in to use. A standard link may confuse the browser.

Can VRML files be viewed outside of the browser?

✔ When you install some VRML plug-ins, you may also install a standalone VRML viewer. You can use these viewers to view VRML worlds separate from the browser and even when not connected to the Internet.

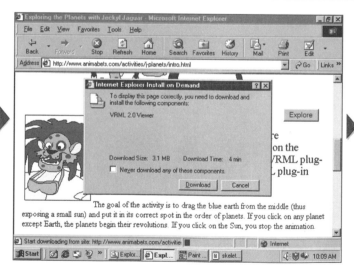

■ Internet Explorer can detect the needed plug-in for this file type and enable you to automatically download it.

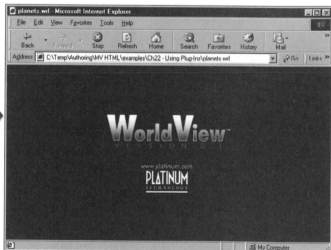

■ The plug-in loads to view the VRML file.

DOWNLOAD AND INSTALL THE FLASH PLUG-IN

Flash is a software package created by Macromedia that enables vector-based multimedia presentations on the Web. Flash files can include animation, sound, and interactive elements.

Flash files are relatively small because they include vector graphics. Vector graphics are

created mathematically from lines and shapes. They can be sized to any size without losing any resolution. This capability keeps their file sizes relatively small.

To view Flash content in a Web browser, you need to download and install the Flash plug-in player. This plug-in player enables your browser to interpret the Flash files

that are referenced in your HTML file.

You can download the Flash plug-in from Macromedia's Web site at www.macromedia.com. Once downloaded, the player automatically installs itself. The player download is only about 107K in size and downloads quickly.

DOWNLOAD AND INSTALL THE FLASH PLUG-IN

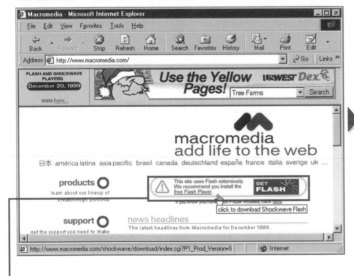

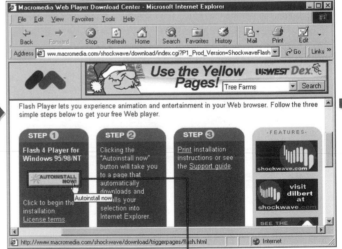

1 Go to the Macromedia site.

2 Go to the Downloads page.

3 Click the Get Flash button.

■ A Web page describing the download steps is displayed.

4 Click the AutoInstall Now button.

What happens if I try to view a Web page with Flash content if the Flash plug-in player is not installed?

✔ When you encounter a Web page that includes Flash content and you have not installed the Flash plug-in player, Internet Explorer detects that the plug-in is missing and asks if you wish to download and install the plug-in. Clicking the Download button in this dialog box automatically begins the download process. After the download completes, you can view the Flash content.

Can I install the Flash plug-in from anywhere else?

✔ Web sites that include Flash content typically include a button that will let you download the Flash plug-in.

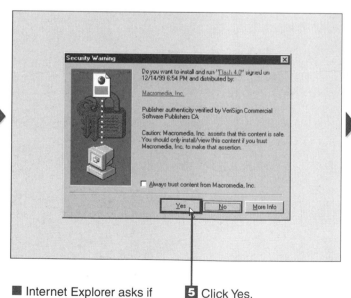

■ Internet Explorer asks if you want to download the player.

5 Click Yes.

■ The Flash plug-in player automatically downloads and installs.

■ A test Flash file on the Macromedia site shows up when the plug-in is fully installed.

CREATE A PRESENTATION: SET UP A FLASH DOCUMENT

The best way to learn about Flash is to see how Flash content is created. In this example, you create a Flash file for a fictitious company. Many of the sections that follow add to this file later.

To create Flash content for your Web pages, you need to purchase the Flash software package. One of the first tasks is to create a new Flash document.

When you open the Flash program, a new movie workspace is automatically loaded and ready to go. Define the movie settings including the background color and dimensions.

These settings can be set using the Movie Properties dialog box. This dialog box can be opened by clicking Modify⇨Movie.

This dialog box also lets you set the movie frame rate, grid spacing, color and units.

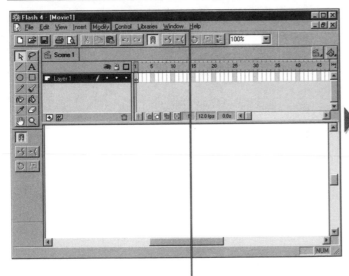

1 Open the Flash program.

■ A new movie file is created.

2 Click Modify.

3 Click Movie.

■ The Movie Properties dialog box opens.

4 Change the width and height to the desired dimensions.

What frame rate should be used?

✔ Frame rates for the Web should be set between 8 and 12 frames per second (fps). A value in this range is sufficient to see the motion of the Flash elements. Higher values are difficult to maintain on lower bandwidth connections.

Does a movie with larger dimensions download slower than one with smaller dimensions?

✔ High-resolution movies do not necessarily download slower. Because Flash content is vector-based, the graphics will be displayed consistently regardless of their size. The number of elements included, not their size, determines Flash file sizes.

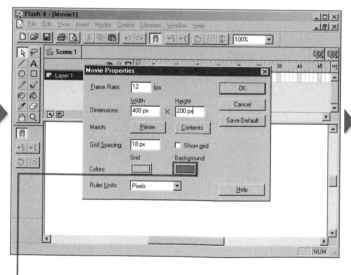

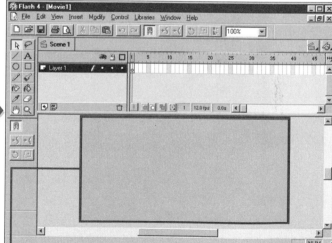

5 Click the Background button to change the background color.

6 Click OK to apply the settings.

■ The movie template is updated to the specified dimensions and background color.

CREATE A PRESENTATION: USE THE FLASH TOOLS

The Flash program includes many different features. Many of these features, called tools, can be selected from the toolbar located at the left side of the Flash window.

These tools let you select objects, add lines, text, ovals, rectangles, freehand curves, and colors.

To use a tool, you need to select it by clicking it. You can then click and drag the tool onto the background to create and position the various Flash elements. The tools all work in a fairly similar way. When you select a tool, the properties for that tool display in the space directly under the toolbar.

In this example, you enhance the presentation that was started earlier in this chapter as you investigate some additional Flash features.

CREATE A PRESENTATION: USE THE FLASH TOOLS

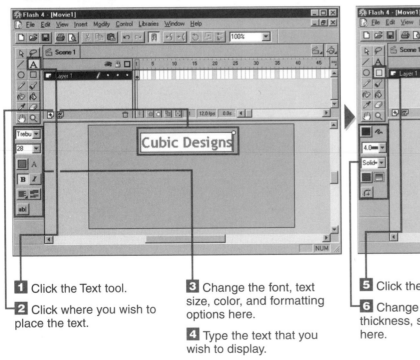

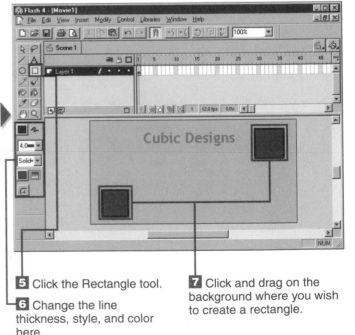

1 Click the Text tool.

2 Click where you wish to place the text.

3 Change the font, text size, color, and formatting options here.

4 Type the text that you wish to display.

5 Click the Rectangle tool.

6 Change the line thickness, style, and color here.

7 Click and drag on the background where you wish to create a rectangle.

What tools are included in the toolbox?

✔ The toolbox includes an Arrow tool for selecting elements and a Lasso tool for selecting multiple items. The toolbox also includes drawing tools for straight lines, ovals, and rectangles; a Text tool; a Pencil and Brush tool; and an Ink Bottle and Paint Bucket tool for coloring lines and elements. Use the Eye Dropper tool for selecting colors, an Eraser tool to clear portions of the drawing, a Pan tool and Zoom tools for looking at different sections of the workspace.

Can the toolbox be moved to the other side of the window?

✔ If you click and drag the border that surrounds the toolbox, you can reposition the toolbox as a dialog box anywhere you wish.

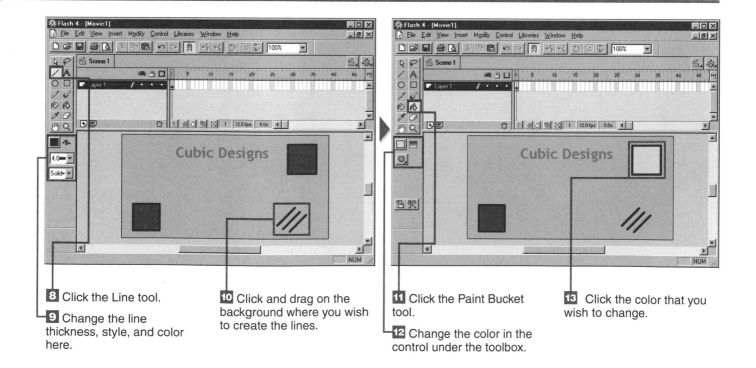

8 Click the Line tool.

9 Change the line thickness, style, and color here.

10 Click and drag on the background where you wish to create the lines.

11 Click the Paint Bucket tool.

12 Change the color in the control under the toolbox.

13 Click the color that you wish to change.

CREATE A PRESENTATION: WORK WITH LAYERS

*L*ayers are used to keep the elements separate. If several elements are created on the same layer, they are combined if similar colors touch. This can cause some difficulty as your elements start to move.

You can create a new layer by clicking Insert⇨Layer. The new

layer appears directly above the old layer, but it has a new name. If you select the layer name, all elements within that layer are selected and highlighted.

The elements in a layer can be hidden, locked, or displayed as an outline by clicking the icons above the layer names.

To delete a layer and all the elements on it, select the layer name and click the garbage can icon below the layer names.

In this example, you learn how to work with flash layers.

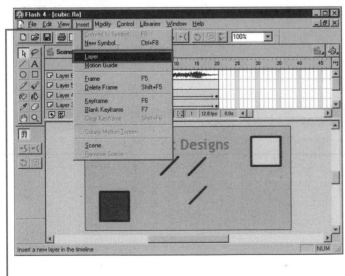

1 Add three new layers by clicking Insert.

2 Click Layer.

■ These layers are named Layer 1 through Layer 4.

3 Click Layer 1 to select it.

■ All the elements that are part of Layer 1 are outlined and highlighted.

How do I rename a layer?

✔ You can rename a layer by double-clicking the layer name and then typing a new name. As your documents get larger and more complex, you may want to rename your layers to help you remember which graphics are on which layer.

What are the icons and dots to the right of the layer names used for?

✔ The icons to the right of and above the layer names are used to hide, lock, and display an outline for each layer. The dots indicate whether the layer is visible, locked, or displayed in outline mode.

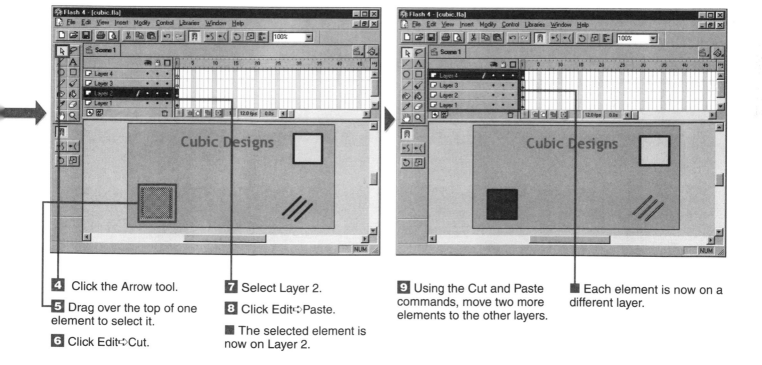

4 Click the Arrow tool.

5 Drag over the top of one element to select it.

6 Click Edit⇨Cut.

7 Select Layer 2.

8 Click Edit⇨Paste.

■ The selected element is now on Layer 2.

9 Using the Cut and Paste commands, move two more elements to the other layers.

■ Each element is now on a different layer.

CREATE A PRESENTATION: SET KEYFRAMES

To animate the motion of graphics about the scene, you need to set keyframes. A *keyframe* defines the location of an element for a different frame. After keyframes are set, you can tween between them.

For example, if some text moves slowly across the screen from left to right, it has one keyframe at the start of the movement that shows where the element is when it starts, and another keyframe at the end of

the motion that defines its position when it stops.

To the right of the layer names is a grid. The columns of this grid represent the frames of the movie.

Keyframes in Flash are set by selecting a frame, moving the element, and then clicking Insert⇨Keyframe. When a keyframe is set, a small black dot becomes visible in the grid to indicate the keyframe.

MASTER IT

How can I tell where the keyframes are?

✔ Keyframes are indicated in the timeline as a solid black dot. Each layer can have a keyframe set for each frame.

In this example, you enhance the presentation that was started earlier in this chapter as you investigate some additional Flash features.

CREATE A PRESENTATION: SET KEYFRAMES

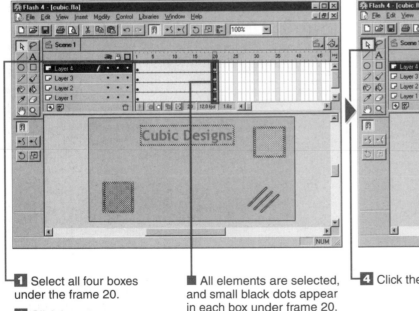

1 Select all four boxes under the frame 20.

2 Click Insert.

3 Click Keyframe.

■ All elements are selected, and small black dots appear in each box under frame 20.

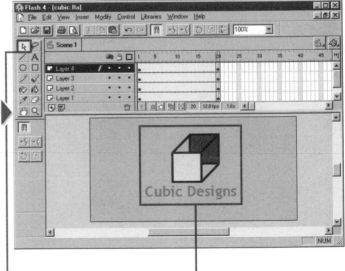

4 Click the Arrow tool.

5 Move each element into a different position.

CREATE A PRESENTATION: SET ELEMENTS IN MOTION

After you have keyframes set that mark the beginning and ending positions of an element, you can have Flash compute all the intermediate positions between these two end positions. This process is called *tweening*.

Before you can tween motion, you need to set keyframes for the beginning and ending positions. You then need to select all the frames between these two locations and click Insert⇨Create Motion Tween. This automatically generates all the intermediate positions to cause the element to move smoothly between the two end positions.

How are tweened motions indicated?

✔ After you use the Create Motion Tween command, the tween motion can be identified as an arrow on the timeline that runs between the beginning and ending keyframes.

CREATE A PRESENTATION: SET ELEMENTS IN MOTION

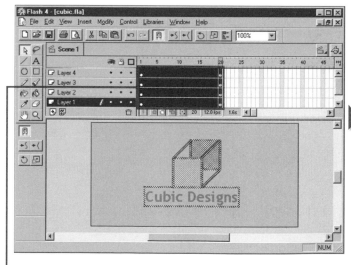

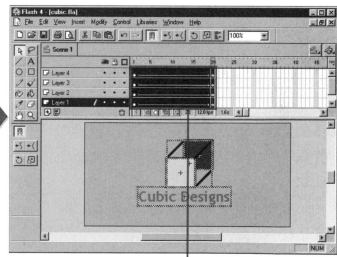

1 Select all the grid boxes for all layers between frames 1 and 20.

2 Click Insert.

3 Click Create Motion Tween.

■ An arrow displays, moving between the keyframe at frame 1 and the keyframe at frame 20.

CREATE A PRESENTATION: VIEW ELEMENTS IN MOTION

You may want to see the motion of the elements to check it. You have several ways in which to check the element motion.

One way to check motion is to drag the red frame cursor. As the frame cursor is dragged, the positions of the elements for the current frame are displayed.

Another way to view the motion is with the Controller dialog box. This dialog box includes simple buttons for Play, Stop, Forward, Step Forward, Rewind, and Step Back. To view the motions, click the Play button, and the motion from the current frame to the last frame will appear.

In this example, you enhance the presentation that was started earlier in this chapter as you investigate some additional Flash features.

CREATE A PRESENTATION: VIEW ELEMENTS IN MOTION

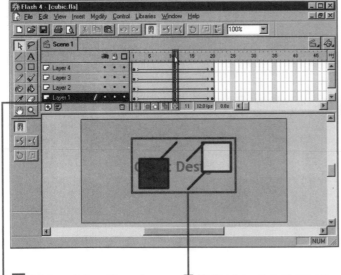

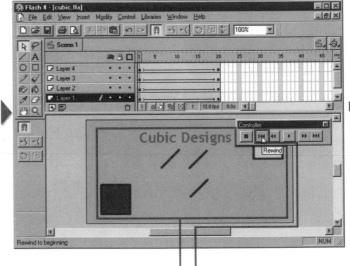

1 Click and drag the red frame cursor from the first frame to the end frame.

■ Notice how the elements move progressively toward their final destinations.

2 Click Window.

3 Click Controller.

4 Click the Rewind button.

■ The elements are all returned to their starting positions.

How do I close the Controller toolbar when I am not using it?

✔ Choosing Window⇨Controller opens the Controller toolbar. This toolbar can be repositioned anywhere on the screen by dragging its title bar. If you click Window⇨Controller again, the toolbar closes. You can also close the Controller toolbar by clicking the X button in the upper-right corner.

Can I view the animation in slow motion?

✔ Using the Step functions in the Controller, you can step forward or backwards through an animation sequence.

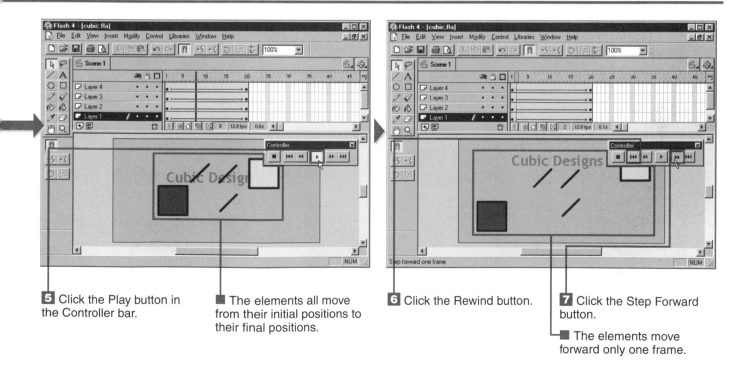

5 Click the Play button in the Controller bar.

■ The elements all move from their initial positions to their final positions.

6 Click the Rewind button.

7 Click the Step Forward button.

■ The elements move forward only one frame.

CREATE A PRESENTATION: TRANSFORM OBJECTS

You can reposition objects by using the Arrow tool, but other transformations are also possible. For example, by using the Modify⇨Transform command, you can rotate, scale, or flip an element.

You must select an element before these commands become active.

You can select elements with the Arrow tool. After an element is selected, select the command to use under the Modify⇨Transform menu.

This causes the transform to either change the position of the element for the current frame or to display

handles that surround the element that can be dragged the desired amount.

In this example, you enhance the presentation that was started earlier in this chapter as you investigate some additional Flash features.

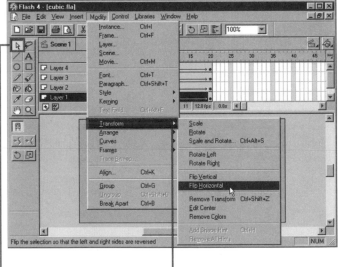

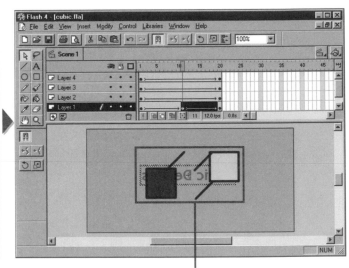

1 Select the first layer.

2 Select the text element using the Arrow tool.

3 Drag the red frame cursor to frame 10.

4 Click Modify.

5 Click Transform.

6 Click Flip Horizontal.

■ The text is flipped and now appears backwards.

Can I specify the amount of Scale or Rotation by using the keyboard instead of the mouse?

✔ Clicking Modify⇨Transform⇨Scale and Rotate opens a simple dialog box that includes scale and rotate fields. You can enter values into these fields by using the keyboard for precise control over the transforms of your elements.

Can all elements be transformed?

✔ Transformations are reserved for visible objects. It makes no sense to transform a sound file. Any object that can be selected in the window can be transformed.

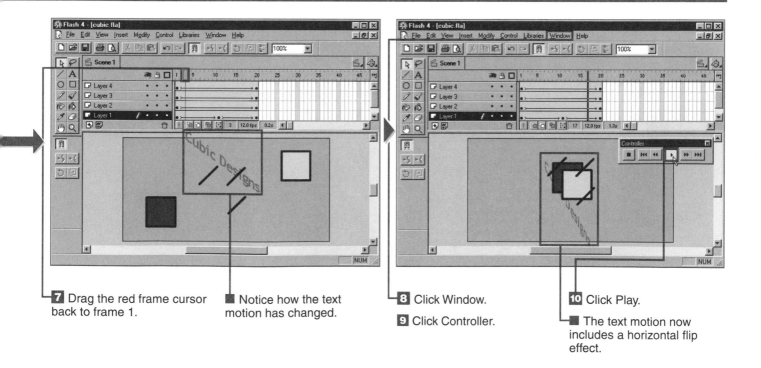

7 Drag the red frame cursor back to frame 1.

■ Notice how the text motion has changed.

8 Click Window.

9 Click Controller.

10 Click Play.

■ The text motion now includes a horizontal flip effect.

CREATE A PRESENTATION: USE LIBRARY ELEMENTS

Although you can import custom graphics and elements into the Flash environment with the File⇨Import command, Flash also includes several libraries of elements that you can use to get started.

These libraries include a vast assortment of objects that can be resized and used in many different ways.

You can also add imported elements to the libraries by using the Library dialog boxes. You access these dialog boxes by choosing Window⇨Library.

Several default libraries of elements are included with Flash, including Buttons, Bitmaps, and Sounds. These default libraries can be opened using the Windows⇨

Libraries command. The actual libraries are installed on your hard drive with the product.

In this example, you enhance the presentation started earlier in this chapter as you investigate some additional Flash features.

CREATE A PRESENTATION: USE LIBRARY ELEMENTS

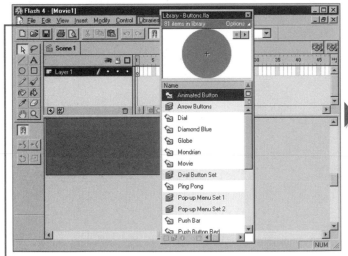

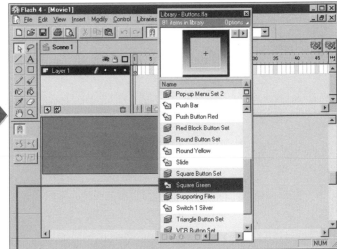

1 Click Libraries.

2 Click Button.

■ The Button Library window opens.

3 Scroll through the available buttons until you find one you would like to use.

How can libraries be organized?

✔ Each library can include folders and elements. Elements can be added to folders by dragging them onto the folder. Double-clicking a folder opens it and reveals its contents. You can delete elements and folders using the Delete icon at the bottom of the window.

Can multiple library objects be stacked on top of one another?

✔ Another way to use the library items is to stack them on top of each other to create new graphical elements. For example, a button can be resized and placed directly behind an image to act as a border to the image.

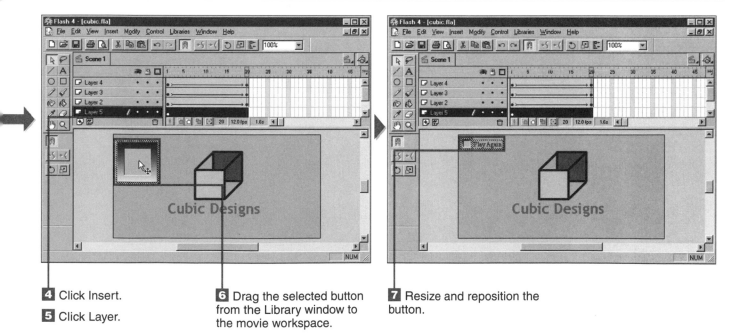

■4 Click Insert.

■5 Click Layer.

■6 Drag the selected button from the Library window to the movie workspace.

■7 Resize and reposition the button.

CREATE A PRESENTATION:ADD INTERACTIVE ELEMENTS

Adding interactivity to the Flash file lets the users interact with your Web page. Interactive elements can make the site more engaging.

Elements in the movie can be made interactive by using the Actions panel of the Instance Properties dialog box.

To see this panel and its interactive options, select an element and click Modify⇨Instance. Doing this opens the Instance Properties dialog box. Within this dialog box, click the Actions tab to view the Actions panel.

The plus sign icon (+) presents a pop-up menu of all the available actions that you can apply to an element to make it interactive.

These actions include Play, Stop, Get URL, Load Movie, Mouse Events, and others.

In this example, you enhance the presentation that was started earlier in this chapter as you investigate some additional Flash features.

CREATE A PRESENTATION:ADD INTERACTIVE ELEMENTS

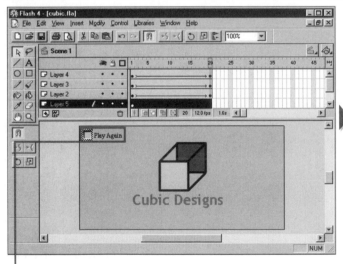

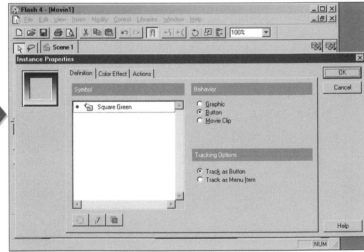

1 Select the elements that you wish to make interactive, such as a button.

2 Click Modify.

3 Click Instance.

■ The Instance Properties dialog box opens.

What mouse event actions are available?

✔ The Actions panel includes several mouse events that can detect and react the movements of the mouse within the Flash movie. These mouse events include Press and Release for detecting mouse clicks, Roll Over and Roll Out for detecting when the mouse cursor is over an element, Drag Over and Drag Out for detecting when elements are being dragged, and Key Press for detecting when certain keyboard keys are pressed.

How can actions be removed?

✔ To remove an action, you simply need to select the action and delete it using the Delete key.

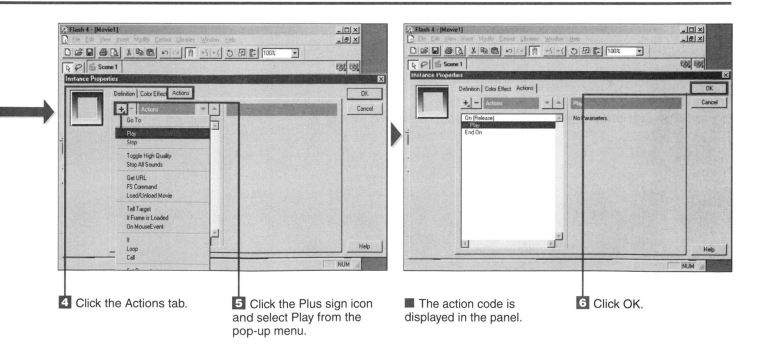

4 Click the Actions tab.

5 Click the Plus sign icon and select Play from the pop-up menu.

■ The action code is displayed in the panel.

6 Click OK.

CREATE A PRESENTATION: ADD SOUND CLIPS

Sounds can be used to add valuable feedback to the user who interacts with the Flash file. If a button makes a clicking sound when the user clicks it, they know that their interaction has been received.

Sound can also be added to Flash movies. These sound files can be imported or included from the default sound library.

Before you add sound to a movie, you should create a new layer to hold the sound element. When you drag a sound file from the library and drop it on the workspace, the sound form is displayed in the current layer starting at the selected frame.

You can modify sounds using the Sound panel of the Frame Properties dialog box. This dialog box can be opened by using the Modify⇨Frame command. The Sound panel includes controls for specifying sound effects and how the sound is synched.

CREATE A PRESENTATION: ADD SOUND CLIPS

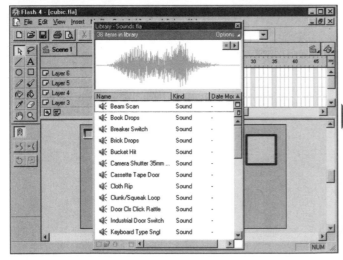

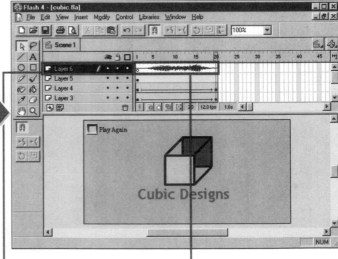

1 Click Libraries.

2 Click Sounds.

■ The Library-Sounds window opens.

3 Click Insert.

4 Click Layer.

5 Select a sound from the library and drag it to the movie workspace.

■ The sound form is displayed in the layer for the active frames.

Can I listen to a sound file?

✔ At the bottom of the Frame Properties dialog box is a Play button that causes the currently selected sound file to be played. A Stop button halts the playing sound.

How do I make a sound loop several times?

✔ Another control in the Frame Properties dialog box is used to control the number of times that the sound loops (plays repeatedly in its entirety). Specifying a value in the Loop field causes the sound to loop that many times. Entering a large value will cause the sound to loop indefinitely.

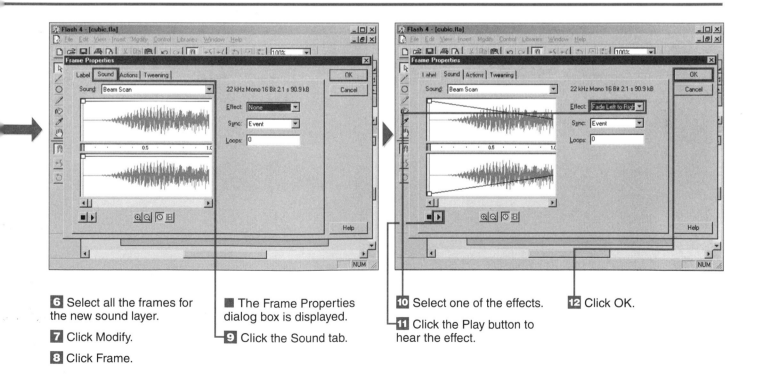

6 Select all the frames for the new sound layer.

7 Click Modify.

8 Click Frame.

■ The Frame Properties dialog box is displayed.

9 Click the Sound tab.

10 Select one of the effects.

11 Click the Play button to hear the effect.

12 Click OK.

CREATE A PRESENTATION: ADD LINKS TO OBJECTS

You can use interactive actions to load new movies, control the action of the current movie, and even interact with other Web pages.

One of the actions available in the Actions panel of the Instance Properties dialog box is the Get URL action. This action retrieves

and loads a specified URL when that frame of the movie is reached, providing a simple way to make an object into a link.

For example, if you create a button and add the Get URL action to it, that button becomes a link to that URL.

Using the Actions panel, you can specify which URL to load. You need to be connected to the Internet to test this action.

In this example, you enhance the presentation that was started earlier in this chapter as you investigate some additional Flash features.

CREATE A PRESENTATION: ADD LINKS TO OBJECTS

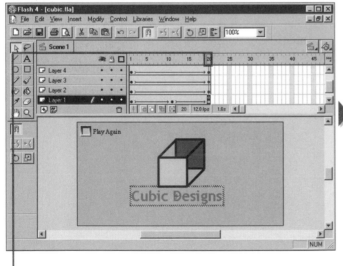

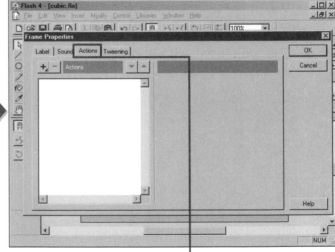

1 Select the text for frame 20.

2 Click Modify.

3 Click Frame.

4 Click the Actions tab.

Can I use the Get URL action to create an e-mail link?

✔ You can also use the Get URL action to create an e-mail link. The only difference needs to be the URL entered in the IRL line. Instead of an *http://* protocol and the domain name, you need to include the *mailto:* protocol and the e-mail address.

When a link in the Flash file is clicked, does the new page replace the current one?

✔ Any links with the Flash file will replace the current Web page with a new one. If you use the Back button to return to the Web page with Flash file, all animations on the Flash document will start over again.

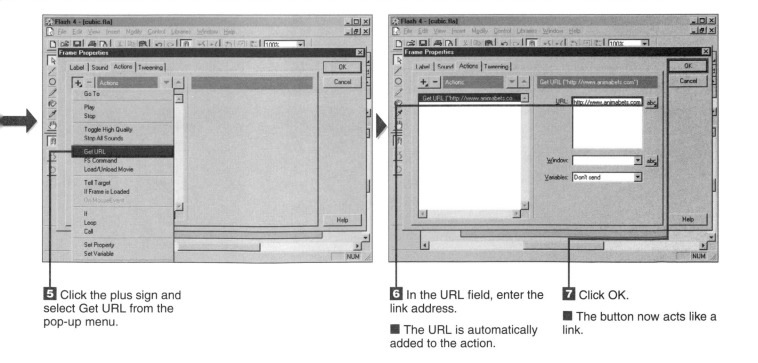

5 Click the plus sign and select Get URL from the pop-up menu.

6 In the URL field, enter the link address.

■ The URL is automatically added to the action.

7 Click OK.

■ The button now acts like a link.

CREATE A PRESENTATION: TEST INTERACTIVE ACTIONS

After you add interactive actions to your Flash movie, you should test those actions. Using the Controller dialog box does not enable these actions, but Flash includes a text mode that you can use to test the interactive nature of your movies.

To enable this test mode, you need to click Control⇨Test Movie. Doing so creates a separate window with the current movie loaded into it. You can return to the workspace by closing this window.

The Control menu also includes other commands for controlling test mode. For example, choosing Control⇨Loop toggles on looping for the movie. You can also select to test the movie at various modem connection speeds, including 14.4, 28.8, and 56 Kbps.

In this example, you enhance the presentation that was started earlier in this chapter as you investigate some additional Flash features.

CREATE A PRESENTATION: TEST INTERACTIVE ACTIONS

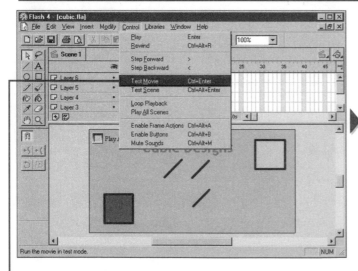

1 Click Control.

2 Click Test Movie.

■ The movie displays in the entire window and starts to play.

3 Click Control.

4 Click Loop.

■ The movie stops after playing through once.

Can I customize the various modem connection speeds to test?

✔ If you click Control⇨Customize, a Customize dialog box opens that enables you to specify a specific modem speed with which to test your movie.

Can I also test my Flash file on high-speed connections like T1, DSL, and others?

✔ Extremely fast, also known as broadband, connection speeds are not of too much concern because users connected at these speeds will not have to wait very long for the Flash files to download. You can set and test these speeds using the Customize option.

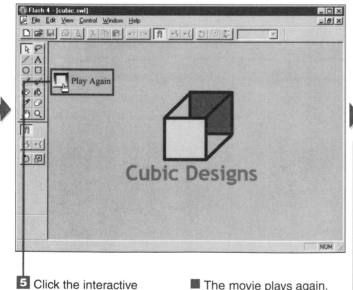

5 Click the interactive button added to the movie.

■ The movie plays again.

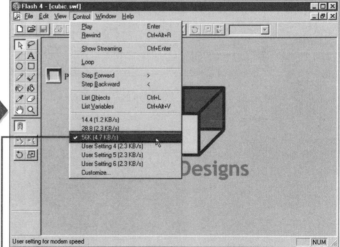

6 Click Control.

7 Click 56K.

■ The movie plays as if it were viewed on a computer with a 56 Kbps modem.

PUBLISH YOUR PRESENTATION

When you finish creating and testing your movie, you are ready to publish it. Publishing is the process of creating the files needed to include and embed the file in your Web page. To do this, you need to tell the Flash program which files it should publish. You can specify these using the Publish Settings dialog box.

This dialog box can be opened by clicking File➪Publish Settings. The Publish Settings dialog box includes a Formats panel in which you can select which file formats you want Flash to generate.

Each file format that you select is added as a new tab to the Publish Settings dialog box. These individual tab panels include the settings for each file format.

When you have the settings ready, click the Publish button to output the files.

For this example, you create the HTML, GIF, and Flash files needed to place the presentation on the World Wide Web.

PUBLISH YOUR PRESENTATION

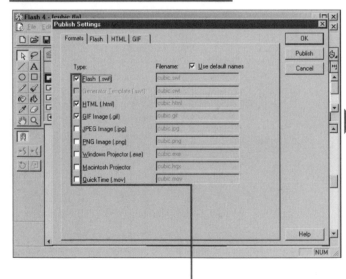

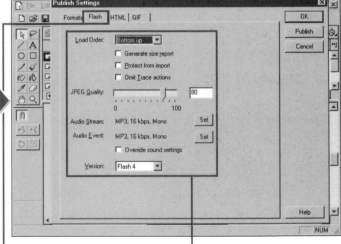

1 Click File.

2 Click Publish Settings.

■ The Publish Settings dialog box opens.

3 Select the file options for Flash to generate for you.

■ A tab is added for each file format that you select.

4 Click the Flash tab.

5 Select the options to use.

■ For this example, the default options work fine.

When I click the Publish button, where are the files saved?

✔ The designated file formats are saved in the same directory as the saved Flash file. From this directory, you can copy them to a server where they can be viewed on the Web.

When files are published, how are they named?

✔ The default is to name the file formats the same as the name of the saved Flash file. You can change this name by entering a unique name in the Formats panel. For example, if you enter the name, MyFlash in the Formats panel, the files will be named MyFlash.html, MyFlash.swf, and myFlash.gif.

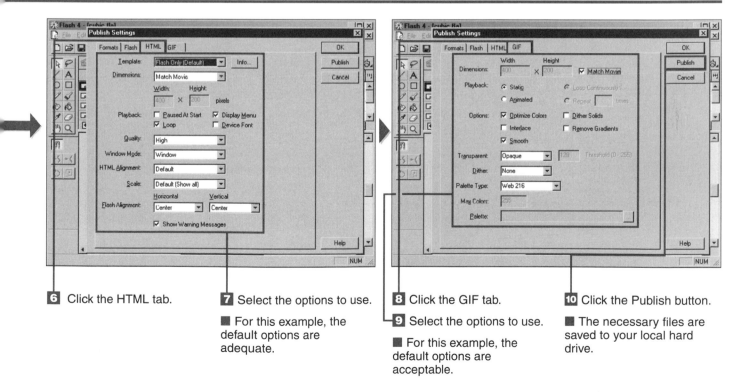

6 Click the HTML tab.

7 Select the options to use.

■ For this example, the default options are adequate.

8 Click the GIF tab.

9 Select the options to use.

■ For this example, the default options are acceptable.

10 Click the Publish button.

■ The necessary files are saved to your local hard drive.

VIEW THE FLASH PRESENTATION IN A BROWSER

After you generate the file formats for the Flash movie, you can open the HTML file in a browser to see the final movie. Your browser needs to have the Flash plug-in installed (see "Download and Install the Flash Plug-in" earlier in this chapter).

The HTML file that is generated by the Flash program contains only the code required to reference and play the Flash movie. If you want to add this code to another HTML file, you need to open the file in an editor like Notepad and copy and paste the code to the desired HTML file.

The GIF files that are generated when the Flash file is published can be used to represent the Flash movie to browsers that do not have the Flash plug-in installed. This can be done by placing an `<img/>` tag within the `<object>` tags. Then, if the Flash file cannot load, an image of the Flash file will be displayed.

This example looks at all the various files that were published, including the GIF and HTML files.

VIEW THE FLASH PRESENTATION IN A BROWSER

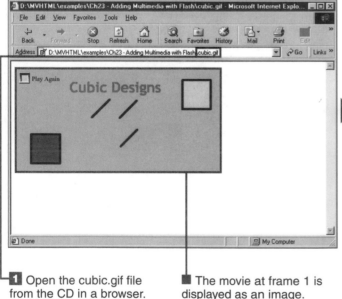

1 Open the cubic.gif file from the CD in a browser.

■ The movie at frame 1 is displayed as an image.

2 Open the cubic.html file from the CD in Notepad.

Can I view the generated files without being connected to the Internet?

✔ If the Flash files are located on your local machine, you can view them in a browser locally without being connected to the Internet. If your Flash movie includes any actions that require a connection, such as the Get URL action, you must be connected for this to work.

Do the Flash SWF and FLA files need to be included in the same directory as the HTML file?

✔ The HTML file references the SWF file, and it needs to be included with the HTML file. The FLA file, on the other hand, is the project file that can be loaded into the Flash program. This file does not need to be included in the same directory as the HTML file. If you need to make changes to the Flash file, you need the FLA file.

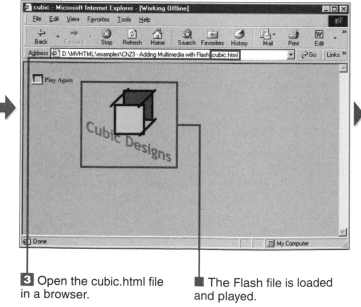

3 Open the cubic.html file in a browser.

■ The Flash file is loaded and played.

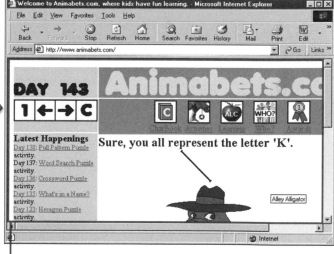

■ When the movie finishes playing, the specified URL is loaded.

USE JAVA APPLETS

Java applets are small programs that can run within a browser. These small programs are written using the Java programming language. The Java programming language is a robust language that is similar in many ways to C++, but Java includes many unique capabilities that make it ideal for writing programs that run on the Web.

The way Java is designed, it can be used on the Web without causing any problems to a user's system. If a user accesses a Web applet that is designed to destroy the user's computer, the Java system does not permit the program access to the user's system files. This security lets users execute Java programs without fearing that they can destroy their system.

The Java Language is Portable, Object-Oriented, and Secure

One of Java's traits that makes it suitable for the Web is its portability. Java programs can be written once and run on multiple different platforms. On the Web, where many different computers are all networked together, Java enables a computer to run the program whether it is a Windows, Macintosh, or UNIX machine.

Java is also *object-oriented,* a programming paradigm that enables a single program to be broken up into smaller pieces. The pieces that are common between multiple programs can be reused rather than being rewritten, which saves programmers time because they can build and use standard libraries of functions that can be reused in a variety of ways.

Compiling Java Applets

Just like writing HTML, you can write Java code using Notepad. These files have the .java extension. However, you cannot view or run Java files in a browser until you compile them.

Compiling is the process of converting Java files into a class file. *Class files* are streamlined files that only can be interpreted by a system program called the *Java Virtual Machine* (JVM). Class files are identified with the .class extension.

The program that is used to compile Java files can be found within the Java Development Kit (JDK). The latest JDK can be downloaded from the Sun Microsystems Java site at www.javasoft.com. After you download the JDK, you must install it to your computer. After the installation finishes, you can compile your Java programs.

The compiler examines the Java file for errors before producing a class file. If any errors exist in the Java file, an error is reported. When all errors are eliminated from the Java file, a class file is generated.

Embedding Java Applets

Java applets can be embedded within a Web page using the <object> tag. This tag points to a Java class file. When the browser encounters an embedded Java applet, the Java Virtual Machine is loaded into memory and the applet is run within the browser.

The <object> tag includes several attributes that can be used to change the dimensions and alignment of the applet.

DOWNLOAD THE JAVA DEVELOPMENT KIT (JDK)

Writing Java files in Notepad does you no good until you compile the files into class files.

To compile Java class files, you must download and install the Java Development Kit (JDK) from the Sun Microsystems Java site at www.javasoft.com/products.

The Sun Java site includes links to the latest JDK. The JDK includes many different utilities that can help you as you develop Java applets. The JDK also includes many libraries of Java code that you can access as you write new programs.

The JDK also includes the Java Virtual Machine (JVM) for the

system that you are developing on. With the JVM installed, you will be able to test the Java files that you create and compile.

Separate JDK versions are available for a variety of platforms including Windows, Macintosh, Solaris, and UNIX. Be sure to download the right version for your system.

DOWNLOAD THE JAVA DEVELOPMENT KIT (JDK)

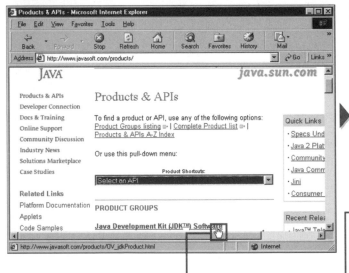

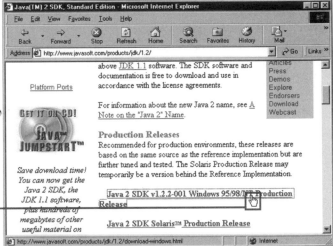

1 Open the Sun Java page containing a link to the JDK.

2 Click the JDK link.

3 Click the link to the operating system that you are using.

Where else can I find the JDK?

✔ You can download the JDK from many places on Web, but the Sun Microsystems Java site is the best place to get the JDK because it is updated frequently. The Sun Java site always has the latest version.

Which JDK version should I use?

✔ Sun Microsystems is continually updating the Java language and the JDK. With each downloaded JDK, make sure that you are aware of the language changes before you start working with the JDK. These changes can be found online at the Sun Java site.

Is the JDK different from the SDK?

✔ The JDK is the bare minimum set of pieces needed to compile and produce class files. The Java Software Development Kit (SDK) includes many additional packages that enhance your development.

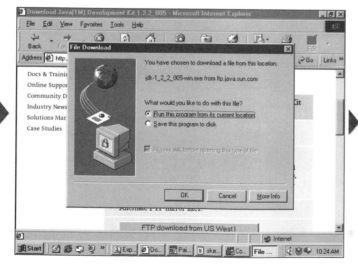

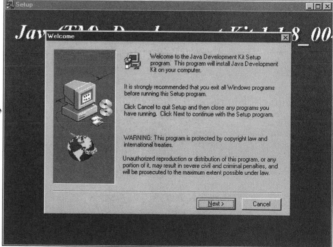

■ The File Download dialog box appears.

4 Select the Run this file from its current location option.

5 Click OK.

■ The JDK installation program runs. Follow the installation instruction to complete the installation.

WRITE JAVA PROGRAMS

Several advanced Java tools enable you to work in an integrated environment. These tools include Microsoft Visual J++, Symantec Visual Café and Borland JBuilder. But these tools are not really necessary. You can write Java programs using a standard text editor, such as Notepad.

Java is a complex programming language that can generate small applets for Web pages as well as full-blown commercial applications.

To learn the language, you must spend some time studying. You can choose from many Java books and online training sites.

After you enter the code, save the file with the .java extension. This helps you to identify the file as Java code to the compiler.

This example is just a small tip of the iceberg of what is possible with Java.

WRITE JAVA PROGRAMS

test1.java - Notepad

```
import java.awt.*;
import java.util.*;
```

test2.java - Notepad

```
import java.awt.*;
import java.util.*;

public class test extends java.applet.Applet {

}
```

1 Open a new file in Notepad and enter two `import` keywords.

2 Type the import library to import after each `import` keyword.

3 Add a semicolon (;) to the end of each `import` statement.

4 Save the file as test1.java.

5 Open the test1.java file in Notepad.

6 Add a public class name that extends the java.applet.Applet class.

7 After the class name definition, add opening and closing brackets.

8 Save the file as test2.java.

Which Java development environments are available?

✔ Many Java-based development environments are available. Microsoft makes Visual J++, Borland has a product called JBuilder, and Symantec's product is called Visual Café. You can find demo versions of these products at the respective company Web sites.

What do the import statements do?

✔ The import statements at the top of the code allow access to specific Java libraries. These libraries include functions that are used within the code. For example, the AWT library includes functions like drawString, which is used to display text to the applet.

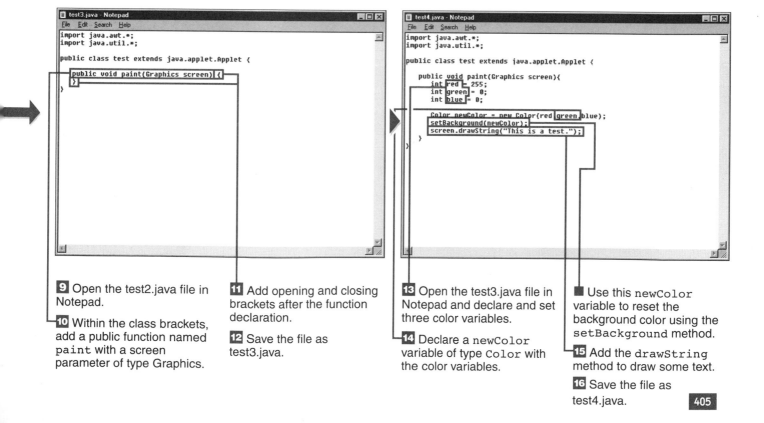

9 Open the test2.java file in Notepad.

10 Within the class brackets, add a public function named paint with a screen parameter of type Graphics.

11 Add opening and closing brackets after the function declaration.

12 Save the file as test3.java.

13 Open the test3.java file in Notepad and declare and set three color variables.

14 Declare a newColor variable of type Color with the color variables.

■ Use this newColor variable to reset the background color using the setBackground method.

15 Add the drawString method to draw some text.

16 Save the file as test4.java.

COMPILE JAVA CODE

After you write some Java code, you need to compile the code into a class file. Compiling the code produces a small portable class file that can be executed within a browser.

A program called javac.exe in the JDK compiles the Java code. You can find it in the \bin directory under the main JDK directory.

The compiler command can be run from a command line like the DOS window. To compile, you need to type the **javac.exe** command followed by the name of the Java file you want to compile.

If the Java file has any errors, the compiler recognizes them and displays an error message. If the Java file does not have any errors, the compiled class file is created with the same name as the Java file.

COMPILE JAVA CODE

1 Click Start⇨Programs⇨ MS DOS Prompt to open a DOS window.

2 Use the cd command to open the directory where the Java file is located.

3 Type the compile directive, **javac.exe**, starting with its path, which is typically something like c:\jdk1.2.2\bin\javac .exe.

4 Type the name of the Java file.

How can I fix a Java program that has errors?

✔ If an error message appears while you compile a Java file, you see the line and place where the error occurred. It also gives you a brief error message that helps you identify the problem. From this information, you can return to the Java file, correct the error, resave the file, and then try to compile it again. The class file cannot be created until you remove all errors.

If the Java file compiles without any errors, does a message appear stating that the compile was successful?

✔ If a Java file is successfully compiled using the JDK, no message is displayed, which can be confusing. If you view the directory, however, you may notice that the class file has been created and does actually exist.

5 Press the Enter key to execute the command.

■ The compiler generates a class file. If an error exists in the Java file, it will be displayed.

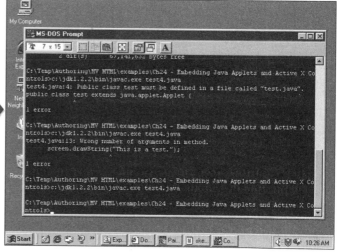

■ If the file successfully compiles, the compiler creates the class file in the same directory as the Java file.

EMBED AN APPLET

Class files can be embedded and executed with the browser. To do this, you need to use the `<object>` tags.

Within the opening `<object>` tag, include the `classid` and `codetype` attributes. The `classid` is set to the keyword `java:` followed by the class file name. The `codetype` defines the

MIME type to the browser. For Java files it is set to application/octet-stream.

The `<object>` tags can also include other attributes like `width` and `height` to set the applet dimensions and the `align` attribute to align the applet to the left or right margin.

If the applet class file exists in a subdirectory, you can use the `codebase` attribute to indicate the name of the subdirectory. For example, `<object codebase="classes/myJava.class"` would embed the class file name myJava.class in the classes subdirectory.

1 Open the HTML file and add a set of `<object>` tags within the `<body>` tags.

2 Type **classid** and **codetype** attributes.

3 Set `classid` to java: and the class filename.

4 Set the `codetype` attribute equal to application/octet-stream.

5 Add some alternative text in within the `<object>` tags.

6 Save the file.

7 Open the file in a browser.

■ The applet loads and runs in the browser.

408

Can I use applets without writing the Java code?

✔ You need the Java files only to compile the class files. If you have the class file, you do not need the Java file unless you want to make changes to the applet. Many Java applet repositories on the Web let you use precompiled Java applets. To embed files obtained from these repositories, you do not need to download the JDK and compile the code.

Can I determine if an object in the browser is an applet?

✔ If you move the mouse cursor over the top of an applet in the browser, the Status Bar at the bottom of the browser displays the message, "Applet Started." This message can be used to help identify applets embedded within the Web page.

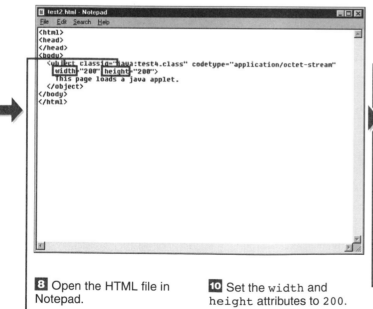

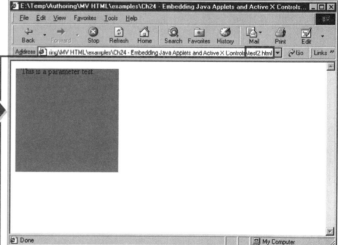

8 Open the HTML file in Notepad.

9 Add the `width` and `height` attributes to the `<object>` tag.

10 Set the `width` and `height` attributes to `200`.

11 Save the file with a new name.

12 Open the file in a browser.

■ The applet loads with the new dimensions.

CHANGE APPLET PARAMETERS

Using parameters, you can make Java applets that include variables that can be modified within the Web page file. If a Java file is coded correctly, you can specify applet parameter values within the Web page file that can affect the output of the applet. These parameter values are sent to

the applet from the HTML file using the <param/> tag. The <param/> tag includes two attributes—name and value. The name attribute is the name of the parameter, and the value is the value that is sent to the applet.

The name attribute needs to match the name of the variable included

in the Java code. All parameters sent to the applet as part of the <param/> tag are received by the applet as a string. These strings need to be converted to a number type if you intend to do calculations with them.

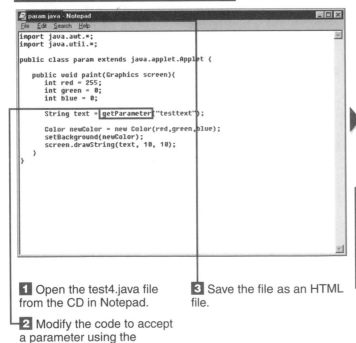

```
import java.awt.*;
import java.util.*;

public class param extends java.applet.Applet {

    public void paint(Graphics screen){
        int red = 255;
        int green = 0;
        int blue = 0;

        String text = getParameter("testtext");

        Color newColor = new Color(red,green,blue);
        setBackground(newColor);
        screen.drawString(text, 10, 10);
    }
}
```

1 Open the test4.java file from the CD in Notepad.

2 Modify the code to accept a parameter using the getParameter function.

3 Save the file as an HTML file.

4 Enter the command in the DOS window to compile the class file for this code.

If I download an applet from a Web repository, how do I find out the acceptable parameters?

✔ When you download an applet off the Web, you can find out what the acceptable parameters are by searching the Java file for the getParameter method. If you do not have access to the Java file, the applet probably includes a Read Me file or some other form of documentation that lists the acceptable parameters.

What is the benefit of using the <param/> tag?

✔ Using the <param/> tag, you can control the applet using parameters that are sent from the Web page. This functionality does not require the Java class to be recompiled for a subtle change. For example, if you send a color as a parameter, the applet can be programmed to use the color parameter as the background color. If you ever want to change the background color, you need only to change the value in the <param/> tag instead of the entire Java class file.

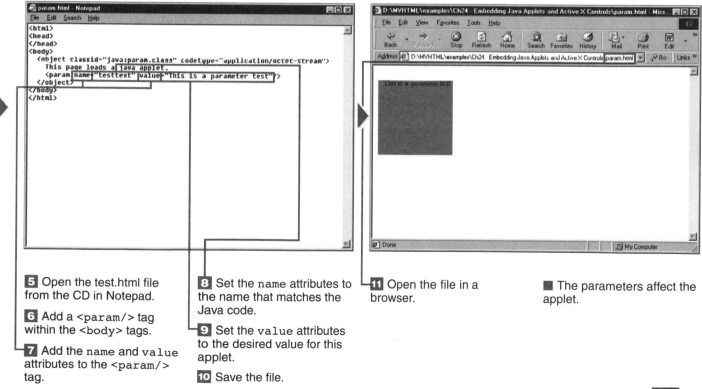

5 Open the test.html file from the CD in Notepad.

6 Add a <param/> tag within the <body> tags.

7 Add the name and value attributes to the <param/> tag.

8 Set the name attributes to the name that matches the Java code.

9 Set the value attributes to the desired value for this applet.

10 Save the file.

11 Open the file in a browser.

■ The parameters affect the applet.

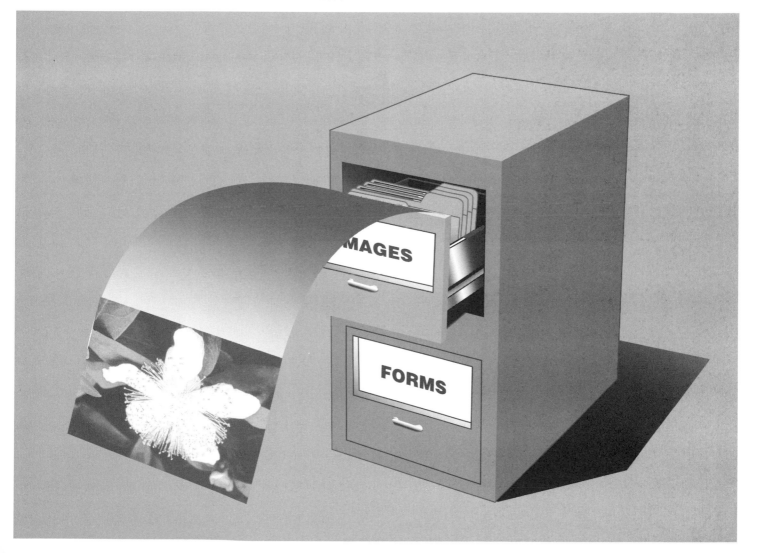

USING JAVASCRIPT EVENTS

Although Java applets, covered in Chapter 23, enables you to embed programmed content within a Web page, these programs are only referenced by the HTML code. JavaScript, on the other hand, is a scripting language that is interpreted by the browser as the page loads. This enables the scripting syntax to be placed alongside the HTML code.

Using JavaScript is advantageous because it is processed locally on the browser. The browser does not have to ask the server to process the JavaScript commands or to send more information. The browser runs all the data and functions within itself.

JavaScript Events

JavaScript *events* are bits of code that link user actions to the scripts that need to be executed. These actions include clicking the mouse, pressing a keyboard key, selecting or changing form elements, and loading and unloading a Web page.

JavaScript events can be positioned within an HTML tags just like the other attributes. Events can be set equal to a small line of JavaScript code or to the name of a JavaScript function declared elsewhere in the Web page.

For example, the onclick event can be added as an attribute to the <button> tag and set equal to the function name blink, like this:

```
<button onclick="blink();"/>
```

This tag not only displays a button on the Web page, but when this button is clicked, the blink JavaScript function executes.

You can use a number of different events within a Web page, and the places where they can be used are different for each event. This chapter covers some of the more common JavaScript events.

Mouse Events

Mouse events are fired when the user clicks or moves the mouse. If the user clicks the mouse button once, the onclick event fires. If the user clicks the mouse button twice, ondblclick is fired.

For more precise details, you can use the onmousedown event to signal when the mouse button is pressed down and the onmouseup event when a mouse button is released.

The onmouseover event detects when the mouse cursor moves over the top of an element. The onmouseout event detects when the mouse cursor moves off an element.

Keyboard Events

The onkeypress event can be used to detect when a key on the keyboard is pressed. The specific key that was pressed can be found in the window.event.keycode object.

Similar to the mouse button clicks, the onkeydown event detects when the key is  first pressed and held down, and the onkeyup event is fired when the pressed key is released.

Selection Events

When an element is highlighted in the browser, the element is said to have *focus*. The onfocus event signals when an element has the focus. Pressing the Tab key can change this focus. When an element loses the focus, the onblur event is fired.

When an element is selected, the onselect event is fired.

Miscellaneous Events

Another common event used with form elements is the onchange event. This event fires whenever the data of the form element is changed.

The onload event detects when a Web page has completely finished loading. Similarly, the onunload event is fired when a Web page is unloaded. This happens when the user leaves the current page or presses the Reset button.

When a Web page that is loading into the browser is cancelled, the onabort event is called.

Two form buttons have specific functions—*submit* and *reset*. These same functions can be detected using the onsubmit and onreset events.

DETECT A MOUSE CLICK

One of the keys to interacting with the user is to detect mouse clicks. When a user clicks a Web page, one usually expects something to happen.

When the user clicks on a Web page element like a form button, a `click` event is triggered. This event is detected by the `onclick`

event. This event can then be used to start another section of JavaScript code.

Web page designers typically add the `onclick` event to form buttons created using the `<input/>` and/or `<button>` tags. The `onclick` event can also be used with the checkbox and radio

button elements and within the `<a>` tag. Form elements like radio buttons and checkboxes are covered in Chapter 17.

This example uses the skeleton.html file from the CD, but you can apply the steps to any situation.

DECTECT A MOUSE CLICK

```
<html>
<head>
</head>
<body>
   <form name="form1">
      <input/>
   </form>
</body>
</html>
```

```
<html>
<head>
</head>
<body>
   <form name="form1">
      <input type="button" name="button1" value="Hello"/>
   </form>
</body>
</html>
```

1 Open the HTML file.

2 Add a set of tags to reflect the object you want the mouse to click.

■ In this case, `<form>` and `<input/>` tags are added.

3 Add the `name` attribute to the `<form>` tag and set it to a reference name.

■ In this case, the `name` attribute is set to `form1`.

4 Add the `type`, `name`, and `value` attributes to the `<input/>` tag.

5 Set the `type` attribute to `button`, the `name` attribute to `button1`, and the `value` attribute to the text that will appear on the button face (`"Hello"` in this example).

When can the onmousedown and onmouseup events be used?

✔ The `onclick` event detects when the mouse button is clicked and released. The `onmousedown` and `onmouseup` events detect the individual actions of clicking and releasing the mouse button. The user could press the mouse and not release it. In this case, the `onclick` event would not detect this action, but the `onmousedown` event would.

Can the browser detect the difference between a single click and a double-click?

✔ JavaScript includes separate events for a single click and a double-click. The event for a single click is `onclick` and the event for detecting a double-click is `ondblclick`.

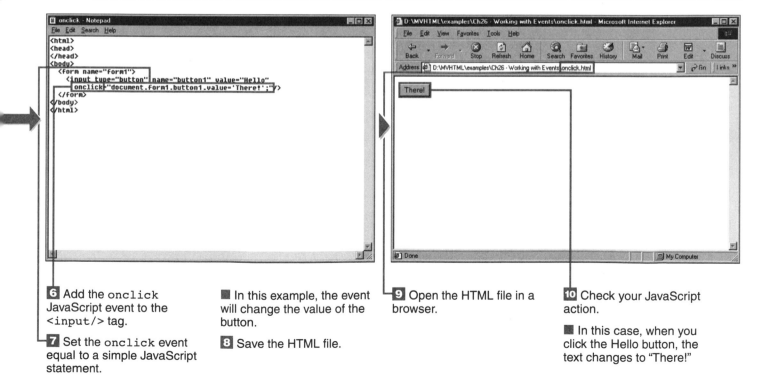

6 Add the `onclick` JavaScript event to the `<input/>` tag.

7 Set the `onclick` event equal to a simple JavaScript statement.

■ In this example, the event will change the value of the button.

8 Save the HTML file.

9 Open the HTML file in a browser.

10 Check your JavaScript action.

■ In this case, when you click the Hello button, the text changes to "There!"

DETECT A DOUBLE-CLICK

Double-clicking is very similar to a single click, except that the user rapidly clicks twice in succession instead of once on the mouse button.

The `ondblclick` event detects double-clicks. You can add this event to all of the same elements as the `onclick` event, including the `<input/>`, `<button>`, and `<a>` tags.

For example, the statement `<input type="button" value="Start "ondblclick="document.write('Hello')"/>` would create a single button. When the user double-clicks this button, the text, "Hello" will be printed to the screen.

The `ondlbclick` event can be used independent of the `onclick` event. You can even use these two events together to make a single button with multiple functions.

This example uses the onclick.html file from the CD, but you can apply the steps to any situation.

DETECT A DOUBLE-CLICK

1 Open the HTML file.

2 Add the `ondblclick` event.

■ If the code includes an `onclick` event, add the `ondblclick` event after the `onclick` event.

3 Set the `ondblclick` event equal to some JavaScript code.

■ This example causes the button value to change again.

4 Save the HTML file.

5 Open the HTML file in a browser.

■ The designated elements are displayed on the page. In this case, the browser displays a single button.

Can two events be added to a single tag?

✔ A single tag can include multiple events. The browser processes these events in the order that they are listed. For example, if a tag includes both an `onclick` and `ondblclick` events, both will be processed when the element is clicked.

If the onclick and ondblclick events are added to a button, will both events be detected if the button is clicked twice?

✔ A button that includes both the `onclick` and `ondblclick` events will detect both in the process of clicking twice. Even though the user clicks twice to fire the `ondblclick` event, the `onclick` event will still fire the first time the button is clicked.

If the user clicks twice slowly, will the ondblclick event be detected?

✔ A double-click is only detected if the user clicks quickly enough to detect a double-click according to the system settings.

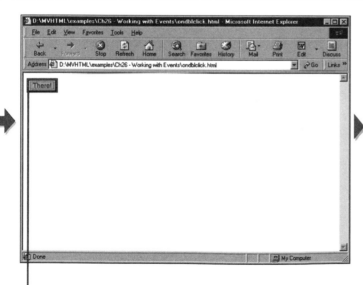

6 If the file contains an `onclick` event, click the object that triggers the `onclick` event.

■ In this example, the text on the button changes.

7 Double-click the object of the `ondblclick` event.

■ In this example, double-clicking the button changes the text again.

CREATE ROLLOVER BUTTONS

You can use *rollover* buttons to help the user navigate a Web page. When the mouse cursor moves over the top of a rollover button, the button changes its appearance.

JavaScript accomplishes this by replacing the original image with a new image by using the onmouseover and onmouseout events.

The onmouseover event is set to display a new image in place of the original, and the onmouseout event is set to display the original image.

These event settings cause the new image to display whenever the mouse cursor is over the top of the button and the original image to display when the mouse cursor leaves the button.

The onmouseover and onmouseout events complement hypertext links, image maps, and images.

This example uses the skeleton.html file from the CD, but you can apply the steps to any situation.

CREATE ROLLOVER BUTTONS

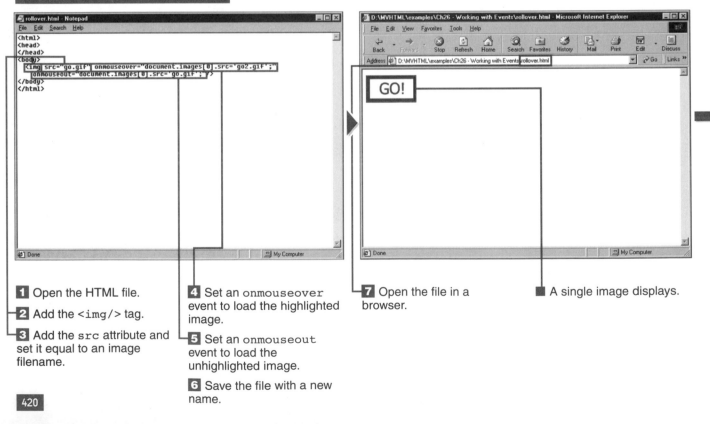

1 Open the HTML file.

2 Add the <img/> tag.

3 Add the src attribute and set it equal to an image filename.

4 Set an onmouseover event to load the highlighted image.

5 Set an onmouseout event to load the unhighlighted image.

6 Save the file with a new name.

7 Open the file in a browser.

■ A single image displays.

Can any events detect when the mouse cursor moves?

✔ In addition to the **onmouseover** and **onmouseout** events, the **onmousemove** event can be used to detect when the mouse cursor is moved over an element. This event can be used to detect when the mouse is sitting idle and when it is being used.

Can any events be used to detect when the mouse button is pressed and held?

✔ The **onmousedown** event detects when the mouse button is pressed and held on top of an element. A similar event is the **onmouseup** event, which detects when the mouse button is released on top of an element. When the user clicks an element, both these events are fired along with the **onclick** event.

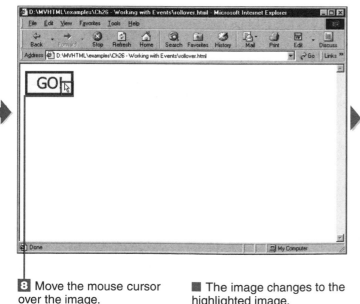

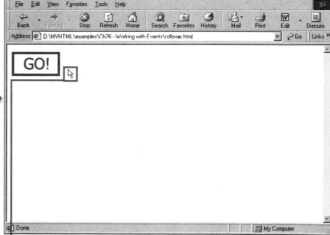

8 Move the mouse cursor over the image.

■ The image changes to the highlighted image.

9 Move the mouse cursor away from the image.

■ The image reverts to its original look.

421

DETECT A KEY PRESS

Text can be entered into a text field or `textarea` element using the keyboard, but you may sometimes want to detect a single key press, such as a key to start a certain function.

When a keystroke on the keyboard is pressed, the `onkeypress` event can detect it. The `window.event.keyCode` object

identifies the actual key that was pressed.

Using this event, you can check for the key that was pressed and react accordingly.

For example, for the statement `<input type="button" value="Start" onkeypress="if`

`(window.event.keyCode ='S')document.write ('Hello')"/>` the onkeypress event checks for the S key. If this key is pressed, the word "Hello" is displayed on the screen.

This example uses the skeleton.html file from the CD, but you can apply the steps to any situation.

DETECT A KEY PRESS

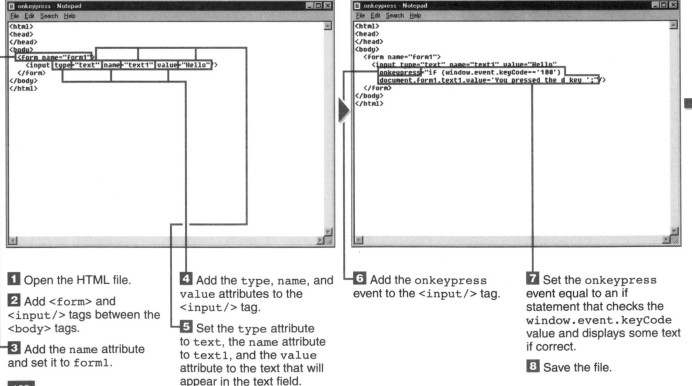

1 Open the HTML file.

2 Add `<form>` and `<input/>` tags between the `<body>` tags.

3 Add the `name` attribute and set it to `form1`.

4 Add the `type`, `name`, and `value` attributes to the `<input/>` tag.

5 Set the `type` attribute to `text`, the `name` attribute to `text1`, and the `value` attribute to the text that will appear in the text field.

6 Add the `onkeypress` event to the `<input/>` tag.

7 Set the `onkeypress` event equal to an if statement that checks the `window.event.keyCode` value and displays some text if correct.

8 Save the file.

How are the onkeydown and onkeyup events used?

✔ The onkeydown and onkeyup events are very similar to the onmousedown and onmouseup events. The user could press a keyboard key and not release it. In this case, the onkeydown event would detect this action, but the onkeypress event would not until the keyboard key was finally released.

Are the onkeydown and onkeyup events fired when the onkeypress event is fired?

✔ The onkeydown and onkeyup events will fire whenever the onkeypress event is fired, except when the onkeydown event is detected before the onkeyup event.

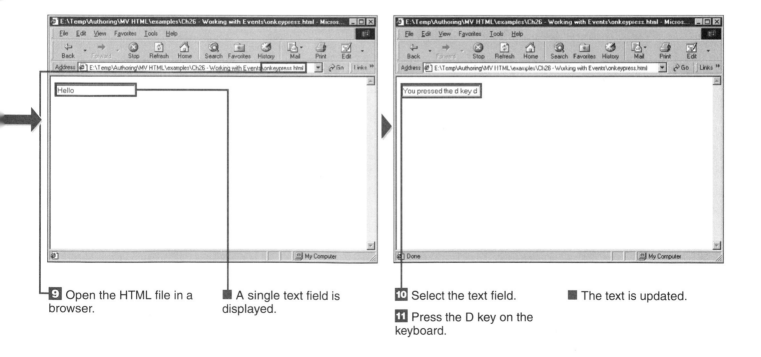

-9 Open the HTML file in a browser.

■ A single text field is displayed.

10 Select the text field.

11 Press the D key on the keyboard.

■ The text is updated.

SET FOCUS

*F*ocus determines which form element has the attention of the keyboard. For example, if a button has the focus and you press the Enter key, the Web page would respond just as if you had clicked the button with the mouse cursor.

Using the Tab key, you can move the focus between different form elements. You can set the order in which elements of a form receive the focus using the `tabindex` attribute. This attribute is discussed in detail in Chapter 17.

As the focus changes, you can detect when an element receives the focus using the `onfocus` event. You can also detect when an element loses focus using the `onblur` event.

The `onfocus` and `onblur` events can be used with the `<select>`, `<input/>`, and `<textarea>` tags, as well as, with framesets.

This example uses the onkeypress.html file from the CD, but you can apply the steps to any situation.

SET FOCUS

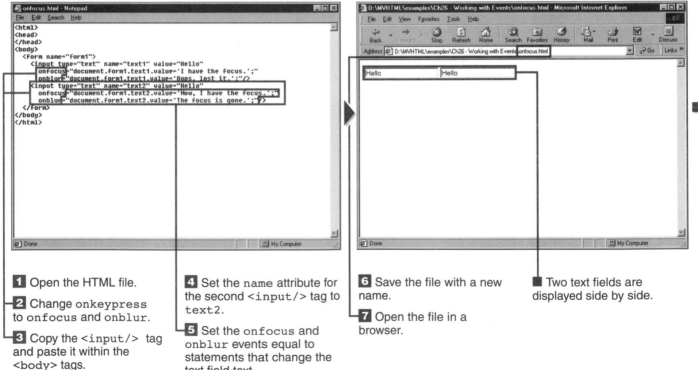

1 Open the HTML file.

2 Change `onkeypress` to `onfocus` and `onblur`.

3 Copy the `<input/>` tag and paste it within the `<body>` tags.

4 Set the `name` attribute for the second `<input/>` tag to `text2`.

5 Set the `onfocus` and `onblur` events equal to statements that change the text field text.

6 Save the file with a new name.

7 Open the file in a browser.

■ Two text fields are displayed side by side.

Where is the onselect event used?

✔ The onselect event can be used with text fields and textarea elements to detect when a section of text is selected. When a section of text is selected, you can replace, delete, or change it.

Can any events detect when a form is reset or submitted?

✔ Two useful events exist that you can use with forms: the onreset and onsubmit events. The onreset event happens when a reset button is clicked, and the onsubmit event happens when a submit button is clicked. Using these events, you can override the default HTML action that happens when these buttons are used.

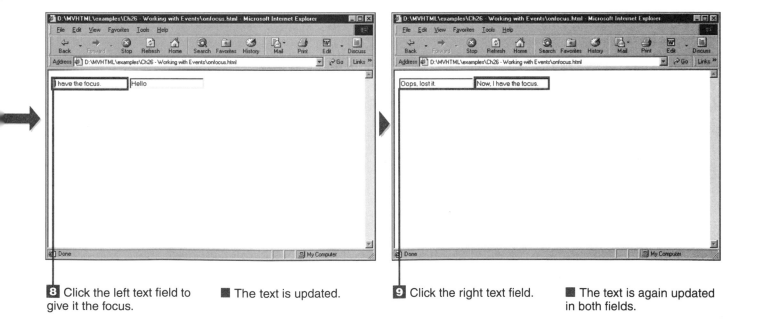

■8 Click the left text field to give it the focus.

■ The text is updated.

■9 Click the right text field.

■ The text is again updated in both fields.

SELECT A PULL-DOWN MENU SELECTION

The onchange event can be used to detect whenever a form element changes. You might find this event handy if your Web page requires the viewer to make choices. For example, if you have a selection list on your page, something like a list of desserts to order, onchange can detect when the user makes or changes their selection.

Chapter 17 describes the selection list element as a way to offer a list of choices to the user.

Another very useful event is the onchange event. This event can detect whenever a form element changes. This can be useful for detecting when a different selection list item is chosen.

The onchange event works with the `<select>`, `<input/>`, and `<textarea>` tags.

This example uses the onkeypress.html file from the CD, but you can apply the steps to any situation.

SELECT A PULL-DOWN MENU SELECTION

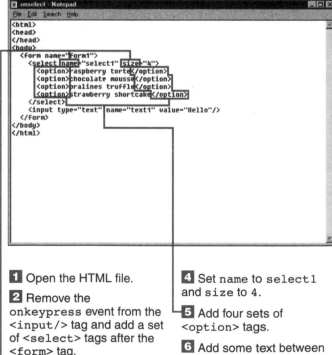

1 Open the HTML file.

2 Remove the onkeypress event from the `<input/>` tag and add a set of `<select>` tags after the `<form>` tag.

3 Type **name** and **size**.

4 Set name to `select1` and size to 4.

5 Add four sets of `<option>` tags.

6 Add some text between each `<option>` tag.

7 Add the onchange event to the opening `<select>` tag.

8 Set the onchange event to some JavaScript that changes the text in the text field.

9 Save the file with a new name.

When does the onchange event happen with text and/or textarea fields?

✔ Within a text or a `textarea` field, you can only make changes when the element has focus. You can put an element in focus by clicking or tabbing to it. The `onchange` event does not trigger until the text or `textarea` field loses focus. It can lose focus by clicking away from the element or pressing the Tab key.

Can other scripting languages be used instead of JavaScript?

✔ JavaScript is the most popular client-based Web scripting language because it is supported on both Netscape Navigator and Internet Explorer, but other scripting languages exist. Setting the `language` attribute to another language such as VBScript enables browsers to use these other languages. VBScript is similar in syntax to Visual Basic, but only the Internet Explorer browser supports it.

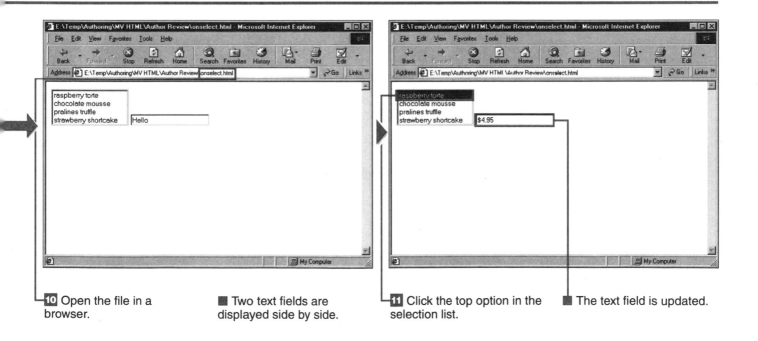

10 Open the file in a browser.

■ Two text fields are displayed side by side.

11 Click the top option in the selection list.

■ The text field is updated.

CREATE A LOADING MESSAGE

As Web pages get more complex, they may take longer to load. This can be confusing to the user who is not quite sure whether the page has fully loaded. Using the onload event, you can notify the user when the page has finished loading.

The onload event is usually placed within the <body> tag.

A similar event to onload is the onunload event. This event happens before the current page is left or when the page is reset using the browser's Reset button.

Using the onunload event, you can provide some last minute details to users before they leave the Web page, such as closing any windows that were opened.

This example uses the skeleton.html file from the CD, but you can apply the steps to any situation.

CREATE A LOADING MESSAGE

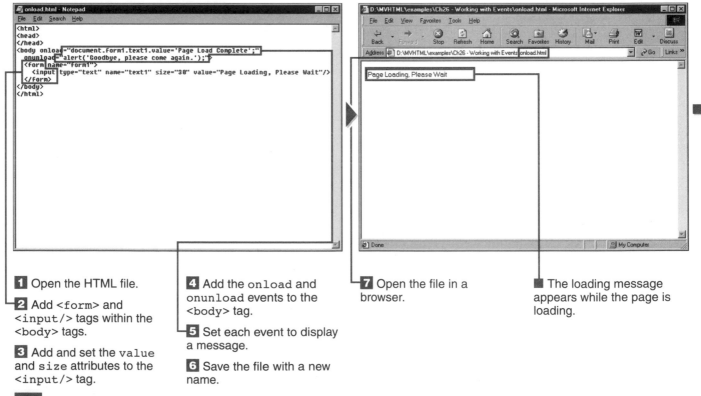

1 Open the HTML file.

2 Add <form> and <input/> tags within the <body> tags.

3 Add and set the value and size attributes to the <input/> tag.

4 Add the onload and onunload events to the <body> tag.

5 Set each event to display a message.

6 Save the file with a new name.

7 Open the file in a browser.

■ The loading message appears while the page is loading.

Does any event fire when a loading Web page is canceled?

✔ Anytime a Web page is loading in a browser, the user can cancel the page by clicking the Stop browser button. This action can be detected using the `onabort` event. This provides a useful way to inform the user what has happened if all the elements have not loaded.

Does any event detect when something goes wrong?

✔ The `onerror` event lets you detect when an error loading elements occurs. If the browser experiences trouble loading an image or a page, then the `onerror` event fires. Using this event, you can present a message to the user that is easy to understand.

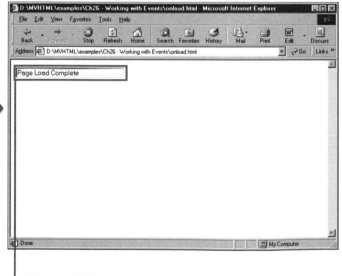

■ After the Web page has finished loading, the message is updated.

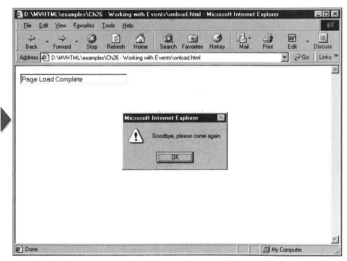

8 Load a separate Web page in the browser.

■ An alert box appears with a message.

ACCESS JAVASCRIPT FUNCTIONS WITH EVENTS

JavaScript events can be set equal to a single JavaScript statement, but they can also access and execute a separate function that is contained within a set of `<script>` tags.

The `<script>` tag accepts the `type` and `language` attributes. The `type` attribute can be set to a

recognized MIME type, such as `text/javascript`. The `language` attribute is another way to specify the scripting language to use. For JavaScript, it is simply set to `javascript`.

The `<script>` tags can appear anywhere within the `<head>` or `<body>` tags.

Functions are declared using the function keyword followed by a function name. The function can be executed by setting its function name equal to an event.

This example uses the skeleton.html file from the CD, but you can apply the steps to any situation.

ACCESS JAVASCRIPT FUNCTIONS WITH EVENTS

1 Open the HTML file.

2 Add a set of `<script>` tags within the `<head>` tags.

3 Add the `type` attribute to the `<script>` tag.

4 Set the `type` attribute equal to `text/javascript`.

5 Add the `changebg()` function.

6 Add a set of brackets after the function statement.

7 Within the function brackets add the line `document.bgcolor`.

8 Set the `bgcolor` line equal to `purple`.

9 Add a semicolon (;) to the end of the line.

10 Save the file with a new name.

Why do functions need to have parentheses after them?

✔ A function can be passed parameters when it is called. The parentheses that follow the function name represent these parameters. If a function does not accept any parameters, the parentheses are blank. Function names always include parentheses, which help to identify them as functions.

Does an event need to call a JavaScript function?

✔ JavaScript events can be set equal to any valid JavaScript code. This code could be a single line of JavaScript, multiple lines of JavaScript, or a call to a function that is defined within a set of `<script>` tags. Within the event, each line of JavaScript must end with a semicolon (`;`), including function calls.

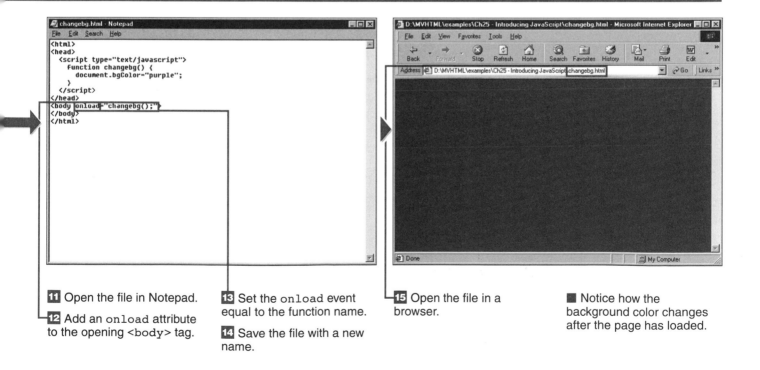

11 Open the file in Notepad.

12 Add an `onload` attribute to the opening `<body>` tag.

13 Set the `onload` event equal to the function name.

14 Save the file with a new name.

15 Open the file in a browser.

■ Notice how the background color changes after the page has loaded.

PLACE SCRIPTS IN A SEPARATE FILE

If your Web site uses several common JavaScript functions on many different Web pages throughout your site, then you could create a single external JavaScript file and have all the Web pages access this single external file.

To link a Web page to an external script file, you can use the `src`

attribute with the `<script>` tag. Set this attribute to the URL of an external file that contains some JavaScript.

The external file does not need to include the `<html>`, `<head>`, or `<body>` tags. It also does not need to include the .html extension. External JavaScript files typically will have a .js extension.

The external JavaScript file can be anywhere on the Web.

This example uses the changebg.html file from the CD, but you can apply the steps to any situation.

PLACE SCRIPTS IN A SEPARATE FILE

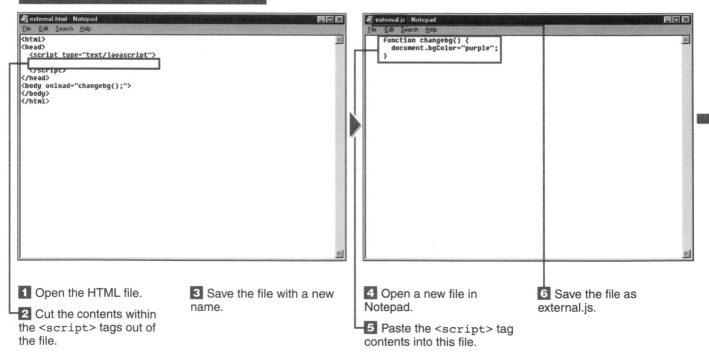

1 Open the HTML file.

2 Cut the contents within the `<script>` tags out of the file.

3 Save the file with a new name.

4 Open a new file in Notepad.

5 Paste the `<script>` tag contents into this file.

6 Save the file as external.js.

Are function names case sensitive?

✔ JavaScript is case sensitive. If you type a function name with a capital letter, you need to include that same capital letter when you call the function. So the functions `hello`, `Hello`, and `HELLO` are all different. If your function is not being recognized correctly, check for a misspelled function name.

Can an external JavaScript file include multiple functions?

✔ External JavaScript files can include many different functions. Any functions included within an external file would be to a Web page as if the functions were included within the `<script>` tags where they were referenced.

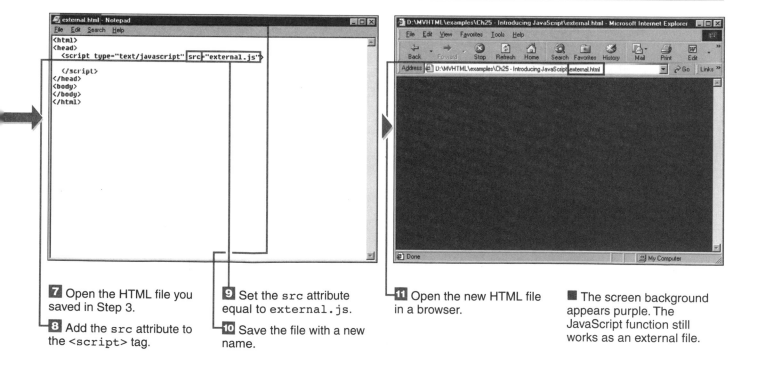

7 Open the HTML file you saved in Step 3.

8 Add the `src` attribute to the `<script>` tag.

9 Set the `src` attribute equal to `external.js`.

10 Save the file with a new name.

11 Open the new HTML file in a browser.

■ The screen background appears purple. The JavaScript function still works as an external file.

OFFER A NO SCRIPT ALTERNATIVE

As part of the browser configuration, users have the option of disabling JavaScript support. If a user has disabled JavaScript support, he or she cannot see any JavaScript that you include in your Web page.

You can handle a browser that has had JavaScript support disabled using the `<noscript>` tags. If the JavaScript cannot be processed, the content included within the `<noscript>` tags is displayed.

For example, a pair of `<noscript>` tags is used to explain to the users that the Web page includes some added functionality that is only visible if JavaScript is enabled on their browser. This reminder would give the users a chance to enable their browser to view the extra functionality.

This example uses the function.html file from the CD, but you can apply the steps to any situation.

OFFER A NO SCRIPT ALTERNATIVE

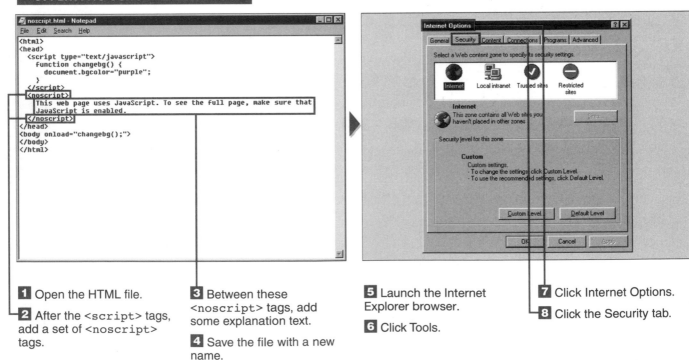

1 Open the HTML file.

2 After the `<script>` tags, add a set of `<noscript>` tags.

3 Between these `<noscript>` tags, add some explanation text.

4 Save the file with a new name.

5 Launch the Internet Explorer browser.

6 Click Tools.

7 Click Internet Options.

8 Click the Security tab.

Can I automatically enable JavaScript on a user's browser?

✔ You cannot control a user's browser configuration, so you cannot alter someone's configuration to enable JavaScript support. The best you can do is to tell them how to enable it and encourage them to enable it.

What other items can be enabled or disabled using the browser preferences?

✔ Many different Web page enhancements can be enabled or disabled using the browser preference settings. Using Netscape's Preferences dialog, you can disable Java, JavaScript, style sheets, and cookies. Using Internet Explorer's Options dialog you can disable Java, Active X controls, scripting, and cookies.

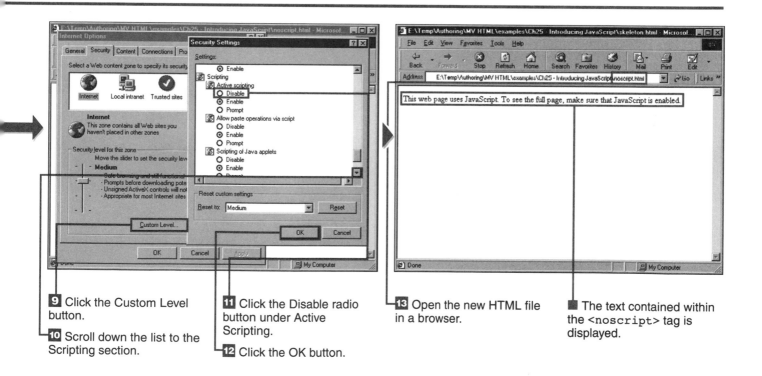

9 Click the Custom Level button.

10 Scroll down the list to the Scripting section.

11 Click the Disable radio button under Active Scripting.

12 Click the OK button.

13 Open the new HTML file in a browser.

■ The text contained within the `<noscript>` tag is displayed.

WORK WITH OBJECTS

A JavaScript *object* is a more complex form of a variable. Objects can hold multiple pieces of data and can represent abstract things like HTML elements and the current date or weather conditions.

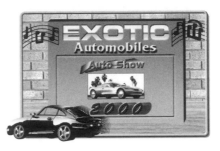

How Objects are Organized

The *Document Object Model* is the structure for how you refer to all the various elements on a Web page. In the Document Object Model, the parent object is the `window` object. The `window` object includes everything that deals with the browser window, such as location and history. You can use the information in the `window` object to control the appearance and function of the Web page.

One of the children of the window object is the `document` object. The `document` object includes all the elements that make up the Web page, such as images and forms. When you use an object property or method, you can retrieve data about the current object or change its behavior.

Objects can include subobjects. On a Web page, for example, the list of subobjects might include a graphic, blocks of text, and a sound file.

Identifying the Object Hierarchy

JavaScript uses a hierarchical naming convention. The basic format is:
`<parent>.<subobject>.<subobject>`

More subobjects can be added, as long as all the objects are separated by periods (.). For example, if a Web page includes a form named form1, and the form includes a text field named text1, the text field can be identified as the `window.document.form1.text1` object.

Properties and Methods

Each Web page object has several properties and methods associated with it.

- *Properties* can be used to tell you the details about the object, such as the length of a text field or the name of a selection list.

- *Methods* are like built-in functions. They perform an action to the object. For example, the scroll() method enables scrolling in a window; the alert() method opens a particular type of dialog box. You can easily identify methods by looking for their parentheses; methods always end with parentheses.

- For some methods, you can pass parameters by including them within the parentheses. If a function does not have any parameters, the parentheses are left empty.

Non-Web page elements

Not all objects are associated with actual Web page elements. For example:

- The Math object includes properties and methods for working with several mathematical functions such as logarithms and trigonometric functions.

- The Date object can be used to work with various aspects involving dates and times.

- The String object enables you to manipulate and control string variables.

VIEW THE CURRENT URL

Certain objects contain valuable information that is useful to know as you develop scripts.

The `location` object, a subobject of the `window` object, identifies the current Web page URL.

To see this information, you can set the `window.location` object to appear in a `text field` object by setting the value of the `text`

field object equal to the `window.location` object.

The `location` object includes several properties that can be used to obtain several different pieces of information about the current URL, including host, hostname, href, pathname, port, and protocol. From this information, you can manipulate the URL to redirect the user to another Web page.

The `location` object also includes a `reload()` method that can be used to reload the current page.

This example uses the skeleton.html file from the CD, but you can apply the steps to any situation.

VIEW THE CURRENT URL

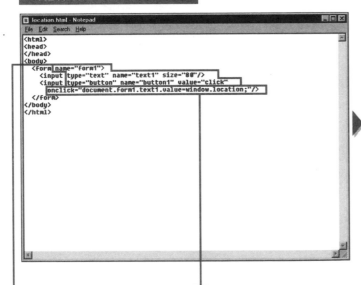

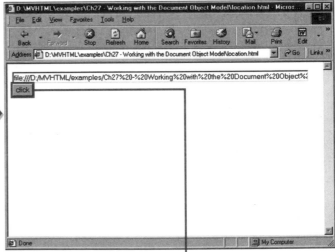

1 Open the HTML file.

2 Add `<form>` and two `<input/>` tags within the `<body>` tags.

3 Add and set attributes to create a text field and a button.

4 Add the `onclick` event and set it to a statement that displays the `window.location` object value in the text field.

5 Save the file.

6 Open the file in a browser.

7 Click the button on the Web page.

■ The current URL is listed in the text field.

438

How can the location object be used?

✔ You can use the location object to print the URL for the current page at the bottom of every page. This can be done by including the `document.location.href` statement within a set of `<script>` tags.

How else can I view the URL of the current Web page?

✔ The `document` object can also be used to view the current URL. The statement for this object looks like `document.URL`. This statement must be included within a set of `<script>` tags or as part of an event statement to be used.

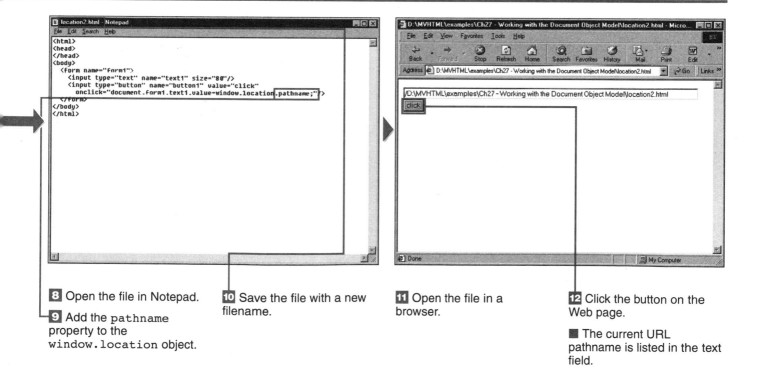

8 Open the file in Notepad.

9 Add the `pathname` property to the `window.location` object.

10 Save the file with a new filename.

11 Open the file in a browser.

12 Click the button on the Web page.

■ The current URL pathname is listed in the text field.

CONTROL PAGE HISTORY

The history object enables you to duplicate the browser's Forward and Back buttons to move between viewed Web pages.

You can use the history object's length property to view the length of the current history list saved by the browser.

The history object also includes several methods. The back() method can cause the previously loaded Web page to appear in the browser. The forward() method displays the next page in the browser. The go() method accepts a number parameter, which can be positive or negative, and moves you forward or backward in the history list.

For example, the statement document.history.go(-2) displays the Web page that is two pages back in the history list.

This example uses the skeleton.html file from the CD, but you can apply the steps to any situation.

CONTROL PAGE HISTORY

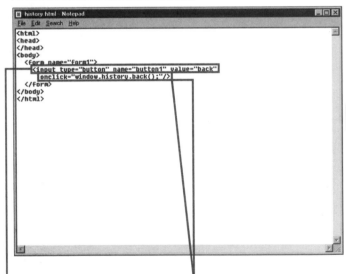

1 Open the HTML file.

2 Add a set of <form> tags with the name attribute set.

3 Add an <input/> tag with the type, name, and value attributes set.

4 Add the onclick event and set it equal to the window.history.back() method.

5 Save the file with a new filename.

6 Open another HTML file in a browser.

How can I test a JavaScript method?

✓ The browser can be used to test JavaScript methods. To do this, enter the word **javascript** in the browser's Address bar, followed by a colon and the JavaScript method. The results of the method will display in the browser. For example, typing `javascript: document.write ("Hello")` causes the word "Hello" to appear in the browser.

Can I reload the current page with the history object?

✓ The `history.go()` method can be used to reload the current page. If the index is set to 0, the current page is the one in the history list that is loaded. This has the same effect as a page refresh. The code looks like `this,document.history(0)`.

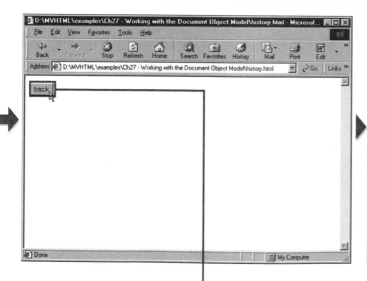

7 Open the file you created in Step 5.

8 Click the button on the Web page.

■ The previous Web page is loaded in the browser.

CHANGE LINKS

Almost all the various Web page elements can be referenced using JavaScript objects. For example, the `links` object holds all the links included on the Web page. You can locate individual links by specifying the *index value* for the link.

These index values are numbered sequentially from the top of the page to the bottom, starting at 0 for the first link.

The index value is specified within square brackets immediately after the link's object name. For example, if you have three links on

the Web page, the first link on the page can be referred to as document.links[0], the second one can be referred to as document.links[1] and so on.

This example uses the history.html file from the CD, but you can apply the steps to any situation.

CHANGE LINKS

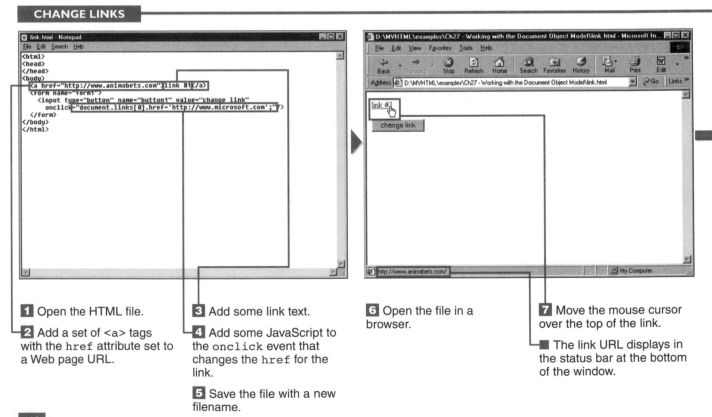

1 Open the HTML file.

2 Add a set of `<a>` tags with the `href` attribute set to a Web page URL.

3 Add some link text.

4 Add some JavaScript to the `onclick` event that changes the `href` for the link.

5 Save the file with a new filename.

6 Open the file in a browser.

7 Move the mouse cursor over the top of the link.

■ The link URL displays in the status bar at the bottom of the window.

If the document object is a subobject of the window object, why doesn't the window object need to be included?

✔ The document object refers to all of the elements on the Web page. Because there are so many document subobjects, the browser knows that the document object is a subobject of the window object and doesn't require that the window object be included.

Why does the links object look similar to the location object?

✔ In many ways, the links object is similar to the location object, except that the URL is the link URL instead of the current Web page URL. The links object shares many of the same properties as the location object, including host, hostname, href, pathname, port, and protocol.

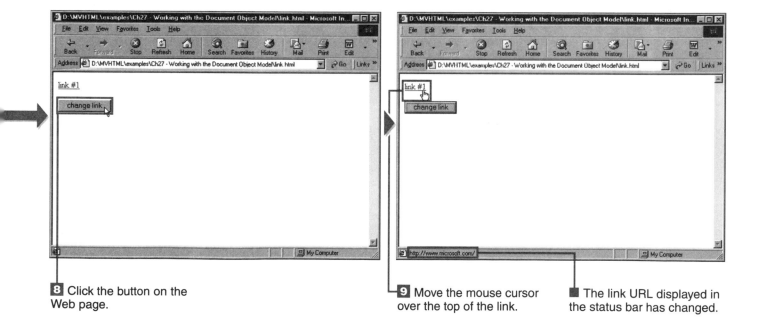

8 Click the button on the Web page.

9 Move the mouse cursor over the top of the link.

■ The link URL displayed in the status bar has changed.

CHANGE IMAGES

The images object can also be used to index the various images included on a Web page. The first image on the Web page is referred to as document.images[0] and the second image is referred to as document.images[1].

Many of the properties for the images object resemble the

<img/> tag attributes. The <img/> tag is discussed in Chapter 11. These properties enable you change an image's attributes by using JavaScript in response to an event.

For example, you can have an image change size as the user moves the mouse cursor over the top of it.

Properties for the images object include border, complete, height, width, hspace, vspace, lowsrc, name and src. Many of these properties match the attributes of the <img/> tag.

This example uses the link.html file from the CD, but you can apply the steps to any situation.

CHANGE IMAGES

```
images.html - Notepad
File  Edit  Search  Help
<html>
<head>
</head>
<body>
  <img src="polar_bear.jpg"/><br/>
  <form name="form1">
  </form>
</body>
</html>
```

```
images.html - Notepad
File  Edit  Search  Help
<html>
<head>
</head>
<body>
  <img src="polar_bear.jpg"/><br/>
  <form name="form1">
    <input type="button" name="button1" value="change image"
      onclick="document.images[0].src='boris_bear.gif';"/>
  </form>
</body>
</html>
```

1 Open the HTML file.

2 Add a set of <img/> tags.

3 Add the src attribute and set it equal to an image filename.

■ In this example, the src attribute is set to an image of a polar bear. (See Chapter 2 for more on attributes.)

4 Add a line break <br/> tag.

5 Add an <input/> tag and values.

■ In this example, an event on button1 has a value that changes the image. (See Chapter 17 for more on <input/> tags.)

6 Add JavaScript that changes the image's attribute file to the desired attribute.

■ In this example, the onclick event triggers the change.

7 Save the HTML file.

What does the complete property do?

✔ Another property of the `image` object is the complete property. This property is a Boolean value that is `false` until an image is completely loaded. When completely loaded, the complete property is set to `true`. Using this value, you can check to see if an image is loaded before changing it. For example, if you have an image loaded that will change, you can check the complete property before allowing the image to change.

Can I dynamically change the other image properties like the width and height?

✔ All listed image properties can be dynamically changed using JavaScript statements. This provides a way to let you do some fun tricks to your images like changing sizes and spacing in response to an event.

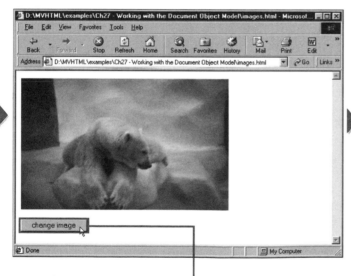

■ 8 Open the HTML file in a browser.

■ 9 Click the Web page button.

■ The new image appears.

USE RADIO BUTTONS

*R*adio buttons are a subobject of the form object, which in turn is a subobject of the document object. Each individual radio button is indexed by the order that it appears in the form. The first radio button has an index value of 0. Controlling radio buttons with JavaScript enables you to get feedback from the user.

For example, a set of four radio buttons named myradio could be referred to in order as myradio[0]

myradio[1], myradio[2], and myradio[3].

Just like the other Web page elements, the object properties are similar to the attribute list for the <input/> tag, including checked, name, type, and value.

The radio button object also includes several useful methods that can be used to automatically select a radio button, such as

- blur() makes the radio button lose the focus.

- click() makes a radio button act like the user clicked on it.

- focus() makes the radio button get the focus.

This example uses the location.html file from the CD, but you can apply the steps to any situation.

USE RADIO BUTTONS

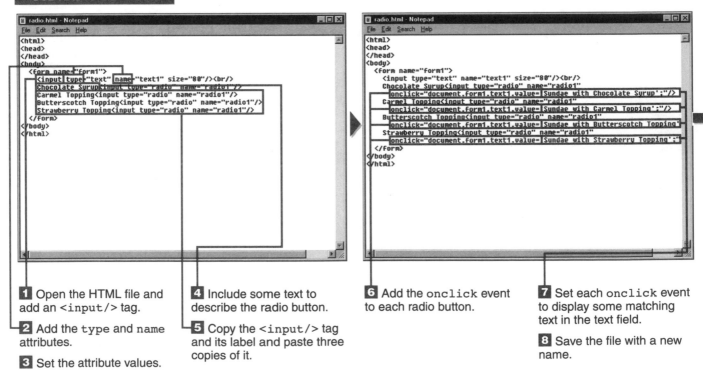

1 Open the HTML file and add an <input/> tag.

2 Add the type and name attributes.

3 Set the attribute values.

4 Include some text to describe the radio button.

5 Copy the <input/> tag and its label and paste three copies of it.

6 Add the onclick event to each radio button.

7 Set each onclick event to display some matching text in the text field.

8 Save the file with a new name.

MASTER IT

Does the checkbox object work in a similar manner to the radio button object?

✔ The `checkbox` object is very similar to the `radio button` object. Checkboxes are also indexed and can be referred to using the index values. The `checkbox` object also shares all of the same methods and properties as the `radio button` object.

How are checkboxes different from radio buttons?

✔ Checkbox buttons are boxes that can be marked as checked or unchecked. They are typically used to set or unset options. Checkboxes are created with an `<input/>` tag whose type attribute is set to checkbox. Each individual checkbox can be selected independent of the others, but only a single radio button in a set can be selected. Both of these elements are discussed in Chapter 17.

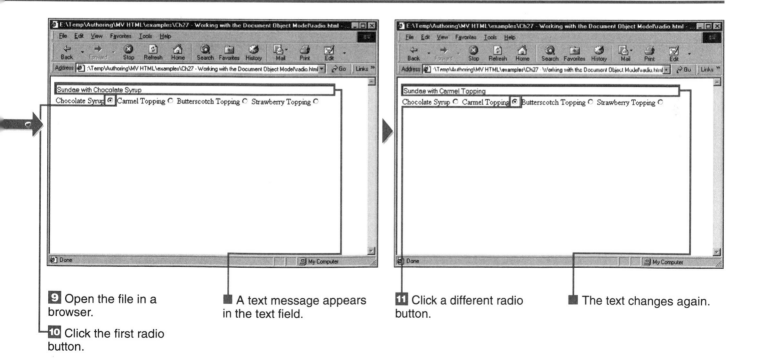

■9 Open the file in a browser.

■10 Click the first radio button.

■ A text message appears in the text field.

■11 Click a different radio button.

■ The text changes again.

WORK WITH SELECTION LISTS

The select object is used to control selection lists. These lists can present a list of objects in a drop-down list. The <option> tags contained within a selection list, however, are referred to as subobjects of the select object.

The select object also includes the name and type properties, as well as a property called length that returns the number of options in the selection list. The selection object also includes the blur() and focus() methods.

Each option object can be referred to by its index value, with 0 being the first option. For example, the first option of a selection list

named mylist found in a form named form1 would be document.form1.mylist.option[0]. The option object also includes the selected, text, and value properties.

This example uses the history.html file from the CD, but you can apply the steps to any situation.

WORK WITH SELECTION LISTS

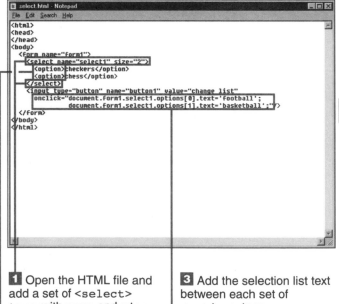

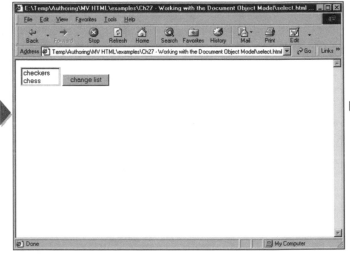

1 Open the HTML file and add a set of <select> tags with name and size attributes.

2 Add two sets of <option> tags.

3 Add the selection list text between each set of <option> tags.

4 Set the onclick event to change the text within both <option> tags.

5 Save the file.

6 Open the file in a browser.

■ A selection list and a button are displayed.

What happens if you try to reference an index value that does not exist?

✔ If you try to reference an index value that doesn't exist, the browser produces an error. The status bar on the browser displays a message indicating that an error has occurred. If you click the error icon in the status bar, the details of the error appear in a dialog box.

What does the selectedIndex property return if no selection list item is selected?

✔ If no selection list item is selected, the `selectedIndex` property returns a −1. You can check for this value to determine if no item has been selected.

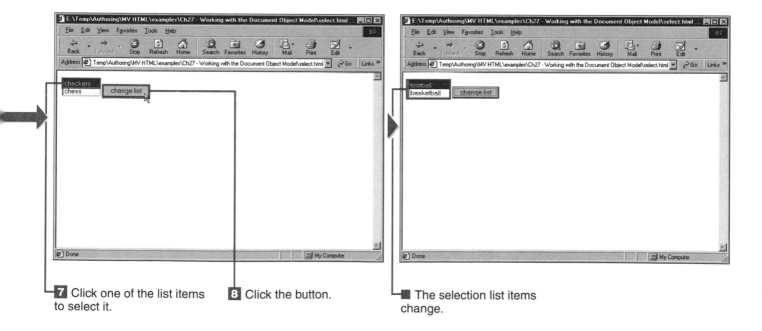

7 Click one of the list items to select it.

8 Click the button.

■ The selection list items change.

USING THE DATE OBJECT

The Date object isn't associated with a Web page element, but JavaScript syntax includes it. This object can be used to display the current time and date.

Before you can use the Date object, you must create it. To create a Date object, you need to give it the variable name (it can be any valid text) and set it equal to the new keyword followed by the

Date() method. For example, mydate = new Date() would create a new Date object called mydate.

After you have created a new Date object, you can use one of many methods to get information about the current date and time. For example, the toLocalString() method returns the value of the current Date object in the local time zone.

The other methods can be used to return only a portion of the date and time information, such as getDate(), getDay(), getHours(), getMinutes(), getMonth(), getSeconds(), getTime(), and getYear().

This example uses the location.html file from the CD, but you can apply the steps to any situation.

USING THE DATE OBJECT

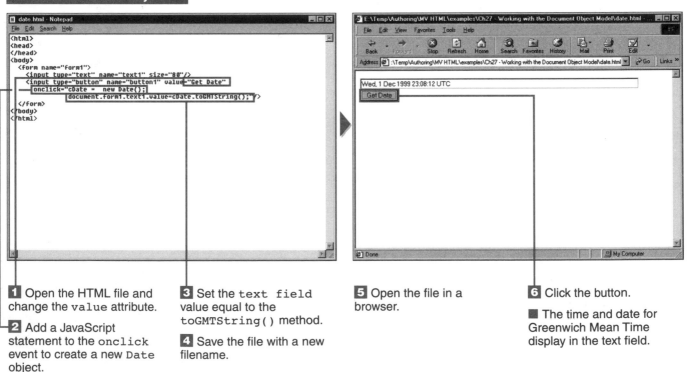

1 Open the HTML file and change the value attribute.

2 Add a JavaScript statement to the onclick event to create a new Date object.

3 Set the text field value equal to the toGMTString() method.

4 Save the file with a new filename.

5 Open the file in a browser.

6 Click the button.

■ The time and date for Greenwich Mean Time display in the text field.

Why do all the date methods return a number?

✔ The date methods typically return just an integer number. These numbers are associated with various date and time information. For example, the `getDay()` method returns a 0 for Sunday and a 6 for Saturday. The `getMonth()` method returns a 0 for January and an 11 for December. The `getTime()` method returns the number of milliseconds that have transpired since January 1, 1970.

How does the Date object keep track of date and time?

✔ The Date object when unformatted holds only a single piece of data—an integer. This integer is the number of milliseconds that have transpired since January 1, 1970. This number for the current time is a rather large number.

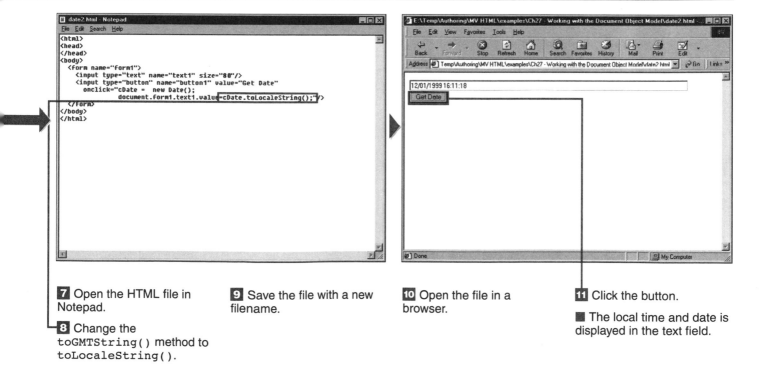

7 Open the HTML file in Notepad.

8 Change the `toGMTString()` method to `toLocaleString()`.

9 Save the file with a new filename.

10 Open the file in a browser.

11 Click the button.

■ The local time and date is displayed in the text field.

USING THE MATH OBJECT

The Math object is another object that is not associated with a Web page element, but is native to the JavaScript syntax.

The Math object includes properties for representing various mathematical values such as Euler's constant (E), base-10 logarithms (LOG10E), natural logarithms (LN10), pi (PI), and the square root of two (SQRT2).

The Math object methods include a variety of advanced mathematical functions. These functions include, but are not limited to, abs(x), ceil(x), floor(x), sin(x), cos(x), tan(x), log(x), min(x), max(x), pow(x,y), random(), and sqrt(x), where x and y are numbers.

The Math object doesn't need to be specified as a subobject of the document or window objects, but it does need to be capitalized. For example, to specify the value of pi, you would use the Math.PI syntax.

This example uses the history.html file from the CD, but you can apply the steps to any situation.

USING THE MATH OBJECT

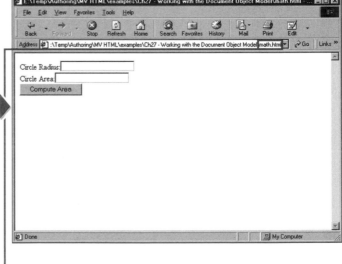

1 Open the HTML file.

2 Add two `<input/>` tags with `type` and `name` attributes.

3 Add descriptive text in front of each `<input/>` tag.

4 Change the JavaScript statement so that the value for the second text field gets set equal to the computed value.

5 Save the file with a new filename.

6 Open the file in a browser.

■ A form with two text fields and a button is displayed.

MASTER IT

How do I use the Math object methods?

✔ Each `Math` object method returns a value based on the number that is passed as a parameter. The number passed in as a parameter could be an actual number or another object. For example, `Math.pow(2,3)` returns a value of 8, which is the value of 2 raised to the 3 power. The JavaScript statement `Math.cos(document.form1.text1.value)` would return the cosine of the value found in the text field named text1 on the form named form1.

Does the Math object keyword always need to be capitalized?

✔ The Math object keyword that appears in front of the properties and methods always needs to be capitalized. JavaScript is case-sensitive and does not work if code is capitalized incorrectly.

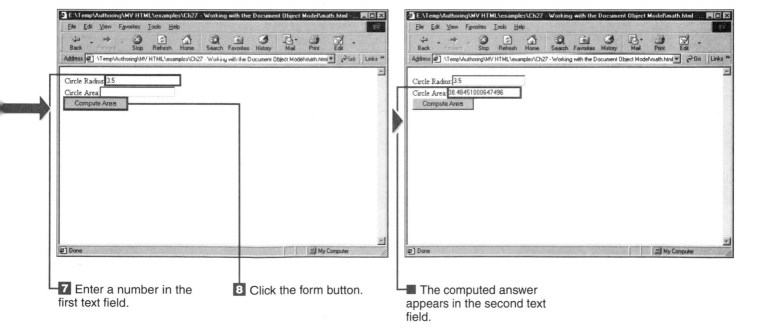

7 Enter a number in the first text field.

8 Click the form button.

■ The computed answer appears in the second text field.

WORK WITH STRINGS

The String object lets you work with text. The String object has a single property—the length property. This property returns the number of characters in the string.

The String object has numerous methods that can be applied to text. A number of these methods can be used to format the text with HTML tags. For example, the

bold() method returns a string of text surrounded by an opening and closing <bold> tags. Other string formatting methods include big(), bold(), fontColor(color), fontSize(size), italics(), link(href), small(), strike(), sub(), sup(), toLowerCase(), and toUpperCase().

Other methods enable you to combine, locate, and extract portions of text. These methods include charAt(index), concat(text), replace(text1, text2), and substring(index1, index2).

This example uses the location.html file from the CD, but you can apply the steps to any situation.

WORK WITH STRINGS

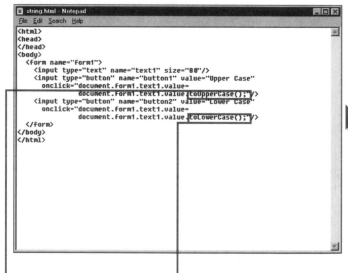

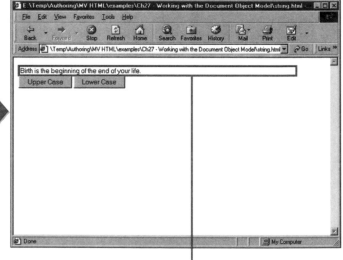

1 Open the HTML file.

2 Change the JavaScript statement associated with the onclick event to update the text field value with the results of the toUpperCase() method.

3 Copy the second <input/> tag and paste it within the <form> tags.

4 Change the JavaScript method toLowerCase().

5 Save the file.

6 Open the file in a browser.

■ A form is displayed with a text box and two buttons.

7 Type some text in the text box.

How can I use a string that doesn't come from a user-filled text field?

✔ To work with strings in JavaScript, you need to first create a `String` object. To do this, you need to list a name for the string and set it equal to new `String()`. The string name can then be used to refer to the object. For example, the JavaScript statement `string1 = new String();` would create a new `String` object and `string1.bold();` would call the `bold()` method for that string.

Can single quotes be used in place of double-quotes?

✔ Single quotes can be used in place of double-quotes. In some places, you will want to use a set of each. For example, if you specify a `document.write` statement within an event, the quotes for the `document.write` statement need to be different from the event quotes.

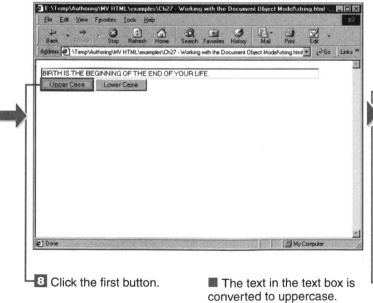

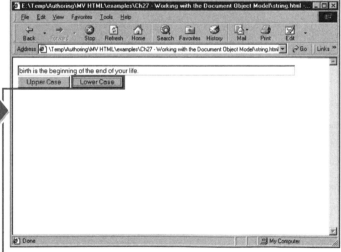

■ Click the first button.

■ The text in the text box is converted to uppercase.

■ Click the second button.

■ The text in the text box is converted to lowercase.

WRITE HTML WITH JAVASCRIPT STATEMENTS

One of the benefits of working with JavaScript is that you can still write standard HTML to the browser screen using JavaScript statements. Although this may seem like a roundabout way to display elements in the browser, the power of this technique lies in being able to output computed values.

The JavaScript statement to write to the browser is the `document.write()` function. Any text or HTML code that is placed within the parentheses in quotes is displayed in the browser in the same manner as if it were loaded from a standard HTML file. Any text that is not included in quotes, such as variable names or other JavaScript objects,

is interpreted as JavaScript statements.

For example, the JavaScript statement `document.write ('<b>hello</b>', name);` would print the word *hello* in bold letters in the browser followed by the value of the JavaScript variable, `name`.

WRITE HTML WITH JAVASCRIPT STATEMENTS

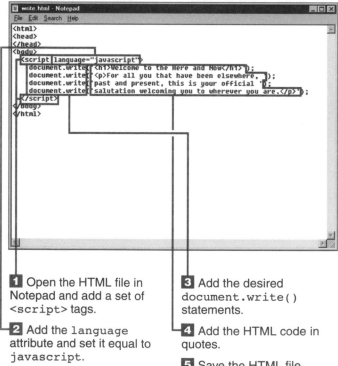

1 Open the HTML file in Notepad and add a set of `<script>` tags.

2 Add the `language` attribute and set it equal to `javascript`.

3 Add the desired `document.write()` statements.

4 Add the HTML code in quotes.

5 Save the HTML file.

6 Open the HTML file in a browser.

■ The HTML code is displayed within the browser.

For normal text, why do I not just have the text wrap around to the next line?

✔ Within a JavaScript statement, each line of text needs to include its own document.write statement. If a hard return is included within a `document.write` statement, the JavaScript statement does not find the end quotation mark and parenthesis, causing the script to fail.

Can I include a line break at the end of a line that is displayed in a browser?

✔ To display each `write` statement on a new line, you can use the `document.writeln()` function. This adds a line break to the end of the line. You could also add the `<br>` tag to the end of the `document. write()` statement.

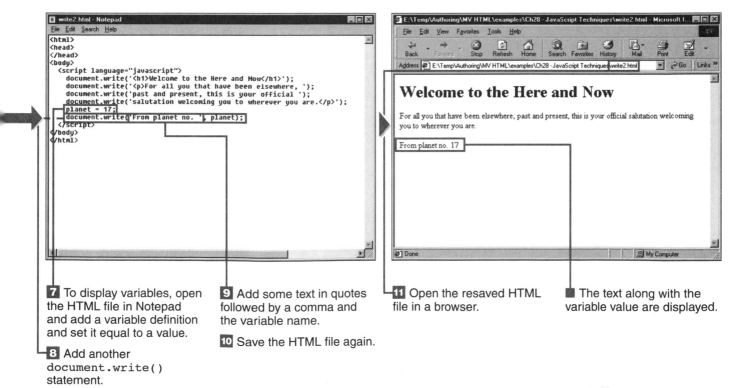

7 To display variables, open the HTML file in Notepad and add a variable definition and set it equal to a value.

8 Add another `document.write()` statement.

9 Add some text in quotes followed by a comma and the variable name.

10 Save the HTML file again.

11 Open the resaved HTML file in a browser.

■ The text along with the variable value are displayed.

DISPLAY RANDOM QUOTES

The `random()` function enables you to generate random numbers that can be used in a variety of ways. For example, you can randomly select an image to load when the Web page loads or randomly change the content to add variety to the Web page.

The `random()` function returns a value between 0 and 1. If you multiply this value by a given variable and then use the `Math.floor()` method to round the value to the next lowest integer, you can create random integer values between 0 and a given variable.

For example, the JavaScript statement `Math.floor(17 * Math.random())` would create a random number ranging between 0 and 17. Using this statement and changing the integer value, you can create a range of random integer values.

An array of values can be specified using the `Array` keyword and placing the values in parenthesis with each value separated with a comma.

DISPLAY RANDOM QUOTES

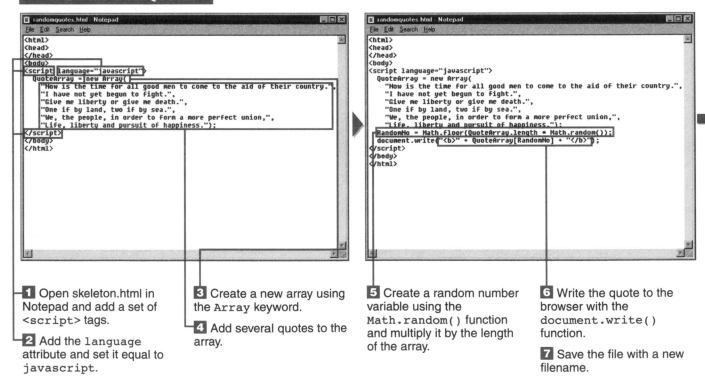

1 Open skeleton.html in Notepad and add a set of `<script>` tags.

2 Add the `language` attribute and set it equal to `javascript`.

3 Create a new array using the `Array` keyword.

4 Add several quotes to the array.

5 Create a random number variable using the `Math.random()` function and multiply it by the length of the array.

6 Write the quote to the browser with the `document.write()` function.

7 Save the file with a new filename.

How can I create a random number between 1 and 17?

✔ You can easily set the range of random numbers by changing the constants in the random number statement. To have the range begin at 1 instead of 0, you will need to add a 1 to the randomly generated number. For example, `Math.floor(17 * Math.random() + 1)` would create a random range from 1 to 17.

Can I use the Math.ceil( ) method instead of the Math.floor( ) method?

✔ The purpose of the `Math.floor()` method is to round the random numbers to integer values. The `Math.ceil()` method rounds numbers up to the nearest integer instead of down. This could also be used to create a range between 1 and the an integer value.

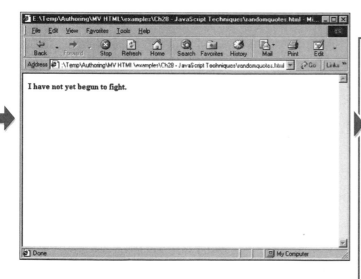

■ 8 Open the HTML file in a browser.

■ A quote is displayed in the browser.

■ 9 Click the Refresh button on the browser.

■ The page is reloaded and another quote is displayed.

DISPLAY TEXT ON THE BROWSER'S STATUS BAR

The browser's status bar displays useful information to the user such as the `href` value of a link when the mouse cursor is moved over a link. This information is displayed automatically by the browser, but you can also display messages on the status bar using JavaScript.

Using the `window.status` JavaScript property, you can set the text that is displayed in the status bar. To do this, you simply need to set the `window.status` property equal to a line of text. This text can also include JavaScript statements.

For example, the JavaScript statement `window.status=`

`"hello and welcome"` would display this above text in the status bar.

If this JavaScript statement is used to display text in the status bar while the mouse cursor moves over a link, the text will display the link's URL.

DISPLAY TEXT ON THE BROWSER'S STATUS BAR

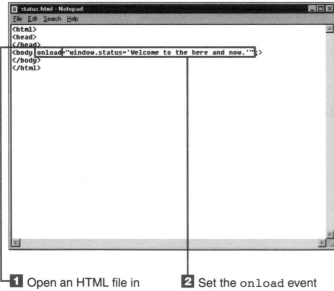

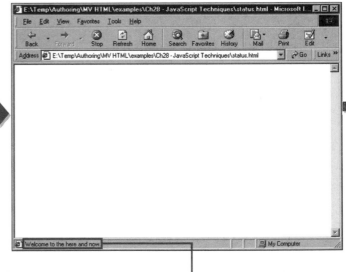

1 Open an HTML file in Notepad and add the `onload` event.

■ This example shows skeleton.html from the CD.

2 Set the `onload` event equal to `window.status=` and the text to display.

3 Save the file with a new filename.

4 Open the file in a browser.

■ A message is displayed in the browser's status bar.

460

What happens to the status bar text if the text string is longer than the browser window?

✔ If the text string displayed in the browser status bar is longer than the browser window, the text string is truncated.

Can I format the text that appears on the status bar with HTML tags such as <b>?

✔ Because the status bar is not part of the browser that is interpreted, any formatting that you send to the status bar will appear as part of the text string. For example, if you include a <b> tag as part of the status bar message, the actual tag will be displayed along with the message.

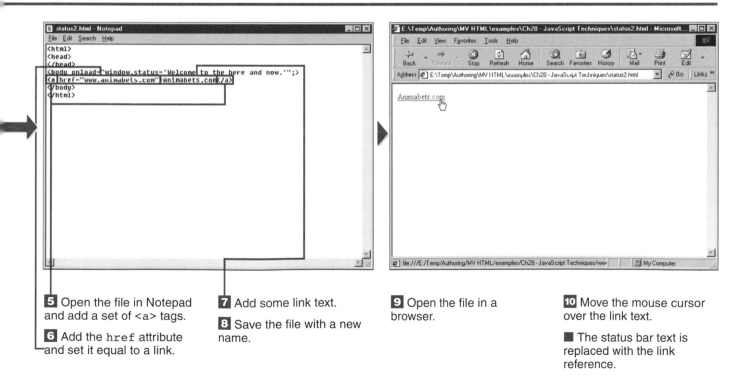

5 Open the file in Notepad and add a set of <a> tags.

6 Add the `href` attribute and set it equal to a link.

7 Add some link text.

8 Save the file with a new name.

9 Open the file in a browser.

10 Move the mouse cursor over the link text.

■ The status bar text is replaced with the link reference.

OPEN A NEW BROWSER WINDOW

Have you ever noticed while browsing the Web that some links spawn a new browser window? JavaScript accomplishes this by using the `window.open()` function.

The `window.open()` function accepts three parameters. The first parameter is the URL of the page that should open in the new window. The second parameter is the name for the new window. This name can then be used to reference the new window.

The third parameter can include several different attributes including `width`, `height`, `toolbar`, `status`, `menubar`, `scrollbars`, and `resizable`. All but the first two attributes listed here can be set to either yes or no.

For example, the JavaScript statement `window.open ("mypage.html", "mywindow", "width=200, height=400, toolbar=no, status=no, resizeable= yes");` would open a new 200 x 400 pixel resizable window with no toolbar or status bar and load the mypage.html file in it.

OPEN A NEW BROWSER WINDOW

1 Open an HTML file in Notepad and add a set of `<script>` tags with the `language` attribute.

2 Add the `window.open()` function.

3 Add the URL of the page to open, and a name for the new window.

4 Add and set the `width`, `height`, and `resizable` attributes.

5 Save the file with a new filename.

6 Open the file in a browser.

■ The Web page is displayed.

MASTER IT

From the original Web page, how do I write text to the new window?

✔ When you create a new window, one of the parameters is to give the new window a name. This name can be used to send output to the new window. For example, the `document.write()` function would write output to the current Web page and `mywindow.write()` would write text to a new window named mywindow.

If I do not specify the width and height attributes, what size will the new window be?

✔ If the `width` and `height` attributes are not specified, the new window will be sized the same as the current window. In many cases, this is preferred, but if you want to use the new window as a navigation list, you should size it smaller.

■ The new window is also opened, displaying the referenced Web page.

7 Click and drag the lower-right corner of the new window to resize it.

Note: If the `resizable` attribute is set to `yes`, the window can be resized.

CLOSE A REMOTE WINDOW

If an extra window is opened, you can fill the window with any HTML page. This window can be used as a remote navigation toolbar for the browser. Enabling an easy way to close the remote window is a good idea.

With many browser windows open, the screen becomes cluttered. You can always close a window by clicking the close icon in the upper-

right corner of the window, but JavaScript also includes a method for closing remote windows.

Using this method is an easier way for the user to close a window

To close a remote window, you can use the `window.close()` function. This closes the current remote window.

The `window.close()` function can be used to close the original browser window, but a dialog box will appear before the window is closed. Windows that have been opened using the `window.open()` method will close automatically when the `window.close()` method is called.

CLOSE A REMOTE WINDOW

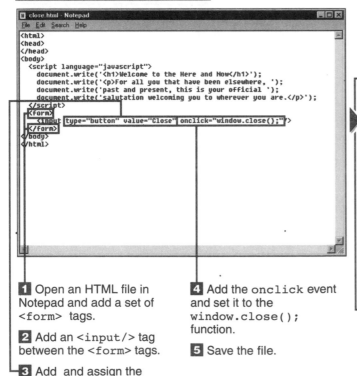

1 Open an HTML file in Notepad and add a set of `<form>` tags.

2 Add an `<input/>` tag between the `<form>` tags.

3 Add and assign the `type` and `value` attributes.

4 Add the `onclick` event and set it to the `window.close();` function.

5 Save the file.

6 Open the file in Notepad.

7 Change the URL for the new window to the name of the file you are editing.

8 Save the file.

Can I close the original browser window with the window.close( ) function?

✔ If you are using the Microsoft Internet Explorer browser, executing the `window.close()` function sends a message to the browser to close the browser. Internet Explorer displays a warning message before it closes the browser. If you click the OK button, the browser closes.

Can I react to a window being closed?

✔ When the `window.close()` method is called, the `onunload` event is fired. This event can be used to execute a script prior to the window being closed.

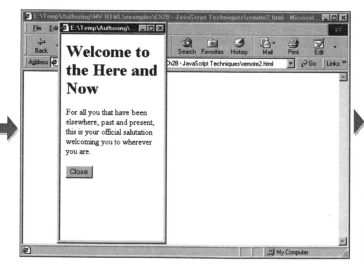

9 Open the file.

■ The Web page and a new window are opened and displayed.

10 Click the Close button in the remote window.

■ The remote window closes.

USING DIALOG BOXES

Perhaps the easiest way to present messages to the user is with dialog boxes. These dialog boxes appear on top of the browser and need to be clicked before the browser will continue to work.

Many programs use dialog boxes to present information to the user.

They can also be used to collect information from the user.

JavaScript includes three different types of dialog boxes:

• The alert dialog box presents a text message to the user and includes a single OK button.

• The confirm dialog box includes a text message along with OK and

Cancel buttons. This dialog returns true if the OK button is clicked or false if the Cancel button is clicked.

• The prompt dialog box includes a text message, a text field for entering text, and OK and Cancel buttons.

All these dialog boxes are functions within the window object.

USING DIALOG BOXES

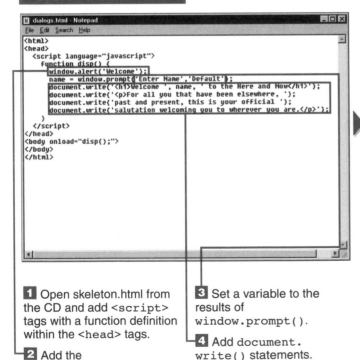

1 Open skeleton.html from the CD and add <script> tags with a function definition within the <head> tags.

2 Add the window.alert() method set to display a message.

3 Set a variable to the results of window.prompt().

4 Add document.write() statements.

5 Add the onload event to the <body> tag and set it the function name.

6 Save the file.

7 Open the file in a browser.

■ An alert box appears.

8 Click the OK button.

Note: The document.write() statement is set to output the prompt dialog text to the browser.

How do I set the default value in the prompt dialog?

✔ The `window.prompt()` function accepts two values within its parentheses. The first value is the text that appears in the prompt dialog. The second value is the default text that appears in the text field of the prompt dialog. You must separate these two values with a comma.

What is returned if the Cancel button is clicked for a prompt dialog box?

✔ If the Cancel button is clicked when a prompt dialog box is opened, a null value is returned. A null value means simply that nothing was returned. If you were to display the value of a prompt dialog box that is returned when the Cancel button is clicked, a string that says, 'null' will be displayed.

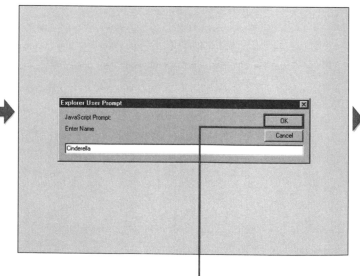

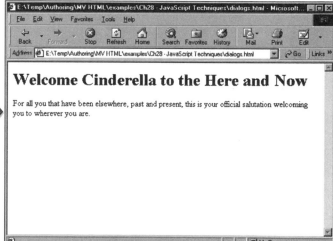

■ A prompt dialog box appears.

■ Type a name in the text box.

■ Click the OK button.

■ The personalized page is displayed.

USING JAVASCRIPT TIMERS

JavaScript can be used to set up timers that will let certain scripts be executed at different times. These can be useful for timing different actions on the Web page.

The function that makes timers possible is the `window.set Timeout()` function. This

function accepts two parameters. The first parameter is a JavaScript statement to execute. This can be a single statement such as `document.bgcolor = 'blue'` or it can call a function that is defined elsewhere in the Web page. It can even include several statements by separating them with semicolons.

The second parameter accepted by the `window.setTimeout()` function is the time value to wait before the JavaScript statement is executed. This value is measured in milliseconds. For example, a value of 5000 causes a delay of 5 seconds, and a value of 10000 causes a delay of 10 seconds.

USING JAVASCRIPT TIMERS

timeout.html - Notepad
File Edit Search Help
```
<html>
<head>
  <script language="javascript">
    function rabbit() {
      document.write("<h1>Oops, that's not a rabbit.</h1>");
      document.write("<img src='dudley.gif'/>");
    }
  </script>
</head>
<body>
</body>
</html>
```

timeout.html - Notepad
File Edit Search Help
```
<html>
<head>
  <script language="javascript">
    function rabbit() {
      document.write("<h1>Oops, that's not a rabbit.</h1>");
      document.write("<img src='dudley.gif'/>");
    }
  </script>
</head>
<body onload="window.setTimeout('rabbit()', 5000)">
  <h1>For my next trick, I'll pull a rabbit out of a hat.</h1>
</body>
</html>
```

1 Open an HTML file in Notepad.

2 Add a set of `<script>` tags within the `<head>` tags.

3 Type **language= "javascript"**.

4 Add a function definition.

5 Add within the function definition, a `document.write()` statement uses an `<img/>` tag to load an image.

6 Add the `onload` event to the `<body>` tag.

7 Set the `onload` event equal to the `window.setTimeout()` method.

8 Add the defined function name and the time value in milliseconds.

9 Add a single heading.

10 Save the file.

Can I set a regularly repeating timeout?

✔ To set a timer to repeat at regular intervals, you can include the `setTimeout()` function inside of a loop. Another way to repeat the time is to use the `setInterval()` function. This function executes the first parameter at a regular interval as specified by the second parameter. The second parameter is measured in milliseconds.

How does the setInterval( ) method work?

✔ If you have created a function called `displayTime()` that displays the current local time in a text field, you can have this field update every second with a JavaScript statement that looks like this: `setInterval (displayTime(), 1000)`.

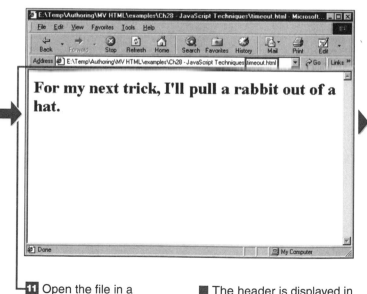

11 Open the file in a browser.

■ The header is displayed in the browser.

12 Wait for the designated time value.

■ The script function is executed after the timeout value is reached displaying an image.

13 Click the browser's Refresh button.

■ The original page is reloaded and the timeout value is reset.

VALIDATE FORMS

Although server-side scripts can be used to validate form data, using JavaScript to validate forms saves an extra trip or two to the server. This can help reduce the network traffic and can make Web pages on lower bandwidth computers appear faster.

By validating the form before it is sent to the server for processing,

you can be sure of the type of data you will be receiving. This can help reduce the number of errors in your data that could cause problems later on.

For example, you can validate a phone number to make sure that it does not include any letters or

validate a range of numbers such as a date value between 1 and 31.

The way to validate form data is different for every type of data, but JavaScript includes many operators and string functions that help you customize the validation routines.

VALIDATE FORMS

validate.html - Notepad
File Edit Search Help

```
<html>
<head>
  <script language="javascript">
    function validate(val) {
      if (val < 1 || val > 4) {
        alert('Please insert a value between 1 and 4.');
      }
    }
  </script>
</head>
<body>
</body>
</html>
```

validate.html - Notepad
File Edit Search Help

```
<html>
<head>
  <script language="javascript">
    function validate(val) {
      if (val < 1 || val > 4) {
        alert('Please insert a value between 1 and 4.');
      }
    }
  </script>
</head>
<body>
  <form name="form1">
    Please rate the service (1-4):
    <input name="text1" type="text" size="4"
onchange="validate(this.value);" />
  </form>
</body>
</html>
```

1 Open an HTML file in Notepad.

■ This example shows skeleton.html from the CD.

2 Add a set of `<script>` tags and a function definition with the `<head>` tags.

3 Add a JavaScript statement that checks the value of the text field and displays an alert dialog if the text field value is unacceptable.

4 Add a set of `<form>` tags within the `<body>` tags.

5 Add some descriptive text and an `<input/>` tag.

6 Add and set the `name`, `type`, and `size` attributes.

7 Add the `onchange` event and set it to the defined function name.

8 Save the file with a different name.

What do the != and || symbols mean?

✔ JavaScript uses several operators in mathematical operations. In addition to the standard mathematical symbols for add (+), subtract (−), multiply (*), and divide (/), the != symbol means "not equal", && means "and," and || means "or,"

What do the < and > symbols mean?

✔ The < symbol means "less than." It compares values to see if one is less than the other. The > symbol means "greater than". It compares values to see if one is greater than the other. These symbols can be combined with an equals sign to check if one number is less than or equal to the other. For example, <= means "less than or equal to," and >= means "greater than or equal to."

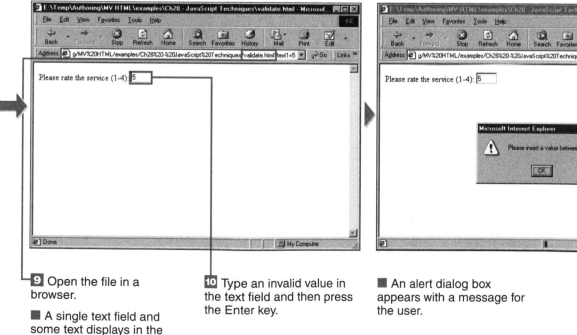

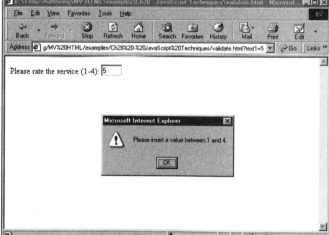

9 Open the file in a browser.

■ A single text field and some text displays in the browser.

10 Type an invalid value in the text field and then press the Enter key.

■ An alert dialog box appears with a message for the user.

USING COOKIES

Cookies are small pieces of data that help maintain the state of the browser. They are written to the user's computer and are indexed by the site that creates it. When the user returns to the site later, the remote server retrieves the data from the user's computer and uses it.

One common use of cookies is to keep information about the user's preferences. Saving a user's preferences in a cookie enables the browser to read the cookie and display the Web page according to the user's specifications the next time that he or she returns.

To write a cookie using JavaScript, you use the `document.cookie` object. By setting this object equal to the piece of data that you wish to save, the cookie is automatically written to the user's computer.

The following example uses the skeleton.html file from the CD.

USING COOKIES

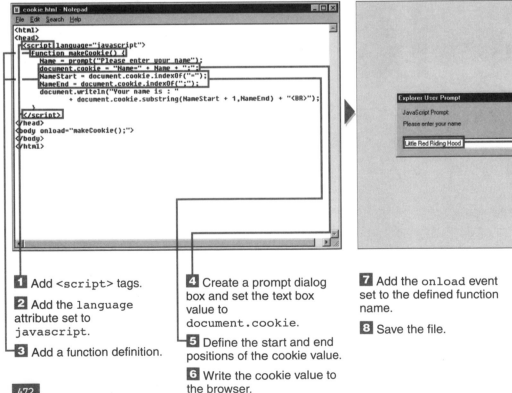

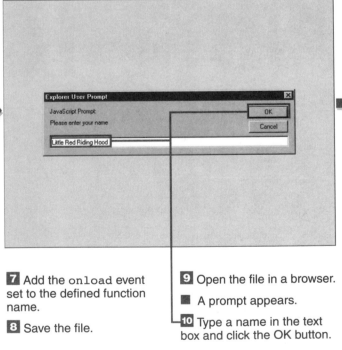

1 Add `<script>` tags.

2 Add the `language` attribute set to `javascript`.

3 Add a function definition.

4 Create a prompt dialog box and set the text box value to `document.cookie`.

5 Define the start and end positions of the cookie value.

6 Write the cookie value to the browser.

7 Add the `onload` event set to the defined function name.

8 Save the file.

9 Open the file in a browser.

■ A prompt appears.

10 Type a name in the text box and click the OK button.

What data exists in a cookie?

✔ The data in a cookie consists of a name and the data. Each piece of data saved in a cookie should have a name and an equal sign so that it can later be identified and retrieved.

Can cookies be disabled in a browser?

✔ The browser includes settings for disabling cookies if you do not want them stored on your computer. For Internet Explorer, you can disable cookies by clicking Tools ➪ Options. This opens the Internet Options dialog box. Select the Security tab and then click the Custom Level button. Under the Cookies heading, select the Disable radio button.

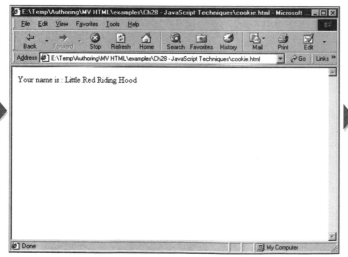

■ The name is appears in the browser.

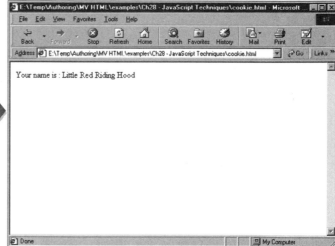

🔟 Close the browser and re-open it.

■ The browser remembers the name value and displays it.

DISPLAY THE LOCAL TIME AND DATE

After a new `Date` object is created, you can use one of many methods to get information about the current date and time.

One very useful `Date` object method is the `toGMTString()` method, which will return the current Greenwich Mean Time. Another useful method is the `toLocalString()`. This method will return the current date and time for the local time zone.

The format for these dates and times lists the day, followed by the date, the month, and then year.

After the year comes the hours, minutes, seconds, and finally the time zone.

For example, Wed, 12 Apr 2000 03:37:38 UTC, would be the date and time format for Wednesday, April 12 of the year 2000 at 3:37 and 38 seconds.

DISPLAY THE LOCAL TIME AND DATE

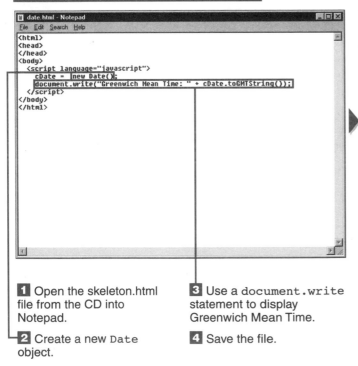

1 Open the skeleton.html file from the CD into Notepad.

2 Create a new `Date` object.

3 Use a `document.write` statement to display Greenwich Mean Time.

4 Save the file.

5 Open the file in a browser.

■ The time and date for Greenwich Mean Time is displayed.

Can I change the date format?

✔ The format of the `Date` object remains the same displaying the day, date, time, and time zone if you use the `toGMTString()` method. This method displays the day and month using three characters, such as `Fri` for Friday and `Apr` for April. For example, this format looks like `Fri, 14 Apr 2000 19:01:54 UTC`. The date format for the `toLocaleString()` method is a little different. This method displays only numbers with the date first and then the time. Slash symbols (`/`) are placed between the date numbers. For example, the format for this method is `04/14/2000 13:05:13`. You can also use the `toString()` method to display the `Date` object. This format looks even more different with the year at the end of the string. For example, this format looks like `Fri Apr 14 13:06:23 MDT 2000`. If you want to use a custom format, you can use the get methods to format the date.

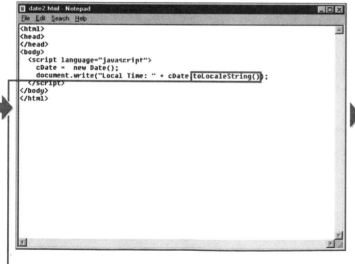

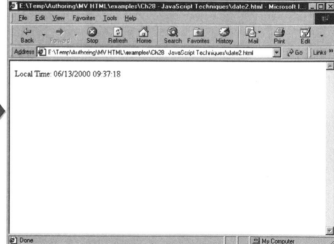

6 Open the HTML file in Notepad.

7 Change the `toGMTString()` method to `toLocaleString()`.

8 Save the file with a new name.

9 Open the file in a browser.

■ The local time and date are displayed.

DETECT A USER'S BROWSER

By detecting the user's browser, you can alter the content as needed for the user's browser.

For example, many of the dynamic HTML syntax are different between browser types. The `navigator` object includes three properties, which return the type of browser. The `appCodeName` property

returns the code name of the current browser. This property is typically `Mozilla`, which is the standard code base.

The `appName` property returns the actual browser name, such as Microsoft Internet Explorer.

What different browser types are there?

✓ The main two browser types include Microsoft's Internet Explorer and Netscape's Navigator, but other browsers exist. These other browsers will have a different identifying name, but the code name will probably be similar.

DETECT A USER'S BROWSER

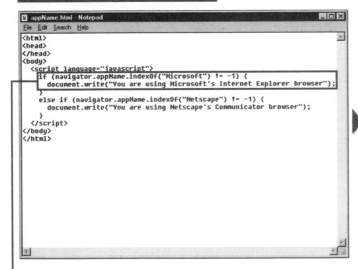

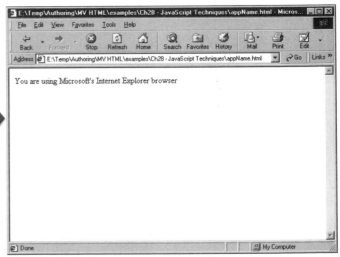

1 Open the skeleton.html file in Notepad.

2 Add an `if` statement to check for the word "Microsoft" within the `navigator.appName` value.

3 Save the file with a new name.

4 Open the file in a browser.

■ The browser type is detected and displayed.

476

DETECT THE BROWSER'S VERSION

The different browser version supports differing levels of HTML. For example, the early 3.0 browser versions only supported HTML Version 3.2.

Later versions supported later HTML specifications. If you use a feature in a later HTML version with a browser that does not support it, the results can be unexpected.

To eliminate any problems, you can check for the current browser version number using the `navigator.appVersion` property.

The following example shows the skeleton.html file, which is included on the CD.

What version numbers can you expect?

✔ The earliest versions to use JavaScript were the Netscape 2.0 and Internet Explorer 3.0 versions. Browsers prior to these versions will not be able to interpret JavaScript code.

DETECT THE BROWSER'S VERSION

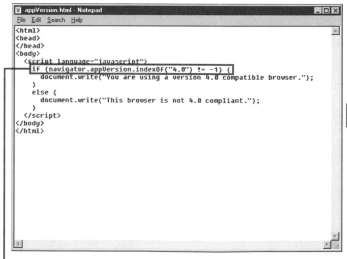

1 Open the HTML file in Notepad.

2 Add an `if` statement to check for the version number.

3 Save the file with a new name.

4 Open the file in a browser.

■ The browser version is detected and displayed.

31) DEFINING MARGINS, PADDING AND BORDER STYLES

32) DEFINING DIMENSIONS AND LIST STYLES

Sunshine VACATIONS

→ About Our Company ←
HEADING 1

Sunshine Vacations provides travelers with the best flights, accomodations and rental cars, across the country and around the world! We go the extra mile to ensure your trip is as enjoyable as possible. The next time you need to book a trip, contact us first and enjoy the security and peace of mind that we provide our customers.

→ Company History ←
HEADING 1

Founded in 1980, Sunshine Vacations has become a leader in the travel industry. We have expanded throughout the United States, and have won many service awards throughout the years. One of the highest honors we have received is an international Customer Service Award, which we won last year!

CENTER
HEADING 1

Left

Center

Right

Justified

USING STYLE SHEETS

One of the key problems that Web page designers have had to face is that carrying over a consistent design from one Web page to another is not easy. *Style sheets* answer this need by allowing all the Web pages to derive their styles from a single definition. This makes updating all the Web pages in an entire Web site significantly easier.

What Style Sheets Can Control

Style sheets can be used to control

- Text styles, like size, color, and formatting (see Chapter 29)

- Page backgrounds (see Chapter 30)

- Image dimensions and borders (see Chapter 31)

- Margins (see Chapter 31)

- List styles (see Chapter 32)

Using Selectors

Styles can be defined for a specified tag called a *selector*. For example, if the selector is `pre`, all `<pre>` tags within the Web page will be formatted with the defined style.

Defining a Style

To define a style, the selector must be listed first, followed by all of the style properties and values within a set of brackets. A colon (:) should separate the style property and the style value. A semicolon (;) separates each separate style property/value pair.

For example, to specify that heading 1 text should be red and centered, the style definition would be `H1{color: red; text-align: center}`, where H1 is the selector.

H1 {color: red; text-align: center}

Including Style Definitions

Style sheet definitions such as the color, text weight, and dimensions, can be referenced from three different places:

- As an external file. External style sheets are referenced using the `<link/>` tag.

- Embedded within the Web page. Embedded style sheets are placed within the opening and closing `<style>` tags. These tags can be placed within the `<head>` tags for a given page.

- Inline. Inline style sheets can be included within a single tag using the `style` attribute.

Definition Hierarchy

If a single selector includes three different style definitions, the definition that is closest to the actual tag takes precedence. So, inline styles take priority over embedded style sheets, which take priority over external style sheets.

USING EMBEDDED STYLE SHEETS

Embedded style sheets provide a way to include all the styles for a given Web page in one central location. A set of `<style>` tags includes all the style definitions for embedded style sheets. These `<style>` tags can be included within the `<head>` tags (see Chapter 5).

The style definition should include a selector. This selector should match a tag within the Web page. Following the selector, all the style property/value pairs should be listed within brackets. A colon should separate the style property from the style value.

Several style properties can be included for a single selector by separating them with a semicolon. For example, the style definition `body {color: blue; background-color: white}` would display all body text as blue and the background color as white.

You can also apply the same style definition to several selectors at the same time by separating the selectors with commas. For example, `h1,h2,h3,h4,h5,h6 {color: green}` would cause all headings to appear green.

This example uses the skeleton.html file from this book's CD, but the steps can be applied to any situation.

CREATE A SIMPLE STYLE SHEET

1 Open the HTML file in Notepad.

2 Add `<style>` tags.

3 Add a selector (p here) followed by brackets.

4 Add the desired property and attribute.

■ Here the `color` property is set to `red`.

5 Save the HTML file.

6 Open the HTML file in a browser.

■ The sections with the designated selector reflect the defined style — in this case, the body text paragraphs with the p selector are all colored red.

Do style sheets limit the number of new style definitions that can be included within the brackets?

✔ Style sheets do not limit the number of style definitions that can be included within the brackets for a given selector. Every new style definition, however, must be separated from the others by a semicolon symbol.

Do embedded style sheets always need to be positioned within the `<head>` tags?

✔ The `<style>` tags can be positioned within the `<head>` tags or between the closing `<head>` tag and the opening `<body>` tag. Some browsers allow the `<style>` tags to be included anywhere within the Web page.

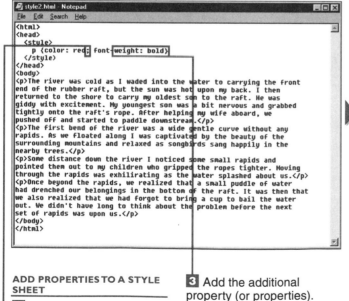

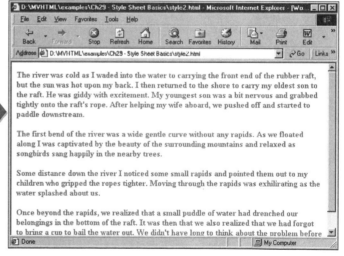

ADD PROPERTIES TO A STYLE SHEET

1 Open an HTML file with a style sheet in Notepad.

2 Add a semicolon after the existing property.

3 Add the additional property (or properties).

■ This example shows the `font-weight:` style set to `bold`.

4 Save the HTML file.

5 Open the HTML file in a browser.

■ The defined property or properties are not displayed. In this example text is now red and bold.

CREATE STYLE SHEET CLASSES

If you define a style for a selector such as paragraph or block quote that appears numerous times throughout the Web page, you can specify a specific instance of the selector using *classes*.

Adding a period and a class name after the selector specifies a

selector class. This class name can be associated with a specific tag with the `class` attribute.

For example, if you specify a style for the p selector and set the class name to `.green`, only paragraphs with the `class="green"` attribute will have the defined style applied.

Each selector can include several different classes.

This example uses the style.html file from this book's CD, but the steps can be applied to any situation.

CREATE STYLE SHEET CLASSES

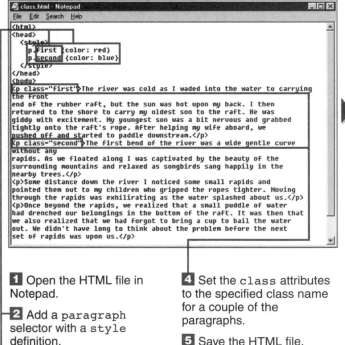

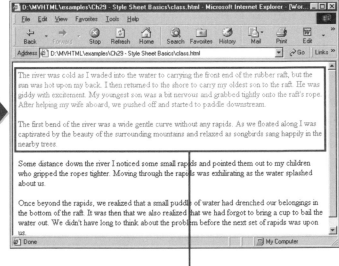

1 Open the HTML file in Notepad.

2 Add a `paragraph` selector with a `style` definition.

3 Add `class` names to each selector.

4 Set the `class` attributes to the specified class name for a couple of the paragraphs.

5 Save the HTML file.

6 Open the HTML file in a browser.

■ The first two paragraphs are colored differently.

Can several selectors with class names be grouped together?

✔ You can define several selectors with the same style definition by separating them with commas. This same technique also works for selectors with class names. For example, `p.first, blockquote.first {color: red}` would color red the text for all paragraphs and blockquote tags with the `class` attribute set to `red`.

Can style sheet class names include numbers as well as letters?

✔ Style sheet class names can include numbers and letters. For example `p.1` and `pre.no17` are both valid class names. Class names cannot include symbols such as brackets and braces.

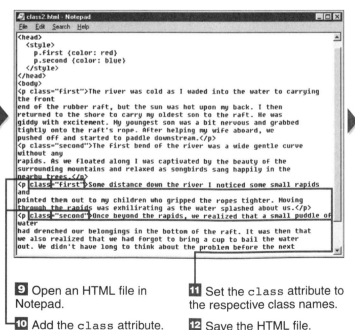

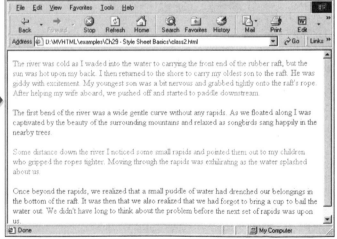

9 Open an HTML file in Notepad.

10 Add the `class` attribute.

11 Set the `class` attribute to the respective class names.

12 Save the HTML file.

13 Open the HTML file in a browser.

■ All paragraphs now have a style applied.

USING EXTERNAL STYLE SHEETS

The real value of style sheets lies in being able to define the style for several pages in one location using external style sheets. With the style definitions contained in an external file that several Web pages reference, you can make changes to many pages at once in one location.

The external style sheet file should include only the style definitions.

The external style sheet does not need to include the `<style>` tags. This file should be saved with the .css extension, which identifies it as a style sheet. The file can be placed and referenced from anywhere on the Web.

To reference an external style sheet, you need to include a `<link/>` tag within the `<head>` tags. This `<link/>` tag should include the following attributes:

- The `rel` attribute identifies the external file as a style sheet and should be set to `stylesheet`.

- The `type` attribute defines the MIME type for the external file and should be set to `text/css`.

- The `href` attribute should be set to the actual filename for the external file.

USING EXTERNAL STYLE SHEETS

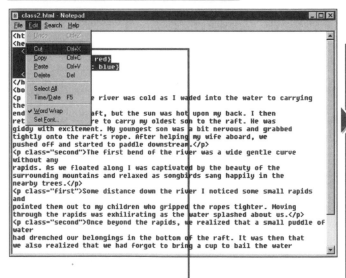

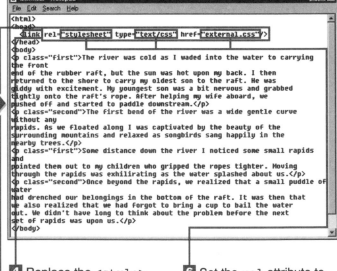

■1 Open the Web page HTML file in Notepad.

■2 Select all the text between the `<style>` tags.

■3 Select Edit⇨Cut.

■ This puts the text on the clipboard so that you can paste it into your new style sheet.

■4 Replace the `<style>` tags with the `<link/>` tag.

■5 Add the `rel`, `type`, and `href` attributes.

■6 Set the `rel` attribute to `stylesheet`, the `type` attribute to `text/css`, and the `href` attribute to the external style sheet filename.

■7 Save the Web page file.

What will happen if the <style> tags are included in the external style sheet?

✔ The external style sheet does not need to include the <style> tags. Because the browser does not interpret the external style sheet, any tags within the file will confuse the styles. If you include the <style> tags, typically the first style definition will be ignored.

What happens if you open the external CSS file in a browser?

✔ If you try to open the external CSS file in a browser, the browser cannot open the file, because the file has a different extension. The only way to use an external CSS file is to reference it using the <link/> tag within another HTML document.

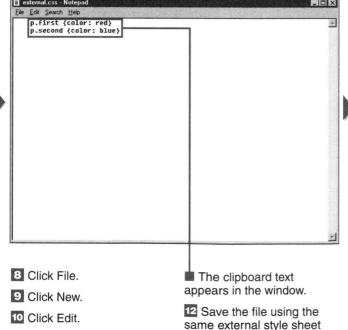

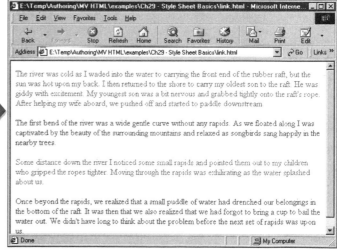

8 Click File.

9 Click New.

10 Click Edit.

11 Click Paste.

■ The clipboard text appears in the window.

12 Save the file using the same external style sheet filename defined in Step 6.

13 Open the Web page HTML file in a browser.

■ The styles are displayed in the browser.

USING INLINE STYLES

O ccasionally, you may want to deviate from the defined Web site style sheet. You can do this by using an *inline style.*

An inline style is applied at the tag level using the `style` attribute. The style properties defined using

the `style` attribute only affect the tag of which the attribute is a part.

For inline styles, the properties and their values are included within the quotes following the `style` attribute. Inline styles need no selector or brackets.

For example, to set the text color for the <body> tag to blue, you'd define the style like this: <body style="color: blue">.

This example uses the skeleton.html file from this book's CD, but the steps can be applied to any situation.

USING INLINE STYLES

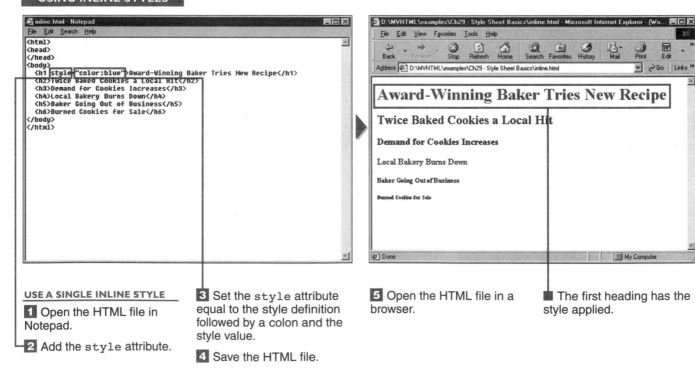

USE A SINGLE INLINE STYLE

1 Open the HTML file in Notepad.

2 Add the `style` attribute.

3 Set the `style` attribute equal to the style definition followed by a colon and the style value.

4 Save the HTML file.

5 Open the HTML file in a browser.

■ The first heading has the style applied.

Do inline styles override all other style definitions?

✔ Inline styles override any other style definitions included within an embedded style sheet or an external style sheet. This make a Web page more difficult to maintain because global changes will be ignored.

Can the style attribute be included with all tags?

✔ The `style` attribute is one of the global attributes that is included with almost all tags. There are a few exceptions though. For example, the `style` attribute cannot be used where styles have no affect such as the `<html>`, `<head>`, and `<title>` tags.

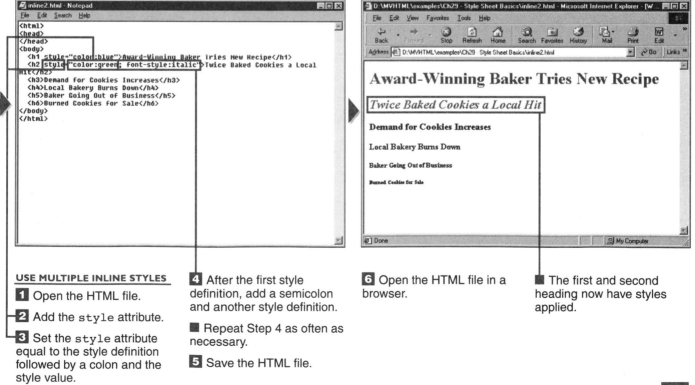

USE MULTIPLE INLINE STYLES

1 Open the HTML file.

2 Add the `style` attribute.

3 Set the `style` attribute equal to the style definition followed by a colon and the style value.

4 After the first style definition, add a semicolon and another style definition.

■ Repeat Step 4 as often as necessary.

5 Save the HTML file.

6 Open the HTML file in a browser.

■ The first and second heading now have styles applied.

APPLY STYLES TO SPECIFIC TEXT

At some point, you may want to identify specific sections of text within another tag for a unique style. For example, if you have a paragraph of text and you want to apply a different style to only select words within that paragraph, you can use the `<div>` and `<span>` tags to identify these sections.

The `<div>` tag is used for larger sections of text. The `<div>` tag is similar to the `<p>` tag, and can include the `align` attribute.

The `<span>` tag is used for smaller sections of text, single words, or even individual letters. The `<span>` tag can be used within other tags without causing a line break.

Both of these tags support the `style` attribute, which makes them useful for applying a unique style to a specific section of text.

This example uses the skeleton.html file from this book's CD, but the steps can be applied to any situation.

APPLY STYLES TO SPECIFIC TEXT

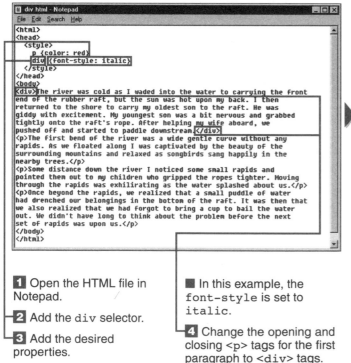

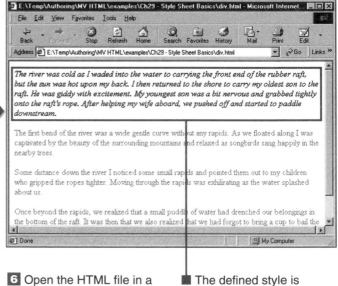

1 Open the HTML file in Notepad.

2 Add the `div` selector.

3 Add the desired properties.

■ In this example, the `font-style` is set to `italic`.

4 Change the opening and closing `<p>` tags for the first paragraph to `<div>` tags.

5 Save the HTML file.

6 Open the HTML file in a browser.

■ The defined style is displayed in the browser. In this case, the first paragraph is now italic.

Can <div> and <span> tags include other elements like images and tables?

✔ The <div> and <span> tags can be used anywhere within the Web page, but the styles will only apply to the applicable elements. For example, the color property is only used to define text color and cannot be used to change the color of an image or table.

How are the <div> and <span> tags formatted differently?

✔ The <div> tag causes a line break to appear automatically at the end of the specified text. The <span> tag does not include a line break.

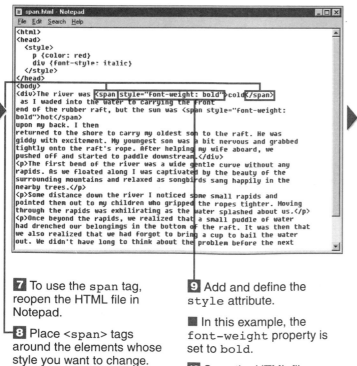

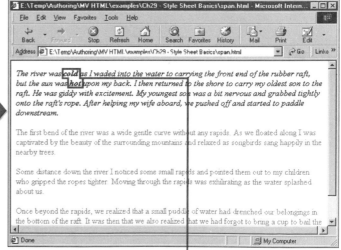

7 To use the span tag, reopen the HTML file in Notepad.

8 Place <span> tags around the elements whose style you want to change.

9 Add and define the style attribute.

■ In this example, the font-weight property is set to bold.

10 Save the HTML file.

11 Open HTML file in a browser.

■ The designated changes appear. In this example, several words now appear in bold.

DEFINE TEXT ALIGNMENT

Although many tags include an align attribute, you have more control and easier maintenance over your Web pages when you use style sheets to align your text.

Using style sheets, you can easily align text. The style property to align text is the text-align property. This property can be set to left, center, right, justify, or to any valid string.

The left, center, and right values align the text to either side or center it in the middle of the browser. The justify value spaces the text so that both sides are aligned.

Setting the text-align property to a string only affects the text within table cells. This value causes the table cells to be aligned to the specified string. Doing this can be useful for aligning dollar values in a spreadsheet-like table.

This example uses the skeleton.html file from this book's CD, but the steps can be applied to any situation.

DEFINE TEXT ALIGNMENT

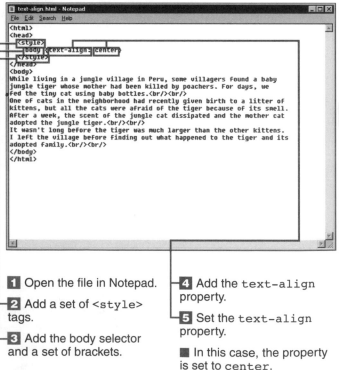

1 Open the file in Notepad.

2 Add a set of <style> tags.

3 Add the body selector and a set of brackets.

4 Add the text-align property.

5 Set the text-align property.

■ In this case, the property is set to center.

6 Save the HTML file.

7 Open the HTML file in a browser

■ All text within the <body> tag now reflects the text-align property value. In this example, the text is centered in the browser window.

If a style sheet tag is set to left-align the text, and the tag also includes the align attribute set to right, which alignment value has priority?

✔ If the style sheet defines the alignment differently than the `align` attribute, the value with the highest priority is the one closest to the tag. In this case, the `align` attribute is closer to the tag than the style sheet definition, so the `align` attribute takes precedence, right-aligning the text.

Are style sheets preferred over the align attribute that is used with some tags such as the <p> tag?

✔ The `align` attribute has been deprecated in favor of style sheets. That means that future HTML specifications will discontinue the `align` attribute. For the time being, however, deprecated attributes can be used, but style sheets are preferred.

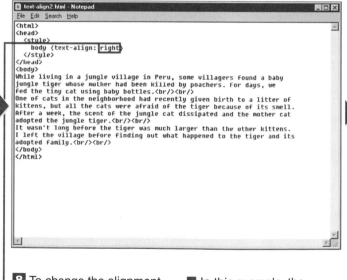

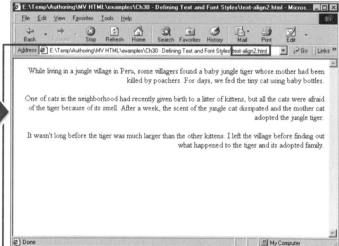

8 To change the alignment, re-open the HTML file in Notepad.

9 Set `text-align` to another value.

■ In this example, the property is set to `right`.

10 Save the HTML file.

11 Open the HTML file in a browser.

■ The alignment reflects the changes. In this case, the paragraphs are all now right-aligned.

DEFINE TEXT INDENTATION

Creating an indented paragraph without style sheets requires a fancy trick such as a graphical spacer because the <p> tag does not include an attribute that can indent the text. Style sheets, on the other hand, make it easy to include paragraph indents. You can also control precisely the exact indent value.

Using the text-indent property, you can control the length of the indent. This property can be set to any valid length and can even include negative values.

Indent lengths can be measured in either pixels or percentages.

- To specify a pixel length, include the number of pixels followed by the letters *px*. For example, text-indent: 20px indents the text 20 pixels from the left edge.

- To specify a percentage measurement, include a percentage symbol (%) after the numerical value. For example, text-indent: 20% indents the text 20 percent of the browser width.

This example uses the skeleton.html file from this book's CD, but the steps can be applied to any situation.

DEFINE TEXT INDENTATION

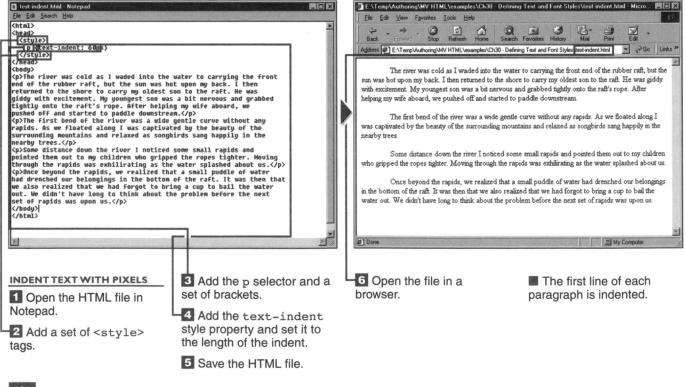

INDENT TEXT WITH PIXELS

1 Open the HTML file in Notepad.

2 Add a set of <style> tags.

3 Add the p selector and a set of brackets.

4 Add the text-indent style property and set it to the length of the indent.

5 Save the HTML file.

6 Open the file in a browser.

■ The first line of each paragraph is indented.

What happens if the text-indent value is negative?

✔ If the text is left-aligned and the indent value is negative, the text extends beyond the left side of the browser window and is not visible. You should be careful when using negative **text-indent** values that the first line of text is still visible.

What happens if I enter a value that is greater than the browser width such as 200%?

✔ If a value is entered for the **text-indent** property that exceeds the browser width, the horizontal scroll bars will appear within the browser. These scrolls bars let the user view the text that is indented beyond the browser width.

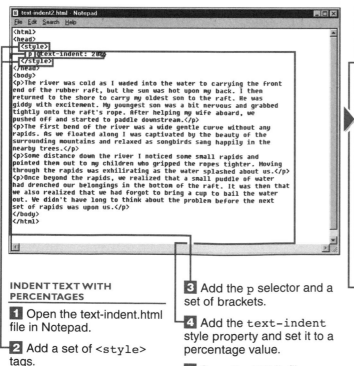

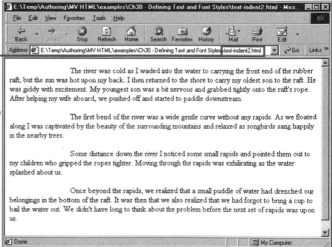

INDENT TEXT WITH PERCENTAGES

1 Open the text-indent.html file in Notepad.

2 Add a set of `<style>` tags.

3 Add the p selector and a set of brackets.

4 Add the `text-indent` style property and set it to a percentage value.

5 Save the HTML file.

6 Open the HTML file in a browser.

■ The first line of each paragraph is indented a percentage of the browser window.

DEFINE LETTER SPACING

Another very useful property that was not easy to accomplish before style sheets was changing the spacing between letters. This is known to typographers as *kerning*.

Kerning letters in a heading enables you to fit the heading in an exact space.

The property that enables the kerning of text is the `letter-spacing` property. This property lets you define the amount of white space that appears between each letter.

Acceptable values for the `letter-spacing` property can be measured in pixels (px), or *em spaces* (em). One em space

measurement equals the width of the letter *m*. For example, `letter-spacing: 1em` places enough space for a letter *m* between each letter.

This example uses the skeleton.html file from this book's CD, but the steps can be applied to any situation.

DEFINE LETTER SPACING

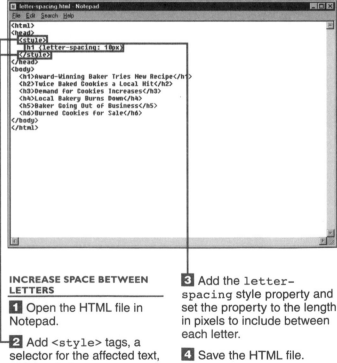

INCREASE SPACE BETWEEN LETTERS

1 Open the HTML file in Notepad.

2 Add `<style>` tags, a selector for the affected text, and brackets.

3 Add the `letter-spacing` style property and set the property to the length in pixels to include between each letter.

4 Save the HTML file.

5 Open the HTML file in a browser.

■ Notice how the distance between each letter has increased.

Can I separate just the space between each word?

✔ The style sheet specification lists property called `word-spacing` that can be used to control the spacing between each word, but the default browsers do not currently support it.

Can I cause the text not to wrap within the browser window?

✔ The style sheet specification also lists a property called `white-space` that can be set to `pre` or `nowrap`. This causes the text to act like it is surrounded by `<pre>` tags or to not wrap within the browser window. Most browsers do not currently support this property.

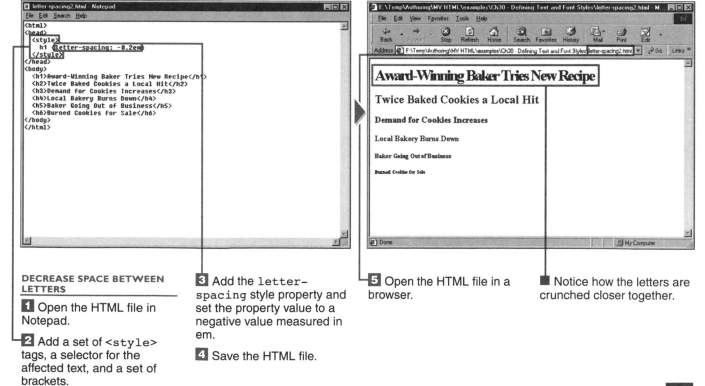

DECREASE SPACE BETWEEN LETTERS

1 Open the HTML file in Notepad.

2 Add a set of `<style>` tags, a selector for the affected text, and a set of brackets.

3 Add the `letter-spacing` style property and set the property value to a negative value measured in em.

4 Save the HTML file.

5 Open the HTML file in a browser.

■ Notice how the letters are crunched closer together.

DEFINE LINE SPACING

Another useful spacing control is to add space between adjacent lines of text in a paragraph. This technique enables you to control the length of a paragraph and the white space that it uses.

The letter-spacing property can be used to add horizontal space

to a section of text, but the letter-spacing property will not space the text vertically. To space the height of each line of text, you can use the line-height property. The line-height property can be set using a number to designate the number of lines to include, such as 2 for double-space. You can also specify

the line height as a percentage of the browser window or using em spaces.

This example uses the skeleton.html file from this book's CD, but the steps can be applied to any situation.

DEFINE LINE SPACING

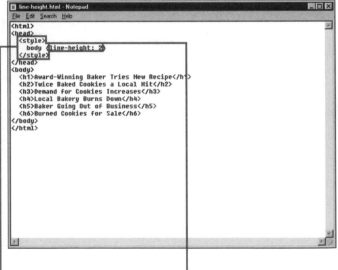

DEFINE LINE SPACING BY NUMBER OF LINES

1 Open the HTML file.

2 Add a set of <style> tags, a selector for the affected text, and a set of brackets.

3 Add the line-height style property and set the property to the number of lines to include between each line of text.

4 Save the HTML file.

5 Open the HTML file in a browser.

■ Notice that the headers are all double-spaced.

Can the line-height values be fractions of a number like 1.5?

✔ When specifying `line-height` values, you can include fractional numbers such as 1.5 and 2.2. The value is simply a multiplication factor. So, a value of 1 does not change the line height from its default value. Values less than 1 crowd the lines of text closer together.

Can I specify the number of pixels to appear between adjacent lines?

✔ In addition to percentage values, such as 1.5, you can also specify the spacing between adjacent lines in pixels. For example, `line-height: 20px` would space each line by 20 pixels. Point values can be specified using the pt ending to the value.

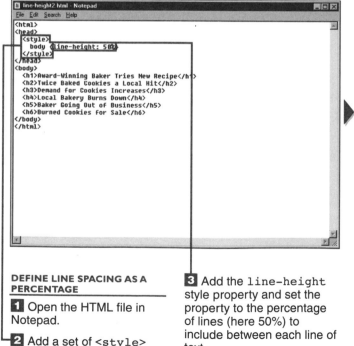

DEFINE LINE SPACING AS A PERCENTAGE

1 Open the HTML file in Notepad.

2 Add a set of `<style>` tags, a selector for the affected text, and a set of brackets.

3 Add the `line-height` style property and set the property to the percentage of lines (here 50%) to include between each line of text.

4 Save the HTML file.

5 Open the HTML file in a browser.

■ All the text within the `<body>` tag is now crunched as directed — in this case, to fit within 50 percent of the browser window.

DEFINE A FONT FAMILY

One of the biggest benefits that style sheets provide is to specify and control the font that is used to display the text. You can specify the font that is displayed by using the `font-family` property.

The `font-family` can accept several font families separated by commas. Specific font names can be included alongside generic font families. Generic font families can include `serif`, `sans-serif`, `cursive`, `fantasy`, and `monospace`.

Any specific fonts need to be included in quotes. Unless you have a specific need, consider using generic fonts. A specified font can only be used if the user's computer can display the specified font. If the specified font is not found on the user's computer, the next specified font is tried. The browser continues to peruse the listed fonts until a usable specified font can be found. These substitutes may not create the impact that you desire.

This example uses the skeleton.html file from this book's CD, but the steps can be applied to any situation.

DEFINE A FONT FAMILY

font-family.html - Notepad

```
<html>
<head>
  <style>
    h1 {font-family: sans-serif}
  </style>
</head>
<body>
  <h1>Award-Winning Baker Tries New Recipe</h1>
  <h2>Twice Baked Cookies a Local Hit</h2>
  <h3>Demand for Cookies Increases</h3>
  <h4>Local Bakery Burns Down</h4>
  <h5>Baker Going Out of Business</h5>
  <h6>Burned Cookies for Sale</h6>
</body>
</html>
```

E:\Temp\Authoring\MV HTML\examples\Ch30 - Defining Text and Font Styles\font-family.html - Micros...

Award-Winning Baker Tries New Recipe

Twice Baked Cookies a Local Hit

Demand for Cookies Increases

Local Bakery Burns Down

Baker Going Out of Business

Burned Cookies for Sale

DESIGNATE A GENERIC FONT

1 Open the HTML file in Notepad.

2 Add a set of `<style>` tags, a selector for the affected text, and a set of brackets.

3 Add the `font-family` style property and set the property to a generic font.

■ In this example, the property is set to `sans-serif`.

4 Save the HTML file.

5 Open the file in a browser.

■ Notice that the first header appears in the designated font — in this case, sans-serif.

What happens if none of the specified fonts are available?

✔ When using the `font-family` property, the browser looks from left to right for the first font family that the user's computer recognizes. If a useable font is not found, the text is displayed in the browser's default font.

Is there a limit to the number of fonts that I can specify within the font-family property?

✔ There is not a limit to the number of fonts that the `font-family` property can hold. The more fonts that are specified, the greater the likelihood that a font family will be found on the user's system. Including more fonts will conversely result in wider variations in the Web page design.

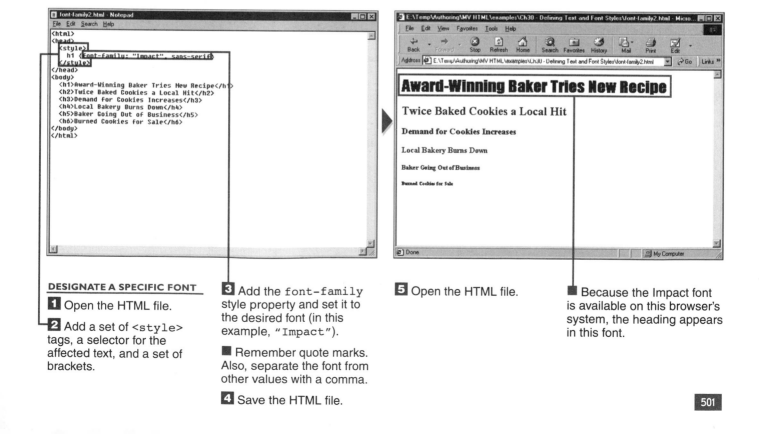

DESIGNATE A SPECIFIC FONT

1 Open the HTML file.

2 Add a set of `<style>` tags, a selector for the affected text, and a set of brackets.

3 Add the `font-family` style property and set it to the desired font (in this example, "`Impact`").

■ Remember quote marks. Also, separate the font from other values with a comma.

4 Save the HTML file.

5 Open the HTML file.

■ Because the Impact font is available on this browser's system, the heading appears in this font.

DEFINE FONT STYLES AND VARIANTS

Although italics can be displayed using the <i> tag, style sheets make it easier for you to globally update all the places within several places where italics are used. Style sheets also include support for some additional formatting variants, such as small capital letters, that are not available using standard HTML tags.

The font-style property can be used to italicize the text. This can be done with two different values. This property can be set to normal, italic, or oblique.

The font-variant property can be used to format the text in a unique way. The font-variant property can be set to normal or small-caps.

This example uses the br.html file from this book's CD, but the steps can be applied to any situation.

DEFINE FONT STYLES AND VARIANTS

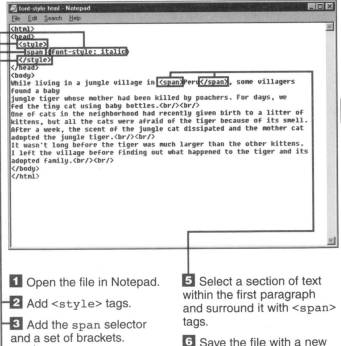

1 Open the file in Notepad.

2 Add <style> tags.

3 Add the span selector and a set of brackets.

4 Add the font-style and set it to italic.

5 Select a section of text within the first paragraph and surround it with <span> tags.

6 Save the file with a new name.

7 Open the new HTML file in a browser.

■ Notice that the section of text marked with the <span> tags is displayed in italics.

How is the oblique value for the font-style property different than the italic value?

✔ The `oblique` value is different from the `italic` option in that the `italics` option uses the actual italic version of the font; the `oblique` manually slants the text without relying on an italicized font.

How often can the small caps value for the font-variant be used?

✔ Specifying a paragraph of text as small caps is unacceptable to many users. This equates to yelling at the user. Small-caps are useful as another way to highlight a specific word or phrase and should be used in design like bold formatting.

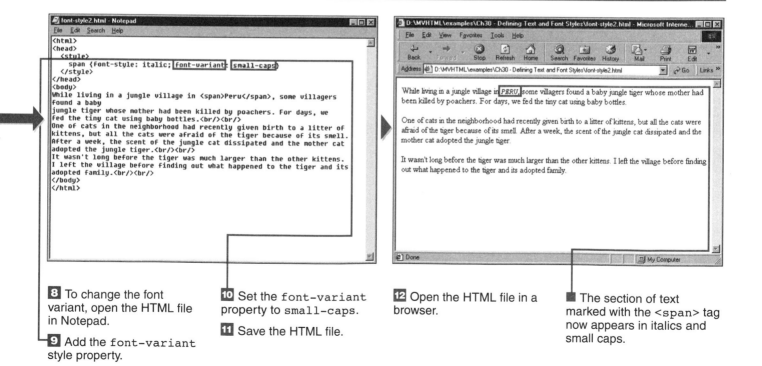

8 To change the font variant, open the HTML file in Notepad.

9 Add the `font-variant` style property.

10 Set the `font-variant` property to `small-caps`.

11 Save the HTML file.

12 Open the HTML file in a browser.

■ The section of text marked with the `<span>` tag now appears in italics and small caps.

503

DEFINE FONT WEIGHT

Although HTML includes a
`<b>` tag for making text
bold, you can use style
sheets to achieve several different
levels of boldness.

Allowing different bold thicknesses
gives the designer several options
for highlighting words. For some
designs, lighter weights work better.

The `font-weight` property is
used to set how thick the text
appears. Acceptable values for this
property include

- Lighter

- Normal

- Bold

- Bolder

The `font-weight` property can
also be set to a number between
100 and 900. A value of 100
appears lighter and a value of 900
appears bolder.

Be careful not to overuse bold
formatting. Using too much bold
text can backfire, making your most
important points (the ones you
bolded) blend into the text as much
as they would in a plain font. Not
only do you lose your emphasis,
you also risk losing your credibility.
The reader may begin to doubt the

importance of the bold points and
conclude that none of the material
is important. In fact, it may become
annoying and cause you to lose
your reader altogether.

Many times bold comes across as
screaming, especially when applied
to a large amount of text. If bold
"screams," all caps "speaks firmly"
and can be a good alternative that
allows emphasis with a more
moderate tone.

This example uses the br.html file
from this book's CD, but the steps
can be applied to any situation.

DEFINE FONT WEIGHT

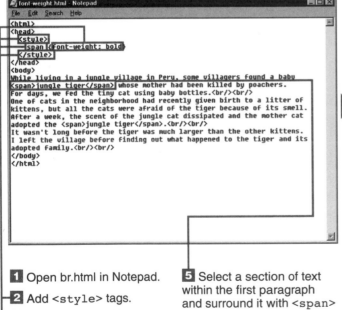

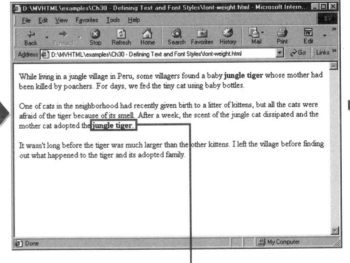

1 Open br.html in Notepad.

2 Add `<style>` tags.

3 Add the `span` selector
and a set of brackets.

4 Add the `font-weight`
property and set it to `bold`.

5 Select a section of text
within the first paragraph
and surround it with `<span>`
tags.

6 Save the file.

8 Open the file in a
browser.

■ Notice that the section of
text marked with the `<span>`
tags is displayed in bold.

How are the numerical values different from the keyword values?

✔ The keyword values include `lighter`, `bold`, and `bolder`. The lighter keyword produces the same results as using the numerical value `100`. The default value of normal is the same as `400`. The `bold` value is the same as `700` and the `bolder` value is the same as `900`.

Can I specify fractional weight values such as 650 or 872?

✔ Implementation depends on the browser, but the standard does not support fractional weight values. Acceptable values must end with two zeros. All other values will be ignored.

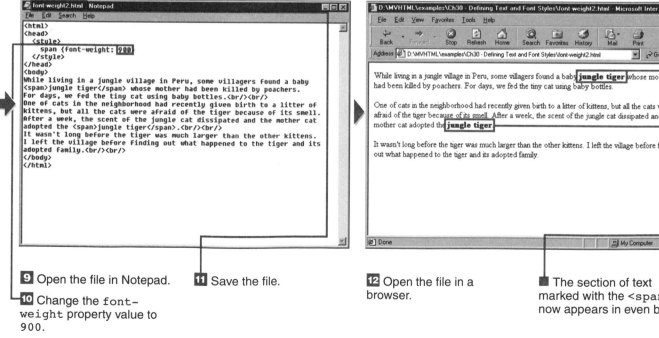

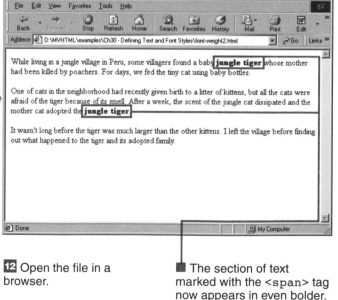

9 Open the file in Notepad.

10 Change the `font-weight` property value to `900`.

11 Save the file.

12 Open the file in a browser.

■ The section of text marked with the `<span>` tag now appears in even bolder.

DEFINE FONT SIZE

Standard HTML has very few options when you want to change the size of a font. Basically, you have to use the `<font>` tag and apply it each time you want a change in the font. Fortunately, you can use style sheets and the `font size` property to quickly set the font size on a Web page. Style sheets and the `font-size` property are the preferred method for setting font size on a Web page.

The `font-size` property accepts several different types of values, including:

- **Absolute sizes.** The absolute values are `xx-small`, `small`, `medium`, `large`, `x-large`, and `xx-large`.

- **Relative sizes.** The relative values are `smaller` or `larger`. These values decrease or increase the font size relative to the default font size.

- **Font point sizes.** This is a numerical value measured in points (pt). The default font size is 12 point or a 3 on the HTML scale size of 1–7.

This example uses the br.html file from this book's CD, but the steps can be applied to any situation.

DEFINE FONT SIZE

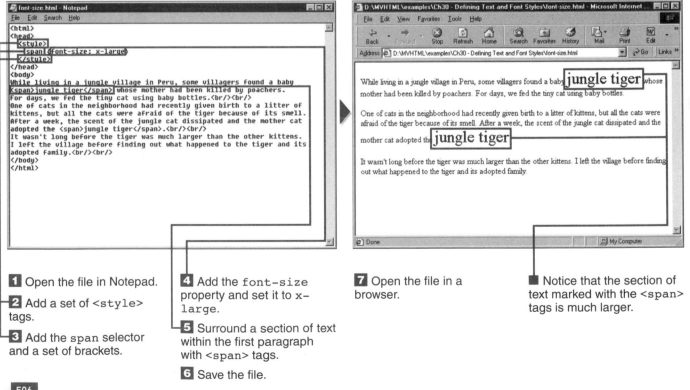

1 Open the file in Notepad.

2 Add a set of `<style>` tags.

3 Add the span selector and a set of brackets.

4 Add the `font-size` property and set it to `x-large`.

5 Surround a section of text within the first paragraph with `<span>` tags.

6 Save the file.

7 Open the file in a browser.

■ Notice that the section of text marked with the `<span>` tags is much larger.

MASTER IT

How can the relative keywords larger and smaller be used?

✔ The relative keywords, `larger` and `smaller`, change the font size from its current size. The font's size is determined by any styles applied to the tags that it encompasses. For example, if the `<body>` tag has a font size applied, any `<span>` tags within the `<body>` tags that use the relative font size keyword are sized relative to the `<body>` tag's font size.

Is this property preferred over setting the font size with the `<font>` tag?

✔ Style sheets are the preferred method for controlling font size. The `<font>` tag has been deprecated in the official HTML specification. Its use will be discontinued in future specifications.

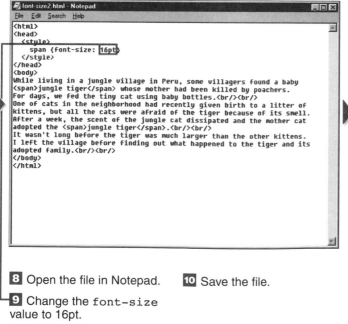

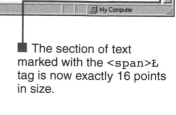

8 Open the file in Notepad.

9 Change the `font-size` value to 16pt.

10 Save the file.

11 Open the file in a browser.

■ The section of text marked with the `<span>`Ł tag is now exactly 16 points in size.

DEFINE FONT COLOR

Text color in standard HTML has traditionally been set using the `<font>` tag. With the `<font>` tag, every individual instance of text color had to be marked. This is difficult to maintain across several Web pages. Using style sheets, though, you can quickly and easily update text color values as needed.

The `color` property is used to set the text color. Acceptable values for the color property include the standard color keywords such as red, blue, and green, or the RGB hexadecimal triplicate values preceded with the number symbol (#). The default color is black.

Consider the color of your background when adjusting the text color. If you set the paint to be the same color as its canvas, users will

not be able to differentiate between the two, viewing only a solid-colored screen without text. Choosing text color for your pages is covered more in depth in Chapter 7.

This example uses the br.html file from this book's CD, but the steps can be applied to any situation.

DEFINE FONT COLOR

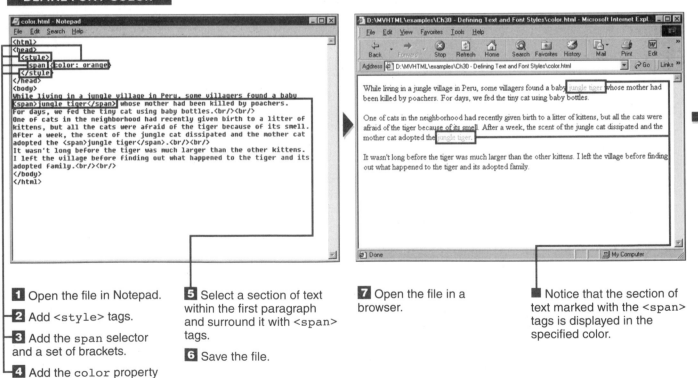

1 Open the file in Notepad.

2 Add `<style>` tags.

3 Add the span selector and a set of brackets.

4 Add the color property and set it to orange.

5 Select a section of text within the first paragraph and surround it with `<span>` tags.

6 Save the file.

7 Open the file in a browser.

■ Notice that the section of text marked with the `<span>` tags is displayed in the specified color.

Text color can also be set using the text attribute in the <body> tag. Which is the preferred way to specify text color?

✔ The advantage of using the text attribute in the <body> tag is that the text attribute correctly displays the text color on older browsers that do not support style sheets. However, style sheets are the preferred way to color text. In fact, if the <body> tag includes the text attribute set to one color and the body selector is set to another color in the <script> tag, the style sheet definition takes precedence.

Should the <font> tag be used to specify text color?

✔ The <font> tag has been deprecated, which means that its use will be discontinued in future specifications HTML. You can still use it, but officially, its use is not recommended.

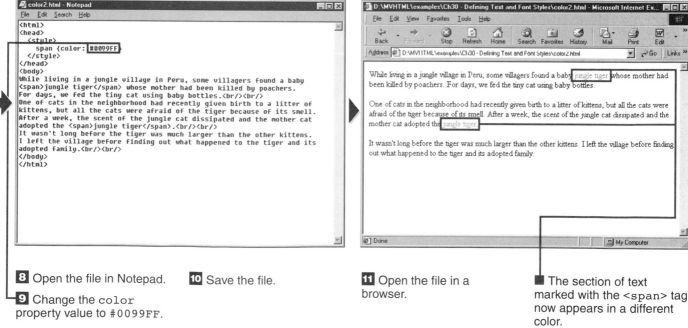

8 Open the file in Notepad.

9 Change the color property value to #0099FF.

10 Save the file.

11 Open the file in a browser.

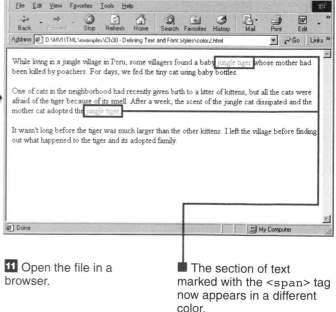

■ The section of text marked with the <span> tag now appears in a different color.

DEFINE MULTIPLE FONT STYLES

You can assign many of the font styles discussed in this chapter to a single selector simultaneously using the font property. This property accepts multiple font style property values to format the text. The prefered order of these values is as follows:

- font-style
- font-variant
- font-weight
- font-size
- line-height
- font-family

A single space should be included between each value.

Some of these property values deserve greater explanation. font-style includes the typeface (for example, Times New Roman) and font slant (that is, italics or normal). You might think that bold would be a font-style attribute, but it is actually a font-weight attribute.

font-variant allows for normal or small caps. Boldness and lightness are defined by font-weight and your order of preference to font families (that is, serif or cursive) is defined in font-family. For example, to define a section of text, the font property can look like this: font {italic bold 20pt 2 "Times Roman" serif}.

This example uses the br.html file from this book's CD, but the steps can be applied to any situation.

DEFINE MULTIPLE FONT STYLES

1 Open the HTML file in Notepad.

2 Add a set of <style> tags.

3 Add the body selector and a set of brackets.

4 Add the font property and set it to italic bold 12pt "Times Roman" serif.

5 Save the file.

6 Open the file in a browser.

■ Notice that the body text has several font styles applied.

Do I need to include an entry for every property covered in the font property?

✔ Although the `font` property can include multiple properties, not all of them need to be included. Any of the properties can be excluded from the `font` property (by simply putting a space between the commas where the property should be), but if they are included, the order should be maintained. If the order is not maintained, the browser gets confused and does not render the font style correctly.

What is the advantage of the font property?

✔ Using the `font` style sheet property is a much simpler way to specify many various font properties, but it can also be confusing because individual property values can be unrecognized.

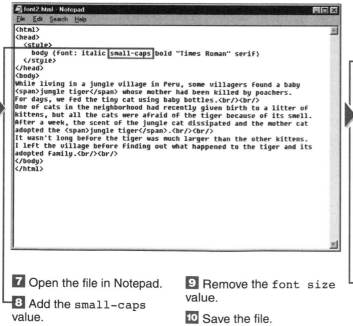

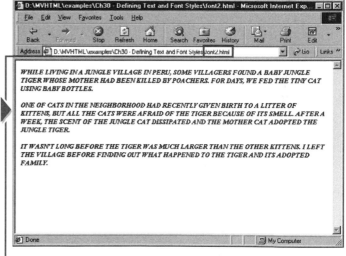

7 Open the file in Notepad.

8 Add the `small-caps` value.

9 Remove the `font size` value.

10 Save the file.

11 Open the file in a browser.

■ The body text font style has now changed again.

DEFINE TEXT DECORATION STYLES

You can use the `text-decoration` property to add several unique formatting options. The value for this property can be set to `none`, `underline`, `overline`, `line-through`, or `blink`.

The `underline` value places a line under the text, and the `overline` is the opposite (applicable to the use of foreign languages), placing a line above the text. The `line-through` value works just like the `<strike>` tag, placing a line through the center of the text. This can be useful when you want to depict changes. The `blink` value causes the text to blink in the browser, a practical tool to grab the user's attention, while avoiding the overuse of bold. The `none` value, of course, adds no unique formatting options or can shut off automatically applied text decorations, such as underlined links. One or more of these text decoration properties can be applied by simply including all values desired.

This example uses the br.html file from this book's CD, but the steps can be applied to any situation.

DEFINE TEXT DECORATION STYLES

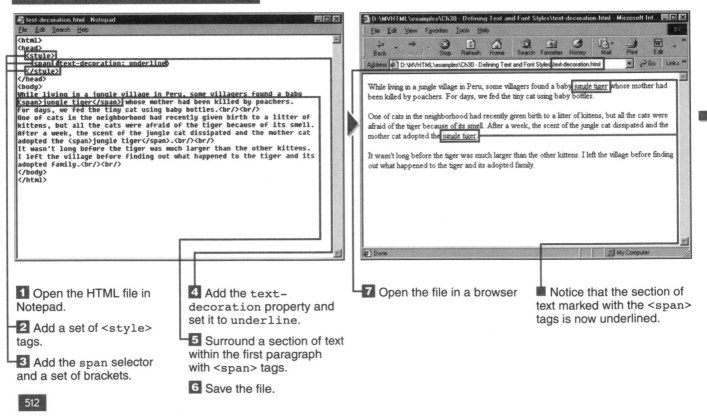

1 Open the HTML file in Notepad.

2 Add a set of `<style>` tags.

3 Add the `span` selector and a set of brackets.

4 Add the `text-decoration` property and set it to `underline`.

5 Surround a section of text within the first paragraph with `<span>` tags.

6 Save the file.

7 Open the file in a browser

■ Notice that the section of text marked with the `<span>` tags is now underlined.

When should the blink value be used?

✔ You should use the blink value cautiously. Many Web users complain whenever blinking text is found on a Web page. Blinking text is very distracting and should only be used creatively so as not to annoy the users.

Should I underline my hypertext links?

✔ When the browser displays hypertext links, it automatically underlines the links. This makes them identifiable as links on black-and-white systems.

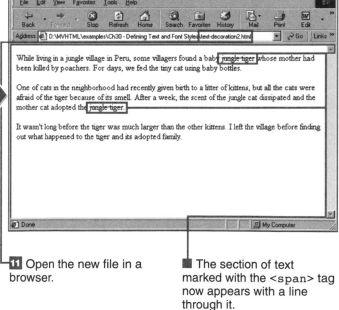

8 Open the same file in Notepad.

9 Change the `text-decoration` value to `line-through`.

10 Save the file with a different name.

11 Open the new file in a browser.

■ The section of text marked with the `<span>` tag now appears with a line through it.

DEFINE TEXT TRANSFORM STYLES

This property can be used to ensure that content is published in the desired format. Text that is published in all capitals is like yelling at the user and should only be used on rare occasions to highlight specific words and phrases.

The `text-transform` property defines how the text is capitalized. The acceptable values for this property include `none`, `capitalize`, `uppercase`, and `lowercase`.

The `capitalize` value capitalizes only the first letter in each

sentence, but `uppercase` and `lowercase` change all the letters.

This example uses the br.html file from this book's CD, but the steps can be applied to any situation.

DEFINE TEXT TRANSFORM STYLES

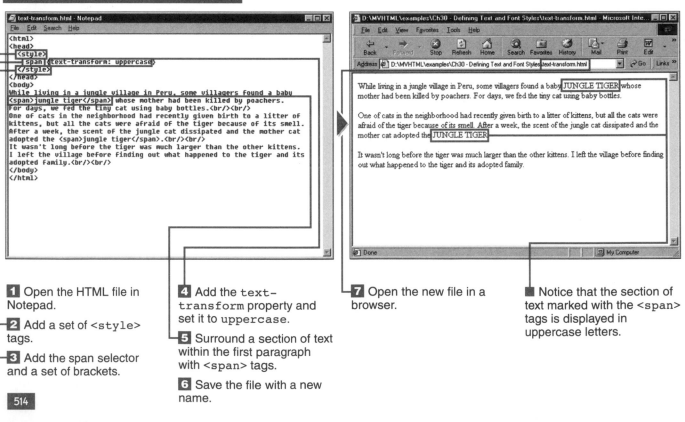

■ **1** Open the HTML file in Notepad.

■ **2** Add a set of `<style>` tags.

■ **3** Add the span selector and a set of brackets.

■ **4** Add the `text-transform` property and set it to `uppercase`.

■ **5** Surround a section of text within the first paragraph with `<span>` tags.

■ **6** Save the file with a new name.

■ **7** Open the new file in a browser.

■ Notice that the section of text marked with the `<span>` tags is displayed in uppercase letters.

Because uppercase text is often considered as if someone were yelling, when can uppercase text be used?

✔ It is generally rude to use uppercase letters for normal text, but using uppercase letters for headings and names is acceptable.

Does JavaScript include similar methods for converting text to all uppercase or all lowercase?

✔ JavaScript has methods that can be used to convert text to upper- or lowercase. You can use style sheets to automatically convert text in a similar manner. These JavaScript methods are covered in Chapter 25.

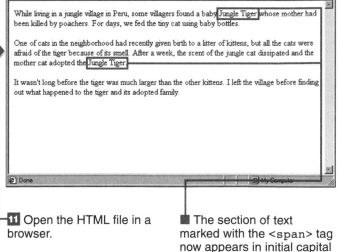

8 Open the same HTML file in Notepad.

9 Change the `text-transform` value to `capitalize`.

10 Save the file.

11 Open the HTML file in a browser.

■ The section of text marked with the `<span>` tag now appears in initial capital letters.

DEFINE BACKGROUND COLOR

You can set the background color of Web pages by using the bgcolor attribute added to the <body> tag. This, however, only sets the color for one page. Using style sheets enables you to set the background color for several pages at once.

The style sheet property that makes this possible is background-

color. This property can accept any valid color name or the keyword rgb followed by the amount or red, green, and blue in parenthesis. The red, green, and blue values can range between 0 and 255, with 0 being no color and 255 being full color.

For example, the style definition, background-color

{rgb(255, 0, 0)} would produce a red page background.

This example uses the skeleton.html file from this book's CD, but the steps can be applied to any situation.

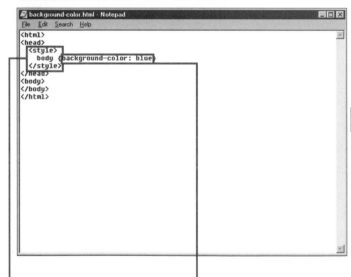

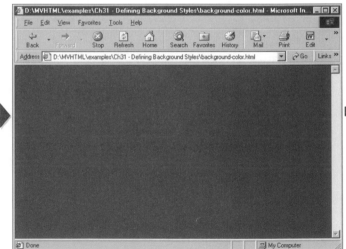

1 Open the HTML file in Notepad.

2 Add <style> tags, a selector, and a set of brackets.

■ This example uses the body selector.

3 Add the background-color style property and set it.

■ In this example, the property is set to blue.

4 Save the HTML file.

5 Open the HTML file in a browser.

■ The page background color now reflects the specified property. In this example, the background is now blue.

If a page includes both a style definition for the background color and the bgcolor attribute in the <body> tag, which determines the color of the page?

✔ If a Web page includes both a style sheet definition and the bgcolor attribute for the background color, the style sheet definition takes priority. For example, if the style sheet includes the background-color property set to blue and the <body> tag includes the bgcolor attribute set to green, the page will appear blue.

Which method of adding background color is preferred?

✔ Specifying background colors using the bgcolor attribute of the <body> tag (covered in Chapter 6) is actually deprecated. Use of the bgcolor attribute will be discontinued in future specifications in favor of style sheets.

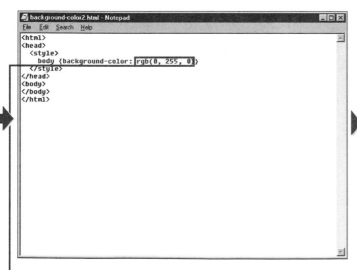

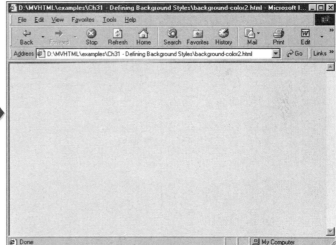

6 To change an established background color, open the HTML file in Notepad.

7 Change the background-color property.

■ In this example, the value is changed to rgb (0, 255, 0).

8 Save the HTML file.

9 Open the HTML file in a browser.

■ The page background color is now changed. In this example the background is now green.

DEFINE ELEMENT BACKGROUND COLOR

The preceding section showed an example of changing the background-color of a Web page with the body selector. What happens if you use another selector?

The background-color style property changes the background color for any selector. The new

background color displays immediately only around the selector element. This feature is not possible using standard HTML.

For example, if the selector is h1, the specified color will only surround the heading text, not the whole page.

This property can only be used with selectors that are displayed in the browser window including headings, lists, and tables, but not images or applets.

This example uses the skeleton.html file from this book's CD, but the steps can be applied to any situation.

DEFINE ELEMENT BACKGROUND COLOR

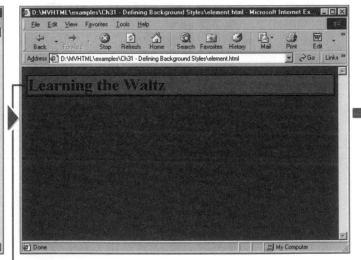

1 Open the HTML file in Notepad.

2 Add a selector (in this case, h1) and brackets.

3 Add the background-color style property.

■ In this example, the property is set to green.

4 If the selected element (in this case, a heading 1) does not yet exist, add tags and text.

5 Save the HTML file.

6 Open the HTML file in a browser.

■ The background color for the header reflects the designated value. In this example, the heading background is green.

■ If you only want to add color to one background, you can stop now. If, however, you want to add color to a second background, proceed with Step 7.

What are the concerns if I use the background-color property to change the background color of a Web page element?

✔ When coloring Web elements, you should be careful to use a color that is complementary to the background color and other colors that are used on the Web page. Conflicting colors can destroy the design of a Web page. You should also be cautious to make sure the background color does not mask the text.

If a nontext element like the img selector includes a specified background color and margins or padding, will the element background be visible?

✔ The margin and padding properties are covered in the Chapter 31. These properties will appear invisible and will not allow the element background color to be displayed. If you wish to surround an image with a color, you can use the border properties discussed in Chapter 31.

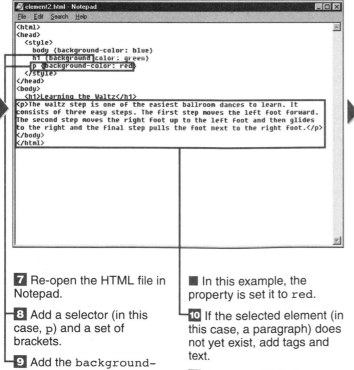

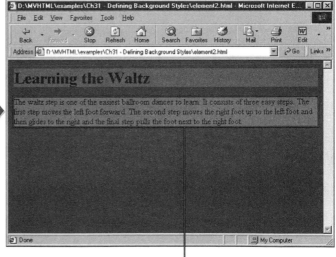

7 Re-open the HTML file in Notepad.

8 Add a selector (in this case, p) and a set of brackets.

9 Add the background-color style property.

■ In this example, the property is set it to red.

10 If the selected element (in this case, a paragraph) does not yet exist, add tags and text.

11 Save the HTML file.

12 Open the HTML file in a browser.

■ The second background now reflects the designated color. In this example, the background of the paragraph text is colored red.

DEFINE BACKGROUND IMAGE

Style sheets can display a background image as well as a background color. The background-image property does this.

Using normal HTML, displaying a background image can be done using the background attribute with the <body> tag. The advantage of style sheets is that when you set up a standard style sheet definition that affects several pages, the background for all these pages could be changed using one reference.

The background-image style property is set to the URL for the image to use. To include a URL with a style sheet property, you need to include the url keyword followed by the actual URL in parentheses.

For example, the property background-image {url(myimage.gif)} loads the myimage.gif image as the background image for the Web page.

This example uses the skeleton.html file from this book's CD, but the steps can be applied to any situation.

DEFINE BACKGROUND IMAGE

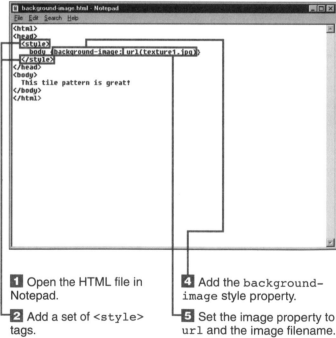

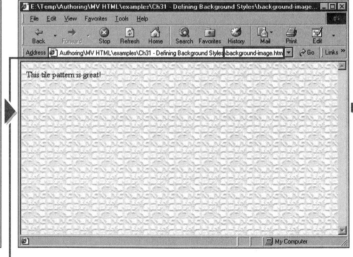

1 Open the HTML file in Notepad.

2 Add a set of <style> tags.

3 Add a selector (in this case, body) and a set of brackets.

4 Add the background-image style property.

5 Set the image property to url and the image filename.

6 Save the HTML file.

7 Open the HTML file in a browser.

■ The specified background now includes an image.

What kind of image types can be included as background images?

✔ Background images can be any accepted graphic format, including GIF, JPEG, and PNG.

Is there any way to position the background image using style sheets?

✔ Style sheets enable you to position precisely the background image using the background-position property. This property and several others that can control the background image are presented in the sections that follow.

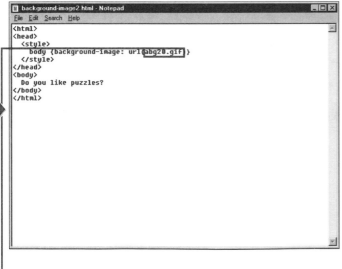

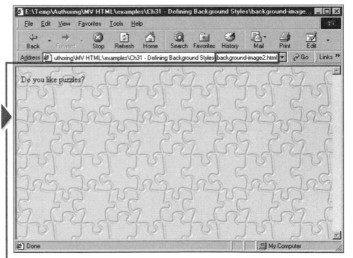

8 To change a background, open the HTML file in Notepad.

9 Change the background-image property filename.

10 Save the HTML file.

11 Open the HTML file in a browser.

■ The background image is now different.

DEFINE BACKGROUND TILING

When a background image is used, the image is by default tiled horizontally and vertically until it fills the entire browser window. Style sheets add the ability to tile the background image only vertically or horizontally. You can also specify that the background image does not tile in either direction.

The *background-repeat* property enables these new features. To tile only in the horizontal direction, you can set the background-repeat property to repeat-x. To tile only in the vertical direction, you can set it to repeat-y, and the no-repeat value causes the background image to not be tiled in either direction. The *x* and *y* values represent the horizontal and vertical distance from the upper-left corner of the browser window.

This example uses the background-image.html file from this book's CD, but the steps can be applied to any situation.

DEFINE BACKGROUND TILING

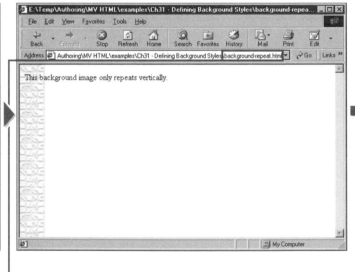

1 Open the HTML file in Notepad.

2 Add the background-repeat property.

3 Set the background-repeat property value.

■ In this example, the property is set to repeat-y, to tile vertically.

4 Save the HTML file.

5 Open the HTML file in a browser.

■ The background image repeats as directed, in this case vertically.

If the background image does not fill the entire browser window using the repeat-x, repeat-y, or no-repeat values, what color is the rest of the browser window?

✔ The space that is not occupied by the background image is colored the default white color. You can use the background-color property in conjunction with the background-image property to color the remaining background space.

Can I add space between the repeating background image and the browser edge?

✔ You can use the background-position property, which is covered in the section "Define Background Position," to position the background image. Another way to add space is to include some white space as part of the background image.

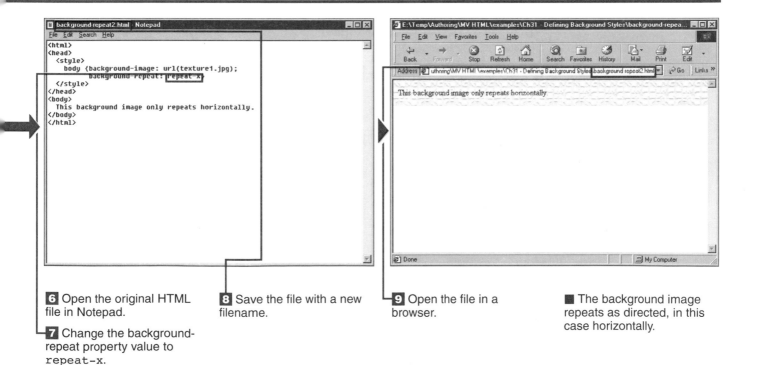

6 Open the original HTML file in Notepad.

7 Change the background-repeat property value to repeat-x.

8 Save the file with a new filename.

9 Open the file in a browser.

■ The background image repeats as directed, in this case horizontally.

DEFINE BACKGROUND ATTACHMENT

Another useful style sheet property that you can use to control how the background images scrolls on the Web page is the `background-attachment` property.

This property has two settings:

- **Scroll.** The scroll setting is the default. The scroll setting causes the background image to scroll along with the browser window.

- **Fixed.** The fixed setting causes the background image to remain in its position when the browser window is scrolled.

This property has no effect if a background image is not specified.

If the background image is used as part of the Web page design, it would make sense to fix the background image within the browser. The scroll setting,

however, provides feedback to the user that the page is scrolling, which can be helpful.

This example uses the skeleton.html file from this book's CD, but the steps can be applied to any situation.

DEFINE BACKGROUND ATTACHMENT

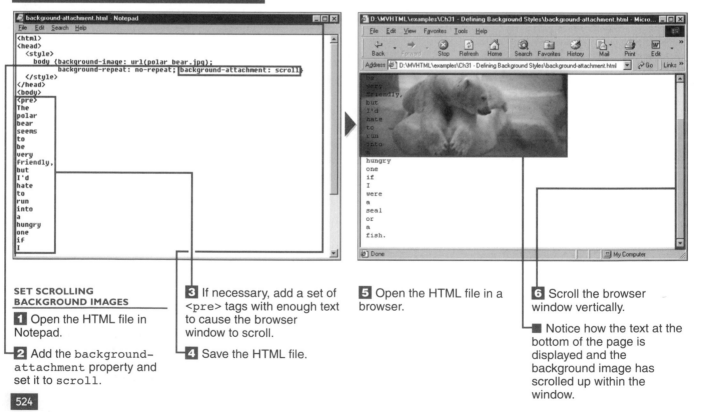

SET SCROLLING BACKGROUND IMAGES

1 Open the HTML file in Notepad.

2 Add the `background-attachment` property and set it to `scroll`.

3 If necessary, add a set of `<pre>` tags with enough text to cause the browser window to scroll.

4 Save the HTML file.

5 Open the HTML file in a browser.

6 Scroll the browser window vertically.

■ Notice how the text at the bottom of the page is displayed and the background image has scrolled up within the window.

Does the background-attachment property work if the background image is added using the background attribute of the <body> tag?

✔ If you include a background image using the background attribute of the <body> tag, the other background image properties, such as background-repeat and background-attachment, still control the background image.

Does this property have any effect if the Web page content fits within the browser?

✔ If the Web page content fits within the browser, the browser will not scroll, so this property will have no effect.

Does this property work if the browser scrolls horizontally?

✔ This property will work the same for content that needs to scroll horizontally as it does for content that scrolls vertically.

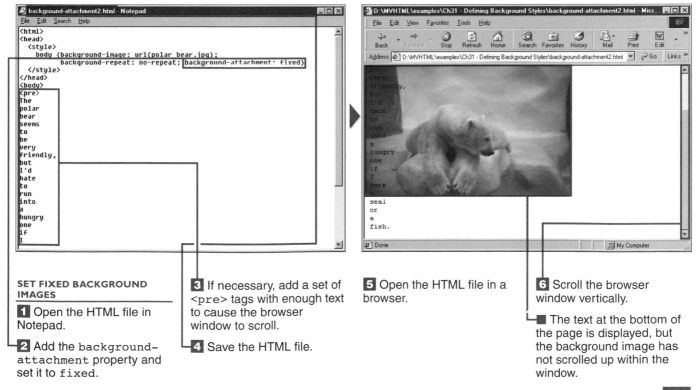

SET FIXED BACKGROUND IMAGES

1 Open the HTML file in Notepad.

2 Add the background-attachment property and set it to fixed.

3 If necessary, add a set of <pre> tags with enough text to cause the browser window to scroll.

4 Save the HTML file.

5 Open the HTML file in a browser.

6 Scroll the browser window vertically.

■ The text at the bottom of the page is displayed, but the background image has not scrolled up within the window.

DEFINE BACKGROUND POSITION

Another feature that is enabled with style sheets is the ability to position the background image on the Web page. You accomplish this with the `background-position` property.

This property can accept the keywords `top`, `center`, `bottom`, `left`, and `right` to position the background image along the browser edges. Two keywords can be used together with the first value used for the horizontal placement and the second for the vertical placement. For example, `background-position: top center` centers the background image at the top edge of the browser window.

You can also specify the number of pixels from the top left corner of the browser window (or percentage values). If only one value is included, the browser assumes that the value is the horizontal direction.

This example uses the background-repeat2.html file from this book's CD, but the steps can be applied to any situation.

DEFINE BACKGROUND POSITION

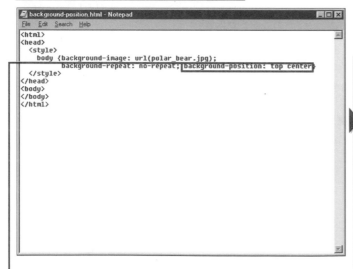

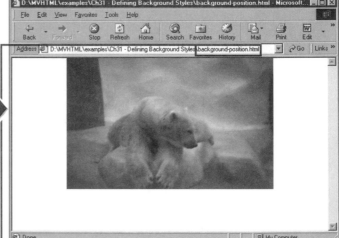

1 Open the HTML file in Notepad.

2 Add the `background-position` property and set it to `top center`.

3 Save the file with a new filename.

4 Open the file in a browser.

■ The background image is positioned centered along the top edge of the browser.

If only one background-position value is included, the value is used for the horizontal direction. What is the default vertical placement?

✔ The default vertical placement is centered in the browser window. So, if the background-position property is set to 20px, the background image is placed 20 pixels from the left edge in the center of the browser.

What happens if you include conflicting background-position values?

✔ If you include conflicting background-position values in a style sheet definition, the browser uses the value that was specified last. For example, if you include top and bottom as values, the background image will be positioned along the bottom edge.

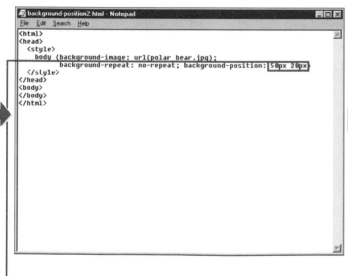

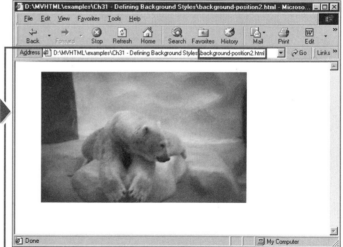

5 Open the HTML file in Notepad.

6 Change the background-position property value to 50px 20px.

7 Save the file with a new filename.

8 Open the file in a browser.

■ The background image is positioned exactly 50 pixels from the left edge and 20 pixels from the top edge.

COMBINE MULTIPLE BACKGROUND PROPERTIES

You can specify several background image properties at once by using the *background* property. This syntax is very handy for creating compact style sheet definitions, but it can be difficult to understand what the definition does.

The order that the properties appear is important and goes like this:

- `background-color`

- `background-image`

- `background-repeat`

- `background-attachment`

- `background-position`

Not all properties need to be included, but the ones that are included need to appear in order. A single space separates each property.

For example, `background {blue url(myimage.gif) repeat-y fixed left top}` would load the image, myimage.gif, on top of a blue background and position it vertically along the left edge of the browser window.

This example uses the skeleton.html file from this book's CD, but the steps can be applied to any situation.

COMBINE MULTIPLE BACKGROUND PROPERTIES

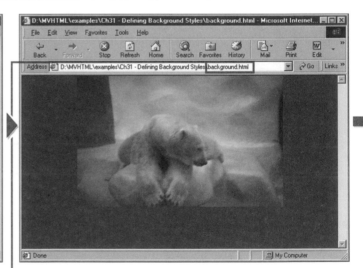

1 Open the HTML file in Notepad.

2 Add a set of `<style>` tags.

3 Add the `body` selector and a set of brackets.

4 Add the `background` style property and set it to `blue url(polar_bear.jpg) no-repeat fixed top center`.

5 Save the file with a new filename.

6 Open the file in a browser.

■ The page background appears as specified.

Can all selectors use the background style property?

✔ All selectors can use the `background` style property. The `body` selector affects the Web page background, and using other selectors affects only those tags. Including the `background` property for some selectors, such as the img or applet selectors would not make sense.

What happens if I list the properties in the wrong order?

✔ If the properties for the background style sheet definition are listed in the wrong order, the browser looks for the first property that it understands and interprets it and any other properties after it. All others are ignored.

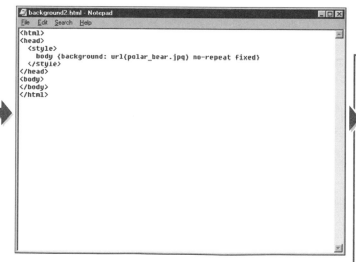

7 Open the HTML file in Notepad.

8 Remove the values `blue`, `top`, and `center` from the `background` property.

9 Save the file.

11 Open the file in a browser.

■ The page background now appears differently.

DEFINE MARGINS

Web page elements, especially text, can greatly benefit from the use of *margins*. Margins help separate the Web page element from the edges of the browser window.

Margins can be set for any Web page element with the `margin` property. This property can accept four values—for the top, right, bottom, and left edges.

As an alternative to four values, you can include two values. These two values set the top and bottom margins to the first value and the right and left margins to the second value.

The values can be measured in pixels (px) or as a percentage (%) of the window. For example, `margin: 20px` would create a margin that is 20 pixels in width.

This example uses the skeleton.html file from this book's CD, but the steps can be applied to any situation.

DEFINE MARGINS

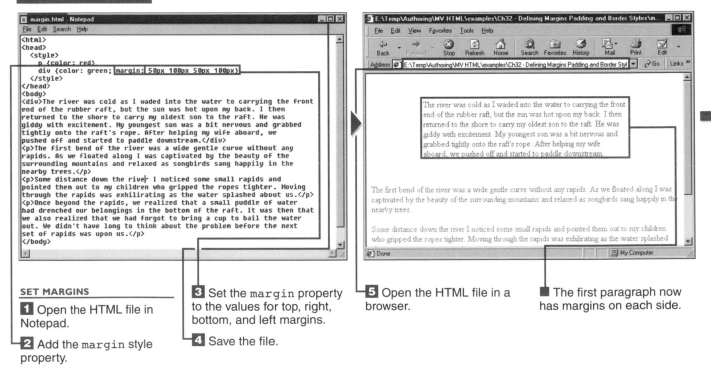

SET MARGINS

1 Open the HTML file in Notepad.

2 Add the `margin` style property.

3 Set the `margin` property to the values for top, right, bottom, and left margins.

4 Save the file.

5 Open the HTML file in a browser.

■ The first paragraph now has margins on each side.

What happens if I include only one or three margin values?

✔ If only one value is listed for the `margin` property, this value is applied equally to all four edges. If three values are included, the top edge gets the first value, the left and right edges get the second value, and the bottom edge gets the third value.

Can I mix percentage values with pixel values when specifying different margins?

✔ If you specify different margin widths for the different edges of a Web element, you can use specifying one margin in pixels and another as a percentage.

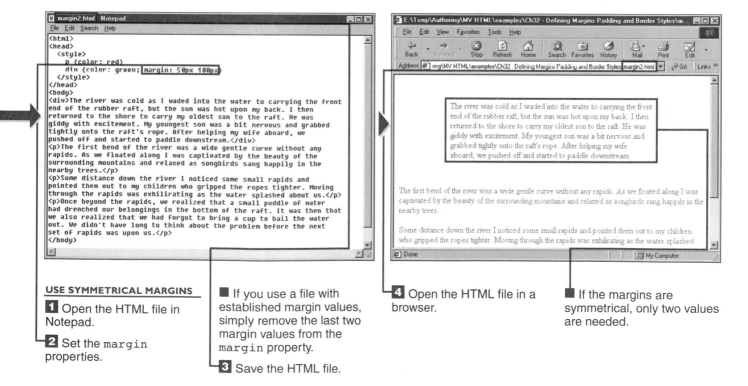

USE SYMMETRICAL MARGINS

1 Open the HTML file in Notepad.

2 Set the `margin` properties.

■ If you use a file with established margin values, simply remove the last two margin values from the `margin` property.

3 Save the HTML file.

4 Open the HTML file in a browser.

■ If the margins are symmetrical, only two values are needed.

DEFINE PADDING

When you want to add some white space between the Web page and the element, you can specify the space to include using the padding properties.

Padding is the space that appears between the Web page content and the element box. Padding is most effective if the background color property is used to display the background of a Web page element.

Padding can be set with the padding property. The padding property, like the margin property, takes four values. These values set the padding for the top, right, bottom, and left edges of the element box.

These values are expressed either as pixels (px) or percentages (%). For example, padding: 20% would add padding space equivalent to 20% of the browser window.

This example uses the skeleton.html file from this book's CD, but the steps can be applied to any situation.

DEFINE PADDING

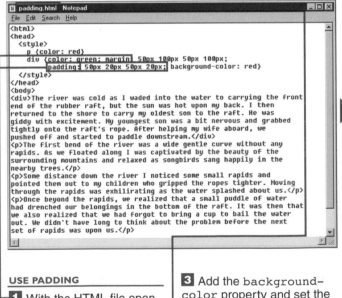

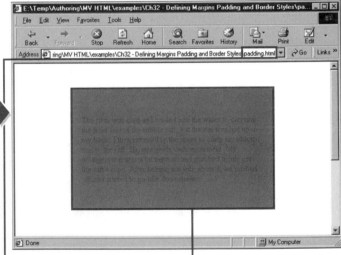

USE PADDING

1 With the HTML file open in Notepad, add the padding style property.

2 Set the padding property to the values for top, right, bottom, and left.

3 Add the background-color property and set the property.

■ The background color is set to red in this example.

4 Save the HTML file.

5 Open the HTML file in a browser.

■ The file reflects your padding and background-color selections. In this example, the first paragraph is shown in a red box, and padding separates the text from the box edges.

Can the padding space be colored a color that is different than the background color?

✔ The padding space is invisible and cannot be set to a color that is different than the element's background. If the Web page element's background color is the same as the Web page color, the margin and padding spaces are indistinguishable.

Can content be placed within the padding space such as text?

✔ Padding space is simply white space and nothing can be placed within the padding area. Tables can be used if you want to add text around a Web element. Tables are covered in Chapter 15.

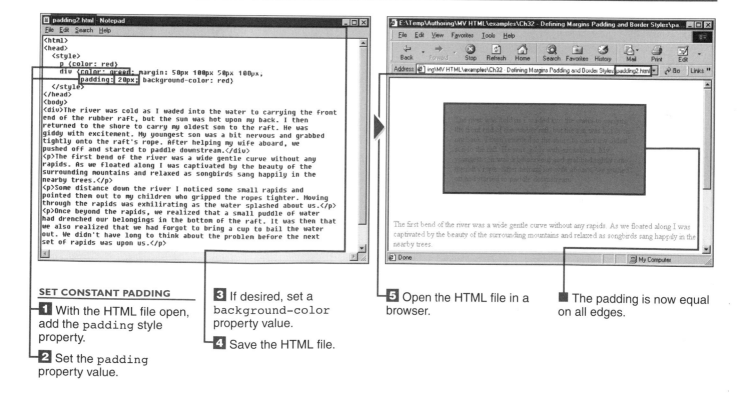

SET CONSTANT PADDING

1 With the HTML file open, add the `padding` style property.

2 Set the `padding` property value.

3 If desired, set a `background-color` property value.

4 Save the HTML file.

5 Open the HTML file in a browser.

■ The padding is now equal on all edges.

533

DEFINE BORDERS

At the edge of a Web page element's box, you can specify a *border*. This border appears between the margin and padding space.

Borders are created using the `border` property. This property can accept a width, a style, and a color. Only the `style` value is required. If the `width` or `color` values are left off, the default width of 5 pixels is used, and the color will match the text color.

Valid border styles include `none`, `dotted`, `dashed`, `solid`, and `double`. You can also use

- `groove`: a shaded border that resembles a groove
- `ridge`: a shaded border that resembles a ridge
- `inset` : a shaded border that is lighter in the lower-right corner.
- `outset`: a shaded border that is lighter in the upper-left corner

Valid width values include `thin`, `medium`, `thick`, or a width measured in pixels (px).

This example shows how to insert a basic border and change border width and color values.

This example uses the skeleton.html file from this book's CD, but the steps can be applied to any situation.

DEFINE BORDERS

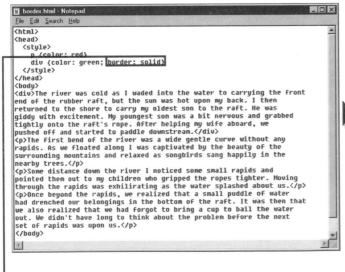

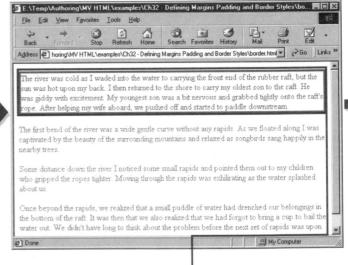

1 Open the HTML file in Notepad.

2 Add the `border` style property and set its style.

3 Save the HTML file.

4 Open the HTML file in a browser.

■ Your border selection is reflected. In this example, the first paragraph now has a border.

Can I specify border width, color, and style independent of the border property?

✔ The border property is actually a shortcut for the border-width, border-color, and border-style properties. You can use these longhand properties to separate the various border properties.

Can I define a separate border style for each edge?

✔ Similar to the border property, you can set the style for each individual edge using the border-top, border-bottom, border-right, and border-left properties. Using only one of these makes a border appear only for that edge. These properties are covered in the next section.

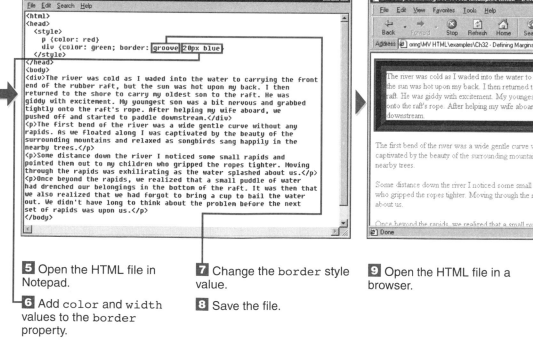

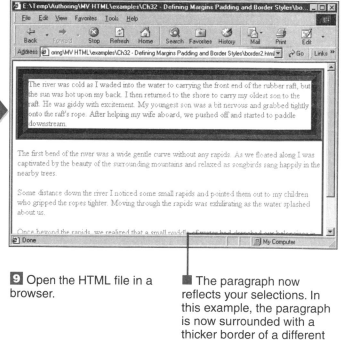

5 Open the HTML file in Notepad.

6 Add color and width values to the border property.

7 Change the border style value.

8 Save the file.

9 Open the HTML file in a browser.

■ The paragraph now reflects your selections. In this example, the paragraph is now surrounded with a thicker border of a different color and style.

DEFINE STYLES FOR A SINGLE EDGE

The margin, padding, and border properties covered elsewhere in this chapter only let you apply the property values simultaneously to all four edges of a Web page element. Style sheets (see Chapter 28) include several additional properties that enable you to apply a style value to a single side independent of the others.

You accomplish this by using this format after each property:

`<style><edge name>`

Replace `<style>` with the desired property, and `<edge name>` with the name of the edge—`top`, `bottom`, `left`, or `right`. Do not forget the dash. For example, to set a margin for the top edge only, you would use the `margin top` property.

Additional properties for the top edge include `padding-top`, `border-top`, `border-color-top`, `border-width-top`, and `border-style-top`. The values for these properties match the

similar non-edge-specific properties. For example, the `padding-top` property works the same way as the `padding` property, but it only applies to a single edge.

Other edges include bottom, left, and right. For example, you can specify `border-color-bottom`, `border-color-left`, and `border-color-right`.

This example uses the div.html file from this book's CD, but the steps can be applied to any situation.

DEFINE STYLES FOR A SINGLE EDGE

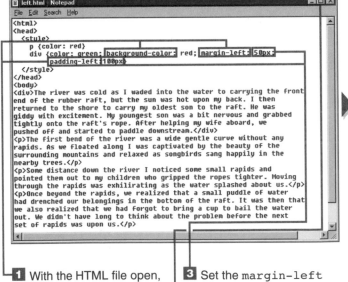

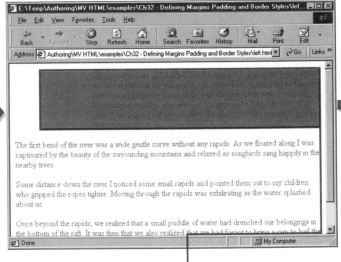

1 With the HTML file open, add the `background-color`, `margin-left`, and `padding-left` style properties.

2 Set the `background-color` property to red.

3 Set the `margin-left` property to the left margin length and the `padding-left` value to the left padding length.

4 Save the file with a different filename.

5 Open the new file in a browser.

■ The first paragraph now has a margin and padding on only the left side.

Why do style sheets include so many redundant properties?

✔ The shortcut properties like `margin`, `padding`, and `border` provide an easy way to quickly add styles to a Web page. The additional properties enable a wider set of features that are not possible using the shortcut properties. This precise control is one of the benefits to style sheets.

Why would I want to include separate styles on each edge?

✔ Web page elements that have a different style for each edge would look very confusing, but including only a single style on one edge could be a very effective design technique.

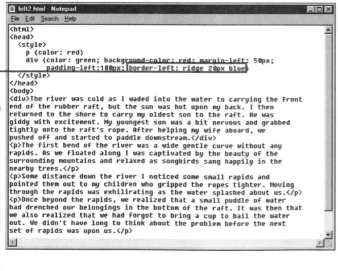

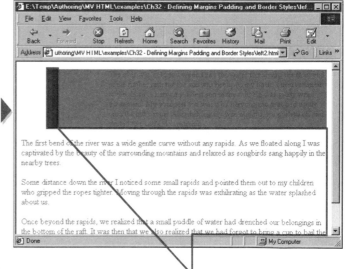

6 Open the new HTML file in Notepad.

7 Add the `border-left` property and set the width, color, and style.

8 Save the file with a new filename.

9 Open the new file in a browser.

■ The paragraph now has a border added to the left edge.

DEFINE HEIGHT AND WIDTH

The size of the box that contains each Web page element can be controlled using style sheets. Under standard HTML, the browser controls the size of the element's box. Controlling the size of the element box gives the Web page creator additional control over where elements get placed on the page.

The style properties that enable this resizing are the width and height properties. Each of these properties accepts length values in either pixels (px) or a percentage (%) of the browser window.

You can also use the auto value to turn the box sizing over to the browser. If the auto value is specified, the size of the element

will be determined by the surrounding elements.

You can use these properties with text elements as well as images and tables.

This example uses the skeleton.html file from this book's CD, but the steps can be applied to any situation.

DEFINE HEIGHT AND WIDTH

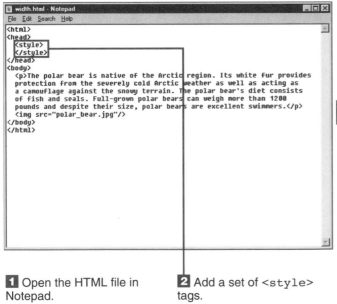

1 Open the HTML file in Notepad.

2 Add a set of <style> tags.

3 Add a selector (in this case, p) for the first element for which you want to define height and width.

4 Add the width and height values to the selector.

■ If you want the browser to define one of the values, replace the value with auto.

Note: The background-color property is included so the paragraph size is visible.

How does the auto value affect images?

✔ If dimensions are added to the width and height properties for an `img` selector, the image is resized to the specified dimensions. If, however, one of the properties is set to auto, the specified dimension is used, and the auto dimension is sized to maintain the image's actual proportions.

Can the width and height properties accept negative values?

✔ These properties cannot include negative values. If the `width` and/or `height` properties include a negative value, the negative value will be ignored.

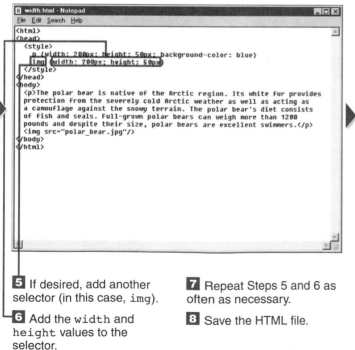

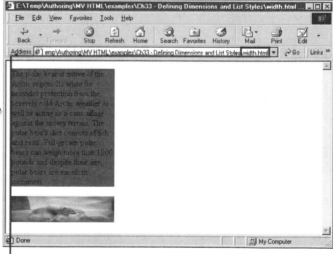

5 If desired, add another selector (in this case, `img`).

6 Add the `width` and `height` values to the selector.

7 Repeat Steps 5 and 6 as often as necessary.

8 Save the HTML file.

9 Open the file in a browser.

■ The elements are sized as specified. If you need to resize an element, simply re-open the HTML file and adjust the width and height selectors.

DEFINE FLOAT AND CLEAR ATTRIBUTES

Web page elements can be positioned to the left or the right by using the `align` attributes. You can also specify for images and tables whether content can be placed to the left or right.

These features can be duplicated using style sheets with two properties:

- `float`. The `float` property can be set to `none`, `left`, or `right`. This property enables

elements to be positioned to the side of the element.

- `clear`. The `clear` property can be set to `none`, `left`, `right`, or `both`. This property keeps elements from being placed to the side of the element.

The advantage with style sheets is that all Web elements including text can be resized, so all Web page elements can have other elements placed to their side.

For example, if you have an image positioned to the left of the browser, any text that includes a definition to float to the right will wrap around the image. If the image includes a clear style definition, the text will not be positioned to its right.

This example uses the skeleton.html file from this book's CD, but the steps can be applied to any situation.

DEFINE FLOAT AND CLEAR ATTRIBUTES

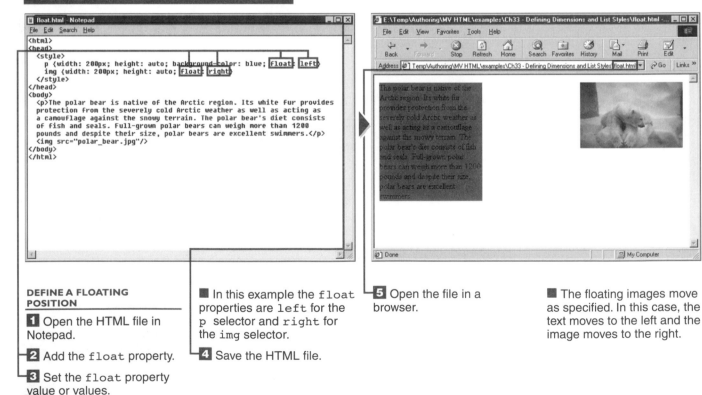

DEFINE A FLOATING POSITION

1 Open the HTML file in Notepad.

2 Add the `float` property.

3 Set the `float` property value or values.

■ In this example the `float` properties are `left` for the `p` selector and `right` for the `img` selector.

4 Save the HTML file.

5 Open the file in a browser.

■ The floating images move as specified. In this case, the text moves to the left and the image moves to the right.

Can elements be placed in the same vertical space as an element that has the clear property set?

✔ If a Web page element has the `clear` property set to `both`, no other element can be placed on the same row. Using the `right` or `left` values, you can have text wrap around one side of an image, but not the other.

If two elements have conflicting float and clear settings, what will happen?

✔ If two elements have conflicting `float` and `clear` settings, the last definition will take priority. For example, if a Web element has both `clear: right` and `float: right` style definitions, the element will be aligned to the right.

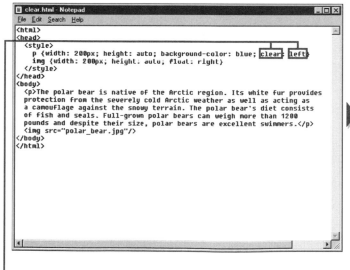

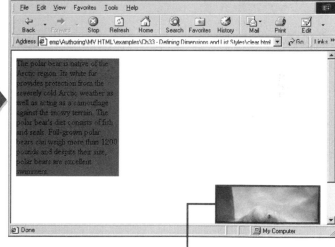

DEFINE A CLEAR POSITION

1 Open the HTML file in Notepad.

2 Add the `clear` property.

3 Set the `clear` property value or values.

■ In this example, the property for the p selector is `left`.

4 Save the HTML file.

5 Open the HTML file in a browser.

■ The elements are moved as specified. In this case, the image is moved from its position to the right of the paragraph to below the paragraph.

DEFINE LIST STYLES

Several style sheet properties work specifically with lists. Using these properties, you can specify the list style, load custom bullet images, and set the positioning of the bullets.

The list-style-type property can be used to set the bulleted or numbered list style. This style

property only makes sense if applied to the li selector.

This property can accept none, disc, circle, square, decimal, lower-roman, upper-roman, lower-alpha, or upper-alpha.

For example, a style definition list-style-type: upper-roman will make all ordered lists in the page appear with uppercase Roman numerals.

This example uses the skeleton.html file from this book's CD, but the steps can be applied to any situation.

DEFINE LIST STYLES

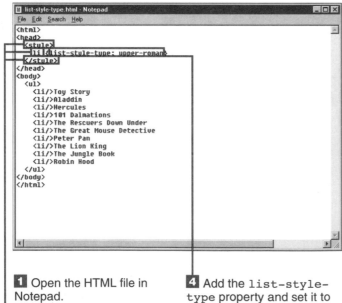

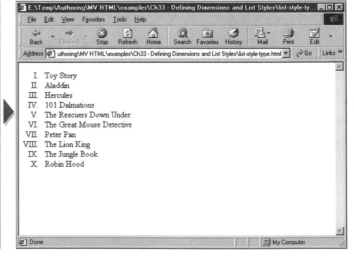

1 Open the HTML file in Notepad.

2 Add a set of <style> tags.

3 Add the li selector and a set of brackets.

4 Add the list-style-type property and set it to the desired value.

■ In this example, the property is set to upper-roman.

5 Save the HTML file.

6 Open the HTML file in a browser.

■ The list displays as specified. In this example, the list uses uppercase Roman letters.

Can bullet types be specified for an ordered list and numbers for an unordered list?

✔ Any of the list types that are accepted by the `list-style-type` property can be used with either ordered or unordered lists. For example, if you have an ordered list, created with the `<ol>` tags, you can set the `list-style-type` property to `circle`, and circular bullets are used for the list.

What will happen if the list-style-type property is used on a non-list element like a paragraph?

✔ If the `list-style-type` property is used on a non-list element like a paragraph, the property will be ignored and have no affect on the paragraph.

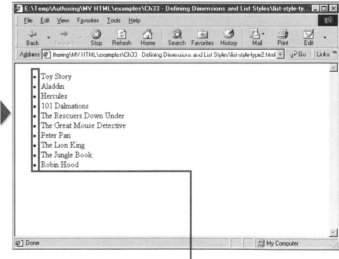

7 To change a list display, open the HTML file in Notepad.

8 Change the `list-style-type` property value as desired.

■ In this example, the value is changed to `disc`.

9 Save the HTML file.

10 Open the HTML file in a browser.

■ The list reflects the changes. In this example, the bullets are now solid circles.

USING IMAGE BULLETS

Chapter 12 shows how to include images in front of the text for a bulleted list as a way to create custom bullets. You can use style sheets to create actual custom bullets in front of a list element.

To use a custom image as a bullet for a list, you use the list-style-image property. This property is set to the url keyword followed by the image filename in parentheses.

For example, if you have created a custom bullet named mybullet.gif, you can include it in a list using the list-style-image: url(mybullet.gif) definition.

The bullet image filename can be a valid URL anywhere on the Web.

This example uses the skeleton.html file from this book's CD, but the steps can be applied to any situation.

USING IMAGE BULLETS

1 Open the HTML file in Notepad.

2 Add a set of <style> tags.

3 Add the li selector and a set of brackets.

4 Add the list-style-image property and set it to url and the name of the bullet image in parentheses.

5 Save the HTML file.

6 Open the HTML file in a browser.

■ The list is displayed using custom bullet images.

Which selectors can be used with these list style properties?

✔ The list style properties can use the `ol`, `ul`, `li`, `menu`, `dd`, `dir`, `dl`, and `dt` selectors. The list containers like `ul` and `ol` will update the style for all elements contained within the selector, but the `li` selectors can be changed independently using classes. Lists are covered in more detail in Chapter 9.

Are there any size restrictions to these custom bullet images?

✔ Custom bullet images can be of any size and of any of the valid image formats including GIF, JPEG, and PNG. More information on these formats can be found in Chapter 11.

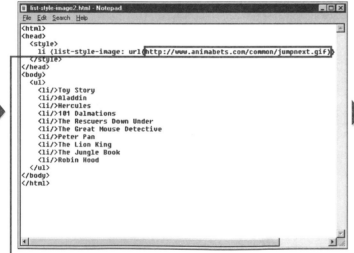

7 To change a custom bullet style, open the HTML file in Notepad.

8 Change the `list-style-image` property value as desired.

■ In this example, the value is changed to `http://www.animabets.com/common/jumpnext.gif`.

9 Save the HTML file.

10 Open the HTML file in a browser.

■ The list bullets are changed as specified. In this example, the bullets are now arrows taken from the Web.

DEFINE LIST POSITION

When list items are longer than one line, they wrap within the browser window and repeat on a second line underneath the first line. Style sheets include a property that you can use to control how the second line is lined up with the first line when the text wraps.

This property is the `list-style-position`-property. The property can be set to either inside or outside. The inside value will cause the second line of text to be positioned underneath the list bullet or number. The outside value is the default value. This value causes the second line of text to be

indented. The indentation aligns the first letter of the second line of text under the first letter for the first line.

This example uses the skeleton.html file from this book's CD, but the steps can be applied to any situation.

DEFINE LIST POSITION

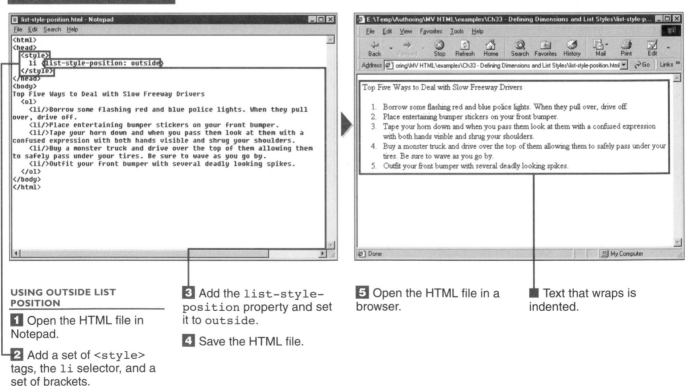

USING OUTSIDE LIST POSITION

1 Open the HTML file in Notepad.

2 Add a set of `<style>` tags, the `li` selector, and a set of brackets.

3 Add the `list-style-position` property and set it to `outside`.

4 Save the HTML file.

5 Open the HTML file in a browser.

■ Text that wraps is indented.

Is there a shortcut property for the list style properties?

✔ The list-style-type, list-style-image, and list-style-position properties can all be included within the shortcut list-style property. The order for these properties is list-style-type, list-style-image, and list-style-position. For example, li {list-style: circle url(mybullet.gif) outside} would load the mybullet.gif image as a custom bullet using indented positioning.

Why would I want to use a shortcut property?

✔ Shortcut properties like list-style are cleaner to use and do not clutter a file with too many separate file definitions. It can, however, be difficult to understand all the properties that are included with the shortcut property. For clarity, separate style definitions are recommended.

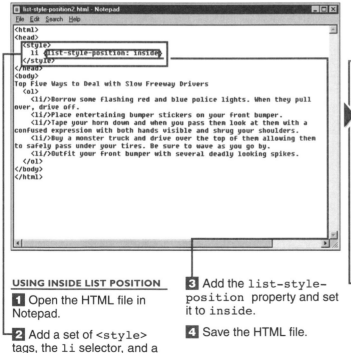

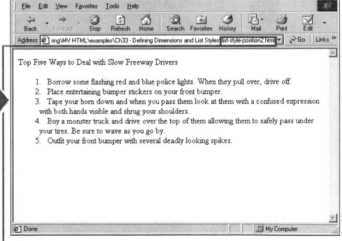

USING INSIDE LIST POSITION

1 Open the HTML file in Notepad.

2 Add a set of <style> tags, the li selector, and a set of brackets.

3 Add the list-style-position property and set it to inside.

4 Save the HTML file.

5 Open the HTML file in a browser.

■ Text that wraps is now positioned under the list number.

SECTION X

35) CROSS-BROWSER DYNAMIC HTML

DYNAMIC HTML FOR INTERNET EXPLORER

Dynamic HTML is an extension to standard HTML that gives you more control over how Web page elements display in browsers. For example, you can use Dynamic HTML to move Web elements about the browser window.

Dynamic HTML uses several complimentary technologies, including style sheets and JavaScript. When the user's browser calls up your page, JavaScript scripts will set the styles and enable the elements to be manipulated interactively.

The difficulty in working with dynamic HTML arises from browser incompatibilities. Microsoft has built-in support for dynamic HTML that has been sanctioned by the World Wide Web Consortium (W3C), the governing body for HTML. Netscape, on the other hand, has developed and supported a different standard and methods. Chapter 34 covers these methods.

This chapter covers the Microsoft approach to dynamic HTML. Keep in mind that many of the techniques discussed in this chapter only work in the Internet Explorer browser.

Naming Elements

Before any Internet Explorer Web page elements can be acted on, they need to be named so that they can be referenced. Although many Web page elements, such as form elements covered in Chapter 17, include a `name` attribute, not all elements allow the `name` attribute.

As an alternative, all elements can accept an `id` attribute, which can be used to name the Web page element. The `id` attribute is one of the standard common attributes that can be used universally by all tags. The `id` can also be used in JavaScript statements to refer to the various Web page elements.

For example, the `id` attribute can be added to the opening paragraph tag like this, `<p id="myStory">`. You can then refer to this element using this `id` value.

Before you can control the visibility of an element, you need to give the element a reference identification. This can be done with the `id` attribute. The value of the `id` attribute can be any text name.

Once you known an element's `id`, you can control the element by using JavaScript statements. These statements can dynamically change the value of the element attributes and styles.

Object Positioning

Another important aspect of control is the ability to precisely position objects. Dynamic HTML enables the positioning of objects by using several style sheet properties. The properties include position, `top`, `right`, `bottom`, `left`, `float`, `clear`, `visibility`, and `z-index`. These properties are explained in more detail later in this chapter.

Using the `top`, `right`, `bottom`, and `left` properties, you can precisely define the distance between each edge of the browser. For example, `top: 200px` positions an element 200 pixels from the top edge of the browser.

The `visibility` property can be used to make elements appear or disappear in response to an event such as a mouse click or moving the mouse over the top of another element.

Because elements can be positioned, they can be overlapped. The `z-index` property can be used to control which elements appear on top of others. This property, like the others, can also be controlled using JavaScript.

When you understand how to give elements a name and how to use the style properties for positioning them, you'll be ready to use some JavaScript to dynamically control element style, position, and even content.

DEFINE THE POSITIONING METHOD

The default positioning method lets the browser control how the Web page elements are placed in the window. Using style sheets, you can specify a different positioning method.

These positioning methods are defined using the `position` property. Acceptable values include

- `static`—the default property; enables the browser to determine the page layout

- `fixed`—keeps elements positioned relative to the surrounding elements

- `absolute`—positions the elements the specified distance from the browser

- `relative`—positions the elements relative to their normal static position as specified

The `absolute` and `relative` positioning methods work along

with the `top`, `bottom`, `left`, and `right` properties. So, these positioning methods will only be affected if the `top`, `bottom`, `left`, and `right` properties are specified.

This example uses the auto.html file from this book's CD, but the steps can be applied to any situation.

DEFINE THE POSITIONING METHOD

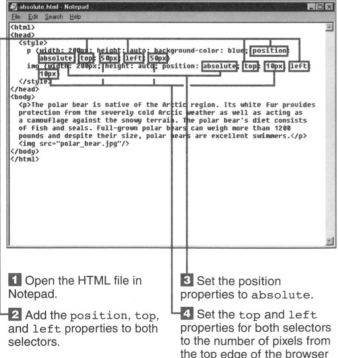

1 Open the HTML file in Notepad.

2 Add the `position`, `top`, and `left` properties to both selectors.

3 Set the position properties to `absolute`.

4 Set the `top` and `left` properties for both selectors to the number of pixels from the top edge of the browser window.

5 Save the file.

6 Open the HTML file in a browser.

■ Both elements are displayed from the upper-left corner of the browser window according to the top and left dimensions.

How do the static and fixed values work?

✔ If the `position` property is set to `static`, the Web page elements are positioned by the browser the same way, as if no style sheets were used. The `fixed` value causes the elements to remain fixed in their position as the browser window scrolls.

Can I use the fixed positioning method to make a single element like an image stay in the same place?

✔ You can set a single image to use the fixed positioning method and then position it in a corner of the browser. This will make the image remain in the corner as the Web page is scrolled.

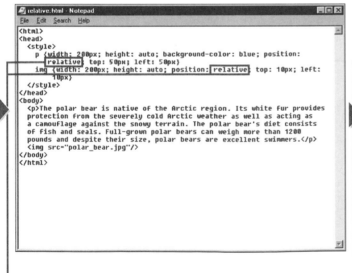

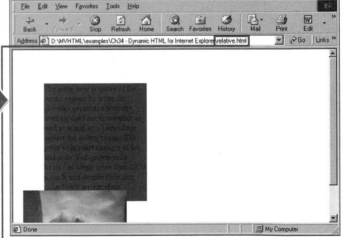

7 Open the HTML file in Notepad.

8 Change the `position` property value to `relative` for both selectors.

9 Save the file.

10 Open the file in a browser.

■ Both elements are displayed from the upper-left corner of where they normally have appeared.

USING RELATIVE POSITIONING

Relative positioning can position elements relative to other elements. For example, if the image is right where you want it, you could position the matching text to appear 20 pixels under the image using relative positioning.

Of the four basic positioning methods, using the *relative* positioning method is more confusing because the element position is based on where it would normally be placed.

The relative positioning method is most useful to push elements a short distance away from the edge or from other elements, just like the hspace and the vspace attributes for the <img/> tag. These attributes are covered along with images in Chapter 11.

For example, if two paragraphs using the width and height properties are positioned side by side, you can use relative positioning to define the space between them.

The relative positioning method works well if the static layout is close to the desired layout and the elements only need a little tweaking.

This example uses the headings.html file from this book's CD, but the steps can be applied to any situation.

USING RELATIVE POSITIONING

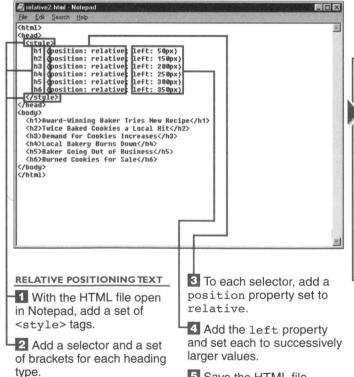

RELATIVE POSITIONING TEXT

1 With the HTML file open in Notepad, add a set of <style> tags.

2 Add a selector and a set of brackets for each heading type.

3 To each selector, add a position property set to relative.

4 Add the left property and set each to successively larger values.

5 Save the HTML file.

6 Open the HTML file in a browser.

■ Each heading is indented further than the one above it.

What happens to elements that are contained within other elements when the parent element is relatively positioned?

✔ Subordinate elements are positioned along with their parent element if the relative positioning method is used. For example, if an image is contained within a paragraph and the paragraph is positioned using relative positioning, the image will also be positioned according to the relative values.

Can an element be absolutely and relatively positioned?

✔ Each element can only use a single positioning method. If two values are included in a style definition, then the later one will be used. For example, if a style definition includes position: relative; position: absolute, then absolute positioning will be used.

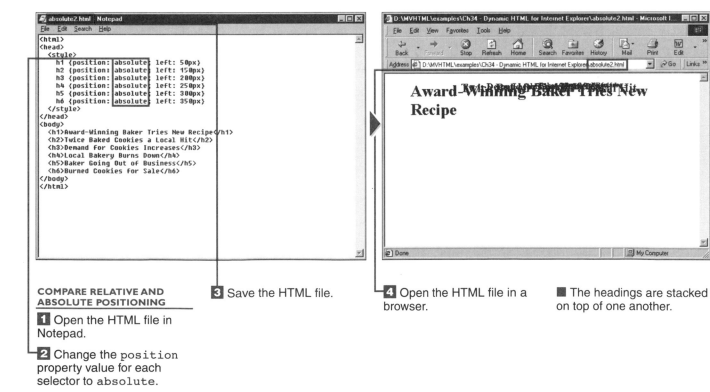

COMPARE RELATIVE AND ABSOLUTE POSITIONING

1 Open the HTML file in Notepad.

2 Change the `position` property value for each selector to `absolute`.

3 Save the HTML file.

4 Open the HTML file in a browser.

■ The headings are stacked on top of one another.

USING ABSOLUTE POSITIONING

The *absolute* positioning method is easy to understand. It simply positions the Web page element a specified distance from the specified browser edge. This method makes it possible to position any element anywhere within the browser window.

The distance from the edge is measured in *pixels* (px). You can also use percentages to make the distance from the edge relative to the browser window size.

The style sheet properties for the various browser window edges include `top`, `bottom`, `left`, and `right`. For example, the definition

`top:-50px; left: 100px` would position an element 50 pixels from the top edge and 100 pixels from the left edge.

This example uses the auto.html file from this book's CD, but the steps can be applied to any situation.

USING ABSOLUTE POSITIONING

ABSOLUTE POSITIONING IMAGES

1 With the HTML file open in Notepad, add the `position` property to both selectors and set them both to `absolute`.

2 Add the `top` and `left` properties.

3 Set the `top`, `bottom`, `left`, and `right` properties to the number of pixels from the top edge of the browser window.

4 Save the file.

5 Open the file in a browser.

■ Both elements are displayed from the upper-left corner of the browser window according to the top and left dimensions.

What happens when an element includes opposing position properties like top and bottom or left and right?

✔ If you accidentally specify opposite position properties, like `top` and `bottom` or `left` and `right` for the same selector, the `top` and `left` properties take priority regardless of their order.

Where is absolute positioning best used?

✔ Absolute positioning works the best for items such as paragraphs and images that are placed and laid out according to the browser window.

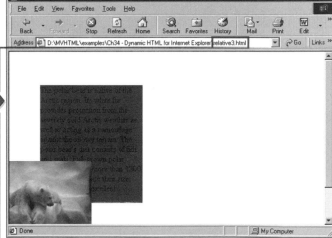

COMPARE RELATIVE AND ABSOLUTE POSITIONING

1 Open the HTML file in Notepad.

2 Change the `position` property value for each selector to `relative`.

3 Save the file.

4 Open the file in a browser.

■ The paragraph is the first element, so it is positioned the same as for the absolute positioning method. The image, on the other hand, is positioned relative to its normal position under the paragraph.

SET LAYER ORDER

Because style sheets enable you to position elements, you can position two elements on top of each other. To give you more control over elements that are overlapped, style sheets include a property that lets you define which element appears on top.

The style property for controlling layer order is the z-index property. This property can be set to auto, which stacks the elements in the order that they appear in the browser, or it can be set to an integer representing the stacking

order. Elements with a low z-index value are displayed underneath elements with a higher z-index value.

For example, if an image of a tiger with a z-index of 5 overlaps an image of a tree with a z-index of 7, the tree image is displayed on top, obscuring the tiger image.

This example uses the absolute3.html file from this book's CD, but the steps can be applied to any situation.

If a transparent GIF image overlaps another image, is the underlying image visible?

✓ If a transparent GIF image is positioned on top of another image, the underlying image is visible through the regions that are transparent in GIF images. This technique can be used to create some interesting effects. GIF images are covered in more detail in Chapter 12.

SET LAYER ORDER

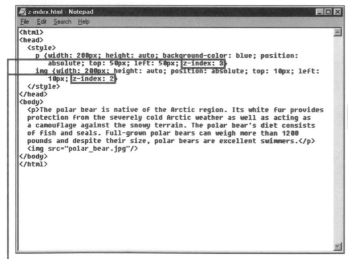

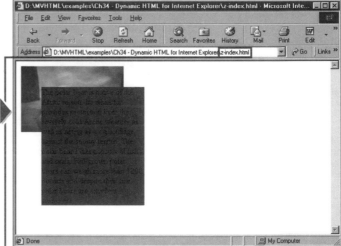

1 With the HTML file in Notepad, add the z-index property to both selectors.

2 Set the z-index values.

■ In this example, the z-index values are 3 for the p selector and 2 for the img selector to 2.

3 Save the HTML file.

4 Open the HTML file in a browser.

■ The elements are displayed in the prescribed order.

DEFINE VISIBILITY

Another style sheet property that is useful when working with positioned elements is visibility. You can use this style property to make the elements invisible.

The visibility property's value can be set to hidden or visible. The default, of course, is visible. Setting the visibility property to hidden makes the element invisible.

Even though elements are hidden, they still affect the layout of the various elements. For example, if any image is displayed at the top of a Web page, all text beneath the image is positioned below where the image would appear if it were visible.

This example uses the relative2.html file from this book's CD, but the steps can be applied to any situation.

Can I hide an element so that it does not affect the layout?

✔ One simple way to hide an element so that it does not affect the layout is to simply remove the element from the Web page. You can do this by deleting the syntax that creates the element or by using comment marks (//) to comment out the element.

DEFINE VISIBILITY

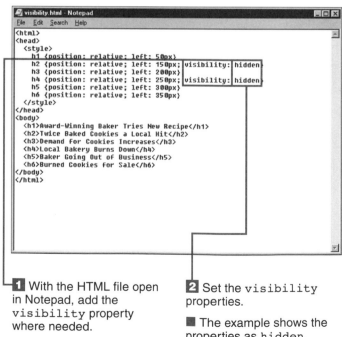

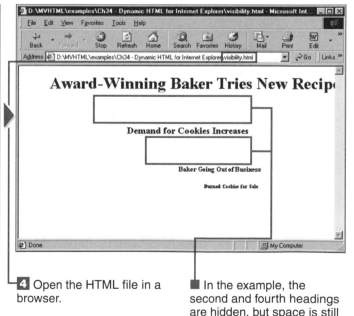

1 With the HTML file open in Notepad, add the visibility property where needed.

■ In this example, the property was added to the second and fourth selectors.

2 Set the visibility properties.

■ The example shows the properties as hidden.

3 Save the HTML file.

4 Open the HTML file in a browser.

■ In the example, the second and fourth headings are hidden, but space is still maintained for them.

DYNAMICALLY CHANGE VISIBILITY

In addition to setting the visibility for a Web page element, you can also dynamically set visibility using JavaScript.

Before you can control the visibility of an element, you need to give the element a reference identification. This can be done with the `id` attribute. The value of the `id` attribute can be any text name.

Once the `id` attribute is set for an element, you can dynamically set the `visibility` property for that element with the `style.visibility` JavaScript statement. The syntax of this statement is as follows:

```
<object>.style.visibility
=<'action'>
```

Replace the code in angle brackets accordingly. For example, setting

the `onclick` event equal to `text1.style.visibility = 'hidden'`-causes the element with the ID of `text1` to be hidden when the `onclick` event is triggered.

For more on JavaScript events, see Chapter 25.

This example uses the absolute3.html file from this book's CD, but the steps can be applied to any situation.

DYNAMICALLY CHANGE VISIBILITY

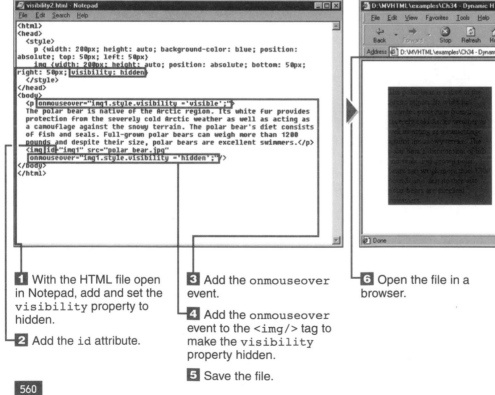

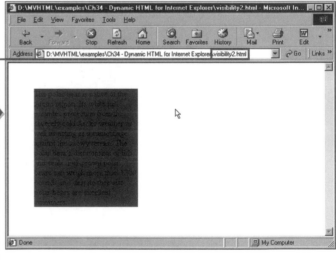

1 With the HTML file open in Notepad, add and set the `visibility` property to hidden.

2 Add the `id` attribute.

3 Add the `onmouseover` event.

4 Add the `onmouseover` event to the `<img/>` tag to make the `visibility` property hidden.

5 Save the file.

6 Open the file in a browser.

■ A single paragraph is displayed in the browser.

Why is the document object not needed in front of the id name?

✔ The document object is assumed for any id name that is included on the current Web page. The document object, therefore, is not needed because the browser is smart enough to know its current context.

Which events are frequently used to control visibility?

✔ The `onmouseover` and `onmouseoff` events are useful events to use to control the visibility of elements. These events enable Web page elements to appear and disappear as the mouse moves around the browser. The `onclick` event is also useful for making Web page elements appear and disappear.

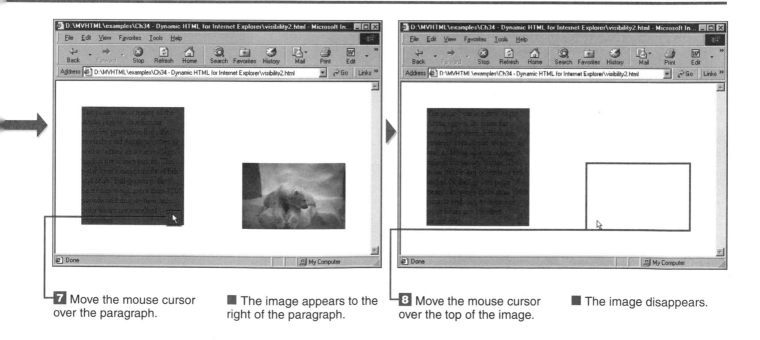

7 Move the mouse cursor over the paragraph.

■ The image appears to the right of the paragraph.

8 Move the mouse cursor over the top of the image.

■ The image disappears.

DYNAMICALLY CHANGE STYLES

Just like you can dynamically control an element's visibility, you can also dynamically control the values of style properties.

All style properties are subobjects under the style object. The style subobject, likewise, is a subobject of the element id.

The style property can be set equal to an accepted value. For example, if a <p> tag includes an id attribute equal to p1, then the JavaScript statement p1.style.text-align = "right" causes the paragraph to be aligned to the right whenever the JavaScript statement is executed.

Statements such as this enable you to control the style definition using JavaScript.

This example uses the para.html file from this book's CD, but the steps can be applied to any situation.

DYNAMICALLY CHANGE STYLES

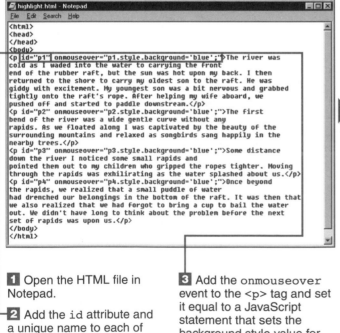

1 Open the HTML file in Notepad.

2 Add the id attribute and a unique name to each of the <p> tags.

3 Add the onmouseover event to the <p> tag and set it equal to a JavaScript statement that sets the background style value for the paragraph to a color.

4 Save the file with a new name.

5 Open highlight.html in a browser.

■ All paragraphs are displayed with white backgrounds.

What happens if a style property is defined within the <style> tags and then later dynamically changed?

✔ If a style property is defined in the <style> tags, externally in a style sheet file, or using a style attribute, the element appears in that style when the Web page is first loaded. If the style is later changed in response to an event, the new style is adopted. If the Web page is reloaded, the original definition is again restored.

Can you control styles that are defined using an external style sheet?

✔ External style sheets offer a starting point for style definitions. You can use JavaScript within the Web page to change any style definitions that were initially loaded using an external style sheet.

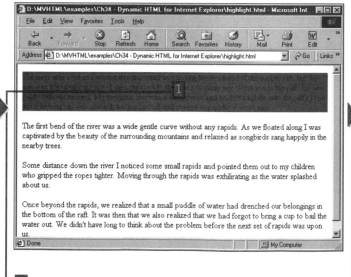

6 Move the mouse cursor over the top of the first paragraph.

■ The first paragraph appears with a blue background.

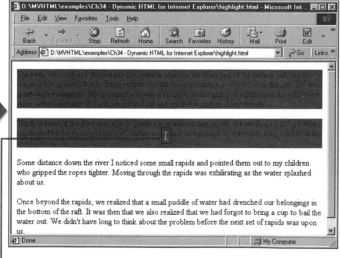

7 Move the mouse cursor over the top of the second paragraph.

■ The first and second paragraphs both appear with blue backgrounds.

DYNAMICALLY CHANGE TEXT

JavaScript can change not only the visibility and style of a Web page element, but also an element's content, such as paragraph text or list elements.

The JavaScript property that makes this possible is innerHTML, which refers to the content that comes within a set of tags.

After the id attribute is set for an element, you can dynamically change the content of a tag using the innerHTML property. The syntax of this statement is as follows:

```
<object>.innerHTML=
<'action'>
```

Replace the code in angle brackets accordingly. For example, setting the onclick event equal to p1.innerHTML = 'new content' causes the element with the id of p1 to be changed to new content when the onclick event is triggered.

For example, the JavaScript statement id1.innerHTML = "hello" would replace the contents within the tags identified with an id of id1 with the word "hello."

The innerHTML property can only be used on tags that include both opening and closing tags.

This example uses the skeleton.html file from this book's CD, but the steps can be applied to any situation.

DYNAMICALLY CHANGE TEXT

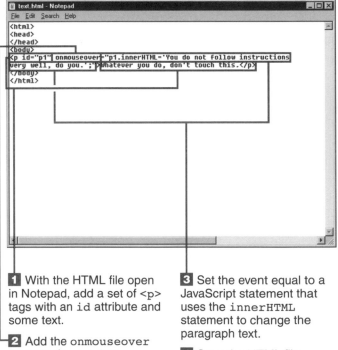

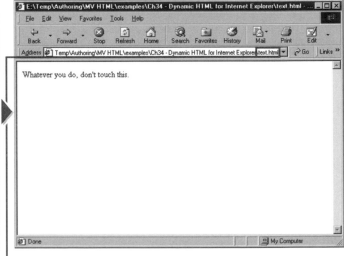

1 With the HTML file open in Notepad, add a set of <p> tags with an id attribute and some text.

2 Add the onmouseover event to the <p> tag.

3 Set the event equal to a JavaScript statement that uses the innerHTML statement to change the paragraph text.

4 Save the HTML file.

5 Open the HTML file in a browser.

■ A single paragraph is displayed.

The paragraph text does not change. What could be wrong?

✔ If the text within the quotes of the JavaScript statement includes a quote mark, the JavaScript statement gets confused and does not work correctly. You can include quote marks using an entity value such as `&lsquo;` This value can be placed within a normal section of text to display special characters.

Why can the innerHTML property only be used with tags that have an opening and closing tag?

✔ The `innerHTML` property changes only the content that exists between the opening and closing tags. A single tag such as `<img/>`, does not have anything to change, so the `innerHTML` property is ignored.

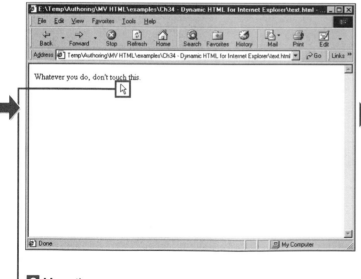

6 Move the mouse cursor over the top of the paragraph.

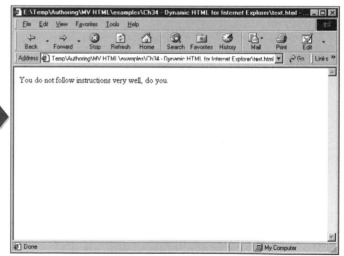

■ The paragraph text changes.

DYNAMICALLY CHANGE POSITION

nother way you can dynamically change the Web page is to reposition elements around the Web page. Dynamically positioning Web page elements can be accomplished by setting the any of the position related style properties such as `style.top` or `style.position` in a JavaScript statement.

You can also control positions based on the movements of the mouse cursor. The mouse cursor's position can be accessed using the `window.event.x` and `window.event.y` properties. The `window.event.x` property measures the distance in pixels from the browser's left edge. The `window.event.y` property measures the distance between the mouse cursor and the top edge of the browser.

For example, the statement `id1.style.top =`

`window.event.y` positions the top edge of an element identified with an `id` equal to `id1` to the vertical position of the mouse cursor.

This example uses the absolute3.html file from this book's CD, but the steps can be applied to any situation.

DYNAMICALLY CHANGE POSITION

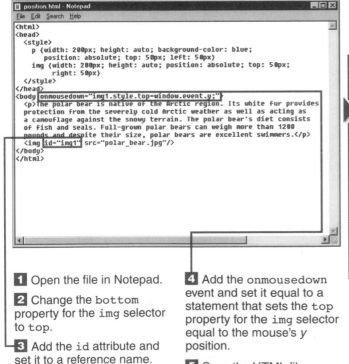

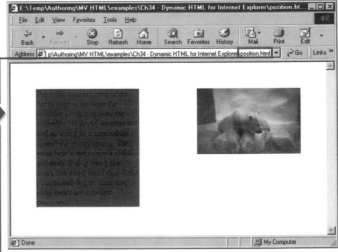

1 Open the file in Notepad.

2 Change the `bottom` property for the `img` selector to `top`.

3 Add the `id` attribute and set it to a reference name.

4 Add the `onmousedown` event and set it equal to a statement that sets the `top` property for the `img` selector equal to the mouse's *y* position.

5 Save the HTML file.

6 Open the HTML file in a browser.

■ A paragraph and an image are displayed.

Will the event.x and event.y values ever be negative?

✔ The `event.x` value is the distance in pixels that the mouse cursor is from the browser's left edge. The `event.y` value is the distance in pixels that the mouse cursor is from the browser's top edge. Any values outside of the browser window are ignored. The `event.x` and `event.y` values will always be positive values.

Can you move the cursor position by setting the event.x and event.y values?

✔ The `event.x` and `event.y` values are read-only values. You cannot control the mouse cursor position by setting these values.

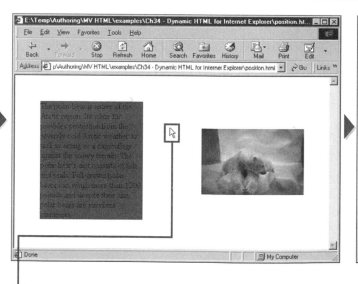

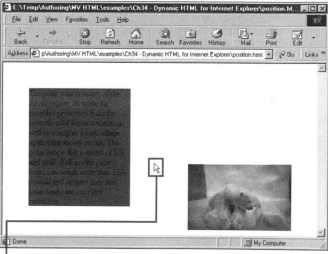

7 Move the mouse cursor anywhere within the Web page.

8 Click the mouse button.

■ The top of the image is positioned at the same height as the mouse cursor's position.

9 Move the mouse cursor to a different location within the Web page.

10 Click the mouse button.

■ The top of the image is positioned at the same height as the mouse cursor's position.

DETECT EVENT ELEMENTS

One way to initiate JavaScript statements is to specify events within HTML elements. If you have a large number of elements, including an event for each one can be difficult. To overcome this, you can use the event.srcElement property to represent the element that triggered the event.

For example, each element that includes an event can call a standard JavaScript function that uses the event.srcElement property to know to which element to apply the style. This generic function does not need to identify each individual element.

The following example uses the skeleton.html file from this book's companion CD.

DETECT EVENT ELEMENTS

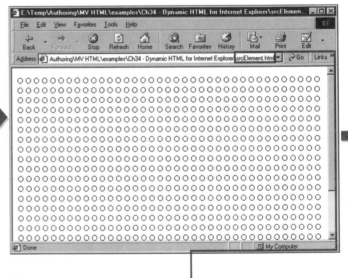

1 Add <span> tags.

2 Type one letter between the <span> tags.

3 Add the onmouseover event set to an empty JavaScript function statement.

4 Copy the set of <span> tags enough times to fill the browser window.

5 Add <script> tags.

6 Add a function declaration with brackets.

7 Within the brackets, add the JavaScript code to identify the current event element and change its color.

8 Save the file.

9 Open the HTML file in a browser.

■ A browser window full of letters is displayed.

What other event properties are there?

✔ The event object includes several other useful properties. The `fromElement` property can be used to detect for the `mouseover` event, the element that the mouse cursor was over before it moved on top of the current element. The `toElement` property is similar, except that it tells which element for the `mouseout` the mouse cursor moved to after leaving the current one.

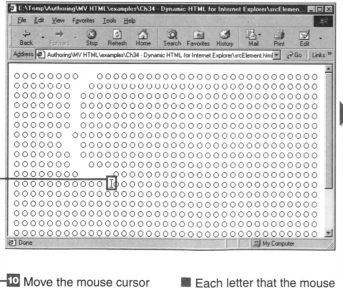

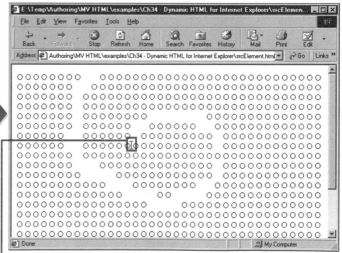

10 Move the mouse cursor over the Web page.

■ Each letter that the mouse cursor is over changes color.

11 Continue to move the mouse cursor over the Web page.

■ Each letter that the mouse cursor is over changes color.

DYNAMIC HTML FOR NETSCAPE NAVIGATOR

Dynamic HTML (DHTML) for the Netscape Navigator browser is handled differently than Dynamic HTML for the Microsoft Internet Explorer browser, but there are many aspects that are similar.

How DHTML is the Same for Navigator and IE

If you are familiar with how Dynamic HTML works for the Microsoft Internet Explorer browser (Chapter 33), you can find many similarities with how Dynamic HTML works with the Netscape Navigator browser.

Many of the same aspects of positioning and dynamic control are possible for both browsers. Chapter 35 shows you a method for dealing with Dynamic HTML for both browsers.

Netscape Navigator recognizes and uses several of the same properties that Internet Explorer uses, including `position`, `top`, `bottom`, `right`, `left`, and `visibility`.

How DHTML is Different for Navigator and IE

Although there are many similar properties between the two major browsers, it is the differences that cause all the trouble.

The major differences between the two browsers are how they handle positioning and layers. The position properties for Netscape Navigator are syntactically different than that for Internet Explorer.

Layers are created using the <layer> tag instead of a style sheet definition.

DHTML Positioning for Navigator

Dynamic HTML positioning on Netscape Navigator is accomplished using a couple of new tags:

- The <layer> tag defines positions absolutely based on the browser's upper-left corner.

- The <ilayer> tag positions elements relative to its inline position.

These layers are like a separate sheet that can be placed on top of one another, made visible or invisible and moved to exact positions.

Using Layers in DHTML

The <layer> and the <ilayer> tags include several attributes for controlling the position and size of the various HTML elements.

Using the width and height attributes, you can define the element's size. The visibility attribute can be set to show or hide. The position of the element from the upper-left corner can be set with the top and left attributes. The <layer> tag also includes the z-index, above, and below attributes for controlling how overlapping elements are viewed.

The content of the layer includes all elements within the opening and closing <layer> tags. This can include text, images, and other HTML elements.

The <layer> tag can also include JavaScript events such as onmouseover, onmouseout, and onfocus.

USING LAYERS

You can use `<layer>` tags to create independent positional layers that contain HTML content for Netscape Navigator.

Netscape Navigator uses the `<layer>` tag to create independent positional layers that contain HTML content. All of the content within the opening and closing `<layer>` tags is included within the layer.

The `<layer>` tag can include the `background` and `bgcolor` attributes for defining the background image and color. These attributes work the same way as they do for the `<body>` tag. The `<body>` tag and its attributes are covered in Chapter 5.

After a layer has been created, you can position it absolutely based on the upper-left corner of the browser window by using the `top` and `left` attributes.

You can set the size of a text layer by using the `width` and `height` attributes. `width` and `height` attribute values are expressed in pixels or as a percentage of the layer.

This example uses the polar_bear.html file from this book's CD, but the steps can be applied to any situation.

USING LAYERS

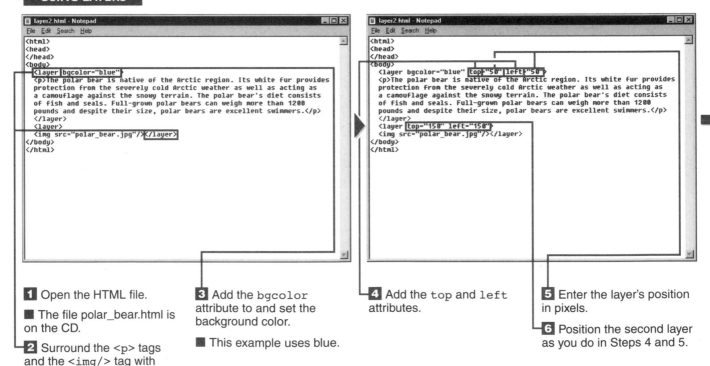

1 Open the HTML file.

■ The file polar_bear.html is on the CD.

2 Surround the `<p>` tags and the `<img/>` tag with `<layer>` tags.

3 Add the `bgcolor` attribute to and set the background color.

■ This example uses blue.

4 Add the `top` and `left` attributes.

5 Enter the layer's position in pixels.

6 Position the second layer as you do in Steps 4 and 5.

What happens when `<layer>` tags are opened in Internet Explorer?

✔ The Internet Explorer browser opens an HTML file that uses the `<layer>` tags, it ignores the `<layer>` tags. All other HTML is viewed as expected.

Can layers be positioned relative to other layers or are all layers positioned absolutely?

✔ Layers created using the `<layer>` tag are positioned absolutely from the upper-left corner of the browser. To use relative positioning, you can use the `<ilayer>` tag, which is covered in the next section.

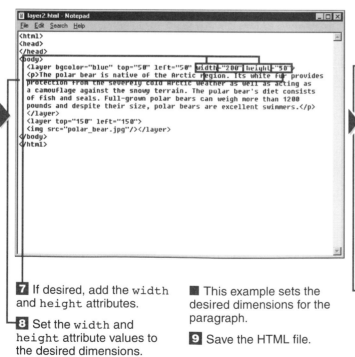

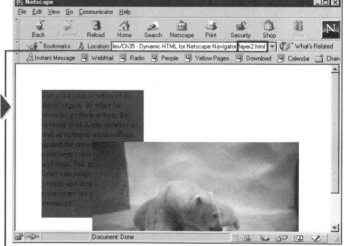

7 If desired, add the `width` and `height` attributes.

8 Set the `width` and `height` attribute values to the desired dimensions.

■ This example sets the desired dimensions for the paragraph.

9 Save the HTML file.

10 Open the HTML file in a browser.

■ If necessary, reopen the HTML file to adjust the `width` and `height` attributes.

USING INLINE LAYERS

As HTML elements are displayed on the Web page in Netscape Navigator, the browser determines their placement. If you want to indent an element a small distance from its original placement, you can use the `<ilayer>` tag.

The *i* in `<ilayer>` stands for "inline." The `<ilayer>` tag offsets the element based on the element's original placement. This means that the element is relative to its default position, so in effect, the `<ilayer>` tag works the same as setting the `position` style property to `relative`. (The `relative` property is discussed in Chapter 33.)

For example, if you have two layers and you want to separate the two layers and indent the lower one by 20 pixels, you can use a tag like `<ilayer top="20"`

`left="20">`. This code makes the second layer appear 20 pixels below the first and indented 20 pixels from the left edge.

The `<ilayer>` tag uses all the same attributes as the `<layer>` tag, including `top`, `left`, `width`, and `height`.

This example uses the skeleton.html file from this book's CD, but the steps can be applied to any situation.

USING INLINE LAYERS

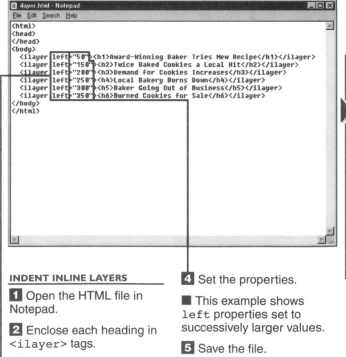

INDENT INLINE LAYERS

1 Open the HTML file in Notepad.

2 Enclose each heading in `<ilayer>` tags.

3 Add properties.

4 Set the properties.

■ This example shows `left` properties set to successively larger values.

5 Save the file.

6 Open the HTML file in a browser.

■ The layers are displayed as directed — in this case, each heading is indented further than the one above it.

Can the top and left attributes be set to negative values?

✔ The positioning attributes, `top` and `left`, can be set to negative values. Negative values will move the element closer to the top or left edge rather than further from it. Elements can be moved beyond the edge. For example, if an element has a `top` attribute set to 1000, it is probably not initially displayed in the browser window because it is positioned so far to the right of the browser.

Is it better to use <layer> or <ilayer> tags?

✔ Both of these tags have their advantages and disadvantages. Standard layers are better for global positioning and laying out the Web page. Inline layers are better for subtle positions like indents and positioning layers relative to other elements.

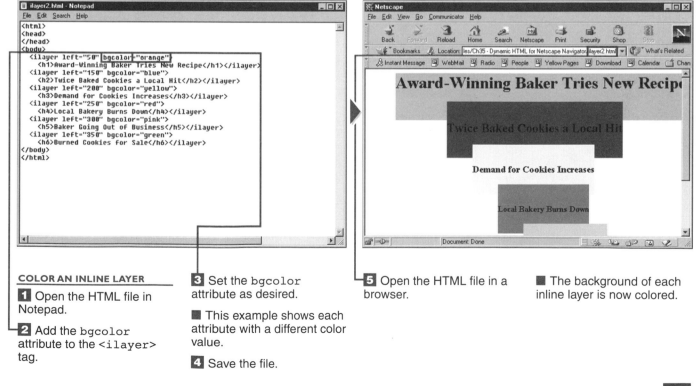

COLOR AN INLINE LAYER

1 Open the HTML file in Notepad.

2 Add the `bgcolor` attribute to the `<ilayer>` tag.

3 Set the `bgcolor` attribute as desired.

■ This example shows each attribute with a different color value.

4 Save the file.

5 Open the HTML file in a browser.

■ The background of each inline layer is now colored.

SET LAYER ORDER

Just as with Internet Explorer (see Chapter 33), you can use Dynamic HTML to position two elements on top of each other for Netscape Navigator users using layers.

Layers enable you to position elements, so you can position two elements on top of each other. When elements overlap, you can set which element appears on top of the other.

Three attributes are used to control the element layer order. These attributes are z-index, above, and below. The z-index attribute can be set to an integer representing the stacking order. Elements with a low z-index value are displayed underneath elements with a higher z-index value. The above and below attributes can be set to the id of another layer. The current layer is placed below or above this layer.

For example, if a blue image with a z-index of 5 overlaps a purple image with a z-index of 7, the purple image is displayed on top, obscuring the blue image. If the blue layer includes the above attribute set to the id value for the purple image, the purple image appears above the blue image.

This example uses the layer2.html file from this book's CD, but the steps can be applied to any situation.

SET LAYER ORDER WITH THE Z-INDEX ATTRIBUTE

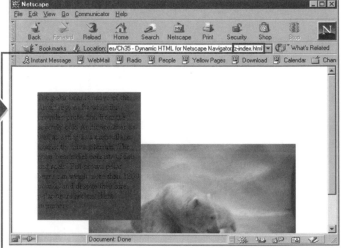

1 Open the HTML file in Notepad.

2 Add the z-index attribute to both <layer> tags.

3 Set the z-index attribute value for the first <layer> tag to an integer value and the z-index attribute value for the second <layer> tag to a value that is less than the other layer.

4 Save the file.

5 Open the file in a browser.

■ The paragraph element is displayed on top of the image.

If you use the above or below attributes and it does not seem to work, what could be wrong?

✔ You can only set the `above` or `below` attributes equal to the `id` values for layers that have already been created. If you set the `above` or `below` attributes to a layer that hasn't been created yet, the attributes will not work correctly.

Do the z-index values need to be consecutive?

✔ The z-index values do not need to be sequential. The layer order will progress from the lowest z-index value to the greatest z-index value. It is a good idea to not number values sequentially. Then you could include an in-between value without renumbering.

SET LAYER ORDER WITH THE ABOVE ATTRIBUTE

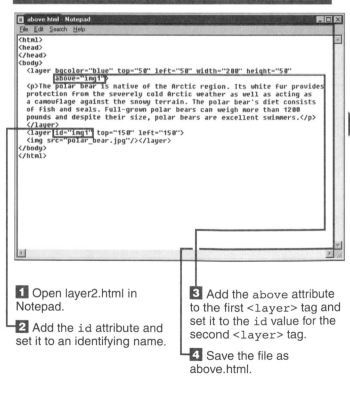

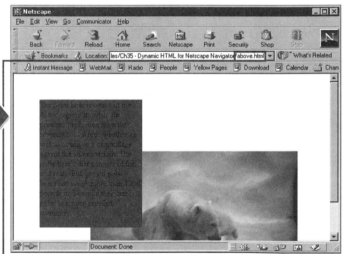

1 Open layer2.html in Notepad.

2 Add the `id` attribute and set it to an identifying name.

3 Add the `above` attribute to the first `<layer>` tag and set it to the `id` value for the second `<layer>` tag.

4 Save the file as above.html.

5 Open the above.html file in a browser.

■ The paragraph element is again displayed on top of the image.

SET LAYER VISIBILITY

As Web page content is added to a layer, you might want to make this content visible or invisible. You can hide a layer at any time using the `visibility` attribute. This attribute can be set to either `show` or `hide` and can be controlled dynamically with JavaScript.

You can use a variety of JavaScript events to make a layer appear or disappear. Some useful events for this property include the `onmouseover`, `onmouseoff`, and `onclick` events. These events and others are covered in Chapter 25.

For example, if a `<layer>` tag includes a JavaScript event such as `onmouseover`, the visibility of an element with an id of `p1` can be set to be `visible` using the JavaScript statement `onmouseover="p1.visibility ='show';"`. This works only if the `p1` layer has already been created.

This example uses the skeleton.html file from this book's CD, but the steps can be applied to any situation.

SET LAYER VISIBILITY

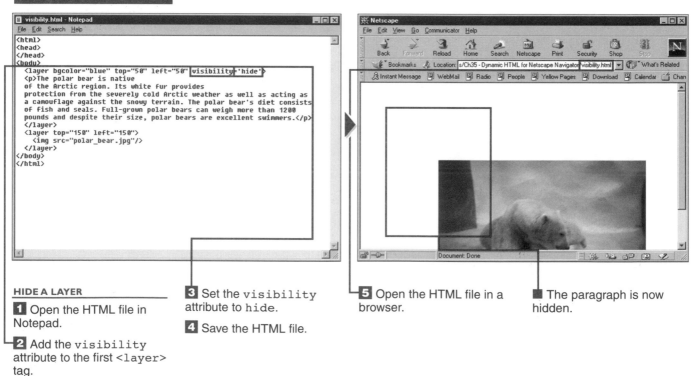

HIDE A LAYER

1 Open the HTML file in Notepad.

2 Add the `visibility` attribute to the first `<layer>` tag.

3 Set the `visibility` attribute to `hide`.

4 Save the HTML file.

5 Open the HTML file in a browser.

■ The paragraph is now hidden.

Can I control layers that have not been identified with an id?

✔ Using the `id` attribute, you can refer directly to the attributes of a `<layer>` tag, but if the layer is not identified with an `id` attribute, you can refer to it using the an index value that matches the order that it appears in the Web page. For example, the third layer in the HTML file can be identified using the `document.layers[2]` object. All layers in a Web page are stored in an array. More information on element arrays and index values can be found in Chapter 25.

How can invisible layers be used?

✔ If you have a several layers created and initially set to be invisible. You can make them appear when the user clicks on or moves the mouse over certain words.

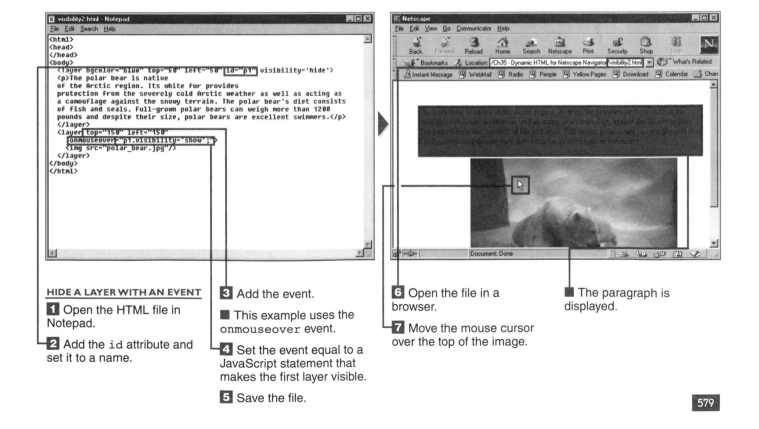

HIDE A LAYER WITH AN EVENT

1 Open the HTML file in Notepad.

2 Add the `id` attribute and set it to a name.

3 Add the event.

■ This example uses the `onmouseover` event.

4 Set the event equal to a JavaScript statement that makes the first layer visible.

5 Save the file.

6 Open the file in a browser.

7 Move the mouse cursor over the top of the image.

■ The paragraph is displayed.

LOAD A WEB PAGE INTO A LAYER

The layer model for Netscape Navigator is useful for creating containers that can hold Web page elements or even entire Web pages.

Using the src attribute, you can specify a separate Web file to load within a layer. This technique provides an alternative to using frames, plus you can overlap several layers.

For example, if a <layer> tag includes a src attribute set equal to myfile.html, the Web file is opened and displayed within the layer.

This example uses the skeleton.html file from this book's CD, but the steps can be applied to any situation.

Can the src attribute be set to load a Web page from anywhere on the Web?

✔ The src attribute can be any valid URL. To load a Web page from the Web into the layer, you simply need to include the http protocol definition along with the path to where the Web page file is located. For example src="http://www.mysite.com/myfile.html" would load into the layer the Web page found at this site. The src attribute can also be set to other types of files, such as GIF or JPEG images.

LOAD A WEB PAGE INTO A LAYER

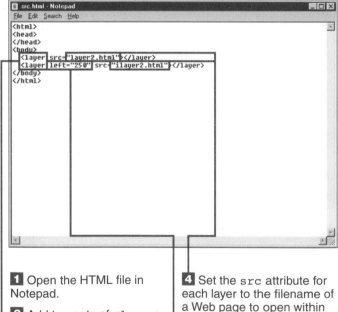

1 Open the HTML file in Notepad.

2 Add two sets of <layer> tags.

3 Add the src attribute to each <layer> tag.

4 Set the src attribute for each layer to the filename of a Web page to open within the layer.

5 Add the left attribute and set it a distance from the left edge.

6 Save the file.

7 Open the file in a browser.

■ The Web pages load and display side by side within layers.

CLIP LAYERS

Although you can resize layers that contain text using the width and height attributes, these attributes have no effect on images. You can, however, change the viewable portion of a layer by using the clip attribute, which includes four values separated by commas. These values define the upper-left and lower-right corners of the viewable region. For example, if a layer included a 100 x 100 pixel image, the attribute clip="40, 40, 60, 60" would display only the center section of the image, the part that begins at 40 pixels down from the top, 40 pixels from the left edge, and continues until 60 pixels up from the bottom, 60 pixels in from the right edge. Image dimensions are discussed in Chapter 11.

This example uses the skeleton.html file from this book's CD, but the steps can be applied to any situation.

What happens if only two values are included?

✔ Although the clip attribute can be set to four different values, you can include only two values and the clip attribute will still work. If only two values are listed for the clip attribute, the upper-left corner is assumed to be at 0, 0. Two values will define the width and height of the clipping region.

Can the clip values be set to negative values?

✔ The clip values can be set to negative values. This will display more of the background around the Web elements in the layer.

CLIP LAYERS

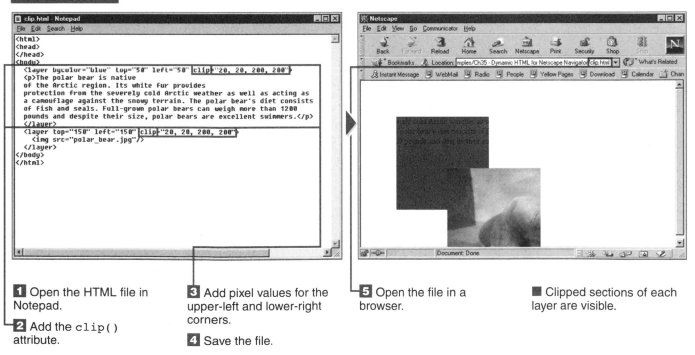

1 Open the HTML file in Notepad.

2 Add the clip() attribute.

3 Add pixel values for the upper-left and lower-right corners.

4 Save the file.

5 Open the file in a browser.

■ Clipped sections of each layer are visible.

DYNAMICALLY CONTROL LAYERS

The layer object also includes several methods that you can use to control the layers using JavaScript.

The moveAbove() and moveBelow() methods pass a layer name within the parentheses and are used to change the layer order. The moveBy() and moveTo() methods pass *x* and *y* pixel values. They can be used to move a layer about the browser window. The resizeBy() and resizeTo() methods also pass two values that represent the width and height that the layer should be resized to.

These methods need to be used within a JavaScript statement. For example, onmouseover="p1. moveTo(200, 200)" would move the layer named p1 to the location 200, 200.

This example uses the layer.html file from this book's CD, but the steps can be applied to any situation.

DYNAMICALLY CONTROL LAYERS

1 Open the HTML file.

■ This example uses layer.html from the CD.

2 Add the id attribute and a unique name.

3 Add an event and set it to a JavaScript statement that uses a method to reposition a layer.

■ This example uses the onmouseover event to trigger the moveTo() method.

4 If desired, add a second event to reposition the layer again.

■ This example adds the onmouseout event and set it equal to a JavaScript statement that uses moveTo() to return the layer to its original position.

5 Save the HTML file.

Which JavaScript events can be used with the <layer> tag?

✔ The `<layer>` tag can use only specific events. These events include `onmouseover`, `onmouseover`, `onblur`, `onfocus`, and `onload`. The elements within the `<layer>` tag can accept different events, but the `<layer>` tag recognizes only these events. JavaScript events are covered in more detail in Chapter 25.

Are the methods covered here part of JavaScript?

✔ Although the window object in JavaScript includes `moveTo()`, `moveBy()`, `resizeTo()`, and `resizeBy()` methods, the methods for layers that are presented in this section are unique to Netscape layers. The `moveAbove()` and `moveBelow()` methods are not part of JavaScript.

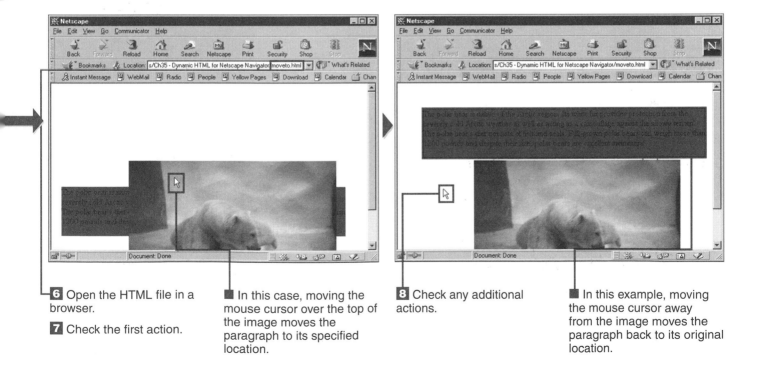

6 Open the HTML file in a browser.

7 Check the first action.

■ In this case, moving the mouse cursor over the top of the image moves the paragraph to its specified location.

8 Check any additional actions.

■ In this example, moving the mouse cursor away from the image moves the paragraph back to its original location.

NEST LAYERS

You can nest layers within each other when you want a layer to inherit the attributes from another or when you want to reduce the number of attributes that need to be included with a layer.

You nest by placing the `<layer>` tag inside of another `<layer>` tag. The original layer is called the

parent, and the nested layer is called the *child*.

The child layer inherits the attributes of the parent, but child layers can include their own attributes that will override the parent attributes. For example, if a parent layer includes a `left` attribute set to 50, all child layers also will be positioned 50 pixels

from the left edge. However, if one of the child layers has a `left` attribute set to 100, that layer is positioned differently than its parent.

This example uses the headings.html file from this book's CD, but the steps can be applied to any situation.

NEST LAYERS

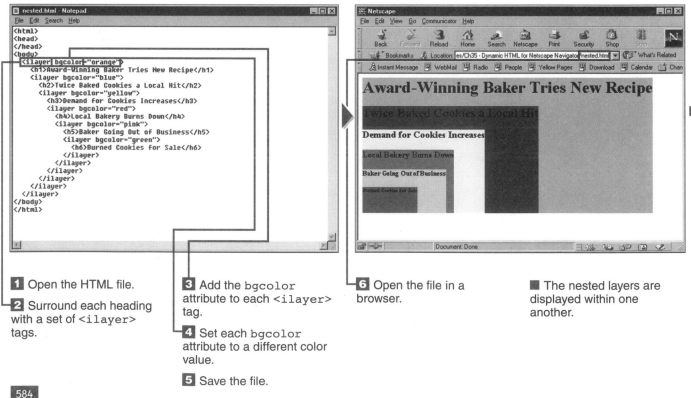

1 Open the HTML file.

2 Surround each heading with a set of `<ilayer>` tags.

3 Add the `bgcolor` attribute to each `<ilayer>` tag.

4 Set each `bgcolor` attribute to a different color value.

5 Save the file.

6 Open the file in a browser.

■ The nested layers are displayed within one another.

If a layer is dynamically moved, do all its children layers move with it?

✔ One of the main advantages of nesting layers is that children layers will follow their parent layers. This can make it easy to move a large structure of layers without having to move each layer individually.

Can you use JavaScript to identify a layer's parent layer?

✔ The layer object includes a property—`parentLayer`—that can be used to determine a layer's parent layer. Every layer has only one parent layer. For example, you can identify the parent of a layer with an `id` of layer 1 using the statement `layer1.parentLayer`.

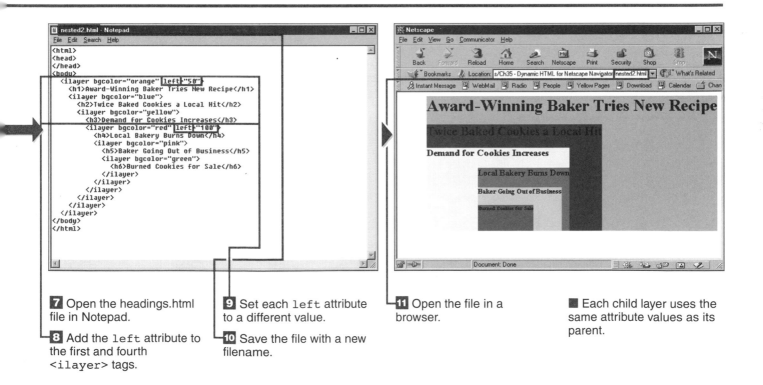

7 Open the headings.html file in Notepad.

8 Add the `left` attribute to the first and fourth `<ilayer>` tags.

9 Set each `left` attribute to a different value.

10 Save the file with a new filename.

11 Open the file in a browser.

■ Each child layer uses the same attribute values as its parent.

DETECT BROWSER TYPE

Dynamic HTML is a great idea that enables Web elements to move around the browser in response to the user. The problem with this technology is that its implementation is different between the two major browsers—Microsoft's Internet Explorer and Netscape's Navigator.

The key to cross-browser dynamic HTML is detecting which browser

your Web page visitors are using to access your site and to present those visitors with the appropriate page.

Although you could check for every browser type and version, that would not be frugal. This example concentrates on detecting only the major browsers—Netscape Navigator or Internet Explorer.

The JavaScript statement that makes this detection possible is `navigator.appName`. This object holds the name of the browser.

This example uses the skeleton.html file found on the book's CD, but you can apply these steps to any file.

DETECT BROWSER TYPE

```
<html>
<head>
</head>
<body>
<script>
document.write("appname: " + navigator.appName);
</script>
</body>
</html>
```

appname: Microsoft Internet Explorer

1 Open the file in Notepad.

2 Add a set of `<script>` tags.

3 Add the `document.write()` method.

4 Add some text and the `navigator.appName` property.

5 Save the file.

6 Open the file in the Internet Explorer browser.

■ The name for this browser is detected and displayed as Microsoft Internet Explorer.

How can you execute a JavaScript statement based on the navigator.appName property?

✔ JavaScript includes an `if` statement that allows you to execute conditional commands. To execute a statement based on the browser, you can include the `navigator.appName` property within an `if` statement like this: `if (navigator.appName == "Netscape")`. From there, include the statement to be executed.

Why does the operator within the if statement consist of two equals signs?

✔ Two equals signs together is actually a comparison operator. That is different from the assignment operator, which is a single equals sign. The comparison operator is used within a JavaScript statement, such as an `if` statement, to compare two statements and the assignment operator is used to assign values to variables.

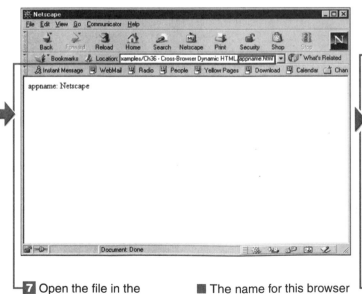

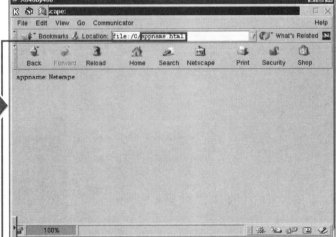

7 Open the file in the Netscape Navigator browser.

■ The name for this browser is detected and displayed as Netscape.

8 Open the file in the Netscape Navigator browser on a different operating system.

■ The name for this browser is detected for this Linux system and displayed as Netscape.

DETECT BROWSER VERSION

You can use the navigator.appVersion property to get more information about the user's browser if you need to know more than just the browser type.

The navigator.appVersion property returns the browser version number in addition to the operating system name.

The browser version number can be used to determine whether the user's browser has the functionality to view your Web page. For example, the 2.0-browser versions do not have the capability to view framed Web pages. By using JavaScript and the navigator.appVersion property, you can check for this variable and show a

different version of the Web pages to users with browsers that have capability limitations. Chapter 5 explains how can send them to a separate Web page.

This example uses the skeleton.html file found on the book's CD, but you can apply these steps to any file.

DETECT BROWSER VERSION

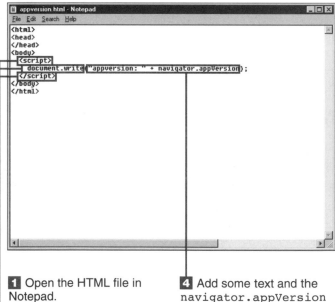

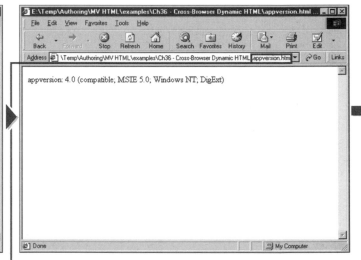

1 Open the HTML file in Notepad.

2 Add a set of `<script>` tags.

3 Add the `document.write()` method.

4 Add some text and the `navigator.appVersion` property.

5 Save the file.

6 Open the file in the Internet Explorer browser.

■ The version number for this browser is detected and displayed as 4.0.

Why does the operator within the if statement consist of two equals signs?

✔ Two equals signs together is actually a comparison operator. That is different from the assignment operator, which is a single equals sign. The comparison operator is used within a Java-Script statement, such as an `if` statement, to compare two statements and the assignment operator is used to assign values to variables.

Do browsers have the same version number regardless of the system?

✔ When Microsoft or Netscape creates a new browser version, they develop it individually for each system. Some versions are released for some systems earlier than other systems, but generally all systems will have the same browser version. Not all browsers are not available for every type of system.

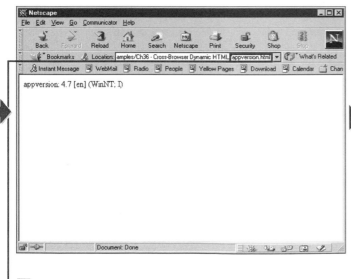

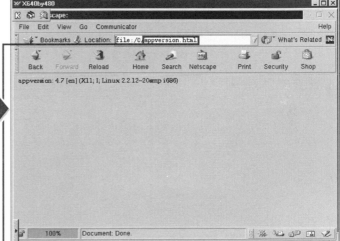

7 Open the file in the Netscape Navigator browser.

■ The version number for this browser is detected and displayed as 4.7.

8 Open the file in the Netscape Navigator browser on a different operating system.

■ The version number for this browser on a Linux system s detected and also displayed as 4.7.

DETECT USER OPERATING SYSTEM

If you just need to know for what operating system the user's browser was compiled, you can get the information by using the `navigator.platform` property.

Possible values that can be returned include `Win32` (for Windows-based computers),

`MacPPC` (for Macintosh Power PC computers), and `UNIX` (for UNIX-based computers).

Knowing with what operating system the user's browser coincides helps when you use some specialized plug-ins. For example, if you want to use a Macromedia Flash file, you should look for a

Windows and Macintosh computers. It also helps you know, when using content such as audio or video files, what file types to present.

This example uses the skeleton.html file found on the book's CD, but you can apply these steps to any file.

DETECT USER OPERATING SYSTEM

1 Open the HTML file in Notepad.

2 Add `<script>` tags.

3 Add the `document.write()` method.

4 Add some text and the `navigator.platform` property.

5 Save the file.

6 Open the file in the Internet Explorer browser.

■ The platform that the browser is running on is detected and displayed as Win32.

Why else would you want to know the type of browser that the user is running?

✔ If you are creating Web pages that offer system-specific solutions or products, you can target the exact information and/or products that the user would be interested in based on their detected system. For example, if your site includes system tips for various computer systems, you can automatically send the user to the Web pages that contain the information for their system.

What other useful properties are part of the JavaScript navigator object?

✔ The `language` property can be used to determine the default language setting. The `mimeTypes` property includes an array of all the supported MIME types for the user's browser. The `plugins` property returns an array of supported plug-ins. The `navigator` object also includes the `javaEnabled()` method, which returns a `true` value if Java is enabled on the user's browser.

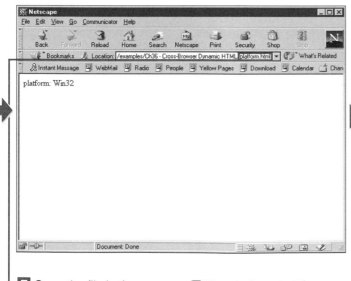

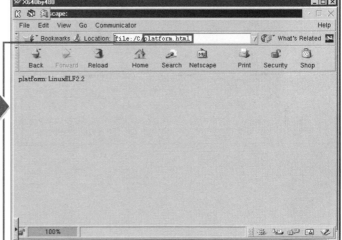

7 Open the file in the Netscape Navigator browser.

■ The platform that the browser is running on is detected and also displayed as Win32.

8 Open the file in the Netscape Navigator browser on a different operating system.

■ The platform that the browser is running on is detected and displayed as LinusELF2.2.

DYNAMICALLY CHANGE STYLES

You can determine in which browser the user views your Web pages via the `navigator.appName` JavaScript property. If you place this property in an `if` statement, you can give the browser different commands based on which browser he or she is using.

Netscape Navigator processes the Web page differently than does Internet Explorer. Netscape Navigator processes the style definitions prior to displaying the HTML; hence, the JavaScript style definitions need to come before the HTML.

Internet Explorer, on the other hand, cannot use an object until the object has been declared; hence, the JavaScript style definitions for Internet Explorer need to be defined after the HTML elements.

For example, the `if` statement could say, in a sense, "If the browser is Netscape, go to this page. If it is Internet Explorer, go to this page."

This example uses the polar_bear.html file found on the book's CD, but you can apply these steps to any file.

DYNAMICALLY CHANGE STYLES

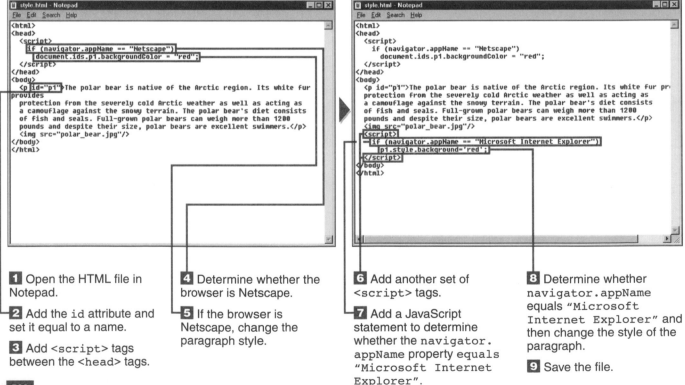

1 Open the HTML file in Notepad.

2 Add the `id` attribute and set it equal to a name.

3 Add <script> tags between the <head> tags.

4 Determine whether the browser is Netscape.

5 If the browser is Netscape, change the paragraph style.

6 Add another set of <script> tags.

7 Add a JavaScript statement to determine whether the `navigator.appName` property equals "Microsoft Internet Explorer".

8 Determine whether `navigator.appName` equals "Microsoft Internet Explorer" and then change the style of the paragraph.

9 Save the file.

MASTER IT

Besides the position of the <script> tags, how else do style definitions differ between Internet Explorer and Netscape Navigator?

✔ Internet Explorer has a more robust implementation of the Document Object Model. Using Microsoft's implementation you can reference any Web page element. All these elements are referenced as part of the document object. You can also see differences in the way that objects are referenced and in the style property syntax. For example, style can be referenced for

Internet Explorer using the element's `id` followed by the `style` keyword and the `style` property. Styles in Netscape Navigator are referenced using the `document.ids` object followed by the `id` name and the `style` property. For example, to reference a style in IE, you would use a statement like, `id1.style.background`, and in Netscape, it would look like, `document.ids.id1.backgroundColor`.

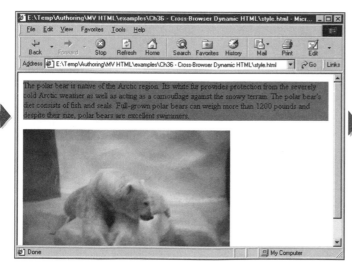

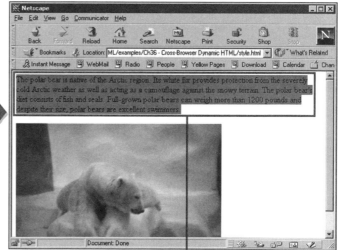

10 Open the HTML file in Internet Explorer

■ The background color of the paragraph is red.

11 Open the HTML file in Netscape Navigator.

■ The background color of the paragraph for this browser is also red.

SET MULTIPLE STYLES

You should keep in mind some intricacies when dealing with dynamic styles so that you can change styles on either browser.

Netscape Navigator does not allow you to use shortcut style properties such as margin, border, and padding; you must use each individual property within a JavaScript statement. Netscape requires a specific syntax, such as,

remembering to remove the hyphen (-), to close up the two words, and to capitalize the second word, such as borderWidth and marginTop.

Internet Explorer, on the other hand, cannot use any style definition that includes a hyphen, such as border-width. You can, however, use shortcut styles such as font and background.

For example, to specify for Netscape Navigator a blue dashed border that is 10 pixels wide, you would use the borderWidth, borderColor, and borderStyle definitions. For Internet Explorer, you would use the border property.

This example uses the style.html file found on the book's CD, but you can apply these steps to any file.

SET MULTIPLE STYLES

1 Open the HTML file in Notepad.

2 Add a set of brackets for the first set of <script> tags.

3 Add several JavaScript statements to set the border style for Netscape Navigator.

4 Change the JavaScript statement for the second set of <script> tags to set the border for Internet Explorer.

5 Save the file.

When are brackets used in JavaScript?

✔ Brackets are not needed if a JavaScript statement such as a function name or an `if` statement includes only one statement. If a function name or an `if` statement needs to execute several JavaScript statements, those statements need to be contained within a set of brackets.

Is there a limit to the number of styles that can be applied to a single Web element?

✔ Using JavaScript, you can apply many separate style definitions to a single Web element. If conflicting style definitions exist, the style that is closest to the Web element will be used.

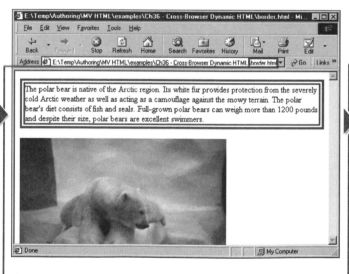

6 Open the file in Internet Explorer.

■ The paragraph's border is displayed.

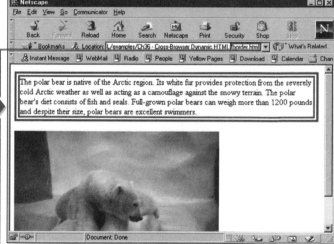

7 Open the file in Netscape Navigator.

■ The paragraph for this browser also includes a border.

POSITION ELEMENTS

Luckily, most of the style sheet positioning properties work the same in both Internet Explorer or Netscape Navigator, so you can use them to position elements consistently on either browser.

The position style sheet property can be used outside of the browser

detection scripts. It works for both major browsers.

To position elements using style sheets, either add a set of <style> tags within the <head> tags of a document or reference an external style sheet via the <link/> tag.

The style properties and their values can be included within the <style> tags as described in Chapter 28, "Style Sheet Basics."

This example uses the border.html file found on the book's CD, but you can apply these steps to any file.

POSITION ELEMENTS

```
<html>
<head>
  <style>
    p {position: absolute; top: 200px; left: 50px}
  </style>
  <script>
    if (navigator.appName == "Netscape") {
      document.ids.p1.borderWidth = "10";
      document.ids.p1.borderColor = "blue";
      document.ids.p1.borderStyle = "dashed";
    }
  </script>
</head>
<body>
<p id="p1">The polar bear is native of the Arctic region. Its white fur pr
protection from the severely cold Arctic weather as well as acting as
a camouflage against the snowy terrain. The polar bear's diet consists
of fish and seals. Full-grown polar bears can weigh more than 1200
pounds and despite their size, polar bears are excellent swimmers.</p>
<img src="polar_bear.jpg"/>
<script>
  if (navigator.appName == "Microsoft Internet Explorer")
    p1.style.border = '10 dashed blue';
</script>
</body>
</html>
```

The polar bear is native of the Arctic region. Its white fur provides protection from the severely cold Arctic weather as well as acting as a camouflage against the snowy terrain. The polar bear's diet consists of fish and seals. Full-grown polar bears can weigh more than 1200 pounds and despite their size, polar bears are excellent swimmers.

1 With the HTML file open in Notepad, add a set of <style> tags.

2 Add a selector and a set of brackets for the <p> tag.

3 Between the brackets, add several style definitions for positioning the paragraph element.

4 Save the file.

5 Open the HTML file in a browser.

■ This shows the default position of the elements.

If a style has conflicting definitions in the <style> tags and the <script> tags, which definition takes precedence?

✔ If a style is defined in both the <style> and <script> tags, the style defined in the <script> tags takes precedence. For example, if the text color is defined as blue in the <style> tags and as green in the <script> tags, the text color will be green regardless of where the <style> tags are located.

Why are all position coordinates based off the upper left corner of the browser?

✔ For all HTML displayed in the browser, the starting point for the text is the upper left corner of the browser. This relates to the English standard for reading, which starts in the upper-left corner. Other languages will use different orientations.

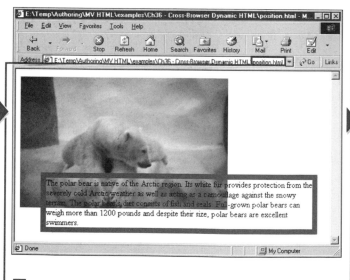

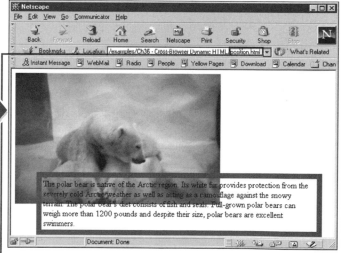

6 Open the HTML file in Internet Explorer.

■ The paragraph's position is changed.

7 Open the HTML file in Netscape Navigator.

■ The paragraph's position for this browser is the same.

36) CHECKING YOUR PAGES

37) UPLOADING WEB PAGES

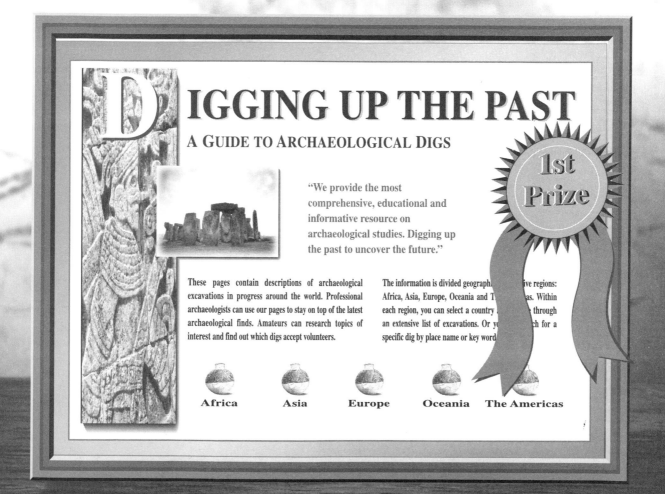

DIGGING UP THE PAST

A GUIDE TO ARCHAEOLOGICAL DIGS

"We provide the most comprehensive, educational and informative resource on archaeological studies. Digging up the past to uncover the future."

These pages contain descriptions of archaeological excavations in progress around the world. Professional archaeologists can use our pages to stay on top of the latest archaeological finds. Amateurs can research topics of interest and find out which digs accept volunteers.

The information is divided geographi[cally into] five regions: Africa, Asia, Europe, Oceania and T[he Americ]as. Within each region, you can select a country a[nd brows]e through an extensive list of excavations. Or yo[u can sear]ch for a specific dig by place name or key word[.]

1st Prize

Africa   Asia   Europe   Oceania   The Americas

CHECK WEB PAGES IN A BROWSER

When you've finished writing the HTML code in Notepad or another HTML editor, you can use a browser to open the page and check for obvious errors. This simple method enables you to catch things like display problems and misspellings before anyone else sees the page.

Because the browser can display local HTML pages saved on your computer's hard drive, you do not have to upload the pages to the server unless the Web page uses a CGI script.

Opening the Web page in both the Internet Explorer and Netscape Navigator browsers is a good idea,

especially if the browsers use features like Dynamic HTML that are different between the two major browsers.

When the page loads, look for misplaced elements. If any syntax is missing, like the end of a tag, the HTML code is visible.

CHECK WEB PAGES IN A BROWSER

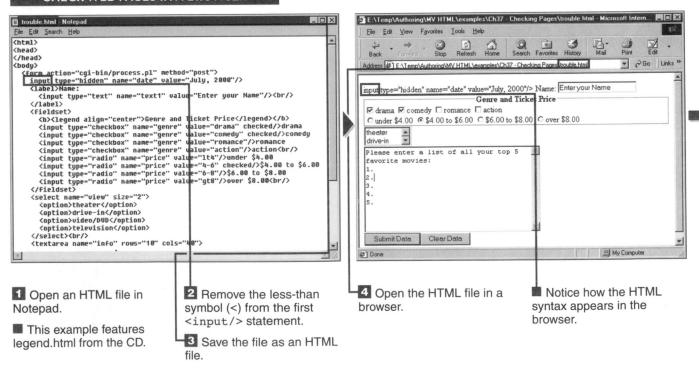

1 Open an HTML file in Notepad.

■ This example features legend.html from the CD.

2 Remove the less-than symbol (<) from the first `<input/>` statement.

3 Save the file as an HTML file.

4 Open the HTML file in a browser.

■ Notice how the HTML syntax appears in the browser.

Are Internet Explorer and Netscape Navigator the only browsers that I should check?

✔ Internet Explorer and Netscape Navigator represent perhaps 90 percent of the browsers used to surf the Web, but you can find different versions of each running on different operating systems that will be worth testing. For example, the current Internet Explorer version is 5, but testing your Web page on Version 4 may show some problems.

Are there any differences between similar browsers on different operating systems.

✔ Two pages viewed using Netscape Navigator on a computer running Windows and a Macintosh computer could be different. The differences have to do with the system fonts and the way pages are displayed. It is beneficial to check your pages on different operating systems if you have accessed to them.

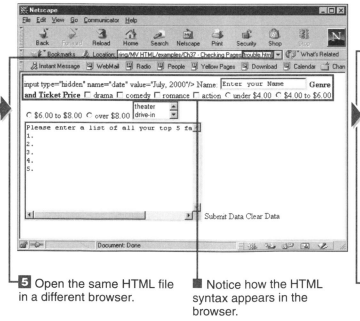

5 Open the same HTML file in a different browser.

■ Notice how the HTML syntax appears in the browser.

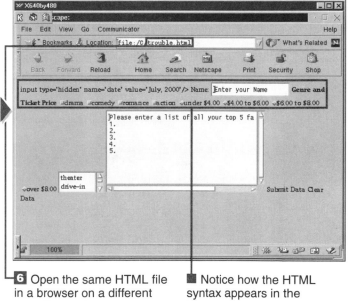

6 Open the same HTML file in a browser on a different operating system.

■ Notice how the HTML syntax appears in the browser.

VALIDATE WEB PAGES

After you have completed your Web page and checked it in a browser, another way to check the page is to use a *validating* utility. These utilities are found on the Web and can be downloaded from a repository such as www.download.com.

Validating utilities compare the Web page syntax in your Web page

file with the accepted specification and show you if there are any syntax errors in your HTML code.

For example, the HTML 4.0 specification requires closing tags for certain tags. If a closing tag is missing, the validation utility will list this as an error.

These validation utilities also make suggestions for better enabling your Web pages to be viewed in a browser.

One such validating service can be found on the W3C's Web site at http://validator.w3.org.

VALIDATE WEB PAGES

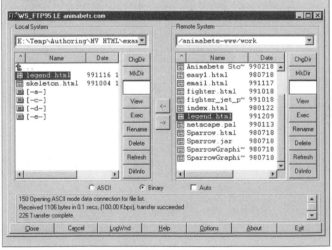

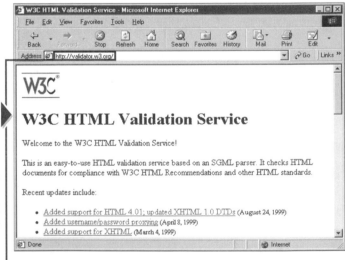

1 Use an FTP program to copy the Web page file to the server.

2 Enter the URL for the W3C HTML Validation Service in a browser.

What other validation utilities are available?

✔ Many such validation utilities are available. Another good validation Web site can be found at www.Weblint.org. Other validation utilities can be downloaded such as CSE HTML Validator, at www. htmlvalidator.com.

Can validation utilities automatically correct your Web page files?

✔ The functionality of the various validation utilities is different. Some utilities can be configured to automatically correct certain errors. You need to give the utility access to your files to make the needed changes.

Can validation utilities be used to check spelling and links?

✔ Many utilities can be used to perform multiple functions such as spell and link checking in addition to HTML validation.

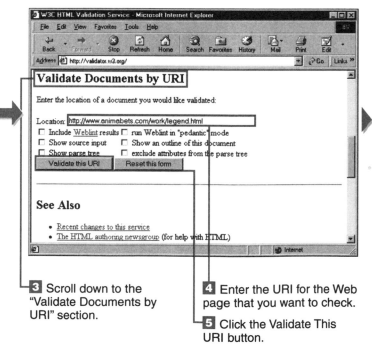

3 Scroll down to the "Validate Documents by URI" section.

4 Enter the URI for the Web page that you want to check.

5 Click the Validate This URI button.

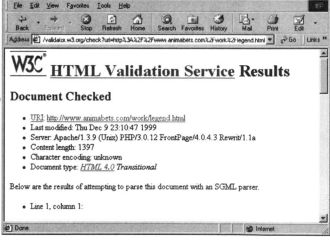

■ The results are displayed on a Web page.

SPELL-CHECK YOUR SITE

If the text on your Web site includes misspelled words, it makes your Web pages appear less appealing. These errors can be easily identified and corrected.

Even if you are not a good speller, there are tools available that help you to identify and eliminate spelling errors from your Web pages.

Although many of the HTML editor packages like FrontPage include spell-checking functions, you can still check your pages if you write HTML using Notepad.

The technique is to copy and paste the HTML code into a word processor with a spell checker and make notes of the spelling errors. You can then return to the HTML

document and correct the spelling errors.

Even if you do not have access to a word processor that includes a spell checker, you can download a generic spell checker.

SPELL-CHECK YOUR SITE

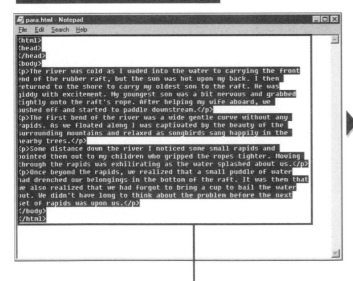

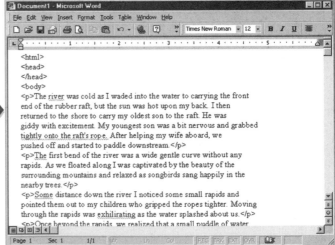

1 Open an HTML file in Notepad.

■ This example uses skeleton.html from the CD.

2 Select the entire section of HTML code.

3 Click Edit.

4 Click Copy.

5 Open a new file in a word processor like Microsoft Word.

6 Paste the HTML code to the new file by clicking Edit⇨Paste.

■ The HTML code appears within the word processor.

Will the spell checker become confused with all the HTML tags and attributes?

✔ The main purpose for spell-checking a Web page is to identify the spelling errors within the text that will display, but the spell checker also identifies misspelled tags. As the spell checker flags tags and properties that are spelled correctly, click the Ignore All button so that the spell checker only questions these words once.

Does it really matter if I misspell some words?

✔ Many users are bothered by misspelled words. Some even take it upon themselves to notify you of the errors by e-mail.

Do common Web utilities include a spell checker?

✔ Many of the common Web utility packages include a spell-checking function in addition to other features.

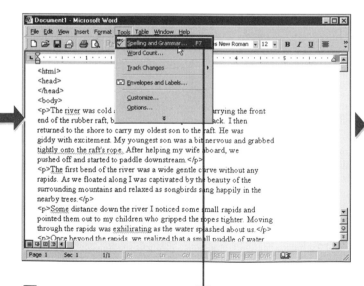

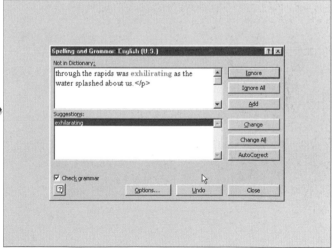

7 Select Tools.

8 Select Spelling and Grammar to start the spell checker.

■ The Spelling and Grammar dialog box opens and identifies any misspelled words.

CHECK LINKS

Checking your links is just as important as checking your spelling and your display. Most of the popular HTML editors include site-management functions such as link checking. However, if you use Notepad to develop your HTML files, you can download separate site-management tools.

One such site-management tool that you can use to check the links is Xenu Link Sleuth. This program is simple but effective, and you can find it at www.download.com.

To check all the links in your site, you simply need to provide Link Sleuth with the root Web page. The program then searches through

your Web pages for hyperlinks, image links, frame links, and any other links. As Link Sleuth finds a link, it checks the link to see if the link is valid and then displays a report. You can then use the report to fix the broken links in your Web pages.

CHECK LINKS

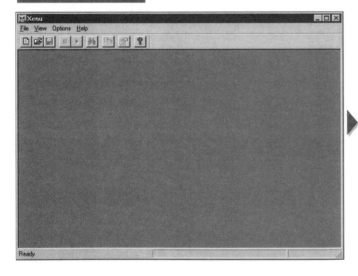

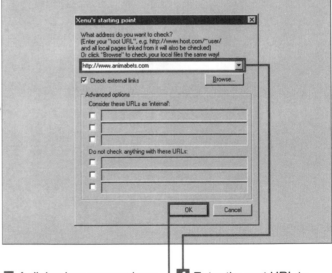

1 Open the Xenu Link Sleuth program.

2 Select File.

3 Select Check URL.

■ A dialog box opens where you can enter the URL to check.

4 Enter the root URL to check.

5 Click the OK button.

What other site-management tools are available?

✔ The Web is full of tools that can help you check all the links on your site. To see the available Web-management tools, search the Web to find an assortment of tools. One of the more useful and popular set of Web utilities is created by Coffee Cup Software. Many of these utilities are included on the book's CD. You can also download these from www.coffeecup.com. In addition to the Coffee Cup Software utilities, the CD also contains many other useful Web utilities.

Do Web editors typically include features like link checking?

✔ Web editors such as HomeSite or FrontPage include many features that make it easy to work with entire Web sites. These features will let you check the links for the entire Web site quickly and easily.

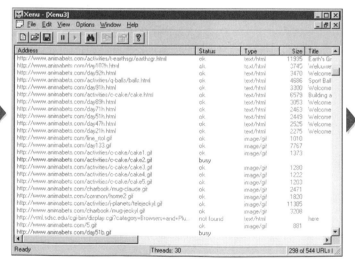

■ The program checks all links throughout the Web site and lists them in the window.

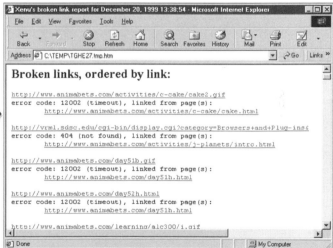

■ After all links have been checked, the program asks if you want to generate an HTML report.

SECURE SERVER SPACE

A server is a computer that is connected to the Internet that holds the Web page files that make up a site. The files, once placed on the server, become accessible to any computer connected to the Internet.

Before you can upload your Web page files to a server where they can be viewed on the Web, you need to secure some server space.

Finding a Host Server

Most Internet service providers (ISPs) offer some server space when you sign up for their service. They typically offer between 5MB and 20MB, which is sufficient for smaller personal Web sites.

You can get free server space from several places on the Web. These sites let you post your Web page files in exchange for allowing advertising to be displayed. The more common way is to pay a hosting company to give you access to space on their server.

Another alternative is to obtain your own domain name, but you need to pay to register the name and also pay for hosting fees.

Different Web hosting companies vary from one another in many ways. You should compare technical support, limits on space and traffic, support for extensions like databases and CGI, and reporting features.

How Server Files are Organized

If you are using server space provided by your ISP, your directories are located as a subdirectory under the ISP's domain name. The directory name is typically your account username.

For example, if my ISP domain is www.bigisp.com and my username is biguser, my server space is in the biguser directory under the user directory for the www.biguser.com domain. After you have uploaded your pages, you can find them on the Web at www.bigisp. com/biguser. If you are using a hosting company, the company's domain name will replace the ISP name.

Critical Information

Accessing the server space requires several critical pieces of information. First, you need to know where the server space is located. This will be listed as a *domain address*. You also need to know the username and password for accessing your server space.

If you have these basic pieces of information, you can send your Web page files to the server using a File Transfer Protocol (FTP) program.

Your browser can also be used to transfer files between the server and your local computer.

OBTAIN A DOMAIN

If you use a hosting company or your ISP, their domain name appears as part of your URL address. If you obtain your own domain, however, users can find your site using an address that you select.

If you wish to obtain your own domain, you need to first see if the domain you want is available. Several places on the Web enable you to check whether your desired domain name is taken. One such place is at www.internic.net/whois.html.

After you have found a domain name that you wish to register, you need to contact a hosting site that can register the domain and provide some server space for you.

Hosting sites charge you depending on the amount of server space that you need. You should also check with the hosting site to see what advanced features they offer such as a CGI bin, database support, automatic site reporting, and others.

OBTAIN A DOMAIN

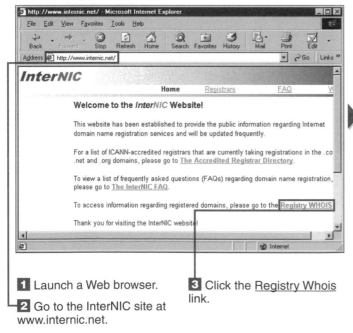

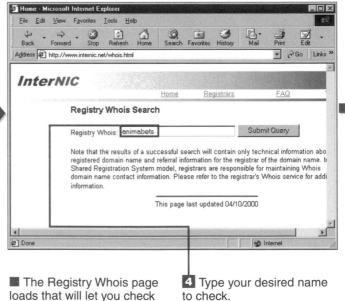

1 Launch a Web browser.

2 Go to the InterNIC site at www.internic.net.

3 Click the Registry Whois link.

■ The Registry Whois page loads that will let you check domain names.

4 Type your desired name to check.

How can there be two domains with the same name?

✔ The domain name is made up of a name and a domain type identifier. This identifier comes after the name and is separated by a period. Many different domain type identifiers exist, but the most common ones include *com* (commercial sites), *net* (networks), and *org* (organizations). There are also identifiers for the various counties such as Canada *(ca),* Japan *(jp),* and England *(uk).*

Is InterNIC the only place to register a domain name?

✔ Most hosting sites can register domain names for you. For example, Network Solutions is a hosting company that lets you search for free domain names on their site. They also submit a registration to InterNIC for you. The benefit of this is that it becomes a single point where you can locate, register and host some server space.

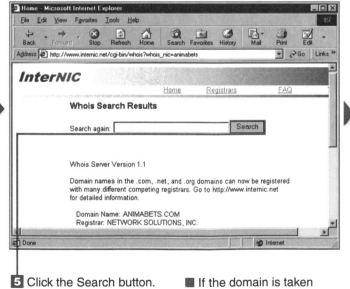

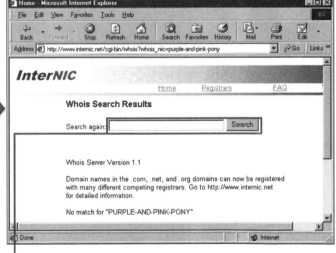

5 Click the Search button.

■ If the domain is taken then a registrant is listed.

6 Enter another domain name to check and click the Search button.

■ The domain is available if no match can be found for the name.

CHECK TOTAL SITE FILE SIZE

If you plan on uploading your Web files to the Web space provided by your Internet service provider, you need to be aware of the space limitations that the provider has designated. Most ISPs charge you an additional fee if you upload more than your allotted space.

Before you upload any file to the Web server, checking the site's available free space first is a good idea. Windows Explorer can show the size of individual files, but viewing the Properties dialog for the parent folder tells you the size of all the files that make up the site.

To check the site's free space, just right-click the parent directory and then click Properties. The Properties dialog box appears, and it shows the cumulative file size for all files contained within that directory.

CHECK TOTAL SITE FILE SIZE

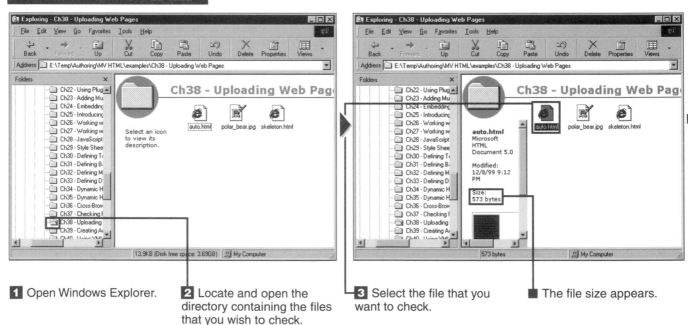

1 Open Windows Explorer. **2** Locate and open the directory containing the files that you wish to check.

3 Select the file that you want to check.

■ The file size appears.

Is there a quicker way to access the Properties dialog box?

✔ The Properties dialog box can be accessed quickly by right-clicking the directory folder and then selecting Properties from the pop-up menu.

Can I see the file sizes for all files in a directory at the same time?

✔ If you click the View⇨Details command in Windows Explorer, all file sizes become visible for the given directory.

Can I mark folders and files as read-only so they cannot be changed?

✔ The Properties dialog box also includes an Attributes section, which includes a checkbox for marking a file as read-only. Files and folders marked as read-only cannot be modified. If you try to save a modified read-only file, Windows notifies you that you must save the file as a different name.

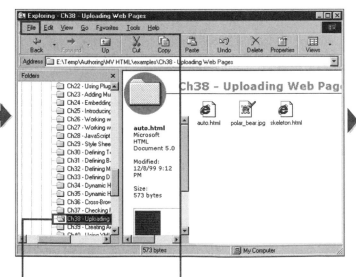

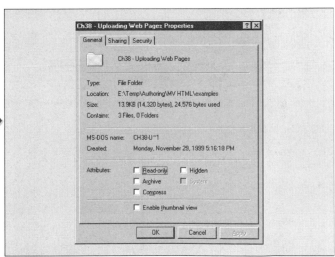

4 Select the directory folder that contains all the files that you intend to upload.

5 Click File.

6 Click Properties.

■ The Properties dialog box shows the total file size for all files in the directory.

SET UP AN FTP CLIENT

You can transport your Web pages from your local computer to the server in one of several ways. One method is to use FTP client software.

Several different FTP client packages are available, but they all work in a similar manner. The FTP client enables you to connect to the server, where it shows you a listing of files and directories on the server, as well as a listing of files on your local computer.

Before you can upload Web pages to the server, you must set up the FTP client so that it can connect to the server. To set up an FTP client, you need to have the site address, a username, and a password. You should obtain this information from the server administrator.

Many different FTP clients, such as CuteFTP and W/S FTP, are available for transfering your files.

SET UP AN FTP CLIENT

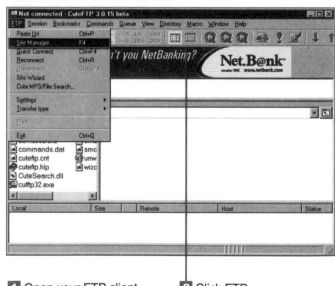

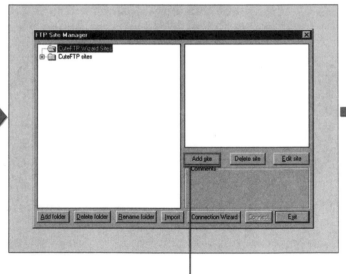

1 Open your FTP client software, such as CuteFTP.

2 Click FTP.

3 Click Site Manager.

■ The Site Manager dialog box appears. This box keeps track of all the available servers to which you can connect.

4 Click the Add Site button.

Can I set up the FTP client to connect automatically?

✔ CuteFTP includes a Connection Wizard that takes you through the several steps required to set up your FTP client. One of the options of this wizard is to automatically connect to a site when the client is launched. Other FTP clients have similar features.

When using CuteFTP, how are the three panes used?

✔ CuteFTP includes four separate panes. The left one displays the contents of your local hard drive, and the right pane shows the contents of the server that you are connected to. The top pane is where messages are displayed. These messages tell you the status of the files and any errors that may occur during the transfer process. The bottom pane shows in one line which files are moving from where to where.

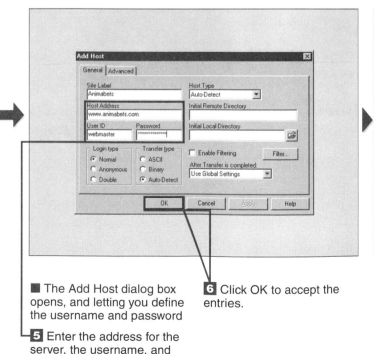

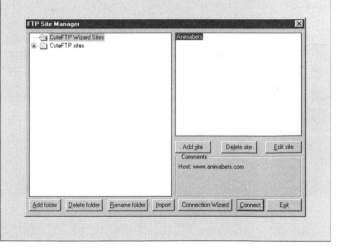

■ The Add Host dialog box opens, and letting you define the username and password

6 Click OK to accept the entries.

■ The Site Manager dialog box now includes the server name.

5 Enter the address for the server, the username, and password.

UPLOAD PAGES WITH AN FTP CLIENT

The first step in uploading your Web pages is to connect to the server. Once uploaded to the server, your Web pages are visible from any computer connected to the Internet. If you have set up the FTP client correctly, getting your Web pages online should be easy.

After connecting, you see a listing of the files and directories on the server, as well as the files and directories on your local computer.

You can then select files on the server to download to your local computer or files on your local computer that you can upload to the server.

You can transfer files in two different formats—ASCII or Binary. *ASCII* transfers are for plain text files such as HTML Web pages. *Binary* transfers are used for graphics and other file types like audio and video files.

UPLOAD PAGES WITH AN FTP CLIENT

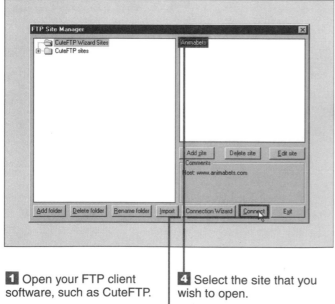

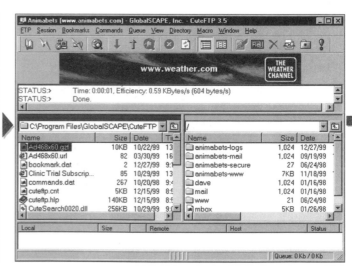

1 Open your FTP client software, such as CuteFTP.

2 Click FTP.

3 Click Site Manager.

4 Select the site that you wish to open.

5 Click the Connect button.

■ Once connected, the server files will be displayed.

■ The local files are displayed in the left pane and the server files are displayed in the right pane.

Is there an easy way to determine whether I need to use the ASCII or Binary transfer methods?

✔ Most FTP clients include an Auto Detect mode that automatically determines which transfer method is needed. Auto Detect sets the transfer method to whichever method is needed. This is especially useful if you are transferring entire directories of files that include HTML Web files and graphics.

What is the Auto transfer setting?

✔ Depending on the type of file, the transfer method could be set to ASCII or to Binary. The Auto setting that appears with many different FTP clients automatically determines the type of transfer setting that you need. This option is a convenient setting.

How do I know if an error occurred in the transfer?

✔ Transfer errors appear in the message pane. Error messages typically appear in red text to make them easy to identify.

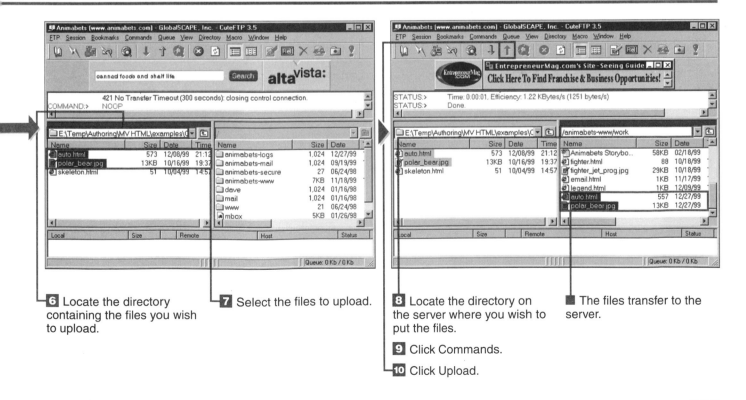

6 Locate the directory containing the files you wish to upload.

7 Select the files to upload.

8 Locate the directory on the server where you wish to put the files.

9 Click Commands.

10 Click Upload.

■ The files transfer to the server.

USING BROWSER FTP

If you do not have an FTP client or you do not want to bother with one, you can use the browser to handle your FTP chores. Because FTP is just another protocol like HTTP, the browser recognizes and interacts with FTP sites.

To access an FTP site, you need to type **ftp://** in the browser's location field followed by the FTP site's domain name. For example, entering **ftp://ftp.microsoft.com** links you to the Microsoft public FTP site.

When connected to an FTP site, the directories appear like folders and the files display as icons. You can upload files by dragging and dropping them onto the browser window. To download files, you simply need to double-click the file icon.

If you need to log on to an FTP site, you can use the File⇨Login As command to open a dialog box where you can enter your username and password.

USING BROWSER FTP

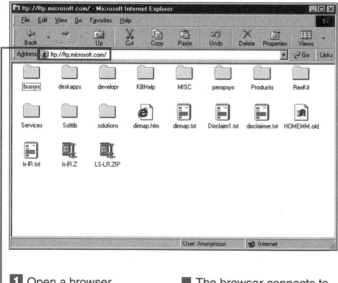

1 Open a browser.

2 Type **ftp://** and the name of an FTP server, such as **ftp.microsoft.com**.

3 Press Enter.

■ The browser connects to the FTP site and the files and directories at that site are displayed.

4 Locate and open the directory that contains the files you wish to download.

5 Double-click the file that you wish to download.

How can I determine the size of the files?

✔ Using the browser as an FTP client works just like the other Windows programs. You can determine the size of a file by right-clicking the file and selecting Properties from the pop-up menu. To see the file sizes all at once, you can change the View to show Details.

What is an anonymous login?

✔ Many sites have public FTP sites that can be accessed without a username or password. These sites require an anonymous login. The username for these sites is simply anonymous and the password is typically your own e-mail address. The next section covers anonymous logins in detail.

Can I include the username and password in the URL?

✔ You can log on to an FTP site without entering a username or password by including the username and password directly before the domain name. The drawback to this method is that the password is visible. This is shown in the next section.

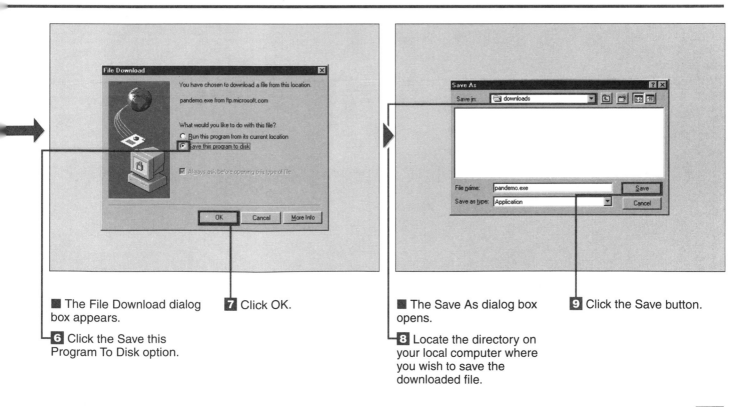

■ The File Download dialog box appears.

6 Click the Save this Program To Disk option.

7 Click OK.

■ The Save As dialog box opens.

8 Locate the directory on your local computer where you wish to save the downloaded file.

9 Click the Save button.

ACCESS A SECURE FTP SITE USING A BROWSER

When you connect to an FTP site using a browser, the browser connects to the public sections of the site as an anonymous login.

Accessing a secure FTP site requires a username and password. The company that hosts your Web space gives you a username and password.

You can add a username and password in front of the domain name for the FTP site to automatically login to the FTP site. The username and password can be listed between the protocol statement and the FTP domain and should be separated with a colon symbol (:). An at symbol (@) should then separate the username

and password from the domain name.

For example, if the username is blink and the password is meow1 for a site, the location field should contain `ftp://blink: meow1 @ftp.mysite.com`.

ACCESS A SECURE FTP SITE USING A BROWSER

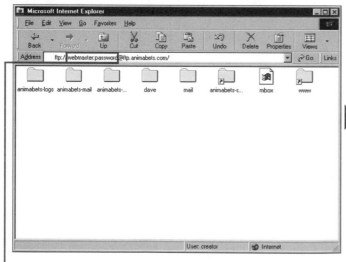

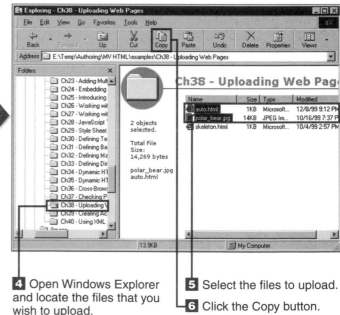

1 Open a browser and type **ftp://** and the name of an FTP server in the Address bar.

2 Add the username and password separated by a colon (:).

3 Add an at symbold (@) after the password.

■ The browser connects to the secure FTP site and the files and directories at that site are displayed.

4 Open Windows Explorer and locate the files that you wish to upload.

5 Select the files to upload.

6 Click the Copy button.

Should I be concerned about the username and password being displayed in the location field?

✔ If you are accessing your FTP site at a location where others can see your password by glancing over your shoulder, you can connect to the main FTP site and then click File⇨Login In As. This command opens a Login dialog box where you can enter the username and password that are not displayed in the browser.

Could a link be made with a username and password included that would enable users access to the FTP site?

✔ If the address of an FTP site that includes a username and password is made into a link, any users clicking the link from a browser would be sent to the FTP site. This would also make the username and password available to any user that viewed the Web page source.

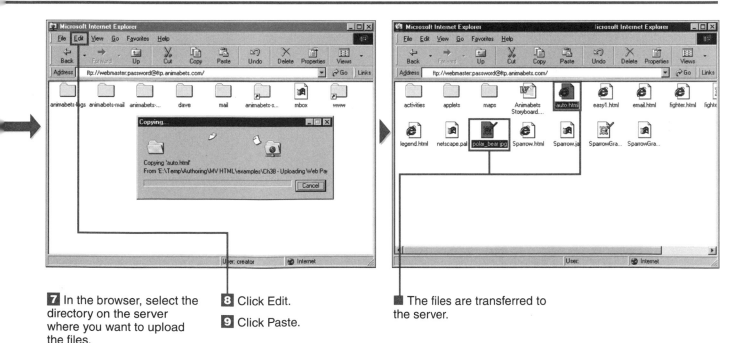

7 In the browser, select the directory on the server where you want to upload the files.

8 Click Edit.

9 Click Paste.

■ The files are transferred to the server.

HTML 4 and XHTML™ 1 • HTML

38) CREATING ACCESSIBLE WEB PAGES

39) USING XML

SUPPORT MULTIPLE BROWSERS

Millions of users surf the Web, and these users use a broad array of browsers. Users' browsers differ, depending on the computer system they are running on, the browser type, the browser version, and the browser size.

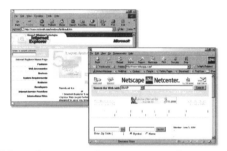

Although Microsoft Internet Explorer and Netscape Navigator represent a majority of browsers that are in use today, many other browsers exist. For example, some UNIX systems use Lynx, which is a text-based browser. Other browsers have been created to read XML, which has not made its way into the popular browsers yet.

Support for older browsers

Many users will visit your Web pages with older browser versions that may no longer be compatible with your Web pages. For example, if you try to view a Web page that uses frames with Netscape Navigator 2.0, the frames aren't visible.

You can handle older browsers by using the alternate tags such as `<noframes>` and `<noscript>` to present information to users of older browsers.

Another technique that ensures that your pages can be understood by a large majority of browsers is to always include alternative descriptive text by using the `alt` attribute.

Check for browser-specific tags and properties

Chapters 33 and 34 present several specific tags and properties that only work in one browser. Although Chapter 35 shows you how to overcome these limitations, you should be very careful when using proprietary tags and properties to not alienate users of a specific browser.

To check for browser idiosyncrasies, you should check your Web pages in both Internet Explorer and Navigator before uploading your pages.

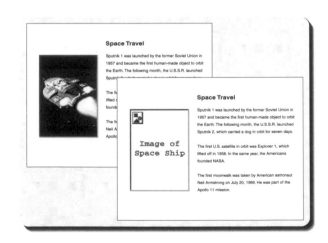

Building resolution independence

When you build your Web pages, you cannot know the size of the user's browser. A work-around to this is to use percentage values in place of pixel widths and heights.

Making pages accessible to disabled users

Style sheets include several properties audio browsers interpret for defining how pages are read to visually impaired people.

You can also use access keys to make links and form elements accessible with the keyboard.

Specifying languages

To make your Web pages more accessible to people of different languages and cultures, you can use the lang attribute to define the language that is used throughout the page.

SUPPORT VARIOUS SCREEN RESOLUTIONS

Computer screen monitors can be set to various resolutions, including 640 x 480, 800 x 600, 1024 x 768 and more. If you build your Web pages so they look great on a browser that is sized to 800 x 600, the user needs to scroll in order to see the entire site on a browser sized to 640 x 480.

With Web TV consoles and Web-enabled PDAs becoming more prevalent, the ability to adapt your Web pages to different screen resolutions is becoming more critical.

The best way to handle various screen resolutions is to use percentage values for all elements that specify width and height.

For example, instead of specifying a table width as `<table width="640">`, use a percentage value such as `<table width="90%">`. This sizes the table based on the size of the browser.

This example uses the width.html file from this book's CD, but the steps can be applied to any situation.

SUPPORT VARIOUS SCREEN RESOLUTIONS

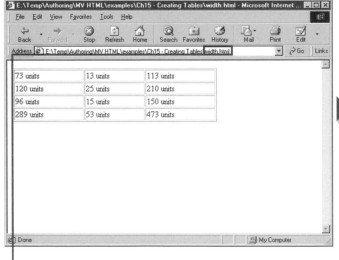

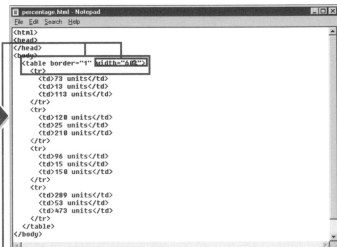

1 Open the HTML file in a browser.

2 Open the HTML file in Notepad.

3 Search the file for any pixel dimensions.

4 Change the pixel values to a similar percentage value.

■ In this example, the width was changed to a value of 60%.

5 Save the file under a new name.

How can I determine the resolution of the user's screen?

✔ Internet Explorer recognizes two JavaScript properties that can be used to determine the resolution of the user's screen. These two properties are `windows.innerWidth` and `windows.innerHeight`.

How can these properties be used?

✔ You can place these two properties within a script to display content based on the size of the window. For example, a statement such as `if (window.innerWidth > 640)` would check to see if the width of the browser window is greater than 640 pixels. The statement `if (window.innerHeight == 480)` would check to see if the height of the browser window is greater than 480 pixels.

What happens if a Web page is larger than the browser window?

✔ If the content of a Web page is larger than the browser window, then the browser displays scroll bars that the viewer can use to see the content that extends beyond the browser window.

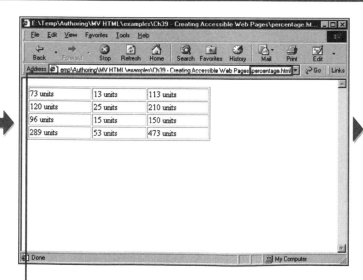

6 Open the new HTML file in a browser.

7 Resize the browser.

■ The relative dimension of the table stays true to the browser window.

MAINTAIN SEPARATE VERSIONS

Because some visitors to your Web site may use older browsers that do not support things like frames, you may want to have different versions of your page that they can access.

Several sites enable support for a broad range of browsers by maintaining several different

versions of their pages. These sites typically have an introduction page that lets the user decide which version to access.

A number of different criteria separates different sites. One common one is using frames. Another is the browser they are using. A third division could be to

select to view a high-bandwidth site or a low-bandwidth site.

If a certain version of the site uses any specific plug-ins, you should list these on the introduction page. Listing them helps the user to decide whether they want to see the page.

MAINTAIN SEPARATE VERSIONS

intro.html - Notepad

```
<html>
<head>
</head>
<body>
 <a href="jet image.html">Low-Bandwidth: Jet Fighter Image (15kb)</a><br/>
 <a href="jet video.html">High-Bandwidth: Jet Fighter Video (261kb)</a>
</body>
</html>
```

E:\Temp\Authoring\MV HTML\examples\Ch39 - Creating Accessible Web Pages\intro.html - Mi...

Address: E:\Temp\Authoring\MV HTML\examples\Ch39 - Creating Accessible Web Pages\intro.html

Low-Bandwidth: Jet Fighter Image (15kb)
High-Bandwidth: Jet Fighter Video (261kb)

1 Open the HTML file in Notepad.

2 Add two sets of `<a>` tags with `href` attributes.

3 Set the first `href` attribute to one page version.

4 Set the second `href` tag to a second page version.

5 Add some descriptive text between each set of `<a>` tags.

6 Save the HTML file.

7 Open the HTML file in a browser.

How can I know which plug-ins are installed for a browser?

✔ All plug-ins installed for a browser are contained within the `navigator.plugins` object array. The `plugins` object includes a `length` property that can be used to determine the number of plug-ins that are included in this array. You can then refer to the plug-in objects by referencing their index. For example, `navigator.plugins[2]` accesses the third element in the array. Remember that JavaScript starts count array elements from 0.

How can I check for a specific plug-in?

✔ If you include a JavaScript statement that uses the `indexOf` method to look for the occurrence of the plug-in name, you can check for a specific plug-in. For example, the following statements would check for the Flash plug-in, for `(j=0;j<=navigator.plugins.length;j++) {if (navigator.plugins[j].indexOf == "Flash")`.

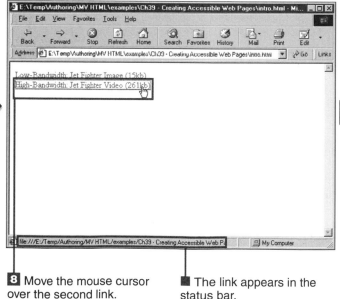

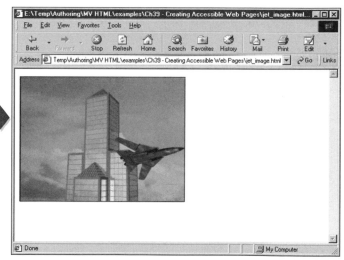

8 Move the mouse cursor over the second link.

■ The link appears in the status bar.

10 Click the first link.

■ The designated item — in this case, the low-bandwidth file — loads into the browser.

USING AURAL STYLE SHEETS

Many vision-impaired people can use the Web by means of aural browsers. These browsers read the page content to the person, but much of the content like images can easily be misinterpreted.

Another way to make your Web pages more accessible is to enable them to the vision-impaired. Aural browsers are becoming available

that read the content of a Web page to the vision-impaired.

To ensure that each element in your Web page can be interpreted, you need to make sure that all graphic images use the `alt` attribute that effectively describes the image.

One problem with reading the content is that these browsers are not aware of how to change the

pitch or emphasis certain words or phrases. These subtle audio clues can be inserted into a document using aural style sheets.

Style sheet properties for reading text include `volume`, `speak`, `pause`, `cue`, `pitch`, `stress`, and others.

USING AURAL STYLE SHEETS

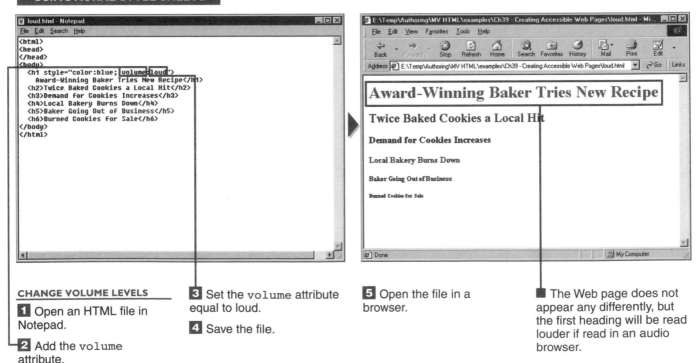

CHANGE VOLUME LEVELS

1 Open an HTML file in Notepad.

2 Add the `volume` attribute.

3 Set the `volume` attribute equal to loud.

4 Save the file.

5 Open the file in a browser.

■ The Web page does not appear any differently, but the first heading will be read louder if read in an audio browser.

What other properties exist for defining aural style sheets?

✔ The `volume` property controls the volume. The `speak` property can be set to `normal` or `spell-out`. The `pause-before`, `pause-after`, and `pause` properties can be used to set pauses. The `cue-before`, `cue-after`, and `cue` properties can be used to play sound effects in the place of icons or bullets. The `play-during` property can play

background sound, the `azimuth` and `elevation` properties can vary the direction of the sound, and the `speech-rate`, `voice-family`, `pitch`, `pitch-range`, `stress`, and `richness` properties can be used to define the style of the sound. Finally, the `speak-punctuation` and `speak-numeral` properties define how punctuation and numbers are spoken.

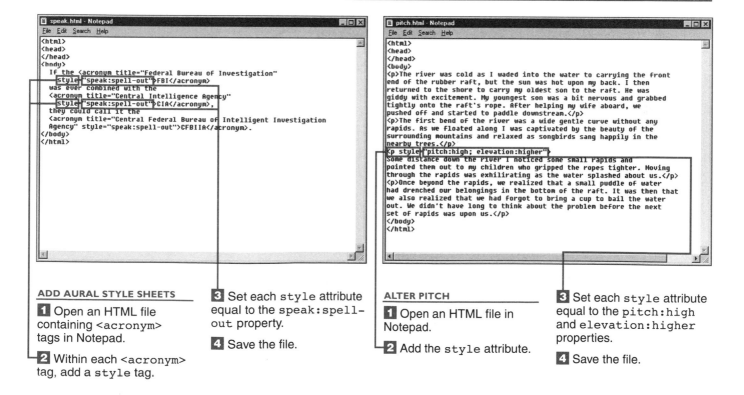

ADD AURAL STYLE SHEETS

1 Open an HTML file containing `<acronym>` tags in Notepad.

2 Within each `<acronym>` tag, add a `style` tag.

3 Set each `style` attribute equal to the `speak:spell-out` property.

4 Save the file.

ALTER PITCH

1 Open an HTML file in Notepad.

2 Add the `style` attribute.

3 Set each `style` attribute equal to the `pitch:high` and `elevation:higher` properties.

4 Save the file.

USING ACCESS KEYS

Another helpful way to make your pages more accessible is to include *access keys*. Access keys are common in the Windows and Macintosh operating systems. These are the keys that you can press to make an operation work. For example, rather than clicking Edit⇨Copy, you can simply press Ctrl+C to perform the same function.

By providing access keys for your Web pages, you enable users to navigate your Web pages more easily by using only the keyboard.

Access keys can be specified for form elements and links using the accesskey attribute. To use a specified access key, you need to press and hold the Alt key (or the Cmd key for Macintosh systems).

You should somehow mark the hotkey so that the user can identify it as an access key.

USING ACCESS KEYS

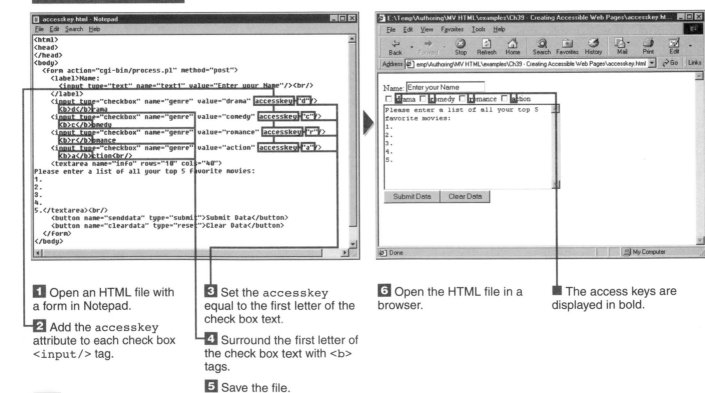

1 Open an HTML file with a form in Notepad.

2 Add the accesskey attribute to each check box `<input/>` tag.

3 Set the accesskey equal to the first letter of the check box text.

4 Surround the first letter of the check box text with `<b>` tags.

5 Save the file.

6 Open the HTML file in a browser.

■ The access keys are displayed in bold.

How can I mark an access key so that users can recognize it?

✔ You can mark access keys several different ways. One way to mark them is to alter the formatting of the access keys. For example, using underline or bold formatting makes the letter stand out. The main thing is to be consistent. You also might want to include a help screen that explains how to use the access keys.

How can I format the text that is included on a button?

✔ Formatting tags like <b> and <i> will only work on regular text that is included on a Web page. You cannot use these formatting tags on the text that is included as an attribute such as a button. One way around this is to make an image with the needed formatting into a button.

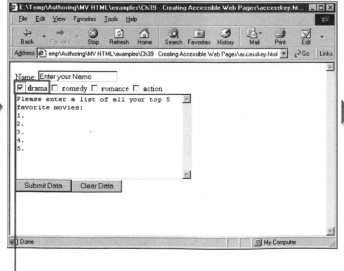

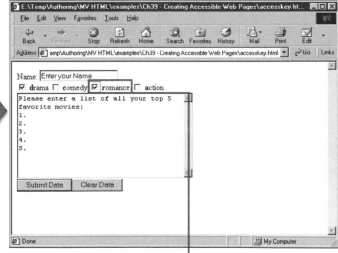

7 Press and hold the Alt key while pressing one of the access keys.

■ Notice how the check box for that access key is selected.

8 Press and hold the Alt key while pressing another access key.

■ Notice how the check box for that access key is selected.

SPECIFY A LANGUAGE

The Web can be found in all corners of the world. Another way to make your Web pages accessible is to create Web pages using different languages.

One of the common attributes that can be used with many HTML elements is the `lang` attribute. This attribute can be used to designate the language that is used for the content inside the tag. This attribute can also be included in

the `<html>` tag for applying a language to the entire Web page.

Using the `lang` attribute does not mean that the browser will automatically translate your content. The current browsers do very little to support this attribute, but foreign language operating systems can be set to look for the `lang` attribute and correctly display the content according to the language rules.

The `lang` attribute is set to a two-letter language code. These language codes include `en` for English, `fr` for French, `de` for German, `it` for Italian, `nl` for Dutch, `el` for Greek, `es` for Spanish, `pt` for Portuguese, `ar` for Arabic, `he` for Hebrew, `ru` for Russian, `zh` for Chinese, and `ja` for Japanese.

SPECIFY A LANGUAGE

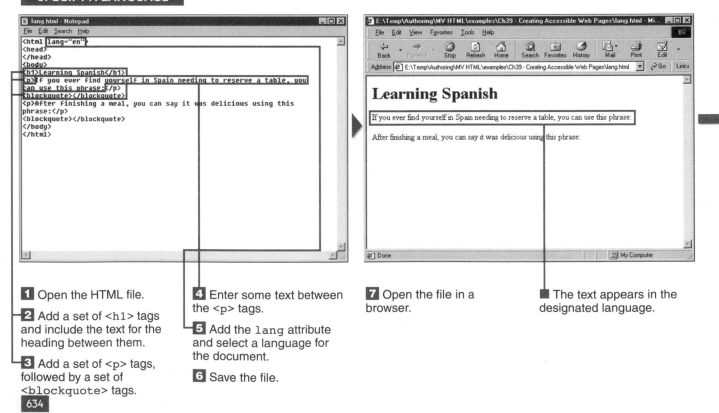

1 Open the HTML file.

2 Add a set of `<h1>` tags and include the text for the heading between them.

3 Add a set of `<p>` tags, followed by a set of `<blockquote>` tags.

4 Enter some text between the `<p>` tags.

5 Add the `lang` attribute and select a language for the document.

6 Save the file.

7 Open the file in a browser.

■ The text appears in the designated language.

How can I control the text reading direction?

✔ Some languages, such as Hebrew and Japanese, read text from right to left rather than than left to right like English. You can specify the reading direction of text using the `dir` attribute. This attribute can be set to `ltr` or `rtl`. The default is `ltr`, which reads the text from left to right.

What is the default setting for the lang attribute?

✔ The default setting for the `lang` attribute is not English, but unknown. Unless otherwise specified, a specific language isn't used.

What language rules besides text reading direction are specific to a language?

✔ In addition to text reading direction, languages differ in how they use punctuation. For example, languages like French, German, and Russian all use diacritical marks that affect the word's pronunciation.

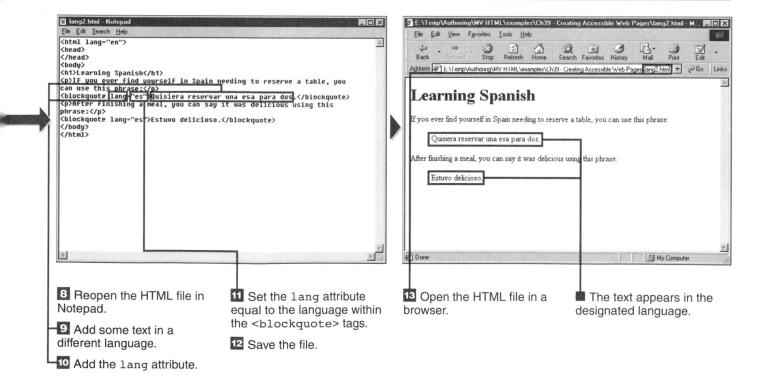

8 Reopen the HTML file in Notepad.

9 Add some text in a different language.

10 Add the `lang` attribute.

11 Set the `lang` attribute equal to the language within the `<blockquote>` tags.

12 Save the file.

13 Open the HTML file in a browser.

■ The text appears in the designated language.

DOWNLOAD THE AMAYA BROWSER

XML functionality is not yet implemented in Internet Explorer or Netscape Navigator, but the World Wide Web Consortium (W3C) has created a browser that can be used to test newly developed Web technologies such as MathML. If you want to create a Web page with newly developed Web technologies like

XML, you can test the page using the Amaya browser that was specially developed by the World Wide Web Consortium.

You can download the Amaya browser from the W3C's Web site at www.w3c.org. The latest version of the installation program is around 4.6MB.

After you download the setup file, you need to run it to install the Amaya browser.

The Amaya browser can be used to view and author Web pages including pages that use HTML, XHTML, MathML, and Cascading Style Sheets (CSS).

DOWNLOAD THE AMAYA BROWSER

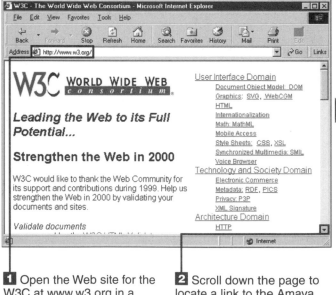

1 Open the Web site for the W3C at www.w3.org in a browser.

2 Scroll down the page to locate a link to the Amaya browser.

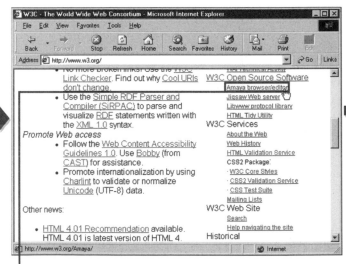

3 Click the link to access the Amaya browser.

Does the W3C have any other software available?

✔ From the W3C site, in addition to the Amaya browser, you can download a Web server named Jigsaw, a protocol library, and HTML Tidy, a utility that can check HTML code and convert HTML documents into XHTML documents.

Is there a cost to use the Amaya browser?

✔ The purpose of the Amaya browser to provide developers with a platform that they can use to test their work. It is available free of charge for this purpose. The software cannot be resold or made commercially available without the authorization of the World Wide Consortium. If you have any questions concerning using the software, consult the licensing agreement that is part of the installation routine.

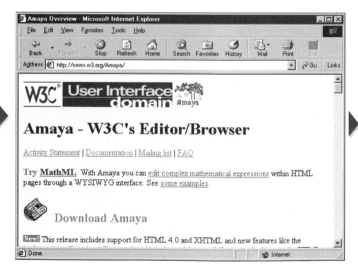

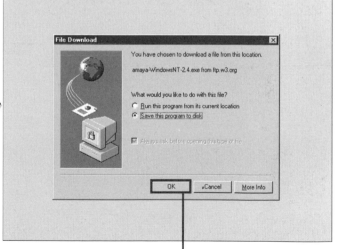

■ The Amaya browser Web page is displayed.

4 Click the link to download the Amaya browser.

5 Select a directory where you wish to save the downloaded file.

6 Click OK to save the file to disk.

MathML: MARKUP FOR MATHEMATICS

The main benefit of XML is to give meaning to data. This enables browsers and other programs to understand not only how Web content should be displayed, but also what kind of data the content is.

Mathematical equations, for example, can be displayed in a browser using text, symbols and graphics, but without the correct markup, the content is not understood by your browser.

To handle this dilemma, an XML application named *MathML* has been created by the W3C. MathML can define mathematical and scientific equations for interpretation and display.

Current versions of Microsoft Internet Explorer and Netscape Navigator browsers cannot display MathML documents, but other browsers such as Amaya can display MathML documents.

This task's example uses two images from the book's CD— math.html and math.xht.

MathML: MARKUP FOR MATHEMATICS

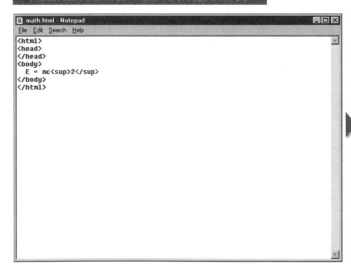

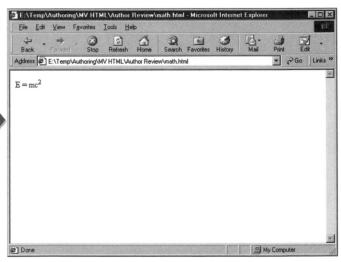

1 Open the math.html file from the CD in Notepad.

2 Open the math.html file in a browser.

■ The simple formula for the Theory of Relativity is displayed.

Why does the XML document look a lot more difficult and complicated than the simpler HTML document?

✔ HTML is simpler because it only deals with displaying content. XML documents are more difficult and complex, but they give meaning to the data that can be used by other programs to manipulate and use the data. XML is more complex, but the rewards for the complexity is worth the trouble.

How can other programs use MathML?

✔ Because the XML markup of mathematical symbols defines the meaning of the math equation, the MathML document could be read by other math programs that could generate results based on the values of the different variables. For example, the mathematical programs Mathematica and Maple can use MathML documents.

3 Open the math.xht file from the CD in Notepad.

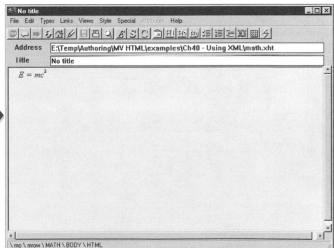

4 Open the math.xht file in the Amaya browser.

■ The Theory of Relativity is displayed in the Amaya browser as an XML document.

CREATE MathML CONTENT WITH AMAYA

In addition to viewing MathML content, you can also create MathML content with Amaya. Creating MathML documents is easy to do using a set of tools that are located within a toolbox. These tools include many of the common mathematical structures like square roots, exponential values, and integrals.

With Amaya open, you need to open the Math toolbox. You can access this toolbox by selecting Types⇨Math⇨MATH.

This toolbox contains several icon buttons that can be used to create different mathematical structures. When the icon buttons in the toolbox are clicked, gray boxes

where the math symbols can be located are displayed. Selecting these gray boxes and typing a variable, number, or symbol can create equations.

When the equation is complete, you can save the file as an XHTML file by selecting File⇨Save As.

CREATE MathML CONTENT WITH AMAYA

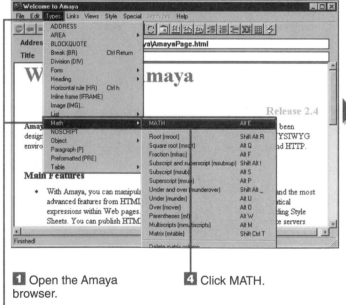

1 Open the Amaya browser.

2 Click Types

3 Click Math.

4 Click MATH.

■ The Math toolbox appears.

How can I select mathematical symbols?

✔ Many mathematical and scientific equations use Greek symbols to represent different variables. You can access a dialog box of the available symbols by clicking the Symbol button in the Math toolbox.

Can mathematical symbols and equations be placed alongside standard HTML?

✔ The Amaya browser allows standard HTML elements such as lists, tables, images and headings co-exist in the same document with MathML equations and symbols. Many of the buttons in the top toolbar let you add standard HTML elements.

Do I need to use the Math toolbox to add mathematical elements to the page?

✔ The Math toolbox is added for convenience. You can also add mathematical elements using the Types⊅Math menu. All the buttons included in the Math toolbox are available as menu commands.

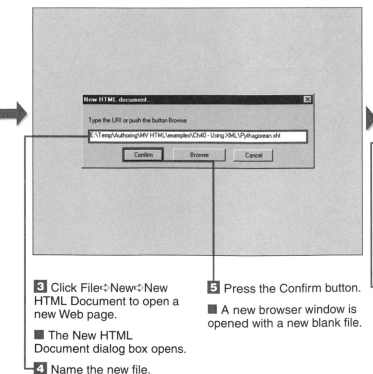

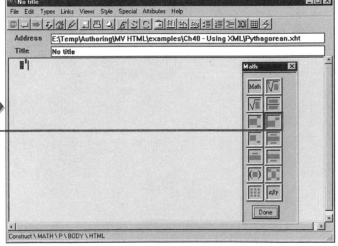

3 Click File⊅New⊅New HTML Document to open a new Web page.

■ The New HTML Document dialog box opens.

4 Name the new file.

5 Press the Confirm button.

■ A new browser window is opened with a new blank file.

6 Click the Superscript button (📷) in the Math toolbox.

■ Two gray boxes are displayed to the right of the cursor.

CONTINUED

CREATE MathML CONTENT WITH AMAYA CONTINUED

The Math toolbox includes tools for creating math equations. Each of these tools represents a separate MathML tag. Some of the tools included are

Square Root (msqrt): Takes the square root of a number.

Fraction (mfrac): Creates a fractional statement.

Subscripts (msub): Adds subscripts to a number.

Superscripts (msup): Adds superscripts to a number.

Parenthesis (mf): Surrounds a statement in parenthesis.

Matrix (mtable): Builds a matrix of numbers.

If you examine the XHTML file in Notepad after saving the MathML document, you may see a number of these tags.

CREATING MATHML CONTENT WITH AMAYA CONTINUED

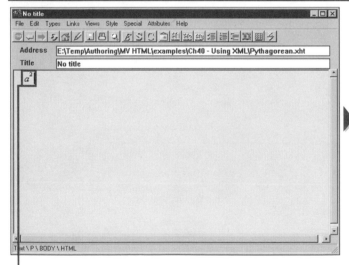

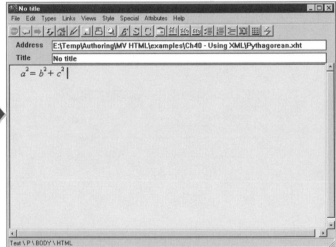

7 Click the lower gray box and then type a variable.

8 Click in the upper gray box and type the power for that variable.

9 Use the Math toolbox icons to complete the equation.

What is the xmlns attribute that is included with the <math> tags?

✔ The `xmlns` attribute is defined in the MathML DTD and is used to reference where the specifications for these tags are located. Using this attribute, the browser knows where to look to find the information on what the data in the document means. The browser uses this information to decide how to display the content.

Can the <math> tag be used to create other types of expressions?

✔ The whole idea behind XML is to represent data correctly. The `<math>` tag could be used to represent other statements such as chemical expressions, but the chemical industry is building a XML standard that would be better to use to create chemical expressions.

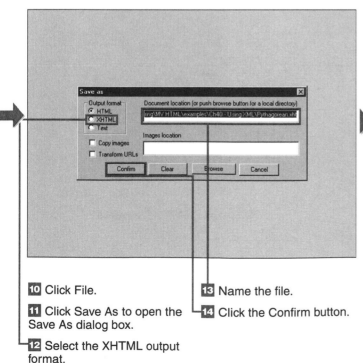

10 Click File.

11 Click Save As to open the Save As dialog box.

12 Select the XHTML output format.

13 Name the file.

14 Click the Confirm button.

15 Open the file in the Notepad.

USING SMIL: SYNCHRONIZED MULTIMEDIA

Another promising XML application is *Synchronized Multimedia Integration Language* (SMIL), pronounced "smile." This application enables users to create advanced online presentations using a variety of multimedia elements.

The SMIL elements can be identified and positioned using standard style sheet properties with the `<layout>` tag. You can also set the duration of each element and whether they are played sequentially or at the same time (parallel).

Multimedia objects that can be included in a SMIL document can include audio, video, images, text, text streams, and animations. The tags for these elements are `<audio>`, `<video>`, `<img>`, `<text>`, `<textstream>`, and `<animation>`.

Like MathML, only a couple of SMIL browsers are currently available, but SMIL multimedia presentations will soon be included in the mainstream browsers.

USING SMIL: SYNCHRONIZED MULTIMEDIA

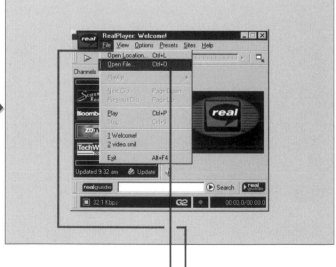

1 Open a SMIL file in Notepad.

■ Notice how the tags differ from the standard HTML tags.

2 Open the RealPlayer G2 player.

■ The RealPlayer G2 can be downloaded from www.real.com.

3 Click File.

4 Click Open File.

Can SMIL be combined with HTML pages?

✔ When browsers that support SMIL become available, you will be able to combine SMIL and HTML in the same document. You will also be able to use the `<text/>` tag within SMIL documents to open HTML pages by setting the `type` attribute equal to `text/html`.

Where can I learn more about the SMIL standard?

✔ The World Wide Consortium's (W3C) web site, located at www.w3c.org includes the latest version of the SMIL specification, as well as, SMIL examples, links to software that use the SMIL specification. Previewing the SMIL Web pages on this site offers a good starting point for learning SMIL.

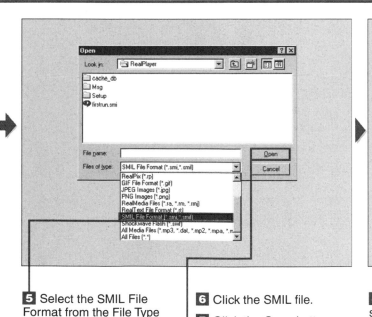

Fighter Jet Fly-By

5 Select the SMIL File Format from the File Type drop-down list.

6 Click the SMIL file.

7 Click the Open button.

8 Click the Play button to see the video.

■ The video file and the image display in order.

APPENDIX

WHAT'S ON THE CD-ROM

The CD-ROM included in this book contains many useful files and programs. Before installing any of the programs on the disc, make sure that a newer version of the program is not already installed on your computer. For information on installing different versions of the same program, contact the program's manufacturer.

System Requirements

To use the contents of the CD-ROM, your computer must be equipped with the following hardware and software:

- A PC with a Pentium 133 MHz or faster processor, or a Mac OS computer with a 68040 or faster processor
- Microsoft Windows 95 or later, Windows NT 4 or later, or Mac OS system software 7.5.5 or later
- At least 16MB of total RAM installed on your computer (we recommend at least 32MB)
- At least 400MB of hard drive space
- A ten-speed (10x) or faster CD-ROM drive
- A sound card for PCs
- A monitor capable of displaying at least 256 colors or grayscale
- A modem with a speed of at least 28.8 Kbps

Installing and Using the Software

Shareware programs are fully functional, free trial versions of copyrighted programs. If you like particular programs, register with their authors for a nominal fee and receive licenses, enhanced versions, and technical support. Freeware programs are free, copyrighted games, applications, and utilities. You can copy them to as many PCs as you like — free — but they have no technical support. GNU software is governed by its own license, which is included inside the folder of the GNU software. There are no restrictions on distribution of this software. See the GNU license for more details. Trial, demo, or evaluation versions are usually limited either by time or functionality (such as being unable to save projects).

For your convenience, the software titles appearing on the CD-ROM are listed alphabetically.

Acrobat Reader, from Adobe

For Windows 95/98 and NT 4.0 or later, Macintosh. Trial version. Acrobat Reader is a program and plug-in that can be used to display, search, and print PDF files.

Author's sample files

For Mac and Windows 95/98/NT 4.0. These files contain all the sample codes from the book. You can browse these files directly from the CD-ROM, or you can copy them to your hard drive and use them as the basis for your own projects. To find the files on the CD-ROM, open the D:\Author Samples folder.

BBEdit, from Bare Bones Software

For Macintosh. Trial version. BBEdit created by Bare Bones Software is an advanced HTML editor that can be used to create Web pages. This demo enables you to use the full version for an evaluation period.

BBEditLite, from Bare Bones Software

For Macintosh. Lite version. BBEdit Lite is a trimmed-down version of the popular HTML editing package that can be used to create Web pages.

CSE HTML Validator Lite, from Windows-AI Internet Solutions

For Windows 95/98 and NT 4.0 or later. Demo version. CSE HTML Validator Lite created by Windows-AI Internet Solutions does not include all the features of the professional version, but it does not expire.

CSE HTML Validator Professional, from Windows-AI Internet Solutions

For Windows 95/98 and NT 4.0 or later. Demo version. CSE HTML Validator Professional created by Windows-AI Internet Solutions can be used to validate your Web pages. This demo enables you to use the full version for an evaluation period.

CuteFTP, from GlobalSCAPE

For Windows 95/98 and NT 4.0 or later. Shareware version. CuteFTP is an FTP client that can be used to transfer files to a Web server.

CuteMAP, from GlobalSCAPE

For Windows 95/98 and NT 4.0 or later. Shareware version. CuteMAP is another image map editor. It can be used to create and save image maps.

Dot Planet ISP, from DotPlanet.com

For Windows 95/98/NT 4.0. Evaluation version. In case you do not have a connection to the information superhighway, the CD includes sign-on software for DotPlanet Internet Access, an Internet service provider.

During the sign-up process, you need to enter the registration number: **502CY.**

After you are signed on, you can access the world wide Web from DotPlanet's home page. You need a credit card to sign up with DotPlanet Internet Access.

Dreamweaver, from Macromedia

For Windows 95/98 and NT 4.0 or later and Mac. Trial version. Dreamweaver is a robust Web page creation tool. It enables you to dynamically edit HTML and JavaScript pages. This demo enables you to use the full version for an evaluation period.

Fusion, from NetObjects

For Windows 95/98 and NT 4.0 or later and Mac. Trial version. Fusion is template-based tool for creating Web sites. This demo enables you to use the full version for an evaluation period.

GIF Animator, from Ulead Systems

For Windows 95/98 and NT 4.0 or later. Trial version. GIF Animator is a package that can be used to create animated GIF images. This demo enables you to use the full version for an evaluation period.

GoLive, from Adobe Systems, Inc.

For Windows 95/98 and NT 4.0 or later and Mac. Trial version. GoLive is a Web site creation and management tool. It integrates well with other Adobe products such as Illustrator and Photoshop. This demo enables you to use the full version for an evaluation period.

GraphicConverter, from Lemke Software

For Macintosh. Shareware version. GraphicConverter is a graphic conversion program that can be used to convert images between different formats.

HomeSite, from Allaire Corp.

For Windows 95/98 and NT 4.0 or later. Thirty-day evaluation version. HomeSite is a Visual HTML editor. It can be used to create Web pages. The evaluation version expires after 30 days.

HotDog Express, from Sausage Software

For Windows 95/98 and NT 4.0 or later. Trial version. HotDog Express is the easier-to-use version of their Web page creation program.

HotDog Professional, from Sausage Software

For Windows 95/98 and NT 4.0 or later. Trial version. HotDog Professional is the professional-level Web page creation program.

HTML Pro, from Niklas Frykholm

For Macintosh. Shareware version. HTML Pro is a Web page editing package that can be used to create Web pages.

Internet Explorer, from Microsoft

For Windows 95/98 and NT 4.0 or later, Macintosh. Commercial version. Internet Explorer is a robust browser that can be used to display Web pages.

Mapedit, from Boutell Communications

For Windows 95/98 and NT 4.0 or later. Shareware version. Mapedit is an image map editor. It can be used to create and save image maps.

Netscape Communicator, from Netscape

For Windows 95/98 and NT 4.0 or later, Macintosh. Commercial version. Netscape Communicator is another popular Web browser that can be used to display Web pages.

Paint Shop Pro, from JASC

For Windows 95/98 and NT 4.0 or later. Evaluation version. Paint Shop Pro is a powerful image-editing package. This demo enables you to use the full version for an evaluation period. Paint Shop Pro includes many tools for creating, editing, and working with Web images.

Reptile, from Sausage Software

For Windows 95/98 and NT 4.0 or later. Trial version. Reptile is a seamless tile-creation package.

Shockwave + Flash Player, from Macromedia, Inc.

For Windows 95/98 and NT 4.0 or later, Macintosh. Commercial version. The Shockwave and Flash Players are plug-ins that can be used to display Flash and Shockwave content within a browser.

APPENDIX

SiteCheck, from Pacific Coast Software

For Macintosh. Shareware version. SiteCheck is a set of utilities that can be used to check the links on your site's Web pages.

SmartSaver Pro, from Ulead Systems

For Windows 95/98 and NT 4.0 or later. Fifteen-day trial version. SmartSaver Pro is a Web image-optimization package that enables you to visually select the file settings for creating optimized images. This demo enables you to use the full version for an evaluation period.

Spider, from InContext Systems

For Windows 95/98 and NT 4.0 or later. Evaluation version. Spider created by InContext Systems is a Web authoring package for creating Web pages.

StuffIt Expander, from Aladdin Systems

For Macintosh. Demo version. StuffIt Expander, created by Aladdin Systems, can create expandable archive files that can be expanded as needed.

StuffIt Lite, from Aladdin Systems

Macintosh. Freeware version. StuffIt Lite, created by Aladdin Systems, can be used to compress and archive files. The lite version is freeware and does not expire.

Web Razor Pro, from Ulead Systems

For Windows 95/98 and NT 4.0 or later. Fifteen-day trial version. Web Razor Pro is a Web image-editing package that includes features for creating GIF animations and optimizing Web images. This demo enables you to use the full version for an evaluation period.

WinZip, from Nico Mak Computing

For Windows 95/98 and NT 4.0 or later. Evaluation version. WinZip is a file compression and archiving package.

Troubleshooting

I tried my best to compile programs that work on most computers with the minimum system requirements. Your computer, however, may differ, and some programs may not work properly for some reason.

The two most likely problems are that you do not have enough memory (RAM) for the programs you want to use, or you have other programs running that are affecting installation or running of a program. If you get error messages like Not enough memory or Setup cannot continue, try one or more of these methods and then try using the software again:

- Turn off any anti-virus software.

- Close all running programs.

- In Windows, close the CD-ROM interface and run demos or installations directly from Windows Explorer.

- Have your local computer store add more RAM to your computer.

If you still have trouble installing the items from the CD-ROM, please call the IDG Books Worldwide Customer Service phone number: 800-762-2974 (outside the U.S.: 317-572-3443).

MASTER VISUALLY HTML 4 AND XHTML 1 ON THE CD-ROM

You can view *Master VISUALLY HTML 4 and XHTML 1* on your screen using the CD-ROM included at the back of this book. The CD-ROM allows you to search the contents of the book for a specific word or phrase. The CD-ROM also provides a convenient way of keeping the book handy while traveling.

You must install Acrobat Reader on your computer before you can view the book on the CD-ROM. This program is provided on the disc. Acrobat Reader allows you to view Portable Document Format (PDF) files. These files can display books and magazines on your screen exactly as they appear in printed form.

To view the contents of the book using Acrobat Reader, display the contents of the disc. Double-click the START.htm icon. In the page that appears, click "The book in electronic format" to access the contents of the book.

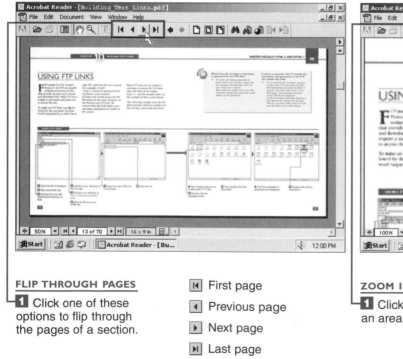

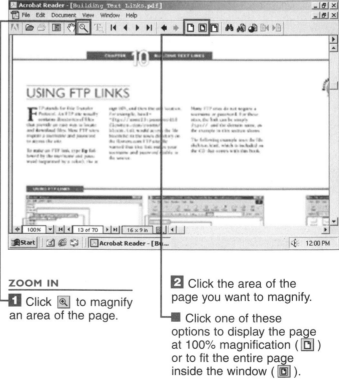

FLIP THROUGH PAGES

1 Click one of these options to flip through the pages of a section.

◄	First page
◄	Previous page
►	Next page
►|	Last page

ZOOM IN

1 Click 🔍 to magnify an area of the page.

2 Click the area of the page you want to magnify.

■ Click one of these options to display the page at 100% magnification (□) or to fit the entire page inside the window (□).

How do I install Acrobat Reader?

✔ Open the ACROREAD folder on the CD-ROM disc. Double-click the RS40ENG.exe file and then follow the instructions on your screen.

How do I search all the sections of the book at once?

✔ You must first locate the index. While viewing the contents of the book, click 🔍 in the Acrobat Reader window. Click Indexes and then click Add. Locate and click the index.pdx file, click Open and then click OK. You need to locate the index only once. After locating the index, you can click 🔍 to search all the sections.

How can I make searching the book more convenient?

✔ Copy the Acrobat Files folder from the CD-ROM disc to your hard drive. This enables you to easily access the contents of the book at any time.

Can I use Acrobat Reader for anything else?

✔ Acrobat Reader is a popular and useful program. There are many files available on the Web that are designed to be viewed using Acrobat Reader. Look for files with the .pdf extension.

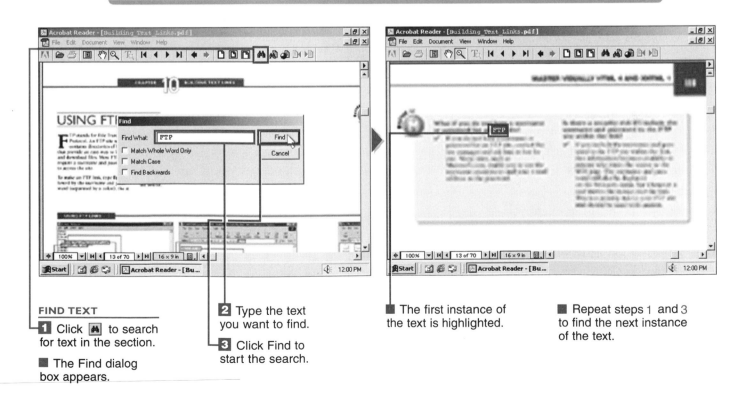

FIND TEXT

1 Click 🔍 to search for text in the section.

■ The Find dialog box appears.

2 Type the text you want to find.

3 Click Find to start the search.

■ The first instance of the text is highlighted.

■ Repeat steps 1 and 3 to find the next instance of the text.

APPENDIX

limitation of liability for consequential or incidental damages, the above limitation or exclusion may not apply to you.

7. U.S. Government Restricted Rights. Use, duplication, or disclosure of the Software by the U.S. Government is subject to restrictions stated in paragraph (c)(1)(ii) of the Rights in Technical Data and Computer Software clause of DFARS 252.227-7013, and in subparagraphs (a) through (d) of the Commercial Computer–Restricted Rights clause at FAR 52.227-19, and in similar clauses in the NASA FAR supplement, when applicable.

8. General. This Agreement constitutes the entire understanding of the parties and revokes and supersedes all prior agreements, oral or written, between them and may not be modified or amended except in a writing signed by both parties hereto that specifically refers to this Agreement. This Agreement shall take precedence over any other documents that may be in conflict herewith. If any one or more provisions contained in this Agreement are held by any court or tribunal to be invalid, illegal, or otherwise unenforceable, each and every other provision shall remain in full force and effect.

GNU GENERAL PUBLIC LICENSE

Preamble

The licenses for most software are designed to take away your freedom to share and change it. By contrast, the GNU General Public License is intended to guarantee your freedom to share and change free software – to make sure the software is free for all its users. This General Public License applies to most of the Free Software Foundation's software and to any other program whose authors commit to using it. (Some other Free Software Foundation software is covered by the GNU Library General Public License instead.) You can apply it to your programs, too.

When we speak of free software, we are referring to freedom, not price. Our General Public Licenses are designed to make sure that you have the freedom to distribute copies of free software (and charge for this service if you wish), that you receive source code or can get it if you want it, that you can change the software or use pieces of it in new free programs; and that you know you can do these things.

To protect your rights, we need to make restrictions that forbid anyone to deny you these rights or to ask you to surrender the rights. These restrictions translate to certain responsibilities for you if you distribute copies of the software, or if you modify it.

For example, if you distribute copies of such a program, whether gratis or for a fee, you must give the recipients all the rights that you have. You must make sure that they, too, receive or can get the source code. And you must show them these terms so they know their rights.

We protect your rights with two steps: (1) copyright the software, and (2) offer you this license which gives you legal permission to copy, distribute and/or modify the software.

Also, for each author's protection and ours, we want to make certain that everyone understands that there is no warranty for this free software. If the software is modified by someone else and passed on, we want its recipients to know that what they have is not the original, so that any problems introduced by others will not reflect on the original authors' reputations.

Finally, any free program is threatened constantly by software patents. We wish to avoid the danger that redistributors of a free program will individually obtain patent licenses, in effect making the program proprietary. To prevent this, we have made it clear that any patent must be licensed for everyone's free use or not licensed at all.

The precise terms and conditions for copying, distribution and modification follow.

TERMS AND CONDITIONS FOR COPYING, DISTRIBUTION AND MODIFICATION

0. This License applies to any program or other work which contains a notice placed by the copyright holder saying it may be distributed under the terms of this General Public License. The "Program", below, refers to any such program or work, and a "work based on the Program" means either the Program or any derivative work under copyright law: that is to say, a work containing the Program or a portion of it, either verbatim or with modifications and/or translated into another language. (Hereinafter, translation is included without limitation in the term "modification.") Each licensee is addressed as "you."

   Activities other than copying, distribution and modification are not covered by this License; they are outside its scope. The act of running the Program is not restricted, and the output from the Program is covered only if its contents constitute a work based on the Program (independent of having been made by running the Program). Whether that is true depends on what the Program does.

1. You may copy and distribute verbatim copies of the Program's source code as you receive it, in any medium, provided that you conspicuously and appropriately publish on each copy an appropriate copyright notice and disclaimer of warranty; keep intact all the notices that refer to this License and to the absence of any warranty; and give any other recipients of the Program a copy of this License along with the Program.

APPENDIX

You may charge a fee for the physical act of transferring a copy, and you may at your option offer warranty protection in exchange for a fee.

2. You may modify your copy or copies of the Program or any portion of it, thus forming a work based on the Program, and copy and distribute such modifications or work under the terms of Section 1 above, provided that you also meet all of these conditions:

   a) You must cause the modified files to carry prominent notices stating that you changed the files and the date of any change.

   b) You must cause any work that you distribute or publish, that in whole or in part contains or is derived from the Program or any part thereof, to be licensed as a whole at no charge to all third parties under the terms of this License.

   c) If the modified program normally reads commands interactively when run, you must cause it, when started running for such interactive use in the most ordinary way, to print or display an announcement including an appropriate copyright notice and a notice that there is no warranty (or else, saying that you provide a warranty) and that users may redistribute the program under these conditions, and telling the user how to view a copy of this License. (Exception: If the Program itself is interactive but does not normally print such an announcement, your work based on the Program is not required to print an announcement.)

These requirements apply to the modified work as a whole. If identifiable sections of that work are not derived from the Program, and can be reasonably considered independent and separate works in themselves, then this License, and its terms, do not apply to those sections when you distribute them as separate works. But when you distribute the same sections as part of a whole which is a work based on the Program, the distribution of the whole must be on the terms of this License, whose permissions for other licensees extend to the entire whole, and thus to each and every part regardless of who wrote it.

Thus, it is not the intent of this section to claim rights or contest your rights to work written entirely by you; rather, the intent is to exercise the right to control the distribution of derivative or collective works based on the Program. In addition, mere aggregation of another work not based on the Program with the Program (or with a work based on the Program) on a volume of a storage or distribution medium does not bring the other work under the scope of this License.

3. You may copy and distribute the Program (or a work based on it, under Section 2) in object code or executable form under the terms of Sections 1 and 2 above provided that you also do one of the following:

   a) Accompany it with the complete corresponding machine-readable source code, which must be distributed under the terms of Sections 1 and 2 above on a medium customarily used for software interchange; or,

   b) Accompany it with a written offer, valid for at least three years, to give any third party, for a charge no more than your cost of physically performing source distribution, a complete machine-readable copy of the corresponding source code, to be distributed under the terms of Sections 1 and 2 above on a medium customarily used for software interchange; or,

   c) Accompany it with the information you received as to the offer to distribute corresponding source code. (This alternative is allowed only for noncommercial distribution and only if you received the program in object code or executable form with such an offer, in accord with Subsection b above.)

The source code for a work means the preferred form of the work for making modifications to it. For an executable work, complete source code means all the source code for all modules it contains, plus any associated interface definition files, plus the scripts used to control compilation and installation of the executable. However, as a special exception, the source code distributed need not include anything that is normally distributed (in either source or binary form) with the major components (compiler, kernel, and so on) of the operating system on which the executable runs, unless that component itself accompanies the executable.

If distribution of executable or object code is made by offering access to copy from a designated place, then offering equivalent access to copy the source code from the same place counts as distribution of the source code, even though third parties are not compelled to copy the source along with the object code.

4. You may not copy, modify, sublicense, or distribute the Program except as expressly provided under this License. Any attempt otherwise to copy, modify, sublicense or distribute the Program is void, and will automatically terminate your rights under this License. However, parties who have received copies, or rights, from you under this License will not have their licenses terminated so long as such parties remain in full compliance.

5. You are not required to accept this License, since you have not signed it. However, nothing else grants you permission to modify or distribute the Program or its derivative works. These actions are prohibited by law if you do not accept this License. Therefore, by modifying or distributing the Program (or any work based on the Program), you indicate your acceptance of this License to do so, and all its terms and conditions for copying, distributing or modifying the Program or works based on it.

6. Each time you redistribute the Program (or any work based on the Program), the recipient automatically receives a license from the original licensor to copy, distribute or modify the Program subject to these terms and conditions. You may not impose any further restrictions on the recipients' exercise of the rights granted herein. You are not responsible for enforcing compliance by third parties to this License.

7. If, as a consequence of a court judgment or allegation of patent infringement or for any other reason (not limited to patent issues), conditions are imposed on you (whether by court order, agreement or otherwise) that contradict the conditions of this License, they do not excuse you from the conditions of this License. If you cannot distribute so as to satisfy simultaneously your obligations under this License and any other pertinent obligations, then as a consequence you may not distribute the Program at all. For example, if a patent license would not permit royalty-free redistribution of the Program by all those who receive copies directly or indirectly through you, then the only way you could satisfy both it and this License would be to refrain entirely from distribution of the Program.

   If any portion of this section is held invalid or unenforceable under any particular circumstance, the balance of the section is intended to apply and the section as a whole is intended to apply in other circumstances.

   It is not the purpose of this section to induce you to infringe any patents or other property right claims or to contest validity of any such claims; this section has the sole purpose of protecting the integrity of the free software distribution system, which is implemented by public license practices. Many people have made generous contributions to the wide range of software distributed through that system in reliance on consistent application of that system; it is up to the author/donor to decide if he or she is willing to distribute software through any other system and a licensee cannot impose that choice.

   This section is intended to make thoroughly clear what is believed to be a consequence of the rest of this License.

8. If the distribution and/or use of the Program is restricted in certain countries either by patents or by copyrighted interfaces, the original copyright holder who places the Program under this License may add an explicit geographical distribution limitation excluding those countries, so that distribution is permitted only in or among countries not thus excluded. In such case, this License incorporates the limitation as if written in the body of this License.

9. The Free Software Foundation may publish revised and/or new versions of the General Public License from time to time. Such new versions will be similar in spirit to the present version, but may differ in detail to address new problems or concerns.

Each version is given a distinguishing version number. If the Program specifies a version number of this License which applies to it and "any later version", you have the option of following the terms and conditions either of that version or of any later version published by the Free Software Foundation. If the Program does not specify a version number of this License, you may choose any version ever published by the Free Software Foundation.

10. If you wish to incorporate parts of the Program into other free programs whose distribution conditions are different, write to the author to ask for permission. For software which is copyrighted by the Free Software Foundation, write to the Free Software Foundation; we sometimes make exceptions for this. Our decision will be guided by the two goals of preserving the free status of all derivatives of our free software and of promoting the sharing and reuse of software generally.

NO WARRANTY

11. BECAUSE THE PROGRAM IS LICENSED FREE OF CHARGE, THERE IS NO WARRANTY FOR THE PROGRAM, TO THE EXTENT PERMITTED BY APPLICABLE LAW. EXCEPT WHEN OTHERWISE STATED IN WRITING THE COPYRIGHT HOLDERS AND/OR OTHER PARTIES PROVIDE THE PROGRAM "AS IS" WITHOUT WARRANTY OF ANY KIND, EITHER EXPRESSED OR IMPLIED, INCLUDING, BUT NOT LIMITED TO, THE IMPLIED WARRANTIES OF MERCHANTABILITY AND FITNESS FOR A PARTICULAR PURPOSE. THE ENTIRE RISK AS TO THE QUALITY AND PERFORMANCE OF THE PROGRAM IS WITH YOU. SHOULD THE PROGRAM PROVE DEFECTIVE, YOU ASSUME THE COST OF ALL NECESSARY SERVICING, REPAIR OR CORRECTION.

12. IN NO EVENT UNLESS REQUIRED BY APPLICABLE LAW OR AGREED TO IN WRITING WILL ANY COPYRIGHT HOLDER, OR ANY OTHER PARTY WHO MAY MODIFY AND/OR REDISTRIBUTE THE PROGRAM AS PERMITTED ABOVE, BE LIABLE TO YOU FOR DAMAGES, INCLUDING ANY GENERAL, SPECIAL, INCIDENTAL OR CONSEQUENTIAL DAMAGES ARISING OUT OF THE USE OR INABILITY TO USE THE PROGRAM (INCLUDING BUT NOT LIMITED TO LOSS OF DATA OR DATA BEING RENDERED INACCURATE OR LOSSES SUSTAINED BY YOU OR THIRD PARTIES OR A FAILURE OF THE PROGRAM TO OPERATE WITH ANY OTHER PROGRAMS), EVEN IF SUCH HOLDER OR OTHER PARTY HAS BEEN ADVISED OF THE POSSIBILITY OF SUCH DAMAGES.

END OF TERMS AND CONDITIONS

INDEX

INDEX

(continued)

(continued)

(continued)

INDEX

(continued)

(continued)

XMetal, 69

xmins attribute, 643

XML (Extensible Markup Language), 50–51, 638–639